The MBA by Distance Learning

Student Handbook

EDINBURGH
BUSINESS SCHOOL

The MBA by Distance Learning

Student Handbook

PITMAN
PUBLISHING

The Graduate School of Business
Heriot-Watt University

PITMAN PUBLISHING
128 Long Acre, London WC2E 9AN

A Division of Pearson Professional Limited

First published in Great Britain in 1995

ISBN 0 273 61234 4

British Library Cataloguing in Publication Data
A CIP catalogue record for this book can be obtained from the British Library

10 9 8 7 6 5 4 3 2 1

Typeset by PanTek Arts, Maidstone, Kent.
Printed and bound in Great Britain by Clays Ltd, St Ives plc

The Publishers' policy is to use paper manufactured from sustainable forests.

Contents

Preface

This book has been written to serve two purposes: first, to provide prospective students of the MBA degree with as much information as possible in terms of programme content and pedagogy, level of difficulty of examinations, administrative procedures and regulations governing the degree; second, to provide existing students with insights into the examination assessment process, with advice on examination techniques, and with additional practice in the taking of examinations through the provision of further essay/case study questions and model answers.

Accreditation

In discussing the question of accreditation, two quite separate issues arise: first, the structure and operation of university education in the UK; second, the principles which govern access to it.

With very few exceptions, UK universities are public institutions largely financed from general taxation. Degrees awarded by these universities receive worldwide acceptance because their holders are found to be well-educated in the disciplines which they have studied. The overall standard of UK Higher Education is maintained by a system of interlocking examiners, with senior faculty from one university taking responsibility for degree examination standards in sister institutions.

Some countries, notably the US, operate a different system, one in which a university is "accredited" by some outside body. This is a process in which items such as faculty numbers, libraries, playing fields and so on are checked off against some acceptable level; i.e. the inputs to the system form the criteria on which the judgement of its worth is based.

The need to be demonstrably of a certain standard arose in the US through the proliferation of small private institutions which took powers to award degrees without having the faculty or resources to maintain university-level standards. In the UK public educational institutions like Heriot-Watt University, of which there are in the UK and Northern Ireland a total of 91, receive these degree-awarding powers from Parliament, usually through the award of a Royal Charter. They do not depend upon rules and regulations determined by private institutions or associations.

Accreditation is not and has never been a feature of the UK University Education system – with the single exception of the Council for National Academic Awards (CNAA), a body which accredited polytechnic institutions lacking their own degree-awarding powers. Over the years, polytechnics have reached required university standards and have themselves been given Royal Charters. As a result, the CNAA, having fulfilled its function, has ceased to exist.

The second issue relating to accreditation is that of access to higher education.

Access has universally been restricted to a comparatively small proportion of a country's population, initially through the belief that only the 'elite' – however defined – could benefit from such an education, and more recently because resource constraints have limited the number of places available. Where the number of applicants exceeds the number of places, a selection process must by applied. It has long been recognised that the usual filter of prior academic attainment provides, at best, an uncertain estimate of eventual student performance. It continues to be used out of necessity and for want of a better alternative.

The ultimate test of a student's worth remains the final examination. Providing that examination is well constructed and meets the standards of the university for the award of a particular type or class of degree, no other criteria need be applied.

Where there are no constraints on the numbers of students admitted to a degree programme, as in one which is entirely distance learning, there is no need to limit student access to such a programme.

It is our contention that prospective MBA students are well able to decide for themselves if a Master's Degree in Business suits their needs and is within their capabilities. They are also able to select, from the multiplicity of programmes on offer, the one that will provide the best return on their investment of time and money after taking all of the significant factors into account.

Feedback from students

It is very important to us to ensure that the overall service we offer is efficient and actually provides student with what they want. In the Distance Learning environment it is difficult to obtain comprehensive information on student satisfaction on the basis of personal contact, so in January 1994 we undertook a large scale survey of student opinion in which a long questionnaire was sent to all students who had taken examinations in the December 1993 Diet. The questionnaire covered all aspects of course provision from the quality of the texts right through to the size of desk that students sit at to take examinations. In order to generate information which was amenable to processing, we asked students to rate the various aspects of the MBA on a 7 point scale, where 1 was a poor opinion and 7 was a high opinion. While the responses made it possible for us to focus on those areas where improvements could be made, in general it would appear that we have got the MBA programme just about right. An indication of the level of satisfaction expressed is reflected in the overall opinion of the courses themselves in relation to a range of characteristics: degree of coverage, enthusiasm for the subject, structure, practical applications, clarity of exposition, level of feedback, usefulness in the student's job, overall opinion of the course, and student interest in the subject matter.

Course characteristic

Coverage	*Enthusiasm*	*Structure*	*Practical*	*Clarity*	*Feedback*	*Useful*	*Interest*	*Overall*
5.6	5.3	5.5	5.2	5.4	4.9	5.2	5.7	5.4

Since the midpoint of the seven point scale is 4.0, it emerged that on average students were well satisfied with the courses in relation to all the characteristics; in fact, only a very small number of students expressed real dissatisfaction with the quality.

We also asked a large number of questions relating to our own organisational procedures, and the main finding was that while in general we achieved high ratings, a few individuals slipped through the net from time to time; given the number of students in the programme it is probably not surprising that this happens, but we do our utmost to ensure that all students receive a high quality of service.

For those students who are considering whether or not to embark on the MBA, the result of asking students why they enrolled for the distance learning method may be of some interest. Again, we asked students to rate their reasons on the seven point scale:

Reasons for taking the Distance Learning MBA (DLMBA)

	Mean rating
The flexibility of the DLMBA	6.5
The transportability of the DLMBA	5.7
The modular approach	5.4
Quality of the texts	5.0
Price	4.7
Open access	4.6
Twice yearly examinations	4.5

The dominant reason for selecting the MBA was its flexibility, followed by transportability. This is primarily because of the demanding working environment of many of our students, and the fact that they come from a highly mobile part of the population. These reasons are closely followed by the modular approach, which enables students to study individual subjects and topics when it suits them best. These results are consistent with our objective of providing an MBA education for individuals who cannot undertake the standard academic course which requires attendance at specified times at a particular insitution, and imposes an inflexible course structure dictated by the academic year.

Part I

Guidance for Students

Introduction

The purpose of this section is to anticipate and answer many of the questions which may arise during your programme. As students in a British degree programme, you may notice some differences in the way things are done compared to university customs in your area. One of the purposes of this section is to identify these differences, and to help smooth the waters between Edinburgh and the distance learners, worldwide.

In various publications which you may receive, several organizations are named. All their addresses and contact numbers are located at the end of this section. Here is a brief introduction to them:

Heriot-Watt University is the source of your MBA programme. The University is well known throughout Europe for the excellent quality of its education, particularly in business and technical fields.

The Graduate School of Business, Edinburgh Business School, Heriot-Watt University handles all of the administrative aspects of the Distance Learning MBA.

Pitman Publishing, a major British publisher of educational materials, publishes the texts for the Heriot-Watt University MBA and coordinates the efforts of the distributors who sell the courses worldwide.

Great Britain is where the University is located. Great Britain encompasses England, Scotland, Wales, and Northern Ireland, so Heriot-Watt University is both British and Scottish.

How many courses to take at a time

The most frequently-asked question by students who have decided to enter the Heriot-Watt MBA programme is, "How many courses should I take at one time?"

The most reasonable way to answer it is to assess your available time. Each compulsory course should take you roughly 150 hours of study time to complete, although the Marketing course contains more written material than the others and will therefore take you longer to work through. Each elective course should take you about 100 hours. The actual length of time will, of course, depend upon the individual student's background in the area. Once you know how much time you can spend per week on your graduate study, you can decide how long you want to take to complete the entire programme. Even the most leisurely approach should allow you to study one course at a time and complete two examinations per year. However, most students want to complete their programmes in less than five years. Many students work on two courses at a time. If you have more time available, you may wish to take three. Your best indicator will be how you get along in your first course, which is why many students decide to begin studying just one course (even if they purchase all nine at once) to gauge their own pace.

Be sure, when choosing the order in which you plan to study your courses, that you consult the examination schedule.

Your first course

When you remove your first course from its slip case, you'll find the main portion of the text in protective shrink-wrap with a number of coloured pages added on top. We suggest that you read through these pages first. They are an excellent summary of University policy in many relevant areas. In addition, there are forms you are asked to fill out (samples of which are on the following pages).

The Application for Registration

Sending in the form

Look through the coloured sheets and find the Application for Registration. This lets Heriot-Watt University know that you are on board. Fill it out and send it in as soon as you determine that you do, in fact, wish to become an MBA student. You need send in only **one** of these forms at the start of your programme (although you will find one in each course). Should you later need to write to the Director of Studies, or to any other University office, you will be in their computer system as a student. Note that you are asked to send in this application *even if you do not hold a Bachelor's degree* and thus are not technically qualified to apply for matriculation. The University will hold this application in their files until you have passed the examinations for any two of the seven compulsory courses. You will then be enrolled as a part-time Master's level student and sent your Student Matriculation Card. The University considers you "part-time", even if your intent is to take four or five examinations at the same sitting. Employers, lenders, and other universities may have different definitions.

It is possible that, based on information which you supply on forms, you may receive a request from Ms Pamela Ferguson, MBA Administrative Assistant, asking for a copy of your college transcript(s). This in no way implies that the University is questioning your qualifications. Most universities require you to send a transcript when you first apply. Heriot-Watt may simply need to know more about its students in order to respond to those agencies which oversee

British higher education. Don't stop your coursework. Just arrange to have a transcript sent directly from your former university(ies).

If you had a Bachelor's degree upon entry, or if you've passed your second examination, and haven't yet received a Student Matriculation Card, you may wish to write to Ms Pamela Ferguson to inquire when you might expect to receive yours.

Occasionally, students ask if they can get a Student ID card as soon as they sign on, whether they are able to matriculate officially or not. Unfortunately, University policy does not permit issuing Student Cards except to Matriculated (enrolled) Students.

Filling out the form

There are a few items on the Application for Registration which might need clarification.

Your surname is your last name.

Where you are asked for your date of birth, note that it says "day–month–year". That is the order in which the British, and most Europeans, give dates. For instance, many North Americans would say January 3, 1995, or write it as 1/3/95. In British usage, 1/3 /95 means March 1, 1995 (which they would write as 1 March 1995)!

Please also note that when the British want you to make a check mark in a box, they say "Please tick".

Also, American and many other degrees do not generally come in "classes". British degrees may be "first class" or "second class" or "honours". American degree holders should just leave that area on the form blank.

Be sure to have someone else certify that the picture is really you.

And read the instructions next to the Matriculation Card portion of the form. Don't fill it out – just attach a picture and sign in the space indicated.

The Student Information Form

Note that the Student Information Form goes to Pitman Publishing in London. By sending in this form you are not just getting on another mailing list. Pitman Publishing will not sell the names thus generated. However, also note that *you have to mail it in an envelope, if you are outside Great Britain, and you must pay international postage.*

Change of address

If you change your address during the course of the programme, please notify Heriot-Watt University, Pitman Publishing, and your local agent. Information relevant to students of the Distance Learning MBA Programme can come from any of these sources, and you want to be certain of receiving any future notices promptly.

APPLICATION FOR MATRICULATION FORM

IF YOU ARE NOT ALREADY A MATRICULATED STUDENT OF HERIOT-WATT UNIVERSITY YOU MUST COMPLETE THIS FORM ONCE IN BLOCK CAPITALS

Serial number

Please affix a current passport-type photograph **The certificate of authenticity has to be completed by someone other than the applicant.**

I certify that the above photograph is a true likeness of the applicant

Signature

Name

Address

Occupation

1. Last name			
2. Other names			
3. Former last name (if any)			
4. Date of birth	**Day**	**Month**	**Year**
5. Title (Dr, Mr, Ms etc.)			
6. Sex (Please tick)		**Male**	**Female**
7. Marital status (Please tick)		**Married**	**Single**
8. Country of birth			
9. County and country of permanent residence			
10. Nationality			
11. (a) Permanent Home Address **Telephone No.**			
11. (b) Correspondence Address (if different) Telephone No.		Fax No.	

NOTE TO STUDENT

Part-time Student Matriculation Card
Please affix a passport-type photograph to the card and add your signature in the space provided. **PLEASE LEAVE THE REST OF THE CARD BLANK**. The University will complete the card and return it to you.

Heriot-Watt University
Part-time student
Matriculation Card

Matriculation number:

Last name:

Other name(s):

Date of expiry:

Signature of student:

Please affix a current passport-type photograph

Please note: Only one of the Application for Matriculation forms need be completed per student.

Please return this form to Edinburgh Business School, The Graduate School of Business, Heriot-Watt University, Edinburgh EH14 4AS.

12. Degrees/Diplomas/other qualifications

Names of university/ college/institution	*Dates From*	*To*	*Title of qualification obtained/to be obtained*	*Class of degree*	*Date awarded/ to be awarded*

13. Please give details of above qualification (e.g. classes, projects)

14. Is English your native language? (Please tick) ☐ Yes ☐ No

The UK Higher Education Statistics Authority (HESA) has requested Heriot-Watt University to collect data on ethnic origin and disability for all students. This is not compulsory but please complete the following if you wish.

15. Ethnicity Please identify your ethnic origin ______________________

16. Disability

(a) Are you registered as disabled? (Please tick) ☐ Yes ☐ No

(b) Please give your disability ______________________

Please attach certified copy of your qualifications for verification.

Declaration:

1. I certify that the information above is correct to the best of my knowledge.
2. I understand that a matriculated student is required to abide by the regulations of the University and to conform to its discipline.

Signature of applicant ______________________ Date ______________

For Heriot-Watt University use only. Classification: PN6_____Course: 31137

Matriculated part-time students are personally liable for all obligations incurred in using this card

EXAMINATION REQUEST FORM

Do not cut up this form
Complete *all three* sections in block capitals. Please provide *three* photographs. Please sign *all three* forms.

Serial No.

Last name: ____________________

Other Name(s): ____________________

Address: (for correspondence) ____________________

____

Preferred Examination Location (please indicate nearest large city): ____________

Signature ____________________

Please affix a current passport-type photograph

- -

Serial No.

Last name: ____________________

Other Name(s): ____________________

Address: (for correspondence) ____________________

____

Preferred Examination Location (please indicate nearest large city): ____________

Signature ____________________

Please affix a current passport-type photograph

- -

Serial No.

Last name: ____________________

Other Name(s): ____________________

Address: (for correspondence) ____________________

____

Preferred Examination Location (please indicate nearest large city): ____________

Signature ____________________

Please affix a current passport-type photograph

- -

Examination Fee Remittance Advice (where applicable)

Payment must be in £ sterling
The examination fee for each course to be examined is £55* sterling. Please enclose £55* or simply quote the serial number of any course purchased before 1 January 1992. ____________

I enclose a cheque (payable to Heriot-Watt University) for £ ____________

Alternatively, please debit my credit/debit card: ACCESS ☐ MASTERCARD ☐ VISA ☐ SWITCH ☐

Card No. ____________ Expiry Date ____________

Signature ____________

Please return this form *complete* to Edinburgh Business School, The Graduate School of Business, Heriot-Watt University, Edinburgh EH14 4AS, UK

* Price subject to review without notice

Please see overleaf for important information.

NOTIFICATION OF CHANGE OF ADDRESS/NAME FORM

Serial Number

(Please use capitals)

Previous Details	**Revised Details as from** ____________ (date)
Title: Dr / Mr / Mrs / Miss / Ms*	Title: Dr / Mr / Mrs / Miss / Ms*
Initials:	Initials:
Surname:	Surname:
Job title:	Job title:
Business / Correspondence Address:*	Business / Correspondence Address:*
Daytime Telephone Number:	Daytime Telephone Number:
Fax Number:	Fax Number:
Home / Correspondence Address:*	Home / Correspondence Address:*

From what organisation did you buy your course manual? Pitman Publishing / Local Distributor or Agent*

If Distributor or Agent, what was the name? ______________________________

(*Please delete as appropriate)

Please return to the address overleaf.

STUDENT INFORMATION FORM

Serial Number

Please complete and return this form to the address overleaf.

This will ensure you are kept fully up-to-date with the latest information from Heriot-Watt University and/or the Publishers, Pitman Publishing, on courses, examinations and other items of interest to you.

(Please use capitals)

Title: Dr / Mr / Mrs / Ms* Initials: Surname:

Job Title:

Business / Correspondence Address:*

Daytime Telephone Number: Fax Number:

Home / Correspondence Address:*

Are you self-funded or company sponsored? Self / Company / Both*

Age* (*optional*): 21–25 / 26–35 / 36–45 / 46+

Sex: Male / Female

Did you purchase your course materials direct from Pitman Publishing? Yes / No*

If "No", what was the name of the Distributor or Agent who supplied you? ______________________

(*Please delete as appropriate)

Please ensure you complete and return the Notification of Change of Address / Name Form enclosed with this pack if and when necessary.

The examinations

Since the examination you take at the end of each course is the source of your grade, we will spend a fair amount of time discussing the examination procedures.

The Examination Form

The coloured pages at the front of your course also include a Notice of Examination Request. Students all over the world will take the examination for Economics, for example, on the same day, as close to the same time as is reasonable. The series of examinations is called a "diet of examinations" in Scotland.

An application to take an examination must be in the hands of the University *by March 1 for the June examinations, and by September 1 for the December examinations.* The reason they need so much advance notice is that at each examination time there is a different array of students, worldwide, planning to take the examinations. The University does not begin to set up examination sites or hire proctors (which they call "invigilators") to administer the examinations until all the requests are in and they can do it efficiently, combining sites when possible. Please do not wait until the last minute to register for your examinations. Dates for examinations are set three or four years in advance, thus you can plan the order in which to take the examinations.

Yes, you must send three photos in with *each* application to take an examination. If you are taking three examinations, you will need nine photos. On occasion, Heriot-Watt must contract with a different proctor for each examination, even if the site at which the examinations are given remains the same throughout the series. Each proctor is responsible for the records and examinations of each sitting and needs to have a photo of each student for verification. Photos must be the same sort of full head shots that are used on passport applications. The three photos on each application must be identical; no snap-shots, please.

Notice that there is a place to suggest Preferred Examination Location. Examinations are given at major colleges and universities all over the world. You may give the name of a nearby city, including the name of the state or province it is in as well. Your preferences will be taken into consideration when the examination sites are being set up, but since Heriot-Watt will be trying to accommodate as many students as efficiently as possible, there is, of course, no guarantee that you will be assigned to the university nearest to you. A word of advice: **Don't** write in a university name where the form asks for your "preferred examination location". Heriot-Watt must follow certain guidelines to be as fair as possible. They can't appear to be serving one student's interests above another. (And there is always the concern that a student might have some connection at the local university testing centre that is being suggested.)

We strongly recommend that you send your examination registration forms by registered mail, requesting a return receipt or an acknowledgement receipt, or that you use a courier service such as UPS or DHL. The University will notify you that they have received your forms; however, this acknowledgement may be sent any time during the month following the deadline to apply. They will, of course, tell you where to go to take your examination, but since those arrangements may take up to eight weeks to complete, you will not know for certain that you are scheduled to take an examination until well past the time when anything can be done to include you if your forms were lost in the mail. If you do not get your return receipt back within three or four weeks, it would be appropriate to communicate with The Graduate School of Business, to make sure they received your forms. Heriot-Watt University **must** have your forms in hand for you to be permitted to take the examination.

Your course has a serial number listed on the examination, registration, and information forms. This number is yours, and will never be reissued to another student. We suggest that you keep a record of your course numbers in a safe place just in case your actual courses or the forms are lost or destroyed. Confirmation of your student status and replacement of the forms will be made easier if you can supply your course numbers.

Scheduling your examinations

The examinations are given during a one week period. This means that two or more examinations can be scheduled for the same day at the same time. Be sure to check the examination schedule before signing up for multiple examinations.

Notice also that these examination dates are set by the University in Britain. Unfortunately, it means that holidays which may occur in other countries all over the world cannot be taken into account in setting up the examinations. There is no way around this. Fortunately, arrangements must be made far in advance of all these examination dates, so you will know if your examination falls on a national holiday. You may well decide to plan your examination taking to avoid those days. Since fewer examination sites may be available on national holidays, you may have to travel further to your examination.

It is essential that you plan well ahead. Deciding when you will take your examination for a course will help you plan your study time, and will act as a strong incentive to keep to your study schedule. For security reasons, examination dates cannot be changed, no matter how valid a student's reason might be. If you cannot take your examination on the given date, you will simply have to postpone it until the next "diet" in six months.

If your examination site is not satisfactory

Occasionally, through oversight, students are assigned to an examination site which is too distant to make a reasonable commute possible. If this happens to you, notify The Graduate School of Business as soon as you can.

Sending examination fees

The fees must be paid in British pounds sterling. Prepare for this payment early on. Do not wait until two weeks before the examination registration closes to figure out how to send in your examination fees! The simplest way to send examination fees is to pay by credit card, if you have a Visa or MasterCard. The amount is charged in pounds in Edinburgh, but the charge appears in your own currency on your statement. If you do not use either card, you might find that making an arrangement with a family member or friend to charge your examination fee is the simplest solution. Note that some forms list VISA or ACCESS. ACCESS is what the Europeans call MasterCard, but just to keep things straight, write in MasterCard before you write your card number down so they are clear about what card you are using.

If you cannot arrange to make your payment by credit card, you will to do some research to determine the most economical way to pay your fees in British pounds. Here are some suggestions: try your local bank first to see if you can obtain a bank draft in pounds sterling to cover the examination fee. Ask what they will charge you for this. Some banks with a lot of international business charge very nominal fees. Others can charge a rather large fee to convert local currency into pounds. Other possibilities include buying an International Money Order at the post office, buying British pound travellers' cheques from American Express or Thomas Cook. *Do not send cash.*

If you decide not to take an examination

Write or fax Ms Pamela Ferguson at The Graduate School of Business (fax number +44–131–451–3002) as soon as you reach your decision. If you notify The Graduate School of Business by 1st May for the June examinations, or by 1st November for the December examinations, your examination fee will be retained by the University and applied to the next diet of examinations you attend. If you notify The Graduate School of Business after this, your examination fee is forfeited. Your Prospectus may say that the cancellation deadline for a refund of examination fees is thirty days prior to the examination, but the new rule, which is now in force, is the 1st of the preceding month.

If you simply do not turn up, you forfeit the examination fee. It is not considered a failure. You can sign up and pay another fee at a subsequent examination series. But The Graduate School of Business would greatly appreciate your notifying them, even if it is a day or two before the examination, that you will not be taking it. They can then notify the testing centre, and perhaps (if you're the only scheduled examination-taker) avoid wasting the time and effort of the examination proctor.

Note that you cannot walk out of the examination once you have seen the examination. Even if you have not started working on it, the examination will be considered a failure.

To re-register for an examination

When you decide to take the examination you missed, write a letter to The Graduate School of Business, giving the serial number of your course and stating that you wish to re-register for an examination. If you failed on your first try, or if you notified them after the deferment deadline, include the fee (£55 for the 1995 diet of examinations). You may include a preferred examination location (as on your examination form). Review the section above on examination registration and sending examination fees. Feel free to telephone your distributor's office if you have questions about the procedure.

Exam protocols

All examinations are three hours long. Government and Industry, Marketing, Strategic Planning, and Negotiation are all essay and/or case study questions; the others are approximately two-thirds essay/case study and one-third multiple choice questions. Consult the sample examination section at the end of your course (and in this book) for more specific information.

Minor changes may be made from examination to examination in order to make levels of difficulty the same. Any major change will be notified to students.

You may use a non-programmable financial calculator in the examinations. The examination proctor can ask to examine the one you've brought. (You can't bring in a programmable one and say you haven't programmed it.)

The University has said, "Statistical tables will be provided where necessary. A formula sheet is provided in Quantitative Methods; formulae for other courses must be memorized. The more complex ones will not be asked for."

Special needs

Heriot-Watt has been outstanding in responding to students with special needs. Such students often choose distance learning programmes because they are unable to attend regular classes. Students with physical handicaps, students who are incarcerated, and students who live in geographically remote locations have all been successfully accommodated. The key is to make your situation known as soon as you begin the programme, by writing to Ms Pamela Ferguson at The Graduate School of Business, detailing your situation, so the University can respond to the constraints under which your examinations may have to be offered.

Blind students can arrange help in taking examinations (having the questions read aloud, for example). They will have to arrange payment for helpers and they may incur additional proctoring fees in the event that a second proctor and a private room is needed to avoid disturbing other students taking the examination. If you have a medical condition, authenticated by a doctor's statement, which would make it impossible for you to complete an examination in three hours, that, too, can be worked around.

Cheating

A student found cheating on an examination will have the grades of all examinations taken to that date annulled. The University is very serious about this. Don't even think about jeopardizing your future in this way.

Grades

Examination results

The results of all examinations will be sent to the student directly, approximately six weeks after the end of the diet of examinations. You cannot telephone for your results. You should allow another week for mail to reach you from Scotland. However, if you took an examination in June and you haven't heard by 1st September, or you haven't had December examination results by 1st March, you may contact the University to inquire.

You should know that there are good reasons why it takes so long to grade these examinations. A unique feature of British university education is the fact that examinations are monitored not only by the faculty in the university at which the student is enrolled, but also by an External Examiner, a distinguished faculty member from another university. This ensures that examinations are equivalent throughout Britain in terms of the content tested and the grading standards applied. The External Examiner reads a random sample of the papers and all marginal cases, so that you are assured of as fair a judgement as possible.

Transcripts

Transcripts are available upon request from the University. Write to The Graduate School of Business for details.

Because of the international nature of the student body, the results are given in categories as follows. A score of 50% correct on an examination is a "Pass". In common with American graduate programmes, only students receiving the equivalent of a letter grade of "B" are considered to have passed. Here are the equivalent percent of correct answers and letter grades:

A = 65% or above
B = 50–64%
C = 45–49%

A transcript of your record, for which there is no charge, will just tell within which percentage range your grade fell (i.e., Economics – 50 – 64%). For £5, you can get an exact numerical score for one course. For £8 they will send you all the exact scores of your examinations (and thus of your course grades) to date. Write to Ms Pamela Ferguson to request these.

Students have asked what the equivalent in semester units would be for each course. Although British universities do not operate under that system, Heriot-Watt University has determined that each course in the Heriot-Watt Distance Learning MBA programme is the equivalent of 4 semester units of graduate study.

Failure

It does happen. This is a rigorous graduate programme, and occasionally a student feels ready for the examination but just has not prepared quite well enough. You do get a second chance, and the fact that you needed two tries to pass the course will not show up on your records. Remember what they call the one who graduates at the bottom of the class in medical school? Right – they call him (or her) "Doctor". You can learn from your experience and do better next time. In fact, students who fail an examination get feedback in the form of an analysis of the essay portions of their examination papers to help understand what needs to be done the next time.

Any student failing one of the core courses should seriously consider buying and using the software which is available for each of those courses, if that has not already been done. The software packages were designed to provide alternative methods of presentation for many of the ideas covered in the courses, and a more hands-on approach which many people find of great help in assimilating and retaining information.

However, there is a cold hard reality to acknowledge here, too. If you fail one of the seven compulsory courses for a second time, the University policy is that there is no third chance. If circumstances which were truly beyond your control caused your failure, it is possible to initiate an appeal process to the University. For example, someone suffering a coronary incident during the examination itself can apply for permission to try the examination again. The University will ask for proof of the circumstances, including a medical certificate relating to the date of the examination (where relevant) to be supplied within one month of the examination date for which you were scheduled. (If you fail an elective course twice, you cannot take that course again, but you can take other electives and complete the degree.) Not withstanding these statements, any student who has demonstrated his or her ability to profit from the programme by obtaining several compulsory passes, will not normally be required to leave the programme by reason of the two-fail rule.

Students may *not* purchase the course a second time and re-register. However, if you have completed any of the courses, you do not leave empty-handed. Because Heriot-Watt is a public, i.e. government-funded university, you may present your transfer credits from the Heriot-Watt programme to another university and probably have at least some courses waived in another MBA programme. Since different universities allow different amounts of credit transfer, be sure to shop around for your best next move.

Transferring credits

Because Heriot-Watt has the Royal Charter, it is considered the equivalent of, for example, an American university with regional accreditation. Thus credits earned through Heriot-Watt should be accepted by any accredited institution of higher learning. However, you should know that universities are highly independent institutions, in many cases making their own rules regarding academic matters. How many credit units may be transferred (or if transfer credits are awarded at all) is up to the individual school. Most departments set a maximum number of credits which can be transferred in and applied towards a degree programme. Since that department will be awarding the degree, they claim the right to do most of the educating that results in the awarding of the diploma. If you anticipate the possibility of using the credits earned in your Heriot-Watt MBA programme for another school's degree, do research your options carefully. Different schools accept different numbers of transfer credits. A few universities are still stubbornly holding on to the idea that education can only happen when students sit in rows in a classroom and are lectured to by a professor. Such schools will not accept units earned through distance learning no matter how rigorous the programme or prestigious the school from which it comes. Fortunately, there are not too many schools with this attitude.

Exemptions

The Heriot-Watt University Distance Learning MBA consists of nine courses. In very select cases, students may be granted an exemption from no more than two of the seven compulsory courses. Note that exemptions are granted *only* for the compulsory courses. You must take two electives from the ones offered. You can use this as an opportunity to refine your knowledge in an area with which you are already familiar, or explore one which is new to you.

Some exemptions are automatic; most are not. If, for instance, you are a Chartered Accountant (British) or a CPA in the US or CGA (in Canada) you will not have to take Quantitative Methods or Accounting. The University has examined the requirements for several other professional qualifications (Certified Financial Planner and Certified Computer Professional) and determined that these do not qualify for exemptions.

Exemptions for specific courses are not easily come by. If you have taken and successfully passed a body of undergraduate courses (two or more in one subject) or one or two graduate level courses which you believe to be the equivalent of Heriot-Watt courses, you may send a copy of your transcript with a letter of explanation to the Director of Studies at The Graduate School of Business, Edinburgh Business School, Heriot-Watt University. (Please see the Application for Exemption form in the prelims to each course.) The more detailed the information you send regarding the course(s) the better your chances of being granted an exemption. Including a detailed syllabus of the course (exactly what was covered), what work outside of class was required, the name of the textbook and any additional books you were required to read, would be a good idea.

Rarely, you would simply be told that you had been granted an exemption. More commonly, the University would invite you to take an exemption examination – to establish your proficiency by taking the regularly scheduled examinations for up to two such courses. In other words, you would take the examination without buying or reading the course material. If you pass the examination, you do not have to pay for or take the course. If you do not pass the examination, you must then buy and take the course. These exemption examinations do not count as one of the two chances a student has to pass the examination for a course. In other words, if you fail this "challenge" examination, you can still take the regular course examination twice.

If the University has any reservations about the quality of the institution issuing your transcript, they may simply require you to take the courses.

Some students have asked if courses which were exempt show up on a transcript: transcripts show courses passed and courses exempted.

Advice to students on the taking of examinations

In the Distance Learning MBA examinations, the "no choice in the selection of questions to be answered" and the rigorous process by which examination questions are approved by external examiners, are designed to ensure that students who receive a passing certificate have mastered the subject in question. The practice final examinations and solutions to questions contained in the texts are designed as self-test instruments to indicate to students how well prepared they are to sit the final examinations. Despite such procedures and in light of the 10,000 examinations attempted (with a pass rate of 74%) plus the cumulated reports of the internal and external examiners, it is becoming increasingly obvious that some advice to students is opportune. Why? Because there appears to be empirical evidence to support the hypothesis that a minority of students are failing in courses, not because the students do not know the material but because of misallocation of scarce time during the sitting of the examinations.

The most obvious evidence of misallocation is the practice of some students of re-writing the questions themselves in the examination booklet. This practice, presumably based on habits inherited from school or university life, consumes scarce examination time and contributes nothing to students' scores. The folly of this practice is reinforced when the student appends a note "insufficient time to complete the examination".

But such appended notes also appear in examination scripts when the questions themselves are not repeated but when a written answer of 8 pages on a case study worth a maximum of 20 points is accompanied by one half of one page of writing for an essay question worth 40 points.

So how should you, as a student, allocate your scarce examination time to achieve the highest mark or maximize the probability of a passing performance?

Surprisingly, given the heterogeneous nature of students, there is a unique solution. The solution requires the use of marginal analysis, familiar to students who have studied the Economics course. For those who have not, consider the following table which records the marks a student will achieve in a two-hour examination for different allocations of examination time between Multiple Choice Questions (maximum score 40 points) and an essay question (maximum score 100 points). Passing performance requires 70 points (50%).

Examination Scores

Multiple Choice Questions		*Essay Questions*		
Time spent (minutes)	*Score*	*Time spent (minutes)*	*Score*	*Total score*
120	33	0	0	33
100	32	20	23	55
80	29	40	38	67
60	25	60	48	73
40	20	80	55	75
20	11	100	58	69
0	0	120	60	60

If two hours are allocated to the Multiple Choice Questions, the total score will be 33 points – a fail; conversely if the Multiple Choice Questions are ignored and the 2 hours are allocated to the essay question the score will be 60 points, also a fail.

The secret of marginal analysis is discovering the best use of, in this example, the last 20 minutes of the two-hour (120 minutes) examination time. Consider, for example, the allocation of 80 minutes to Multiple Choice Questions and 40 minutes to the essay, yielding a total score of 67 points. Is this optimal? No. If you spend 20 minutes less on Multiple Choice Questions you lose 4 points (29 – 25); but the additional 20 minutes allocated to the essay raises your essay score from 38 to 48, i.e. a gain of 10 points. Thus your total score increases by 6 points from the reallocation and a marginal fail of 67 points becomes a pass of 73 points. You can do even better, scoring 75 points in total, if you allocate a further 20 minutes to the essay, gaining 7 more points (55 – 48) at the cost of 5 points in the Multiple Choice Questions (25 – 20). The same principle holds for the 3-hour examinations with more than 2 sections.

But, you may argue, with some justification, "I do not know how many additional points I would gain by reallocating time, at the margin, among questions". Unfortunately we do not know either, but we can tell you that only 5 students, out of 10,000 examination scripts examined, have passed in a subject in which they did not answer a case or essay worth 20% of the total points.

Now there is a high probability that during the examination day:

- you would be able to answer some questions unasked better than the questions set;
- the written examination process is not the ideal measuring rod of your understanding and potential;
- family or business pressures have upset your preparation and concentration; or
- you are nervous and uncertain about everything.

Be that as it may you still have to tackle examinations set by the University whose last wish is to fail you if you are proficient in the subject but who must ignore all "extraneous" factors to preserve the validity of the Heriot-Watt University MBA degree.

So what advice can we offer?

1. Do not write out the questions asked *unless* this focuses your concentration and produces a better answer – highly unlikely.
2. Write a brief outline of your answers. This can serve two purposes: it can help to avoid duplication and it can allow you to transfer an idea which you had thought would fit one question to another.
3. Concentrate on the question asked, i.e. avoid extraneous material in your answers to cases and essays.
4. With Multiple Choice Questions do not leave any question unanswered. Since it takes time to read the question and evaluate the options and time is scarce, many Multiple Choice Question examiners believe it pays students to choose the option they believe correct at the first reading. Only if time permits when the cases/essays are completed should the "doubtful" Multiple Choice Questions be revisited.
5. Write clearly and concisely.
6. In many cases diagrams and mathematics serve as useful shorthand methods of communication. When using diagrams, remember to label the axes and graphs.

Deadline for completion

From the day you pass your first examination, you have seven years to complete the MBA. For new students, this may seem impossibly far away, and in fact most will finish much sooner than that. However, some students in graduate school at Heriot-Watt or almost any other school may find themselves with that deadline looming closer and closer because of a demanding job, illness, family situations, or for other reasons. If you encounter the kind of emergency which puts an overwhelming obstacle in your path, you can apply for a leave of absence from the programme. However, it would be best if you just filed this information away as a sign that the University does try to work with students who find themselves in difficult situations. Seven years is plenty of time to complete your programme: with foresight, efficiency, and a little good fortune, you will be done long before the deadline.

Graduation

Graduation is not an automatic process once you've finished your last examination. You must fill out a form the University will send you once the Senate of the University reviews your records and votes to award the degree (a process which cannot be rushed). Return the form with the Graduation Fee. Finishing with a December examination means you'll be ready to graduate in July. But even if you qualify for a November graduation, you are welcome to put off your appearance on campus until the following summer and to participate in the summer Convocation, and combine it with a vacation. You can graduate *in Absentia*, but you still have to pay the fee, or you won't be listed in their records as having completed graduation. They will mail you your diploma after the graduation ceremonies if you choose not to attend.

The graduation ceremony is quite a splendid and gala one, and can be the focus and centre point of a wonderful holiday in Scotland. Edinburgh is a beautiful old city, and only a few hours by train or car from the grandeur of the Highlands and Islands.

Changes in the MBA programme

Some students have expressed concern about the possibility that the University will change its rules and regulations "mid-stream", such as requiring an additional course, or making substantial changes in the content of a course. The University will make no significant changes to the Distance Learning MBA Programme without a seven-year notice, so that anyone already in the programme will not be affected by the changes.

Financial aid

Perhaps you have already begun your MBA programme by buying a course on your own, but are beginning to wonder if you should have looked harder for some financial help. If you are employed, it cannot hurt to approach your employer (or the personnel or training officer) and discuss the possibility of tuition reimbursement. Even companies without formal tuition aid plans may still be willing to consider paying, since there may be considerable tax advantages for them in so doing.

Many tuition plans are run strictly by reimbursement: the student pays the required fees, takes the courses, and presents evidence of satisfactory completion. The reimbursement is a kind of reward. Each student passing an examination receives a certificate affirming successful completion of that particular course which can be used to claim reimbursement if support is being given on a per-course basis.

The certificates of completion you receive for each course examination successfully passed may also be of help. If you need to approach a bank somewhere along the line to acquire a loan to get that home computer you want, clear evidence in hand of your success to date may stand you in good stead.

Distance learning: suggestions and resources

Students who are new to distance learning may feel anxious about being “on their own”. At least in a residential programme, if you don’t understand something, you can wait until the next class meeting and ask the teacher, or perhaps consult with a fellow student.

Distance Learning (at least in the British model) is not the same as “taking correspondence courses”. Over ten years and hundreds of thousands of pounds went into creating the Heriot-Watt University Distance Learning MBA as a stand-alone programme. That means you have, in your course materials, everything you need to prepare yourself to pass the final examination. The programme is not set up to offer students the opportunity to enter into a correspondence relationship with the professors who wrote the materials or who teach it on an on-going basis on campus.

The courses are entirely self-contained, which means you can pass the examinations with just what is given in the text material you have received. However, some of the texts do contain references for further reading which are given to enable students to develop their understanding of particular concepts beyond what is needed for examination purposes.

The student help line

If you have a specific question about a particular point raised in your text (for example, it seems to contradict something else you have just learned in the book) you can use the Student Help Line to help resolve it.

And here, a word to the wise: many students are used to just picking up the telephone and calling someone to ask a question. You would do much better to write or fax your question to Ms Pamela Ferguson at The Graduate School of Business. With a written question in hand, Ms Ferguson can locate the appropriate person, get an answer in writing, and get back to you. That is the way the system was set up to work, and it works best that way. A fax will get to the right person just as quickly and more reliably than a telephoned message can. Often, questions related to course content are referred directly to one of the course authors, who may be at a university in the US, France, or elsewhere in the world.

If you would just like to know more about the subject you are studying, a number of alternatives are available.

The software option

If you have not purchased the software to supplement your text, consider doing so. The software relates directly to the work you are doing with the same emphases, vocabulary, and structure.

In addition, there are always books available from university libraries and bookstores. If you find yourself within range of a university which offers an MBA, you might benefit from a browse in the business section of their bookstore. Seeing what other textbooks have to say about a particular area which either interests or troubles you in your own programme can be very revealing. But we want to stress that additional texts are not needed to complete your Heriot-Watt MBA successfully.

Previous years' exams

These are contained in this book.

The student link network

If you're feeling isolated, consider participating in the Student Link Network. A modest number of students have joined the Student Network through Pitman Publishing in England. If you'd like to join that list, write to Ms Yvonne Mitchell at Pitman Publishing. She will be happy to send you a list of the names, addresses, and phone numbers of all students who have agreed to be a part of this network.

Other approaches

We've heard from a few students, particularly ones with little university work, that the mathematical components of the courses were harder than expected. The simple fact is that business runs by the numbers. To be an effective manager in a business of any size, you will need to be able to understand, collect, manipulate, arrange, interpret, and present data in numerical form. Whether you are writing a business plan for a new venture or helping higher management evaluate personnel, there will be times when you need to have a tool kit of mathematical applications to help convey information (and convince people whom you wish to convince).

One student, owner of a small business, who found herself taking far too long to feel comfortable with the work required in Quantitative Methods, came up with an excellent idea. She telephoned the business school at her local university and asked if they might recommend a graduate student who would be willing to tutor her. Graduate students are generally eager to supplement their fellowships by using the very stuff they are studying, and our student was given a list of names to call. She found someone who was sympathetic to her request and who, she felt, enabled her to work through the Quantitative Methods course twice as fast and with a much higher degree of comprehension than working alone.

Once you have mastered the material in the Quantitative Methods course, you should be well-equipped to deal with whatever maths you encounter in the rest of your MBA programme. Time spent on Quantitative Methods is well spent.

If numbers pose no particular challenge for you, but you feel you would like more help in general: help in setting up your study schedule, advice on doing this whole process well, some hints on staying motivated – addressing those concerns early on is an excellent idea.

Preparing for examinations

Students who have no special concerns about working through the text material may wonder if there is anything else they should know about preparing for examinations.

The best advice is, of course, to work efficiently through the textbook, leaving at least one week before the examination date for a thorough review. The material has been arranged to help reinforce your learning of the important points. Take advantage of Review and Discussion questions to assess your learning as you go along, and return to these questions during your examination preparation.

When studying for your examination, use the Table of Contents and Summary Points for each chapter to refresh your memory concerning the area to be addressed.

The Practice Final Examinations and Worked Solutions, at the back of your loose-leaf text and contained in this book, are your best guide to what to expect. It is worth the time and effort to set yourself up as if you were really in the examination setting. Give yourself three hours to do the examination. Go over the answers carefully when scoring your results. If you are really concerned about your ability to perform effectively in the examination, you may wish to schedule your study so that there is plenty of time between finishing the text and taking the practice examination, to go over portions of the material which were not clear or which you had difficulty retaining.

Remember that there are thousands of people all over the world taking and passing these examinations. You will want to do your best, but you might consider that your first examination is really a learning experience. If you do not do as well as you had hoped, you will get another chance.

Answer all the questions!

It seems so obvious, but the University has found that many of those who fail the examinations do so not because they are unfamiliar with the material, but simply because they do not answer all the questions. If an examination has five essay
questions, there are people who write good answers to two or three of the five, and do not answer the other two or three at all. The answer, of course, is to budget your time at the start of the examination, and stick with your budget. If there are five essay questions in three hours (180 minutes), you might decide to spend 30 minutes on each, and then have a final 30 minutes to go back and modify or expand on some of the answers. Again, taking practice examinations will give you a much better sense of how to use your test time well.

Organizing your study time

Tell people what you are doing. Tell your friends, your family, your co-workers, if that is comfortable, and even your employer. Tell them that it is important to you, that it is for a limited time, and that you will do your best to maintain all your obligations during the course of the programme. There will, however, be times when you will have to make choices and the hard ones are not "Do I take my Finance examination or go to my sister's wedding?" Big conflicts usually surface in time to deal with them. Emergency situations (such as an illness or an accident) which require you to postpone an examination and/or take time out from your studying can be accommodated by working things out between yourself and the University. You have seven years to complete the programme from the date of your first "Pass" on your first examination and you should be able to do it in far less time.

The difficult conflicts are the little ones: time studying is time away from family, from routine contact with friends, from your own little pleasures and rewards. You will have to give up something to do this. It may even be that for a time you have to give up doing extra work on your job. Letting your employer know why you're not working on a Saturday, or working overtime, is a good idea.

Once you are established publicly as a serious student, you need to stick to it. Set yourself a schedule. It will make things easier on those who used to be able to get your attention at any time. When you overhear someone say, "Don't bother Daddy now; he's busy studying," or "Forget Susan for Saturday; she does her MBA stuff on weekend mornings," you will know you are being taken seriously. Now you really have to do it!

If at all possible, arrange a regular place to study. Have a good light, a comfortable chair, and a place to keep your materials. When you go there, you will soon find yourself preprogrammed to do your work. It is worth a lot of effort to arrange a door between yourself and possible distractions, if at all possible.

Do not neglect your physical health during your graduate programme. You are taking on the equivalent of a part-time job and you need the energy to do it well. If you are out of shape and worn out by the end of your regular workday, you will simply fall asleep over your open text. Learning new material takes attention, and you need to be able to pay attention well in the limited time you have for study.

Consider setting up a way to get regular exercise for the time you will be involved in the MBA programme. If it is not a thing you do presently, you will come out of the programme with an MBA *and* a good start on a long life to enjoy the benefits of your advanced degree. Your fitness programme can be as simple as a brisk forty-five-minute walk three times a week. Or you can decide to get really serious about it: define the time you could spend on fitness. Shop around for a gym, exercise studio, or even a personal trainer to help you make maximum use of that time, and commit yourself to sticking with a routine as long as you are doing your MBA.

Ultimately, the best advice is simply to keep in touch with your own progress as you go through a course. Keep a regular study schedule, either by studying for a certain number of hours or covering a certain number of pages of material per week. Admit when you have difficulty and look for help. Remember that learning from printed materials and taking examinations can be challenging if you have been away from school for some years. These efforts call upon skills you may have shelved years ago. But they can be relearned. Thousands of people, worldwide, are advancing themselves in their business careers through the Heriot-Watt Distance Learning MBA programme. You are among a distinguished group. Receiving your degree will confirm your place among that elite group of self-motivated, capable, well-trained business people.

Going on to a doctorate

Some students have inquired about the possibility of studying for a doctoral degree after the MBA. In the UK, the MBA is not regarded as a suitable degree for preparation for doctoral studies. Most schools consider the MBA a "terminal degree". Most people in business consider mastery of the field a sufficient academic qualification. It is considered at least as important to prove oneself by achieving a measure of success in the business world. But prospective students ask whether they can go on for a Doctorate with a Heriot-Watt MBA. Some are just trying to keep all the options open. If business success does not follow in a few years, such students might wish to consider teaching. At university level a Ph.D. is necessary for most entry-level teaching positions. However, the US model of a taught programme followed by a dissertation and defence is seldom found in the UK. Doctorates are customarily research degrees, and have as a pre-requisite a research degree at Master's level (M.Sc. or M. Phil.).

Heriot-Watt University in Scotland, in common with most UK universities, does not offer a distance learning Doctorate. Individual departments offer facilities to doctoral students whose research proposals are approved by the faculty. Such students would also, as a rule, be expected to do some undergraduate teaching.

In terms of further study in the US and Canada, you should know, however that the situation described in the previous section, Transferring Credits (see p.1/16), is even more pronounced with regard to applying a Master's from one school towards a Doctorate from another. The School of Business or Business Department of each university is in charge of choosing the students to whom they offer admission. There is usually a subsidiary person, or a committee, charged with considering whether to allow transfer credits into a doctoral programme on a case-by-case basis. These days many schools admit students directly into a doctoral programme from the Bachelor's level. The students are expected to complete the equivalent of a Master's degree in coursework and, often, a series of written and oral examinations. At that point (which is usually at least two years along in the process), the Master's degree is awarded and the student begins independent, guided research on the project which will result in a dissertation some years down the line. A student who begins a doctoral programme with a Master's in hand may find that although credits are granted there may be no allowance for the courses taken. Schools often claim the right to do the educating which leads to the granting of their degrees. In addition, some schools will not even consider awarding transfer credits until you have completed a full year of coursework and they can evaluate the quality of your work on their own terms. You can try bargaining, but they hold all the cards and it is unwise to begin the difficult and demanding route through graduate school in an adversarial relationship with your department. Do your research and bargaining before you enroll and get the best deal you can.

Finally, consider the idea that in thinking about a Doctorate, you are actually thinking about going into a different line of work. You want an MBA to further your business career. The Doctorate is actually the entry into the field of academia, which can be a very different country. The people in charge of that country by and large feel that if you want to join their ranks, you ought to undergo the kind of training they did, which includes entering completely into the academic process in a residential programme for a period of time. Since, as an academic you would be training other potential academics, the idea may be that there are things you need to learn about the whole academic system, not just about the subject you're hoping to teach, that you need to know to do your job well. They may have a point. So you may find that your distance learning credential will need much more defence in academia than in business. Your perseverance and ability to learn independently will be respected, but you will have to prove that you can also fit in to an institutional (university) setting.

Studying on campus

All of the MBA programmes offered by Heriot-Watt University assume that students will be employed. This means that on-campus programmes take place on Mondays and Fridays. Full-time students attend both full days; part-time students attend classes on either of these days, or a combination of them. The academic year runs from September to July.

If you wish to attend on campus, you must make a regular application (due by 1st March in the year you wish to attend). If you've passed two core courses in the Distance Learning MBA, no GMAT is required.

You should know, however, that on-campus electives count for only half as much as Distance Learning ones (so you'd have to take four to meet the Distance Learning programme requirement).

Also, if you're considering transferring from the Distance Learning Programme to on-campus study to finish your MBA you will, of course, be given exemption from the courses you've already completed, but "exemptions granted to distance learning students on the basis of previous academic qualifications cannot be used in the full- or part-time programmes". So says the official policy.

You should explore on-campus possibilities by letter, directly with the University.

For further information

To send in your Student Information Form, to report any defect in the material (including missing pages, etc.), to purchase other Pitman books:

Heriot-Watt MBA Department
Pitman Publishing
128 Long Acre
London WC2E 9AN
United Kingdom

For more general academic matters, write to

The Director of Studies
The Graduate School of Business
Edinburgh Business School
Heriot-Watt University
Riccarton, Edinburgh, EH14 4AS
United Kingdom
Fax: 44–131–451–3002

For information on doctoral programmes and other graduate programmes of Heriot-Watt University, request the Guide to Postgraduate Study and Research from

The Registrar
Heriot-Watt University
Riccarton, Edinburgh, EH14 4AS
United Kingdom
Telephone: 44–131–449–5111
Fax: 44–131–449–5153

MBA statistics

Number of students and examination performance

By March 1995 about 10,000 individuals had purchased a total of about 33,000 courses in 100 countries. The geographical distribution of purchasers is as follows:

The geographical distribution of purchasers (as at March 1995)

Country	%
United Kingdom	22
Europe	8
South Africa	12
USA & Canada	17
Australasia	6
Hong Kong	15
Singapore	4
Malaysia	4

Over 13,000 individual subject examinations had been taken in the eight diets up to December 1994. The overall pass rate was 74%, and this increased to 84% for matriculated students.

The MBA software

Introduction

The Graduate School of Business, Edinburgh Business School (which incorporates the institution formerly known as The Esmée Fairbairn Research Centre) has been in the forefront of developments in the field of educational software for many years, and has carried out a great deal of research into the cost effectiveness of educational software in the context of other innovative teaching techniques. The development of the software for the MBA by Distance Learning has drawn on this research and development experience, and has also benefited from the experience of the MBA authors in developing and implementing software in management training programmes. On the basis of our experience, extending over a period of 20 years, the three areas in which software has the potential to be cost effective are simulations, data handling and hypotheses testing, and reinforcement.

Simulations

The advantage of simulations is that they enable aspects of a subject to be taught which are virtually impossible to teach in the conventional manner. This is of particular importance in subjects where there is a great deal of interdependence, for example in macroeconomics, which is concerned with understanding how the economy works, and in strategy, which is concerned with reconciling the many influences which determine company performance over time. Interdependence leads to extended logical chains, such as "the government has decided to increase the money supply in order to reduce the interest rate so that investment expenditure will be stimulated, however, this will lead to an outflow of 'hot money' which will cause the exchange rate to fall, which in turn will lead to an increase in exports which, given the economy is at full employment already, is likely to lead to excess demand and inflationary pressures, and this is complicated by the fact that imports are expected to increase due to a reduction in trade barriers, which in turn will..."

Once a lecturer begins to expound in this manner, students quickly lose the thread, but this approach is encountered in the beginning of most economics courses and many management courses with an economic content. A good corollary is the attempt to teach chess without having access to a board or chessmen. Why the teaching profession continues to pursue inappropriate techniques is an issue which remains unresolved.

The effectiveness of simulations is based on the principle of learning by doing. The student is placed in the position of managing director of a company, or Chancellor of the Exchequer (or Secretary of the Treasury) in charge of government economic policy, and has to make decisions to achieve stated objectives. It is living through such events, and attempting to make sense of them using relevant ideas and theories, which has a powerful learning effect. Many instructors have found that the simulation approach acts as a springboard to higher order learning objectives, such as synthesis and evaluation, thus adding a dimension to teaching which is difficult to achieve using conventional methods.

Data handling and hypotheses testing

Despite the fact that managers are bombarded daily with numbers, it is usually difficult to obtain series of figures which can be used analytically, and to have at hand the type of statistical tools which enable the data to be investigated in a rigorous fashion. The result is that managers are typically ignorant of many important aspects of the environment within which they operate.

Managers often do not appreciate that it is not sufficient simply to have access to facts, but it is necessary to be able to apply statistical approaches to data in order to arrive at meaningful conclusions. The hypothesis testing element of software enables students to apply relatively sophisticated approaches to rationalising data and to testing hypotheses. This is not simply an end in itself, but can greatly contribute to a rational and structured approach to real life problems. For example, when deciding on changes to a company's employee remuneration package, managers often lay stress on the value of company cars, free sports facilities, subsidised canteen food and various other non-financial benefits; however, the primary question which should be addressed is "What combination of benefits would make employees happiest?". It may very well be that employees would prefer to forego all benefits in kind and receive any additional money in their pay packets. How would a manager determine if this were the case? Clearly an employee opinion survey is necessary, together with methods of analysing the resulting data to determine which is the optimum allocation of the available wages fund.

As in the case of simulations, there is a significant learning by doing element in hypotheses testing. The student will quickly discover that the techniques are not difficult to comprehend, but because statistical results are always open to different interpretations it is rare that anything can be proved beyond any doubt.

Reinforcement

In subjects such as Quantitative Methods and Finance, much learning is achieved by working through examples. While this is an essential element in the learning process, software makes it possible to pursue many more examples than would be possible by working each out individually. One of the features of reinforcement software is the use of graphics to **animate** the concepts and permit the student to "see" the impact on the relationships of altering key variables. This enables aspects of a topic to be pursued in a manner which is impossible otherwise. For example, many problems in real life can be thought of in terms of solving relationships which refer to the same variables; in economics, the quantity of a good purchased depends on its price (demand) and the quantity firms are willing to produce also depends on price (supply). At what point are demand and supply equal? This problem involves solving **simultaneous equations**, the very mention of which is usually sufficient to fill managers with dread. But a graphical presentation shows the **solution** simply as where the two lines meet; the student can change the position and the shape of the two lines to explore the impact on the solution of different types of relationship.

The role of the software

The role which the software plays in the course package must be seen in the context of the range of educational options offered. The overriding principle is that different students learn in different ways, therefore the course packages should be regarded as a menu of options from which the student can choose. The text for each course contains a body of material which must be covered, or knowledge of which must have been assimilated by the student previously, by any course purporting to teach that subject. Where appropriate the text is supplemented by multiple choice questions and cases. The software is designed to provide an additional vehicle for learning basic concepts, and in some cases to teach areas well nigh impossible using conventional approaches.

The ability to assimilate the concepts contained in the courses and apply them to real world situations will depend on the aptitude and experiences of the student involved. For example, the student with high quantitative skills and mathematical abilities should, like a counterpart in conventional MBA courses, have little trouble with the Quantitative Methods course, and will typically find the multiple choice questions and cases adequate. Other students, however, who have "blind spots" when equations and numbers are mentioned, have benefited tremendously from the software packages.

Since the software is optional, the text can be studied independently of the software. Indeed, the software is not referred to in the text. The link between the text and the software is from software to text. It would be confusing for students who did not opt to use the software to have references to the software in the text.

Part 2

Complete Contents of the Courses

The compulsory courses

Accounting A distance learning programme

The Accounting programme is written by Niall Lothian, Grant Thornton Professor of Accounting and Head of Department of Accountancy and Finance at Heriot-Watt University, and John Small, Deputy Principal and Professor of Accountancy and Finance at Heriot-Watt University.

Professor Lothian has taught at IMEDE in Lausanne and is currently a member of the visiting faculty of INSEAD, Fontainebleau. He has conducted seminars and managerial briefings in Europe, Africa and China, the latter under the auspices of the United Nations Industrial Development Organisation.

Professor Lothian has also been consultant to British Government agencies such as The Ministry of Defence and The Cabinet Office and to a number of international companies including Digital, Sun, Philips and Swire.

Professor Small is Chairman of the Accounts Commission in Scotland. The Accounts Commission is responsible for arranging the audit of Local Government in Scotland and ensuring the proper steps are taken to achieve economy, efficiency and effectiveness. He is a member of Council of the Chartered Association of Certified Accountants and was its President in 1982/83. He has been Chairman of the Education Committee of the International Federation of Accountants. He is an honorary member of the Arab Society of Certified Accountants.

Module 1
An Introduction to Accounting and the Accounting Equation

Module 2
The Profit and Loss Account

Module 3
The Balance Sheet and Cash Flow Statements

Module 4
Financial Statements and Inflation

Module 5
The Framework for Financial Reporting

Module 6
Interpretation of Financial Statements

Module 7
Emerging Issues and Managerial Options in Financial Reporting

Module 8
An Introduction to Cost and Management Accounting

Module 9
Cost Characteristics and Behaviour

Module 10
Allocating Costs to Jobs and Processes

Module 11
Costs for decision-making

Module 12
Budgeting

Module 13
Standard Costing

Module 14
Accounting for Divisions

Module 15
Investment Decisions

Module 16
New Developments in Management Accounting

Economics A distance learning programme

The author, Professor Keith G Lumsden, MA, PhD, FRSE, is Director of The Graduate School of Business, Edinburgh Business School, Heriot-Watt University, Edinburgh and Director of Studies for Heriot-Watt University MBA by Distance Learning .

The concept of a distance learning MBA was the brain-child of Professor Lumsden while he was at Stanford University, California where he taught in the Graduate School of Business for 15 years. He pioneered many of the techniques which form the basis of the MBA courses, particularly self-assessment questions and problems, case studies, databases and computer simulations. He has published 14 books and over 60 articles in professional journals. Professor Lumsden consults with major companies throughout the world. He is currently engaged in organising and teaching in executive seminars and programmes for many international companies.

Module 1
Economic Concepts, Issues and Tools

Module 2
An Overview of Economics

Module 3
Demand

Module 4
Supply

Module 5
The Market

Module 6
Economic Efficiency

Module 7
Organization of Industries

Module 8
Public Goods and Externalities

Module 9
Income Distribution

Module 10
International Sector

Module 11
Macroeconomics Overview

Module 12
Potential Output

Module 13
The Circular Flow of Income

Module 14
Simple Model of Income Determination

Module 15
Expanded Model of Income Determination

Module 16
Fiscal Policy

Module 17
Money, The Central Bank and Monetary Policy

Module 18
The Quantity Theory and the Keynesian Theory of Money

Module 19
Integration of the Real and Monetary Sectors of the Economy

Module 20
Inflation and Unemployment

Module 21
The World Economy

Finance A distance learning programme

The Finance programme is written by Kenneth J Boudreaux, Professor of Economics and Finance, at the AB Freeman School of Business, Tulane University, New Orleans.

Professor Boudreaux is an eminent scholar in finance, known widely for his ability to combine cutting-edge knowledge of the field with understandable explanations to professionals. In addition to being a successful researcher and university professor, he has for the past two decades lectured extensively to executives on topics in finance, in all parts of the world. Professor Boudreaux is the co-author of *The Basic Theory of Corporate Finance*, a widely-used graduate-level text, and has published significant scholarly research on issues in corporate finance, securities markets and corporate restructuring. His research is frequently cited in journals of finance and economics worldwide.

Module 1
The Basic Ideas, Scope and Tools of Finance

Module 2
Fundamentals of Company Investment Decisions

Module 3
Earnings, Profit and Cash Flow

Module 4
Company Investment Decisions Using the Weighted Average Cost of Capital

Modlue 5
Estimating Cash Flows for Investment Projects

Module 6
Applications of Company Investment Analysis

Module 7
Risk and Company Investment Decisions

Module 8
Company Dividend Policy

Module 9
Company Capital Structure

Module 10
Working Capital Management

Module 11
International Financial Management

Module 12
Advanced Topics: Options and Agency

Marketing A distance learning programme

The Marketing course is written by Professor Harper Boyd Jr and Professor Orville C Walker Jr.

Professor Boyd has served on the faculties of such prominent universities as Northwestern, Stanford, INSEAD and Tulane. He is currently serving as a Distinguished Professor of Marketing at the University of Arkansas at Little Rock. He has worked closely with a variety of business firms around the world in a number of different capacities. He has a global background, having taught in some 25 different countries. He has published extensively – 40 books and 100 articles – and has received many honours.

Professor Orville C Walker is the James D Watkins Professor of Marketing at the University of Minnesota, USA. He has published 5 books and over 40 articles in professional journals on a wide range of topics including consumer behaviour, distribution and retail management, sales force motivation, marketing strategies and the implementation of marketing programmes. In 1981 he was the joint winner of the O'Dell Award for the best article published in the Journal of Marketing Research and in 1989 the joint winner of Harold H Maynard award for making the most significant contribution to marketing theory in an article published in the Journal of Marketing. Besides his graduate and undergraduate teaching, Professor Walker has taught in many programmes for company executives.

Module 1
Marketing and the Marketing Management Process

1.1 Summary of chapter contents

1.2 Statement of chapter objectives

1.3 Summary outline of chapter contents

* Introduction
* Marketing activities and their characteristics
* Relationships of marketing to business strategy and operations
* Development of marketing systems
* Marketing's role in society is to facilitate exchange
* Market functions and institutions
* Marketing management

1.4 Replacement materials

1.5 Review questions

Module 2
The Strategic Role of Marketing

2.1 Summary of chapter contents

2.2 Statement of chapter objectives

2.3 Summary outline of chapter contents

* Introduction
* Corporate, business and marketing strategies
* Strategic decisions at the corporate level
* Strategic decisions at the business unit level
* The role of marketing in formulating and implementing strategies

2.4 Replacement materials

2.5 Review questions

Module 3
Analysing the Macroenvironment

3.1 Summary of chapter contents

3.2 Statement of chapter objectives

3.3 Summary outline of chapter contents

* Introduction
* Characteristics of the macroenvironment
* The demographic/economic environment
* The political/legal environment
* The technological environment
* The sociocultural environment
* Strategic environmental issue management – a four stage process

3.4 Replacement materials

3.5 Review questions

Module 4
Consumer Markets and Buying Behaviour

4.1 Summary of chapter contents

4.2 Statement of chapter objectives

4.3 Summary outline of chapter contents

* Introduction
* Consumer purchasing decisions
* The high-involvement, complex decision-making process
* Low-involvement purchase decisions
* Psychological and personal influences on consumer decision-making processes
* Social influences on consumers' decision-making processes

Module 5
Organizational Markets and Buying Behaviour

Module 6
Market Segmentation

Module 7
Industry and Competitor Analysis

* Industry structure analysis
* Use of strategic groups in analyzing intra-industry competition
* Bases of competition
* Individual competitor analysis

7.4 Replacement materials

7.5 Review questions

Module 8
Industry Dynamics and the Product Life Cycle

8.1 Summary of chapter contents

8.2 Statement of chapter objectives

8.3 Summary outline of chapter contents

* Introduction
* Overview of the product life cycle concept
* Characteristics and implications of the product life cycle stages
* Investment implications of the product life cycle
* Industry driving forces and the product life cycle

8.4 Replacement materials

8.5 Review questions

Module 9
Market Research and Market Measurements

9.1 Summary of chapter contents

9.2 Statement of chapter objectives

9.3 Summary outline of chapter contents

* Introduction
* Marketing research
* Market measurement – the demand estimation process
* Market potential versus market forecasts
* Definition and uses of market potential
* Measurement of actual potential
* Relative market potentials
* Sales forecasting
* Decision support systems (DSS)

9.4 Replacement materials

9.5 Review questions

Module 10
Market Targeting and Positioning Decisions

Module 11
Business Strategies and Marketing Programme Decisions

Module 12
Product and Services Decisions

- Servicing
- Product line strategy decisions
- Services

12.4 Replacement materials

12.5 Review questions

Module 13
Developing and Testing New Products and Services

13.1 Summary of chapter contents

13.2 Statement of chapter objectives

13.3 Summary outline of chapter contents

- Introduction
- The new product development process
- Objectives and strategies for new products
- New product ideas and the idea screening process
- Product design
- New product testing
- Commercialization
- Applying the new product development process to services

13.4 Replacement materials

13.5 Review questions

Module 14
Pricing Decisions

14.1 Summary of chapter contents

14.2 Statement of chapter objectives

14.3 Summary outline of chapter contents

- Introduction
- Strategic pricing issues
- The price setting process
- Initiating and responding to price changes

14.4 Replacement materials

14.5 Review questions

Module 15
Distribution Decisions

15.1 Summary of chapter contents

15.2 Statement of chapter objectives

15.3 Summary outline of chapter contents

* Introduction
* Channel functions and institutions
* Recent trends among channel institutions
* Channel design alternatives
* Channel design decisions
* Channel management decisions

15.4 Replacement materials

15.5 Review questions

Module 16
Promoting Mix Decisions

16.1 Summary of chapter contents

16.2 Statement of chapter objectives

16.3 Summary outline of chapter contents

* Introduction
* The promotional mix
* The communciation process
* Framework for developing an effective promotional mix

16.4 Replacement materials

15.5 Review questions

Module 17
Advertising, Sales Promotion and Public Relations Decisions

17.1 Summary of chapter contents

17.2 Statement of chapter objectives

17.3 Summary outline of chapter contents

* Introduction
* Advertising objectives
* The source
* The message
* Advertising media
* Feedback
* Advertising budgets
* Sales promotion
* Public relations

17.4 Replacement materials

17.5 Review questions

Module 18
Personal Selling Decisions

18.1 Summary of chapter contents

18.2 Statement of chapter objectives

18.3 Summary outline of chapter contents

* Introduction
* Strategy objectives
* Types of sales jobs
* Steps in the selling process
* Planning the sales programme
* Implementing the sales plan
* Evaluation and control

18.4 Replacement materials

18.5 Review questions

Module 19
Strategies for New Market Entries

19.1 Summary of chapter contents

19.2 Statement of chapter objectives

19.3 Summary outline of chapter contents

* Introduction
* How new is new?
* Objectives of new product and market development
* Market entry strategies: pioneers versus followers
* Strategic marketing programmes for pioneers

19.4 Replacement materials

19.5 Review questions

Module 20
Strategies for Growth Markets

20.1 Summary of chapter contents

20.2 Statement of chapter objectives

20.3 Summary outline of chapter contents

* Introduction
* Strategic issues in growth markets

Module 21
Strategies for Mature and Declining Markets

Module 22
Strategies for Global Markets

Module 23
Implementing Business and Marketing Strategies

23.1 Summary of chapter contents

23.2 Statement of chapter objectives

23.3 Summary outline of chapter contents

* Introduction
* Relationships between business and marketing strategies
* Administrative relationships and strategy implementation
* Organizational structure, processes and strategy implementation
* Alternative organizational designs
* Marketing action plans

23.4 Replacement materials

23.5 Review questions

Module 24
Monitoring and Controlling Marketing Programmes

24.1 Summary of chapter contents

24.2 Statement of chapter objectives

24.3 Summary outline of chapter contents

* Introduction
* Profitability analysis
* Strategic control and marketing audits
* Product market entry action plan control
* Sales analysis
* Global marketing control
* Contingency planning

24.4 Replacement materials

24.5 Review questions

Appendix 1: Answers to review questions and rationale for selected multiple choice questions

Appendix 2: Practice final examinations

Organisational Behaviour A distance learning programme

The main author of this programme, Professor Robert C Dailey, is Professor of Management at Drake University, Iowa.

Before taking up his present position, Professor Dailey was on the Faculty of the Freeman School of Business, Tulane University. He has prepared and taught courses in management, organisational behaviour, organisational development, organisational theory, interpersonal behaviour, human resource management and behavioural science research. These courses have been taught to undergraduates, MBAs, PhDs, executive MBAs and master of science students. He received the Howard Wissner Award for excellence in teaching at Tulane Unversity.

His publications have appeared in several journals. In addition he is the author of *Understanding People in Organisations*. He has completed over 50 consulting projects in American corporations and hospitals.

The author of Module 2, Professor Tony Keenan, is Professor of Business Organisation, Heriot-Watt University.

The author of Module 10, Dr Monir Tayeb, is a lecturer in International Business and Organisational Behaviour at Heriot-Watt University.

Module 1
The Basics of Organisational Behaviour

Module 2
Human Resource Management

Module 3
Contemporary Theories of Motivation

Module 4
Organisational Control and Reward Systems

Module 5
Job Design and Employee Reactions to Work

Module 6
Understanding Work Group Dynamics and Problem-Solving

Module 7
The Influence Processes in Organisations: Power, Politics, Leadership and Entrepreneurship

Module 8
Managing Transitions: Organisational Culture and Change

Module 9
Organisational Design

Module 10
Japanese Management Style

Quantitative Methods A distance learning programme

The Quantitative Methods programme is written by David Targett, ICL Professor of Information Systems at the School of Management, University of Bath, and formerly Senior Lecturer in Decision Sciences at the London Business School.

His books, including *Coping With Numbers* and *The Economist Guide to Business Numeracy*, have stressed communication rather than technical rigour and have been sold throughout the world. He has written over fifty case studies which confirm the increasing intregration of Quantitative Methods with other management topics. One of his many articles, a study on the provision of management information, won the Pergamon Prize in 1986. He was part of the team that designed London Business School's highly successful part-time MBA Programme of which he was the Director from 1985 to 1988.

Module 1
Introducing Statistics

Module 2
Basic Mathematics

Module 3
Data Communication

Module 4
Data analysis

Module 5
Summary Measures

Module 6
Sampling Methods

Module 7
Distributions

Module 8
Statistical Inference

Module 9
More Distributions

Module 10
Analysis of Variance

Module 11
Regression and Correlation

11.3 Mathematical preliminaries
* The equation of a straight line
* Residuals

11.4 Simple linear regression

11.5 Correlation
* Correlation coefficient

11.6 Checking the residuals

11.7 Regression on a microcomputer
* Inspect the scatter diagram
* Calculate the regression coefficients
* Calculate the correlation coefficient
* Examine the residuals

11.8 Some reservations about regression and correlation

11.9 Concluding remarks

Review questions

Case studies

Module 12
Advanced Regression Analysis

12.1 Introduction

12.2 Multiple regression analysis
* Similarities and differences between simple and multiple regression
* Dummy variables

12.3 Non-linear regression analysis
* Curvilinear regression
* Transformations

12.4 Measuring closeness of fit
* Measuring closeness of fit
* Testing that the residuals are random
* Deciding which variables to retain (in multiple regression)
* The accuracy of predictions

12.5 Regression analysis summary

12.6 Concluding remarks

Review questions

Case studies

Module 13
The Context of Forecasting

Module 14
Time Series Techniques

Module 15
Managing Forecasts

Strategic Planning A distance learning programme

Professorial Fellow of The Graduate School of Business, Edinburgh Business School, Heriot-Watt University, Alex Scott (MA, MSc, PhD) is a pioneer in developing and carrying out research into new educational techniques, including studies into the efficacy of innovative techniques in teaching beginning economics.

Utilising employee surveys he has helped develop techniques designed to identify factors contributing to job satisfaction and effective management in companies. He has carried out economics research into efficiency in education, efficient use of energy, energy and the environment and the cost to the taxpayer of government industrial aid programmes.

He is at the forefront in the application of computers in teaching economics and business, and in collaboration with Professor Keith Lumsden has produced several highly successful software packages; Running the British Economy is the most widely used software package in economics worldwide and has had a major impact on economics teaching at school, university and business levels; Stratship and Stratplan are business simulations widely used on international management development programmes and by the United Nations in teaching managers in developing countries.

Module 1
Introduction to Strategy, Planning and Structure

Module 2
Modelling the Strategic Planning Process

2.1 The modelling approach
* The components of a model
* Benefits and costs of the modelling approach
* A functional model

2.2 Strategy makers
* Strategy and the evolution of the company
* Strategists

Review question

Stratplan Appendix
* Allocating time
* Structuring the decision process
* Resolving points of view

Module 3
Company Objectives

3.1 Setting objectives

3.2 The gap concept
* External versus internal gap factors
* Gaps and resources
* Gaps and incentives

3.3 Credible objectives

3.4 Quantifiable and non-quantifiable objectives

3.5 Aggregate objectives

3.6 Disaggregated objectives

3.7 The principal agent problem

3.8 Means and ends

3.9 Behavioural versus economic and financial objectives

3.10 Economic objectives

3.11 Financial objectives
* Discounting and present value
* Net present value
* Capitalized value
* Choice of interest rate: the cost of capital
* Return on investment
* Shareholder wealth

3.12 Social objectives

3.13 Ethical considerations

Module 4
The Company and the Economy

Module 5
The Company and the Market

Module 6
Internal Analysis of the Company

Module 7
Making Choices Among Strategies

Module 8
Implementing and Evaluating Strategy

The elective courses

Decision-making Techniques A distance learning programme

The Decision-making Techniques programme is written by David Targett, ICL Professor of Information Systems at the School of Management, University of Bath and formerly Senior Lecturer in Decision Sciences at the London Business School.

Professor Targett has many years' experience teaching executives to add numeracy to their list of management skills and become balanced decision-makers. His books, which include *Coping with Numbers* and *The Economist Guide to Business Numeracy*, have been sold throughout the world. One of his many articles, a study on the provision of management information, won the Pergamon Prize in 1986. He was part of the team that designed London Business School's highly successful part-time MBA Programme of which he was the Director from 1985 to 1988. During this time he extended the international focus of the teaching by leading pioneering study groups to Hong Kong, Singapore and the United States of America.

Module 1
Decision Analysis

1.1 Introduction

1.2 Prerequisite ideas
* Decision trees
* Payoffs
* Expected monetary value (EMV)

1.3 Applications
* Oil explorations
* Technological problems
* Medical research

1.4 Carrying out decision analysis
* Stage 1: Draw the tree
* Stage 2: Insert payoffs
* Stage 3: Insert probabilities
* Stage 4: Roll-back procedure
* Stage 5: Summarize the optimal path and draw up the risk profile

1.5 The value of additional information
* Expected value of sample information
* Expected value of perfect information

Module 2
Advanced Decision Analysis

Module 3
Linear Programming

Module 4
Extending the Ideas of Linear Programming

Module 5
Simulation

Module 6
Network Planning Techniques for Large Projects

Module 7
Decisions and Information Technology

Government, Industry and Privatization
A distance learning programme

The Government, Industry and Privatization Course is written by Professor Sir Alan Peacock, DSC, MA, DUniv, DEcon, DSc, FBA, HonFLSE, FRSE, and Professor Martin Ricketts, BA, DPhil, FRSA.

Professor Sir Alan Peacock and Professor Martin Ricketts are top-rank economists who are uniquely qualified to offer a guide through the maze of problems encountered by companies in their economic relations with governments.

Alan Peacock, currently Honorary Research Professor in Public Finance, The Esmée Fairbairn Research Centre, Heriot-Watt University, Riccarton, Edinburgh, is one of the UK's best-known experts on the economics of public finance and has published over 30 books and monographs and 200 professional articles. He has held senior posts at The London School of Economics (1948–56) and at the Universities of Edinburgh (1956–78) and Buckingham (1978–84). He was the first Vice-Chancellor of the independent University of Buckingham (1983–84). He has been awarded honorary degrees by eight universities, is one of the few economists who is a Fellow of the British Academy, and is an Honorary Fellow of the London School of Economics.

He has had a long career as an economic adviser to the UK Government, to seven other Governments and to such international organisations as OECD, IMF and the UN. For three years (1973–76) he served full-time as Chief Economics Advisor, UK Department of Trade and Industry and chaired the Committee on Financing the BBC (1985–86), which has had a major influence on the future structure of broadcasting. His services have been recognized by the award of a Knighthood for public service in 1987. He has also had business experience as a partner in an economic consultancy, as a non-executive director of a publishing firm and latterly of a banking concern. He has also advised several companies on economic policy questions. He was awarded the Scottish Special Free Enterprise Award in 1987.

Professor Martin Ricketts has been successively Lecturer, Reader and is now Professor of Economic Organisation at the University of Buckingham. Previously he was a research worker on industrial policy with the Federation of British Industries. He is a BA in Economics of Newcastle University and a DPhil of the University of York. He specialises in industrial economics and public finance. He has held a number of visiting posts abroad, notably as Visiting Professor at the Virginia Polytechnic University, USA and at the University of Catania, Italy. He was appointed Economic Director of the National Economic Development Office (NEDO) on secondment from Buckingham for a period of two years.

He has been much in demand as an economic adviser, receiving assignments from a trade association, the Anglo–German Foundation and the Centre for Policy Studies (founded by Margaret Thatcher). He was recently invited to become a member of the Advisory Council of the Institute of Economic Affairs and is also a Fellow of the Royal Society of Arts. He masterminded the IEA's major *Survey of Economists' Attitudes* to technical and policy questions which is the latest of his long line of professional publications.

Module 1
The Bargaining Economy

1.1 Introduction
* Limitations on government actions

1.2 Reasons for government control of industry
* The normative approach
* The positive approach

1.3 Method of analysis
* Information requirements
* Feedback effects

1.4 The information problem
* Moral hazard
* Adverse selection

1.5 Private interests and government policy
* Regulatory capture
* Interest group pressure

Review questions

Module 2
Structure and Growth in Government

2.1 Introduction

2.2 The economic role of government
* The budget

2.3 The relative size of government
* Government expenditure on goods and services as proportion of GDP
* Total government current expenditure as proportion of GDP
* Government employment as proportion of total employment

2.4 Growth of government in relation to the economy
* Growth in government spending
* Growth in government employment

2.5 The causes of government growth
* Demand factors
* Supply factors

2.6 Consequences of growth in government

Review questions

Module 3
Regulation (1): Competition Policy

3.1 Introduction

3.2 Regulation and market structure
* Natural monopoly

Module 4
Regulation (2): Environmental Policy

Module 5
Government Purchasing

5.1 Introduction

5.2 The market environment

* Bi-lateral monopolies
* Alternative government procurement policies

5.3 Some economics of government purchasing policies

* The government as monopsonist
* The government in a position of bi-lateral monopoly
* The problem of uncertainty

5.4 Conclusion

Review questions

Module 6
Government Control of Private Industry: Subsidies

6.1 Introduction

6.2 The choice of aims

* Three structural policies

6.3 Forms of financial inducement

* Types of financial instrument
* Economic coverage
* Direct and indirect subsidies

6.4 Some economics of subsidies

6.5 Government subsidies in an open economy

6.6 Conclusions on subsidy management

Review questions

Module 7
The Government as Producer (1): Non-marketed Output

7.1 Background

7.2 The economic analysis of bureaucracy

* Bureaucracy as monopoly

7.3 Difficulties in testing the model

7.4 Improving government production efficiency

* Auditing government expenditures
* Introducing market forces
* Contracting out

7.5 Conclusion

Review questions

Module 8
The Government as Producer (2): Marketed Output of Public Enterprises

Module 9
Privatization and Deregulation

International Trade and Finance A distance learning programme

Hugh Fleming is a lecturer in Economics at Heriot-Watt University. He has specialised in International Finance and taught the subject for some twenty years. He is involved in the Heriot-Watt MBA programme, teaching macroeconomics. Mr Fleming is involved in executive management programmes in which he regularly lectures on financial issues in the world economy.

Andrew Scott is currently a Senior Lecturer in the Economics of the European Community at the Europa Institute, University of Edinburgh. He was previously a lecturer in Economics at Heriot-Watt University, where he specialised in International Trade. Mr Scott has been an adviser to the Statistical Office of the European Community and to the Economic and Social Committee of the European Communities.

Module 1
The Structure of International Trade

Module 2
Explanations of International Trade

Module 3
Trade Policy

Module 4
International Commercial Diplomacy

Module 5
Trade and Economic Development

Module 6
International Economic Integration

Module 7
Financing of Trade

Module 8
International Capital

Module 9
Exchange Rate Determination

Module 10
Exchange Rate Systems

Module 11
The European Monetary System

Module 12
International Lending and Borrowing

Module 13
The International Monetary Fund

Negotiation A distance learning programme

The Negotiation programme is written by Professor Gavin Kennedy, BA, MSc, PhD, FCInstM, Managing Director of Negotiate Ltd., and a Professor at The Graduate School of Business, Edinburgh Business School, Heriot-Watt University, Edinburgh.

Professor Kennedy taught at the University of Strathclyde Business School for eleven years and was a Professor in the Department of Accountancy and Finance, Heriot-Watt University, Edinburgh from 1984–88. He ran the UK's first Negotiating Workshop at Brunel University, London in April 1972.

Module 1
What is Negotiation?

Module 2
Distributive Bargaining

Module 3
Preparation for Negotiation

Module 4
Debate in Negotiation

Module 5
A Proposal is not a Bargain

Module 6
Bargaining for an Agreement

Module 7
Styles of Negotiation

Module 8
Alternative Approaches to Negotiation

Strategic Information Systems A distance learning programme

The Strategic Information Systems programme is written by David Targett, ICL Professor of Information Systems at the School of Management, University of Bath and formerly Senior Lecturer in Decision Sciences at the London Business School.

Professor Targett has many years' experience teaching executives to add numeracy to their list of management skills and become balanced decision-makers and to understand the strategic role of information. His style is based on demystifying complex techniques and demonstrating clearly their practical relevance as well as their shortcomings. He is the author of the Decision-making Techniques programme and the Quantitative Methods programme in the Heriot-Watt Business School MBA Series, and his books, including *Coping with Numbers* and *The Economist Guide to Business Numeracy*, have been sold throughout the world. One of his many articles, a study on the provision of management information, won the Pergamon Prize in 1986.

He was part of the team that designed London Business School's highly successful part-time MBA Programme of which he was Director from 1985 to 1988. During this time he extended the international focus of the teaching by leading pioneering study groups to Hong King, Singapore and the United States of America. He has taught on all major programmes at the London Business School and has developed and run management education courses involving scores of major companies including: British Rail, Citicorp, ICI, ICL, Marks and Spencer and Shell.

Summary

Information Technology (IT) is the equipment used to handle information and data. Information Systems (IS) are formed when such devices are linked so that information can flow between people, functions and organizations. IS can now do more than just provide basic data: they can transform industries, organizations, products and management styles. IS are therefore strategic, with the potential to affect the overall direction of an organization and to create competitive advantage. As a result, IS are no longer solely the concern of specialist computer departments. This course looks at what general managers need to know about IS, both positively to exploit what it has to offer, and negatively to avoid disasters. It also provides background by defining the strategic role of IT.

Module 1
A Strategic Overview

1.1 Introduction

1.2 Is IT strategic?

1.3 Examples of strategic IT

- The airline industry
- Retail banking
- The tyre industry

Module 2
Technical Issues in IT

Module 3
Identifying Opportunities: The Business Benefits of IS

Module 4
Developing and Aligning an IT Strategy

Module 5
Deciding Whether to Invest

Module 6
Implementation and Management

Module 7
Auditing and Monitoring

Strategies for Change A distance learning programme

The editors of the text are Howard Kahn and Janis Paterson.

Dr Howard Kahn lectures on Organisational Behaviour in the Department of Business Organisation of Heriot-Watt University, Edinburgh, Scotland. He has wide commercial and consultancy experience, and has written a number of texts and articles on the topic of occupational stress.

Janis Paterson lectures in Human Resource Management in the Department of Business Organisation of Heriot-Watt University, Edinburgh. She has been adviser on pay systems and remuneration to numerous government agencies and private organisations.

Dr D Jane Bower lectures in Technology Management in the Department of Business Organisation of Heriot-Watt University, Edinburgh.

Alasdair M MacLeod is an Honorary Lecturer and Research Fellow in the Department of Business Organisation of Heriot-Watt University, Edinburgh.

Professor Douglas Pitt is Dean of the Business School of Strathclyde University, Glasgow, Scotland.

Dr Monir Tayeb is a Senior Lecturer in Cross-cultural Studies in the Department of Business Organisation of Heriot-Watt University, Edinburgh.

Richard C Warren is a Principal Lecturer in Industrial Relations and Business Ethics in the Department of Business Studies of Manchester Metropolitan University, England.

Module 1
New Directions in Managing Human Resources

Janis Paterson

Module 2
Sress at work

Howard Kahn

Module 3
Changing Organizational Perspectives

Douglas Pitt

Module 4
Intergrating Technological and Organizational Development

D Jane Bower

Module 5
Human Resource Management and the Environment

Monir Tayeb

Module 6
Managing Quality

Alasdair M MacLeod

Module 7
Ethics and Business

Richard C Warren

Part 3

Examination Assessment

This section contains examples of actual student responses to selected examination questions in each subject together with model answers and examiners' comments.

Please be aware that the occasional spelling or grammatical error which you will find in student answers are not penalised providing the meaning is clearly expressed. This section has been written to provide an insight into the minds of the University's examiners and the approaches which they adopt to the grading process.

The Quantitative Methods examiner has given details of the errors made most commonly by students in the case studies.

The examiner in Strategic Information Systems has analysed each part of the case study before going on to criticise the student's answer in detail.

Examples of questions and model answers only are provided for the most recent elective course Strategies for Change. At the time of going to press (Spring 1995), no examinations had been taken for this course.

All the approaches adopted by the various examiners have a single purpose – to improve students' examination performance. For this effort to be successful it will be necessary for students to make a detailed study of the individual questions and answers and of the examiners' comments.

The compulsory courses

Accounting

Case study

In your role as a director of Whittington Beers plc, you have been closely reviewing the operating performance of one of your principal competitors, United Breweries plc.

Over the past few years, you have computed the following range of ratios for United Breweries plc. You also have available the average ratios for the brewing industry for 1994.

Ratio	*1990*	*1991*	*1992*	*1994 average*
Current (times)	1.10	1.05	0.97	1.35
Quick (times)	0.85	0.75	0.75	0.95
Profit margin (%)	10.15	11.58	7.63	12.17
Return on total assets (%)	8.80	12.25	4.24	5.72
Return of owners' equity (%)	12.16	11.08	8.45	12.15
Fixed to current assets (%)	225.6	350.5	378.8	365.2
Debt (%)	65.1	52.6	44.7	55.6
Times interest earned	12.3	11.2	10.1	14.2
Average collection period (days)	71.0	70.0	63.0	70.0
Inventory turnover (times)	18.7	18.6	17.2	18.5
Earnings per share (pence)	20.8	24.8	25.6	22.3
Dividend yield (%)	1.12	1.46	1.78	2.15

The 1994 published accounts are now available to you, providing an opportunity to update the ratios for both 1993 and 1994.

United Breweries plc	**1994 £m**	**1993 £m**
Profit and Loss Account		
Sales	1 514	1 487
Cost of sales	760	813
Gross margin	754	674
Operating costs	571	465
Profit on ordinary activities before taxation	183	209
Taxation	(49)	(62)
Profit on ordinary activities after taxation	134	147
Dividends	(73)	(69)
Profit retained for the year	61	78

Balance Sheet

Fixed Assets	1952	1749
Current Assets		
Stocks	103	90
Debtors	237	231
Cash at bank	100	124
	440	445
Creditors due within one year	(638)	(543)
Net current liabilities	(198)	(98)
Total assets less current liabilities	1754	1651
Creditors due in excess of one year	(331)	(320)
	1423	1331

Capital and Reserves

Share capital	376	371
Share premium	26	–
Retained profits	1021	960
	1423	1331

Additional information is also available from the published accounts.

(i) Operating costs includes £26m of interest payable in 1994 (1993 – £23m).

(ii) Share capital comprises wholly Ordinary Shares of 50 pence each in nominal value. Early in 1994, a further 10m Ordinary Shares were issued at a price of 310 pence per share, giving rise to a share premium balance of £26m.

(iii) The market price of United Breweries' share was 350 pence at the end of financial year 1994 (1993 – 400 pence).

Your colleagues on the Board of Directors (of Whittington Beers plc) believe that United Breweries plc may be prepared to engage in talks to discuss a possible agreed takeover bid by Whittington Beers plc.

Required:

1. Using the information in the 1994 published accounts, update the tabulation of ratios for United Breweries plc – for both 1993 and 1994. **(24 marks)**

2. Identify any factors in United Breweries performance over the five year period which give particular cause for concern, especially in relation to the current industry average. **(6 marks)**

3. Identify any factors in United Breweries' performance over the five year period which give positive indicators as to possible future performance. **(5 marks)**

(Total of 35 marks)

Actual student answer

Question 1

Ratio			£m 1994		£m 1993	
Current	=	$\frac{\text{Current assets}}{\text{Current liabilities}}$	$= \frac{440}{638}$	= 0.689	$\frac{445}{543}$	= 0.819
Quick	=	$\frac{\text{Current assets–inventory}}{\text{Current liabilities}}$	$= \frac{440-103}{638}$	= 0.528	$\frac{445-90}{543}$	= 0.653
Profit margin	=	$\frac{\text{Profit after interest \& tax}}{\text{Sale}}$	$= \frac{134}{1514}$	= 8.85%	$\frac{147}{1487}$	= 9.88%
Return on total assets	=	$\frac{\text{Profit after interest \& tax}}{\text{Total assets}}$	$= \frac{134}{2392}$	= 5.6%	$\frac{147}{2194}$	= 6.7%
Return on owner's equity	=	$\frac{\text{Profit after interest \& tax}}{\text{Owner's equity \& revenue}}$	$= \frac{134}{1423}$	= 9.4%	$\frac{147}{1331}$	= 11.04%
Fixed to current assets	=	$\frac{\text{Fixed assets}}{\text{Current assets}}$	$= \frac{1952}{440}$	= 443.6%	$\frac{1749}{445}$	= 393.0%
Debt	=	$\frac{\text{Debt total}}{\text{Debt assets}}$	$= \frac{969}{2392}$	= 40.5%	$\frac{863}{2194}$	= 39.3%
Times interest earned	=	$\frac{\text{Profit before interest}}{\text{Interest}}$	$= \frac{134+26}{26}$	= 6.15	$\frac{147+23}{23}$	= 7.39
Average collection period	=	$\frac{\text{Debtors}}{\text{Sale} \div 365}$	$= \frac{237}{1514 \div 365}$	= 57 days	$\frac{231}{1487 \div 365}$	= 57 days
Inventory turnover	=	$\frac{\text{Sales}}{\text{Inventory}}$	$= \frac{1514}{103}$	= 14.7 times	$\frac{1487}{90}$	= 16.5 times
Earnings per share	=	$\frac{\text{Profit after interest \& tax}}{\text{Number of shares}}$	$= \frac{£134\,000\,000}{752\,000\,000}$	= 17.8 p	$\frac{£147\,000\,000}{742\,000\,000}$	= 19.8 p
Dividend yield			$= \frac{17.8}{350}$	= 5.08%	$\frac{19.8}{400}$	= 4.95%

Some companies have started calculating profit before tax on the basis that timing of tax implication makes it more difficult to compare with previous periods but in answering this question, the traditional approach of profit after tax has been used.

(Marks awarded 20)

Question 2

There is a general decline in the performance of the company when compared with average for this industry. Current ratio has steadily declined over the last five years indicating increase in creditors payable within a year and decline in current assets. Quick ratio has also reduced markedly over the last 5 years. This tends to suggest that should the business be liquidated immediately, the company cannot meet its current liabilities. Average for the industry is near normal 1. Profit margin has also declined significantly indicating an increase in operating costs. Margin is down by approximately 30% in 1994 against industry average of 12.17%. Fixed to current assets is significantly higher than industry average indicating increased investment in fixed assets or reduced current assets comparing to industry. Return on total assets has declined in 1992 but has started picking up again in 1993 and 1994.

Reduced profitability is also affecting times interest earned when comparing against industry's average, with substantial drop in five years which must be causing concern to the lenders.

(Marks awarded 4)

Question 3

Dividend yield has substantially increased in 1993 and 1994 when comparing with previous period over two times the industry's average. This goes in line with issuing of shares at premium. Presumably the market looks at the company's position that it is going through investment phase with increase of 11.6% fixed assets in 1994 compared with 1993.

(Marks awarded 1)

Examiner's comments

1. With 24 marks available for this part of the question, this candidate performed the computational tasks particularly well, making errors in only two of the ratios requested. Both of the errors – in the times interest earned ratio and the dividend yield ratio – stemmed from a misunderstanding of the definitions of these ratios. However, 20 marks out of a possible 24 marks represents a commendable achievement.
2. Although the candidate has satisfactorily identified 4 out of 6 "causes" for concern, the presentational impact of his answer could have been improved by listing the factors, rather than enmeshing them in a paragraph of narrative discussion. The candidate failed to recognise the patchy performance of return on owners' equity and the increasing inventory turnover ratio. This limited his marks to only 4, out of 6 available.
3. The final part of the question lent itself readily to the use of listing to identify the positive indicators. Again, the candidate chose to use a narrative paragraph to convey the answer.

   This was the poorest part of the total answer with the candidate recognising only the company's major commitment to fixed assets as a positive sign for the future. The identification of rising dividend yield as a positive factor was discounted on the grounds that the candidate did not know how to compute dividend yield (*see* 1.1 above). The candidate failed completely to identify the improved return on total assets, the decreasing debt ratio and the falling average period of debtors. The result was the candidate gained only 1 mark out of 5 available.

The computational aspects of the case were performed well, creating the basis upon which the candidate's overall mark of 25 out of 35 was achieved. It was disappointing that the candidate failed to score better on the interpretative sections of the case, where the analysis of the computations was extremely limited.

Economics

Question

Examine critically the role of prices in determining the allocation of resources and distribution of income in a capitalist economy highlighting both the strengths and weaknesses of such a system. **(40 marks)**

Actual student answer

In a capitalist economy, subject to legal constraints, households are free to spend their income on any variety of goods and to offer their resources as they choose. Similarly firms are free to hire and fire labour and other factor inputs and to produce any goods and services they like. Besides the legal constraint, one limiting factor, of course, is that resources relative to wants that need to be satisfied are grossly limited. Choices then have to be made as income spent on product A is no longer available to be spent on any other product and similarly a resource utilised in the production of A is no longer available for production of any other goods/services.

In the capitalist economy, the choice as to what to produce and consequently how resources are allocated and income distributed is determined not through some central planning body but through the price mechanism, price here being determined freely through the interaction between the forces of supply and demand.

Individual consumers who are rational utility maximisers acting independently within this market system specify through their dollar power their preferences for particular goods and services. As the price of these goods and services go up, it provides signals to firms who are in business to maximise profit, what to produce.

This process can be illustrated by the following figure:

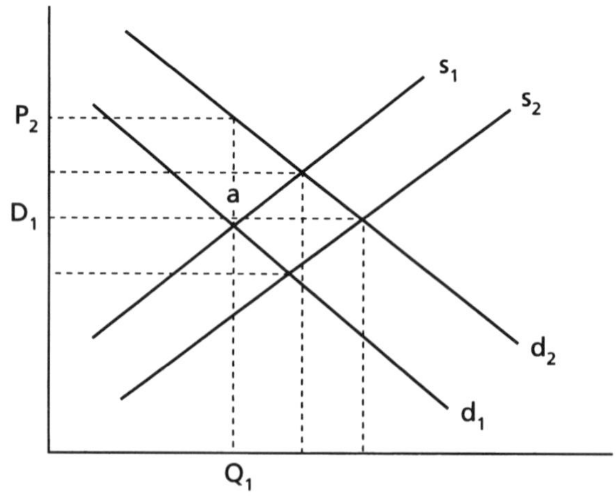

Figure 1 Price mechanism

Assuming that market opens with demand curve d_1 and supply curve s_1, at point "a" where they intersect, the equilibrium price and quantity would be p_1 and q_1 respectively. Now supposing that following a change in consumer preference for the particular good/service in question, the demand curve shifts from d_1 to d_2 pushing up price to p_2 within the market period. This price increase information, assuming perfect information within the market, would be known by all the players in the market. Profit maximising firms would respond to this price information by employing more of the variable factor of production in the short term. In the long term, when all factors of production can be varied, more firms would react to this price information and would move resources into this sector. This resource allocation would continue until the supply curve shifts from s_1 to s_2 and a new equilibrium price and quantity is established in the market.

The price mechanism also operates in the factor market thereby influencing the distribution of income. Firms hire out factor inputs in response to higher demand for the goods and services for which those inputs are required. A higher demand for a particular good then implies a higher demand for the particular inputs that go into its production and a higher demand for a factor of production would mean those factors would command higher prices. Thus the higher the demand for a factor of production and the larger the amount of the factor owned by a household or individual, the higher would be the income. The reverse is also applicable meaning for instance, households with no skills and thus less demand for their labour would have low income. The advantages of the price mechanism are enormous ensuring:

- efficient allocation of resources, and
- economic efficiency.

Consistent with human self-interest, of course, the price mechanism operates only under conditions of perfect competition and in the real world perfect market conditions do not exist. For instance, no way do we have perfect information available to all players in the market. Besides there are some inherent weaknesses in the system:

1. It does not ensure the adequate provision of public goods required by all in the economy, e.g. national defence.
2. It does not take account of negative externalities meaning high levels of pollution in capitalist countries of the West.
3. The use of persuasive advertising means consumers are never sovereign as implied.
4. In the capitalist countries where it operates, it creates severe inequalities of income, rich living alongside people below the poverty line.
5. It promises low inflation and low unemployment. The experience of these Western capitalist countries does not confirm this. **(Marks awarded 28)**

Examiner's comments

The answer demonstrated a good understanding of how markets for goods and services and factors of production operate in both the short and long term, and how prices and factor rewards are determined.

While not utilising the mathematics of the marginal equivalency conditions, a useful approach for analysing economic efficiency, the student was able to identify several areas of market failure, e.g. public goods, externalities and inequitable income distribution, but lost marks by not demonstrating why such factors caused market failure nor how they could be overcome. In this area economies of scale and monopoly were conspicuous by their absence.

Further marks were lost by lack of analysis of why an inequitable distribution of income, explained by the student on "efficiency grounds", was a weakness of the price mechanism. The student did demonstrate a knowledge of the economist's assumptions underlying the "model" of the free enterprise system and pointed out their non fulfilment in the real world. The essay was well-structured, clearly written and logically presented.

The score of 28 out of 40 reflects a good answer; the omissions mentioned above plus lack of detailed analysis accounted for the missing points.

Model answer

Your answer should demonstrate how prices are determined in competitive markets by the forces of demand and supply and show the critical role prices play in the behaviour of consumers attempting to maximise utility and in the behaviour of firms attempting to maximise profits. Your analysis should also show how market forces determine factor prices, i.e. wages, salaries, rent, interest and dividends resulting in the distribution of income.

The strength of the capitalist system can be shown by demonstrating how economic efficiency will prevail if the marginal equivalency conditions are fulfilled. You should analyse those areas of economic activity where collective or government action is required if economic efficiency is to prevail. In this context public goods, externalities and economies of scale should be analysed showing why their presence prohibits economic efficiency being attained. In addition, you should argue that while the income distribution which emerges in the capitalist system is not concerned with economic efficiency, it is a weakness of the system if it produces a distribution which is socially unacceptable.

Finance

Question: Investment appraisal

Daley Healthcare is a company operating in the healthcare business. It wants to become involved in the market for care of the elderly, which in Britain is a growing and profitable sector of the healthcare industry. Daley Healthcare has two options: it can open up a nursing home or it can open up a residential home.

A nursing home is more expensive to set up and run, as the level of care provided is similar to that of a hospital, except that no surgical operations are undertaken. A residential home is less expensive to set up and operate because the staffing and equipment needs are less than that of the nursing home. From an investment point of view nursing homes can be attractive as the fees charged to the patients are much higher than those charged in a residential home.

Daley Healthcare has identified a suitable location to build its chosen home. It will cost £3 million to build a nursing home (Option A) and to equip it to the necessary standards. The residential home will only cost £2 million to build and equip to the necessary standards (Option B). The nursing home will be able to accommodate 40 patients but the residential home, due to the less intensive nature of its care, will be able to take 50 patients. The fees charged to patients are expected to be £400 per week for the nursing home and £210 per week for the residential home.

The staffing arrangements differ for the two homes. The nursing home requires 4 qualified nurses and 8 care assistants; the residential home requires 9 care assistants only. The salaries of the staff are £14 000 per annum for nurses and £10 500 for care assistants (assume the salaries are paid at the end of the year).

The local government council is willing to grant Daley Healthcare a 10-year concession to run the nursing or residential home, after which time it would pass into the control of the council, and the company's investment would be ended. In addition, the nursing or residential home has to reapply for its licence to operate as a healthcare establishment. The costs involved in renewing the licence each year are £100 000 for the nursing home, and £30 000 for the residential home. Daley Healthcare would be responsible for all these costs. The council would pay for all the other costs involved in running the home during the 10 years.

Daley Healthcare has conducted a feasibility study and commissioned market research on this market and this has incurred expenses of £50 000. This research was completed by 31 December 1993.

There are quoted companies on the stock market operating in these areas. Companies operating in the nursing home sub-sector and residential home sub-sector typically have a nominal opportunity cost of capital of 17% and 16% respectively. The expected inflation rate is assumed to remain 3.5% per annum into the foreseeable future, affecting all cash flows and revenues.

The set up costs are assumed to occur in year 0 (i.e. 1.1.94 to 31.12.94), and assume that revenues and costs start in the next time period, year 1 (i.e. 1.1.95) for calculation purposes assume end period cash flows. Also assume 100% occupancy for 52 weeks per year for the full 10 years.

Please ignore tax in this analysis.

NB For all the questions, please show your workings. No marks will be awarded for a numerical answer without any explanation.

Required:

1. Calculate the real discount rate for assessing the projects. Show all working. **(6 marks)**

2. Estimate the cash flows of the two projects (nursing home and residential home). Please make clear headings for the different categories of cash flows. **(10 marks)**

3. What is the Net Present Value (NPV) of each project when both raise prices exactly in line with the rate of inflation? You are limited to choosing just one project. Which one, if either, would you choose? **(10 marks)**

4. Assuming that the nursing home can increase its prices by 2.5% above the rate of inflation, all other revenues and costs will continue to rise at the rate of inflation, the residential home revenues and costs will rise by the rate of inflation, what is the NPV of the nursing home project now? Which project would you choose now, if either? **(12 marks)**

5. What difference does it make if real cash flows are discounted by nominal discount rates as opposed to real discount rates? **(4 marks)**

6. The feasibility and market research reports each incur substantial early costs. What is the appropriate method of treating these costs when calculating the new Net Present Value (NPV) of the projects? **(4 marks)**

7. What other investment appraisal techniques might have been used to assess the projects? Which method is to be preferred? Give two reasons for your choice. **(9 marks)**

(Total of 55 marks)

Actual student answer:

Option A

Cashflow / Date	Set-up cost (£000s) (1)	Healthcare income (£000s) (2)	Healthcare salaries (£000s) (3)	Licence fee (£000s) (4)	Net cashflow (1)+(2)+(3)+(4) (£000s) (5)	Discount rate 13% (6)	(5)×(6) NPV (7)
1.1.94	(3 000)				(3 000)	1	(3 000)
1.1.95		832	(140)	(100)	592	0.8850	523.92
1.1.96		832	(140)	(100)	592	0.7831	663.59
1.1.97		832	(140)	(100)	592	0.6931	410.32
1.1.98		832	(140)	(100)	592	0.6133	363.07
1.1.99		832	(140)	(100)	592	0.5428	321.34
1.1.00		832	(140)	(100)	592	0.4803	284.34
1.1.01		832	(140)	(100)	592	0.4251	251.66
1.1.02		832	(140)	(100)	592	0.3762	222.71
1.1.03		832	(140)	(100)	592	0.3329	187.08
1.1.04		832	(140)	(100)	592	0.2946	174.40
Total							212.43
						(12%)	

Option A: prices increased by 2.5% above inflation

Cashflow / Date	Set-up cost (£000s) (8)	Healthcare income (£000s) (9)	Healthcare salaries (£000s) (10)	Licence fee (£000s) (11)	Net cashflow (8)+(9)+(10)+(11) (£000s) (12)	Discount rate 13% (13)	(5)×(6) NPV (14)
1.1.94	(3 000)				(3 000)	1	(3 000)
1.1.95		832	(140)	(100)	592	0.8850	523.92
1.1.96		852.08	(140)	(100)	621.80	0.7831	479.88
1.1.97		874.12	(140)	(100)	634.12	0.6931	439.51
1.1.98		895.97	(140)	(100)	655.97	0.6133	402.31
1.1.99		918.37	(140)	(100)	678.37	0.5428	368.22
1.1.00		941.33	(140)	(100)	701.33	0.4803	336.85
1.1.01		964.86	(140)	(100)	724.86	0.4251	308.14
1.1.02		988.99	(140)	(100)	738.99	0.3762	281.77
1.1.03		1 013.71	(140)	(100)	773.71	0.3329	257.57
1.1.04		1 039.05	(140)	(100)	799.05	0.2946	235.40
Total							633.56
						(12%)	

Option B

Cashflow / Date	Set-up cost (£000s) (1)	Healthcare income (£000s) (2)	Healthcare salaries (£000s) (3)	Licence fee (£000s) (4)	Net cashflow (1)+(2) + (3)+(4) (£000s) (5)	Discount rate 13% (6)	(5) × (6) NPV (7)
1.1.94	(2000)				(2000)	1	(2000)
1.1.95		546	(94.5)	(30)	421.5	0.8929	376.36
1.1.96		546	(94.5)	(30)	421.5	0.7972	336.02
1.1.97		546	(94.5)	(30)	421.5	0.7118	300.02
1.1.98		546	(94.5)	(30)	421.5	0.6355	267.86
1.1.99		546	(94.5)	(30)	421.5	0.5674	239.16
1.1.00		546	(94.5)	(30)	421.5	0.5066	213.53
1.1.01		546	(94.5)	(30)	421.5	0.4523	190.64
1.1.02		546	(94.5)	(30)	421.5	0.4039	170.24
1.1.03		546	(94.5)	(30)	421.5	0.3606	151.99
1.1.04		546	(94.5)	(30)	421.5	0.3220	135.72
Total							381.56

Question 1

The real discount rate
(1 + nominal rate) = (1 + real rate) (1 + inflation rate)

Option A: (1 + 17%) = (1 + real rate) (1 + 3.5%)
real rate = 13%

Option B: (1 + 16%) = (1 + real rate) (1 + 3.5%)
real rate = 12%

Question 2

Working

(a) *Annual Income* Option A = £400 × 52 weeks × 40 patients = £832 000
Option B = £210 × 52 weeks × 50 patients = £546 000

(b) *Annual Staff Salaries* Option A = (£14 000 × 4) + (£10 500 × 8) = £140 000
Option B = £10 500 × 9 = £94 500

(c) market research = sunk cost ⇒ I not counted.

Question 3

The net present value is calculated in previous table column (7).

Option A: NPV = £212.43
Option B: NPV = £381.56

If only one project should be chosen. Option B should be chosen because it produces a high NPV of £381.56.

Question 4

Option A, new NPV = £633.56

Now the new Option A should be chosen.

Question 5

If real cash flows are discounted by nominal discount rates, the NPV will be *understated* and good projects will be rejected.

The correct method is using real cash flows discounted by real discount rates.

Question 6

Since this is a sunk cost, this cost should be *ignored* in the cashflow.

Examiner's comments

1. This is a question designed to test whether the student recognises that inflation must be taken into account when discounting the cash flows. If the real cash flows are discounted by nominal interest rates this may result in good projects being rejected as the discount rate would be set too high. The real discount rate should be calculated as follows: (1 + r) = (1 + m)/(1 + I), where (1 + r) is the real rate of interest, (1 + m) is the nominal rate of interest and (1 + I) is the inflation rate.

Nursing home cost of capital		= 17%		
Inflation		= 3.5%		
Residential home cost of capital		= 16%		
Nursing home:	(1.17)/(1.035)	= 1.13	=	13%
Residential home:	(1.16)/(1.035)	= 1.12	=	12%

If real cash flows are used in the following analysis, these discount rates should be applied.

So the student should discount the real cash flows by 13% and 12%. Most students did this correctly, but some inflated the cash flows throughout and then discounted by 17% and 16% which arrives at the same result.

The student in this case has applied the correct formula and calculated the correct interest rates.

2. This part of the question asked the student to calculate and show the cash flows of the two projects under consideration. This student has worked out the cash flows necessary in the correct manner. The correct answer for this and the next two parts is laid out in the answer grid on pp. 3/18–3/19.

   The aim here was to get the student to identify and lay out the relevant cash flows for the project. This was a case of reading the question carefully and including only the cash flows that affected the project directly. This meant excluding the feasibility study. Once the correct cash flows had been identified, the student would project them for the ten-year life of the project.

   The student in this example has correctly identified and labelled the cash flows.

3. Once the student had correctly worked out the cash flows, he then had to apply the correct discount rate. In this case the student has demonstrated full knowledge of the NPV technique and has applied the correct real discount rate to the real cash flows, and has worked through the process correctly and indicated the proper choice, that of the residential home as it had the higher NPV.

   NPV calculations are shown in columns 6 and 7, using the real discount rate

   NPV of nursing home = £206 762 (£3 206 762 – £3 000 000)
   NPV of residential home = £374 053 (£2 374 053 – £2 000 000)

   Choose the residential home.

4. This proved to be the hardest part of the question, and a number of students failed to attempt it. The problem was one of increasing the revenues of the nursing home while holding everything else constant. The revenues were increased by 2.5% per annum and resulting cash flows after the usual subtractions would be discounted at 13% to get the new NPV. The new NPV is £626 790 which is now higher than the residential home, so the nursing home is the preferred choice now.

   The NPV of the nursing home with rising real revenue is shown in columns 8, 9, and 10.

   The new NPV of the nursing home is £626 790, (£3 626 790 – £3 000 000), the residential home NPV stays at £374 053.

   This time choose the nursing home as it has the higher NPV.

   The marks awarded for Questions 2, 3, and 4 reflect the different stages and levels of difficulty. A possible ten points were available for working out the cash flows, which could be regarded as the basic workings of the question. Ten points were awarded for the calculation of the NPV, these points are awarded separately to reward evidence of knowledge of the NPV technique. A further twelve points were available for Question 4, where students had to adapt the NPV to changing circumstances.

5. If the students had read all the parts of the questions before starting, then this question would have provided a prompt to those who might have been unsure of how to go about answering the whole question. The aim of the question was for the student to articulate what the effects would be if the wrong interest rates had been used.

   This student has briefly summed up the basic position but has not written anything further.

If nominal discount rates (the observable ones which include inflation's influence and are therefore higher than the associated real rates) are used with the real cash flows, there will be a bias towards rejecting good projects along with the bad.

6. This question aimed to make the student comment on those costs that are irrelevant to the calculation of the NPV, to distinguish between those costs that are directly associated with the project and those that are not.

   The feasibility and market research reports have been carried out and must be paid for whether the projects go ahead or not. They are *sunk costs*, and should *not* be included in the cash flow analysis.

   In this example answer the student has only written one and a half lines for his answer, so the mark is 2.5 out of a possible 4. The student has identified the sunk costs and they should be ignored, but has not expanded on that position, so he cannot receive full marks for the answer.

7. The last question gave the student a chance to describe the various investment appraisal techniques. This part was especially important to those who had struggled with the calculations earlier. There were a possible nine marks available here.

   Other investment appraisal techniques that may be used are: internal rate of return (IRR), discounted payback, profitibility index (PI), accounting rate of return.

   The NPV approach is viewed as more sound than the IRR method because it assumes reinvestment at the cost of capital rather than the project's IRR. IRR cannot cope with negative cash flows (taxes) at the end of projects. Payback period tends to discriminate against long term projects and can exclude projects with a greater NPV. Payback ignores cash flows beyond the payback period. Accounting rate of return takes no account of the timing of cash flows or the size and life of the investment. Also it is based on accounting profits rather than cash flows. NPV is the only safe method of ensuring the firm's objective of maximising wealth.

   In the paper we are looking at here the student has failed to answer this part of the question, but he has passed the question overall as he has scored heavily on the technical part of the question.

   Overall the question was completed well by the student. He has demonstrated full competance in calculating and adapting the NPV technique, he knows exactly what he is doing. On the other hand when it came to articulating on the NPV technique, he has done less well than might have been expected. This could be due to a lack of time, or a difficulty with the language.

   On the division of marks in the question, there was a total of 55 marks available, 38 marks for calculations and a practical demonstration of the student's knowledge of the technique, and 17 marks available for descriptive information about the technique.

   The reasoning for the split was that students should only pass the question if they could show a reasonable technical grasp of the NPV method. On the other hand, if all they could do was complete the calculations correctly, but not write anything, they should still pass the question, as the question was a fair test of the technique. Students did receive credit for however much of the question they had completed.

Answer sheet for question 2

(Please enter your own headings for items which are relevant for the calculation of cash flow.)

Option A

Cashflow categories:	*Revenue* (1)	*Labour costs* (2)	*Health certificate* (3)	*Set-up costs* (4)	*Cashflow* (5)	*13% Real discount factor* (6)	*Real discounted cashflow* (7)
1.1.94				3 000 000		1	
1.1.95	832 000	140 000	100 000		592 000	0.884615	523 692
1.1.96	832 000	140 000	100 000		592 000	0.782544	463 266
1.1.97	832 000	140 000	100 000		592 000	0.692251	409 812
1.1.98	832 000	140 000	100 000		592 000	0.612376	362 526
1.1.99	832 000	140 000	100 000		592 000	0.541717	320 696
1.1.00	832 000	140 000	100 000		592 000	0.479211	283 693
1.1.01	832 000	140 000	100 000		592 000	0.423918	250 959
1.1.02	832 000	140 000	100 000		592 000	0.375004	222 002
1.1.03	832 000	140 000	100 000		592 000	0.331734	196 387
1.1.04	832 000	140 000	100 000		592 000	0.293457	173 727
	8 320 000	£1 400 000	£1 000 000		£5 920 000	total =	£3 206 762 £206 762

Option B

Cashflow categories:	*Revenue* (1)	*Labour costs* (2)	*Health certificate* (3)	*Set-up costs* (4)	*Cashflow* (5)	*12% Real discount factor* (6)	*Real discounted cashflow* (7)
1.1.94				2 000 000			
1.1.95	546 000	94 500	30 000		421 500	0.892241	402 847
1.1.96	546 000	94 500	30 000		421 500	0.796095	359 437
1.1.97	546 000	94 500	30 000		421 500	0.710309	320 704
1.1.98	546 000	94 500	30 000		421 500	0.633767	286 146
1.1.99	546 000	94 500	30 000		421 500	0.565473	255 311
1.1.00	546 000	94 500	30 000		421 500	0.504538	227 799
1.1.01	546 000	94 500	30 000		421 500	0.45017	203 252
1.1.02	546 000	94 500	30 000		421 500	0.40166	181 350
1.1.03	546 000	94 500	30 000		421 500	0.358378	161 808
1.1.04	546 000	94 500	30 000		421 500	0.31956	144 371
	5 460 000	£945 000	£300 000		£4 215 000	total =	£2 374 053 £374 053

(Please enter your own headings for items which are relevant for the calculation of cash flow.)

Cashflow categories:	*Revenue up by real 2.5%* (8)	*Adjusted cashflow* (9)	*Real discounted adjusted cashflow* (10)	(11)	(12)
1.1.94					
1.1.95	832 000	592 000	523 692		
1.1.96	852 800	612 800	479 543		
1.1.97	874 120	634 120	438 970		
1.1.98	895 973	655 973	401 702		
1.1.99	918 372	678 372	367 486		
1.1.00	941 332	701 332	33 086		
1.1.01	964 865	724 865	307 283		
1.1.02	988 987	748 987	280 873		
1.1.03	1 013 711	773 711	256 667		
1.1.04	1 039 054	799 054	234 488		
	£9 321 214	£6 921 214	£3 626 790	NPV = £626 790	

Cashflow categories:	*Revenue up by real 2.5%* (8)	*Adjusted cash flow* (9)	*Real discounted adjusted cashflow* (10)	(11)	(12)
1.1.94					
1.1.95					
1.1.96					
1.1.97					
1.1.98					
1.1.99					
1.1.00					
1.1.01					
1.1.02					
1.1.03					
1.1.04					

Marketing

Question

In 1990 expenditure on tea in the UK rose by 16% on the previous year to a record £625 million (higher than the expenditure on coffee). Traditional tea accounts for 96% of retail sales. More than 80% of it is sold in tea bags, a trend boosted by the introduction of round tea bags.

A leading tea company wishes to benefit from the increasing sales of premium teas and is introducing a new brand to meet the demand for decaffeinated tea.

As Marketing Research manager

1. Prepare the outline of a marketing research plan to test the feasibility of the produced new product.
2. Detail how the most appropriate test marketing methods might be determined.

Actual student answer

Question 1 Outline marketing research plan – decaffeinated tea

Introduction

The increase in demand for decaffeinated tea requires the company to undertake a market research plan to investigate the attractiveness of the market.

This report outlines the steps to be taken to test the feasibility of the proposed new product.

Stages in the market research plan

(i) Environmental analysis

The following areas need to be investigated:

- current offerings in the market
- competition levels in terms of number of competitors, size of competitors and relative market share
- analysis of market potential
- analysis of target market characteristics.

A brief review of the above will give the researcher a feel as to the way the research should continue.

(ii) Discussion of research with management

Management have already decided that a new product is a possibility. They are asking the researchers to test its feasibility.

Management should outline the following to allow the researchers to fully grasp the tasks to be undertaken:

- reasons for introducing new product (relevant data trends)
- type of target market (characteristics)
- objectives of the research.

At this stage it is imperative that the researchers are clear as to what the management hope to achieve from the research, i.e. it is clear what they have to do. A common problem at this stage is that the management fail to correctly specify the research objectives.

(iii) Define research methodology

There are basically two approaches which can be adapted. They are:

(1) *Exploratory research* – This approach investigates the problem or proposal in more detail. Examples of this type of research in the context of decaffeinated tea would include:

- Discussion groups with tea drinkers. The groups could be based on age, social class, etc. The researcher would question the group on what it thought of the decaffeinated tea concept.
- Consumer surveys, e.g. question people in a shopping mall about how they feel about decaffeinated tea.

(2) *Conclusive research* – This approach tests whether the new product fulfils the benefits sought by a target audience. In this context "does the new decaffeinated tea taste the same as normal tea?" A variety of tests could be used here including:

- laboratory tests – experts taste and compare
- blind unpaired tests – consumers compare new product with normal tea and are asked if they can tell the difference
- test marketing – encourage identified groups to try the product at home. Ask them for their conclusions.

(iv) Define the sample

The researchers must decide how the sample is to be structured so that results of tests can be extrapolated to the full population. As such, probability sampling would be more useful than non-probability sampling which would not allow extrapolation.

In this instance the sample would only contain tea drinkers. The sample could be split based on age, amount of consumption, social class, etc. Then once it has been stratified, select on a random basis from each sub-sample.

Ensure sample is representative and unbiased.

(v) Collect data

Data can basically be collected via:

- questioning, or
- observation (represents only 1% of data collected for all types of test).

In this instance it is likely that questionnaires would be used to ask the following style of questions:

- Is the colour the same as normal tea?
- Does it smell like normal tea?
- Does it taste like normal tea?
- Other relevant questions.

(vi) Tabulate and analysis data collected

Tabularise data collected.

Analyse data to decide if decaffeinated tea was acceptable in the sample and whether they would purchase it as an alternative to normal tea or would it result in increased generation?

Produce a forecast of the likely take up and hence sales volume for the total market based on research results.

Ensure that data transfer between collection and tabulation has been done correctly. If this is not the case then conclusions could be invalid.

(vii) Take appropriate action

The following options will be possible:

(i) Scrap new product as target market don't like it.

(ii) Refine product before proceeding.

(iii) New product is successful, hence test market.

Question 2 Most appropriate test marketing methods – decaffeinated tea

Introduction

This report assumes the new decaffeinated tea product has passed initial screening and fulfilled the market research objectives.

This report outlines the next stage which is test marketing to test the national marketing plan and ultimately provide a forecast of natural sales for the first year of production.

Types of test marketing methods

(i) Small versus large scale

There are basically two scales of market testing. The first are small scale tests which are "relatively" cheap and assist in preventing competitors from observing the marketing plan and the new product offering. The advantage of this approach is the avoidance of competitors performing reverse engineering on the product and then introducing a “me-too” (i.e. copy) of the new product soon after the new product is produced. There are, however, a number of disadvantages associated with this approach. They include:

- artificial environment could affect results
- results may use too small a sample to allow extrapolation to natural market.

A large scale full market test usually involves the marketing plan being tested in a given geographical area or areas and the results being extrapolated to the full market. A recent example of this approach was seen when Persil’s new washing-up liquid was tested in Carlisle. This approach has a number of advantages.

- real environment should ensure more accurate results
- allows greater analysis by researchers of adoption process reaction to advertising message and repeat buying process
- observation of how sales are generated against competitors and their reactions.

The main disadvantages associated with this approach are as follows:

- very high cost
- time scale needs to be long enough to allow at least two or three re-buy decisions to be taken. This allows competitors time to do reverse engineering on the product and observe the sales potential of the new product
- advertising and promotion campaign becomes easy to observe by competitors. This allows competitors in particular the opportunity to copy sales promotion techniques.

Types of tests

(i) Small scale

- Laboratory tests – in this case could have a mock-up café and observe adoption process for new product. Test advertising message – mock-up TV programmes, mock-up magazine adverts.
- Consumer tests – free samples to selected households to obtain feedback. Testing advertising message and retention.

(ii) Large scale

- Test marketing plan in a selection of towns, cities, etc.

Analysis of most appropriate test marketing method

To prevent competitors getting early access to the new product, laboratory and consumer tests should be undertaken to ensure the product fits the needs of the consumer. Once the product is fully developed it can then go to stage two.

Due to the artificial nature of small scale, a large scale test is probably imperative due to this being a high involvement but nature purchase. The test should consider the following:

Product

- Do consumers re-buy? If not, why not?
- Is the product durable for storage purposes?

Price

- Are consumers willing to pay the price?
- What are competitors' prices?
- Do competitors react to price changes?

Distribution

- Are all outlets stocking the product in the test area?
- Is there adequate she!f-space?
- Are there stock outs? Why?

Promotion

- Do consumers remember the message?
- Are consumers aware of product attributes?
- Is there brand loyalty?
- Are coupons being redeemed?
- Are other sales promotions working?

Conclusion

For tea, which is a high involvement product, full market testing is essential to ensure the product has been correctly positioned.

The product's promotional campaign has to be tested to achieve an objective of brand loyalty which will help to off-set the impact of "me-too" products which may follow.

Large scale testing is expensive but imperative in this case.

Examiner's general comments regarding answering marketing questions

Throughout the answer paper the examiner is looking for the candidate to display a sound knowledge of marketing, including strategic marketing and marketing research practice Both the case study approach and the essay give the student an opportunity to show the application of theory to practice. Thus, in the case studies, if the candidate can introduce pertinent recommendations in the light of personal experience this will be credited, as will the use of relevant examples in the essay question.

While the examiner is seeking a marketing approach to the answer provided, there is not any preconceived "right" approach. Rather, the candidate's logical approach and supporting justification for selecting a particular strategy to answer the problem will be carefully considered.

It should be noted that a common error on the part of some students is to mis-read the question. More specifically, many students mis-read "marketing research plan" as "marketing plan"; in error, they provide the outline of a *marketing plan* instead of the *marketing research plan* specified in the question.

Model answer

1. Define the nature of marketing research. This is an assessment of the market trends for a particular product or service through the use of desk research and field research undertaken by both persons who may be internal and/or external to the firm. It would be likely to include investigation of potential, actual customers and non-customers, as well as competitor analysis.

   Outline the marketing research plan. This should define

   - the objectives of the marketing research
   - the type of marketing research techniques that might be used to help management decision making in new product development
   - the resources available for the marketing research in terms of finance, personnel and time.

   The use of a formal marketing information system (MIS) would also be helpful and a marketing database could be introduced.

2. Discuss the specific marketing research techniques that would be likely to be useful for consumer new product development. These would be likely to include desk research and field research. The techniques could be qualitative and/or quantitative techniques in nature. Qualitative techniques might include group discussions and in-depth interviewing; quantitative techniques would be likely to include customer surveys, product trials (possibly using hall tests), and home placements and various forms of test marketing. Indicate, in terms of finance, time scale and human resources, the resources likely to be available for your recommendations to be implemented.

Examiner's comment on the actual student answer

The student set out the answer in a clear manner, using the report style which is appropriate to the question as given, i.e. "prepare the outline of a marketing research plan".

In the sample answer the student then took the managerial approach to the question. Desk research regarding the background to the market was assessed through the environmental analysis. At the introductory stage, discussions were held with management to specify the nature of the market research inquiry. Importantly the objectives of the research were determined.

The answer proceeded to examine the methodology of the marketing research to be used. This started with exploratory research, predominantly qualitative in nature (group discussions and general consumer surveys). Some mention of in-depth interviewing would have been helpful. Conclusive research, quantitative in nature, followed, namely, laboratory tests, blind-paired tests and test marketing. It would have been helpful if these techniques could have been further detailed, for example, hall tests using sip testing, etc.

Discussion of the sampling method to be used was useful, as was the method of data collection and the analysis of that data.

The student then developed the second part of the question, by detailing critical elements of the test marketing methods selected. Issues such as the selection of test regions, areas, cities and the controls to be used in the test market were also briefly considered.

Improved marks would have been achieved if more consideration had been given to specifying the resources likely to be available to implement the marketing research plan in terms of finance, time scale and human resources.

Overall the student provided an appropriate approach to the question and displayed sound knowledge of the critical issues of the question.

Organisational Behaviour

Question 1

Define the term "performance appraisal". Examine why organisations need to assess the performance of their employees and identify how the appraisal process affects the individual at work.

Actual student answer

Performance appraisal is defined as a systematic process of assessing the effectiveness of employees for human resource management.

The results or feedback gathered from this assessment are an effective way of identifying training needs and also a source to determine the employee's qualities and performance. Rewards or compensation methods can also be derived from this exercise.

However, the results' validity, reliability and consistency have always been the main concerns. The validity of the feedback/data is defined as the effectiveness of the data. Reliability is concerned about the stability of a measure over time of different raters. Consistency is the regularity of measure as compared with the rates evaluated at different time periods.

Other aspects of the appraisal which are most commonly found include errors as indicated below:

- Halo effect, which is the tendency of an appraiser to rate an appraisee the same on all performance dimensions because of a general impression.
- Similarity effect which is the tendency of an appraiser to rate an appraisee based on the appraiser's expectation.
- Leniency effect which is the tendency of an appraiser to rate an appraisee on an average rating.
- Central tendency which refers to an appraiser who rates an appraisee on a uniform or standard rating.
- Bias of the appraiser on the appraisee's rating.
- Recency effect reflects the tendency of an appraiser rating an appraisee on events which occurred during the period before the appraisal.

There are several methods to conduct the performance appraisal objectively as follows:

- *BAR (Behavioural Anchored Rating) assessment*
  This method is based on behavioural assessment of an employee. Questionnaires are aimed at identifying the employee's tasks and how the job is done in relation to other areas or persons. Ratings of 0–10 are allocated for the various feedbacks.

- *Absolute rating method*
  Answers to questionnaires are in a dictotomy method with no alternatives, e.g. Yes or No. This method is only applicable to routine jobs which are machine paced that do not involve many external factors or are not greatly influenced by too many variables.
- *Graphic*
  Ratings are given to answers relating to the employee's personality traits which are related to the job. However, due to the nature of questionnaires which are negatively tuned towards degrading an employee, it is not a good appraisal system.

The appraisal process is a necessity to any organisation who are involved in a multiplicity of operations. Through this process the needs of the employee can be ascertained and subsequently attended to by the type of training, jobs, and rewards and advancement.

Employee's job range and depth may be improved due to the salient qualities ascertained from the appraisal. In this process, the job can also be enriched, enlarged or rotated depending on the employee's capabilities and attitude.

All in all, the employee's performance can be guided by the organisation, particularly human resource management to achieve maximum productivity.

Examiner's comments

In the first part of the question, candidates are required to produce either of the two definitions in the main text. One definition may be found in module 2 on page 38 ("appraisal is the systematic assessment of how effectively each job is being performed"), the other in module 4 on page 83 ("appraisal is a process which generates valid information about employee work effectiveness for the purpose of making informed human resource decisions"). The student's answer, although briefer than the text book version, is acceptable because it covers the main issues of assessment and work effectiveness.

In the second part of the question, candidates are required to describe and comment on the reasons why organisations need to assess employee performance. The information for this may be found on page 83 of the text and covers the following issues:

- To identify desirable on-the-job behaviour
- To evaluate employees' work for its contribution to organisational goals
- To give feedback to employees about their work performance
- To increase employee motivation
- To provide data for use in making decisions about salaries, promotion and training
- To make employees aware of the performance standards required.

In the student's answer the candidate notes these points in one short paragraph without adding any explanatory comments. However, these issues need to be developed and the information to do this may be found in module 2, pages 38 and 39. The student's answer lacks substance and depth.

In part 3 candidates are required to merely identify the ways in which the appraisal process affects the individual. These are listed on page 83 of the course and include:

- Needs fulfilment
- Job satisfaction
- Organisational commitment
- Job involvement
- Satisfaction with supervisors
- Satisfaction with pay
- Achievement of promotions
- Greater responsibility
- Self-awareness.

In the above question, the candidate fails to deal with this part of it adequately. Most of his answer introduces issues which are not relevant to the question. It is important before attempting to answer a question to read it carefully.

Question 2

What do we mean by "organisational culture"? Consider the factors which contribute to the development of a company's organisational culture and identify the liabilities associated with a strong organisational culture.

Actual student answer

Organisational culture is the shared values and beliefs of the workforce which create norms for employee behaviour.

Culture is notoriously difficult to define, as different people view it in different ways (depending on whether they are external or internal to the organisation), and the "true" culture is often only evident after an event such as an organisational crisis.

Culture is the "organisational way of life".

Culture develops slowly over time, and it is therefore important that the organisation "nurtures and directs" culture in a planned manner. One important point to note is that although culture develops slowly, an organisational crisis (a disaster precipitated by technology, people, structures or economics which severely damages people, natural and social environments) may shock culture into a sudden change of direction (e.g. the Union Carbide disaster in Bhopal, India), and we must therefore plan for this.

As a starting point, it is important that culture is developed in line with changing structures, strategies, processes, markets and leadership for the organisation to be effective/successful.

Sources of culture change may be external or internal, and result from technology, economics, people, society or organisational mechanisms. We must monitor these sources of crisis/culture change, evaluate their effects and prepare solutions.

It is generally accepted that two main factors contribute to the development of culture:

- The role of the CEO/leader
- An effective and robust socialisation process.

The CEO plays a fundamental role in planting the "seeds" of culture into the organisation. A classic example is McKnight, the founder of 3M, who has left a legacy of a culture which advocates innovation.

Socialisation is the process by which culture is transmitted from one generation to another.

Pascale of Stanford University posits that the development of culture revolves around:

- Careful selection of new employees, to ensure that the "profile/characteristics" of new employees fit with culture.
- Realistic job previews to ensure that prospective employees feel comfortable with the culture.
- Indoctrination and debasement to create humility in employees to make them more "open" to organisational norms.
- Train all new employees "in the trenches" so that they understand the core aspects of the organisation.
- Develop promotion/reward systems which focus on performance excellence as dictated by organisational norms.
- Identify employees with high potential, label them as protégés and assign them to mentors.
- Use folklore and stories to reinforce the culture.
- Top management act as role models to give "authoritative" model for excellence.

All the above points, when used and are present in organisations will develop the culture. Prerequisites are that management:

- value the importance of employees' contribution to organisational effectiveness;
- are comfortable with the "human" aspects of the business;
- embrace their positions as "role model" and believe in and accept the importance of culture.

I would once again end with the emphasis on planning culture developments, especially in terms of being pro-active in relation to crisis situations.

How managers handle a crisis situation will have a fundamental, often irreversible, effect on the culture of the organisation.

Liabilities associated with a strong culture are as follows:

- It is possible that strong cultures may hinder change, and this can be dangerous especially where the change relates to strategies, leadership or the market place.

- In respect of take-overs of firms with strong cultures, the acquiring firm will expect the firm to adapt its culture in line with the acquiring firm this is likely to cause problems (e.g. a non-unionised firm which takes over a strongly oriented, unionised firm).
- Cultures which do not "fit" with strategies and objectives cause the organisational performance to drop. This can be seen especially where cultures are allowed to develop in an unplanned/haphazard way.
- Because of geographical or unit differentiation, strong sub-cultures may emerge, and these will result in the above problems.
- Strong cultures (or sub-cultures) may result in undesirable organisational outcomes such as "empire-building", taking the focus away from organisational effectiveness.
- Lastly strong cultures which advocate lack of planning etc., will cast an "invulnerability culture" into the organisation. This can have catastrophic effects as the happening of an organisational crisis will affect not only the direction of the culture, but will increase the shock effect of any crisis.

It is now widely recognised that culture is fundamental to the long term success of the organisation, and generally speaking a culture which is fairly strong, and has its direction planned in line with strategy, structures, leadership and the market, is preferable.

Examiner's comments

The first part of the question requires candidates to state precisely what organisational culture is. A definition can be found on page 197 of the main text. In the above answer the candidate gives a correct definition at the beginning of his answer. He gets added marks because he warns the reader that although he has done what was asked in the question he has reservations about the definition, noting the difficulty of defining it. This shows that he has thought about the definition and has a point of view.

In the second part of the question, candidates are required to think about and note down the relevant factors. This is meant by the word "consider". In the above answer the candidate notes, correctly, that there are two major factors, which he identifies as "The Role of the CEO" and the "Socialisation Process" and then goes on to explain each of the components of these. You can find this information on pages 201 and 202 of the main text. Note that he does not proceed to write long descriptions of each item and that here and elsewhere he uses practical examples to illustrate the point he is making. There is no need to describe these examples in detail because this would add nothing to the issues under discussion. At the end of the list he reminds the reader again of the reason for the list and this gives him the opportunity to introduce an issue which links the second part of the question to the third part.

In the third part of the question candidates are required to specify the problems associated with a strong culture and make a few notes of explanation of why these are considered liabilities. This information can be found on pages 200 and 201 of the main text. In the above answer the candidate has concentrated on the "reason why" and the "implications of" each of these elements and this analytical approach gives added value to the answer.

The above answer covers all the required issues. Nothing of any importance has been missed. Neither are there any errors in interpretation of the facts and issues. In assembling the points, putting them together and showing the inter-relationship between them the candidate has produced a well structured and succinct answer and avoided repetition. It is not enough to list facts without any explanations or introduce issues in a random fashion. An answer has to be structured.

Quantitative Methods

Case study 1

At a crop research institute, four different varieties of wheat are grown so that the yields can be investigated. As it is thought that the location in the field (such as amount of sunshine, wind, etc.) may also have an effect on yield, the field is divided into 4 equal strips. Yield figures are shown in the table below:

	Yield			
	Wheat strain			
Location	A	B	C	D
1	11	15	11	11
2	15	17	14	14
3	15	18	14	13
4	13	16	15	12

1. Produce a two-way analysis of variance table for the above data. **(11 marks)**

2. Is there a significant difference in the average yield for the different varieties of wheat? **(4 marks)**

3. Is there a significant difference in the average yield produced by the different locations in the field? **(4 marks)**

4. Write a report on your findings. What qualifications would you wish to make to your conclusions? **(6 marks)**

(Total of 25 marks)

Case study 2

A local newspaper has a weekly section which advertises property for sale. Editorial comment is also included in this section. For their first issue in June the editors wish to comment on changes in property prices since the beginning of the year. It has been suggested that a property index should be calculated.

Properties sold in this area fall into three main categories: detached houses, other houses and flats. The table below shows the data for the first three months of the year (prices are given in £000s and refer to the average price).

Month	*Detached houses*		*Other houses*		*Flats*	
	Price	*Quantity*	*Price*	*Quantity*	*Price*	*Quantity*
Jan	82	30	61.8	100	45.1	232
Feb	95	40	62.1	124	47.5	376
March	87	32	62.9	152	50.3	512

1. Write a short report on the trends observed in the above table. **(5 marks)**
2. Calculate three different types of aggregate price index for February using January as the base month.

   Comment on the advantages and disadvantages of each of the indices you have produced. **(12 marks)**
3. Recommend the most suitable type of index for use in the property index, giving your reasons. **(2 marks)**
4. If the newspaper decided to make such an index a permanent feature, outline briefly the other factors that would need to be taken into account. **(6 marks)**
(Total of 25 marks)

Case study 3

1. Describe briefly the characteristics of the normal distribution. **(5 marks)**
2. Outline the importance of the normal distribution in statistical inference. **(4 marks)**
3. In a factory producing soft drinks, there is a canning process to fill the cans. The content of the cans is normally distributed with mean 442.5 ml and standard deviation of 1.2 ml. The cans are all marked as containing 440 ml.
   (a) What percentage of the cans contain more than 444 ml? **(5 marks)**
   (b) If the firm is found to have sold a can containing less than the stated content, the firm can be prosecuted. In a production run of 8,000 cans, how many cans would contain less than the stated content? **(6 marks)**
   (c) Between what limits does 92% of the production fall? **(5 marks)**
(Total of 25 marks)

Case study 4

A brewery produces several different kinds of beer, together with its latest product, a low-alcohol beer. It supplies the retail market which includes shops, supermarkets and off-licences with its products. For this market the beer is usually sold in bottles or cans; these may be sold individually, or as multi-packs (4 or 6 cans), or in crates. The brewery also supplies the licensed trade such as hotels, restaurants, clubs, bars and pubs. In this sector, the beer may be supplied in cans, bottles, crates or casks.

The brewery needs to plan its future production, and requires forecasts of its sales in the different markets. The firm also needs to forecast sales for its various products and for the different types of packaging and distribution.

Describe how a suitable forecasting system could be developed for the brewery.

(Total of 25 marks)

Examiner's comments on actual student answers

The answers provided by students to the case studies in this paper have revealed the following areas of difficulty:

Case study 1

- Calculation of the sum of squares between treatments

  $$\text{SST} = \text{Number of blocks} \times \sum_j \left(x_j - \overline{\overline{x}}\right)$$

  Frequently students omitted the number of blocks, in this case four.
- Calculation of the sum of squares between blocks

  $$\text{SST} = \text{Number of treatments} \times \sum_i \left(x_i - \overline{\overline{x}}\right)$$

  Frequently students omitted the number of treatments, in this case four.
- The easiest way of calculating the error sum of squares is by subtraction. The error sum of squares should always be positive.

  Error SS = Total SS – Treatment SS – Block SS
  = 66 – 36 – 24 = 6
- In the ANOVA table the degrees of freedom were often incorrectly calculated. The degrees of freedom for the treatments, blocks and total should be calculated first, the error degrees of freedom can then be calculated by subtraction.

  Error df = Total df – Treatment df – Block df

Source	*Degrees of freedom formula*	*Degrees of freedom value*
Treatments	c–1	3
Blocks	r–1	3
Error	(rc–1)–(c–1)–(r–1)	9
Total	rc–1	15

- This example required a *two-way* ANOVA and should have contained the following rows:

  Treatments
  Blocks
  Error
  Total

  Using two separate one-way ANOVAs would not be acceptable.

- The mean squares were frequently calculated incorrectly. They should always be positive.

$$\text{Mean square treatments} = \frac{\text{Sum of squares between treatments}}{\text{Treatment degrees of freedom}}$$

$$= \frac{\text{SST}}{\text{Treatment df}} = \frac{36}{3} = 12$$

- The F-ratio was frequently calculated incorrectly. It must be positive.

$$\text{F-ratio for treatments} = \frac{\text{Mean square for treatments}}{\text{Error mean square}}$$

$$= \frac{12}{0.67} = 17.91$$

$$\text{F-ratio for blocks} = \frac{\text{Mean square for blocks}}{\text{Error mean square}}$$

$$= \frac{8}{0.67} = 11.94$$

- Interpretation of the F-ratios

  Even many of the students who had accurately calculated all the information in the ANOVA table could not interpret the results of the analysis correctly. The interpretation of the results of hypothesis tests is very important. There is not much point in collecting data for a significance test, performing the calculations but then not knowing how to interpret the results. This is a common problem in the Quantitative Methods examinations.

  In a two-way ANOVA there are two pairs of hypotheses, one for the Treatment means, the other for the Block means. In both cases the hypotheses are:

Null Hypothesis:	The population means are equal
Alternative Hypothesis:	The population means are not equal

  The *F-ratio observed* (Fobs) is compared with the *Critical F-ratios* (F5% or F1%) given in the tables. Students may find it helpful to draw a sketch diagram to illustrate their data. For example:

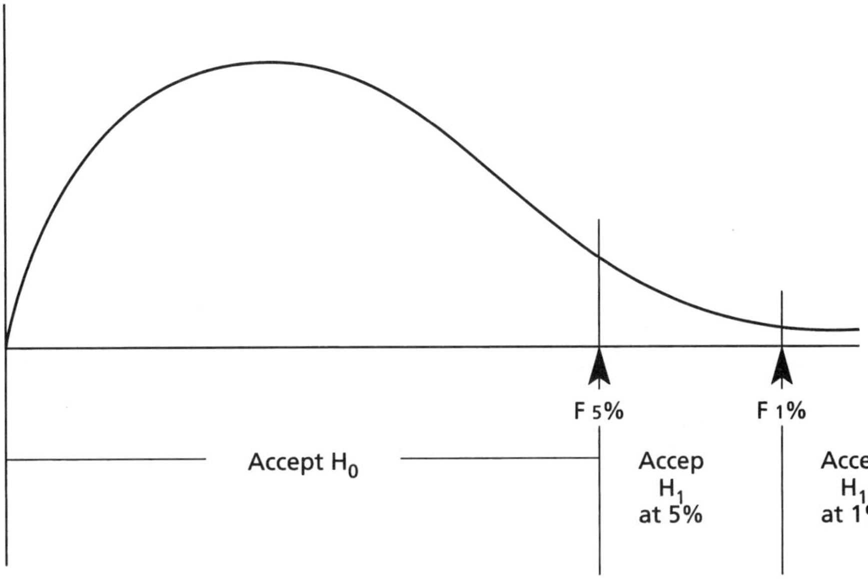

The value of F observed should also be shown. If this value falls in the tail of the distribution, the alternative hypothesis should be accepted, otherwise the alternative hypothesis should be rejected.

The outcomes can be summarised as follows:

If	Fobs < F5%	Reject alternative hypothesis
If	F5% < Fobs < F1%	Accept alternative hypothesis at 5% level of significance
If	F1% < Fobs	Accept alternative hypothesis at 1% level of significance

Testing the treatments (varieties):

Null hypothesis: Treatment population means are equal
Alternative hypothesis: Treatment population means are unequal

F-ratio observed = 17.91 with 3 and 9 degrees of freedom.

To find the critical values in the F-distribution tables you need the column headed 3, and the row labelled 9. This produces the values for the critical F-ratios.

Critical F at the 5% level of significance = F5% = 3.86

Critical F at the 1% level of significance = F1% = 6.99

Illustrating this in a diagram:

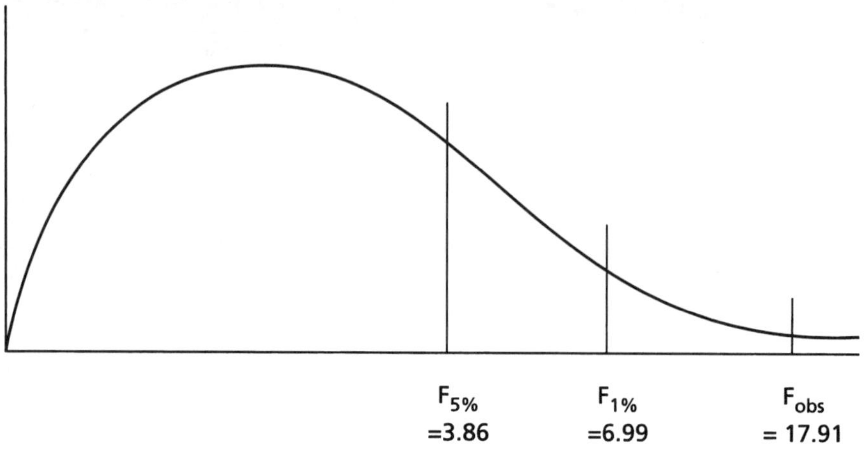

Fobs > F1% hence the alternative hypothesis should be accepted at the 1% level of significance.

The observed F-ratio of 17.91 is more extreme than the critical value of F at 1%, and there is only a probability of <0.01 that a value of 17.91 would occur from this F-distribution. Since this probability is very small we conclude that our observed value of 17.91 has been produced by a population with a different distribution. There is a probability of <1% that we are drawing the wrong conclusion, this is indicated by the statement "at the 1% level of significance".

Returning to the example, we conclude that there is a significant difference in the treatment means at the 1% level of significance. Putting this another way, the average yields from the four varieties are significantly different at the 1% level of significance.

Testing the blocks (locations):

Null hypothesis: Block population means are equal
Alternative hypothesis: Block population means are unequal

F-ratio observed = 11.94 with 3 and 9 degrees of freedom

To find the critical values in the F-distribution tables you need the column headed 3, and the row labelled 9. This produces the values for the critical F-ratios.

Critical F at the 5% level of significance = F5% = 3.86

Critical F at the 1% level of significance = F1% = 6.99

Illustrating this in a diagram:

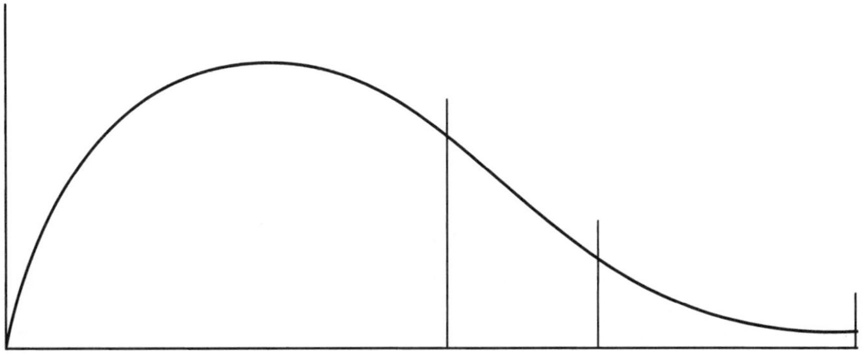

The observed F-ratio of 11.94 is more extreme than the critical value of F at 1%, and there is only a probability of <0.01 that a value of 11.94 would occur from this F-distribution. Since this probability is very small we conclude that our observed value of 11.94 has been produced by a population with a different distribution. There is a probability of <1% that we are drawing the wrong conclusion, this is indicated by the statement "at the 1% level of significance".

Returning to the example, we conclude that there is a significant difference in the block means at the 1% level of significance. Putting this another way, the average yields from the four locations are significantly different at the 1% level of significance.

- Many candidates were unable to explain their findings in words even if they had come to the correct numerical conclusion. If you are commenting on the outcome of the analysis of variance as in the two sections above remember that the results refer to the averages or means.

Do look at the data and comment on the obvious patterns in it. Also look for outliers, i.e. unusually high or low values. Many of these features should be obvious from an initial inspection of the data and should be looked for before any formal calculation is undertaken.

Case study 2

1. In the first question of this case study candidates were asked to comment on the trends in the data. These trends should have been obvious from an inspection of the data, but some candidates were reluctant to provide any commentary. The marks for this section are indicated and students are unwise to omit a section such as this.

2. In the second question of the case study three examples of aggregate price indices were needed. This should indicate that the indices would need to take account of each of the three different types of housing. Many students ignored this and calculated indices for each type of housing separately. Candidates also often omitted to comment on the advantages and disadvantages of the index they had calculated.
3. In the third question some students again omitted to either make a recommendation or to justify their choice.
4. In the fourth question students were asked to outline the other factors that should be taken into account in the construction of a property index. Again several students seemed reluctant to express their views. You should be able to apply the general principles and features of index series to a specific example.

Case study 3

1. Most students made a good attempt at this question. Marks were generally lost in questions 2 and 3(b).
2. In question 2 many students were unable to explain the importance of the normal distribution in statistical inference. The Central Limit Theorem, the distribution of the sample means and consequently the normal distribution are essential to our understanding of statistical estimation and in hypothesis testing. Without such information we would be unable to calculate confidence intervals or perform many of the statistical tests.
3. Most candidates correctly recognised that question 3 used the normal distribution and the standard normal deviate z. The z values were in general calculated correctly, but some candidates seemed unsure as to which area under the normal distribution curve they had calculated or required. Candidates would again benefit from drawing a small diagram to illustrate the areas involved.

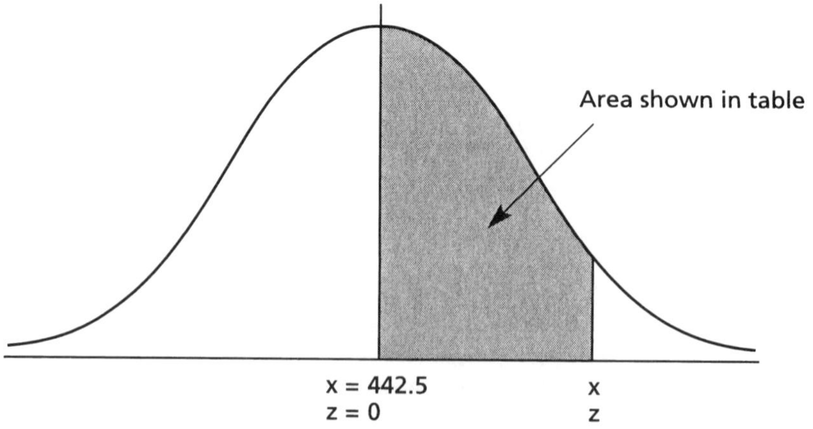

4. In question 3(b) many candidates were unclear as to the area required. The value of 440 ml is *less than* the population mean of 442.5 ml, and therefore the area in the *left tail* is required.

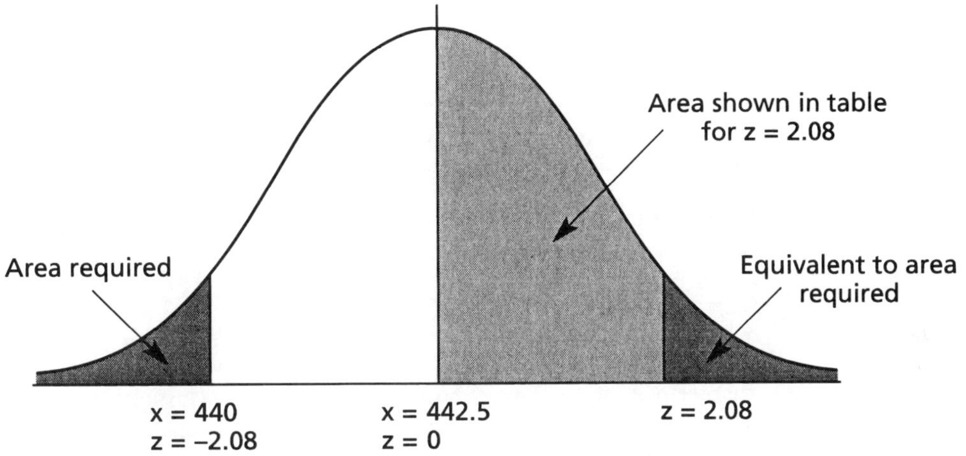

Case study 4

Many candidates simply stated the forecasting guidelines as given in the text. This was not sufficient to gain a good mark for this question. The question was set in the context of the brewing industry and the answers needed to explain how a forecasting model could be used specifically in this industry and its environment. Obviously the guidelines could be used to provide a foundation for the answer, but candidates need to think about and comment on the relevance and limitations of each guideline to the particular case study.

Summary

Candidates generally answered questions well. The major weaknesses were in interpreting the results of hypothesis tests, relating theory to practical cases (index and forecasting) and in commenting on trends and patterns in data.

In calculations candidates should show their working, and should comment on any unusual values that they obtain. The use of sketch diagrams might help some candidates in the interpretation of hypothesis tests and in the use of the normal distributions.

Strategic Planning

Case study I

THE FINANCIAL TIMES
INFLATION RETURNS

The past two years have seen the fastest growth in the economy in 20 years, with real GNP increasing by over 4% each year. But there are signs that this is causing extreme inflationary pressures, the unemployment rate has dropped to its lowest level for 12 years, and wage claims are up to 12%.

MEMO, Acme Plc
From: Managing Director
To: All Board Members

The accounting department has expressed severe misgivings about the performance of the Liqueur and the Blend. The marketing department suggests that we need to look at the performance of our products against the background of a growing economy. It seems to me that the Malt commands a strong competitive position reflected in its high profitability. We have spent a lot trying to generate market share for the Liqueur, but despite the fact that sales have risen by 20% in the past two years, market share has stayed very low. The Blend has been around for a long time, but the market is likely to decline as tastes change in favour of the Malt and the Liqueur.

Information on the accounts and products for Acme Plc is contained in Appendix 1 on page 3/45.

1. Compare the views of a marketing specialist and an accountant on the three products. **($5\frac{1}{3}$ marks)**
2. How would you reallocate company resources to increase profits in the short and the long term, bearing in mind the newspaper report and the memo? **(14 marks)**
3. Imagine that the company decides to issue 1 million shares. What information would you use in deciding how much to pay for a share? Approximately how much would you be willing to pay? **(14 marks)**

(Total of $33\frac{1}{3}$ marks)

Case study 2

The TV guide price war

The events in 1991 show how competitive pressures come into play when a legal monopoly is terminated. Until the end of February 1991 in the UK television programme listings were published weekly by two magazines: *TV Times* (which only published commercial channel listings) and *Radio Times* (which only published British Broadcasting Corporation channels, which are funded by an annual licence fee); beside providing listings, these magazines contain the types of article found in all popular magazines: articles about stars, personalities, programmes and films, letters to the editor, horoscopes and so on. When the monopoly was terminated *TV Times* was selling about 3.2 million copies per week, and *Radio Times* sold about 2.4 million copies per week. *Radio Times* was priced at 50p, which it did not change for the rest of 1991; *TV Times* was also priced at 50p. When the monopoly was removed both *TV Times* and *Radio Times* started to publish both commercial and BBC channel listings.

The history of sales in the early stages of competition is set out in Table 1, and illustrated in the diagram below.

Table 1 Sales of TV guides (millions)

	TV Times	*Radio Times*	*TV Plus*	*What's on TV*	*TV Quick*	*Total*
February	3.10	2.35	0.50			5.95
March	2.20	2.10	0.40	0.70		5.40
April	1.60	1.70		0.70	2.00	6.00
May	1.65	1.70		0.75	2.70	6.80
June	1.70	1.70		0.90	1.30	5.60

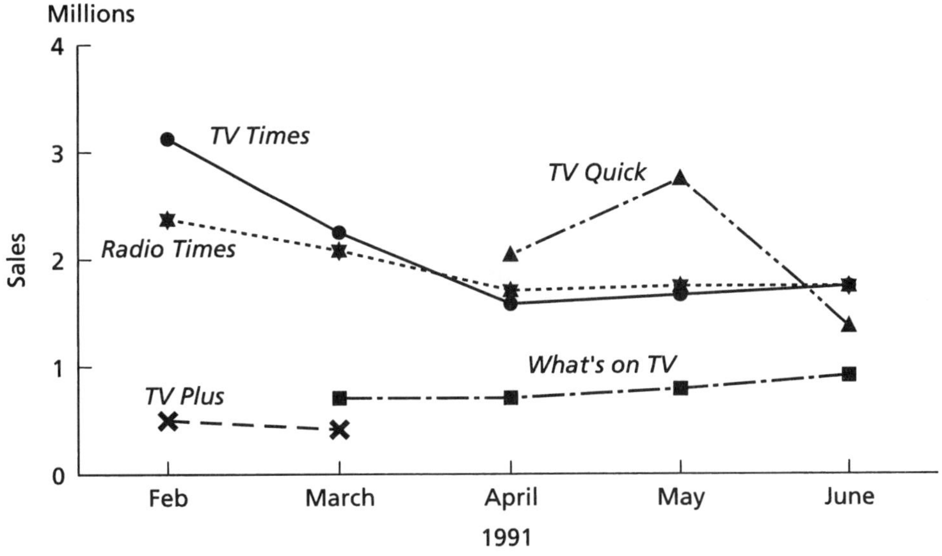

Source: *Sunday Times* 16 June 1991

The first entrant to the market was *TV Plus*, priced at 50p, which took less than 0.5 million sales and lasted one month before going into liquidation.

The second entrant was *What's on TV*, which went on sale at 25p. Soon afterward the price was increased to 35p, then reduced to 10p. It then put the price back up to 35p.

Sales of *What's on TV* started at 0.7 million in March and rose marginally for the next four months.

By the end of April the sales of both *TV Times* and *Radio Times* had fallen to about 1.6 million, despite the fact that *TV Times* had reduced its price from 50p to 25p for two short periods in March and April. This was partly due to the fact that the next entrant appeared on the scene with a bang in April: *TV Quick*. It was estimated that *TV Quick* spent about £20 million in initial advertising; during April it was the biggest individual spender on TV advertising in the UK, and it came on to the market priced at 10p for 10 weeks. It started with sales of 2 million, and quickly increased to 2.7 million, taking market leadership away from *TV Times* and *Radio Times*. *TV Quick* then quadrupled its price to 40p, and sales immediately fell by half to 1.3 million.

Assess the strategic moves by the new entrants, and the effectiveness of the response by *Radio Times* and *TV Times*. **(Total of $33\frac{1}{3}$ marks)**

Case study 3

What differences in the approach to strategy are there likely to be in small compared to large diversified companies? Frame your answer in terms of a strategy process model.

(Total of $33\frac{1}{3}$ marks)

Appendix 1

Acme Plc
Operating account at end year: production cost, and revenue (\$000)

		SALES REVENUE	10119
COST OF GOODS SOLD	6825		
		GROSS PROFIT	3294

Operating account at end year: overheads and operating surplus (\$000)

Factory Rents	200		
Owned Factory Overheads	100		
Hiring & Redundancy cost	750		
Company Marketing	800		
TOTAL OVERHEAD	1850		
		OPERATING SURPLUS	1444

Cash flow for year (\$000)

OUTLAY		INCOME	
Material Purchase	3000		
Loan Interest	750	Interest on Assets	100
Wage Cost	2820		
Line Cost	1470		
Product Marketing	1400		
Total Overhead	1850	Sales Revenue	10119
Total Outlay	11290	Total Income	10219
		Net Cash Flow	−1071

Balance Sheet at end year (\$000)

FIXED ASSETS			
Factory	4000		
TOTAL FIXED ASSETS		4000	
CURRENT ASSETS			
Raw Materials	4000		
Finished Goods	2964		
Cash	1000		
TOTAL CURRENT ASSETS		7964	
TOTAL ASSETS			11964
OWNERS EQUITY		6964	
DEBT			
Loan	5000		
TOTAL DEBT		5000	
TOTAL LIABILITIES			11964

Report on products for year

	Malt	Liqueur	Blend
Composition of Demand			
Orders	7560	2550	1500
Warranty demand	151	128	30
TOTAL DEMAND	7711	2678	1530
Working time (%)	100	117	100
Labour attrition rate (%)	2	6	2
Price (\$/unit)	900	800	850
Competing price (\$/unit)	900	1000	850
Account at end year			
Wage cost (\$000)	1540	720	560
Line Cost (\$000)	770	420	280
Materials Used (\$000)	976	825	250
Product Marketing	200	800	400
TOTAL COST (\$000)	3486	2765	1490
Unit Cost (\$/unit)	446	838	745
Cost of Goods Sold	3442	2243	1140

	Malt	Liqueur	Blend
Composition of Supply			
Output	7810	3300	2000
Inventory	500	2000	200
TOTAL SUPPLY	8310	5300	2200
Distribution of Supply			
Warranty Replacements	151	128	30
Sales to orders	7560	2550	1500
Actual market share (%)	28.0	5.0	5.0
Excess supply (Inventory)	599	2623	670
SALES REVENUE (\$000)	6804	2040	1275
GROSS PROFIT (\$000)	3362	−203	135

Actual student answers

Case study 1

Question 1

Different disciplines offer different views on products and which direction the company should go in generally. Accountants are concerned with units, cashflow and profitability whereas marketing managers look at product life cycles; business cycles; marketing expenditure; competitive reactions; GNP elasticity; segmentation; differentiation and market share.

In the context of Acme plc an accountant's view is that the Malt is generating 49% gross profit which is more than 100% of the gross profit of the company as a whole. This is due to Liqueur having a negative gross profit and Blend only generating 11% gross profit. Accordingly, Liqueur should be abandoned because it is draining resources and unless gross profit can be improved for the Blend it too should be abandoned.

For both Malt and Blend, workers are at 100% working time which suggests a stable labour force at the top of the experience curve, whereas Liqueur is working at 117% causing a higher level of attrition, i.e. 6% compared with 2% for Blend and Malt. The price of Liqueur is below the competing price, this together with high labour costs and marketing costs has resulted in profit margins being eroded.

In terms of turnover, Malt comprises 67% of company turnover; Liqueur 20% and Blend 13% which suggests that Liqueur does have a market but production will need to be improved and marketing costs reduced if it is to make a profit.

The Blend is not making a significant contribution to company profitability and, unless turnover and profit can be increased, it should be abandoned.

A marketing specialist would view the products differently. In terms of the BCG Relative Share Growth Matrix, the Malt is a cash cow, i.e. generating significant profits with a high market share in a mature market. Liqueur is probably a question mark, i.e. relatively small market share in a growing market. Blend is a dog, i.e. small market share in a mature/declining market.

Based on the above, the marketing specialist would advocate keeping Malt and Liqueur but abandon Blend. More resources must be directed to Liqueur in order to capture a higher market share in a growing market. This increased output will result in workers moving up the learning curve thereby improving productivity and reducing the attrition rate and labour costs. Although Malt is the core business in the short term, in the long term the company must seek new products as demand for Malt declines. This can be achieved through Liqueur if a higher market share is gained. Once the market for Liqueur stabilises, marketing expenditure can be reduced as no new customers will be anticipated. A stable market will allow the company to achieve the economies of scale to match demand thereby generating profit and positive cashflows.

Question 2

In deciding how to allocate resources within the company we must look at the environment; the industry; competition and internal factors. The points to be considered are as follows:

Environment/Economy

- GNP has been increasing causing high inflation and low unemployment
- wage costs are increasing as a result of inflationary pressures
- economy is growing.

Competition/Industry

- liqueur market growing but the company's market share is not (suggests the company is losing sales to competitors)
- Blend is a declining market
- Malt is a mature market.

Company

- the company is generating a gross profit percentage of 33% and an operating profit percentage on sales of 14%
- the company commands a strong competitive position in the Malt market but has not yet captured sufficient market share in the Liqueur market
- high labour costs are being incurred in the production of Liqueur due to working overtime and the high attrition rate.

If unit costs for Liqueur fall by 5% and market share is increased to 10% this could generate a turnover of £4 285 000 and a gross profit of £20 000. This, obviously, is still not sufficient to generate long term profitability. However, as the market stabilises the company can start to charge the competing price and reduce marketing expenditure by some £500 000. The revised profitability position would be as follows:

Sales (units)	2 678 × 2 =		5 356
× Sales price			1 000
Sales revenue			£5 356 000
Costs of sales			
Total cost as per question		£2 765	
Less marketing		(500)	
		£2 265	
÷ 3.3 – Unit cost		686	
5% saving in productivity		£652	
Unit cost × Sales costs			
652 × 5 356			3 492 112
Gross profit			£1 863 888
Gross profit %			35%

This, of course, is based on the current market size. As the market increases, 10% will generate more than 5 356 units, but it should be noted that competitors will also be striving to increase their market share and as such the competing price may fall as supply increases more than demand.

These factors can all be combined into a Strengths, Weaknesses, Opportunities and Threats (SWOT) framework as follows:

Strengths

- commanding position in malt market
- potential to generate profits in liqueur market
- experience in the industry
- experienced labour force for malt and blend.

Weaknesses

- high stock level in all three products
- prior liquidity position (generated $1 071 000 in the year)
- high debt to assets ratio (42%)
- liqueur is a loss making product
- Blend is in a declining market.

Opportunities

- economy is growing and demand/consumer spending is high
- expectations are that the economy will continue to grow
- liqueur is a growing market.

Threats

- high inflation rates
- high wage costs
- losing market share to competitors in the liqueur market.

The ranking of the above factors will vary depending on whether or not the decision maker is a prospector, defender, reactor or analyser, i.e. a prospector will be looking for new opportunities and adopt an aggressive approach; the defender may wish to sit back and defend his current market position; the reactor will do "nothing" whilst the analyser will seek to expand based on internal information only.

In the short term, I would abandon Blend and reallocate resources to Liqueur. It is essential that the company generates efficient market share to convert the question mark into a star and ultimately a cash cow as the Malt market declines.

The company is currently experiencing a cashflow problem in that outlays exceed income and it has a high debt ratio. Emphasis must be placed on reducing inventories to such a level that management is satisfied that it can meet demand out of existing inventory levels and output. Obviously the level of stock ultimately held will be dependent upon management's attitude to risk.

Despite generating an operating surplus of £1.4m this is not reflected in the cash flow due to buying materials in excess of demand as discussed above. Accounting procedures are such that cost of sales equals the cost of goods sold which is not necessarily equal to material purchases plus labour and line costs.

In the long term, the company can reduce costs on marketing as the liqueur market stabilises, however the company will need to look at developing other products as the market for liqueur and malt declines.

Management may prefer to "sit on" malt and liqueur and wait until a new product comes on line thereby avoiding development costs and the high risks involved in developing new products or it may decide to research and develop its own products. The latter strategy will result in higher risk but ultimately higher returns.

Although the economy is growing it will ultimately reach a peak and start to decline. As inflation increases government may restrict the money supply causing interest rates to rise. Given the company's high debt ration I would not develop any products yet but stabilise and attempt to achieve a high degree of competitive advantage in both the malt and liqueur markets.

Question 3

In valuing shares, the shareholder will look at the potential growth of the company; the risk involved and the current economic and competitive environment. The value of the share is based on the discounted value of the expected future income stream, i.e.:

$$\text{Share value} = \frac{\text{Profits}}{\text{Discount rate}}$$

In valuing the share, I would look at the past history of profits and assess future profitability based on recent reports; forecasts, etc. I would need to assess risk based on the track record of company management and the non-diversifiable risk is the risk associated with holding shares in Acme Plc and cannot be diversified away.

The discount factor applied would be based on two factors:

- Risk free rate – based on existing market interest rate and expectations
- Risk premium – based on past dividend record of company; management and past profitability record.

There are ultimately three approaches to valuing shares:

- Net asset approach – based on value of net assets in the balance sheet
- Earnings basis – based on earnings potential of company
- Dividends basis – based on expected dividend payment.

The net asset basis would produce a value of approximately \$6 964 000, i.e. \$11 964 000 minus 5 000 000 equals 6 964 000.

The earnings basis would look at the existing profitability level of \$1.4m and try and estimate future profitability. How are profits going to grow? GNP is forecast to increase by 4% but wages will increase by 12%. If we assume profits will grow by 4% on the basis that resource allocation and increased productivity will match the wage increase, this will give long term profits of:

$$[1.4 \times 1.04 + 1.4 \times (1.04)^2 + 1.4 \times (1.04)^3 + 1.4 \times (1.04)^4]$$

The cost of capital will comprise the current interest rate plus a risk premium. I will assume a 15% cost of capital. Given the state of the economy I will forecast a planning time horizon of 4 years only, by which time the value of the company will need to be reassessed.

Based on the above the value of the company is as follows:

$$\frac{1.4 \times 1.04}{1.15} + \frac{1.4 \times 1.04^2}{1.15^2} + \frac{1.4 \times 1.04^3}{1.15^3} + \frac{1.4 \times 1.04^4}{1.15^4} = \$4.38$$

$$\text{Residual value} \quad = \quad \frac{1.4 \times 1.04^4}{0.15}$$

$$1.15^5 = 5.428$$

plus Present value	4.380
	9 808m

The value of shares equals $9 808m divided by the number of shares, i.e. $9.80.

I would be willing to pay up to $9.80 per share.

As no dividends are paid, the third basis is not appropriate.

The company would look at the value of each product when valuing the company but a shareholder would not have this information and can therefore only use the methods outlined above.

Case study 2

In reviewing the effectiveness of the strategic moves of the new entrants it is important to establish the market structure of the industry. Initially *TV Times* and *Radio Times* had a monopoly of the market, i.e. each company published their own channels only.

In February 1991 this monopoly was broken and new entrants were allowed into the market, i.e. barrier to entry were removed thereby opening the market.

The magazine is in essence a homogeneous product in that each tells the same story – which programmes are on television.

There are many buyers of this product and they each have universal availability of information in prices of these products. Accordingly the market has moved from a monopolistic structure to almost perfect competition. I say almost because as yet, the companies are not faced with a horizontal demand curve where there is a “unique” price. Each company is charging different prices for their magazines thereby having elements of an oligopolistic market in that when prices rise demand falls; when price falls demand rises. These structures can be expressed diagramatically as follows:

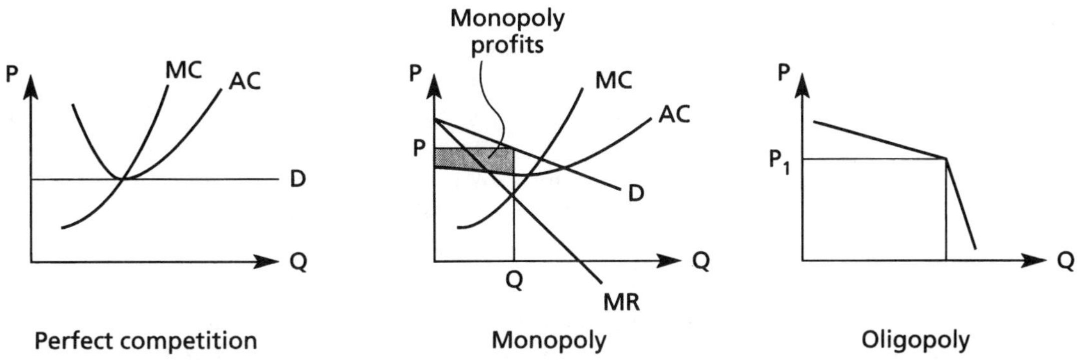

In perfect competition each company is faced with a horizontal demand curve with no economies of scale or barriers to entry. A monopolist on the other hand can influence price and generate profits above the opportunity cost of capital. As the monopoly market "breaks up", the demand curve (D) moves down and the average cost curve (AC) moves up as competition for resources increases thereby increasing pick prices. As the demand curve moves down it will become tangential to the average cost curve and no monopoly profits will be made.

In an oligopolistic market, above price P_1 the demand curve is elastic meaning that an increase in price results in a fall in demand. Below P_1, the demand curve is inelastic resulting in a fall in total revenue if price is reduced due to competitors matching the fall in price.

The strategic mass of each company can be assessed as follows:

TV Plus
Entered at 50p. This was the going rate but as yet *TV Plus* did not have any existing customers. It did not succeed because it was entering a mature market with no perceived product difference when compared with *Radio Times* or *TV Times* and no price difference. It can be located in the perceived price/differential matrix as follows:

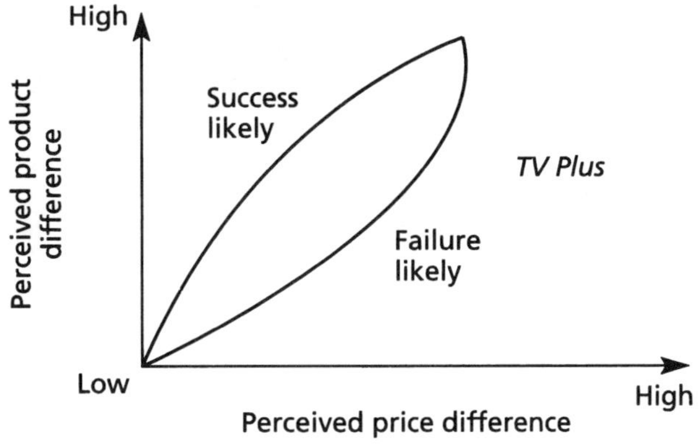

What's on TV

This company recognised the need to establish itself in this mature market and therefore went in at a price 50% below the going rate in an attempt to win customers from competitors. This appeared to be successful in that it attracted sales of 0.7 million. In an attempt to establish the elasticity of the market to changes in prices it increased its price by 10p then reduced its price significantly to 10p. Neither strategy proved successful in that demand remained at approximately 0.7 million. During March and April, *TV Times* reduced its price to 25p but this still had no effect on the sales of *What's on TV* despite the fact that a new competitor – *TV Quick* – entered the market in April.

Having established that the market was not responsive to changes in price, i.e. it was inelastic between the price ranges of 10p and 35p, in order to maximise revenue it set its price at 35p. This enabled the company to maintain its sales levels as well as maximise revenue. The company obviously felt that a price higher than 35p would not generate any increase in demand and may in fact lead to a fall in total revenue due to the fall in demand leading to a loss in turnover more than could be generated from the existing customer base at the higher price, e.g.

35p × 0.7 = £245 000

40p × 0.5 = £200 000   a fall of £45 000.

TV Quick

Adopted a large marketing campaign initially in order to attract customers. This generated sales of 2 million at a price of 10p. This strategy can only be pursued for a short period due to the fact that it is unlikely to be generating profits at this price. In a mature market such as this the strategy of aggressive selling via high marketing expenditure and reduced price may appear "strange" at first. If the product was a "star" in attempting to capture a high market share in a growing market this strategy would appear plausible but even in this mature market the strategy seems to have been successful.

In June, once demand and price had stabilised, *TV Quick* was generating revenue of £520 000 (1.3 × 40p) compared with £315 000 for *What's on TV* and £850 000 for *TV Times* and *Radio Times*. Thus, the aggressive strategy of *TV Quick* is generating more turnover than *What's on TV*. It shall be noted, however, that *TV Quick* has incurred substantial marketing expenditure (£20m) and has gone for a period of 10 weeks in a loss-making position. This strategy will only be successful if the lost revenue and high marketing spend incurred initially is more than compensated for by the larger market share gained at the price of 40p.

TV Times and Radio Times

Both companies have kept their price at 50p (with the exception of *TV Times* during March and April when the price was reduced to 25p). Accordingly neither company has really made an attempt to compete with the new entrants. They appear to be content at losing market share but keeping the same price.

Even the reduction in price by *TV Times* to 25p did not seem to affect demand in any way. Turnover for both companies has fallen from the peak in February to around 1.7 million. Even although this has resulted in a fall in demand of 45% for *TV Times* and

28% for *Radio Times*, each company is still generating more revenue than any of the new entrants. Initially profits on *TV Times* and *Radio Times* should be significantly higher than the new entrants due to an experienced labour force but this advantage will be eroded as the other workers move up the learning curve.

Case study 3

Strategic planning can be viewed as a "flow" process whereby:

Objectives are set

↓

Payouts and shortfalls are forecast

↓

Potential strategies identified

↓

Best strategy risk selected

↓

Organise and complement

↓

Control and re-appraise

↓

Feedback

Strategic planning is a dynamic process as evident above. Feedback allows the organisation to assess how well it has done and what it must do in the future to improve profitability and market performance. A more detailed model will identify which tasks should be carried out at each process, i.e.

Strategists	Set objectives			Who decides what to do
				↓
General environment	Competitive position	Internal factors	Industrial and international environment	Analysis and diagnosis
				↓
Generic strategy alternatives	Strategy variations	Strategy choice		Choice
				↓
Resources and structure	Resource allocation	Evaluation and control		Implementation

Although strategic planning is based on the company it is individuals who make decisions and these decisions are constrained by the organisation and its traditions. In a small company the strategic decisions are normally carried out by the owner/manager and the process tends to be informal. The models outlined above are unlikely to be followed to any great extent. The owner/manager will identify where he wants the company to go and reallocate resources accordingly. He will monitor progress on a regular basis and amend plans and/or resource allocation accordingly.

A larger organisation, e.g. same product but is vertically integrated, will have a more formalised strategy process. The owner/manager will still carry out the strategy decisions but operating decisions will be delegated through policy.

For the large diversified organisation a formal system of strategic planning will be undertaken. Management will be monitored using measurable criteria such as Return on Investment. Both policy and strategy decisions will be delegated and these may be further delegated depending on the degree of diversification and market domination.

Whereas in a small organisation the owner/manager is the strategist – the objective setter, in a larger organisation it may not be evident who is the ultimate strategy maker. At the corporate level the Chief Executive Officer may set the objectives for the company as a whole. Then, each operating unit will also set objectives with the aim of achieving the ultimate corporate objective. Each business unit will be monitored on a regular basis against this objective.

In a small company the owner/manager will carry out the whole strategy process from setting objectives to feedback. In a large organisation analysis and diagnosis will be carried out by each department, e.g. the general environment will be assessed by the economists and marketing specialists. The internal factors will be assessed by accountants; financial specialists; manpower specialists; production; research, etc. Regardless of how the company is structured, i.e. functional or divisional, it is probable that these "experts" exist.

Once the diagnosis has been carried out, the choice of which strategy to pursue may be dependent upon the Chief Executive Officer (CEO) or may be decided at a Board Meeting by a majority vote.

Who implements the strategy may, once again, be undefined. The CEO may disaggregate the company objectives into realistic, achievable and relevant objectives at the business unit level. Once done the business unit manager will use these disaggregated objectives as a goal towards which his unit must strive. The manager will allocate resources accordingly.

Finally, feedback will be the responsibility of everyone within the organisation. How this reaches the "top" will depend on how the organisation is structured. A "flat" organisation may involve managers going straight to the CEO whereas a more hierarchical organisation may involve formal reporting to a manager who then reports to his superior and so on.

It can be seen from above that the approaches to strategy can vary quite substantially depending upon the size of the organisation. To date there has been no empirical evidence to suggest that a particular approach is more effective than any other. Nor has there been any evidence to suggest a combination of personnel characteristics which yields the most effective strategy maker. In essence, strategic planning can be viewed as a multi-dimensional role carried out by many individuals working at different levels in the organisation.

Model answers

Case study 1

1. Compare an accountant and a marketer

The accountant is concerned with efficiency of resource allocation and would look at the ratios: price to unit cost, profit to production cost, profit per unit sold, sales per employee, inventories, etc.; the analysis would be based on historical data and trends. The marketer is concerned with the development of products with a competitive advantage and would look at product position and prospects for the future. The marketer would look at product life cycles, and attempt to place the three products in the BCG matrix, and would conclude that the Malt is a cash cow, the Blend is a dog, and the Liqueur is a question mark, i.e. it has a small market share in a fast growing market. The accountant and the marketer would have similar views about the Malt and the Blend, but would differ on the Liqueur. Of course, not everyone would agree that accountants are so narrow minded.

Accounting conventions can be misleading: e.g. the hiring costs may be due to attrition on Liqueur, and hence should be allocated to that product. The COGS approach can conceal poor performance in terms of current resource allocation.

2. Reallocate resources

There is a great deal of scope for answering this question. The macroeconomic situation is ominous: the high growth in sales for the Liqueur have probably been partly due to a high GNP elasticity, and it is likely that the government will take action to deflate the economy as a result of worsening inflation. Tight labour markets have two implications. First, it may be difficult to avoid overtime working in the future because labour will be scarce; second, an increase in labour cost of 12% could have serious implications for profitability.

When reallocating resources the general principle is to evaluate the impact of changes on marginal cost and marginal revenue.

In the short run there are various overhead costs which could be reduced. For example, hiring and redundancy cost is likely to be a one off and material purchases are far higher than material consumption. The price of the Liqueur could be increased to the competing level (depending on price elasticity), and marketing expenditure on the Blend reduced to at least the same level as for the Malt ("harvest" the Blend for the remainder of its life cycle). Resources currently allocated to the Liqueur could be reduced to get rid of the inventory – bearing in mind the likely prospects for GNP growth; in the extreme, the Liqueur could be abandoned.

In the long run the objective is to utilise resources more efficiently and transform the Liqueur into a cash cow. At the same time, there is a need to ensure that more products are developed for the future portfolio, and at the moment nothing is being spent on R&D. The problem is that these long term objectives are not necessarily consistent with short term profit maximisation.

Sensitivity analysis can be carried out to indicate the rough impact of measures such as increasing the price of the Liqueur, reducing marketing expenditure, introducing JIT and so on.

3. Share price

The share price is determined by the expectation of future cash flows, and is found by discounting expected cash flows using the cost of capital. Each share would generate \$1.4 in operating surplus at the moment. Assuming the cost of capital is 10% this would give a share price of \$14 approximately. However, the expected future cash flows depend on the company's prospects; the market will make use of all information available such as ratios, the company's track record, gearing, cash flow, which will provide an indication of likely future profits and the degree of risk associated with the company. The candidate has already made some suggestions for improving profitability, and the sensitivity analysis will suggest a maximum price which he would be willing to pay given this "insider" view of the company.

Case study 2

The market environment

This is an example of monopoly being replaced by competition among the few, or oligopoly. Some candidates argued that the homogeneous product, coupled with the ease of entry and knowledgeable consumers actually approximate to a perfect market. In this case firms could expect to make the opportunity cost of capital, and all monopoly profits would disappear. Other candidates represented the "big picture" in terms of supply and demand: the supply curve for TV guides moved out to the right, and since demand is inelastic the equilibrium price fell. By June the price had fallen from an average of 50p to about 44p (the average of the four prices).

The more or less fixed market size (subject to short run fluctuations) means that in strategic terms the oligopoly was a zero sum game. Gains in market share could only be made at the expense of competitors, and of course consumers must be given some reason to switch from one TV guide to another. Thus individual producers were likely to be faced with a "kinked" demand curve.

Despite the fact that the TV guides are homogeneous in terms of their main content, there is scope for differentiation in terms of the articles accompanying the listings. Then the TV guides start to encroach on the general magazine market; in fact, at the height of the *TV Quick* advertising campaign the total market size appeared to increase. There was therefore some scope for differentiation and market segmentation; the perceived price and quality matrix can be used to identify the prospects for each of the competitors.

The problems confronting new entrants were formidable. The two existing competitors, *TV Times* and *Radio Times*, had large market shares and hence had the potential benefits of economies of scale and experience effects, together with a degree of consumer loyalty. Some candidates pointed out that advertising revenues were not included in the data, and if these were significant they could help account for the behaviour of competitors.

TV Plus

TV Plus appeared to have no particular strategy; it entered as undifferentiated in terms of quality or price and could not generate sufficient sales to generate profits; it is likely that it incurred much higher costs than *TV Times* and *Radio Times*, and had little financial backing.

What's on TV

What's on TV could be classified as a prospector, and adopted a low cost strategy. It was differentiated on price alone, and apparently tried to test the market by varying price significantly. The outcome suggests that demand was inelastic in the range 10p to 35p.

TV Quick

TV Quick attempted to enter the market as a highly differentiated low cost producer. The objective was to grab market share and then increase the price and hope for a low elasticity of demand. Some candidates felt that the act of quadrupling the price was catastrophic, since demand fell by about half. However, demand was inelastic, and the fact that half as many were sold at four times the price meant that total revenue increased. Compare the revenue generated by the two prices: at 10p the revenue on 2.7 million copies was £0.27 million per week, while at 40p the revenue on 1.3 million copies was £0.52 million per week. Clearly the higher price is preferable, and the losses made up to that point can be regarded as the cost of establishing a 20% market share. This suggests a total revenue of about £26 million per year, which puts the initial £20 million advertising budget in perspective. For example, if *TV Quick* made 20% gross profit on sales revenue, this would generate about £5 million profit per year, giving a pay back period on the initial advertising outlay of about 4 years. This makes no allowance for the losses incurred in the period when price was set at 10p, and any advertising revenue should be included in the final evaluation.

TV Times* and *Radio Times

There are many ways of classifying their response. One argument is that they had no strategy because they were used to a monopoly and were paralysed by a bureaucratic management; this would be particularly true of the *Radio Times*, with its long term association with a government owned service. If they had had any foresight, they would have attempted to erect barriers to entry at an early stage. However, because of their monopoly position they might not in fact have been low cost producers, and may have had to take action to become more efficient after the advent of competition.

Another view is that *Radio Times* adopted a Defender stance in the sense that it did not indulge in the price war because of the zero sum nature of the contest, and decided that a market share loss was the lesser of two evils; on the other hand, *TV Times* was a Reactor, and entered the price war before realising what the *Radio Times* had seen from the beginning. *TV Times'* foray into the price war possibly cost it a great deal in foregone revenue without achieving a significant impact on market share.

Case study 3

A strategy process model is intended to clarify the elements of strategy making, and usually takes the form of objective setting, analysis and diagnosis, strategy choice, implementation and control, evaluation and feedback.

There is plenty of scope for discussion on where differences are likely to arise in the two types of organisation; the quality of the argument rather than being "right" or "wrong" is the important feature of the answer. Some candidates argued that all companies, whatever their size or composition, ought to do much the same under each of the elements, and that differences were really a matter of degree, or that the elements were more apparent in a large company because procedures are more formalised.

Objective setting
There is centralised control in the small company, and with the limited product range there is likely to be a more definable set of objectives. The large company devolves a great deal of strategy making to the SBUs. There is a difference between corporate and SBU policy which does not exist in the small company, and the means/ends distinction is particularly important. It is necessary to disaggregate objectives and make them meaningful and achievable to those who implement them.

Analysis and diagnosis
The large company is likely to have more specialists and a lot more information available than small companies. Analyses by functional experts may be conflicting and the CEO must integrate them. Some candidates argued that large companies are more likely to be affected by general economic factors, changes in competition, etc.

Strategy choice
Techniques such as SWOT ought to be employed by both; some candidates argued that the options are not so clear cut for the large company, since it has to make decisions for a number of products in a number of markets. There may be conflicts of interest among the SBUs.

Implementation and control
The large company has less direct control over its resources, and it may be difficult to relate resource use and deployment back to the original strategy choice. This makes it necessary to utilise sophisticated monitoring systems, financial controls, internal pricing and so on. The principal agent problem is particularly apparent in the large company, starting with the separation of ownership and control and pervading all levels of the organisation. It can be argued that there is more flexibility in small companies because there are fewer formal controls, a smaller hierarchy and less bureaucracy.

Feedback
Because of the size, complexity, hierarchy and bureaucracy of a large company communication is a particular problem. Unless there is a formalised structure for communication it may not occur.

Examiner's comments

Case study 1

Question 1
There was a clear statement of the fact that different specialists consider different types of information and can place different interpretations on the same information. The individual products were reviewed in the light of the approaches of both accountants and marketers, and the data were used to demonstrate why they would arrive at different conclusions.

Question 2
The prospects for a company are dependent on external and internal factors, and the answer starts with a review of these. This is followed by a sensitivity analysis, which is then fed into a SWOT analysis. The candidate points out that the actual choice of strategy will depend on the characteristics of decision makers (prospector, defender or whatever) and attitudes to risk. The main criticism of this answer is that the conflict between short and long term profit maximisation was not recognised explicitly.

Question 3
This was a clear statement of company valuation, and the important point was made that the information available to a shareholder would be different from that available to the company itself. The candidate attempted to incorporate the "insider information" relating to the potential improvements arising from the recommendations in Question 2.

Overall, the candidate answered the three sections very well, and produced a number of revealing insights; while there was scope for improvement, the Section was well worth 80%.

Case study 2

The candidate began with an excellent review of the economic background to the change in the market. The candidate did not recognise the "zero sum game" characteristic of the market, and did not attempt to categorise the approaches taken by the competitors in terms of defenders, prospectors, etc. However, this analytical approach, which applied concepts from economics and marketing, was worth 70%.

Case study 3

The candidate set out the strategy process model very clearly and attempted to identify differences between large and small companies using this structure. A number of relevant issues were discussed, including the informal approach in small companies, specialisation of functions in large companies, objective setting and feedback. The answer ended with an interesting point on empirical evidence. Issues which were not addressed include the principal agent problem and potential conflicts among SBUs in large diversified companies. However, given the scope of the answer, and the fact that a good attempt was made to discuss the issues raised (whether the arguments are "right" or "wrong" is not important), a mark of 65% was awarded.

Overall assessment

Every Strategic Planning paper is considered in its entirety to determine whether the student has demonstrated an adequate knowledge of the subject. In this case the candidate had demonstrated analytical ability, had integrated concepts from different disciplines, had shown an understanding of strategy techniques and theories, and had exercised original thinking to come up with interesting insights. The aggregate mark of 72% reflects a "very good-to-excellent" level of performance.

The elective courses*

International Trade and Finance

Essay question

In what ways are firms exposed to exchange rate risk? Analyse the different ways in which they may deal with such risk. **(Total of 40 marks)**

Actual student answer

As exchange rates fluctuate, the firms dealing at an international scale may be favourably or adversely affected by exchange rate fluctuations.

Degree of risk due to foreign exchange fluctuations depends on two factors.

1. Environmental complexity – This refers to the number of different currencies in which a firm deals, e.g. if a firm deals only with the US and invoices in US dollars, then its environments are less complex than a firm which deals with all countries in the EU with 12 different currencies. So the larger the number of currencies, the greater is the environmental complexity and the greater is the risk. However, risk also depends on another factor which is:

2. Environmental change – This refers to the extent the foreign exchange of the currencies fluctuate. If a firm is dealing in currencies, whose values are relatively stable, then the firm has less risk.

So the degree of risk a firm has depends on the number of currencies a firm deals in and fluctuations in the exchange rates of these currencies.

The foreign exchange risk can arise from three types of exposure. These are:

- Transaction exposure
- Economic exposure
- Translation exposure

Let's explain each in turn.

Transaction exposure
This refers to the extent to which future value of a firm's domestic cashflow is affected by exchange rate fluctuations.

* Decision-making Techniques and Government, Industry and Privatization have not been included in this section of the book.

This exposure arises when a firm is exporting and/or importing and deals are denominated in foreign currencies. The risk from this type of exposure can be understood by the following example: if a firm exports and invoices in domestic currency, then the currency inflow is domestic and there is no risk of loss due to exchange rate fluctuation. If the same firm also imports and pays in foreign currency, its outflow is in foreign currency, so it is exposed to foreign exchange risk. If the exchange rate of foreign currency rises, it has to pay more domestic currency to get the required amount of foreign currency. So its costs of imports will go up. The situation explained is typical of many firms, but a firm can find itself in one of the following situations as shown in Table 1.

As can be seen from Table 1, the degree of transaction exposure depends on how much a firm's transactions are in foreign currency. If more, then there is more transaction exposure. Also the volume of transaction is determinant of transaction exposure.

Table 1

Situation	*Currency inflow*	*Currency outflow*	*Exposure*	
			Inflow	*Outflow*
1. A firm deals only in domestic market	Domestic	Domestic	Nil	Nil
2. Export invoice in domestic and import paid in foreign	Domestic	Foreign	Nil	Yes
3. Export invoice in foreign and import paid in foreign	Foreign	Foreign	Yes	Yes
4. Export invoice in domestic and imports paid in domestic	Domestic	Domestic	Nil	Nil
5. Export only, invoice in foreign	Foreign	Domestic	Yes	Nil
6. Import only, invoice in foreign	Domestic	Foreign	Nil	Yes

There are ways in which a firm can avoid risk from the transaction exposure. These are:

Leading and lagging

If a firm is to receive a payment in foreign currency and the exchange rate of domestic currency against foreign is higher, the firm will receive less domestic currency for each foreign unit of currency. To avoid this, a firm can ask its customer to delay (lag) the payment until exchange rates are favourable or the firm may receive the payment and keep it in a foreign currency account and convert it in domestic only when exchange rates are favourable. Similarly a firm may speed up (lead) a payment to avoid adverse effects on cash inflow.

This option depends on whether a firm has the choice to speed up or delay payment. This method can be used for inter-company transfer where payment time may not be more important than the profitability of the company as a whole.

Currency of invoice

If a firm's transactions are dominated in domestic currency then there is less transaction exposure and loss risk.

This option depends on whether the firm's customer or supplier agree to be invoiced and paid respectively in domestic currency. If the domestic currency is desirable then they will be happy to accept.

Forward contract

A firm can enter into a forward contract to buy or sell a given amount of currency. This way it can lock the exchange rates of the currencies and avoid the risk of fluctuations. A forward contract is a binding contract, so a firm must buy or sell the given amount specified in the contract at a given price. So unless a firm is certain that it needs the given foreign exchange in a certain period, it should not enter into a forward contract. There is no need to pay the whole amount to buy or sell foreign currency. A deposit is required which depends on the credibility of the firm. Usually it is 10% of the value of the contract. If the value of contract is low, the service charge may be high, so it is not suitable for smaller firms.

Currency futures

These differ from the forward contract in the following ways:

(i) Contract size is standardised, i.e. for £2 500 in forward contract you can have any amount of contract.

(ii) Only few currencies are traded. In forward contracts most currencies are traded.

(iii) Contract matures on third Wednesday of March, June, September and December, whereas the forward contract can mature at any date.

(iv) Future contracts are sold through clearing houses.

(v) Future contracts are only traded in specific market, e.g. IMM.

Currency futures are usually used for speculation purposes; only 1% of those mature at maturity date. But if a firm has the similar need which can be met by taking the standardised contract, this option should be considered. It has the following advantages:

- low service charge
- good for small firms.

Currency option

A currency option is a right to buy or sell a currency but not an obligation. So if the spot rate of exchange is favourable at the date of maturity of contract, the holder of the option will not exercise the option and buy or sell the currency at spot rate.

A call option is where the holder has the right to buy a currency.

A put option is where the holder has right to sell the currency.

Currency option offers flexibility to a firm while locking up of exchange rates. There are two types of option: American option, in which the right not to exercise can be taken at any date during the option period; or European Option where right to exercise can be taken at the maturity date of contract.

The above are the methods to deal with transaction exposure.

Economic exposure

This refers to how the present value of a firm's cash flow is affected by foreign exchange.

If a firm is selling a product in a domestic market and the rate of exchange of domestic currency appreciates then they can be cheaper. So foreign competitors may come into the local market to take the firm's share of the domestic market.

Similarly, it can work in a domestic firm's favour. If the exchange rate of foreign currency appreciates or the domestic rate depreciates, it may allow the domestic firm to export more.

If a firm is in a situation in which its domestic market is taken by low cost foreign competitors, it can overcome this strategically.

(i) The domestic firm may find market niches and tailor its product to their needs, so it can better satisfy the needs of the niche market and have more loyal customers.

(ii) The domestic firm can diversify the product range and operate in different markets to overcome economic exposure.

Also, domestic government policies, tariff quotas and other restrictions can help a firm overcome the risk of economic exposure.

Translation exposure

If a firm has subsidies in many countries, the fluctuation in exchange rate will make the assets' valuation different in different periods. If domestic currency is high against a foreign currency (the home of the subsidiary) then when the group balance sheet is prepared it will show less value of assets of the foreign subsidiary (the loss due to the high exchange rate of domestic currency).

So there can be different asset valuation in different years which will affect the group's asset, capital structure ratios, profitability ratios, etc.

The translation exposure depends on the number of subsidiaries a fixed parent firm has and in the number of countries. The parent firm can convert the foreign assets at date at which the exchange rate is favourable, or it can show its subsidiaries' assets at an agreed price with decrease/increase due to exchange rate in a given period accounted separately in the group balance sheet.

There are three types of exposure, transaction, translation and economic, which create risks for any loss due to foreign exchange fluctuation. There are different methods for dealing with each type of exposure and risk. The choice depends on the situation of a firm.

Examiner's comments

I gave this essay 30 marks which equates to 75%, and therefore I clearly considered it to be a good answer. Why was it worth a high mark? Why did I not give a higher mark?

Let me take the second question first. Unlike some of the physical sciences there are no absolute certainties in economic life. There are always some "grey areas" which will arise in any analysis of an economic problem; we do not have 100% correct solutions. Yet even if this premise is accepted, why was the essay graded at 75% and not 88%? As I shall try to show, there are some points in the candidate's answer which are questionable and there are one or two omissions.

First, however, why did I consider it a good answer? If you relate the candidate's essay to the suggested solution it is clear that all the relevant issues are considered. The candidate correctly identifies the three possible types of exposure and demonstrates an understanding of the techniques whereby a firm may seek to reduce or even eliminate exchange rate risk. In particular the candidate makes clear that it is the present value of future cash flows which is important. In addition to the technical merits of the answer, I also consider it to be well structured, and I believe this to be important in presenting an economic argument. The reader of any report does not want to be jumping back and forth across the document; structure is important. In this instance the writer, having introduced the concept of transaction exposure, discusses the ways in which it may be tackled before introducing the concepts of economic exposure and translations exposure. This is precisely the right sequence since the various hedging instruments – forward contract, futures, options, etc. – are directly related to the problems of transaction exposure, not of economic or translation exposure. I should make clear that a candidate who deals with the three types of exposure first and then discusses hedging techniques would not in any way be penalised, but this particular structure earns, if you like, some bonus points.

There are, however, one or two limitations in the answer. In discussing transaction exposure the writer does not make clear that exposure is not necessarily synonymous with risk. If a firm has transactions involving two foreign currencies then it is faced with transaction exposure. The degree of risk, however, can vary depending on the degree to which movements of the exchange rates of the two currencies are correlated with the domestic currency. Thus, if the amount of exposure to the two foreign currencies were identical and movements in the exchange rates of the currencies against the domestic currency were perfectively negatively correlated, then there would be no risk. A potential 10% loss on one currency would be matched by a 10% gain on the other. The writer also argues that the volume of transactions is a determinant of transaction exposure, though as Table 1 correctly illustrates there is no exposure if invoicing is in domestic currency. (I should say that this may be viewed as perhaps a rather trivial oversight.)

In discussing leading and lagging the writer betrays a certain naïvety. It is suggested that a firm could ask its customer to lag payment. Clearly if it is in the firm's interest to have the payment lagged it must be equally true that it is in the customer's interest to lead the payment!

The section on economic exposure is perhaps the weakest part of the essay. The writer does not adequately distinguish between firms who have no trading transactions at all and those who do have trading transactions, but no transaction exposure, i.e. all transactions invoiced in domestic currency. In both cases they are faced with economic exposure since exchange rate changes may affect market share in the domestic economy for both sets of firms and market share in foreign markets for the second set of firms. (This latter case is demonstrated in table 7.3 in the main text).

Negotiation

Case study

Read the following case study and answer the questions below.

Michel Satran is an electronic engineer who has developed from his own resources a completely new processor for mini-computers. From a technical point of view the processor is a long way ahead of anything in production and, also, anything in progress by the major players in this market, who are sticking with refining existing technology. What Satran does not have is capital to turn his prototype into a mass product for the market.

Satran has been turned down by the usual sources of banking funds (they are very risk-averse, having made major losses during the recession and through defaulting Third World debtors). He is now engaged in negotiations with Rich Investment Bank (Jersey) Ltd, who see the potential for the new processor as balancing the undoubted risks, and who are willing to advance the necessary funding (US$ 15 million) if they can secure their investment. They have suggested that they hold a majority share of the equity of Satran's company. They have asserted that they are only interested in making a profit from their involvement and have no long-term plans to maintain their holding.

Satran plans to exploit his invention, possibly by licensing it to one or two of the major producers of computers with, perhaps, some in-house production in France and joint ventures with Far East manufacturers. Satran is considering the proposal to give to Rich Investment Bank a majority of his company's equity, because he is desperate to gain access to funding. He is convinced that once the new processor is adopted as standard it will produce millions of dollars profit for all concerned.

M Satran has asked you, as a consultant negotiator, to assist in the negotiations to find a way to secure the funding and protect his and Rich Investment Bank's legitimate interests. He is also interested in any general advice you can give in forthcoming negotiations.

1. Where is Satran vulnerable in the proposal from Rich Investment Bank (Jersey) Ltd? **(8 marks)**

2. What are Satran's longer term interests? **(8 marks)**

3. What proposal could you suggest to reconcile Satran's and Rich Investment Bank (Jersey) Ltd's interests? **(8 marks)**

4. What are the basic elements of an agreement that he should consider when deciding whether to license his product? **(8 marks)**

5. What kind of BATNA could Satran develop to strengthen him in his negotiations? **(8 marks)**

(Total of 40 marks)

Actual student answer

1. Where is Satran vulnerable in the proposal from Rich Investment Bank? Rich Investment Bank will loan the money $15m if they can secure their investment by holding a majority share in the company.

   Satran would be vulnerable on several points, but he could be protected, following negotiations on:

   (a) With Rich Investment holding a majority share of the company they could sell out at any time – new owner could dump Satran and carry on without him.

   (b) Under what conditions will they operate the loan? What are their repayment terms? What if Satran cannot always meet his commitment?

   (c) Is there an arrangement for Satran to buy back shares at a pre-planned price?

   (d) Can Satran arrange that he is to be the sole purchaser of the shares comprising the loan?

   (e) Will he be given first refusal to purchase the shares?

   Satran should negotiate for the loan, secured by shares in his company under the following conditions. As the Bank is only interested in getting a return on its investment, a future price for the shares could be calculated tied to the project. Increase in profit leads to increase in price so the bank is adequately compensated for its investment. Furthermore, Satran is to be the sole purchaser, at least until he has a majority share holding – say initially the allotment is 20–80%, Satran 20%, Bank 80%; after Satran has reached 51% the market for the shares can be opened up, but Satran still given first refusal.

2. Satran's long-term interest is to eventually own his own company and be the first to market his computer as he sees fit.

   His interests would be as follows:

   (a) Own and control his own company.

   (b) Be free of the Bank.

   (c) Exploit his invention by:

   - Licensing agreement with major manufacturer
   - In-house production in France
   - Joint ventures with Far East manufacturers

   (d) Have his process adopted as a standard and earn him a fortune.

   (e) Protect himself from exploitation by the Bank.

3. A proposal is an unspecific offer followed by an unspecific condition or specific condition.

   Satran could propose if the Bank would consider giving him the money at "say 10%", the percentage of the Company share they could hold may be discussed.

If they let him have the $15,000,000 the Company is probably worth $20m, including its technology. They could let him have 51% of the share (his entry point for Bank – exit could be 30%). Further proposals would cover Satran's opportunity to repurchase the shares, restricted sale and a planned valuation of the shares tied to profit over time. As the bank is only interested in earning a profit and not running a company, a scale of value could be worked out that is fair to both sides.

Finally, Satran must protect himself from the Bank selling the loan or shares to a third party that could take over the business and fire Satran to exploit his idea. This could be done by:

(a) Holding an option for the Bank shares

(b) Agreement that he is the sole partner

(b) He is to be given first refusal for any sale of the shares.

The proposal by Satran and the Bank could be: if the Rich Investment Bank would consider lending Satran $15m on security of shares in his proposed company then discussions could take place on Satran's programme to repay the loan and regain the shares. Furthermore, Satran is the only person able to purchase the shares according to an agreed formula until such time as he owns 51% of the company.

4. The basic element in any agreement is protection against exploitation by either party.

   In a licence agreement, protection must cover:

   - Security of technology against pirates.
   - A guarantee that full fees will be paid and a means of auditing the fees agreed.
   - Form of calculating payment of fee – a lump sum annually as a licence fee? A percentage of sales? A dual system, a licence fee plus portion of sales?

   Other elements may cover:

   - Territory of sales distinctively.
   - Pricing of products – fixed price or price range.
   - Discount for quantity etc.
   - Penalty for undercutting.
   - Sale on shared territory – sole distribution.

   An agreement is the formal stage of a negotiation. It is the conclusion of a bargain, both sides are satisfied they have got all they can.

   Satran should be sure the agreement is so worded that he is protected from exploitation by the other party in any licence agreement he enters into.

5. Satran could collect data that would show the bank if they did not make the loan they were missing out on a marvellous opportunity.

   His accountant could show the $15m investment could [do] well in 2 years, once the product is accepted by the market [it could] be worth $150m, if the major competition became interested they may be prepared to pay a much larger sum, rather than see their market lost – Satran could say – OK, no money – no business.

Satran's alternative may be to go to the opposition and say – join me or someone else will. They may not be able to resist and offer a better deal than the bank.

Satran has a product. It possibly has great potential – his BATNA could be: "I'm offering you an opportunity and if you don't take it someone else will." Or he could offer to sell his product and secure a licence fee to save himself a lot of hassle.

Examiner's comments

1. Satran's vulnerabilities in the proposal from Rich Investment Bank (Jersey) Ltd refers to the possibility that his interests and the bank's might diverge in the future and that in these circumstances, Satran might be disadvantaged by the Bank's unilateral actions. The examinee's answer shows that s/he is aware of the type of issues that could arise if Satran was to concede to their requirement that they take a majority shareholding in the new company.

   In the extreme, the Bank could "sell out at anytime" or they could "dump Satran and carry on without him". This is positive evidence that the candidate understands the question. A step or two more is required to demonstrate the nature and consequences of the vulnerabilities to which Satran is exposing himself.

   For example, in between these two extreme actions there is plenty of scope for Satran being over-ruled by the majority shareholder on both strategic issues (such as marketing) and operational issues (monthly budgets etc.). Satran could fall out with the Bank on myriads of such issues and effectively end up frustrated at his loss of operational control, or even marginalised once the technology is transformed into a sellable product. Which of them, Satran or the Bank, has the managerial control of the day-to-day operations needs to be addressed. This is likely to arise whatever the shareholding arrangements and is a vulnerability common in situations where one party provides the funding of a project. One arrangement, which is common in venture capital deals, is for the borrower to agree to certain covenants which, if breached, create an opportunity for the lender to require remedial action, including, in the extreme, the right to take over the project by installing professional management. The borrower and the lender agree milestones of progress towards a saleable product which, if met, leaves operational control in the hands of the borrower. Some evidence of thoughts along these lines would clearly gain marks for the answer.

   The examinee, however, addresses the central question of the shareholding in parts (b), (c), (d), (e) and suggests methods of reducing the vulnerability. One might ask why Satran concedes that the loan is taken into the new company as equity as well as being paid for through interest? In effect, the lender is both equity stake holder, with his funds at risk like any other shareholder and is also a creditor earning income from the loan. The examinee is seeking ways to make the Bank's demands work rather than challenging the notion that they can both lend money and expect interest on their lending, plus have the right to a share of the profits as a shareholder and have effective control of the business. The Bank in this situation is taking less risk than Satran.

   This leads to questions such as raised in (b) of what happens if Satran cannot meet an obligation (temporarily)? The Bank could take over everything, which could be close to or beyond a critical technical stage when the product is about to be successful.

Satran could lose whatever security he has pledged for the US $15m loan (his house etc.), and, of course, all rights to his invention. He is vulnerable, therefore, if he accepts onerous security terms and very tight milestones of progress.

The examinee's suggestions in (c), (d) and (e) are workable and for that s/he earns positive points. Satran could indeed have an arrangement to buy back shares at a preplanned price to regain control, eventually, of his company; he can also arrange in the contract to be the sole purchaser of the Bank's equity; and he could arrange for a "first refusal" clause. The question is not whether this is possible but whether the Bank would agree to clauses which might effectively lock it into the investment and block their real intentions, should they have them, getting hold of an investment with great potential through taking advantage of Satran's predicament. However, the examinee is asked to give advice as Satran's consultant and not the Bank's! Though Satran should consider the possible motives of the Bank when assessing their detailed proposals.

2. Other people's longer term interests are speculative but they drive to some extent their short term behaviour – where they do not, then it is a lottery whether there is going to be long term. An interest is a reason why somebody does or wants to do something or wants something to happen or not happen. Interests drive their objectives and goals. They justify their wants.

   The Bank's percentage shareholding is an issue; Satran not losing control is an interest. Satran's problem is that he cannot satisfy his interests (however he defines them) without entering into some sort of arrangement with the Bank. He cannot unilaterally dictate terms to the Bank and, therefore, must make some compromises. Once he has the funding he still cannot satisfy his interests, the sense of retaining control of a profitable company, without producing a saleable product. His immediate task is to so negotiate the immediate issues so that he does not compromise his ability to satisfy his longer term interests. Negotiators must consider this perennial problem when contemplating potential issues and positions.

   In Satran's case, his long-term interest must be to maximise his return from his invention. This does not mean necessarily that he intends, or even needs, to maximise his financial return over the lifetime of his product. He could be in it for the glory not the money! His personal long-term goal could be, for example, to earn enough profit from his invention to become financially independent to the extent that he is able to pursue his private interests as an inventor (or enjoying things, such as cruising or going fishing). The sum required for these longer term private interests could be a great deal less than the sum required to maximise the financial return from his invention. If "glory" is more important to Satran (recognition through a Nobel Prize, perhaps) his "sell-out" price could be relatively low to a multi-billion dollar buyer while still remaining "high" in the mind of Satran.

   The question seeks at least a definition or some statement of what an interest is in general, illustrated by some examples relevant to Satran's case. The examinee provides several examples of Satran's goals, beginning with the control of his company and his freedom to "market his computer as he sees fit".

   The examinee's list incorporates two goals (2 and 5) which are the same: "free of the Bank" and "protect himself from exploitation by the Bank". This is a common slip in examinations which are answered under time pressure and most examiners would regard it as a lapse and not a punishable error, though too many of these sorts of slips create the impression of an examinee padding a scarcity of knowledge on a topic to make the answer look better than it is. (It pays to re-read your answers to cross out such "slips".)

Of the list, some doubts must remain as to whether the examinee is clear on the role of an interest. For example, if the question "Why" is asked of each of them, their incompleteness is revealed. Why (item 1) does Satran want to "own and control his own company?" Is that an end in itself? Presumably because not owning the company prevents him from doing or achieving something. That "something" is his longer term interest. Likewise with item 2 – being "free from the bank" – not being free prevents him doing or achieving something. Again with item 3 – "exploiting his invention," and item 5.

In the case of item 4 – "have his process adopted as standard" – the above comments apply but with the exception that the second part – "earn him a fortune" – identifies a possible longer term interest. Having his process adopted as standard could be satisfied whoever owns the process. If this was an interest then Satran does not need to own it himself. If he believes that the process will only be adopted as standard if he owns the company, can get free of the bank and can exploit the invention, and that these are necessary steps to achieving his ultimate goal of earning a fortune, then the examinee has identified his longer term interest, which incidentally justifies the positions he takes on the ownership and other issues.

3. The Bank has asserted that they are only interested in making a profit on their investment and have no longer term plans to maintain their holding. Making a profit from investments is a familiar goal of venture capitalists. They appear to be concerned with the security of their investment and have proposed an equity stake to meet their concerns. There are other ways they can achieve this end and it is not clear why an equity stake in an unproven company and its products assures them of their security concerns. An equity stake only provides security if they assess the potential of Satran's product to be relatively certain – if it flops, their equity is worthless. Therefore, if they want a majority stake they must assess a failure as a relatively low risk. As a consultant it would be the examinee's task to put this reasoning to Satran.

   There is a risk of the product succeeding but in a time horizon unsuited to the Bank, therefore, the suggestion of an equity stake has a rationale – they could sell their stake to an interested buyer who is convinced that the process is going to be successful but has different time horizons for realising the investment to the Bank's. This amounts to the Bank wanting an exit route (most venture capitalists seek to agree an exit route to be implemented within a 3-to-5-year horizon). They also look for a high return on their investment (30–45 per cent, even higher). In the main they are not lending against asset backed security (that is the role of normal banks, which have rejected Satran's requests, presumably because his assets – house etc., – are insufficient to cover $15 million). Venture capitalists lend against the potential value of the proposition. We can be sure that if Rich Investment Bank (Jersey) Limited is prepared to consider a loan of $15 million then their assessment of Satran's product and its profitable future, is highly positive. This strengthens Satran's negotiating position, though having been rejected by other sources of funds and being emotionally committed to his invention, he may not be aware of this (which is, of course, the proper role of an independent consultant to point out to him).

A proposal is a tentative suggestion to resolve a problem, which in this case is to match the different interests of both Satran and the Bank. The examinee has outlined some ideas which address the supply of shares to the Bank as security for the loan with a buy-back clause through profits from the successful exploitation of the invention. In terms of a proposal format is this a proposal?

The condition (the Bank considers the loan) is linked to what appear to be further conditions (Satran's programme of repayments to buy back the shares on an exclusive basis etc.). The Bank might ask: what is in it for us? Surely, some interest payments are required; some rights to cover their security etc.? In short a proposal must address the other party's positional requirements which express their interests.

A proposal consists of two elements: the condition (what the other party must do) and an offer (what the proposer is offering in exchange). As it stands the examinee's proposal does not address the interests of the Bank. It is unlikely to be acceptable in its current form. The examinee has not reflected the aims of the question in his/her answer (a common error in examinations and the avoidable cause of disappointing results for many examinees).

As a suggestion, the following might be considered to be a proposal meeting the terms of the question:

> If the Bank makes the loan available then I will consider an interest payment programme at a rate to be agreed, with an equity option of 10 per cent of the company for the Bank to be exercised at a nominal price of $1 a share at any time between years 5 and 10, and to treat the Bank's investment as a non-voting preference share holding with first claim on dividends until paid off in 2005.

In this proposal, Satran does not jeopardise his interests and makes a fair move towards meeting the Bank's interests. He also covers his vulnerabilities. Other proposals containing different contents are of course acceptable, provided that they are in the correct format.

4. Licensing a product is a means to growth without the expense of financing it yourself. The licencees provide the capital out of their own resources. The licence protects the owner of the intellectual property, or brand name, embodied in the product. For the licensee the benefit is access to a proven product without the heavy expense and risk of inventing a substitute or building a new brand. The licence permits them to make or import, use or distribute the product within a defined territory or within their own products. In Satran's case, his new processor would be licensed for use in the products of original equipment manufacturers (OEMs) either as direct purchases from his European plants or for local manufacture by the world's big players.

   Satran has to make some strategic decisions on how he intends to licence the production or use of his processors. Is he going for an exclusive deal with one computer manufacturer who will be the only manufacturer to have the new processor or will he make his processor available on general licence to any manufacturer that wants to purchase a licence? The choice depends on his estimates of the likely profit streams from each option. He could go for a version of both: an exclusive licence for a (short) number of years, followed by a general licence thereafter. A player may want a head start over rivals and be prepared to pay an initial premium for it. If the licence is exclusive this could inhibit widespread use and motivate designers to find a way round the patent. It is not the case that the best designed invention exclusive to a product necessarily wins in the market (e.g. Betamax versus VHS). Making a processor generally available may mean a lower per unit royalty but a much larger volume of revenue (e.g. MS DOS), than an exclusive restricted processor (e.g. AppleMac).

If Satran goes ahead with a user deal for "one or two" computer manufacturers (retaining production of the processor in combination with an in-house plant in France and producer licences in the Far East), he would require to negotiate minimum sales targets with the computer manufacturers (otherwise sales revenues would be limited). To assist this goal he could negotiate an exclusive use deal with the manufacturers that require them to use his and only his processor in their computers. Likewise, with the processor producers in the Far East – they can only produce his processors and nobody else's. They, too, might be given minimum sales revenue targets per year.

Satran's goal of his processor becoming the standard does not sit easily with even short term exclusive deals. To make it the standard requires not only that it is (and remains) the best available, but that it is available to all producers of computers. His processor could drive the alternatives out of the market, at least for a short time until something better is invented. To achieve this there is a massive requirement for volume production and this places the onus on Satran to ensure volume production by sufficient multiple licensing deals with manufacturers across the globe up to the capacity of the market. He could auction licences to this level of demand or permit an open market, allowing competition to determine capacity, provided that whoever produces his processor pays a royalty to his company. His French plant would enable him to take a share of world production and from the revenue finance Research & Development to improve his processor.

This leaves the amount of the royalty from each processor produced under licence. Here there are several considerations. What proportion of world demand can be produced by his French plant? Net of distribution costs this provides an income stream likely to be larger than the per unit royalty from the licensed output. But to gain world domination in product sales, the finance costs of domestic production may be prohibitive, hence royalty income from licensing must be attractive if standardisation is to occur, even though it might be lower than the profit from producing a (small rather than large) proportion of potential world sales. By licensing other manufacturers, the constraint on the amount of royalty is that it must not be lower than the profit of domestic manufacturing net of distribution and finance costs, but it must be high enough to make it worthwhile for a licensed manufacturer to earn a profit from volume sales to computer producers. Satran might wish to set pricing policy (below/above which the manufacturer cannot sell the processor). The outcome would depend on the relative bargaining power of the manufacturer and Satran in the existing circumstances. He could set the royalty as a percentage of the selling price or as a fixed amount per unit sold irrespective of its price or as a fixed annual payment irrespective of volume produced.

The question of the protection of Satran's intellectual property must be included in a licence deal, including the requirement that licensed manufacturers and users notify Satran's company of breaches of his patent that come to their attention (through imitators trying to sell them the substitutes, perhaps) and that they join Satran in any legal action to protect his patents.

The examinee's answer appears to wander about a lot from the subject. Why a basic element of a licence agreement for Satran to consider is to protect either party from exploitation is not clear. This is also repeated in the last line, indicating to the examiner that s/he is filling space rather than demonstrating understanding of the issues. Some of the points above have been identified by the examinee but not enough to consider this as an excellent answer.

5. The BATNA acronym refers to the Best Alternative to a Negotiated Agreement. It was formulated in this way by Roger Fisher and Bill Ury in their book *Getting to Yes*, and was aimed at reminding negotiators that they should widen their focus when faced with an outcome which is below their expectations and apparently beyond the willingness of the other party to improve upon. If negotiators' focus is too narrow they might either reject a deal which upon reflection might suggest is the very best they could obtain, or accept a deal which upon reflection they could actually improve upon.

   By assessing one's BATNA before, and during, a negotiation, the negotiator is assessing the options that might be available and providing him/herself with a more realistic course of action than deadlocking over, or meekly accepting, the last offer on the table. The judgement is simple: if the negotiator's BATNA is worse than the deal, take the deal; if the BATNA is better, keep pressing for an improvement.

   The examinee has stated the meaning of BATNA and has illustrated some things that Satran could do. Depending on how Satran reviews his options throughout the negotiations he could deadlock when what the Bank offers is the best available compared to offers from other sources, or accept a deal under pressure (Satran is "desperate") that is definitely worse than other outcomes.

   The fact that the Bank's offer contains several vulnerabilities for Satran suggests that he be advised to review his positions in case he is being influenced too much by emotions that are depressing his resistance to the Bank's deal.

   First, you should advise him, normal banks lend on a different basis to venture capitalists, who know how to take advantage of an applicant's ignorance of this point. They do not lend to distressed propositions (they are not lenders of last resort, i.e. usurers and loan sharks). They lend against solid propositions that will make them richer not poorer. Their rejection of an offer is not a tactic – it is a sound judgement based on experience, financial acumen and the most detailed research. If they make an offer to lend it is only because they see themselves succeeding because the proposition is a good one. This does not mean that they will not try to "exploit" the gullible to make themselves richer still. Hence, part of Satran's BATNA is to take this into account when evaluating what is on offer. He should also consider that the Bank's first offer, as is true of all negotiators, is unlikely to be their last. In short, Satran can improve his position.

   Obviously one BATNA with the Rich Investment Bank (Jersey) Ltd is to explore with other venture capitalists their proposals. Satran is an applicant not a supplicant. The fact that traditional banks have turned him down is irrelevant once he explores the options with venture capitalists – of which there are many in Jersey and elsewhere. This is a different lending market, which is highly competitive and therefore to Satran's advantage. Not many propositions of Satran's potential comes before any one venture capitalist. Perhaps one proposition in five hundred would attract a willingness to lend $15 million to it.

Satran's BATNA must include the offers he has/can receive from other venture capitalists. While time is not on his side (somebody else might invent something similar to his processor), there is a judgement to be made about how realistic it is that a pre-emptive discovery by somebody will occur. Satran does not need to make a decision immediately. Of course, it may not look that way so far along the process of raising capital and after many disappointments. But he must not let subjectivity get in the way of cool assessment of his options. Sign in haste, repent at leisure, is perhaps a useful little BATNA to remember.

Satran could, as the examinee suggests, issue an ultimatum – "join me or else" – and it might prompt movement. This would depend on what proposals he is making to them. He could also provide evidence of the benefits of his proposal but this ignores the positive analysis that has already been made by the Bank which has prompted them to make an (inadequate and dangerous) offer in the first place.

If, coolly, Satran considers the possibilities, and has been turned down by every venture capitalist there is, and the Rich Investment Bank's deal is by far the best available, he should either accept it and get on with satisfying his goals, or forget the whole thing and do something else.

Strategic Information Systems

The following question is taken from the June 1994 diet of examinations. The examination consisted of

(i) 6 True/False questions (6 marks),

(ii) 19 multiple choice questions (38 marks), and

(iii) a single case study (100 marks). The analysis is based upon a student's actual response to the case study question – chosen from one of the five best marks returned at this diet.

Case study

A division of G, a large engineering company produces computerised industrial controls. A typical example would be a system for running an automated manufacturing plant. Sales are made throughout the world including recent major deals in Russia and Central Europe.

The technical documentation associated with the controls is extensive and increasingly complex. In addition, a substantial amount of documentation has to support the process of bidding for new contracts and the associated presentations. The existing system for producing all this documentation relies on stand-alone word-processing for text and cut-and-paste for the charts, diagrams and graphics.

The management of the product documentation section and that of the central Business Systems Group were aware that the latest publishing technology could make document publishing much more efficient. In addition, imminent legal changes meant that documentation had to accompany products rather than follow them. The documentation process was, therefore, going to be critical in meeting delivery dates.

There was no standard procedure for justifying new IT investment within the company, although a rigorous proposal document had to be prepared. This was essentially economic, dealing with cost and manpower reductions and other efficiency benefits. The exhaustive quantification was based on a four-year write-off period. The proposal had to be approved by the Business Systems Group, the Site Director and the Group General Manager.

The proposal envisaged the following benefits:

- faster production to meet product delivery date
- manpower cost reduction/avoidance by reducing clerical staff by almost half
- reduction in outside printing costs of £57 000 by bringing all printing inhouse
- improved control of projects by bringing printing in-house
- storage cost reductions by printing on demand instead of to store
- income increase by doubling price of manuals because of their better presentational quality.

In addition, the following unplanned benefits were achieved:

- The system was a significant factor in gaining a large Russian contract because of the speed with which the proposal documentation was prepared.
- Cost reduction were achieved even though the throughput was almost doubled.
- The system acted as a catalyst to a re-organisation of the management structure.

The general user reaction has been favourable and the system has had a real business impact. "The Russian contract would probably not have been achieved without it."

Required

1. Describe McFarlen's Strategic Grid, explaining what the axes represent and giving examples for each cell. **(20 marks)**
2. Where is organisation G on the Strategic Grid? Give reasons for your decision. **(20 marks)**
3. What are the limitations of the Grid in assessing the importance of IT to an organisation? **(10 marks)**
4. Describe the Index Matrix of IT benefits. explaining what the axes represent and giving examples for each cell. **(20 marks)**
5. To which "Era" of IT application does organisation G's system belong and which cell of the matrix best describes the benefits the system is likely to bring" Give reasons. **(20 marks)**
6. For what purposes might organisations use the matrix? **(10 marks)**

(Total of 100 marks)

Examiner's general comments

It is instructive, in light of the answers received from students, to reflect upon the requirements of the question, however obvious this may seem.

First, using Question 1 as an example it should be noted that the question asks for at least three distinct components to the student's reply: (i) The McFarlen Strategic Grid must be described, (ii) the axes should be marked and their representation should be explained, (iii) each cell of the grid should be annotated with an example, in addition to the implied requirement of a label.

This breakdown may seem obvious, as would a breakdown of the other requirements, but a significant proportion of students failed to perform this apparently obvious step and hence failed to give themselves a chance of returning a "good" answer.

Second, many students chose to answer the general requirements of questions 1 and 4 with respect to the information stated in the case study. Perhaps the question should have been explicit in asking for answers to be returned with respect to the general definition of the subject concepts, but those students who answered with respect to the case study generally provided rather contrived answers.

Finally, note the allocation of marks within the case study. In this example questions 2 and 5 are worth 20 marks each. Both ask for the company to be positioned in a grid. Simply choosing a cell will not result in the award of many marks. Students should look at how the requirements are quantified and respond accordingly.

Examiner's guidelines to model answers

Question 1

The McFarlen Grid, as described in section 1.5 of the main text, is used to determine an organisation's position with respect to its *dependence* on IT and the *impact* that the use of IT has within the organisation. It is a 2×2 grid breaking each factor into a *high* or a *low* rating. The student answer (see p. 3/80) captures all the relevant description of section 1.5. The question also asks for examples in each of the 4 cells.

DEPENDENCE	High	Factory	Strategic
	Low	Support	Turnaround
		Low	High
		IMPACT	

The McFarlen Grid

The text describes the following representative organisation types:

Factory Cell: Credit card companies with large billing systems at the core of their business.

Support Cell: Management consultancies who need IT for business support tasks such as word-processing and electronic mail, both of which can be done without IT.

Turnaround Cell: Retail chains have not traditionally been reliant on IT, but the move towards EDI (electronic data interchange) and preferred partnerships puts IT on to the critical path of the business.

Strategic Cell: The ubiquitous example is American Airlines with its success in exploiting IT (for its reservations) in order to create an industry standard product.

Question 2

All the information required to answer this question objectively is also contained in section 1.5 of the text.

Organisation G is in the *Support* cell. It does not appear to rely heavily on the use of IT at the present time, and IT is not one of the most important activities that the business must get right.

The best answers will arrive at this conclusion, or some other objectively argued conclusion, if they use McFarlen's six positioning questions:

1. Are there ways to use IT to create defensible barriers?
2. Is there an opportunity to induce switching costs?
3. Are there opportunities to change the ground rules of competition?
4. Can IT change competition from cost-based to competition-based on sustainable product differentiation?
5. Can IT be used to link in suppliers?
6. Are there ways to use technology as a product?

Arguably G's answer to all of these questions would be "no"; therefore G is in the *Support* cell.

Question 3

This question is not explicitly answered in any single section of the main text but the necessary answer appears in general comments liberally sprinkled through various sections of the book, including sections concerning other similar grid-based approaches and tools. The limitations are common in many cases.

The requisite observations are: (i) that it is difficult to make a precise allocation of an organisation to any single cell; (ii) that the grid can only be used as a guideline or for increasing IT awareness; (iii) that different parts of a large organisation may fall into different cells; and (iv) that rapid changes over time can be hard to represent.

Question 4

The Index Matrix of IT Benefits is the subject of Module 3 of the text and it attempts to identify and categorise IT benefits. The axes along which the matrix is built represent the impact level of IT in an organisation (with three categories – the Individual, Function and Organisation) and the class of benefits obtainable (categories – Efficiency, Effectiveness and Transformation).

The nine cells of the matrix describe the development of Information Systems as falling into three eras:

1. Era I: first applied to functional areas and offering efficiency and, later, effectiveness benefits.
2. Era II: IT applied to the individual, principally through the advent of the PC.
3. Era III: the current era has moved IT into new areas, which are inducing transformations which have an impact on the organisation as a whole.

BENEFIT	Individual	Function	Organisation
Efficiency	Task Mechanisation II	Process Automation I	Boundary Extension III
Effectiveness	Work Improvement II	Functional Enhancement I	Service Enhancement III
Transformation	Role Expansion III	Functional Redefinition III	Product Innovation III

BENEFICIARY

Expanded details for the individual cells are unnecessary here since the names in the cells are quite self-explanatory, but examples are asked for in the question.

Era I

- Process automation: Automating a payroll function to save on staff costs.
- Functional enhancement: Automating stock control can provide better services to customers with respect to stock outs, availability and delivery.

Era II

- Task mechanisation: Word processing mechanises clerical activities in the office.
- Work improvement: Desk-top publishing automates a manual process and improves end quality.

Era III

- Role expansion: Networking computers to facilitate document exchange, for example, has led to a need for managers in new co-ordinating roles.
- Functional redefinition: Distribution systems for retail outlets are transformed through the ability to receive EPOS information on a daily basis.
- Boundary extension: EDI has enabled manufacturers to have computer links to their suppliers, in turn leading to more control over distribution and delivery of components.
- Service enhancement: Insurance brokers linked to insurance company databases can efficiently access policy details suited to a client's particulars.
- Product innovation: In the case of American Airlines, IT transformed its airline reservation system, leading to the development of a new business area in which it did not previously compete.

Question 5

This is another question to which it is difficult to give a definitive answer since there is no single correct cell of the matrix into which G neatly fits. The system introduced into G brings a number of benefits but they are almost certainly benefits to *functions* within G and they do not bring about any obvious *transformation*. Hence the most likely cells which categorise G are "Process Automation" and "Functional Enhancement".

Question 6

The Index Matrix can help organisations in a number of areas: (i) in understanding the business purposes of the systems introduced; (ii) to check that no obvious potential benefits are missed; (iii) to create awareness of what systems can do for the business; (iv) to prepare for investment appraisals.

A coherent, consistent and objective argument is required for all answers.

Actual student answers – worth 76%

Question 1

F W McFarlen's Strategic Grid is a 2 × 2 matrix of an organisation's dependence on IT and its reliance on IT for conducting its core business functions. Developed by McFarlen of Harvard Business School, the matrix represents an overview of the organisation's positioning of IT. It is not meant to be a definitive statement of the dynamic process of Strategic Information Systems.

The grid is a template on which to assess the current position regarding the two axes.

Level of dependence on IT		Low	High
	High	Factory	Strategic
	Low	Support	Turnaround

IMPACT
How critical is it to the organisation?

The level of dependence axis represents the extent to which the company relies upon it to opelate its different functions and the extent to which it automates the processes done by each function.

The impact axis is concerned with the importance of IT's role in the functions critical to the success of the organisation.

The cells above contain "descriptors" which suggest the type of use or result from a company being in each cell.

The "support" cell is where a low dependence and low critical impact of IT meet. An example of this is a company's PAYE records – not a core activity and the process is automated. In "G's" case the old word-processing function is probably a good example.

The "Factory" cell is where there is a high level of dependence but a low impact on core activities. The typical example (and the one from which it derives its descriptor) is the case of manufacturing. The use of IT in the manufacturing process is important but not critical. There are other ways of doing it. It is not the IT that is being manufactured. An example from "G's" case would be a factory using one of its computerised control products.

The "Strategic" cell is where impact and the level of dependence are high. A good example here is, the American Airlines system. The well documented case shows how the airline moved into the "Strategic" cell by automating its reservations service *and* putting it into the travel agents via IT *and* selling the system to both users and service providers.

The "Turnaround" cell is where the IT strategy has progressed to a level where the business now has the opportunity with lateral thinking to move to the strategic opportunity cell. Information systems for the efficient running of the organisations are in place and they represent an important element of the core business. A dealing room system is an example where it may in future be possible to move into information services as a separate line – or forecasting perhaps.

The Strategic Grid is a "snapshot"of the current position and can be viewed across time.

Examiner's comments: Question 1

On reflection the allocation of 20 marks is generous in this case since the Grid is relatively simple in concept, it occurs early in the text and underpins much of the rest of the course, and because the examples are well used through the text. This question does serve as a good opener to the case study however.

This particular answer is very comprehensive and reflects a good understanding of the intent of the Grid.

Question 2

"G" has undergone a change in the way it produces its support material for its products. Not only has the company changed the actual physical side of preparation and printing but also the input into the makeup of the manuals.

Dependence	High	Factory	Strategic
	Low	Support	Turnaround "G"
		Low	High
		Impact	

The original word-processing units were stand-alone and firmly in the "Support" cell. The change of integration with functions involved in production and the improvements to tendering would suggest that these were "Factory" cell type situations. However, the fact the documentation production was now required at the time of delivery transformed their role into one of more importance. They were, as the legal requirement indicates, critical to meeting those dates. The improvement to the service offered to the customer resulted in their being in part responsible for not failing (this is put in a double negative because one cannot say that the product was sold on the basis of the documentation alone). This shows the new relevance to the company of their IT structure for these reasons the G organisation could consider themselves in the "Turnaround cell".

Examiner's comments: Question 2

The argument given is plausible and it follows the detail of the question. The answer only merits an average rating however, mainly because it failed to use the six positioning questions offered by McFarlen. The use of these questions would have completed the argument. They would not necessarily have resulted in a perfect match between this argument's conclusion and that in the solution guidelines, but this is not strictly necessary since this case, and any other similar case, cannot suggest definitive position-based answers. It is important for the student to note this since many students tend to give vague answers in an attempt to hedge options. It is better to be positive, and perhaps risk begin unaligned with the model solution, provided that the argument is persuasive.

Question 3

The limitations of FW McFarlen's grid are based on the general nature of the view of the company.

It is a *static* view in that it gives a picture of where a company is at any one point but does not enable the user to track the development of IT strategy.

There are only two variables which can be subject to interpretation differences, biases of judgement.

The variables are not measureable in a quantities sense and so are subject to interpretation problems.

The level of dependence does not take into account the individual function dependence and likewise the impact measure is only relevant to the organisation as a whole. The breakdown of the PAYE system is not a core problem in terms of production – but unless it is resolved in a large organisation there could be large scale problems within a fairly short time scale.

The positioning might be better done by a system of weighted factors relevant to the organisation.

The final limitation is that it does not point the way forward, offer any solutions and is very general in its application.

McFarlen resolved this last point by looking at ways company could try and move to a "Strategic" position by formulating six questions on the role of IT in the organisation:

1. Are there defensible market entry barriers from the use of IT?
2. Can "switching costs" be induced by the use of IT?
3. Can the "rules of the game" be changed by the use of IT?
4. Can IT change the basis of "competitive advantage"?
5. Can suppliers be linked into the system with the use of IT?
6. Can IT be used as a product?

The Strategic grid answers none of these important questions but it does enable an organisation to take stock of where it is at this point in time regarding its use of IT.

Examiner's comments: Question 3

This is a reasonably good answer in light of the fact that this question requires the student to make a good case, since the text does not do this explicitly. The problems noted in question 2 with respect to McFarlen's positioning questions have been partly answered by their inclusion here. They would obviously have been better used in question 2, and explicit answers to these questions for this case would have been welcome, but their inclusion here does complete expectations for this argument as well as the previous one.

Question 4

The Index Matrix from the Index Group is a 3 × 3 matrix representing a framework for placing current and planned IT uses to see the likely benefits and beneficiaries of such systems. It uses the general areas of structure of the company and the objectives of efficiency effectiveness and transformation. It provides a static view of the IT benefits and allows the progress from one cell to another to be tracked across time. An organisation does *not* follow a set pattern of movement within in the Matrix.

Index matrix
beneficiary

		Individual	Function	Organisation
	Efficiency	Task mechanism	Process automation	Boundary extension
Benefits	Effectiveness	Work improvement	Functional enhancement	Service enhancement
	Transformation	Role expansion	Functional redefinition	Product innovation

The matrix is representative of 3 "Eras" of progress in the IT strategy and are represented by :

- ERA 1
- ERA 2
- ERA 3

The Benefits axis is representing the level of gain from the use of IT in the organisation – this is split into three areas of efficiency effectiveness and transformation. The Beneficiary axis is split into the corporate areas of the operation that will gain that benefit – the individual the function and the organisation as a whole.

The "descriptors" in each cell help to identify the benefits and explain the implications.

- ERA I
  Process automation (Function/Efficiency)
  Example – Stand-alone PAYE System
  Functional enhancement (Function/Effectiveness)
  Example – Use of laptops by salespeople leading to better targeting
- ERA II
  Task mechanism (Individual/Efficiency)
  Example – Upgrading of word-processing software for typists to use templates for letters

Work improvement (Individual/Effectiveness)
  Example – Better report presentations

- ERA III

Role expansion (Individual/Transformation)
  Example – New responsibilities for an individual
Functional redefinition (Individual/Transformation)
  Example – Introduction of new sales structures leads to market research being incorporated into salespersons' software Boundary extension (Organisation/Efficiency)
  Example – Placing of terminals in customers' premises for purpose of ordering
Service enhancement (Organisation/Effectiveness)
  Example – Installation of new EDI Equipment to customer/supplier, improving levels of service
Product innovation (Organisation/Transformation)
  Example – Use of CAD for bathroom design and then the transmission when the design becomes separate product to installation

Examimer's comments: Question 4

Again a quite comprehensive answer. It contains the essential description of the axes and includes examples for each cell. The description is particularly good as it mentions phrases such as "... areas of structure of the company ...", "... a static view of the benefits of IT ..." and "... an organisation does not follow a set pattern of movement ...". This captures the purpose and use of the matrix quite neatly. The examples are not all taken from the text, but each example offered is perfectly valid as an answer, which suggests that the student has a deeper understanding of the course than simply recalling the text would suggest.

Question 5

Index matrix for G

		Individual	Function	Organisation
	Efficiency		Old word-processor units	
Benefits	Effectiveness		Faster production of documents to meet delivery	Better proposal documents Better delivery Improved manual production
	Transformation		In house printing Management restructure	

The "G" organisation's system now belongs in Era 3. There have been a number of benefits for the individual and the functional areas, but the over-riding benefit has been for the organisation as a whole. The proposed management restructure will enable the organisation to develop further the IT strategy to gain the untapped potential of the system – such as involving customers in the initial design stages, better specification of products, etc. The cell most suited to describe the benefits of the system would be the Era 3 Organisation/Effectiveness cell of "Service Enhancement". The system allows G to produce manuals for a product to meet the delivery dates. This enables the customers to receive the product more quickly if desired (at least this will be the case when the imminent legal requirement comes into force). The improved speed of production of the proposal document is also a significant competitive advantage as shown by the Russian order. This enabled the purchaser to decide more quickly and so again represents an improvement to service.

There appears to be no more to the product innovation cell as yet but the impressive performance of the new system and the proposed management reorganisation might achieve the necessary lateral thinking.

Examiner's comments: Question 5

The student's response to this part of the question does not choose a single cell of the Index Matrix as suggested in the question. The case study itself however does not lend itself to a single, definitive choice of cell in answer to this question. If this were not the case then the whole question would probably prove to be a poor case study since it would not be capable of supporting differing, but objective, arguments.

The student's choice of cell is "Service Enhancement", i.e. the *Organisation* as the beneficiary and *Effectiveness* as the benefit. This is perfectly plausible since, as argued, "the system allows G to produce manuals for a product . . . enabling the customer to receive the product more quickly". This would appear to conform to the definition of this cell in the text.

The diagram included supports the student's argument well since it is obvious that the student recognises the Era I benefits (which is the suggested model answer) but that G has progressed beyond this point in its use and exploitation of IT. It is perfectly understandable that a student answer will tend to look for more in the problem than is perhaps there. The answer to Question 2 above also positioned the company in the "lowest" level cell, as does this. Perhaps this student and most others were reading the question for rather more detail than actually intended. In the absence of a definitive answer, "wrong" conclusions can be well argued and therefore receive good marks.

Question 6

Organisations using the Index Matrix (and the associated Transformation Graph) are looking at the opportunities from implementing IT strategies. The identification of such opportunities requires a look at the current position which the Index Matrix provides. It is a snapshot of the company at one period of time but can be used to track progress across time as shown by the arrows on the figure that is drawn earlier in the answer. By understanding the current position of the system within the organisation an evolving strategy can be implemented, up to a point, then lateral thinking may be required.

It is of relevance when undertaking a strategic alignment process for establishing the initial IT platform.

Organisational restructuring and managing for change require that individual and functional needs are met. The Index Matrix can help identify where changes can be expected.

In a contingency plan the alternative IT strategies can be of importance and again the relative merits can be viewed in a general way with the Index Matrix.

Evaluation techniques for Strategic Information Systems often rely on items which are difficult to quantify. The constraints on the evaluation techniques might be such that methods have to measure benefits and costs in a non-monetary way. This might be aided by using the Index Matrix.

Competitive analysis is another area when deciding on an overall business or SBU strategy. To enable you to choose a strategy that is suitable to take advantage of your strengths and your competitor's weaknesses, it is prudent to find out where the competitor is in terms of IT strategy. The Index Matrix can again be used.

As with the Strategic Grid the Index Matrix application is not a strict science. The results, whilst informative, are only part of the exercise. The actual analysis of the organisation IT system is beneficial in itself – perhaps generating new ideas and uses for the system.

Examiner's comments: Question 6

As with the McFarlen Grid, the Index Matrix is introduced into the main (section 3.2) text and clearly explained, though its potential use is not necessarily self-contained in one neat paragraph of text. The potential uses and benefits are hinted at throughout Module 3 and in other areas of the course book. This student's answer tends to discuss the strategic rather than the operational implications but it does contain sufficient points concerning the potential use of the matrix. With the exception of the potential for preparation for investment appraisal, all other points included in the model answer are covered or at least hinted at. In this type of question and in Question 3 above the student has been asked to think of reasons not explicitly obvious in the text. This reply is reasonably detailed yet crisp and does not indicate a very laboured response (as was common in other replies).

Strategies for Change

Question 1

Two personality characteristics which are believed to affect the individual employee's response to and ability to cope with stress at work are *locus of control* and *Type A Behaviour.* Explain what is meant by each of these terms and their relationships with stress.

Model answer

Locus of control refers to the extent to which an individual believes that the control they have over their own life lies within themselves or lies within environmental forces outside their control. Someone who strongly believes that he or she controls events is said to have a *high internal locus of control,* while someone who believes that he or she is at the mercy of events (or fate) is said to have a *high external locus of control.*

An individual's perception of control has been shown to affect their response to stress. For example, all other things being equal, workers who are able to work at their own pace, and decide on the tasks they will carry out show fewer symptoms of stress than workers who do not have these aspects of control over their work. As a further example, where an employee is criticised by their manager for the poor quality of their work, and believes that this is because of their lack of ability to do the work to the required standard, they will become depressed, and the quality of their work will be negatively affected. The employee in this case attributes the criticism to an internal cause (themselves) which is unlikely to change in the short term. However, where the employee believes that they are being criticised because their manager has had a bad day, they are more likely to complete the job and get out of their manager's sight!

The employee in this case attributes the criticism to an external cause (their manager) and it is unlikely to be repeated (unless their boss has another bad day). Increasing an employee's control over their work can reduce occupational stress and improve performance. Also, workers who (incorrectly) believe that they have inadequate control over their work, can be helped by stress management techniques such as cognitive restructuring and assertiveness training.

An individual who is described as possessing a *Type A* Personality and exhibiting *Type A behaviour* is characterised by a number of components. First, they are driven by a sense of time urgency. They seek to achieve more and more within a reducing period of time. Thus they become impatient by what they see as time wasters, which could be standing in a queue, or sitting in a traffic jam, and they often move quickly and talk rapidly. Secondly, these personalities have a strong desire to succeed, and are highly competitive. In so doing, they often fail to take account of the feelings of others. This can extend from work, to their family situation, and to leisure activities. Winning (often at all costs) becomes paramount. Thirdly, Type A behaviour is noted for its high level of hostility. Type A individuals often become resentful and suspicious of others, and they are easily angered by colleagues at work.

Type A individuals are more stressed because of the way they perceive their environment. Because they are jealous of others they get little support from their colleagues. Because they are more affected by the everyday stressors which occur at work, they are unable to cope with them. Because they are driven to succeed, and resent interruptions and interference, they are more likely to experience occupational stress and are likely to be able to deal with it adequately. Type A behaviour can be changed by appropriate counselling, biofeedback, etc.

Question 2

Why is customer focus such a key element in the strategy of all organisations committed to TQM? Discuss.

Model answer

Customer – rather than competitor – focus is of primary importance.

TQM ideally has to begin with the external customer. After all it is he who pays the bills! Thus the key focus of TQM has to be to design, develop and implement a customer–value strategy essentially concerned with identifying and satisfying customer requirements. This strategic approach is singularly different from one which concentrates on competitors – what they are doing and how they are doing it. Though a study of this nature can be beneficial in enabling the organisation to improve its process, almost inevitably the implication is that the organisation concerned has chosen to adopt a "follower" strategy. The likely consequence of making this choice is to deny the organisation the opportunity of bringing new products or services to the market. Significantly such a strategy is likely to have detrimental consequences on the organisation's ability to generate superior, or even an adequate, financial performance.

Customer focus is a challenging approach to embrace and implement.

Substantial evidence exists to support the view that many organisations pay lip service only to the notion that the Customer is King. Furthermore, recent studies reported by Durham Business School have revealed that many organisations have introduced TQM *without* identifying their customers' real needs. David Kearns (of Xerox) had, some years earlier, expressed his disbelief that such an approach was conceivable since it:

> Assumes you own the customer, that you know what he wants better than he does and that he will remain loyal to you no matter how you abuse him.

Kearns spelt out three objectives in developing "Leadership through Quality"; the second stressed that Xerox people must provide customers with innovative products and services that fully satisfy their requirements. He continues:

> When we speak of customers we mean customers in the broadest sense of the word. Every Xerox person has customers, internal or external, for his or her work.

Critically, it is how customers perceive supplier quality that is important *not* the view the supplier takes of his own performance. Royal Mail found it difficult initially to accept that their measurement of First-Class mail delivery performance was based on false premises. It wasn't that their actual measurements were incorrect. They had simply failed to appreciate that their customers' perception of delivery service quality involving "end-to-end" measurement, was the only view that counted. Now Royal Mail "always start with focus on the customer"

There is a positive relationship between the way customers perceive a company's quality relative to the competition and the company's return on investment.

Buzzell & Gale's findings reinforce the view not only that quality – or lack of it – exerts an important influence on an organisation's financial performance but that in making this assessment, customers' perceptions are of key importance.

The emphasis given currently to attracting new customers by many organisations, especially financial institutions, is often misguided. Incontrovertible evidence points to the high costs of attracting new customers as against the modest cost of ensuring that existing customers are truly satisfied with the service they currently receive.

MacFarlane Group Clansman are clear that their guiding credo, "Do what the customer tells you", is an important factor in the company's ability to continue, even during the recent recession, to turn in increased profits year by year.

Contrast the customer focus such an approach demands with that given by car servicing outlets whose shocking quality standards, as reported by "Which" must inevitably be reflected in their financial performance. Small wonder that motor manufacturers, whose quality standards are on the whole vastly improved, are more and more reducing the motorist's dependence on service outlets by increasing the intervals between servicing through better design etc.

How a visionary approach to quality paid off is illustrated by the report of how SAS's Carlzon turned round SAS's loss of $8 million in 1981 to a profit of $54 million in little more than a year through thoroughly effective customer focus. He made sure that he was "really selling what the customer wanted to buy".

Customer focus brings with it commitment to constant change.

This is demonstrated in several ways, through, for example.

- Continuous improvement – KAIZEN
- Training and education of all work people, so as to bring out and develop qualities they, perhaps, did not know they possessed:
  - self-reliance
  - ability to work in teams
  - ability to address problems and to take decisions.

Carefully nurtured, such an approach can generate a groundswell of satisfaction in the workforce – "They really are listening to what we have to contribute."

Question 3

Do the makers of gambling machines have a moral obligation to prevent people from becoming addicted to gambling?

Analyse this question using the three ethical theories outlined in the text (consequentialist, duty and virtue theory).

Model answer

There are no "model" answers in business ethics but perhaps some of the following points might be included in your answers.

Consequentialist theory

Looking at the question from the perspective of utility produces the following considerations favouring preventative action by the makers of gambling machines. Trying to combat gambling addiction will reduce frustration and annoyance in the places where the gambling machines are sited. This increases the well-being of everyone who works there and of the recreational players as well. It may even increase the turnover in the long run, because potential players who were previously deterred by the sight of aggressive gambling addicts will now begin to play the machines. Furthermore, combating gambling addiction will improve the image of the gambling machine makers and this will diminish the pressure from government regulations and pressure groups. And doing something against addiction will without doubt be to the advantage of the players at risk and the addicts. It will also increase the well-being of the relatives and friends of the gambling addicts, since their misfortune will at least be reduced to some extent.

The argument from utility against combating gambling addiction concentrates on two issues. The first is that it will lead to a drop in the daily turnover of the gambling machine owners; after all, addicts spend a lot of money on gambling. The second is that trying to prevent gambling addiction means investing time and effort in training personnel and mounting publicity campaigns. So trying to combat gambling addiction will be in the interests of the players, the addicts, their families and friends, and the people who work in the arcades where there are gambling machines, but it will cost the makers and owners of these machines money and effort. On balance the utility calculation probably tilts the scale in favour of trying to combat the undesirable effects of gambling addiction on the part of the makers of these machines. A lot will depend upon what action can be taken and whether others will share the costs.

Duty theory

Following Kant's notion of categorical imperative, it is our duty to treat others as ends in themselves and not merely as means to an end. From this it can be inferred that it is our duty that we do not harm or injure others from our acts. So in business it is the duty of a manufacturer to exercise a duty of care to prevent others from being injured by the products they produce. Consequently, in the case of gambling machine makers, they should take into account the capacity of the persons who will play on the gambling machines, for example persons who are immature, inexperienced, ignorant or mentally defective. So on the basis of this duty, the makers of gambling machines should pay some attention to protecting those who are vulnerable to gambling addiction when they come into contact with these machines.

On the other hand, Kant also stresses the importance of the moral autonomy of the individual and the duty to take personal responsibility for one's actions. Playing gambling machines is an act of free will and for the mature individual this is an important liberty that they should be able to exercise. Likewise the making of gambling machines is not illegal and is an act of a free entrepreneur in a market society. So if those vulnerable to gambling addiction are protected, then it is the duty of the maker of gambling machines to allow individuals to make their own decisions about whether to play on the machines.

Virtue theory

This approach considers what is in the best interests of the common good and for those who wish to live by virtuous conduct. Because the gambling machine owners make use of society in order to produce their machines, they have responsibilities towards that society. A growing number of gambling addicts will lead to harmful social side effects in society, so taking some form of preventative action will help to reduce these negative consequences for the common good. On the other hand, the virtuous person should try to exercise the virtue of temperance and curb their impulses to gamble in an addictive fashion, and not lose control of their own will, and to work with others in society to see that the harmful effects of gambling addiction are minimised.

In conclusion, a case for the makers of gambling machines to exercise some moral responsibility towards gambling addicts can be made from all three theories. However, these responsibilities are limited and are to be complemented by the need for individuals to exercise responsibility in the face of temptation, and that society helps to protect and make regulations for those who cannot exercise full moral autonomy.

Part 4

Practice Examinations with Answers

The compulsory courses

Accounting

PRACTICE FINAL EXAMINATION 1 – WITH MCQs

The duration of the examination is 3 hours. The marks value is shown below. You may allocate your time as you see fit. The pass mark is 50%.

There is no choice in the selection of questions to be answered.

In the multiple choice questions, no marks are deducted for wrong answers.

The examination is in two sections:
A Multiple Choice Questions
B Cases

Section A: Multiple Choice Questions
30 questions each worth 1 mark. Total marks available in section A — 30 × 1 = 30

Section B: Cases
3 case questions with Question 1 worth 30 marks, Question 2 worth 25 marks and Question 3 worth 15 marks. Total marks available in Section B — = 70

Total marks available — = 100

Pass mark = 50% of 100 = 50

Section A: Multiple Choice Questions

The following information applies to Questions 1–5.

At 30 November, the accounting equation of Bruntsfield Machines Limited is:

Cash £5 300 + Debtors £8 350 + Motor vehicle £10 500 + Raw material inventories £3 650 + work-in-progress inventories £4 000 = Owners' equity £19 800 + Creditors £7 000 + Bank loan £5 000

During December, the following transactions occur:

I Creditors of £2 500 are paid.
II Plant, costing £6 500, is purchased for cash.
III Labour costs of £2 000 are paid in converting the work-in-progress inventory into finished goods.
IV Payments of £800 are received from debtors.
V 75% of the finished goods inventory is sold for £7 500, on credit.

1. What is the amount of cash following the completion of these transactions?

   A Cash of £600
   B Cash of £2 600
   C Overdraft of £2 900
   D Overdraft of £4 900

2. The directors consider that, in the current economic climate, it is prudent to make a 5% provision for doubtful debts. What is the amount of debtors following this provision?

   A £7 173
   B £14 297
   C £14 675
   D £15 097

3. What is the amount of total Current Assets following the completion of these transactions and the adjustment required in Question 2 above?

   A £17 497
   B £19 447
   C £20 247
   D £24 347

4. In preparing the accounting equation, it is noted that no allowance has been made for depreciation of motor vehicles and plant. It is decided that motor vehicles should be depreciated in four equal annual installments, with plant written off at 20% per annum irrespective of acquisition date. What is the total amount of fixed assets following these depreciation charges?

   A £5 200
   B £12 750
   C £13 600
   D £13 075

5. Following these transactions and the adjustments required in Questions 3 and 4, what is the revised amount of owner's equity?

   A £18 122
   B £18 875
   C £22 622
   D £27 522

The following information applies to Questions 6–8.

At 1 April, Thomas Black and Co. performed their annual stocktaking, counting 35 refrigerators, 25 of which had been purchased at £110 each and 10 for £120 each. Over the next six months, the company made the following purchases.

Month	*Refrigerators purchased*	*Unit price*
May	10	£125
June	6	£130
July	5	£130
August	10	£135
September	5	£130

For the six months, sales amounted to 62 refrigerators, for a total value of £10,750.

6. If the first-in, first-out (FIFO) method of inventory valuation is used, what is the amount of cost of sales?

   A £4 680
   B £7 440
   C £7 460
   D £7 640

7. If the average cost method of inventory valuation is used, what is the amount of closing inventory?

   A £1 016
   B £1 094
   C £1 170
   D £1 190

8. If the last in, first out (LIFO) method of inventory valuation is used, what is the gross profit margin?

   A 19.72%
   B 28.93%
   C 29.90%
   D 30.79%

9. Which of the following defines working capital?

   A Fixed assets less current liabilities.
   B Trading profits less dividends.
   C Fixed assets plus retained profits.
   D Current assets less current liabilities.

10. In a Cash Flow Statement, which of the following is an inflow of cash?

    A increase in inventories
    B purchase of fixed assets
    C sale of ordinary shares
    D increase in debtors

11. In financial statements, Goodwill is defined as:

I the amount paid by a purchaser in excess of a company's net assets.
II the value assigned to a company's brand names.
III the excess of a quoted company's market capitalization over its net assets.
IV the management's external valuation of a company.

Which of the following is correct?

A I only.
B I and II only.
C III only.
D III and IV only.

12. Aberclyde Sailing Club has a financial year which runs to 30 June each year. The annual subscription has been fixed at £300 for the years to 31 March 1992, 1993, and 1994. At 31 March 1992, twenty members had paid their annual subscriptions in advance. At 31 March 1993, all 300 members were fully paid-up, but ten had paid their subscriptions in advance for the year to 31 March 1994.

What is the amount of subscription revenue for the year to 31 March 1994?

A £84 000
B £87 000
C £90 000
D £96 000

13. Silvergate Systems Limited has budgeted sales of £350 000 for next year. Their plan is to cut their inventory level by £33 000 over the year. Their current mark-up is 30% on cost.

What is the amount of purchases next year?

A £212 000
B £236 231
C £245 000
D £302 231

The following information applies to Questions 14 and 15.

During the year, Pine Products plc has acquired Garden Huts Limited for £5m, giving rise to goodwill on acquisition of £1.8m. In considering the accounting treatment of goodwill, the options are to:

I capitalize, but write-off over four years
II capitalize, but write off over ten years
III write-off £1.8m to reserves.

The current year profits of Pine Products plc are £4m and it has 800 000 ordinary shares.

14. If option II is selected, what is the earnings per share in the current year?

A £4.38
B £4.60
C £4.78
D £5.00

15. If option III is selected, what is the earnings per share in the current year?

A £(1.25)
B £4.50
C £4.80
D £5.00

16. Which of the following is correct?

A Management accounting has no rigid rule enforcement on asset valuation and revenue recognition.
B Management accounting is strictly governed by statements of standard accounting practice.
C Financial accounting is not compulsory, but few companies succeed without a system.
D Management accounting is highly structured around the accounting equation.

The following information applies to Questions 17 and 18

	Actual	*Budget*	*Job 423A*
Direct labour (£)	10 000	12 000	3 000
Direct material (£)	16 000	15 000	2 750
Factory overhead (£)	35 000	40 000	
Labour hours	6 000	5 000	150
Machine hours	7 500	8 000	250

17. If a machine hour rate is used for factory overhead, what is the amount charged to Job 423A?

A £750
B £1 167
C £1 250
D £2 000

18. If a direct labour hour rate is used for factory overhead, what is the total cost of Job 423A?

A £6 950
B £8 200
C £15 750
D £16 250

The following information applies to Questions 19–21

Weasel Limited produces a single product. Its costs are as follows:

	Variable per unit	*Fixed per period*
Product costs	£15	£35 000
Period costs	£10	£60 000

19. If the product sells for £50 and the firm sells all it produces during the period, how many units must be sold to break even?

A 1 000
B 1400
C 2400
D 3 800

20. If the firm sells 5 000 units per period, what price should be charged to earn £5 000 in profit?

A £44
B £45
C £50
D £51

21. If fixed period costs increase by £10 000, what is the revised number of units for break-even operation given that the selling price can be increased to £60 per unit?

A 2 500
B 3 000
C 3 150
D 3 325

22. In the accountant's break-even model of cost behaviour, which of the following is correct if the volume of output is increasing?

A Unit fixed cost is increasing.
B Total variable costs are decreasing.
C Unit selling price is increasing.
D Unit fixed cost is decreasing.

The following information applies to Questions 23–25.

Argyll Mugs Limited forecasts a monthly fixed factory overhead of £24 000 with a normal monthly output of 1 200 mugs. For the final six months of the year, the following data have been accumulated:

	Mugs manufactured	*Mugs sold*
July	1 300	800
August	1 200	1 200
September	900	1 200
October	1 000	1 000
November	1 500	1 200
December	1 300	1 000

There is no opening inventory of mugs on 1 July.

23. In how many months will the net profit under absorption and variable costing be identical?

A Not in any month.
B In one month.
C In two months.
D In four months.

24. In how many months will the net profit under variable costing exceed the net profit under absorption costing?

A In one month.
B In two months.
C In three months.
D In four months.

25. If actual fixed overhead for November is £25 000, what is the amount of overhead over- or under-recovery for that month?

A Under-recovery of £1 000.
B Over-recovery of £1 000.
C Under-recovery of £5 000.
D Over-recovery of £5 000.

The following information applies to Questions 26–29.

Troon Products Limited is a contract printer for the Bank of Caledonia, for which it produces pay-in slips in batches of 1 000 units. For this batch size, the following standard has been prepared:

	£
2 kg of material at £20 per kg	40
3 hours of direct labour at £12 per hour	36
6 hours of overhead at £30 per machine hour	180
	256

During May, 100 batches were produced with the following cost information:

Materials used 210 kgs at £21 per kg

Direct labour	320 hours, costing £3 900
Applied overhead	620 machine hours

26. What is the material efficiency variance?

    A Adverse variance of £200.
    B Adverse variance of £210.
    C Adverse variance of £410.
    D Adverse variance of £105.

27. What is the material price variance?

    A Adverse variance of £200.
    B Adverse variance of £210.
    C Favourable variance of £210.
    D Adverse variance of £410.

28. What is the labour efficiency variance?

    A Nil.
    B Adverse variance of £60.
    C Adverse variance of £240.
    D Adverse variance of £246.

29. What is the labour rate variance?

    A Adverse variance of £56.
    B Adverse variance of £60.
    C Favourable variance of £60.
    D Adverse variance of £300.

30. If divisional performance is assessed only by ROI then it is possible that divisional managers will produce dysfunctional decisions. Examples may include:

    I A policy of non-replacement of ageing fixed assets.
    II A decision to freeze recruitment of new staff.
    III A reluctant agreement to a head office directive on transfer pricing policy.
    IV A rejection of projects which earn ROI in excess of the company's cost of capital.

    Which of the following are examples of dysfunctional behaviour?

    A I and II only.
    B I, II and III only.
    C II and III only.
    D I and IV only.

Section B: Cases

1.

The board of directors of Huntley Products Limited is considering the following investment proposal:

Proposal		*Cost (£)*
A	Installation of mainframe computer system	180 000
B	Purchase of extra warehouse space	200 000
C	Research and development of a new product	100 000
D	Creation of a formal staff training system	40 000
E	Introduction of approved quality assurance scheme	70 000

Each project will provide benefits in terms of lower cash outflows, over the next five years, as follows:

Proposal A: anticipates cost savings of £66 000 per annum over each of the next five years.

Proposal B: expects annual cash flows to be reduced by £145 000 in only the first two years of this period, with no benefits thereafter.

Proposal C: since this relates to the development of a new product, no benefits are expected till year 3, but thereafter at the rate of £73 000 per annum.

Proposal D: is looking for annual cost savings of £16 000 in each of these five years.

Proposal E: substantial savings of £70 000 per annum are expected to accrue over this period.

Each proposal is structured into two equal phases of cost incurrence and cash flow benefits. If necessary, the board is prepared to undertake the first phase of any proposal without pushing on to the second phase.

The current funds available for this investment are limited to £300 000 and therefore, it is not possible to carry out all proposals at this time.

The internal rate of return on each project is:

Proposal	IRR%
A	24.32
B	28.79
C	22.05
D	28.65
E	26.82

The board have decided that the minimum return on any project must be 10% per annum.

However, the directors are unsure how to proceed to evaluate these proposals.

Required:

1. Carry out an assessment of the proposals, with a view to advising the directors of the criteria applicable in ranking the investment proposals. **(22 marks)**

2. Prepare a list of other factors which the directors may need to consider before coming to a final conclusion. **(8 marks)**

(Total of 30 marks)

Notes

1. Ignore taxation.
2. The present value of £1, at 10% discount rate is:

End of Year	*Present value*
1	0.909
2	0.826
3	0.751
4	0.683
5	0.621

2.

Executive Cars plc have produced their Annual Report and Accounts for the year to 31 December 1990.

Consolidated Profit and Loss Account	*1990*	*1989*
	£m	*£m*
Turnover	830.4	746.5
Cost of sales	646.2	577.8
Gross profit	184.2	168.7
Distribution costs	(20.6)	(19.7)
Administrative expenses	(56.8)	(41.2)
Operating profit	106.8	107.8
Net income from investments	14.0	13.5
Profit on ordinary activities before taxation	120.8	121.3
Taxation	(37.4)	(33.7)
Profit on ordinary activities after taxation	83.4	87.6
Dividends	(17.2)	(24.1)
Retained profit	66.2	63.5

Consolidated Balance Sheet	*1990*	*1989*
	£m	*£m*
Fixed assets	237.4	176.6
Current assets		
Inventory	104.7	87.0
Debtors	43.2	48.4
Cash at Bank	271.6	156.2
	419.5	291.6
Creditors: amounts falling due within one year	(346.2)	(234.2)
Net current assets	73.3	57.4
Total assets less current liabilities	310.7	234.0
Creditors: amounts falling due after more than one year	(77.5)	(67.0)
	233.2	167.0
Capital and reserves		
Called-up share capital	45.2	45.2
Share premium	2.8	2.8
Profit and loss account	185.2	119.0
	233.2	167.0

Share capital comprises 180.9m ordinary shares of 25 pence each. Following the publication of these results, market price stands currently at £5.80 per share, compared to £4.50 a year ago.

Required:

Your father has a holding of 10 000 ordinary shares in Executive Cars plc. He is disappointed with the lack of growth in operating profits, together with the large cut in dividends. He asks your advice on the strength of the company in comparison with 1989 results.

Carry out a full ratio analysis on the accounts of Executive Cars plc, paying particular attention to the areas of liquidity, profitability and efficiency. Provide a commentary on the ratios you calculate. **(18 marks)**

Conclude your analysis by advising your father on the key stock market ratios, outlining your overall impression of the company's performance. **(7 marks)**
(Total of 25 marks)

3.
Inverfrost Products Limited manufactures a single product – a special chemical – Alphastar. The company has always operated a standard costing system to control the variable cost aspects of the product.

The standard cost for Alphastar is:	£
Direct materials	
Raw material Kl – 2 kg at £1 per kg	2.00
Raw material B3 – 1 kg at £3 per kg	3.00
Direct labour – 3 hours at £4 per hour	12.00
Variable overheads – 3 hours at £6 per direct labour hour	18.00
	35.00

The company's annual budget envisages sales of 40 000 units of Alphastar at £80.00 each, spread evenly over the year.

The first quarter of the financial year has just been completed with the following results:

	£	£
Sales (9 000 units at £85.00)		765 000
Direct materials		
Kl – 18 000 kg at £1 per kg	18 000	
B3 – 8 500 kg at £3.50 per kg	29 750	
Direct labour (28 000 hours at 4.50 per hour)	126 000	
Variable overheads	165 000	
		338 750
Contribution margin		426 250

The management are modestly pleased with the actual results for the quarter, but are disappointed that sales have fallen short of the budgeted level. They are also concerned that, whereas some costs seem under control, others are significantly different from those laid down in the standard.

Required:

Prepare a full variance analysis of variable cost elements. Ignore sales variances.

(10 marks)

From the information available, suggest possible explanations for the variances identified.

(5 marks)
(Total of 15 marks)

Solutions to Multiple Choice Questions/Section A

Question	*Answer*	*Question*	*Answer*
1.	D	16.	A
2.	B	17.	C
3.	B	18.	A
4.	D	19.	D
5.	A	20.	B
6.	B	21.	B
7.	B	22.	D
8.	B	23.	C
9.	D	24.	A
10.	C	25.	D
11.	A	26.	A
12.	C	27.	B
13.	B	28.	C
14.	C	29.	B
15.	D	30.	D

Case 1

1.

Proposals		A		B		C		D		E	
Year	*NPV factor*	*Cash flows*	*NPV*	*Cash flows*	*NPV*	*Cash flows*	*NPV*	*Cash flows*	*NPV*	*Cash flows*	*NPV*
0	1.00	(180 000)	(180 000)	(200 000)	(200 000)	(100 000)	(100 000)	(40 000)	(40 000)	(70 000)	(70 000)
1	0.909	66 000	59 994	145 000	131 805	–	–	16 000	14 544	70 000	63 630
2	0.826	66 000	54 516	145 000	119 770	–	–	16 000	13 216	70 000	57 820
3	0.751	66 000	49 566	–	–	73 000	54 283	16 000	12 016	70 000	52 570
4	0.683	66 000	45 078	–	–	73 000	49 589	16 000	10 928	70 000	47 810
5	0.621	66 000	40 986	–	–	73 000	45 333	16 000	9 936	70 000	43 470
			70 140		51 575		50 015		20 640		195 300
Investment			180 000		200 000		100 000		40 000		70 000
Ratio (NPV/Investment)			0.39		0.26		0.50		0.52		2.79
Ranking			4		5		3		2		1

Note: For such investment comparisons, IRR% are of limited value due to their very nature as ratios.

The ratio (NPV/Investment) enables the proposals to be compared in terms of their usage of the limiting factor of scarce investment funds. This ranking mechanism highlights the excellent return available on Proposal E, in comparison with the other proposals.

The scarce funds for investment must be allocated in accordance with the ranking mechanism. The fact that the proposals can be undertaken in two equal phases means that it is possible to commence the first phase of Proposal A within the investment budget currently available.

Therefore, the directors are advised to select the investment proposals, as follows:

Funds available		£300 000
Proposal E	Quality assurance	70 000
Proposal D	Training	40 000
Proposal C	New product	100 000
Proposal A	Mainframe computer (50% project only)	90 000
		£300 000

2. The directors may also wish to take account of some of the following qualitative factors in making their final decision on the selection of investment proposals.

   Risks and uncertainty
   Sensitivity analysis
   Technological risks/obsolescence
   Legislative provisions
   Management morale
   Employee industrial relations
   Capacity constraints

Case 2

Liquidity ratios	*1990*	*1989*
1. *Current ratio*		
Current assets / Current liabilities	419.5 / 346.2	291.6 / 234.2
	= 1.21	1.25
2. *Quick ratio*		
(Current assets – stock) / Current liabilities	(419.5 – 104.7) / 346.2	(291.6 – 87.0) / 234.2
	= 0.91	0.87

Comments
The company has maintained a solid current ratio in 1990, boosted by a significant increase in cash balances which have offset the rise in creditors. Although the current

ratio is lower than the "rule of thumb" yardstick of 2, the size of the cash balances means that, even at 1.2, it reflects a comfortable working capital position.

There may be some concern about the growth in cash levels, which seems to have occurred at the expense of creditors. It may be questioned whether creditors are being over-stretched and whether cash can be better utilized in other, more productive directions, e.g. in fixed assets. The quick ratio has improved marginally, buoyed by the higher cash balances. At 0.91, it is close to the yardstick figure for the quick ratio. With the high proportion of cash, it represents a healthy liquidity position.

Profitability ratios		*1990*	*1989*
1. *Profit margin*			
$\frac{\text{Profit after interest + tax}}{\text{Sales}}$		$\frac{83.4}{830.4}$	$\frac{87.6}{746.5}$
	=	10.05%	11.74%
2. *Return on total assets*			
$\frac{\text{Profit after interest + tax}}{\text{Total assets}}$		$\frac{83.4}{237.4 + 419.5}$	$\frac{87.6}{176.6 + 291.6}$
	=	12.7%	18.7%
3. *Gross profit margin*			
$\frac{\text{Gross profit margin}}{\text{Sales}}$		$\frac{184.2}{830.4}$	$\frac{168.7}{746.5}$
	=	22.19%	22.6%
4. *Return on equity*			
$\frac{\text{Profit after tax}}{\text{Capital employed}}$		$\frac{83.4}{233.2}$	$\frac{87.6}{167.0}$
	=	35.77%	52.46%
5. $\frac{\text{Admin. expense}}{\text{Sales}}$		$\frac{56.8}{830.4}$	$\frac{41.2}{746.5}$
	=	6.8%	5.5%
6. $\frac{\text{Distribution costs}}{\text{Sales}}$		$\frac{20.6}{830.4}$	$\frac{19.7}{746.5}$
	=	2.48%	2.64%

Comments

Although gross profit margins have held up fairly well at 22.19%, there are clear signs of concern with declining overall profitability. Both return on total assets and return on equity have fallen sharply in 1990. Investigation must focus on the increase in administrative expenses, significantly up from 5.5% to 6.8% of turnover.

Efficiency Ratios		*1990*	*1989*
1. *Inventory turnover*			
Sales / Inventory		830.4 / 104.7	746.5 / 87.0
	=	7.93 times	8.58 times
2. *Average collection period*			
Debtors / Sales per day		43.2 / 830.4 ÷ 365	48.4 / 746.5 ÷ 365
	=	19 days	24 days
3. *Fixed assets turnover*			
Sales / Fixed assets		830.4 / 237.4	746.5 / 176.6
	=	3.5 times	4.2 times

Comments
The decline in the inventory turnover ratio, from 8.58 to 7.93 in 1990, reflects some genuine concern about rising inventory levels in the balance sheet. Attention requires to be focused on the realizable value of this inventory in the future.

There are, however, positive signs with a substantial improvement in the average collection period from 24 days to 19 days, indicative of a more effective credit control function.

On the other hand, there has been a disappointing fall in the fixed asset turnover ratio from 4.2 times to 3.5 times. The additional investment in fixed assets has not produced equivalent benefits in higher turnover.

Stock market ratios

1. *Earnings per share (EPS)*			
Profit after tax / No. of ordinary shares		83.4 / 180.9	87.6 / 180.9
	=	46.1 pence	48.4 pence
2. *Price/earnings ratio*			
Market price / EPS		580 / 46.1	450 / 48.4
	=	12.58	9.3

3. *Dividend yield*

Dividend per share / Market price		£17.2m ÷ 180.9 / £5.80	£24.1 ÷180.9 / £4.50
	=	1.64%	2.96%

4. *Dividend cover*

Net profit / Dividend		83.4 / 17.2	87.6 / 24.1
	=	4.85 times	3.64 times

Comments

Earnings per share is slightly down, reflecting the fall in profitability. Despite this fact, the P/E ratio has risen, possibly due to other factors. With dividend yield also declining, it may well be the right time to advise the disposal of shares in this company.

It seems that the company has decided to restrict its dividend pay-out, perhaps to conserve cash for the future, although its cash balances are strong.

Case 3

Variance analysis

Materials-KI

Price variance	= (SP – AP)AQ
	= (£1 – £1)18 000
	= Nil variance
Efficiency variance	= (SQ – AQ)SP
	= ([9 000 × 2] – 18 000)£1
	= Nil variance
Materials-B3	
Price variance	= (SP – AP)AQ
	= (£3 – £3.50)8 500
	= £4 250 adverse
Efficiency variance	= (SQ – AQ)SP
	= ([9 000 × 1] – 8 500)£3
	= £1 500 favourable
Direct labour rate variance	= (SR – AR)AT
	= (£4 – £4.50)28 000
	= £14 000 adverse
Efficiency variance	= (ST – AT)SR
	= ([9 000 × 3] – 28 000)£4
	= (27 000 – 28 000)£4
	= £4 000 adverse

Variable overheads		
Spending variance	= Standard cost of actual time taken for units produced	*less* Actual costs incurred
	= (28 000 × £6)	*less* £165 000
	= £168 000	*less* £165 000
	= £3 000 favourable	
Efficiency variance	= Standard cost of flexible budget time allowance for units produced	*less* Standard cost of actual time taken for units produced
	= (9 000 × 3 × £6)	*less* (28 000 × £6)
	= £162 000	*less* £168 000
	= £6 000 adverse	

Summary

From the variance analysis, several causal factors emerge in explanation of the company's performance.

1. On the cost side, the majority of the difficulties have arisen in labour cost and the associated variable overheads. A total labour adverse variance of £18 000 seems likely to have stemmed from using too highly qualified and well-paid staff for jobs with which they were unfamiliar, giving rise to a massive adverse rate variance of £14 000 and an adverse efficiency variance of £4 000.

2. Some of the negative aspects of direct labour performance have spilled into variable overheads with an overall adverse variance of £3 000.

3. On the materials side, Kl was used exactly as per the standard. Material B3 seems to have suffered a large price rise from the supplier, producing an adverse price variance of £4 500. In turn, the favourable efficiency variance of £1 500 might well be the consequence of the higher price of B3 as greater care was taken in its use.

PRACTICE FINAL EXAMINATION 2 – WITHOUT MCQs

Case Studies

Question 1

Glendale Foods Limited purchases mushrooms for canning and subsequent sale to supermarket chains. All mushrooms are carefully inspected upon receipt in the factory and graded into large or button mushrooms. Any poorer quality mushrooms are set aside for canning as mushroom soup.

For the month of November, the management accountant has compiled the following data in respect of each case of 100 cans of each product.

	Large £	*Button* £	*Soup* £
Selling Price	106	124	58
Costs			
Materials	56	56	26
Labour	28	42	14
Variable factory overhead	8	8	8
Fixed factory overhead	4	4	4
	96	110	52
Profit	10	14	6
Profit (%)	9.4	11.3	10.3

During November, budgeted sales were achieved in each of the product lines, as follows:

Large 1 500 cases
Button 1 500 cases
Soup 2 100 cases

The costs of both variable and fixed factory overhead have been calculated by dividing total monthly costs by the sales volume achieved. However, the management accountant believes that it would be more relevant to link variable factory overhead to direct labour costs, since there is a closer causal relationship.

The sales director believes that the company has an opportunity to increase its market share in December. He estimates that a price reduction of £1 per case would have the effect of increasing the sales volume of the product line selected by 40% over November levels. In view of their high profitability and high selling price, he favours the implementation of the price reduction on only button mushrooms.

Required:

1. ***What is the level of profit earned in November?*** **(2 marks)**

Current Profitability in November

Product	*Output (cases)*	*Profit per case* £	*Total profit* £
Large	1 500	10	15 000
Button	1 500	14	21 000
Soup	2 100	6	12 600
	5 100		48 600

2. ***It is decided to change the method of computing variable factory overhead to link it to direct labour costs. Revise the total cost per case for each product to include the new approach.*** **(6 marks)**

Variable factors overhead – 5 100 cases × £8 per case = £40 800

Total direct labour cost

			£
Large	–	1 500 × £28 per case	42 000
Button	–	1 500 × £42 per case	63 000
Soup	–	2 100 × £14 per case	29 400
			134 400

$$\text{Overhead allocation rate \%} = \frac{\text{Variable factory overhead}}{\text{Direct labour cost}}$$

$$= \frac{£40\,800}{£134\,400}$$

$$= 30.36\%$$

Product	*Direct labour cost* £	*Variable factory overhead* £	*Output (cases)* £	*Cost per case* £
Large	42 000	12 750	1 500	8.50
Button	63 000	19 126	1 500	12.75
Soup	29 400	8 924	2 100	4.25
	134 400	40 800		

	Large £	*Button* £	*Soup* £
Product			
Original total cost	96.00	110.00	52.00
Less:			
Original variable factory overhead	(8.00)	(8.00)	(8.00)
Add:			
Revised variable factory overhead	8.50	12.75	4.25
Revised total cost	96.50	114.75	48.25

3. ***Assess the viability of the sales director's proposal for a price reduction on cases of button mushrooms. Include in this appraisal the results of the change in the approach to variable factory overhead.*** **(7 marks)**

Further analysis is hampered by the treatment of fixed costs, which have been allocated to the product lines on a volume basis. Total fixed costs are £20 400 (5 100 cases × £4 per case). To assess the sales director's proposal, it is essential to focus on the contribution per product, using the revised variable factor overhead costs.

	Large	Button	Soup
	£	£	£
Per case			
Selling Price	106.00	124.00	58.00
Variable costs			
Materials	56.00	56.00	26.00
Labour	28.00	42.00	14.00
Factory overheads	8.50	12.75	4.25
	92.50	110.75	44.25
Contribution	13.50	13.25	13.75
Ranking	2	3	1

Contribution analysis reveals that sales of soup generate the highest contribution per case, altering the impression arising from the original presentation of November data.

Effect of sales director's proposal

Sales of cases of button mushrooms will increase to 2 100 from 1 500, but the contribution per case will decline to £12.25 due to £1 price reduction.

	£
Revised total contribution (2 100 × £12.25)	25 725
Less: Original total contribution (1 500 × £13.25)	19 875
Increase in profit	5 850

Therefore, the proposal is certainly viable and attractive in its own right.

4. ***Consider the application of the sales director's proposal to the other two product lines. If implemented, which of the three product lines would generate the highest incremental profit?*** **(6 marks)**

The contribution analysis, by product, revealed the error in the sales director's presumption that the most profitable range was the button mushroom. In fact, both large mushroom and soup generate higher contributions per case and therefore, additional 40% volume of either of these lines will also increase profits.

Large mushrooms	£
Revised total contribution (2 100 × £12.50)	26 250
Less: Original total contribution (1 500 × £13.50)	20 250
Increase in profit	6 000

Mushroom soup	£
Revised total contribution (2 940 × £12.75)	37 485
Less: Original total contribution (2 100 × £13.75)	28 875
Increase in profit	8 610

Since mushroom soup has the highest contribution per case, it is no surprise that it will also generate the highest incremental profit following a 40% increase in volume.

5. ***Assess the proposal, as applied to all three product lines, in terms of its effectiveness in increasing turnover levels.*** **(4 marks)**
(Total of 25 marks)

Market share can only be measured in terms of increasing sales revenues as a result of the higher volume at the lower price.

Product	*Original sales £*	*Revised sales £*	*Increase + %*
Large	1 500 × £106 = **£159 000**	2 100 × £105 = **£220 500**	+38.7
Button	1 500 × £124 = **£186 000**	2 100 × £123 = **£258 300**	+38.9
Soup	2 100 × £58 = **£121 800**	2 940 × £57 = **£167 580**	+37.6

Solely from the perspective of increasing market share, it is indeed the Button mushrooms which would give the largest increase in revenue and hence, market share. However, it is not a conclusive edge and hence, it would seem likely that the increased profitability would be a more important deciding factor.

Question 2

Denver Gold Mining Co. Inc. has a wholly-owned subsidiary, Alaskan Silver Inc., which operates a silver mine in Anchorage, Alaska. As part of a strategy to focus on its core activities, Denver has decided that it wishes to sell Alaskan Silver Inc. to realise cash to fund new investments in gold mining in Mexico.

The management of Alaskan Silver Inc. are interested in a management buy-out, but they are aware that the silver mine has only a further four years of extraction life remaining. To assist the management in determining a reasonable price to pay Denver, the company accountant has assembled the following information.

(i) Sales of silver are forecast to be $650 000 in the next year, rising by 10% and then a further 3.5% in the following two years, before falling back to $650 000 in the final year.

(ii) Following the closure of the silver mine, the directors estimate that they will be able to sell the useful fixed assets for $45 000. In addition, there will be an obligation to make final redundancy payments of $90 000 and to contribute $65 000 towards the return of the site to an environmentally acceptable status.

(iii) Alaskan Silver Inc. has a current bank overdraft of $55 000.

(iv) The production director has forecast cost of sales, as a % of sales value, as follows:

Year	*%*
1	70
2	70
3	75
4	80

(v) Selling and distribution costs are projected to comprise $45 000 per annum in fixed costs, plus a variable element of 5% of sales value.

(vi) Working capital (excluding the bank overdraft) is expected to decrease by $40 000 per year for each of the four years, with the residual being received in the year following the cessation of mining. At present, working capital includes:

	$
Stocks	125 000
Debtors	185 000
Creditors (excluding bank overdraft)	115 000

(vii) Cost of sales includes an annual provision for depreciation of $45 000 on fixed assets.

In preliminary discussions with the Bank of Vancouver, the directors of Alaskan Silver Inc. have been advised that the cost of borrowing the funds to acquire the company is likely to be 8% per annum.

Denver Gold Mining Co. Inc. is prepared to listen to offers for the subsidiary – in excess of $560 000 as a single lump sum payment.

Notes

(1) Ignore taxation

(2) At 8%, the present value of £1 is

Year	
1	0.926
2	0.857
3	0.794
4	0.735
5	0.681

Required:

1. ***Prepare a report to the directors of Alaskan Silver Inc. advising them of your assessment of the maximum acceptable purchase price to pay Denver.*** **(20 marks)**

2. ***If Denver was prepared to accept payment in four annual installments of $140 000, which effect would that have on your advice to the management of Alaskan Silver Inc.? Incorporate your conclusions in your report.*** **(8 marks)**

Report to: The Directors of Alaskan Silver Inc.

Subject: Proposed Management Buy-Out

In order to assess the potential acquisition of your company from Denver Gold Mining Inc., it has been necessary to carry out a full investment appraisal, based on the forecasts provided by your accountant.

Whilst the full detail of the appraisal is included in Appendix I, my view is that the present value of the investment is $518 000 and therefore, I would recommend that you do not accept Denver's price of $560 000. It may be that the group's desire to strip out non-core activities may outweigh their initial valuation and therefore, they may be prepared to enter negotiations with a willing buyer to come to a price more acceptable to you.

However, the option of an installment basis payment plan is considerably more attractive. In Appendix II, I have included that possibility along with the original forecasts with the result that the proposal generates a positive net present value of $54 000. Therefore, in considering your approach to the negotiations, it will be useful for you to have in mind that, whatever the price agreed, a phased repayment will be of considerable advantage to you, equivalent to an effective reduction in the price agreed.

3. ***Any investment proposal gives rise to issues of risk and uncertainty. Consider how these aspects can be built into a realistic assessment of a potential investment.***

(7 marks)
(Total of 35 marks)

(See main text – Section 15.10 – 15.14.)

Appendix I

	Year 0	*Year 1*	*Year 2*	*Year 3*	*Year 4*	*Year 5*		*$'000*
Inflows								
Sales	–	650	715	740	650	–		
Depreciation	–	45	45	45	45	–		
Working Capital	–	40	40	40	40	35		
Fixed Assets	–	–	–	–	–	45		
	–	735	800	825	735	80		
Outflows								
Bank Overdraft	55	–	–	–	–	–		
Cost of Sales	–	455	501	555	520	–		
Selling and Distribution								
– Fixed	–	45	45	45	45	–		
– Variable	–	33	36	37	33	–		
Redundancy Costs	–	–	–	–	–	90		
Environmental Costs	–	–	–	–	–	65		
	55	533	582	637	598	155		
Net flows	(55)	202	218	188	137	(75)		
Discount Factor	1.00	0.926	0.857	0.794	0.735	0.681		
Present Value	(55)	187	187	149	19101	(51)	=	$518 000

Appendix II

	Year 0	*Year 1*	*Year 2*	*Year 3*	*Year 4*	*Year 5*
Net Flows	(55)	202	218	188	137	(75)
Payment to Denver	–	(140)	(140)	(140)	(140)	–
Revised Net Flows	(55)	62	78	48	(3)	(75)
Discount Factor	1.000	0.926	0.857	0.794	0.735	0.681
Present Value	(55)	57	67	38	(2)	(51)

Net Present Value = $54 000

PRACTICE FINAL EXAMINATION 3 – WITHOUT MCQs

Case Studies

Question 1

In your role as a director of Whittington Beers plc, you have been closely reviewing the operating performance of one of your principal competitors. United Breweries plc.

Over the past few years, you have computed the following range of ratios for United Breweries plc. You also have available the average ratios for the brewing industry for 1994.

Ratio	*1990*	*1991*	*1992*	*1994 Average*
Current (times)	1.10	1.05	0.97	1.35
Quick (times)	0.85	0.75	0.75	0.95
Profit Margin (%)	10.15	11.58	7.63	12.17
Return on Total Assets (%)	8.80	12.25	4.24	5.72
Return of Owners' Equity (%)	12.16	11.08	8.45	12.15
Fixed to Current Assets (%)	225.6	350.5	378.8	365.2
Debt (%)	65.1	52.6	44.7	55.6
Times Interest Earned	12.3	11.2	10.1	14.2
Average Collection Period (days)	71.0	70.0	63.0	70.0
Inventory Turnover (times)	18.7	18.6	17.2	18.5
Earnings per share (pence)	20.8	24.8	25.6	22.3
Dividend yield (%)	1.12	1.46	1.78	2.15

The 1994 published accounts are now available to you, providing an opportunity to update the ratios for both 1993 and 1994.

United Breweries plc	*1994* *£m*	*1993* *£m*
Profit and Loss Account		
Sales	1 514	1 487
Cost of sales	760	813
Gross margin	754	674
Operating costs	571	465
Profit on ordinary activities before taxation	183	209
Taxation	(49)	(62)
Profit on ordinary activities after taxation	134	147
Dividends	(73)	(69)
Profit retained for the year	61	78
Balance Sheet		
Fixed Assets	1 952	1 749
Current Assets		
Stocks	103	90
Debtors	237	231
Cash at bank	100	124
	440	445

Creditors due within one year	(638)	(543)
Net current liabilities	(198)	(98)
Total assets less current liabilities	1 754	1 651
Creditors due in excess of one year	(331)	(320)
	1 423	1 331
Capital and Reserves		
Share capital	376	371
Share premium	26	–
Retained profits	1 021	1 331
	1423	960

Additional information is also available from the published accounts.

(i) Operating costs include £26m interest payable in 1994 (1993 – £23m).

(ii) Share capital comprises wholly Ordinary Shares of 50 pence each in nominal value. Early in 1994, a further 10m Ordinary Shares were issued at a price of 310 pence per share, giving rise to a share premium balance of £26m.

(iii) The market price of United Breweries' share was 350 pence at the end of financial year 1994(1993 – 400 pence).

Your colleagues on the Board of Directors (of Whittington Beers plc) believe that United Breweries plc may be prepared to engage in talks to discuss a possible agreed takeover bid by Whittington Beers plc.

Required:

1. ***Using the information in the 1994 published accounts, update the tabulation of ratios for United Breweries plc – for both 1993 and 1994.*** **(24 marks)**

	1994	*1993*
Current Ratio		
$\frac{\text{Current assets}}{\text{Current liabilities}}$	$\frac{440}{638}$	$\frac{445}{543}$
	= 0.69 times	= 0.82 times
Quick Ratio		
$\frac{\text{Current assets – stock}}{\text{Current liabilities}}$	$\frac{440 - 103}{638}$	$\frac{445 - 90}{543}$
	= 0.53 times	= 0.65 times
Profit Margin		
$\frac{\text{Profit after tax}}{\text{Sales}} \times 100$	$\frac{134}{1514} \times 100$	$\frac{147}{1487} \times 100$
	= 8.85%	= 9.89%

Return on Total Assets

$$\frac{\text{Profit after tax}}{\text{Total assets}} \times 100 \qquad \frac{134}{1\,952 + 440} \times 100 \qquad \frac{147}{1\,749 + 445} \times 100$$

$$= \frac{134}{2\,392} \times 100 \qquad \frac{147}{2\,194} \times 100$$

$$= \underline{5.60\%} \qquad = \underline{6.70\%}$$

Return on Owners' Equity

$$\frac{\text{Profit after tax}}{\text{Owners' Equity}} \times 100 \qquad \frac{134}{1\,423} \times 100 \qquad \frac{147}{1\,331} \times 100$$

$$= \underline{9.42\%} \qquad = \underline{11.04\%}$$

Fixed to Current Asset Ratio

$$\frac{\text{Fixed assets}}{\text{Current assets}} \times 100 \qquad \frac{1\,952}{440} \times 100 \qquad \frac{1\,749}{445} \times 100$$

$$= \underline{443.6\%} \qquad = \underline{393.0\%}$$

Debt Ratio

$$\frac{\text{Total creditors}}{\text{Total assets}} \times 100 \qquad \frac{638 + 331}{1\,952 + 440} \times 100 \qquad \frac{543 + 320}{1\,749 + 445} \times 100$$

$$= \frac{969}{2\,392} \times 100 \qquad \frac{863}{2\,194} \times 100$$

$$= \underline{40.5\%} \qquad = \underline{39.3\%}$$

Times Interest Earned

$$\frac{\text{Profit before tax + Interest}}{\text{Interest}} \qquad \frac{183 + 26}{26} \qquad \frac{209 + 23}{23}$$

$$= \underline{8.04 \text{ times}} \qquad = \underline{10.09 \text{ times}}$$

Average Collection Period (days)

$$\frac{\text{Debtors}}{\text{Sales per day}} \qquad \frac{237}{1\,514/365} \qquad \frac{231}{1\,487/365}$$

$$= \underline{58 \text{ days}} \qquad = \underline{57 \text{ days}}$$

Inventory Turnover (times)

Sales / Stock		1 514 / 103	1 487 / 90
		= 14.7 times	= 16.5 times

Earnings Per Share

Profit after tax / No. of Ordinary Shares		£134m / 752m	£147m / 742m
		= 17.8 pence	= 19.8 pence

Dividend Yield

Dividend per share / Market value per share	× 100	£73m/752m / £3.50	£69m/742m / £4.00
		= 9.71 pence / £3.50	9.30 pence / £4.00
		= 2.77%	= 2.33%

2. ***Identify any factors in United Breweries performance over the five-year period which give particular cause for concern, especially in relation to the current industry average.*** **(6 marks)**

Causes for concern

(i) The substantial decline in both Current and Quick ratios indicate that there are increasing liquidity problems, manifest in a net current liabilities position.

(ii) The profit margin ratio is extremely volatile over the period, finishing well down on the industry average.

(iii) Return on owner's equity has been patchy over the past few years, mainly in decline and considerably lower than the industry average.

(iv) Times interest earned ratio has been gradually weakening over the period and is well down on the industry average.

(v) Inventory turnover has also demonstrated a pattern of increasing over the period, indicative of poor inventory control and suggesting the real possibility of slow-moving stock.

(vi) Earnings per share has fallen back badly over the past couple of years and is now well down on the industry average.

3. ***Identify any factors in United Breweries' performance over the five-year period which give positive indicators as to possible future performance.*** **(5 marks)**
(Total of 35 marks)

Positive indicators for the future

(i) Return on total compares favourable with the industry average – 5.6% in 1994 against 5.72%. Indeed, in previous years, it has been substantially better around 11–12% level – a hopeful sign for the future.

(ii) A major commitment to field assets has been made over the period, reflected in the growing fixed to current asset ratio, which has almost doubled in the period. The comparison with the industry average suggests that the process has gone far enough and the company should be looking to reduce capital expenditure over the next few years.

(iii) The company's debt position has improved substantially since 1990 – down from 65.1% to 40.5%, way ahead of the industry average of 55.6%. Again, this suggests that the cash flow has been sufficiently strong to allow this to occur.

(iv) The success in reducing their average collection period from debtors has been quite remarkable – down from 71 days to 58 days, against a current industry average of 70 days.

(v) There have been gradual improvements in dividend yield over the period, resulting in a dividend yield higher than the industry average in both 1993 and 1994.

Question 2

Denver Drinks Inc. manufactures three soft drinks products – cola, orange and lemon. Over the past few years, the company has been expanding its market size in the mid-west states, to the extent that any future growth is restricted by the machine hours available within the current factory.

At present, the company has no plans to increase the size of the factory or move to new premises.

For the coming, month, the budgeted management accounts show the following information:

	Cola	*Orange*	*Lemon*	*Total*
	$'000	*$'000*	*$'000*	*$'000*
Sales	720.0	600.0	340.0	1 660.0
Direct Materials	115.2	105.0	51.0	271.2
Direct Labour	180.0	126.0	78.2	384.2
Prime Cost	295.2	231.0	129.2	655.4
Manufacturing Overhead				
Variable	64.8	69.0	27.2	161.0
Fixed	171.2	133.9	74.9	380.0
	236.0	202.9	102.1	541.0
Selling and Administrative Overhead				
Variable	72.0	54.0	23.8	149.8
Fixed	62.9	50.6	28.5	142.0
	134.9	104.6	52.3	291.8

Operating Profit	53.9	61.5	56.4	171.8
Total Machine Hours allocated for each product	400	375	305	1 080

Additional information is also relevant:

(i) The machinery available in the factory can be switched readily from one product to another, so that each percentage change in the machine hours devoted to a particular product will have an equivalent effect on the volume of production of that product. Assume that there is no opening stock.

(ii) The company's sales and marketing manager estimates that the maximum accessible market for each of the products, over the coming month, is:

	$'000
Cola	1 440
Orange	1 175
Lemon	675

(iii) Fixed manufacturing overhead has been absorbed into product costs on the basis of prime costs.

(iv) Fixed selling and administration overhead has been allocated to the products on the basis of the floor space occupied by the machinery in the factory.

The company's General Manager has studied the budgeted management accounts and believes that the information available confirms his view that manufacturing should be concentrated on the Lemon drink, which has the highest operating profit per machine hour.

Required:

1. ***Review the General Manager's proposal and outline any weaknesses you can identify.*** **(5 marks)**

The General Manager's proposal is fundamentally flawed because of its dependence on the accuracy of the operating profit figure per machine hour for each of the products. However, the operating profit figure is itself the result of an arbitrary allocation process in respect of both fixed manufacturing overhead and fixed selling and administrative overhead.

The General Manager's proposal would involve the following allocation of machine hours:

Product	*Maximum Market $'000*	*Machine Hours Required*	
Lemon	675.0	753	
Orange	523.2	327	Balance available
	1 198.2	1 080	

As a result, total sales value would decline substantially from its current level of $1 660 000 and no production or sales of the cola range would be made. Proper analysis of this problem requires the application of the contribution techniques, linked to the limiting factor of machine hours, as in (2) below.

Using the information in (2) below, the General Manager's proposal would result in:

Product	*Machine Hours Allocation*	*Contribution per Machine Hour $*	*Total Contribution $*
Lemon	753	524	394 572
Orange	327	656	214 512
	1 080		609 084
		Less: Fixed Costs	522 000
		Net Profit	87 084

As a result, net profit would have fallen from the current level of $171 800 to $87 084 – not an endorsement for the desirability of the General Manager's proposal.

2. ***Prepare the optimum production schedule for the month.*** **(10 marks)**

	Cola $'000	*Orange $'000*	*Lemon $'000*
Sales	720.0	600.0	340.0
Variable Costs			
Direct Material	115.2	105.0	51.0
Direct Labour	180.0	126.0	78.2
Manufacturing Overhead	64.8	69.0	27.2
Selling and Administration Overhead	72.0	54.0	23.8
	432.0	354.0	180.2
Contribution	288.0	246.0	159.8
Machine Hours	400	375	305
Contribution per Machine Hour	720	656	524

Allocation of Machine Hours/Production Schedule

Product	*Maximum Market $'000*	*Machine Hours*	
Cola	1 440	800	
Orange	448	280	(restricted)
	1 888	1 080	

Note: There are insufficient machine hours available to produce the lemon product.

3. ***Prepare a revised set of management accounts, based on the optimum production schedule.*** **(10 marks)**
(Total of 25 marks)

Revised Management Accounts

	Cola *$'000*	*Orange* *$'000*	*Lemon* *$'000*
Sales	1 440.0	448.0	1 888.0
Variable Costs			
Direct Material	230.4	78.4	308.8
Direct Labour	360.0	94.1	454.1
Manufacturing Overhead	129.6	51.5	181.1
Selling and Administration Overhead	144.0	40.3	184.3
	864.0	264.3	1 128.3
Contribution	576.0	183.7	759.7
Less: Fixed Costs			522.0
Net Profit			237.7

Economics

PRACTICE FINAL EXAMINATION 1 – WITH MCQs

The examination is in 3 sections
Section A: Multiple Choice Questions
Section B: Case Study
Section C: Essay Questions

Section A: Multiple Choice Questions
30 questions each worth 2 points.
Total points available in Section A — $30 \times 2 = 60$

Section B: Case Study
Total points available in Section B — $= 20$

Section C: Essay Questions
2 questions each worth 40 points.
Total points available in Section C — $2 \times 40 = 80$
Total points available for examination — $= 160$
Pass mark = 50 per cent of 160 — $= 80$

Section A: Multiple Choice Questions

1. The labour force in a car plant has approached management with the following proposition. "We shall raise average labour productivity (cars per worker) by 5 per cent if you agree to increase our wages by 5 per cent." Assuming all additional cars produced can be sold at current prices, what would happen to the payments to all other factors of production if management agreed? They would:

   A increase by 5 per cent.
   B be unchanged.
   C decrease by 5 per cent.
   D decrease by more than 5 per cent.

2. Suppose that the highly competitive market for electronic calculators is in equilibrium today. If the government decided that every school pupil should be given a calculator, bought at government expense, and at the same time the average total cost of producing calculators were to decrease because of another technological breakthrough in the electronics industry, what would be the joint effects of the government decision and the technological breakthrough?

   A An increase in the equilibrium price of calculators and an increase in the equilibrium quantity.
   B An increase in the equilibrium quantity of calculators; the equilibrium price might rise, fall or be unaltered.
   C A decrease in the equilibrium price of calculators; the equilibrium quantity might rise, fall or be unaltered.
   D A decrease in the number of firms in the industry, and an increase in the equilibrium price of calculators.

3. It has been said that the fundamental fact of scarcity is no longer applicable to the UK economy.

   Which of the following is correct? This statement is:

   A true, because the welfare system in the UK ensures that the basic needs of the poor are met.
   B true, because goods such as tea and coffee, which are not produced in the UK, can be imported from abroad.
   C false, because not all wants of all UK citizens are fully satisfied.
   D false, because a significant number of families in the UK have incomes below what is generally accepted as the poverty level.

4. The table below shows how the factors of production may be combined to produce 100 units of a certain good. Using only the information in the table, which one of the methods can be dismissed by the producer on the grounds of technical inefficiency?

	Land	*Units of labour*	*Capital*
A	10	20	10
B	10	30	6
C	10	40	6
D	10	50	4

5. Which one of the following quotations is *not* an example of the "law" of diminishing marginal utility?

   A "The second glass of beer tastes just as good as the first."
   B "There's a limit to how much ice cream you can eat in a day."
   C "After a while, even TV gets boring."
   D "All work and no play makes Jack a dull boy."

6. A consumer's typical demand curve for a good is downward sloping to the quantity axis because at higher prices the consumer:

   I encounters a leftward shifting supply curve for that good resulting in lower equilibrium quantity.
   II buys less of the good in place of other goods which are now relatively less expensive.

   Which of the following is correct?

   A I only
   B II only
   C Both I and II
   D Neither I nor II

7. The local government has been exploring schemes to make the region more attractive to industry. It has produced the following estimates.

Project	*Description*	*Increase in employment*
Housing estate	Construction of 300 houses	500 jobs
Industrial estate	Construction of 10 advance factories	2 000 jobs
Motorway	Construction of internal motorway system	500 jobs

To achieve economic efficiency which of the following policies should be adopted?

A Undertake only project "Industrial estate".
B Undertake project "Motorway" or "Housing estate" but not "Industrial estate".
C Insufficient information exists to determine which, if any, of the projects should be undertaken.
D Undertake all three projects.

8. Perfect weather conditions in Brazil have produced a bumper coffee crop this year. Although the whole crop could be sold at a price which would more than cover the cost of storing and delivering it, a Brazilian economist has suggested that sufficient coffee be burned to prevent the price of Brazilian coffee beans from falling.

Compared to selling all of the bumper crop what must be the effect of adopting the economist's proposal?

A A reduction in Brazilian coffee growers' real income.
B A reduction in world real income.
C An increase in Brazilian coffee growers' real income.
D An increase in Brazilian real income.

9. Figure 1. shows two production frontiers for catching mackerel, i.e. the maximum amount of fish which can be caught with two different amounts of a fixed factor of production (boat) and with different amounts of a variable factor of production (labour). The rental costs of the boats are \$100 and \$200 respectively. All units of labour are identical.

I A movement from x to y exhibits increasing marginal returns to labour.
II A movement from x to z exhibits increasing returns to scale.

Which of the following is correct?

A I only
B II only
C Both I and II
D Neither I nor II

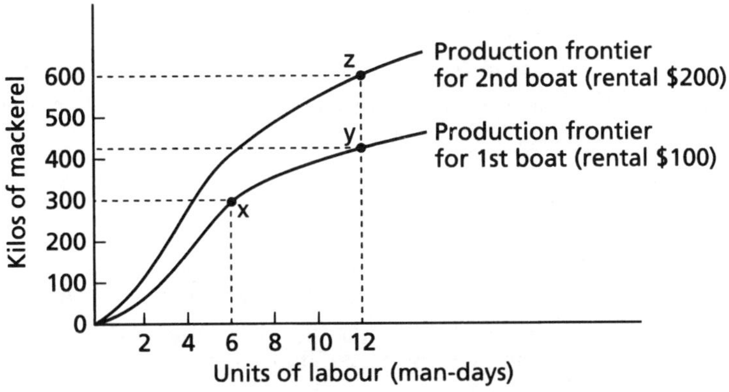

Figure 1

10. People buy more fuel when prices are reduced and less when they are raised. Suppose that advertising does not increase the amount of fuel bought but does influence the choice of brand. Suppose also that fuel of any one grade is for practical purposes a homogeneous product across brands and that any change in industry cost is passed on in part to the public in higher or lower fuel prices. Which of the following would necessarily be true?

    A If all fuel refiners increase advertising expenditure, refining industry total profits will increase but the general public will be worse off.
    B If all fuel refiners increase advertising expenditure, refining industry total profit will decrease and the general public will be worse off.
    C If one fuel refiner increases his advertising expenditure, that refiner's profit will decrease but other refiners' profits will increase.
    D If one fuel refiner increases his advertising expenditure, that refiner will have higher profit, higher sales and lower costs per gallon sold than other refiners.

11. When travelling to the airport from the city most people use the airport bus or travel by taxi. In response to rising fuel costs taxi fares have risen though the bus fare has remained unaltered. If some travellers change their mode of transport in response to the change in fares, what impact will this have on taxi and bus revenues?

    A Taxi revenues will rise, bus revenues will remain unaltered.
    B Taxi revenues will fall, bus revenues will remain unaltered.
    C Bus revenues will rise, taxi revenues may rise, fall or remain unaltered.
    D Bus revenues will rise, taxi revenues will rise.

12. For several decades the Eastfield iron foundry has been processing iron ore and has been an important employer in the local area. Until recently no one complained about the ash particles, the bulk of which fell on vacant land. However, a farmer who bought the vacant land and is now cultivating it has complained to the government that the ash particles are polluting his fields and causing wheat yields to be less than they would otherwise be. If the government wishes to promote efficient resource use in the area, which of the following policies should it adopt?

A Force the iron foundry to stop polluting the area or put it out of business.
B Allow the iron foundry to continue as it is but charge the owners for any resultant decrease in the value of the farmer's output.
C Refuse to intervene and let market forces resolve the conflict between the farmer and the foundry owners.
D Provide the farmer with an alternative field and compensate him for any loss of income incurred.

13. Approximately one half of a city's university students live in rooms/flats which they rent in the private market. The others live in university rooms/flats. Average housing expenditure does not vary significantly between the two groups. In the light of government cutbacks in university finance the university has decided to convert the student accommodation to offices and seminar rooms. The 3 000 students who will be affected have been told they will have to find their own accommodation in the private housing market in the city. Other things being unchanged, such as population, what effect will the university's decision have on the market for private rental housing when the university housing service ceases?

A An increase in rent followed later by an increase in the quantity of private rental housing supplied.
B A decrease in the number of non-student tenants and simultaneously a decrease in rent.
C A decrease in rent as home owners and landlords anticipate the increased student demand.
D No effect, because the students who occupy university housing will not be able to afford private housing.

14. It is rumoured that the government intends to increase the sales tax on alcohol and tobacco from 5 per cent of the selling price to 20 per cent and to use this tax revenue to subsidize gas and electricity production, i.e. lower their prices. If the government does carry out such a plan:

I the average consumer will have a lower real income because the cost of living will be higher.
II income inequality will be increased if people with lower incomes spend a greater proportion of their incomes on alcohol and tobacco but no higher a proportion on gas and electricity than higher income groups.

Which of the following is correct?

A I only
B II only
C I and II
D Neither I nor II

15. A government announced that it does not intend to launch any more satellites; the ten it has launched so far are more than adequate for its needs. On average each satellite cost $1 million; they are all monitored from a single station whose running costs are $50 000 per annum. A group of businesses with plants abroad and a private university with isolated students have requested permission to use one of the satellites to

"bounce" messages to their plants and students. Such a use of the satellite will not affect any government use and will not incur any additional government cost. Given that the government goal is efficient allocation of resources, how much should the government charge the businesses and the university for using the satellite each year?

A Zero.
B Zero to the university and a share of the $50 000 to each of the businesses.
C A share of the $50 000 to both the University and to each of the businesses.
D A share of the $50 000 and a share of the $1 million to the university and to each of the businesses.

16. One year the serfs in a feudal manor produced only $500 worth of ploughs together with $2 000 worth of wheat, all of which they used to produce $3 000 worth of flour, all of which in turn they used to produce $4 000 worth of bread. The feudal lord took half the bread as his dues and exchanged it for other goods from outside the manor such as cloth, meat and drink.

What was the gross output (gross product) of the manor for the year?

A $4 500
B $6 500
C $9 500
D $11 500

17. The following table shows Money GNP and Real GNP in a hypothetical closed economy for three years:

Year	*Money GNP ($m)*	*Real GNP ($m)*
1989	113	113
1990	115	112
1991	120	114

Assuming a constant number of workers it follows that:

I the supply of money increased by $7 million between 1989 and 1991.
II output per worker was higher in 1991 than in 1989.

Which of the following is correct?

A I only
B II only
C Both I and II
D Neither I nor II

18. In any given year some businesses sell more goods and services than they produce, some sell exactly what they produce while others sell less than they produce. However, in the national income accounts in a closed economy total expenditure for final goods and services is always equal to total output.

Which of the following is correct?

This apparent disparity is explained by the fact that:

A what is produced must be sold eventually.
B in the national income accounts total expenditure is defined to exclude depreciation.
C in the national income accounts total expenditure is defined to include any change of inventories.
D the businesses which sell more than they produce always cancel the businesses which sell less than they produce.

19. A government hopes this year to balance the budget (i.e. make government expenditure (G) and tax receipts (T) equal), achieve full employment, and distribute gross national product (GNP) among consumption expenditure (C), investment expenditure (I) and government expenditure (G) in the proportions 60 per cent/20 per cent/20 per cent. The Chief Economic Adviser has warned the government not to make a public statement to this effect. On which of the following is his professional advice based?

A The fact of 20 per cent of GNP being devoted to government expenditure is incompatible with a balanced budget.
B Only by remote chance will values of GNP, C, 1, G and T occur which will achieve the three objectives.
C Balanced budgets are incompatible with full employment.
D It is not possible to influence the distribution of GNP between C, I and G.

20. In a hypothetical economy a group of economists estimated that the value of the marginal propensity to consume was 2/3. An increase in government expenditure of $10 000 million resulted in an increase in real national income of $20 000 million. The reasons why the increase was not $30 000 million are:

I the marginal propensity to import decreased.
II the economy was close to full employment when government expenditure was increased.
III the increase in demand for money caused interest rates to rise and private investment to fall.

Which of the following is correct?

A II only
B II and III only
C I, II and III
D Not I nor II nor III

21. Suppose a significant decrease in the GNP of other European Community countries led to a decline in United Kingdom exports and suppose that the government, because of this, increased the interest rate from 8 per cent to 14 per cent but made no other change in policy.

Which of the following is correct?

From the policy adopted it can be inferred that the government was more concerned about:

A the rising unemployment rate than the rising inflation rate.
B the falling value of sterling than the rising unemployment rate.

C the falling investment rate in export industries than the rising inflation rate.
D the rising unemployment rate than the falling value of sterling.

22. "The more money there is in the economy the more people spend. The more people spend the higher is GNP. Therefore, the greater the supply of money, the better off people must be."

Which of the following is correct?

A The statement is correct because increases in the money supply lead to decreases in interest rates which in turn lead to increases in investment.
B The statement is incorrect because real GNP is limited by the economy's potential to produce goods and services.
C The statement is correct because increases in the money supply lead to increases in interest rates which in turn lead to increases in consumer saving.
D The statement is incorrect because the supply of money has no effect on consumer, government or investment expenditure.

23. "Since there is a limit to the amount of goods and services a nation can produce in a given year, any expansion of a nation's currency will mean a diminution in the real value of the currency."

Which of the following is correct? The quotation is:

A incorrect, since even in the short run the exchange rate determines the value of a nation's currency.
B incorrect, since an increase in the money supply may lead to increased demand for goods and services and given available resources an increase in real output.
C correct, since even in the short run all money supply increases in the UK have been associated with corresponding price level increases.
D correct, since a nation's wealth or resources are in fixed supply at any point in time.

24. Unemployment reached an all time high in the United Kingdom economy in the early 1930s. Many people have argued that had World War II never happened the Great Depression might have continued. In the absence of the War the following policies would have been appropriate for decreasing unemployment:

I a decrease in the money supply to increase interest rates and stimulate savings.
II an increase in income taxes to decrease consumption and increase investment.
III a decrease in government expenditure to free more resources for use in the private sector.

Which of the following is correct?

A I only
B II only
C I and II only
D Not I nor II nor III

25. If at the beginning of a year an economy were operating at full employment and if during the year aggregate demand were to remain constant but potential output (full employment output) were to increase, which of the following must occur?

A An increase in the inflation rate.
B An increase in the unemployment rate.
C An increase in interest rates.
D An increase in the balance-of-payment deficit.

26. Between March and September the exchange rate of the pound against the dollar fell from \$1.50 to \$1.40. At the same time the interest rate in the US rose from 8 per cent to 12 per cent. If there were no inflation in the US, how would this affect a UK holiday-maker who went for a week's holiday to the US with £500 in March compared to one who went with £500 for a week's holiday in September?

A The March holiday-maker would be able you buy more for his £500.
B The September holiday-maker would be able to buy more for his £500.
C The effect would depend on whether the £500 was exchanged for dollars in the UK or in the US.
D It is impossible to say who was better off because of the rise in interest rate.

27. The West German economy was operating at full employment. Its high wage rates attracted employed skilled workers from Turkey to work in Germany. These workers sent home the bulk of their wages which were spent by their families in Turkey.

The effect of the migration of labour to West Germany was to:

I increase potential (full employment) output in West Germany.
II reduce potential (full employment) output in Turkey.
III increase real output in West Germany.

Which of the following is correct?

A I only
B II only
C I and III only
D I, II and III

28. A government decided to abandon import controls and as a result there was a sudden increase in the value of imports. What impact would the increased imports have on the country's National Income? It would

A increase by an amount equal to the value of the additional imports.
B reduce because imports are leakages from the circular flow of income.
C be unaffected because the amount paid for the additional imports was exactly equal to their value.
D increase by an amount equal to the value of the additional imports times the multiplier.

29. A government increases expenditure on investment in the coal and steel industries by \$40m and discovers that this forces up interest rates which in turn leads to a decrease in private investment expenditure of \$40m. Assuming no other offsetting changes in the economy, what is he impact of the increase in government expenditure?

An increase in:

A real GNP.
B the budget deficit (reduction in the budget surplus).
C potential (full employment) GNP.
D the money supply.

30. A simple "textbook" economy is described by the following:

C = 20 + 0.5Y, where
C = consumption expenditure
Y = national income

I = 10	I = gross investment expenditure
G = 10	G = government expenditure
X = 10	X = exports
Z = 10	Z = imports
M = 300	M = money supply

What is the value of the equilibrium level of national income?

A 80.
B 100.
C 120.
D 300.

Answers to Multiple Choice Questions

1. The effect of selling 5 per cent more cars at the current price is to increase total revenue by 5 per cent. It is therefore possible to increase the payments to all factors of production, including labour, by 5 per cent.

Correct response is A.

2. The government decision to buy every school pupil a calculator would shift the demand curve to the right. The reduction in the costs of producing calculators, i.e. a lowering of the average total cost curve, would shift each firm's short-run marginal cost curve to the right and consequently shift the industry short-run supply curve to the right. Whether the new equilibrium price would be higher, the same or lower than the original price will depend upon the relative shifts of the demand and supply curves. Thus the joint effect on price cannot be determined from the information given. However, both curves will intersect to the right of the original equilibrium position.

Correct response is B.

3. No country today has sufficient resources to satisfy all the wants of every member of its population; this is the "fundamental fact of scarcity". The fact that society's basic needs, however defined, might be being met or that commodities not produced in the UK can be imported from abroad does not imply that scarcity no longer exists. Even if every family in the UK were above the poverty level however defined, scarcity would still remain.

Correct response is C.

4. Since no prices are provided, it is not possible to compare A and B since A uses less labour and more capital than B. However, it is possible to compare B and C since they use the same quantity of capital, but C uses more labour; B is therefore more efficient than C, which can be dismissed on the grounds of technical efficiency. B and C is the only pair which it is possible to compare in this way.

   Correct response is C.

5. Any statement which suggests diminishing additional utility derived from additional consumption is consistent with the "law" of diminishing marginal utility. Diminishing marginal utility is consistent with a limit to the amount of ice cream which can be eaten in a day, with boredom watching TV after a time, and with dullness from spending too much time working. However, to say that the second glass of beer tastes just as good as the first suggests that the utility is the same for the second as for the first glass of beer, and is not consistent with diminishing marginal utility.

   Correct response is A.

6. A demand curve shows the quantity of a good which a consumer would buy at different prices *cet. par.*; this is independent of the conditions of supply, therefore statement I is incorrect. As the price increases the quantity typically decreases for a number of reasons, one of which is that other goods become relatively more attractive; this is the substitution effect. Thus statement II is correct.

   Correct response is B.

7. In deciding which policy contributes most to economic efficiency it is necessary to compare marginal costs and marginal benefits of each. Since no cost information is provided it is not possible to draw a conclusion.

   Correct response is C.

8. The Brazilian economist's advice was probably based on his belief that the demand for coffee is price inelastic, i.e. that the bumper crop could only be sold as the result of a price reduction which would lead to a decrease in total revenue. However, no such definite information on the market is provided. The only definite outcome of burning the coffee would be to reduce the total consumption goods available to the world, i.e. to decrease world real income.

   Correct response is B.

9. The output of the first 6 man-days, as shown by X, was 300 kilos; the addition of a further 6 man-days, as shown by Y, added just over 100 kilos, thus the marginal product of labour decreased between X and Y; statement I is incorrect. The movement from X to Z involves doubling both the input of labour and capital; if there were increasing returns to scale, output would more than double. However, the output of mackerel also doubled from 300 to 600 kilos, exhibiting constant returns to scale. Statement II is incorrect.

   Correct response is D.

10. The effect of increased advertising is to increase the cost of production and alter the distribution of expenditure between brands, while leaving total expenditure unchanged. Thus, if all refiners increased their advertising, there would be a redistribution of consumer expenditure between brands, depending on how much additional advertising each refiner carried out, and industry total profit would decrease; when the increased advertising costs were passed on in price increases the general public would become worse off. A is therefore incorrect and B is correct. Since the amount of brand-switching in response to changed advertising is unknown, it is not possible to predict the effect on an individual refiner of a change in his advertising.

    Correct response is B.

11. Since more people now use the bus and the fares are unchanged, bus revenues will rise. The effect of increased taxi fares on total revenues depends on the price elasticity of demand. Since this is unknown, taxi revenues may rise, fall or be unaltered.

    Correct response is C.

12. The social cost of producing iron is greater than the private cost by the decrease in the farmer's output; consequently, because of this externality, setting output at the level where marginal revenue equals private marginal cost is not economically efficient. The solution is to include the decrease in the farmer's output as a cost to the firm, i.e. to charge it according to how much output the farmer loses as a result of iron production. The firm's private marginal cost will now be equal to marginal social cost and the iron foundry will set its output at a lower profit maximizing level. Consequently B is correct. None of the other responses contributes to equalizing private and social cost.

    Correct response is B.

13. The impact of the university's decision will be a shift to the right of the demand schedule for rented accommodation. The stock of rented accommodation is fixed in the short run, therefore this will result in an increase in the market rent. In the long run potential landlords will be attracted into the private renting sector because of the higher rents obtainable, and thus there will later be an increase in the quantity of private rental housing supplied.

    Correct response is A.

14. For any given consumer the greater the proportion of income spent on alcohol and tobacco the greater will be the amount of tax paid and, since the smaller will be the amount of income available for all other purchases, including gas and electricity, the less will be the amount of the subsidy received. Thus, if people with lower incomes spend a greater proportion of their incomes on alcohol and tobacco than do people with higher incomes, but not a higher proportion on gas and electricity, then the scheme will increase income inequality. Thus II is correct. Real income is determined by the nation's resources and you might argue that distortions caused by the tax subsidy programme would cause real income to fall. However, this fall would not be because the cost of living would be higher; this cost of living, e.g. the consumer price index, or GNP deflator could be rising, constant or falling. Thus I is incorrect.

    Correct response is B.

15. The use to which the businesses and the university wish to put the satellite does not exclude any other use, therefore the opportunity cost is zero; furthermore, there are no negative externalities, thus the marginal social cost is zero. A necessary condition for economic efficiency is that price equals marginal social cost, which in this case is zero.

    Correct response is A.

16. The value of final or gross output in economy was \$500 worth of ploughs and \$4 000 worth of bread. The wheat and flour are intermediate goods and to include them in the value of gross output would be double counting. What the feudal lord did with his share of gross output does not affect the value of gross output.

    Correct response is A.

17. The fact that money GNP has risen faster than real GNP indicates rising prices. This could be associated with an increasing money supply, increasing velocity of circulation of money, or both. There is no proof that the money supply increased by £7 million. Statement I is therefore incorrect. Output per worker is real GNP divided by the number of workers; since real GNP increased between 1989 and 1991 and the number of workers did not, it follows that output per worker was higher in 1991 than in 1989.

    Correct response is B.

18. Total expenditure on final goods and services includes expenditure on goods sold from inventories; however, investment expenditure is calculated net of additions to or deductions from inventories. Consequently the net calculation of total expenditure is equal to the value of final output.

    Correct response is C.

19. In order to balance the budget, the government has to predict national income and on the basis of the prediction calculate total tax revenue from the selected tax rate. This total tax revenue must be equal to the selected government expenditure plus transfers; transfers depend partly on the unemployment rate, and hence on the actual value of national income. However, disposable income, and hence national income itself, depends on transfers, therefore it is extremely complicated to calculate in advance the appropriate values for tax rates and government expenditure. The calculation is made even more complex if government expenditure is to be 20 per cent of national income; furthermore, consumption expenditure must be 60 per cent of national income, again adding to the complexity of the calculation. To ensure that investment expenditure is 20 per cent of national income it is again necessary to make a prediction of national income and the rate of interest which will have the desired effect. Given that the government can only make one set of policy decisions for a given year it is extremely unlikely that the three objectives will be attained. Thus B is correct. Government expenditure of 20 per cent of GNP is not incompatible with a balanced budget which in turn is not incompatible with full employment. Thus A and C are incorrect. Since monetary and fiscal policy can influence the distribution of GNP among C, I and G, D is incorrect.

    Correct response is B.

20. The calculated MPC of 2/3 suggests an expenditure multiplier of 3, but the actual multiplier was only 2. One possible explanation for the multiplier turning out to be less than expected is an increase in leakages, for example an increase in the marginal propensity to import. Statement I suggests a reduction in the marginal propensity to import and is therefore incorrect. Full employment or potential output sets a limit to actual output; thus if the gap between actual and full employment output were less than £30 000 million the multiplier would not have been able to work through fully, therefore statement II is a possible explanation. The increased government expenditure caused an increase in aggregate demand and an increase in output, thus causing an increase in the demand for money. Since the supply of money was not increased it is possible that the price of money, i.e. the interest rate, increased, causing private investment and consumption expenditures to fall thus reducing the net effect of the multiplier; statement III is therefore a possible explanation.

    Correct response is B.

21. The decline in exports would lead to a reduction in aggregate demand, causing the unemployment rate to be higher than would otherwise be the case. Increasing the interest rate would cause a reduction in investment and consumption expenditures which would reduce aggregate demand further adding even more to the unemployment rate. A reduction in UK exports would cause a decrease in the demand for sterling, the value of which would fall; an increase in the UK interest rate would make the UK relatively more attractive for savers, therefore the demand for sterling would increase, causing the value of sterling to rise. Thus from the policy adopted it can be inferred that the government was more concerned about the falling value of sterling than the rising unemployment rate.

    Correct response is B.

22. While it is possible to increase aggregate demand by increasing the supply of money, potential output sets an upper limit to real GNP, therefore it does not always follow that the greater the supply of money the better off people will be.

    Correct response is B.

23. An increase in the money supply will make interest rates lower than they otherwise would have been and investment and consumption expenditures higher than they otherwise would have been. If the economy is already at full employment, i.e. if actual output equals potential output, the excess demand will cause inflation and consequently a reduction in the value of the currency. However, if there are unemployed resources, real output will increase without necessarily causing an increase in the price level.

    Correct response is B.

24. An increase in interest rates would reduce aggregate demand, thus increasing unemployment, therefore statement I is wrong. The reduction in consumption arising from an increase in income tax would also reduce aggregate demand and increase unemployment; given there are substantial unemployed resources already, it is not necessary to reduce consumption in order to make resources available for investment,

therefore statement II is wrong. A decrease in government expenditure would also reduce aggregate demand and increase unemployment; again, since there are unemployed resources there is nothing to be gained from freeing additional resources for use in the private sector, therefore statement III is incorrect.

Correct response is D.

25. The economy develops a goal between actual and potential output during the year, thus some resources become unemployed. Consequently there will be an increase in the unemployed rate. There may be increases or decreases in the inflation rate, interest rate and balance of payments deficit, but a change in any is not guaranteed by a gap between actual and potential GNP in a given year.

    Correct response is B.

26. In March the holiday-maker would be able to buy £500 × 1.50 = \$750. In September he would be able to buy £500 × 1.40 = \$700. If there were no inflation in the US, clearly the holiday-maker would be able to buy more in March with \$750 in September with only \$700. The location at which the dollars were bought has no bearing on the value of dollars. Since the holiday-maker went to the US to spend money, not to invest it, the increase in interest rates in the US would not affect him.

    Correct response is A.

27. The upper limit to the potential GNP of any country is determined by the quantity and quality of the labour force, the capital stock and the level of technology. Thus if West Germany were able to expand its labour force through immigrant labour from Turkey, West Germany's potential GNP would increase. As the migrants were in employment, actual GNP would also increase. Thus I and III are correct. Conversely Turkey would experience a fall in its potential GNP when its labour force declined as workers moved to West Germany. Thus II is correct.

    Correct response is D.

28. NI = NE = C + 1 + G + X – M where NI = National Income, NE = National Expenditure, C = Consumption Expenditure, I = Investment Expenditure, X = Export Expenditure and M = Import Expenditure.

    Imports are leakages from the circular flow of income because expenditure on imports result in income being generated in countries abroad, not in the domestic economy. As a result the increase in imports will make national income lower than it otherwise would have been.

    Correct response is B.

29. The increase in government expenditure has crowded out an equal value of investment expenditure, therefore the net effect on real output is zero. The budget surplus or deficit is found as follows: budget surplus or deficit = total tax revenue – government expenditure – transfers. Since tax rates and national income are unchanged, total tax revenue is also unchanged. The increase in government expenditure therefore leads to either a budget deficit or a reduction in the budget surplus.

    Correct response is B.

30. Y = C + I + G + X – Z

Substituting the values given:

$$\begin{aligned} Y &= 20 + 0.5Y + 10 + 10 + 10 - 10 \\ \text{therefore } Y &= 0.5Y + 40 \\ \text{therefore } 0.5Y &= 40 \\ \text{therefore } Y &= 80 \end{aligned}$$

Correct response is A.

Section B: Case Study

The only time fishing boats can enter or leave the harbour is at morning high tide which occurs between 6.00 and 7.00 am. In practice, boats have 24 hours both to travel to and from the fishing grounds and to catch fish. The fishing grounds are 30 miles from the harbour. The faster the boat travels to and from the fishing grounds the more time is available for fishing and the greater is the amount of fish caught. However, the faster the boat travels the greater the amount of fuel consumed. This relationship between speed and fuel consumed is non-linear as shown in the table below.

Speed (miles/hr)	*Gallons for 60 mile voyage*
6	10
7	11
8	13
9	16
10	20
11	25
12	31
13 (max speed)	38

When the boat reaches the fishing ground it drifts, thus using no fuel.

If each hour of fishing yields fish worth $10, if the fuel cost is $1 per gallon and the goal of the boat owner is profit maximization, how fast should the boat sail to and from the fishing grounds? Explain your answer in detail.

Case Analysis

This is a case ideally suited to marginal analysis.

The boat will maximise profit by increasing speed up to the point at which the marginal cost of increasing speed is just equal to the marginal revenue from the increased catch. Thus it is necessary to calculate travel time for different speeds which, subtracted from 24 hours, will yield fishing time. Each hour of fishing time is constant and worth $10. But each additional hour of fishing time has a cost, namely the increase in fuel costs.

The table below shows the relationship between speed, travel time, fishing time and fuel consumption.

Speed (miles/hr)	*Travel time (hrs)*	*Fishing time (hrs)*	*Fuel consumption (gallons)*
6	10.00	14.00	10
7	8.57	15.43	11
8	7.50	16.50	13
9	6.67	17.33	16
10	6.00	18.00	20
11	5.45	18.55	25
12	5.00	19.00	31
13	4.62	19.38	38

One laborious method of calculating the optimal speed to estimate the total cost of fuel for each speed and the value of the total catch for each hour of fishing time. By subtracting the difference the profit maximizing speed becomes evident.

Marginal analysis is much more efficient. Choose any speed, say 10 miles per hour and compare the consequences with a speed of 11 miles per hour. The additional fuel cost is 5 gallons × $1 = $5. The increase in fishing time is 0.55 hours (18.55–18.00). The additional 0.55 hours produces a catch worth $5.5 ($10 × 0.55). Therefore it is worth while increasing speed from 10 to 11 miles per hour.

Increasing the speed from 11 to 12 miles per hour adds costs of $6 ($31–$25). The increase in fishing time of 0.45 hours yields an increase in revenue of only $4.5. Since the marginal cost ($6) exceeds the marginal benefit ($4.5) the increase in speed from 11 to 12 miles per hour will decrease profit.

Consequently the profit maximizing speed is 11 miles per hour.

Section C: Essay Questions

Essay 1

If too much or too little economic activity is undertaken by, or regulated by government in a market economy, neither economic efficiency nor an equitable distribution of income will be achieved. Discuss.

Answer to Essay 1

Your discussion should describe in detail how the market system operates, the meaning of economic efficiency and the assumptions underlying the behaviour and motivation of households and resource owners. This requires analysis of utility maximising consumers, profit maximising firms, operation of markets and the meaning of equilibrium in both the short and long run. The crucial role of prices should be highlighted as a major determinant of household well-being, a signalling device to resource owners in the allocation of factor inputs and as the link in the marginal equivalency conditions. The role of government, a body of citizens of the market economy representing the interests of the citizens, in establishing the "rules of the game" in the market economy should be discussed.

Market failures involving public goods, externalities, economics of scale and income distribution should be analysed. The analysis should include why the price mechanism will not result in economic efficiency in the presence of these factors and how government "interference", while not guaranteeing economic efficiency, can bring the economy closer to an efficient allocation of resources.

Government action which produces prices and output which would not prevail through market forces should be compared with, and evaluated against, the market solution. Such an analysis could include price ceilings, price floors, subsidies, taxes and transfers. The role of government in using monetary and fiscal policy in the pursuit of desirable macroeconomic goals should be included in your discussion. You should also point out that the motivation of governments as vote seekers may prompt actions which benefit a vocal minority at the expense of the silent majority.

Essay 2

In many of the capitalist nations of the world today a significant output or employment gap exists, i.e. actual GNP is significantly less than potential GNP. Economics textbooks suggest that monetary and/or fiscal policy can eliminate output gaps. Resolve this apparent paradox.

Answer to Essay 2

Your analysis should include the determinants of growth in potential GNP, i.e. the growth in the quality and quantity of the capital stock and growth in the quality and quantity of the labour force. It should also show how technological change is embodied in investment goods and training and education of the labour force and how growth in potential GNP is independent of changes in actual GNP.

The determinants of actual GNP should be discussed, i.e. consumption, investment and government expenditure, exports and imports. Your analysis should include the circular flow of income and expenditure and should show how GNP changes as each of the components changes. The instability of some of the components of GNP can be shown to be a cause of fluctuations in GNP. The fluctuations in GNP compared with the relative stability of potential GNP produces output and inflationary gaps. Induced expenditure should be distinguished from autonomous (exogenous) expenditure, a source of economic instability.

The policy tools available to the government consisting of fiscal policy (changes in government expenditure and taxation) and monetary policy and their efficacy in different economic situations should be analysed. In this context you should also point out the disagreements which exist between the different schools of thought as to the appropriateness of the different policy instruments and their potential impact on output and employment. You should point out that desirable macroeconomic goals such as a low inflation rate, a balanced budget and stable exchange rates may conflict with the goal of a low unemployment rate and consequently an employment gap may be the penalty to be borne for achieving other goals. The Phillips Curve, for example, suggests a trade-off between inflation and unemployment. You should evaluate the arguments about the Phillips Curve and distinguish between short run and long-term macroeconomic goals.

PRACTICE FINAL EXAMINATION 2 – WITHOUT MCQs

Case Study

Throughout the Middle Ages, to charge interest for the use of money was improper under Catholic Church doctrines and was prohibited by law in many countries with violation sometimes punishable by death. Such laws were commonly waived by borrowers and lenders because of the obvious benefits to both of borrowing/lending. With the Protestant Reformation and the commercial and industrial revolutions, official antagonism to lending at interest faded rapidly. Yet today some countries, and states within countries, have laws limiting the interest rates than can legally be charged on loans. To safeguard borrowers against greedy lenders it is often argued by politicians that such legislation is required.

Suppose a country is composed of many states each of which can legislate maximum interest rates chargeable on loans and further suppose that one of those states imposes a 1.5% per month (18% per annum) rate of interest that department stores, credit card companies, car dealers, banks and others can charge borrowers. Further suppose that the rate of 18% per annum is well below the going rate for many borrowers, especially high-risk, low-income individuals and families.

What do you predict will be the result of such legislation? Who will gain and who will lose? How will neighbouring states be affected?

Solution

The new state law is fixing the price ceiling (interest rate of 18%) on loans below the free market price. Suppose the supply and demand curves for credit in the state are as follows:

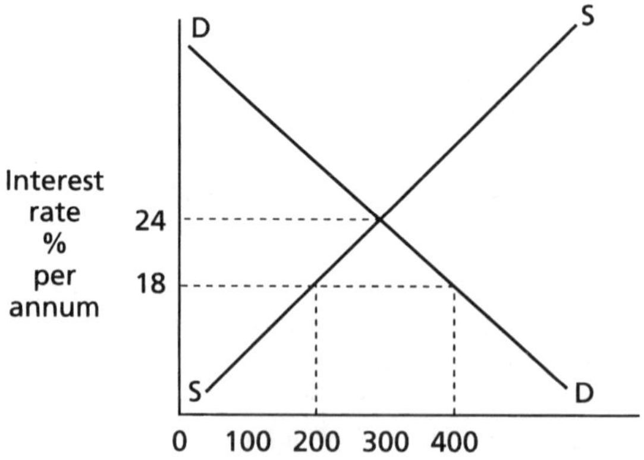

Figure 2

The free market rate would be 24% per annum and £300m would be offered and borrowed per month. The slope of the supply curve indicates that lenders would offer more loan money at higher rates and less at lower rates. Why? At higher rates it will pay to lend to higher risk borrowers. The demand curve indicates that more will be borrowed the lower the interest rate. Why? The interest rate helps determine whether or not people can afford to buy a new refrigerator or car, the lower the interest rate the lower the monthly payments and the effective price of the product to people buying on credit.

On the imposition of the 18% ceiling, lenders will lend only £200m per month but customers will want to borrow £400m, i.e. there will be an excess demand of £200m.

The first effect of the law is that some consumers get cheaper credit but others who were borrowing at 24% get nothing at all – £100m less is lent and an additional £200m of demand remains unsatisfied. There are going to be angry consumers who are refused credit and unhappy lenders who are alienating present and potential customers. The limited supply of credit will go to the well established, low-risk customers of the lenders Those likely to suffer will be new customers, low income and higher risk families.

Rejected borrowers who live near the state boundaries can be expected to take their business to neighbouring states which have no interest rate ceiling and/or "black" markets may develop risking penalties if discovered. In addition there is a possibility that the supply curve may shift to the left if major lenders decide to stop doing business in the state and move to neighbouring states thereby increasing profit and avoiding the criticisms of unhappy borrowers.

Essay Questions

Essay 1

In all leading capitalist economies today there is no shortage of "junk" food, expensive sports cars, useless jewellry, trash literature, pollution and poverty, but there is a shortage of good schools, cheap hospitals and adequate clothing and housing for the poor. The capitalist system may suit the rich and powerful but does little for the ordinary working man and woman and even less for those who can not find employment.

Why do you agree or disagree with the above statement?

Solution

The two main issues which an answer should address are economic efficiency and economic equity. In a capitalist economy how market forces determine which goods and services are produced, how incomes are determined and how prices of goods/services in factor markets are determined, should be detailed. The reason that "junk" food and expensive sports cars are provided is because households indicate to suppliers by bidding with "money" votes that those are goods they desire and profit motivated businesses respond by producing them. There are "market failures" however, e.g. public goods, externalities (pollution) which necessitate collective or government action if economic efficiency is to be attained.

While the capitalist system has been responsible for dramatically increasing the living standards over time of the vast majority of people in capitalist economies, it is true that all capitalist economies have their poor and many of the poor have neither wealth nor highly marketable labour force skills and depend upon government transfers as their main source of income. Whether the existing levels of transfers for the poor are adequate is a value judgement. The quoted statement contains pejorative expressions such as "shortage", "expensive", "useless", "good schools", "cheap hospitals", "adequate clothing", "ordinary working man and woman", which your analysis should show are not meaningful.

Essay 2

Prepare a report for any of the major capitalist economies of the world specifying:

(i) a comprehensive set of macroeconomic goals;

(ii) how such goals might be achieved by the use of the policy tools available over a five year period; and

(iii) the potential problems which might arise to reduce the effectiveness of these policy tools.

Solution

Most accepted comprehensive macroeconomic goals while not exclusive, include:

- low rates of unemployment
- low rates of inflation
- stable exchange rates
- specified distribution of GNP among its component parts.

In developing nations, attracting foreign investment and protecting infant industries may also be goals.

Whatever set of macroeconomic goals you identify, part (ii) of your answer should spell out in detail how the tools of monetary and fiscal policy can help bring about the achievement of these goals over time.

Part (iii) of your answer should analyse problems such as trade-offs between competing goals, lags in the system which make both the identifying of a problem and its cure difficult, exogeneous shocks over which policy makers have no control, instability of relationships within the economy and the complexities which arise the more dependant a given economy is on the world economy.

PRACTICE FINAL EXAMINATION 3 – WITHOUT MCQs

Case Study

In an Eastern European country in which private companies are rapidly emerging, the government of that country is coming under pressure from domestic shoe manufacturers about the large imports of fashion shoes. The government respond by announcing it will either impose a tariff on imports of shoes or set a quota limiting the number of shoes which can be imported into the country each year. As an economist the government hires you to write a report analysing:

(i) the benefits and costs of protecting the domestic shoe industry;

(ii) the impact of a tariff compared to a quota on shoes.

Solution

Your analysis should include legitimate arguments for the imposition of trade restrictions, e.g. the infant industry argument, anti-dumping strategy and countervailing duties policy. You should show that while domestic shoe manufacturers will benefit from the imposition of a tariff or quota, the losers will be those citizens who will have to pay a higher price for the imported shoes Additionally, those firms which export goods from the Eastern European country in question will experience a decrease in sales due to reduced foreign demand, i.e. less of the Eastern European country's currency will be available for its exports as a result of the reduced sales of fashion shoes.

The impact of a tariff will be an upward/leftward shift of the supply curve of imported shoes, a higher equilibrium price, reduced sales but higher tax receipts for the government.

The impact of a quota will be similar to that of the tariff with one important exception – there will be no tax advantage to the government. A method will have to be found to allocate the quota among shoe importers. If the government auctions, i.e. sells to the highest bidder, the quota rights, it will benefit by a sum equivalent to the tax receipts in the tariff case.

In both the tariff and the quota situations, the buyers of imported shoes are less well-off compared to the free trade situation.

Essay Questions

Essay 1

Examine critically the role of prices in determining the allocation of resources and distribution of income in a capitalist economy, highlighting both the strengths and weaknesses of such a system.

Solution

Your answer should demonstrate how prices are determined in competitive markets by the forces of demand and supply and show the critical role prices play in the behaviour of consumers attempting to maximize utility and in the behaviour of firms attempting to maximize profits Your analysis should also show how market forces determine factor prices, i.e. wages, salaries, rent, interest and dividends resulting in the distribution of income.

The strength of the capitalist system can be shown by demonstrating how economic efficiency will prevail if the marginal equivalency conditions are fulfiled. You should analyse those areas of economic activity where collective or government action is required if economic efficiency is to prevail. In this context public goods, externalities and economies of scale should be analysed showing why their presence prohibits economic efficiency being attained. In addition, you should argue that while the income distribution which emerges in the capitalist system is not concerned with economic efficiency it is a weakness of the system if it produces a distribution which is socially unacceptable.

Essay 2

In running an economy to achieve commonly accepted desirable macroeconomic goals, governments and central banks would be well advised to concentrate on policies affecting potential output rather than concentrate on policies affecting actual output. Explain why you agree or disagree with the statement and detail the policies you would advocate governments and central banks should pursue.

Solution

Potential output is determined by the quality and quantity of a nation's capital stock and the quality and quantity of the labour force. In the short-run in a mature capitalist economy, there is very little the government or central bank can do to alter the growth rate of potential output. In the longer run the government can encourage private investment incorporating the latest technological innovations but the resulting impact on the growth rate of potential output will not be large. The government may be able to have a greater impact on the growth rate of potential output by altering income tax rates thus affecting labour incentives and the work rate, altering school leaving and retirement ages, and changing immigration/emigration practices, all of which could affect the quality and quantity of the labour force.

In countries like China, moves towards privatization and the large inflow of foreign capital have increased the growth rate of potential output significantly.

Government and central banks' fiscal and monetary polices can affect actual output to a much greater extent than they can affect potential output. Your analysis should specify desirable macroeconomic goals and demonstrate the appropriate policies to achieve such goals. Such analysis should include potential trade-offs and the problems encountered in dealing with lags, unpredictable and unstable relationships, exogenous shocks and the complexities faced by individual economies closely integrated within the international economy.

Finance

PRACTICE FINAL EXAMINATION 1 – WITH MCQs

The examination is in 3 sections
A True/False Questions
B Multiple Choice Questions
C Essay/Problem Questions

Section A: True/False Questions
20 questions each worth $1\frac{1}{2}$ points. Total points available in Section A $20 \times 1\frac{1}{2} = 30$

Section B: Multiple Choice Questions
30 questions each worth 2 points. Total points available in Section B $30 \times 2 = 60$

Section C: Essay/Problem Questions
2 questions each worth 45 points. Total points available in Section C $2 \times 45 = 90$
Total points available for examination $= 180$
Pass mark = 50% of 180 $= 90$

Section A: True/False Questions

1. £1.00 today is worth more than £1.00 expected to be received tomorrow because £1.00 can be invested today.
2. NPV and IRR are totally different techniques, using different information.
3. Financial markets are probably the most competitive markets in existence.
4. Shareholders may not always wish the firm to undertake all investments which have positive NPVs to the firm.
5. Depreciation is not a cash flow, therefore can be ignored in estimating cash flows of an investment project.
6. One of the most common mistakes made in estimating project cash flows is that analysts forget to subtract interest payments.
7. With mutually exclusive investments, if the IRR of the incremental cash flow exceeds the hurdle rate, the investment with the higher non-discounted cash flow should be accepted.
8. It may be in the best interests of a firm's shareholders to accept a project which has a negative NPV if it interacts with the cash flows of another project in such a way as to produce a higher NPV overall.
9. With well-functioning financial markets, there is no reason to think that borrowing is better than lending in times of high inflation.
10. For the potential to reduce risk by diversifying between two assets, the correlation between them must be negative.
11. When one investment has twice the systematic risk of another, the required return of the riskier should be twice as high.

12. The ß of a geared or leveraged company's equity will always be larger than the ß of the firm's assets.

13. If cash dividends are more heavily taxed than capital gains, we may expect to see companies which pay high cash dividends being subject to higher required returns.

14. Since all clienteles for particular dividend policies have probably been adequately served by companies seeking to maximise share price, it really would affect no one's wealth if your company were to change its dividend policy.

15. In a frictionless "M and M" world, the only thing that would cause a company to choose one debt level over another is the likelihood of encountering bankruptcy.

16. The only positive reason for companies to issue debt is because of tax advantages. We know this because prior to the composition of company income taxes, only equity was issued.

17. Agency and other constraints on the benefits of borrowing must have important effects because we do not see all firms borrowing to the full extent for which the taxation authorities will allow interest to be deducted.

18. The best strategy for accounts receivable is one that offers the greatest likelihood of being paid.

19. Options sell for more than exercise value because options tend to increase in value regardless of the direction of price change in underlying assets.

20 If managers themselves own shares of the company, their incentives to consume company resources disappear because each £1.00 of such consumption reduces share price accordingly.

Section B: Multiple Choice Questions

For each question choose one option only.
(Quantitative results are rounded to the nearest unit, for example £134.56 would be shown as £135.)

1. The financial market asks and pays interest of 9 per cent per year, and you have currently the expectation of receiving £2 000 per year, paid now and at the end of the next two years (three cash flows). What is the maximum amount of money you can spend from this source (including that from transacting with the financial market) at the end of the first year?

   A £2 180 C £6 000
   B £5 985 D £6 015

2. You have been offered the opportunity to purchase an annuity which promises an initial payment to you of £1 000 at the end of this year and each following year for 17 years (including the first payment). If comparable-risk, comparable timing invest-

ments are presently offering 11 per cent interest, what would you be willing to pay now for this annuity?

A £7 000 C £8 380
B £7 549 D £17 000

3. The following investments are available. Their free cash flows for each period are shown, and the appropriate discount rate is 12% per period.

	£'000s			
	t_0	t_1	t_2	t_3
Investment#				
#1	(1 500)	845	670	500
#2	(2 600)	105	200	3 500

Using the NPV technique, which investment(s) should be undertaken?

A #1 only
B #2 only
C Both #1 and #2
D Neither #1 nor #2

4. You expect to receive £1 000 per annum for 50 years and wish to value that expectation at a 10 per cent discount rate, but your present value tables do not have enough periods, and your pocket calculator cannot exponentiate. So you are facing a quite tedious calculation to find the exact value. By how much would you err in using a simple perpetuity valuation?

A $£10\,000/(1.10)^{50}$
B A huge amount since an infinite amount of money will be ignored.
C $£1\,000/(1.10)^{50}$
D 50 (£1 000/1.10)

5. What is the effect when a company undertakes an investment with a positive NPV?

A Shareholder wealth goes up by that amount
B Managers wealth goes up by that amount
C Bondholder wealth goes up by that amount
D Wages and salaries go up by that amount

6. The price/earnings ratio of a company

I always provides useful information about the company's prospects
II provides useful information about the company's prospects when compared to firms in other industries

Which of the following is correct?

A I only
B II only
C Both I and II
D Neither I nor II

7. What do Free Cash Flows of an investment project which are appropriate to be discounted with the project's WACC include?

A All expected payments between the firm and its capital suppliers.
B All changes in the payments between the firm and its capital suppliers induced by the project.
C All changes in the payments between the firm and its capital suppliers induced by the project, were the project to be financed only with equity.
D All changes in the payments between the firm and its capital suppliers induced by the project, were the project to be financed only with equity, but incremented with the expected interest tax shields.

8. Payback Period as an investment decision technique

I is undesirable because it ignores discounting and cuts off consideration of cash flows beyond the payback point.
II even if improved by adding discounting and explicit consideration of all cash flows, cannot be made to work in all cash flow conditions.
III is appealing due to its simplicity.

Which of the following is correct?

A I only
B II only
C I and II only
D I, II and III

9. NPV must be chosen as the technique for evaluation instead of IRR only when

I there are multiple sign changes in projected cash flows.
II projects are mutually exclusive.

Which of the following is correct?

A I only
B II only
C Both I and II
D Neither I nor II

10. The CBR and PI techniques of investment analysis

I each give the same indication of investment acceptability which indication agrees with NPV, if investments are independent.
II are at times superior to NPV in that they give an additional idea of the return relative to the investment or cost.

Which of the following is correct?

A I only
B II only
C Both I and II
D Neither I nor II

11. IRR is more likely to give incorrect indications of investment ranking among a group of mutually exclusive investments when the investments

I are of significantly different magnitude.
II are of significantly different duration.
III have very different NPVs.

Which of the following is correct?

A I only
B II only
C I and II only
D I, II and III

12. Which of the following is correct?
Capital rationing situations tend to occur when companies

A are trying to raise more money than capital suppliers can afford to provide.
B have not planned correctly and run out of funds toward the end of a fiscal year.
C discover more good projects than is typical.
D have complicated management structures which cause problems in information flows.

13. Suppose that your firm is considering two alternative roofing materials for a new plant it is building. The plant is expected to last indefinitely, but the roofing material will of course require occasional refurbishment. Fibreglass shingles will last an expected 25 years, whereas slate's expected lifetime is 32 years. Fibreglass costs £130 000 to install, and has annual maintenance costs incurred at year ends which will average £11 000, whereas slate costs £216 000 and has annual maintenance of only £2 000. Because of differing underpayment structures, once the company decides on a roofing material, it must stick with it, or incur additional large costs of renovation. If a 10% discount is appropriate what should the company do?

A Choose neither because they both have negative NPVs.
B Choose slate because its equivalent annual cost is less than £25 000, compared to Fibreglasses in excess of £25 000.
C Choose Fibreglass because the present value of its costs is less than £230 000 compared to slate's in excess of £230 000.
D Choose Fibreglass because its equivalent annual cost is less than £25 000 compared to slate's in excess of £25 000.

14. Inflation is best handled in investment decision-making by

I estimating real cash flows and applying real discount rates.
II estimating nominal cash flows and applying nominal discount rates.
III estimating cash flows using current prices and using currently observable discount rates.

Which of the following is correct?

A I only
B II only
C III only
D Neither I, II nor III

15. The reason why a portfolio's risk cannot be reduced to zero by diversification is that

I mathematical techniques of combining securities into optimal portfolios are not well enough understood.
II there is a common influence among most investments which causes their returns to be positively correlated.
III many investments are difficult to discover, especially the ones with negative correlations to others.

Which of the following is correct?

A II only
B II and III only
C III only
D I, II and III

16. Investment A has an expected return of 14% and a standard deviation of 5% while investment B has an expected return of 10% and a standard deviation of 3%. Which of the following is true if you were to put half of your wealth into each investment?

A The risk of the portfolio will be 4% and the expected return 12%.
B The risk of the portfolio will be at least 4% and the expected return will be 12%.
C The risk of the portfolio will be no greater than 4% and the expected return 12%.
D The question does not provide enough information to make any of the comments about risk in A, B or C.

17. The ß you have decided is appropriate for your firm's equity investment in a new manufacturing facility for fertilizer is 1.16. If the risk-free rate is 9% and the excess of the market's expected return above the risk-free rate is 8%, what return will you require on the equity investment?

A Approximately 17.0%
B Approximately 17.4%
C Approximately 18.0%
D Approximately 18.3%

18. Which of the following is correct?

Diversification on the part of an equity-financed company so as to reduce cash flow variability is generally

A desirable due to the portfolio effects of risk reduction.
B undesirable due to the fact that opportunities for risk-reducing investments are rare and expensive.
C neutral if shareholders are not well diversified.
D neutral if shareholders are well diversified.

19. Which of the following is correct?

The "passive residual" dividend policy of a company says dividends should

A equal the profits of the firm because profits belong to shareholders.
B equal the retained earnings of the company because this amount is what is "left over" after all other company transactions.

C be based upon shareholder needs for cash for consumption purposes.
D be equal to the amount of cash flow left over after all good investments have been funded.

20. A reasonably stable dividend policy is consistent with

I the wish to satisfy a shareholder clientele of "widows and orphans" who depend upon that cash flow for their personal consumption needs.
II efficient signalling of value-altering news events by the company.
III legal requirements of portfolio admission by certain financial institutions.

Which of the following is correct?

A II only
B I and III only
C II and III only
D I, II and III

21. Debt in a company's capital structure may alter the company's cost of capital and shareholder wealth, relative to what these would have been without debt. Among the sources of such alterations are

I equity's increased risk due to debt's senior claim on company cash flows.
II debt's capital cost being less than equity's due to debt's senior claim.
III interest deductibility.

Which of the following is correct?

A I only
B III only
C I and II only
D II and III only

22. Suppose that the only tax in an economy was company income tax, and that there were no other "frictions" (such as transactions costs, bankruptcy costs, or other agency costs).

Which of the following is correct?

Optimal capital structure for companies in this economy would likely be

A very little debt, since shareholders would not be paying personal income taxes.
B a reasonable balance of debt and equity, such that in difficult economic times the odds of defaulting on interest and principal promises were acceptable.
C as much debt as they could issue with deductible interest.
D zero debt because interest would not be tax deductible.

22. Suppose that Intelligent Micro Designs PLC is seeking your advice about financing a proposed research and development project. IMD's business is designing computer motherboards, accomplished through a very talented group of design engineers. IMD can raise either equity or debt capital. IMD currently has a very low proportion of debt in its capital structure, and has shown an impressive history of earnings increases. Interest and principal payments on the company's proposed borrowings

seem to be modest relative to the company's net cash flows. What could your recommendation be?

A That IMD should issue equity rather than debt because of very high bankruptcy or financial distress costs.
B That IMD should issue debt because it has not exploited sufficiently debt's tax benefits.
C That IMD can issue either debt or equity without differentially affecting its shareholder wealth.
D That IMD should issue a complex debt instrument like a convertible bond.

24. What is the primary trade-off which occurs in managing Accounts Receivable (Debtors)?

A In order to get creditworthy customers you must give them especially good credit terms.
B Good customers sometimes take longer to pay than is best for the company.
C The costs of finding out who will be good customers can be more than the money saved by avoiding poor credit risks.
D Increasing revenues by reducing credit standards versus having secure receivables with lower sales revenues.

25. Inventories

I are costly to hold, but allow revenues to be higher.
II should be kept at the absolute minimum that allows the firm to operate.
III can be made cheaper to hold if the firm reorders less often.

Which of the following is correct?

A I only
B II only
C I and III only
D II and III only

26. Suppose that the current one year interest rate in the US is 9.4% and the UK rate is 11%. Further suppose that the spot exchange rate of dollars for pounds is 1.5 \$/£. What should your prediction of the one year forward rate for \$/£ be?

A 1.351
B 1.50
C 1.478
D 1.665

27. Your firm is building a plant and beginning to sell on credit terms in South Aerok, and is concerned with the potential risks arising from the indications of growing inflation in that country. Your suggestion about hedging this risk should be

I hedge the receivables.
II hedge the plant.

Which of the following is correct?

A I only
B II only
C Both I and II
D Neither I nor II

28. A call option has a striking price of £4.50 and the shares upon which it is based are selling for £4.65. There are several months until the option expires. What will the premium of the call option be?

A Zero because share price is above option value, and exercise would simply produce the "in the money" gain of £0.15.
B Negative, because "in the money" options may go "out of the money" between now and expiration.
C Positive, because "in the money" options stand to benefit more than they lose from price volatility.
D Either positive, negative or zero depending upon the values which appear for the parameters of the Black–Scholes option valuation formula.

29. Which of the following is correct?

The common shares of a geared or leveraged company can legitimately be considered

A a put option because they can be sold at anytime.
B a call option because they allow the repurchase of the bonds of the company.
C a put option because they allow the shareholders to sell the assets of the firm to its bondholders
D a call option because they allow the shareholders to buy the assets of the firm from bondholders.

30. For an "agency problem" to be solvable, necessary conditions of the situation are

I an overall gain in value from solving the problem.
II an incentive for the agent to participate in the solution.

Which of the following is correct?

A I only
B II only
C Both I and II
D Neither I nor II

Section C: Essay/Problem Questions

Points available for each part of the question are given in the right hand margin.

Problem 1

You are given the following information about the market for risk-free government bonds (all of which pay interest at the end of the year):

- There is a 9% coupon bond maturing in two years (it has remaining payments at the end of this and the next year), and it is currently selling for £1 017.07.
- There is a three year 10% coupon bond the price of which you do not know, but the coupon from the first interest payment (the end of this year) is selling in the market for £91.74.

Points

- The three year spot interest rate is 7%.
- There is a four year 11% coupon bond currently selling for £1 164.24.

Please answer the following questions about the bond market (in answering, you may round to the nearest £0.01 and to the nearest 0.01%):

(a) What is the price of a one year 8% coupon bond now in the market? 4

(b) What is the current price of the three year 10% coupon bond? 6

(c) What is the four year spot rate currently in the market? 5

(d) What is the one-period forward rate beginning one period hence? 4

(e) Suppose that you owned the four period 11% coupon bond, and were approached to sell the third coupon payment (the £110 which is expected for the end of year three). At what price would you agree to sell now? 3

(f) With the same assumptions as (e), at what price would you now agree to sell the same coupon two years hence? 7

(g) Suppose that there is another four year risk-free bond in the market, which promises to pay:

End of Year 1	*End of Year 2*	*End of Year 3*	*End of Year 4*
£973.38	£110	£110	£110

What would be the current price of this bond? 5

(h) If your calculator is capable of producing Yield to Maturity, calculate it for both four year bonds. If you do not have access to such a calculator, make an educated guess as to the relative sizes of the YTMs of these two bonds, and explain in either case the reason why the bonds' YTMs are such as they are. 11

TOTAL 45

Problem 2

You are considering "going short" (issuing or "writing") a call option on one share of UK Aero plc. The call option has an exercise price of £18, and one share of UK Aero is currently selling for £17. Your opinion is that at the end of the single period until option expiration, only two UK Aero share prices have any probability of occurring, either £13.60 (probability of 0.35) or £22.10 (probability of 0.65). The risk free market interest rate is 10%, and all other market conditions are as specified in the section in Module 12 on the binomial model of option valuation.

(a) How much money would you collect for issuing the option right now? Construct an explanation to an intelligent but uninitiated student as to why the market is willing to give you money for issuing an option that lets the holder buy something for £18 which is currently selling for £17. 16

(b) Suppose that you were concerned about the risk of issuing a "naked option", and wished to hedge your issuance of this option. Portray the exact transaction or set of transactions which would make your position risk-free. 18

(c) Suppose that you in fact were seeking the risk-return characteristic exhibited by the issuance of this call option, but the option was not available. Illustrate the transaction(s) you could undertake so as to produce the same risk and return exposure as you would have derived from issuing the option. 11

TOTAL 45

Section A: Answers to True/False Questions

1. This is true because the £1.00 invested today at interest will accrue to more than £1.00 in the future.
2. This is false because there are many similarities between NPV and IRR, in that they use the same data, are both discounted cash flow methods, and usually give the same final indications of investment desirability.
3. This is true because financial markets are not only countrywide, but effectively worldwide, and deal in a product which is largely homogeneous: future cash flow expectations. No single participant is large enough to affect that market with its own sales or purchases (save some large governments); information flows quickly, inexpensively and with little bias; and there are few impediments to the free flow of capital across securities or national borders. No other market is as close to a perfectly competitive ideal.
4. This is true because there may be times, especially when the firm is geared and in some financial distress, that bondholders would benefit at the expense of shareholders if a positive NPV investment were undertaken.
5. This is false because ignoring depreciation will cause cash flow estimates to deal incorrectly with tax effects of depreciation.
6. This is false because they should not subtract interest payments at all. Interest payments are cash flows to capital suppliers, and thus are correctly included (not subtracted) in FCF* to which the WACC is applied.
7. This is false because of the use of the word "accepted". It is true that the higher non-discounted NPV investment is better than the other, but not necessarily true that it is acceptable (its IRR may be less than the hurdle rate).
8. This is true because investment projects which have economic (causal) cash flow interactions must be considered only with such interactions specified. In other words it is irrelevant if an investment taken alone has a negative NPV; as long as that investment adds to the positive NPV of another.
9. This is true because markets are very good pricers of existing expectations, and though it is likely that either the net borrower or net lender will benefit at the expense of the other, in order to know in advance which it will be, requires that one be capable of predicting inflation and interest rate changes better than the financial markets. Though markets may not always be terribly good at that, we have found no better alternative.
10. This is false because risk is reduced by diversification as long as correlation is not perfectly positive. This includes all positive correlations less than 1.0.

11. This is false because it would assume that the SML always has a slope equal to 1.0. There is no reason to think that to be a general situation, and in fact there is evidence that the SML changes slope in reaction to changes in the risk-free rate and expected market return.

12. This is true because the equity of an ungeared firm will be the equity of its assets, and since gearing increases the risk of equity, moving from an ungeared to a geared firm will increase equity's risk and ß (responsiveness to overall market return changes).

13. This is true because in order to attract a clientele that pays taxes, such firms would be forced to offer the same aftertax return as other firms with lower dividend payouts and higher capital gains. To duplicate the aftertax return a higher pretax return may be necessary. (If there was a significant clientele that did not pay taxes, or that had very high transactions costs of turning capital gains into necessarily consumable cash, this general proposition may not hold.)

14. This is false because it is costly for clienteles to move from one firm's shares with a particular policy to a different firm's shares with another policy.

15. This is false because bankruptcy is costless in such a world, and would present no detriment to borrowing versus equity.

16. This is false because we know there are other positive reasons (such as agency costs of equity) for issuing debt, and in fact corporate borrowing did exist before the appearance of company income taxes.

17. This is true because mere tax advantage would argue that firms borrow more than we actually see them borrowing.

18. This is false because such a strategy is costly to implement in terms of making judgements about customers, and there is probably some balance of bad customers who are worthwhile putting up with so as to get the higher revenues from all customers.

19. This is false because options both increase and decrease in value as underlying asset values change (calls move in the same direction, and puts move in the opposite direction). The distinguishing feature of options in this context is that the value movements are positively biased (e.g. calls do not decline as much as underlying assets).

20. This is false because each £1.00 of consumption of corporate assets produces £1.00 of benefit to managers, while managers' share value will only decline by £1.00 times the proportions of all shares held by managers.

Section B: Answers to Multiple Choice Questions

1. The correct answer is D. There are several techniques of finding the correct answer, but they have in common the goal of finding the value of all three cash flows at the end of the first year. This could be accomplished by discounting the end-of-third-year cash flow to the end of the second year, adding the undiscounted second year cash flow, and adding the end-of-first year cash flow with one year's accrued interest:

$$£6\,015 = £2\,000\,(1.09) + £2\,000 + \frac{£2\,000}{(1.09)}$$

The same result would occur if all cash flows were first discounted to present value and then accrued outward at interest for one period, or any of a number of other alternatives. Using present and future value tables would also produce the same result, save that multiplicative "factors" (e.g. 0.9174) would be used instead of discounting (e.g. dividing by 1.09) as shown.

2. The correct answer is B. The annuity present value table indicates that a seventeen year annuity at 11% interest has a factor of 7.5488. Multiplying this by £1 000 yields the correct answer.

3. The correct answer is C. The two investments each have an NPV of £144:

$$\#1\quad £144 = -£1\,500 + \frac{845}{(1.12)} + \frac{670}{(1.12)^2} + \frac{500}{(1.12)^3}$$

$$\#2\quad £144 = -£2\,600 + \frac{105}{(1.12)} + \frac{200}{(1.12)^2} + \frac{3\,500}{(1.12)^3}$$

4. The correct answer is A. If the correct cash flow expectation is fifty years of £1 000 per year, a perpetuity will miss an infinite number of £1 000 per annum cash flows beyond year fifty. At year fifty, the value of those is simply their perpetuity value of £10 000. The *present* value of that £10 000 is of course found by the process in A. (Incidentally, the present value is £85.19, or 0.852% – less than one percent – of the £10 000 estimated value, a very small error.

5. The correct answer is A. A correctly calculated project NPV, being based upon residual cash flows and a capital cost which accounts for all required returns to capital suppliers, produces the net increase in wealth of shareholders the residual claimants of the corporation.

6. The correct answer is D. The price earnings ratio of a company can on the proper comparison provide information about the future prospects of a firm, but can yield misleading or incorrect impressions if used carelessly. One such misuse is that mentioned in C, namely cross-industry comparisons.

7. The correct answer is C. A is incorrect because it implies that all of the firm's cash flows are included in a project's NPV. B is incorrect because it would include all financing cash flows including interest tax shields, and D is incorrect in part for the same reason.

8. The correct answer is D. Payback period's shortcomings are well described in I, II is correct because the various discounting and other improvements to payback still relegate it to uses which are at best specialised, and III is correct because payback is seductively simple.

9. The correct answer is D. IRR can be made to work in any situation if one is wise enough to recognise the additional analysis which is required to make it work. In situations of mutual exclusivity, IRR will give good decisions if implemented in an incremental cash flow context. In situations of multiple sign changes, explicit assumptions of reinvestment flows will allow IRR to function. And if multiple discount rates occur across time, a market yield from comparable cash flow securities can provide a hurdle rate. These are, however, formidable conditions, and given that NPV always works,

and is a good bit easier to calculate, especially in the situations listed above. IRR may not be an optimal choice of technique.

10. The correct answer is A. The CBR and PI techniques work correctly to indicate acceptability of investments when there is no economic relatedness among proposals, and each can be considered alone for a "yes" or "no" verdict. The techniques are not in any sense superior to NPV as B implies, and though PI may be useful as a crude first approximation ranking device in certain capital rationing situations, it certainly is not reliable enough to be used as is implied in B. C is contradicted by A.

11. The correct answer is C. The problems which arise with IRR are in divergent patterning of mutually exclusive project cash flows. Both different sizes and timings of cash flows fit that definition. Thus A and B are incorrect. D is incorrect because IRR's confusion is not generally related to the size of NPVs of competing projects.

12. The correct answer is D. Capital rationing is not having enough money to pursue all desirable projects. A is incorrect because capital markets have more money than any single firm could ever find projects (if capital markets will not provide enough money, it is because they disagree as to the desirability of projects, not because of any shortage of funds). B is incorrect because financial markets stand ready at any time to provide funding for good projects. C is incorrect for the same reason. The text indicates that capital rationing is a reaction to an information shortfall in either the market or the company, and thus D is consistent with the latter.

13. The correct answer is B. This is a problem in which the investments are "repeatable" or "renewable". The correct technique (other than specifying all cash flows into the future until the two alternatives have a common terminal point, an unrealistic calculation in this case, since the first common terminal point is 800 years in the future!) is to find each alternative's "equivalent annual cost". To do this first you find each alternative's NPV in its first cycle, and divide the result by the annuity factor for that particular duration:

    For fibreglass:

$$\begin{aligned} NPV_f &= (25 \text{ year annuity factor} \times £11\,000) + £130\,000 \\ &= (9.077 \times £11\,000) + £130\,000 \\ &= £229\,847 \end{aligned}$$

    For slate:

$$\begin{aligned} NPV_8 &= (32 \text{ year annuity factor x } £2\,000) + £216\,000 \\ &= (9.526 \times £2\,000) + £216\,000 \\ &= £235\,053 \end{aligned}$$

    The equivalent annual costs are:

$$\begin{aligned} EAC_f &= NPV_f/25 \text{ year annuity factor} = £229\,847/9.077 \\ EAC_f &= \underline{£25\,322} \\ EAC_8 &= NPV_8/32 \text{ year annuity factor} = £235\,053/9.526 \\ EAC_f &= \underline{£24.674} \end{aligned}$$

    Thus slate is cheaper in a present value sense, because its higher installation cost is offset by the longer duration between installations and the lower annual maintenance. A is incorrect because the negative NPVs are appropriate due to these being "cost minimising" investments.

14. The correct answer is B. Nominal cash flows discounted with nominal discount rates is the superior technique due to the difficulties of estimating real discount rates. Though A could be made to work in concept, in reality its application is prohibitively difficult. C is incorrect because it amounts to something like using nominal discount rates on real cash flows, which will bias NPVs downward.

15. The correct answer is A. As the text described, most investments are influenced by a "common factor" which is usually described as the "market". This common factor produces a situation wherein investments have some lower limit on the extent to which diversification reduces risk. Some newer models of market equilibrium (such as the APT) have seemed to uncover more than one "common factor". I is incorrect because we have plenty of mathematical skills to do such analyses. III is simply incorrect.

16. The correct answer is C. A portfolio's risk can never be any higher than the linear combination of the risks of its component assets. When assets within a portfolio are perfectly positively correlated, portfolio risk is a weighted average (linear combination) of the risks of the component assets. When correlation is less than perfectly positive. portfolio risk will be less than the linear combination. Correlations cannot be greater than perfectly positive. A and B are incorrect for the above reason. D is incorrect because we can confidently ascribe to C.

17. The correct answer is D. This is simply an application of the SML:

    Required Return = $rf + (E(rm)–rf)ß$
    Required Return = 0.09 + (0.08) 1.16
    Required Return = 0.1828 or 18.3%

18. The correct answer is D. Diversification for the purpose of portfolio risk reduction only helps shareholders if shareholders are not themselves already well diversified. To the extent that a firm has debt in its capital structure, it may help due to bankruptcy risk reduction, but hurt due to "coinsurance" of debt claims (increasing their value at the cost of equity).

19. The correct answer is D. A "passive residual" dividend policy means that dividends are fully driven by other decisions the company makes. In other words, after all other policies (including how much cash should be held by the company in bank accounts) are carried out, and if any cash is left over, it may be paid as a dividend. Retained earnings of the company do not follow this definition, because retained earnings are in effect channelled into investments, so B is incorrect, and A and C are obviously not "passive" dividend policies since they are driven by some other concern.

20. The correct answer is D. Shareholder consumption preferences, signalling, and legal-professional portfolio constraints can all influence a company's wish to maintain a reasonably stable dividend across time.

21. The correct answer is B. The only relevant factor in the list is interest deductibility, which causes debt to be more attractive then equity, other things held the same. I is incorrect because equity's higher risk (and required return) is offset by debt's lower cost. II is incorrect for the mirror-image reason of I.

22. The correct answer is C. With interest-deductible debt, no other taxes and no other frictions or agency costs, the shareholder maximising capital structure would be to issue as much debt as carries interest deductibility. Though other deductibilities (like depreciation) might cause less than all of the interest tax shield to be utilised, the company will be no worse-off than it would have been with equity, and on most occasions would pay less taxes. B is incorrect because we have assumed away all of the problems caused by too much debt in the capital structure, and A is nonsense, as is D.

23. The correct answer is A. Most of IMD's value is in intangible assets, made up of its engineering skill. In times of financial distress (generated by declines in the computer industry, which do happen) such assets quickly lose a good bit of their value as employees leave for greener pastures. Debt suppliers, foreseeing this, would require much higher interest rates as compensation for this asset intangibility. B is incorrect because though IMD could perhaps gain interest tax shields, such tax benefits may be otherwise available (through R&D credits, for example), which do not carry bankruptcy costs. C and D propose tactics which would be applicable to firms in other situations. C is an irrelevancy suggestion which IMD does not represent. D would be applicable if bondholders felt that IMD could "shift risks" of investments after borrowing.

24. The correct answer is D. Receivables management is primarily a trade-off between acquiring more sales by easing credit terms and thereby delving more deeply into the pool of questionable customers, versus having lower sales but with faster and more reliable payments. There is no empirical evidence which would support A or B, and C, though correct, is not the primary trade-off of receivable management.

25. The correct answer is A. Physical inventories allow the firm to respond to the requirements of markets more flexibly. However, inventories, including cash, are assets and require financing, and thus cannot be expanded without eventually reaching uneconomic size. II is wrong because it offers too stringent a standard by the above description of the role of inventories. III is opposite to the truth.

26. The correct answer is C. As the Module points out, the ratio between interest factors (1.11/1.094) = 1.01463 must be the same as the ratio between spot and forward exchange rates (1.5/One year forward rate) = 1.01463; therefore the one year forward rate must equal 1.5 ÷ 1.01463 or 1.478. The other rates shown are inconsistent with this required economic relationship.

27. The correct answer is A. Real assets tend to increase in value along with inflation, so there is no need to hedge the plant. Financial assets (such as receivables), however, have future payoffs stated in nominal currency terms, and if inflation is unexpectedly high, future receipts in both the foreign and domestic economy will be less valuable than anticipated when received. Thus A is the only correct answer of those listed.

28. The correct answer is C. An option allows the holder to benefit from positive events (in this case increases in price of the underlying security) in greater degree than to lose from negative events. Specifically, increases in stock price above £4.65 will produce gains in current £0.15 exercise value on "£-for-£" basis, while reductions in stock price below £4.64 cannot reduce exercise value below £0.00. Thus the premium (the amount by which option value exceeds exercise value) must be positive; the option must be selling for more than £0.15. A and B are incorrect because they predict non-

positive values, and D is incorrect because premiums must be either positive or zero (and will only be zero if there is no time until expiration).

29. The correct answer is D. When a company borrows money by issuing bonds, it (in economic effect) is selling the assets of the firm to the bondholders (the bondholders have first claim on those assets in the case of default) in exchange for the money borrowed. Shareholders however (in effect) retain an option to repurchase the assets of the firm from bondholders upon the firm paying the bonds, contractual interest and principal (and otherwise abiding by the terms of the bond indenture). A is incorrect because the option characteristic of common stock has nothing to do with the shares' marketability, B is incorrect, because shareholders may not in fact be able to buy back the bonds (and even if they could it would not be the characteristic which allows shares to be considered options). C is closer to being correct than A or B, and in some contexts may be another way of looking at share value. But in the sense explained by the Module, is not as good an answer as D.

30. The correct answer is C. Both of these conditions are required. If there is no overall gain, there is no value increase to be allocated between principal and agent, and thus no prospect of inducing a change in behaviour. Even with such an increase in overall value, however, the agent must somehow be allocated a part of the gain or there is no incentive for the (decision-making) agent to change behaviour.

Section C: Answers to Essay/Problem Questions

Problem 1 — *Points*

The problem implies the following price and cash flow information, along with the 7% three year spot rate:

Now	*End of Year 1*	*End of Year 2*	*End of Year 3*	*End of Year 4*
£1 017.17	£90	£1 090		
?	£100	£100	£1 100	
£91.74	£100			
£1 164.24	£110	£110	£110	£1 110

(a) The price of the one year 8% coupon bond depends upon the receipt of £1 080 one year hence, discounted at the one year spot rate. The one year spot rate is not given, but can be deduced from the price of the end-of-first-year coupon of the three year bond. Since the £1 080 cash flow from the one year bond and the £100 cash flow from the three year bond have the same risk and timing, they must be subject to the same discount rate: 4

$$£91.74 = \frac{£100}{(1 + i_1)}$$

$$(1 + i_1) = \frac{£100}{£91.74} = 1.09$$

$$i_1 = 9\%$$

With a 9 % one year spot rate, the current price of the one year 8% coupon bond is £1 080/1.09 = £990.83.

(b) The price of the three year 10% coupon bond is a function of its known cash flows discounted with the one, two and three year spot rates. From (a) we now have the one year spot rate, and the three year spot rate is given in the problem as 7%. So the remaining unknown is the two year spot rate. It can be deduced by analysing the two year 9% coupon bond:

$$\text{£}1\,017.07 = \frac{\text{£}90}{(1+i_1)} + \frac{\text{£}1\,090}{(1+i_2)^2}$$

$$= \frac{\text{£}90}{(1+0.09)} + \frac{\text{£}1\,090}{(1+i_2)^2}$$

$$= \text{£}82.57 + \frac{\text{£}1\,090}{(1+i_2)^2}$$

$$\text{£}934.50 = \frac{\text{£}1\,090}{(1+i_2)^2}$$

$$(1+i_2)^2 = \frac{\text{£}1\,090}{\text{£}934.50} = 1.1664$$

$$(1+i_2) = 1.08$$
$$i_2 = 8\%$$

With a two year spot rate of 8%, the price of the three year 10% bond is:

$$\text{£}? = \frac{\text{£}100}{(1+i_1)} + \frac{\text{£}100}{(1+i_2)^2} + \frac{\text{£}1\,100}{(1+i_3)^3}$$

$$\text{£}? = \frac{\text{£}100}{(1+0.09)} + \frac{\text{£}100}{(1+0.08)^2} + \frac{\text{£}1\,100}{(1+0.07)^3} = \underline{\text{£}1\,075.40}$$

(This question can also be solved using forward interest rates.) 6

(c) If the current price of the four year bond is known, and if the first three spot rates are known, it is simple algebra to find the four year spot rate:

$$\text{£}1\,164.24 = \frac{\text{£}110}{(1.09)} + \frac{\text{£}110}{(1.08)^2} + \frac{\text{£}110}{(1.07)^3} + \frac{\text{£}1\,110}{(1+i_4)^4}$$

$$= \text{£}100.92 + \text{£}94.31 + \text{£}89.79 + \frac{\text{£}1\,110}{(1+i_4)^4}$$

$$(1+i_4)^4 = \frac{\text{£}1\,110}{\text{£}879.22} = 1.26248$$

$$(1 + i_4)^4 = 1.06$$
$$i^4 = 6\%$$ 5

(d) The one year forward rate one year hence, ${}_1f_2$, can be found most easily by working with the cash flows and prices of the two year bond:

$$£1\,017.07 = \frac{£90}{(1 + i_1)} + \frac{£1\,090}{(1 + i_1)(1 + {}_1f_2)}$$

$$= \frac{£90}{(1.09)} + \frac{£1\,090}{(1.09)(1 + {}_1f_2)}$$

$$= £82.57 + \frac{£1\,090}{(1.09)(1 + {}_1f_2)}$$

$$(1 + {}_1f_2) = \frac{£1\,090}{£934.50\,(1.09)} = 1.07$$

$${}_1f_2 = 7\%$$ 4

(e) You have already calculated that answer in (c). The value is £89.79. 3

(f) This question is asking for a "forward price" of the year three £110 coupon, expected to exist as of the end of the second year. To find this value you must discount the year three cash flow by the forward interest rate for that year, ${}_2f_3$. This latter forward rate has not yet been calculated (unless you solved one of the earlier answers with forward rates instead of spot rates). The simplest way to calculate ${}_2f_3$ is to recall that:

$$(1 + i_3)^3 = (1 + i_2)^2\,(1 + {}_2f_3)$$

$$(1 + {}_2f_3) = (1 + i_3)^3 / (1 + i_2)^2$$

$$(1 + {}_2f_3) = (1.07)^3 / (1.08)^2 = 1.0502$$

$${}_2f_3 = 5.02\%$$

Therefore the end-of-year two forward price of the end of year three £110 coupon of the four year bond is:

$$£? = £110 / (1 + {}_2f_3) = £110 / 1.05 = £104.74$$ 7

(g) Pricing this bond requires only that the specified cash flows be discounted at the appropriate spot or forward rates:

$$£? = \frac{£973.38}{(1.09)} + \frac{£110}{(1.08)^2} + \frac{£110}{(1.07)^3} + \frac{£110}{(1.06)^4}$$

$$£? = £1\,164.24$$

Note that this price is the same as that of the four year 11% coupon bond. 5

(h) The four year 11% coupon bond's YTM is 6.23%, whereas the bond in (g) has a YTM of 7.97%. (These YTMs are of course, the **constant** discount rates which would produce the correct market prices of the bonds.) If you did not have access to a calculator that could find the YTMs easily, you should have said that the YTM of the 11% coupon bond must be expected to be **less** than the YTM of the other four year bond. The reason why the yield of the coupon bond is less than the yield of the other bond is that the pattern of cash flows presented by the coupon bond is such that much of that bond's present value is generated by its final cash flow (£879.22 of its £1 164.24 value), whereas the other bonds' value is generated almost equally across time. Since the coupon bonds' value comes from a cash flow being operated upon by a much lower discount rate than the average (note that in this market, rates are lower farther in the future). the YTM which is at funny "value weighted average" of the spot rates, must be less for the coupon bond due to the importance to its value of the lower-rate-generated portion, compared to the other bond. Both bonds are, of course, subject to the exact same set of spot and forward market interest rates. The differences in YTM is caused solely by differences in cash flow patterns. 11

TOTAL 45

Problem 2

(a) The call option which you issue will bring you cash (assume no brokerage fees) equal to the value of the option. To value the option first you must find $\mathbf{uS_0}$ and $\mathbf{dS_0}$. With share price increasing from £17 to £22.10, the former is 1.3 and the latter is 0.80 with a decline from £17 to £13.60.

$$\mathbf{C_u} = \max\{0, \mathbf{uS_0} - \mathbf{X}\} = \max\{0, 1.3(£17) - £18\} = £4.10$$
$$\mathbf{C_d} = \max\{0, \mathbf{dS_0} - \mathbf{X}\} = \max\{0.8(17) - £18\} = £0$$

$$\mathbf{Y} = \frac{\mathbf{C_u - C_d}}{\mathbf{S_0(u - d)}} = \frac{£4.10 - £0}{£17(1.3 - 0.8)} = \mathbf{0.48235\ldots}$$

and

$$\mathbf{Z} = \frac{\mathbf{uC_d - dC_u}}{\mathbf{(u - d)(1 + rf)}} = \frac{1.3(£0) - 0.8(£4.10)}{(1.3 - 0.8)(1 + 0.10)} = \mathbf{-£5.96364\ldots}$$

$$\mathbf{YS_0 + Z} = 0.48235\ldots(£17) - £5.96364\ldots = \mathbf{£2.236\ldots}$$

The value of the call option is £2.236. This is the amount of cash that you would receive from writing the option. Note that the exercise value is zero, yet you are paid a positive amount for issuing the option. The reason you are given this money for issuing this option even though it is "out of the money" is that you have promised to sell something for a fixed price (£18) which has at least some probability between now and option expiration of being worth £22.10.

The buyer of the option is purchasing the chance of gaining the spread between exercise price (£18) and £22.10 (netting £4.10) or, if share price instead goes down, simply walking away and not exercising the option. The market values this "lottery ticket" at £2.236. 16

(b) The condition for a "perfect hedge" from the Appendix to Module 2 is:

$$\mathbf{uS_0 - mC_u = dS_0 - mC_d} \qquad \text{[A.12.1]}$$

The hedge comprises the information as to how many options to write in connection with the purchase of one share of the underlying stock:

$$\mathbf{m} = \frac{\mathbf{S_0(u-d)}}{\mathbf{C_u - C_d}} \qquad \text{[A.12.2]}$$

$$= \frac{£17(1.3-0.8)}{£4.10-£0.00} = \mathbf{2.07317\ldots}$$

This tells us that we can form a perfectly hedged portfolio by buying one share of equity and simultaneously writing 2.07317 call options. But we have already issued only one call option, so we could either issue another 1.07317 call options or purchase less than one share. Of course the partial share would bear the same ratio of one per 2.07317 options. If we were to write only one option we would purchase 0.48235 (the inverse of the hedge ratio) shares to hedge perfectly. To test that assertion,

for an increase in share price:

$\mathbf{uS_0 - mC_u}$ = £22.10 – (2.07317) £4.10 = **£13.60** [one share]

or = £22.10(0.48325) – £4.10 = **£6.58** [one option]

for a decline in share price:

$\mathbf{dS_0 - mC_d}$ = £13.60 – (2.07317)£0.00 = **£13.60** [one share]

or = £13.60(0.48325) – £0.00 = **£6.58** [one share]

The portfolio is perfectly hedged: if UK Aero's shares go up and the option has its higher payoff, the portfolio returns £13.60 if hedged by issuing a total of 2.07317 options with a purchase of one share, or goes up £6.58 if hedged by issuing only one option but purchasing 0.48325 shares. If UK Aero's shares decline and the option is worthless (unexercised), the portfolio returns either £13.60 or £6.58 the same depending upon the hedge transaction, but the same amount as it would if share price had increased. 18

(c) You have already actually done the calculations for that answer. Remembering that **Y** is the number of underlying shares to issue so as to form the "call equivalent" portfolio, and **Z** is the amount of lending (if positive), the transaction which would duplicate the issuance of the option would be to *sell* **Y** shares and *borrow* **Z** (if positive):

Since:

$$\mathbf{Y} = \frac{\mathbf{C_u - C_d}}{\mathbf{S_0\,(u-d)}} = \frac{£4.10 - £0}{£17\,(1.3-0.8)} = \mathbf{0.48235\ldots}$$

and

$$\mathbf{Z} = \frac{\mathbf{uCd - dCu}}{\mathbf{(u-d)\,(1+rf)}} = \frac{1.3(£0) - 0.8(£4.10)}{(1.3-0.8)(1+0.10)} = \mathbf{5.96364\ldots}$$

You can sell 0.48235. .. shares and lend (since negative) £5.96364 at the risk free rate. Your payoff is then:

if share price increases:

– **Y** (**u**S_0) + **Z**(1 + rf) = –0.48325 . . . (£22.10) + £5.96364. . . (1.10)
= £4.10

And if share price declines:

– **Y** (**u**S_0) + **Z**(1 +rf) = –0.48325 . . . (£13.60) + £5.96364 . . . (1.10)
= £0.00

Note that these payoffs are exactly the same (if you have not rounded the results) as those for the option payoffs. 11

TOTAL 45

PRACTICE FINAL EXAMINATION 2 – WITHOUT MCQs

Essay Question

Working Capital Management

You are given the following, information from the accounts of K & S Company. Comparable figures, on a percentage basis, are given for the industry.

Profit and Loss Account for Year Ending

	31 Dec. 1992		**31 Dec. 1993**		**31 Dec. 1993**	
	£m	*£m*	*£m*	*£m*	*Industry %*	
Sales		9.95		11.32		100%
Cost of Sales						
Opening Stock	2.23		2.62		8%	
Purchases	8.27		9.26		84%	
	10.50		11.88		89%	
Closing Stock	2.62	7.88	2.42	9.46	10%	81%
Gross Profit		2.07		1.86		22%
Expenses		1.1		1.2		7%
Interest		0.2		0.4		3%
Net Profit before tax		0.77		0.26		8.5%
Tax (@ 30%)		0.23		0.08		2%
Net Profit after tax		0.54		0.18		6.5%

Balance Sheet as at	31 Dec. 1992		31 Dec. 1993		31 Dec. 1993	
	£m	*£m*	*£m*	*£m*	*Industry %*	
Fixed Assets		4.25		4.85		29%
Current Assets						
Stock	2.62		2.42		14%	
Debtors	2.15		2.60		9%	
Other	1.42		1.1		6%	
	6.19		6.12		29%	
Less: Current Liabilities	2.80		3.20		14%	
		3.39		2.92		15%
Net Assets		7.64		7.77		44%
Represented by:						
Ordinary Shares of £0.50		4.00		4.00		17%
Retained Profits						
Opening	3.10		1.59		13%	
Current Year	0.54		0.18		6%	
		3.64		1.77		
10% Debenture 2009		0.00		2.00		8%
		7.64		7.77		44%

Required:

1. ***List ten standard ratios (or similar statistics) that can be calculated from the accounting information listed above and which are useful for financial analysis.*** **(10 marks)**

$$\text{Current Ratio} = \frac{\text{Current Assets}}{\text{Current Liabilities}}$$

$$\text{Quick Ratio} = \frac{\text{Current assets} - \text{Inventory}}{\text{Current Liabilities}}$$

$$\text{Profit Margin} = \frac{\text{Net profit after taxes}}{\text{Sales}}$$

$$\text{Return on total assets} = \frac{\text{Net profit after taxes}}{\text{Total assets}}$$

$$\text{Return on owners equity} = \frac{\text{Net profit after taxes}}{\text{Owner's equity}}$$

$$\text{Return on inventory} = \frac{\text{Net profit after tax}}{\text{Inventory}}$$

$$\text{Debt ratio} = \frac{\text{Total debt}}{\text{Total assets}}$$

$$\text{Times interest earned} = \frac{\text{Profit before tax} - \text{interest}}{\text{Interest charges}}$$

$$\text{Fixed to current ratio} = \frac{\text{Fixed Assets}}{\text{Current assets}}$$

$$\text{Inventory turnover} = \frac{\text{Sales}}{\text{Inventory}}$$

$$\text{Average collection period} = \frac{\text{Debtors}}{\text{Sales per day}}$$

$$\text{Fixed asset turnover} = \frac{\text{Sales}}{\text{Fixed assets}}$$

2. ***Calculate the ratios you have listed in Question 1, above for K & S Company over the two years and also calculate the ratios for the industry.*** **(20 marks)**

Financial Ratios	*Company 1992*	*Company 1993*	*Industry 1993*
Current Ratio	2.21	1.91	2.07
Quick Ratio	1.28	1.16	1.07
Profit Margin	5.42%	1.61%	6.50%
Return on total assets	5.16%	1.66%	11.21%
Return on owners equity	7.05%	3.15%	18.06%
Return on inventory	20.6%	7.44%	46.4%
Debt Ratio	26.82%	47.40%	37.9%
Times interest earned	4.85	1.65	3.83
Fixed to current ratio	68.66%	79.25%	100.00%
Inventory Turnover	3.80	4.68	7.14
Average collection period	78.87	83.83	32.85
Fixed Asset Turnover	2.34	2.33	3.45

3. ***Evaluate and comment on K & S's recent performance compared with the rest of that industry and suggest possible action to be taken by K & S in light of what the ratios are indicating.*** **(15 marks)**

(Total of 45 marks)

The financial ratios calculated showing K & S's recent performance over the two years 1992 and 1993 indicate a company that is definitely experiencing serious problems. What follows is not intended to be a complete analysis, but picks up some areas that need to be highlighted in the answer.

If we examine the ratios, comparing them year to year and against the industry we get a deteriorating situation. The most alarming falls have been in the profitability ratios where the return on total assets and the return on owners equity have fallen from 5.16% to 1.66% and 7.05% to 3.15% respectively. The original return figures were already poor compared to the rest of the industry but have since fallen further. K & S is not making its assets work as hard as the rest of the industry. The return on the owners capital has fallen so far relative to the rest of the industry that investors will surely be demanding that urgent action be taken as swiftly as possible. Sales have increased reasonably over the year, but profits have taken back. This may be an indication that the company is desperate to hang on to what market share it has at the expense of profits. This is further highlighted in the falling profit margin figures where margins have fallen from 5.42% to 1.61%.

The company liquidity ratios are weakening but they are not too out of line with the industry averages, but a lot of the current assets of the company are made up of debtors and this is an increasing proportion, and the debt collection time is getting longer as well as being about 2.5 times the industry average.

With the capital structure ratios, the picture emerges of K & S having more current assets than its competitors in the industry. Management needs to justify this to its investors, otherwise action must be taken to reduce the level of current assets.

The company has taken on long term debt which has contributed to the much higher gearing level. The questions that might be asked are, is this an appropriate long term rate of interest to be locked into? And is this higher gearing level acceptable?

The banks and creditors may suspect the business is not being run efficiently, putting its future in jeopardy.

The stock and debtors position is poor, the collection period is much poorer than the industry. Credit control is weak. There has to be concern that a growing proportion of these debts will be unrecoverable.

The whole company has put in a very lacklustre performance.

The key to improving the company's currently weak financial state is to manage working capital more efficiently. Debtors have increased from 2.15 to 2.6 in the P & L, representing a 16.28% increase whereas sales only went up by 13.77%. In particular the 84 days of debtors outstanding needs to be reduced. The levels of stock should be reduced, and if possible margins to be rebuilt.

If stock and debtors were reduced you would free up more money that could reduce the debt situation, which would help the long term solvency position.

Case Study

Investment Appraisal

Daley Healthcare is a company operating in the healthcare business. It wants to become involved in the market for care of the elderly, which in Britain is a growing and profitable sector of the healthcare industry. Daley Healthcare has two options: it can open up a Nursing Home or it can open up a Residential Home.

A nursing home is more expensive to set up and run as the level of care provided is similar to that of a hospital, except that no surgical operations are undertaken. A Residential Home is less expensive to set up and operate because the staffing and equipment needs are less than that of the nursing home. From an investment point of view nursing homes can be attractive as the fees charged to the patients are much higher than those charged in a residential home.

Daley Healthcare has identified a suitable location to build its chosen home. It will cost £3 million to build a Nursing Home (Option A) and to equip it to the necessary standards. The Residential Home will only cost £2 million to build and equip to the necessary standards (Option B). The Nursing Home will be able to accommodate 40 patients but the Residential Home due to the less intensive nature of its care will be able to take 50 patients. The fees charged to patients are expected to be £400 per week for the Nursing Home and £210 per week for the Residential Home.

The staffing arrangements differ for the two homes. The Nursing Home requires 4 qualified nurses and 8 care assistants; the Residential Home requires 9 care assistants only. The salaries of the staff are £14 000 per annum for nurses and £10 500 for care assistants (assume the salaries are paid at the end of the year).

The local government council is willing to grant Daley Healthcare a 10 year concession to run the Nursing or Residential Home, after which time it would pass into the control of the council, and the company's investment would be ended. In addition, the Nursing or Residential Home has to reapply for its licence to operate as a healthcare establishment. The costs involved in renewing the licence each year are £100 000 for the Nursing Home, and £30 000 for the Residential Home. Daley Healthcare would be responsible for all these costs. The council would pay for all the other costs involved in running the home during the 10 years.

Daley Healthcare has conducted a feasibility study and commissioned market research on this market and this has incurred expenses of £50 000. This research was completed by 31 December 1993.

There are quoted companies on the stock market operating in these areas. Companies operating in the nursing home sub-sector and residential home sub-sector typically have a nominal opportunity cost of capital of 17% and 16% respectively. The expected inflation rate is assumed to remain 3.5% per annum into the foreseeable future, affecting all cash flows and revenues.

The set up costs are assumed to occur in year 0 (i.e. 1.1.94 to 31.12.94), and assume that revenues and costs start in the next time period, year 1 (i.e. 1.1.95) for calculation purposes assume end period cash flows. Also assume 100% occupancy for 52 weeks per year for the full 10 years.

Please ignore tax in this analysis.

NB For all the questions, please show your workings. No marks will be awarded for a numerical answer without any explanation.

Required:

1. ***Calculate the real discount rate for assessing the projects. Show all working.*** **(6 marks)**

   Nursing home cost of capital = 17% Inflation = 3.5%.
   Residential home cost of capital = 16%.
   The real discount rate should be calculated as follows:
   Nursing home: (1.17)/(1.035) = 1.13 = 13%.
   Residential home: (1.16)/(1.035) = 1.12 = 12%.
   If real cash flows are used in the following, analysis, these discount rates should be applied.

2. ***Estimate the cash flow of the two projects (Nursing Home and Residential Home). Please make clear headings for the different categories of cash flows.*** **(10 marks)**

   Cash flows are shown in columns 1, 2, 3, 4, 5 of the answer grid.

3. ***What is the Net Present Value (NPV) of each project when both raise prices exactly in line with the rate of inflation? You are limited to choosing just one project. Which one, if either, would you choose?*** **(10 marks)**

   NPV calculations are shown in columns 6 and 7, using the real discount rate.
   NPV of nursing home = £206 762 (£3 206 762 – £3 000 000).
   NPV of residential home = £374 053 (£2 374 053 – £2 000 000).
   Choose the residential home.

4. ***Assuming that the Nursing Home can increase its prices by 2.5% ABOVE the rate of inflation, all other revenues and costs will continue to rise at the rate of inflation, the Residential Home revenues and costs will rise by the inflation, what is the NPV of the Nursing Home project now? Which project would you choose now, if either?*** **(12 marks)**

   NPV of nursing home with rising real revenue is shown in columns 8, 9, and 10.
   The new NPV of the nursing, home is £626 790 (£3 626 790 – £3 000 000) the residential home NPV stays at £374 053.
   This time choose nursing home as it has the higher NPV.

5. ***What difference does it make if real cash flows are discounted by nominal discount rates as opposed to real discount rates?*** **(4 marks)**

   (Please also see pp. 148–9 of the FINANCE text.)
   If nominal discount rates (the observable ones which include inflation's influence and are therefore higher than the associated real rates) are used with the real cash flows, there will be a bias towards rejecting good projects along with the bad.

6. ***The feasibility and market research reports each incur substantial early costs. What is the appropriate method of treating these costs when calculating the Net Present Value (NPV) of the projects?*** **(4 marks)**

The feasibility and market research reports have been carried out and must be paid for whether the projects go ahead or not. They are SUNK COSTS, and should *not* be included in the cash flow analysis.

7. ***What other investment appraisal techniques might have been used to assess the projects? Which method is to be preferred? Give two reasons for your choice.*** **(9 marks)**
(Total of 55 marks)

Other investment appraisal techniques that may be used are; Internal Rate of Return (IRR), Discounted Payback, Profitability Index (PI), Accounting Rate of Return.

The NPV approach is viewed as more sound than the IRR method because it assumes reinvestment at the cost of capital rather than the project's IRR. IRR cannot cope with negative cash flows (taxes) at the end of projects. Payback period tends to discriminate against long term projects and can exclude projects with a greater NPV. Payback ignores cash flows beyond the payback period.

Accounting rate of return takes no account of the timing of cash flows or the size and life of the investment. Also it is based on accounting profits rather than cash flows.

NPV is the only safe method of ensuring the firm's objective of maximising wealth.

Answer sheet to Case Study: investment appraisal, Question 2

Please enter your own headings for items which are relevant for the calculation of cash flow.

Cash-flow categories	Revenue (1)	Labour costs (2)	Health certificate (3)	Set-up costs (4)	Cash flow (5)	13 % Real discount factor (6)	Real discounted cash flow (7)
1.1.94				3000000		1	
1.1.95	832000	140000	100000		592000	0.884615	523692
1.1.96	832000	140000	100000		592000	0.782544	463266
1.1.97	832000	140000	100000		592000	0.692251	409812
1.1.98	832000	140000	100000		592000	0.612376	362526
1.1.99	832000	140000	100000		592000	0.541717	320696
1.1.00	832000	140000	100000		592000	0.479211	283693
1.1.01	832000	140000	100000		592000	0.423918	250959
1.1.02	832000	140000	100000		592000	0.375004	222002
1.1.03	832000	140000	100000		592000	0.331734	196387
1.1.04	832000	140000	100000		592000	0.293457	173727
	8320000	1400000	1000000		5920000	total	£3206762
						=	£206 762

Cash-flow categories	Revenue (1)	Labour costs (2)	Health certificate (3)	Set-up costs (4)	Cash flow (5)	12 % Real discount factor (6)	Real discounted cash flow (7)
1.1.94				2000000			
1.1.95	546000	94500	30000		421500	0.892241	402847
1.1.96	546000	94500	30000		421500	0.796095	359437
1.1.97	546000	94500	30000		421500	0.710309	320704
1.1.98	546000	94500	30000		421500	0.633767	286146
1.1.99	546000	94500	30000		421500	0.565473	255311
1.1.00	546000	94500	30000		421500	0.504538	227799
1.1.01	546000	94500	30000		421500	0.45017	203252
1.1.02	546000	94500	30000		421500	0.40166	181350
1.1.03	546000	94500	30000		421500	0.358378	161808
1.1.04	546000	94500	30000		421500	0.31956	144371
	5460000	945000	300000		4215000	total	£2374053
						=	£374053

Please enter your own headings for items which are relevant for the calculation of cash flow.

Cash-flow categories	Revenue up by real 2.5% (8)	Adjusted cash flow (9)	Real discounted cash flow (10)	(11)	(12)
1.1.94					
1.1.95	832000	592000	523692		
1.1.96	852800	612800	479543		
1.1.97	874120	634120	438970		
1.1.98	895973	655973	401702		
1.1.99	918372	678372	367486		
1.1.00	941332	701332	33086		
1.1.01	964865	724865	307283		
1.1.02	988987	748987	280873		
1.1.03	1013711	773711	256667		
1.1.04	1039054	799054	234488		
	£9321214	£6921214	£3626790	NPV = £626 790	

Cash-flow categories	Revenue up by real 2% (8)	Adjusted cash flow (9)	Real discounted cash flow (10)	(11)	(12)
1.1.94					
1.1.95					
1.1.96					
1.1.97					
1.1.98					
1.1.99					
1.1.00					
1.1.01					
1.1.02					
1.1.03					
1.1.04					

PRACTICE FINAL EXAMINATION 3 – WITHOUT MCQs

Essay Questions

Question 1 Investment Appraisal at Klossen

Klossen is a fast-growing and highly profitable subsidiary of Lekestuen, a toy company listed on the Stock Exchange. Mr Bamse, the Managing Director of Klossen, has asked the Product Development, Finance and Marketing departments of Lekestuen to collaborate to provide plans for possible new projects Klossen may undertake.

Today, on 31 December 1993, the three departments have just provided Mr Bamse with detailed plans for 9 new projects. The detailed information given to Mr Bamse is reproduced in the table below.

Together with the numerical estimates, the following information was given:

(i) Projects A and C will provide competing products. The Marketing department reports that there will only be a market for **either** project A **or** C, but not for both.

(ii) Project F is a possible addition to project E. Consequently, while project E can be undertaken on its own, project F can only be undertaken if project E is also accepted.

(iii) None of the projects can be delayed until 1995, except project D which can **only** be started in 1995.

The company will not be able to issue additional shares until they receive approval from the shareholders at a General Meeting. The Board of Directors at Lekestuen are confident such an approval will be received at the General Meeting at the end of 1994. As a consequence, while equity capital will be restricted in 1994, there will be no capital restrictions from 1995 onwards.

In addition to the temporary restrictions on equity capital, the Board of Lekestuen does not want to raise additional debt, which would alter the capital structure of the company. As a result, there will be a fixed limit on investments for 1994.

Lekestuen has a beta value of 0.875. The risk-free rate of interest is 5% and the risk premium on the market is 8%. All the new projects Klossen may undertake have the same risk characteristics as Lekestuen's existing activities.

Klossen has been allocated an investment quota of £3.4 million for 1994, none of which has been allocated yet. In 1995 they will receive sufficient capital to be able to finance all profitable investments.

Please ignore taxation in the analysis.

Possible New Projects for Klossen

Start of period Net Cash Flows in £1000

Year	*1994*	*1995*	*1996*	*1997*	*1998*	*1999*
Project						
A	(1 000)	(200)	100	400	800	1 500
B	(200)	100	100	100	100	
C	(1 700)	720	720	720	720	720
D		(2 000)	600	700	800	900
E	(1 000)	250	250	250	250	250
F	100	400	400	400	(650)	
G	(2 700)	1 100	1 100	1 100	1 200	1 300
H	(700)	420	420	420		
I	(600)	300	300	300	300	300

(Negative cashflows in brackets)

NB For all the questions, please show your workings. No marks will be awarded for a numerical answer without any explanation of what data you have used in the calculation.

Required:

1. ***Calculate the appropriate cost of capital for Klossen.*** **(8 marks)**

As the new projects are in the same line of business and carry the same risk characteristics as Lekestuen's existing projects, the Capital Asset Pricing Model can be used to calculate the cost of capital as follows:

$R_i = R_f + ß_i(R_m - R_f)$

We are told that the risk-free interest rate is 5%, ß is 0.875 and the risk premium ($R_m - R_f$) is 8%. R_i, or the cost of capital, is therefore 12%.

2. ***Which measure of the desirability of the investments should Klossen use in selecting which projects to undertake? Why?*** **(5 marks)**

For a further discussion of Company Investment Analysis, please refer to Chapter 6 of the text.

When unlimited funds are available, all projects with a positive NPV should be selected. Here, however, the funds for 1994 are restricted to £3.4 million. We therefore have to make sure that we obtain maximum NPV from the limited funds available. Rather than using the NPV directly, we should use the Profitability Index (PI).

"The PI is the ratio of the cumulated present values of future cash flows (the numerator which sums from time 1 forward) to the present cash flow (the denominator, which is the time 0 or present cash flow) of an investment."

Projects with a PI above 1 will have a positive NPV and are therefore acceptable. Projects should be selected in descending order on the basis of the PI until the whole investment quota is filled, or until there are no more +NPV projects.

Please note that the profitability index should only be used where the cash flow today is a net outlay. One should therefore not calculate the PI of Project F. However, Project F is an addition to Project E, and these projects can therefore be evaluated together. Project EF has the following net cash flows:

1994	(900)
1995	650
1996	650
1997	650
1998	(400)
1999	250

As the initial cash flow is negative, the Profitability Index can now be calculated to be 1.610. Also note that the profitability index is not applicable to Project D. The first cash flow of this project is in one years time, **after** the end of the capital rationing. As this project has a positive NPV (of £210), it should be selected.

3. ***Following the answer to Question 2 above, please calculate this measure for each of the projects.*** **(15 marks)**

The profitability index of Project A can be calculated as the sum of

$$\frac{(-200)}{1.12} + \frac{100}{(1.12)^2} + \frac{400}{(1.12)^3} + \frac{800}{(1.12)^4} + \frac{1\,500}{(1.12)^5} = 1\,545$$

divided by minus the initial cash outflow (–1 000). The PI of Project A is thus 1 545/–(–1 000) = 1.545.

The PI can be calculated in a similar way for the other projects to give the following PI values:

Project	*PI*	*NPV*
A	1.545	545
B	1.519	104
C	1.527	895
D	*	210
E	0.901	(99)
F	*	648
EF	1.610	549
G	1.534	1 442
H	1.441	309
I	1.802	481

4. ***Which projects should Klossen undertake? What would be the total NPV of the chosen projects?*** **(10 marks)**

The most desirable project is Project D, as this project has a positive NPV but no cash outflow in 1994.

Projects should then be selected in descending order of PI, starting with project I with a PI of 1.802. This takes up £0.6 million of the investment quota, leaving £2.8 million to be allocated.

While Project E has a negative NPV, combined with Project F the NPV is positive, and the PI is 1.61. This is the next highest PI, and these two projects should therefore be selected. Combined, these two projects take up £0.9 million in 1994, leaving £1.9 million to be allocated.

Project A has a PI of 1.545, and should be selected next. Please note that Project C can then not be selected, as Projects A and C are mutually exclusive. Project A takes up £1 million of capital, leaving £0.9 million of the investment quota.

Project G has the next highest PI, but his project has an initial cash outflow of £2.7 million, way in excess of the available quota. This project should therefore not be selected.

Project B has a PI of 1.519, with a capital outlay at C_0 of £0.2 million, leaving £0.7 million investment capital. Lastly, Project H with a PI of 1.441 should be selected, and this fills the investment quota of £3.4 million.

To summarize, using PI, projects D, I, E, F, A, B and H should be selected, giving a total NPV of £2 198 000. This solution has been accepted.

It should be noted, however, that when you have to skip some high PI projects (either due to insufficient capital being available or projects being mutually exclusive), relying blindly on the PI solution may cause problems. In this instance, we have rejected Project C as A had a higher PI. Would it be better after all to include Project C instead of A? Projects A (high PI) and H (low PI) together require £1.7 million of investment, and produce a combined NPV of £545.4 + 308.8 = £854,200. Project C on its own (medium PI) also requires £1.7 million investment, but produces a NPV of 895 400. Thus, by replacing Projects A and H by Project C, the total NPV can be increased by £41 200; from £2 198 000 to £2 239 200. The optimum solution is thus projects D, I, E, F, B and C.

5. ***If the Board of Directors of Lekestuen could be persuaded to change the allocation of resources so that Klossen's investment quota for 1994 was increased to £3.8 million, what would be the optimum solution? What would be the total NPV of the selected projects?***

(9 marks)
(Total 47 marks)

If the investment quota rise to £3.8 million, the process of selecting the best projects becomes slightly more complicated. One would again start with Project D, as this project requires no capital in 1994. Following the same procedure as in 4 above, one would select the projects as follows:

Project	PI	C_0	Remaining Investment Quota	NPV
D	*	0	3 800	210
I	1.802	(600)	3 200	481
E+F	1.610	(900)	2 300	549
A	1.545	(1 000)	1 300	545

The next highest PI is Project G, but again we do not have sufficient funds to undertake this project. One alterative would be to undertake Projects B and H (or replacing A and H by C), leaving the solution and the total NPV unaltered from Question 4. This, however, leaves £0.4 million of the investment quota unused. Would the total NPV rise by including the large Project G even if we have to reject some of the smaller projects with higher PI ratios?

Having already selected Projects D, I, E, F and A, we are £1.4 million short if we want to include Project G. Deciding which projects to abandon is a process of trial and error. If we include Project B and G rather than Project I and A, the total NPV would be:

D E F B G
210 + (99) + 648 + 104 + 1 441 = £2 304 700

Consequently, excluding Projects I and A, and including Projects B and G instead, the total NPV will increase by £65 500 from £2 239 200 to £2 304 700.

Question 2

PART 1: ARBITRAGE

(a) ***Please explain what is meant by the "arbitrage principle" (also referred to as "the law of one price").*** **(5 marks)**

The process of arbitrage is related to the law of one price; the same asset cannot be priced differently in two different markets. The process of arbitrage is discussed in several parts of the text, most fully in Section 9.3.1. Arbitrage and Prices – A Digression. Arbitrage can be defined as follows:

"Arbitrage. A process whereby an investor buys and sells securities and adjusts his financing arrangements so as to take advantage of market inequalities in risk and return. It is the main mechanism whereby the market is brought into an equilibrium where the returns on securities are commensurate with the risk attaching to them. Arbitrage may be found in markets other than that for securities, e.g. the commodity market or the foreign currency market."

BROCKINGTON, R., (1986). *A Concise Dictionary of Accounting and Finance*, M&E Professional Dictionaries, Pitman Publishing Ltd.

(b) ***Using brief examples, please explain how the principle of arbitrage applies to the following areas of financial theory:***

(i) ***Miller and Modigliani's discussion of Company Capital Structure.*** **(8 marks)**

For a full discussion, of capital structure theories and arbitrage, please refer to Section 9.3 of the main text and the example of the two companies Geared and Ungeared.

In their 1958 article, Modigliani and Miller argued that in a perfect capital market (where there are no information asymmetries, no transactions costs, no taxation, and where both companies and individuals can borrow and lend at the same risk free rate of interest), company capital structure is irrelevant. If two companies are identical in every respect apart from its capital structure, the total value (debt + equity) of the two companies must be identical (the debt reduces the value of the shares). Otherwise, arbitrage will take place whereby shares in the overvalued company is sold to acquire shares in the undervalued company until the total value (debt + equity) of the two companies is identical. As individuals can borrow themselves, they will not be prepared to pay a premium to companies that borrow - there is a "home made" alternative.

As stated in the text (page 222), "Arbitrage is a transaction wherein an instantaneous risk-free profit is made . . . Arbitrage opportunities cannot be expected to exist for any significant time in a market with well-informed investors. Market prices must adjust to cause all equivalent future cash flows sold in whatever form as single securities or as portfolios of holdings, to sell for the same price."

Even in real capital markets where transactions costs, taxation and different borrowing costs are present, the process of arbitrage is important in ensuring that price anomalies in the market are corrected.

(ii) ***The Purchasing Power Parity Theory of Foreign Exchange Rates.*** **(8 marks)**
(Total 21 marks)

This point is clearly spelled out in the introduction to Section 11.2.1 Exchange Rates and the Law of One Price:

*"How do exchange rates come to bear the relationship to each other that they do? The answer is something called **the law of one price**, or its generalisation, **purchasing power parity**. These related ideas are quite straightforward. They say simply that the same thing cannot sell for different prices at the same time. This is nothing more than our old ally, the assumption that in free markets arbitrage opportunities cannot long exist."*

In other words, if the price of products varies widely between countries, arbitrage will take place whereby the product is bought in the market where it is cheap and sold where it fetches a higher price, until the price in the two different markets is the same.

It should be noted that in practice, however, a number of restriction to free trade (e.g. transaction and transportation costs, taxation, tariffs and quotas), interfere with the free flow of goods (services are often even more difficult to export). This makes purchasing-power parity a poor explanation for short-term exchange rate movements. Many researchers still believe the Purchasing Power Parity theory holds, although it may take several years for prices to fully adjust.

PART II: OPTION PRICING THEORY

(a) ***According to the Black–Scholes option pricing theory, the value of an option is determined by 5 factors.***

(i) ***What are the five factors that determine the value of a call option?*** **(7 marks)**

(ii) ***How do these factors influence the value of a call option, and in what circumstances?*** **(10 marks)**

According to the Black–Scholes option pricing model, option prices are determined by 5 factors, which for a call option are as follows:

The *higher* the **exercise price**, the *lower* the value of the call option, as the share price has to rise more before the option becomes "in the money". The higher the exercise price, the more you have to pay if you exercise your option.

The *higher* the **current market price of the share** (in relation to the exercise price), the *higher* the value of the call option. The higher the share price has risen, the more valuable the right to buy the shares at a fixed price.

The *higher* the **volatility** of the share, the higher the possibility that the share price will rise above the exercise price. Thus the *higher* the volatility of the underlying share, the *higher* the value of the call option.

The value of a call option is *higher* for options with a *long* (or higher) **time to maturity**. As was the case with volatility, the longer the duration of a call option, the higher the possibility that the share price will rise sufficiently to make the option "in the money" and thus worth exercising.

Lastly, the *higher* the **risk free interest rate**, the *higher* the value of a call option. By buying a call (rather than the shares), you are paying a fraction of the full cost of the share. The cash currently saved can be invested in the market gaining interest. The higher the interest rate, the greater the benefit of deferring the full payment.

(b) ***From both the purchaser and seller's point of view, what are the main differences between a call option and a futures contract to buy shares?*** **(7 marks)**

The main difference between an option and a futures contract, is that the purchaser of a futures contract is forced to complete the transaction even if completion is to the detriment of the purchaser, for example, if the shares could be purchased more cheaply in the open market. The holder of a call option would not be required to completed the transaction.

The potential loss to a purchaser of a call option is limited to what she/he paid for the option. If she/he enters into a futures contract to buy shares, the potential loss is larger; if the shares become worthless, she/he has to pay the contracted amount for each share.

There are also important differences between futures and options contracts from the seller's (or what is known as the "writer's") point of view. Writing an option, the maximum profit the seller can make is what she/he receives from selling the options. The buyer will not exercise the option if the value of the shares is lower than the exercise price. The potential loss is unlimited (as the value of the underlying asset may rise infinitely above the exercise price).

When selling a futures contract, the potential gain is restricted to the contracted delivery price (if the underlying asset becomes worthless). The potential loss is still unlimited.

(c) ***With regard to option pricing, what is meant by the terms "in the money" and "out of the money"?*** **(4 marks)**

A call option is said to be "out of the money" if the current value of the underlying asset (the asset on which the option contract is written, e.g. company shares) is below the striking or exercise price. An option being out of the money on expiry will be worthless (but as explained below, will usually have positive value prior to expiry). For a put option the reverse will be the case; the option is out of the money if the current value of the underlying asset is above the exercise price.

A call option will be "in the money" if the current value of the underlying asset is above the exercise price.

(d) ***Why is the value of an "out of the money" option likely to be above zero?*** **(4 marks)**

(Total of 32 marks)

The value of an option can never be negative. As was pointed out under Question (b) above, the owner of an option is not obliged to exercise the option. Thus, if the value of the underlying asset is lower than the strike price on expiry of the option, the option will not be exercised – it will be worthless. However, prior to expiry, there is a chance, however small, that the value of the underlying asset will rise above the exercise price, thus making it beneficial to exercise the option. The more volatile the underlying asset, the higher the probability that the price will move sufficiently to make an out of the money option become in the money.

The only time the option will be worthless prior to expiry, is if the share price falls to zero. The share price will only fall to zero if there is no possibility of the share ever becoming worth anything again (otherwise the share would still be worth something). If the share price can never rise above zero, the call option will be worthless. However, if the share price is above zero, the option will be worth something.

Marketing

PRACTICE FINAL EXAMINATION 1

Case Studies

Answer all 3 questions.

Marks for individual parts of the question are shown in the questions.

Total marks for paper = 100

The pass mark is 50%

Case Studies

Case Study A: The World Class Shipping Company

The World Class Shipping Company served the North Atlantic trade through containerization. It was one of the first companies to provide door-to-door service versus the then traditional port-to-port approach. World Class provided a variety of special equipment, advised about the least expensive and fastest land routings, and even offered a fast customs clearance service. Its sophisticated communications system made it possible to have a high-quality approach to problems posed by shippers, forwarders, and consignees. These services coupled with convenience and dependable sailing schedules had made World Class a highly successful company which held the leading market share for both the east and west-bound North Atlantic containerized trades. Corporate headquarters were located in New York and corporate staff directed the company's marketing activities through offices located in the US, Canada, the UK and Europe.

Germany was the largest European exporter to the US and the second largest importer from there. Regularly scheduled container ships carried over half the German North Atlantic cargo tonnage to and from the States and Canada. Most companies used more than one line to balance risks. Typically, less than 100 shippers provided more than half the volume of a shipping line. If a shipper sold ex-works, either the consignee asked for a particular line or the cargo was turned over to a forwarder. When goods were sold on a CIF (cost, insurance, and freight included, port of destination) basis, then shippers were more involved. Only about 25 per cent of shipments were done on a CIF basis and, thus, forwarders were important in dealing with the shipping lines. About 15–20 forwarders dominated the German market and handled an estimated 50 per cent of all shipments on a tonnage basis.

World Class marketed containers and RORO (roll-on, roll-off) space in Germany. Its market share there was about 14 per cent west-bound versus 22 per cent east-bound, both substantially less than from other areas because a small number of competitors dominated the market. The company's two major competitors were a German carrier with some 40 per cent share west-bound and an American company with about a 25 per cent west-bound share. World Class and its two major competitors all had essentially the same frequency of sailings and transit times and called at the same European and US ports. Only World Class offered a RORO service.

The Company's major sales effort in Germany was handled by the Werther Agency which was paid a commission of 2.5 per cent of sales. This Agency represented 14 other lines, all of which were conventional, non-containerized lines, most of which did not serve the North Atlantic. The agency employed 15 on-the-road salesmen who sold the services of all lines represented by Werther. They called mainly on traffic managers and occasionally on the large freight forwarders. They did as much work as possible by phone.

In recent years the German office had been under pressure to increase sales, decrease expenses, and increase profits – but little progress had been made along these lines. For the most part, company management had relied on members of its German office staff to call upon large accounts. Company executives were concerned about the reaction of forwarders to any increased attention to large accounts.

1. Why does failure to penetrate the German market have the long-term possibility of weakening the company's overall competitive viability? **(25 marks)**
2. How would you segment the German market, including that concerned with "terms of sale"?) **(15 marks)**
3. What, if any, action should the company take regarding the Werther Agency? **(10 marks)**

Case Study B: The Eubank Company

The Eubank Company was founded to exploit commercially a new technology which by changing the crystalline structure of metals generated a "new" set of alloys. The company had developed many novel products and applications ranging from ball bearings to top-secret materials for defence contracts. The company's average annual growth rate had been in excess of 30 per cent. All company products were developed through its own research efforts. The major product lines were concerned with electrical wiring, tubing, castings, and cables. Sales were about $20 million annually which were sold to a wide variety of users, although the 20 largest customers accounted for about one-third of all sales.

A single manufacturing facility took care of the company's production needs. Conflict, therefore, often took place since, for example, the plant might be asked to produce different alloys for two customers on an urgent basis. When this happened, manufacturing would be asked to work overtime. In a similar situation, if R&D time was needed to design a new application for a customer with perhaps a significant potential, then R&D would set aside less pressing projects.

Eubank had originally handled its sales through manufacturers' representatives. Rapid expansion had made a direct sales force expedient, and 3 regional offices and 14 branch sales offices were opened which in total employed 38 salespersons.

The company had an informal organizational structure. From its inception Eubank had been run as a small operation by a close-knit group of top managers, most of whom were engineers. In addition to the president, there were managers in charge of manufacturing, R&D, marketing and sales, finance, and each of the product groups. Management assignments involving different areas of responsibility were frequent – territorial imperatives were held to a minimum. The emphasis was on informality, willingness to change, experimentation and mutual decision-making.

The company's president had over the past year become increasingly concerned about his organizational structure, and especially so, given the anticipated rapid increase in sales and new products. He, therefore, hired a consultant and directed him to study the situation and recommend what type of organization was needed.

1. Describe the various alternative types of organizational structures and, in the process, indicate the conditions under which each would be best suited as well as their strengths and weaknesses. **(20 marks)**
2. Which type of organizational structure should Eubank adopt? Why? **(5 marks)**

Case Study C: Universal Products

The Universal Products Company of Birmingham, UK, produced a line of industrial chemicals, adhesives, detergents, and cosmetics with detergents representing about half its total revenues. Some company brands of household detergents had been sold successfully for a long time, while others had been modified or dropped as market conditions changed. New products were very important in the industry and were constantly being developed by the company. The established policy for a new consumer product was for it to obtain a 15 per cent share of the British market one year after introduction. In an effort to ensure the success of its new products, this company thoroughly tested the product concepts involved and the physical product itself. It also believed strongly in the use of test markets.

The company's labs had recently developed a new liquid all-purpose household cleaner (APCH) which contained a different chemical mix than competing products now on the market. This "mix" enabled the new product to perform "better" in laboratory tests against leading APCH brands in removing stains in bathrooms and kitchens. The APCH market was growing at an annual rate of 20 per cent and, since the company had no APCH entry, it was important that the new product prove successful.

Preliminary marketing research had already determined that a need of considerable magnitude existed for this type of new APCH product. Small-scale consumer tests had been used to select the package design (including colours) and a name. These research projects plus the results of its lab tests had convinced the company that the new product did not need to undergo any consumer use tests (e.g. blind paired comparison tests) and should be test-marketed immediately.

1. What is test marketing? What should be the purpose of such a test for Universal's new APCH product? **(5 marks)**
2. Should Universal use a laboratory test market before undertaking a full-scale test-market operation? Before answering this question, describe what such an undertaking is designed to test and how it is carried out. **(15 marks)**
3. What would Universal hope to learn from a full-scale test market? Be specific in terms of what marketing variables should be measured and what information pertaining to these variables should be obtained. **(15 marks)**

Answers to Case Studies

Case Study A: World Class Shipping Company

1. The German market represents a large part of the company's potential market and yet it accounts for only a small percentage of total revenues. Thus, by permitting their large German competitor to gain and hold a very large share of such an important market, it may be setting the stage for the competitor to use its German revenues and cost base to compete more aggressively against World Class in other markets. This is a real possibility, since competition between lines is typically based on a port-to-port basis for both outgoing and incoming shipments. At the very least the east-bound tonnage market segment (US to Europe) would be jeopardized. Think of all the containers that come in from the US that cannot be used for shipments to the US.

2. The market can and should be segmented by end use (type of product shipped) within size account. This would enable the company to take advantage of any special equipment needed (e.g. containers specially lined to hold certain chemicals) including the use of RORO for which the company is the sole supplier. Despite this, the company holds only a 40 per cent share of eastbound automobile shipments and 12 per cent of machinery shipments.

   "Terms of sale" represents a somewhat different type of segmentation. If the consignee pays the cost of shipping from a German port or factory, the consignee selling represents a viable possibility. This is true because the shipper typically turns over the shipment to a forwarder, since this is the easiest thing to do and he has no cost responsibility. Forwarders under such conditions have little incentive to develop the best "house-to-house" routing since they are paid on a commission basis. If the shipper pays the shipping cost, then he is more likely to be interested in the total routing costs. Consignee selection in Germany (the reverse of what was discussed earlier) is another possibility as is selling to freight forwarders.

   Note: Award 5 marks for discussion (listing) of elements other than those concerned with "terms of sale" which is also worth 5 marks.

3. The Werther Agency has few resources to employ in any effort to increase share. Their salesmen have other lines to sell and they do not have the skill to sell major accounts which require a total system's approach including the use of land transport. Such large accounts are relatively few in number and can/should be handled by trained company salesmen who can study the client's needs and develop a transport system which can best service them. The large freight forwarders should be treated as large accounts and targeted by company salesmen who should note that World Class had divested itself of small accounts.

   Note: Award 5 marks for decision to drop Werther and use a sales organization which sells direct to large accounts.

Case Study B: The Eubank Company

1. There are four main types of organizational structure – functional, product, market and matrix. Each is discussed below and each is worth 5 points – 1 for describing it, 2 for stating the conditions under which it is most applicable and 2 for the kind(s) of business strategy they are best suited for.

A *Functional organizational*

This simple and bureaucratic type of organization at the SBU level has each of its functional area managers reporting to the general manager. Within the marketing department managers of such marketing areas as sales, marketing research and advertising report to the vice-president or director of marketing. At each level, the top manager coordinates the activities of all the functional areas reporting to him or her. There is little specialization by product or customer type.

This type of organization is best suited for businesses whose products and markets are similar in nature, few in number and operating in relatively stable environments. They are best suited to low-cost defender SBUs attempting to maximize their efficiency and profitability in mature or declining industries.

B *Product management organizations*

This form of organization requires an additional layer of managers in the marketing department. Each manager has the responsibility to plan and manage the marketing programmes – and to coordinate the activities of other functional departments (especially production) for a specific product or product line.

It is especially appropriate for an SBU which is attempting to serve a relatively complex environment with a large number of product-market entries which are aimed at different market segments (but who may also compete with one another). Because the product management form of organization is less bureaucratic than the functional structure, it is well suited for pursuing differentiated defender and analyser strategies – particularly so if it operates in industries with complex and unstable market and competitive environments.

C *Market management organizations*

Such structures have managers of major individual markets which have different requirements and preferences for the same type of product. Thus, product managers are replaced by market managers responsible for planning and coordinating programmes for one or more products aimed at a particular market segment. This form of organization is best suited to the same kinds of strategies as a product type organization – differentiated defender and analyser.

D *Matrix organizations*

This type of structure brings together two or more different types of specialist within a particular coordination structure. One such type is the product-market form which brings together specialists on the product and specialists on the markets served. Matrix organizations are most appropriate when a business fills an extremely complex and uncertain environment. It is well suited for prospector businesses and managing new-product development within analyser or differentiated defender businesses.

2. Eubank should consider adopting a product type organization at the present time. Longer term it will probably need to think seriously about a product market type of matrix organization. Thus, Eubank should appoint a product manager for each of its four product lines. The product managers would plan the sales and profits (both short- and long-term) for their assigned product line, the development of new products including R&D projects, pricing, and sales efforts. The marketing director would coordinate these plans and assign priorities with respect to the use of the company's

manufacturing facilities and R&D resources. Later, when volume is sufficient, the company can set up SBU structures built around individual product lines which will probably serve several distinct market sectors. These units would be self-contained with their own manufacturing and marketing/sales activities. R&D would probably remain centralized. **(5 marks)**

Case Study C: Universal Products

1. What is test marketing? This is a procedure which seeks to test on a small-scale basis the commercial viability of a marketing plan for a new or modified product. What should be the purpose of such a test for Universal's new APCH product? Its purpose should be not to test the new product *per se* but to estimate the sales and profitability potentials for the new product *and* to identify and correct problems with the marketing plan and the product itself before its full-scale introduction.

   Note: Of the 5 points, award 2 for the definition of test-marketing and 3 for a discussion of its purpose.

2. Should Universal use a laboratory test-market before undertaking a full-scale test-marketing operation? Before answering this question, describe what such an undertaking is designed to test and how it is carried out.

   Note: Of the 10 points available, award 2 for describing what a lab test is, 4 for how it is carried out, and 4 for your decision as to whether to use such a test.

   A laboratory test market (often referred to as pretest market research) is designed primarily to measure the process by which a consumer adopts a new product – i.e. the three major steps of awareness, trial and repeat buying.

   Typically, the procedure consists of having respondents, who are thought to be representative of the target audience, view commercials about the new product which are imbedded in a TV programme. They then are given the option of buying the product in a simulated store which is also stocked with competing brands. Respondents take the purchased product home and those who bought the test-product are interviewed later to determine their extent of satisfaction (including preference over their regular brand) and repurchase intentions. Respondents are often given the chance to repurchase the test brand (using their own money), which is then delivered to them.

   Since the company knows very little about the adoption process for their new product, and especially so in connection with how a given TV commercial can impact awareness and trial, it should take a lab test. In particular it needs to know whether the way the product is presented in the commercial sufficiently differentiates it from competitive brands and whether the product lives up to its claims in actual use.

3. What would Universal hope to learn from a full-scale test-market? Much depends here on how much confidence management has in its proposed national marketing plan. If management is concerned about its trade offer, then it should include provisions for testing alternative trade offers in the test market research.

   The ultimate objective of any test market is to obtain an estimate of sales for the first year of national operation as per some level of promotional expenditure. In addition, the research should attempt to measure the following:

A *Advertising effectiveness*
The need here is to determine the rate at which target consumers become aware of the new product, the amount of time they retain the message, and their degree of knowledge about the product's characteristics.

B *Effectiveness of an introductory offer*
Research should gather information concerning whether they know about the offer and whether they took advantage of it.

C *Effectiveness of trade offer*
This information can be provided by the sales force who can report on any difficulties experienced in getting cooperation from the trade.

D *Share of total market*
This requires the research to obtain volume data for the new product, competing brands, and the product class or type in either or both dollars and units. It is important to know whether total sales are increased or whether the new product's sales derive solely from those of other brands.

E *Characteristics of buyers, rate of adoption, and repeat-purchase rates.*

F *Reasons for failing to adopt the new product or for discontinuing it.*

Note: Of the 10 marks available, award 2 marks for mentioning the need to estimate the sales and profits to be derived from the new product in the first year, 2 each for E and F above, and 1 each for A–D above.

PRACTICE FINAL EXAMINATION 2

Case Studies

Case Study 1

The world's watch makers are coping well with the recession. No large company has gone out of business and global production rose in 1991. In most Western countries, consumers now take much more trouble over the choice of their watches than they did. The arrival of the Swiss plastic Swatch 10 years ago (over 100 million had been produced by May 1992) provided the catalyst for change and led to watches attracting much more attention. Top quality gold watches have been more successful than most fashion items in the recessionary conditions, so much so that some manufacturers have waiting lists of years for their most prized pieces.

By comparison Hong Kong has produced large numbers of watches over the past 10 to 15 years, but these have been mainly digital and the market for those is falling.

A potential new watch giant is, however, starting to flex its muscles in India. Titan Watch opened in 1985 and by the end of 1991 Titan had well over 60% of the Indian Quartz watch market. It planned to enter the UK and French markets by 1993, placing a strong emphasis on design, market research and advertising which will be vital to the establishment of a new brand. These will not be cheap watches but rather a range designed by some of Europe's top designers.

What advice would you as Marketing consultant give the Marketing Manager for Swatch Watches to help him (or her) to prepare for this potent threat? **(30 marks)**

1. Undertake Political, Economic, Social and Technological environment (PEST) analysis for the industry (and assess the repercussions for Swatch watches).
2. Undertake Strengths, Weaknesses, Opportunities and Threats (SWOT) analysis for Swatch watches (especially concentrating on competitor analysis).
3. Outline possible strategy alternatives for Swatch watches:
   - Fortress defence
   - Confrontation
   - Flanker
   - Differentiated defender.
4. In the light of (1) and (2) above make recommendations of favoured strategies to follow.
5. Undertake marketing research to monitor potential and actual customer demand.
6. Develop the marketing mix components to support the favoured strategies selected in (4) above. Discuss the recommended nature of the marketing mix components; that is, the appropriate product characteristics, pricing policies, promotional mix and supporting channels of distribution.
7. Indicate the resources likely to be available for your recommendations in terms of finance, time scale and human resources.

Case Study 2

Soft drinks sales in the UK in 1991 exceeded £5 000 million. The UK is the largest market for soft drinks, with the average Briton drinking 400 cans a year. The market has been boosted by low-calorie products, which now account for almost a third of total sales. Britons consumed

Million litres of soft drinks

1989	7 100
1990	7 600
1991	7 900 (estimated)

(*Source*: Euromonitor, 1990, Soft drinks: the international market)

Assume you are the Marketing Manager of a major soft drinks producing firm. A new soft drink is to be introduced.

Prepare a Marketing Research Plan to ensure minimum risk for the introduction of the new product. Mention should be made of the sources of information that you might use. **(30 marks)**

1. Define the problem. Set the objectives of the Marketing Research Plan (to determine most favoured new product).

2. Outline the specifications for implementing the plan. These should include:
   - financial resources (how much will be spent on the proposed marketing research?);
   - time scale (how long will the marketing research take?);
   - staffing (who will undertake the marketing research: own staff or outside marketing research agency staff, or combination of both?).

   What controls will be used to monitor the progress of the proposed marketing research?

3. Outline marketing research methodology:
   - desk research
   - field research

   Qualitative techniques:
   group discussions
   in-depth, focused personal interviews.

   Quantitative techniques:
   surveys using personal face-to-face interviewing, telephone interviewing and/or postal surveys.

   hall tests
   test marketing
   mini-van testing.

Essay Question

How far do the promotional methods used for mass consumer market products differ from those for industrial products?

Discuss. **(40 marks)**

Definition of promotional methods/techniques:

- advertising
- sales promotion
- personal selling
- public relations.

Definition of mass consumer markets.

Definition of industrial markets.

Application of use of promotional methods to each type of product market.

Use of examples to support discussion given credit.

PRACTICE FINAL EXAMINATION 3

Questions

Question 1

The international toy industry, worth an estimated US $30 000 million per annum at producers' prices, is one of the world's fastest changing industries, with novelty an important selling point.

Consider a major toy manufacturer based in Europe with sales around US $1 000 million per annum. Presently it sells through a combination of conventional sales force direct to supply chain intermediaries (wholesalers, cash and carry operators, retailers) and, if appropriate, through sales agents' networks.

The Sales Manager has brought in a consultant to review present sales operations. You, as the consultant, are asked to recommend areas that should be considered to improve control of the overall selling, activity. These could include:

- sales organization
- control
- motivation, and
- remuneration. **(30 marks)**

Solution

Consultant's review of present sales operations

The consultant should start by examining the toy manufacturer's sales trends over the last five years. This is likely to involve an assessment of total sales, in terms of actual sales and profits achieved, broken down by region or district, by type of outlet, by product group and any other relevant segmentation category.

This analysis will enable the consultant to examine the effectiveness of the present sales organization, to assess if, and where, restructuring should occur in the future.

The sales organization could be based upon a number of different sales methods which could be: exports direct from European base to US retailer and/or end user US sales agents, distributors or sales force. These will be selling to wholesaler/independents, cash and carry operators, retailers, or perhaps, by direct mail order to the end consumer.

Close examination of sales trends would enable the consultant to determine which sales methods and/or channels of distribution are most effective. It is possible that a combination of sales methods and channels of distribution will be required to be used.

Critical areas which also should be examined by the consultant include sales organization control methods, motivation of persons in the sales organization and the methods of remuneration of those persons involved.

Control methods would include sales planning, sales organization reporting methods (including salesmen's reports) which should be linked into the firm's Marketing Information System and monitoring sale organization performance (e.g. number of sales calls achieved, frequency of sales calls, repeat business achieved, etc.).

Motivation and remuneration are likely to be closely linked. Remuneration can be by commission only (probably used for sales agents), salary and commission, or salary only. It is likely that sales agents will be on commission only, while distributors may well have salary and commission arrangements (as do many conventional sales force people). In some instances salary only arrangements will be used.

Question 2

In the US disposable nappies account for about 85% of all nappy sales, which amount to approximately US $3 500 million (£1 850 million) per annum. Procter and Gamble sales of its brands "Luvs" and "Pampers" had worldwide sales of US $4 320 million in 1990. However, environmentalists are concerned at the impact of disposing of these nappies.

A major nappy manufacturer wishes to develop a nappy to meet the criticisms targeted at traditional disposable nappies.

Outline a Marketing Research plan to ensure that the product development takes into account the concerns of market influencers that determine market demand. Some comment regarding cost and time should be made. **(30 marks)**

Solution

Marketing Research plan

Objectives of the plan should be defined. These could be centred around the need to develop a new product, an environmentally friendly disposable nappy to meet the criticism of products presently on the market This new product has to meet the demand of the present customers, and, if possible, also enlarge the market to include other potential customers not presently customers for the established product.

Resources
The controls should be discussed in terms of:

- finance
- time scale
- persons to be involved (internal and external to the firm).

Finance is difficult to assess, but for the analysis of secondary sources, the research into product image (qualitative and quantitative) and the test marketing, finance in excess of £500 000 might well be required.

Time scale might be for a Marketing Research plan for 1 to 2 years ahead, say.

Persons to be involved could include internal Marketing Research staff, together with those from a Marketing Research Agency.

Research methodology

Desk research (using secondary sources)
Using the Marketing Information System (MIS) within the firm, the sales trends for the present nappy market should be assessed and analysed. For example, how many are sold? where? by whom? What type of nappy? What is the sales trend for disposable and conventional nappies? What are the profit margins involved? Who are the major suppliers/

competitors in the market? What new product development is presently being conducted by the competitors in the market? What is the nature of customer demand? Is there really a strong demand for the environmentally friendly product? Will potential customers be prepared to pay a premium price for such a product?

Field research

Once initial desk research has been completed it would probably be appropriate to undertake some qualitative research to attempt to determine the precise nature of the demand for the environmentally friendly nappies. This could be undertaken by a series of group discussions with targeted user groups and/or in-depth interviews with potential customers and "experts" in the market.

This would be followed by quantitative research to establish the demand for the product in quantitative terms, i.e. how many persons are likely to purchase the proposed new product?

The methods used to collect this information would probably be by surveys undertaken through face-to-face personal interviews, telephone interview or, perhaps, postal survey.

After the background market data was obtained through the above field research techniques, and assuming that the suitable product has been developed by the Research and Development section, it is likely that the proposed new product will require to be test marketed to establish its viability in "a miniature sample" of the total population.

This would involve selecting the appropriate test region, TV area, shops to enable the test market to take place. If finance allowed, it might be appropriate to use two, or even, three comparable "markets".

The test should have a duration that would allow the test product to be purchased not only by first time buyers, but also by repeat buyers (perhaps allowing at least three repeat purchases). Thus it may well have to last at least three months, and perhaps, up to six months.

At this stage the firm will have to decide whether to proceed with the full commercialization of the new product on a national basis, or whether to abandon the proposed new product. It is anticipated that this will be towards the end of two years of the Marketing Research programme.

Question 3

What do you consider to be the main differences between consumer and industrial markets?

How would you expect the management of the marketing mix to reflect these differences?

(40 marks)
(Total of 100 marks)

Solution

Main differences between consumer and industrial markets

Consumer markets tend to service large populations (e.g. number of UK households is approximately 25 million) with products of relatively low individual prices and levels of sophistication. The end-user/consumer is normally the purchaser, using his/her own money. Manufacturers or service suppliers can not usually target directly each potential customer, but rather have to provide the product or service through a series of intermediaries, thus, the typical product, say baked beans, would be supplied to the end-user via the distributor – jobber – retailer. The supply chain would be likely to be:

Manufacturer – Wholesaler – Jobber – Retailer – End-user (consumer).

Industrial markets tend to serve relatively small numbers of customers with products and services of high individual price values and levels of sophistication (e.g. fork lift trucks). The end-user/consumer is not usually using his/her own personal money to purchase the product, but rather is using money "belonging" to the corporate entity. There are usually few intermediaries between the manufacturer/service supplier and the end-user, i.e. the supply chain is typically: Manufacturer – End-user.

The marketing mix components are:

- Product characteristics
- Pricing methods
- Promotional methods
- (Place) Channels of distribution.

Consumer market marketing mix components
Products and services for the consumer market tend to be relatively low technology and do not require the end-user/consumer to be technically well qualified.

Pricing strategies will target market penetration or market skimming. Prices will be relatively low per unit and much research will be undertaken to track successful price levels, using psychological and sociological consumer behaviour research.

Promotional methods will seek to compensate for the relatively large number of intermediaries between the supplier and end-consumer. It will seek to influence the end-user consumer behaviour pattern to help the selling activities of the intermediaries. It will be targeted at the mass consumer market. Media used will, for "above the line" promotion, primarily be TV, radio, cinema and posters. Sometimes direct mail will be used. "Below the line" promotional methods would include coupons with money off benefits, give-a-way goods, competitions, etc.

Channels of distribution will primarily be the retailer in its various guises supported by wholesalers and jobbers if appropriate; increasingly, these latter activities are being subsumed into the role of the retailers.

Industrial markets marketing mix components. These, by contrast to those for consumer markets, are geared towards the needs of the more sophisticated, more technologically aware end-user.

Product characteristics are usually highly sophisticated, frequently one-off specialist products which may well have been developed in conjunction with the end-user. The latest technological development may well be incorporated.

Pricing strategies will be tending towards a long term relationship with the potential and actual customer. They are frequently based on "cost-plus" assessments, and may well include being linked to the manufacturer helping to raise the desired levels of credit/loans etc., through the financial institutions. Sometimes contract bidding is used to establish price. There may be considerable room for negotiation regarding the nature and final pricing package agreed.

Promotional methods are targeted towards a limited number of end-users. The "above the line" promotion is likely to be targeted towards trade press/journals, although some corporate advertising may take place on TV. They will tend to be less "extravagant" in expenditure than for consumer markets "Below the line" promotion will concentrate on literature materials, exhibition attendance and support of trade/research seminar, etc.

Channels of distribution will primarily be direct to the end-user; extended supply chains are seldom appropriate.

Conclusion
Markets are becoming less obviously differentiated and frequently are moving closer together.

Organisational Behaviour

The Organisational Behaviour examination is in 3 sections

A True/False Questions
B Multiple Choice Questions
C Essay/Problem Questions

Section A – True/False Questions
35 questions each worth 1 point. Total points available in Section A — $35 \times 1 = 35$

Section B – Multiple Choice Questions
30 questions each worth 1 point. Total points available in Section B — $30 \times 1 = 30$

Section C – Essay/Problem Questions
3 questions each worth 70 points. Total points available in Section C — $3 \times 70 = 210$
Total points available for examination — $= 275$
Pass mark = 50% of 275 — $= 137$

PRACTICE FINAL EXAMINATION 1

Section A: True/False Questions

Answers to all questions follow examination.
Each question is worth one point.

1. Increases in capital intensity per employee are accompanied by decreases in the importance of employee's needs in the organization.
2. An employee with an external locus of control believes that he could influence the work rules in his organization.
3. Employees who continually test the limits of authority and argue for changes in work rules in highly structured work circumstances would possess characteristics which illustrate the Machiavellian Personality.
4. The manager with a high need for achievement will generally delegate authority to his subordinates because he has confidence that they will successfully perform the task at hand.
5. In employees' early career stages, job satisfaction is less important than organizational commitment as a determinant of the desire to leave the job.
6. The motivator-hygiene theory predicts that absenteeism is greater when employees believe that work hygienes are sufficient but job motivators are absent.
7. Performance on the job and satisfaction with supervision are both examples of first level outcomes in the expectancy theory of work motivation.

8. Behavioural shaping is evident when a supervisor only praises his employees when they perform a new task correctly the first time they attempt it.
9. Behaviour modification programmes are generally most effective when management takes full responsibility for developing them without significant input from employees.
10. A meaningful and valid performance appraisal system should increase employees' expectancies and instrumentalities regarding performance and rewards.
11. The level of employee goal achievement will be higher when goals for employee development are set participatively.
12. When organizational rewards are distributed on the basis of seniority, the instrumentalities for performance–reward outcomes among new employees will deteriorate.
13. A gainsharing programme could continue to provide employee bonuses during periods of declining sales and inventory build up.
14. Herzberg's job design principles suggest that employees should have more authority for determining work methods.
15. Task significance, task identity and skill variety are elements of job depth.
16. Employees with low growth need strength who perceive limited core job dimensions would respond favourably to a job enrichment programme conducted by their employer.
17. Enriching the work of a team of employees can follow the same principles as enriching the jobs of individual employees.
18. A highly cohesive work group will be productive when its norms coincide with the organizations specifications for effective group performance.
19. Only highly cohesive work groups experience the symptoms of groupthink.
20. In general, process losses are greater in newly formed heterogeneous work groups which are not cohesive than in seasoned, homogeneous work groups which are very cohesive.
21. The nominal group technique works best in groups which have been operating for a long period of time.
22. Reward and referent power are both related to the levels of job satisfaction and cohesiveness in a work group.
23. In general, the decisional roles for managers are more important than the interpersonal and informational roles.
24. Fiedler's contingency theory of leadership specifies that there is a "one best way', to be an effective leader.
25. It is easier for a leader to change situational favourableness than it is for him to change his orientation towards his least preferred co-worker.
26. When a manager is selecting a product divisional arrangement instead of a functional arrangement, he is performing organizational design.

27. It would be fair to say that job enrichment would have the biggest impact on the departmentalization aspect of organizational design.

28. The matrix design requires excellent management information systems to provide a balanced focus on project activities and requirements in functional divisions.

29. Decentralized organizations are more commonly found in business environments which are uncertain and dynamically changing.

30. When an organization increases its vertical information processing capacity it is centralising its hierarchy.

31. Developing and installing a quality circle programme would increase the vertical information processing capacity in an organization.

32. Extended environment responses to organizational crises consist of such actions as performing unannounced inspections and installing social support groups for employees.

33. Since organizational culture is randomly transmitted from one generation of employees to the next, it is a waste of time and effort to make features of organizational culture a part of the socialization process for new employees.

34. Organizational diagnosis refers to those activities which identify the true causes of malfunctions in the organization.

35. T-group methods present work groups with simulations of effective and in effective group problem solving to uncover ways to make the groups more effective at decision making.

Section B: Multiple Choice Questions

Each question is worth one point.

1. Which of the following components of a manager's job are most often rewarded by the organization?

   A human and conceptual.
   B technical and human.
   C technical and conceptual.
   D organizational and conceptual.

2. Which of the following most improves job satisfaction once basic maintenance needs for employees are satisfied?

   A challenging-demanding jobs.
   B increased clarity in job descriptions.
   C lengthening time delays between performance and feedback about performance.
   D improved employment benefits.

3. Which of the following is most realistic?

   A high job satisfaction causes high job performance.
   B high job performance causes high job satisfaction.

C the relationship between job performance and job satisfaction is mediated by rewards and perceived equity.
D high job performance cannot occur in conjunction with low job satisfaction.

4. Which of the following is correct? Managers can develop organizational commitment by all of the following EXCEPT

A supervising closely and requiring the employee to focus on the task at hand.
B creating work designs which emphasize team-work.
C acknowledging performance with meaningful rewards and prompt performance feedback.
D participatively creating goals which achieve important organizational outcomes and simultaneously develop the employees' skills.

5. Which of the following is correct? A company policy that all employees are given uniforms free of charge which must be worn on the job is a

A motivational factor.
B high-content factor.
C hygiene factor.
D job-centred factor.

6. In the short run, which factor is LEAST related to the need for achievement?

A taking moderate risks in completing the job.
B requesting immediate feedback about performance.
C needing a promotion or a pay rise.
D pursuing meaningful goals at work.

7. Which of the following is correct? Expectancy is:

A a subjective belief that some level of effort on the job will lead to a given level of performance.
B a subjective belief that a given level of effort will lead to a desirable reward.
C a subjective belief that a given level of performance will lead to a particular set of rewards.
D the degree to which an employee believes that his superior will provide clear task instructions.

8. Which of the following is correct? Helping an employee improve his performance "one step at a time" by positively reinforcing his behaviours which successfully move closer to the desired performance goal is called:

A scheduling behaviour.
B extinguishing behaviour.
C behavioural shaping.
D stretching the ratio of reinforcement.

9. A football player, threatened with suspension from the game, stops using foul language with the game's umpires. He therefore avoids any unpleasant consequence. What is this is an example of:

A positive extinction.
B negative reinforcement.
C punishment.
D shaping behaviour.

10. Which of the following statements does not support behaviour modification theory?

A The theory focuses on changes in psychological states.
B The theory emphasizes the importance of providing timely feedback to employees about their performance.
C The theory stresses the measurement and analysis of observable employee behaviour.
D The theory relates to employees' beliefs about connection between performance and rewards.

11. Which of the following is correct? Skill-based compensation:

A discourages employees from seeking training.
B is used to make part of the employee's compensation contingent on his acquisition of new job-related skills.
C rank orders positions in the firm relative to their difficulty and educational requirements.
D ties the acquisition of new job-related skills to increases in the cost of living.

12. Which of the following is correct? Gainsharing programmes:

A attempt to control labour costs through a formal system which helps employees install labour-saving innovations.
B tend to work only when an enterprise is benefiting from expanding sales.
C do not require employees to achieve better understanding of how their work units contribute to the cost of goods sold.
D do not require a history of good labour management relations in companies to be successful.

13. An employee has just designed a new piece of software and completed the debugging process on it. Which core dimension is MOST related to the above statement?

A task identity.
B feedback.
C skill variety.
D task significance.

14. If employees experience feedback about their performance by completing various steps in their work, which of the following should they experience?

A responsibility for task completion.
B meaningfulness of work outcomes.
C knowledge of results.
D job satisfaction.

15. A characteristic of autonomous work groups is that

I the groups make decisions about changes in work methods.
II the groups negotiate production schedules with manager.
III the groups are responsible for cross training their members.

Which of the following is correct?

A I only
B II only
C I, II and III
D Not I, II or III

16. Which of the following is correct? All of the following are properties of group norms EXCEPT:

A a member may privately disagree with some aspect of work methods in the group.
B the leader spends more time supervising the group if it has strong, focused norms.
C norms develop for central and important beliefs of the group's members.
D some members of a group have more rights to deviate from established group norms than other members do.

17. Which of the following is correct? When members of a group assume that all other members are in favour of the group's course of action, we say that the group is suffering from:

A mindguarding.
B self-censorship.
C illusion of unanimity.
D illusion of invulnerability.

18. Nominal groups

I are highly structured.
II focus on personalities of group members.
III pressure members to reach consensus in decision making.

Which of the following is correct?

A I only
B I and II only
C I, II and III
D I and III only

19. Which of the following activities resolves interpersonal conflict among group members?

A process.
B task.
C job.
D maintenance.

20. Employees comply initially with authority because they assume that people in a position of power have a right to exercise the position's authority. Which of the following describes that right? It is:

A ethical.
B personal.
C legitimate.
D logical.

21. Which of the following is correct? Developing a network, limiting access to information, taking risks and being creative, and creating obligation in others are examples of:

A how employees gain power.
B expert power.
C need for achievement.
D creating role conflict.

22. Which of the following is correct? Leadership consideration behaviour is most closely related to:

A initiating structure behaviour.
B building strong relationships with subordinates.
C having employees participate in decision making.
D entrepreneurial behaviour.

23. According to the path-goal theory of leadership behaviour, a leader's job is to:

I clarify the path to work goals.
II reduce or remove obstacles in the path of employees who are trying to perform well enough to obtain valued rewards.
III where appropriate, involve employees in decisions.

Which of the following is correct?

A I only
B III only
C I and II only
D I, II and III

24. Neutralizers of the effectiveness of the leader's initiating structure behaviour are:

I subordinates' expertise and job knowledge.
II task confusion and conflicting work expectations.
III flexible rules and non routine work demands.

Which of the following is correct?

A I only
B I and II only
C II and III only
D Not I, II or III

25. Which of the following forms of departmentalization help develop specialists or experts?

A product.
B matrix.
C functional.
D territory.

26. Which of the following is NOT true of territorial organizational designs?

A Attention is focused on regional operations.
B Regional managers are probably responsible for the profitability of their operations.
C It is good for the centralized control of business operations.
D It helps managers develop broadly-based management.

27. Which of the following is correct? The matrix design would be least effective when:

A special projects need to be done.
B the organization needs to energized.
C the company's market is stable and unchanging over time.
D co-ordination needs are complex in the company.

28. Which of the following is correct? If employees are unaware of a company's values and beliefs, the company

A develops enduring standards of production.
B has top managers who are unaware of their roles in formulating and transmitting organizational culture to employees.
C uses informal groups to explain company practices to new employees.
D fails to use informal groups to explain policy to new employees.

29. Diagnosis in organizational development is

I expensive.
II time consuming.
III vulnerable to management's desire for quick action.

Which of the following is correct?

A I only
B I and III only
C II and III only
D I, II and III

30. Which of the following groups help members understand how they are perceived by other members of the group?

A T-groups.
B Quality circles.
C Project groups.
D Team building groups.

Section C: Essay Questions

Each question is worth 70 points.

1. "Organizations have to meet the challenge of change by adopting several strategies". Describe these strategies. Consider what qualities a good, planned change programme has and outline the steps in the planned change process.
2. Identify the important features of employee participation in managerial decision-making and discuss the issues which managers must take into account if they wish to use participation more effectively.
3. Define Performance Appraisal. Identify the errors which can affect the appraisal process and consider what steps need to be taken to create a reliable performance appraisal system.

Section A: Answers to True/False Questions

These have been grouped together under Section Headings to assist the student.

The Basics of Organizational Behaviour

1. **False.** More capital intensity per employee may lead to smaller work forces but it will not diminish the importance of satisfying employee needs in organizations. Indeed, organizations are more likely to experience labour market shortages for employees with the skills necessary in organizations which rely on capital intensive production systems to produce their goods and services. These conditions will generate increased attention to the needs of entry level employees in such organizations.
2. **False.** A pattern of beliefs which signifies a person's inability to influence organizational practices characterises an external locus of control. Individuals who possess this pattern of beliefs, may believe that they are powerless to influence events in their work settings.
3. **False.** When work rules are clearly specified and the work situation is highly structured by close, attentive leadership, the Machiavellian employee generally conforms to existing work expectations. However, when the work situation is unstructured and few work rules exist, this employee will try to turn the work situation to his personal ends.
4. **False.** Delegating authority is a difficult aspect of management for the manager with a high need for achievement. This individual is so task focused that he often believes that he is the only one who can effectively perform a task quickly. Thus, for other than interpersonal reasons, the high achievement manager may simply perform a task himself rather than delegate it.

Contemporary Theories of Motivation

5. **False.** Organizational commitment takes longer to form than facets of job satisfaction. Therefore, job satisfaction will be a much more potent predictor of job quitting behaviour than organizational commitment for relatively new employees.

6. **False.** If hygienes are adequate, then employees believe that the organization is adequately providing for their lower-order needs. The absence of job motivators does not mean that they will avoid coming to work on a regular basis.

7. **False.** Only performance is a first level outcome. Satisfaction with supervision is a second level outcome.

8. **False.** Behavioural shaping refers to the administration of rewards as employees' work behaviour more closely approximates the desired work behaviour.

9. **False.** Managers who develop behaviour modification programmes in organizations risk failure if they do not seek employee advice concerning performance feedback, reasonable performance targets or goals, and identification of rewards which are meaningful to them.

Organizational Control and Reward Systems

10. **True.** A valid performance appraisal system will clarify employees' expectations that their levels of effort will lead to acceptable performance, and in turn, raise their beliefs that acceptable performance leads to meaningful rewards. These two outcomes are contingent on the fact that employees possess the abilities to perform the job adequately.

11. **True.** Employee intentions about personal development goals (goal acceptance and goal commitment) would be extremely low under the condition of employer-centred goal setting.

12. **True.** The most dependable motivational basis for distributing rewards in terms of expectancies and instrumentalities is performance.

13. **True.** Gainsharing programmes focus on cost control and productivity. Both of these outcomes centre on the efficiency of the production process which may be unrelated to market conditions in the short run.

Job Design and Employee Reactions to Work

14. **True.** Herzberg's job design principles generally reinforce the importance of higher order needs at work. Allowing employees to select work methods (delegation of authority) reflects the importance of needs such as autonomy, self-esteem and self-actualization.

15. **False.** These three core job characteristics more accurately reflect job range. Autonomy and performance feedback from specific job features are the primary elements of job depth.

16. **False.** The fact that employees had low growth need strength would probably doom the job enrichment programme. The employer would find a thorough analysis of its hiring and selecting practices to be much more beneficial.

17. **True.** While the job enrichment task may be more complex at the team level, the same principles for expanding job range and job depth apply at both the individual and work group levels.

Understanding Work Group – Dynamics and Problem Solving

18. **True.** The degree of similarity between group performance norms and organizational performance standards determines the relationship between group cohesiveness and group performance.

19. **True.** Groupthink is a problem which occurs only in highly cohesive groups. The members of such groups must value their membership more than the critical evaluation of alternatives which may solve the problem(s) facing the group.

20. **False.** The process losses in a new heterogeneous group would consist of disagreements about how to proceed and the nature of group roles. The primary process loss in a seasoned group which is cohesive would probably be groupthink. Both types of process losses could be of the same magnitude for both groups.

21. **False.** The nominal group technique can work well in any group provided that it has not yet formed a framework of norms which would subvert the rules followed in the nominal group process. The technique would work better in a group which had not formed a hierarchy of authority, thus minimising the impact of directive leadership on the decision-making process.

The Influence Process in Organizations: Power, Politics, Leadership and Entrepreneurship

22. **True.** The extent to which group members believed that their group leader possessed referent and reward power would increase members' perceptions that the benefits of membership exceed the costs of membership.

23. **True.** The decisional roles are most closely related to the control of the organization's economic assets. Failure in these roles threatens the organization's survival much more quickly than failure in other roles.

24. **False.** This statement applies to the Ohio State Leadership Theory which states that effective leaders demonstrate both consideration and initiating structure behaviours.

25. **True.** Fiedler proposes that a leader's orientation toward his least preferred co-worker (LPC) is a very durable dimension of the leader's personality. It would be easier to change the leadership situation by giving the leader more power, making the task more understandable or changing the composition of the group being led.

Organizational Design

26. **True.** This is a decision about departmentalization which is a key aspect of organizational design.

27. **False.** It would have the biggest impact on division of labour. Since division of labour refers to the degree of job specialization in an organization, it follows that the principles of job enrichment would alter this aspect of job design the most.

28. **True.** Common problems in matrix designs are "starving" project groups of resources or overlooking reoccurring work processes in functional units.

29. **True.** Organizations which face rapidly changing competition and complex, yet shortening product life cycles must create decision making authority at the level where most product development problems occur. Decentralization is the process of delegating authority for decision making to lower managerial levels.

30. **False.** It is not possible to increase vertical information processing capacity by making the organization's hierarchy more centralized. A hierarchy is simply a chain of command. It is neither centralized nor decentralized.

31. **True.** Quality circles involve employees and their supervisors in solving quality problems in the production of goods and services. This represents a form of delegation of authority for quality to groups of production employees.

Organizational Culture: the New Indicator of Corporate Excellence

32. **False.** These responses are repeated strategic planning and immediate external environment responses respectively.

33. **False.** Organizational culture is most directly controlled by the top executives in an organization. Since they are powerful role models and mentors, it makes perfect sense to have them participate in the transmission of organizational culture to newly-hired employees.

34. **True.** Diagnosis is a set of activities designed to separate the symptoms of malfunctions from the causes of malfunctions in the organization.

35. **False.** These are team building methods. T-groups emphasise the improvement of relations between group members and between the individual member and the rest of the group.

Section B: Answers to Multiple Choice Questions

These have been grouped together under Section Headings to assist the student.

The Basics of Organizational Behaviour

1. **C.** Organizations place the greatest value on the manager's technical and conceptual skills. These skills determine who gets hired and who gets promoted. The skill most often neglected in hiring and promotion decisions is human resource management.

2. **A.** Since the employees lower-order or maintenance needs are satisfied, choices B and D can be ruled out because they refer directly to lower-order need satisfaction. Choice C is illogical since it emphasises the importance of job challenge which is a higher order need related to self-actualization.

3. **C.** Choices A, B and D have been ruled out as meaningful explanations because they are too simplistic. Current thinking in organizational behaviour favours the role of rewards and perceived equity as moderators of the job performance–job satisfaction relationship.

4. **A.** The definition of organizational commitment emphasises these factors: (1) willingness to expend personal effort on behalf of the organization; (2) a personal belief in the values of the organization; (3) the desire to preserve membership in the organization. These three qualities would be heavily supported by choices B, C and D.

5. **C.** The only two accurate expressions in the choice set are motivational factor and hygiene factor (from the two-factor theory of job motivation). Since uniforms would have little impact on the employee's ability to satisfy higher order needs at work, uniforms must represent a hygiene factor.

Contemporary Theories of Motivation

6. **C.** Choices A, B and D are all behavioural characteristics of an employee with a high need for achievement. While pay rises and promotions would be very important to this individual in the long run, he would be much more involved with the level of intellectual challenge, meaningfulness and risk in a task during the short run.

7. **A.** Expectancy is the subjective belief that a given level of effort (motivational force to perform) will result in a given level of performance. Choice B is meaningless because it does not specify the nature of the first level outcome. Choice C refers to instrumentality while choice D is unrelated to the concept in the question.

8. **C.** Behavioural shaping refers to reinforcement for behaviour which increasingly conforms to a pre-established standard. As the behaviour approaches the standard, only improvements are acknowledged. The other three choices refer to other aspects of behaviour modification.

9. **B.** Since the avoidance behaviour is strengthened, negative reinforcement has occurred. The football player has learned how to avoid the unpleasant consequence of suspension from the game.

10. **A.** Behaviour modification predicts and controls behaviour without reference to inner states of mind. In many ways, the individual's environment is given credit for strengthening or weakening behaviour by virtue of the consequences it provides in the wake of behaviour. The other three choices are highly applicable to behaviour modification.

Organizational Control and Reward Systems

11. **B.** Skill-based compensation provides an economic incentive for acquiring as many job-based skills as possible. In effect, the organization gives a pay rise or a bonus when an employee completes a training programme which makes him a more versatile employee. Choice A is irrelevant while choice C refers to an element of job analysis. Choice D is also meaningless.

12. **A.** Gainsharing programmes use team work and innovation to lower labour costs by finding more efficient and effective ways to produce goods and services. Employees earn team-based bonuses when their work units produce a given level of output at a given level of quality with fewer man-hours. The typical bonus cycle is one month.

Job Design and Employee Reactions to Work

13. **A.** Doing a job from beginning to end represents the reverse of job specialization in the terminology of the job characteristic model, task identity. The other three choices represent other job characteristics in that model.

14. **C.** This question ties core job dimensions to critical psychological states in the job characteristic model. The psychological state which goes with feedback is knowledge of results.

15. **C.** Autonomous work groups have all three characteristics. These three are not exhaustive. The module describes many other forms of autonomy which may be assigned to autonomous work groups.

Understanding Work Group – Dynamics and Problem Solving

16. **B.** A key function of norms in groups is to summarize and streamline the influence process. If a group has a rigorous structure of norms then the leader would have to spend less time closely supervising the behaviour of team members. Choices A, C and D are all properties of group norms.

17. **C.** When a group loses its ability to evaluate alternatives it is too cohesive. Conformity in member behaviour is stressed too heavily in the group. This condition leads to groupthink. The assumption of consensus by individual members under conditions of groupthink represents the illusion of unanimity.

18. **A.** Nominal groups are groups formed for the purpose of following a very structured procedure designed to identify the fundamental features of a problem. It is highly structured to (1) ensure that all members participate; (2) prevent dominance by key group figures; and (3) prevent pressures for conformity.

19. **D.** Maintenance activities are any behaviours by group members which prevent process losses triggered by interpersonal conflict and disagreements. Formalising the role of interpersonal conflict resolver allows the group to get back to performance related matters.

The Influence Process in Organizations – Power, Politics, Leadership and Entrepreneurship

20. **C.** Legitimate authority is the power assigned to a position by virtue of its place in the organization's hierarchy or chain of command. This type of authority or power adheres to the position and not the individual occupying the position. The right to exercise the authority extends from the position in question. The other answers have no direct logical relationship to the principle described above.

21. **A.** The practices described in the question refer to methods used by individuals to gain power in organizations. The other choices refer to behavioural concepts which are not directly related to the topic of power acquisition in organizations.

22. **B.** Leadership consideration behaviour is defined as behaviour which attends to the personal needs and welfare of subordinates. Such actions include open door policies, encouraging *esprit de corps* in groups and helping subordinates with personal

problems. These kinds of behaviours would certainly create strong relationships with subordinates. The other three choices do refer to legitimate leader behaviours but they do not directly relate to leadership consideration.

23. **D.** All of these leader behaviours are implications of the path-goal theory of leadership. These outcomes can be achieved by the selection of the four behaviours available to the leader in the theory.

24. **A.** Subordinates' expertize and their job knowledge make it unnecessary for a leader to rely solely on initiating structure behaviour. Choice is another way of saying that employees can create their own successful work methods.

Organizational Design

25. **C.** Functional designs group jobs together by common work activities. Once an employee is assigned to a particular organizational function he will have ample opportunity to learn all the nuances of work in that function. This design provides the greatest opportunity for an employee to specialize in a particular aspect of work in the organization.

26. **C.** Territorial designs specialize in creating marketing expertize in sub-units which are geared to meet the needs of different customer groups in various geographic locations. Because the business units develop geographic specializations in their business and flexibility in a highly centralized design, territorially-oriented units are effective because they are differentiated from other production or sales units in the organization.

27. **C.** Matrix designs purposely create heterogeneous project or product teams to handle the turbulence which occurs in business environments which are dynamic, uncertain and unstable. These designs are highly effective when special projects need to be done or the organization needs to be energized because it is not effectively designed to meet the business challenges in its environment.

Organizational Culture: the New Indicator of Corporate Excellence

28. **B.** Top management is primarily responsible for transmitting organizational culture to all employees, whether they are new or seasoned veterans. They must do this by setting a good example and by personalising the values of the enterprize. A company with a strong culture would develop enduring standards of production and it would never rely solely on informal groups to explain company practices to new employees.

29. **D.** Diagnosis in organizational development helps the organization separate the causes of organizational problems from the symptoms of those problems. If the diagnosis is thorough it will be costly, time consuming and vulnerable to managers' needs for quick results. This can lead to treating the symptoms of problems instead of their true causes.

30. **A.** T-groups or training groups have as one of their goals the improvement of personal understanding of how other group members perceive the focal person. Improved self-awareness of one's motivations and behaviours in the group setting is a primary focus of this organizational development procedure. Project groups are

formal groups which last as long as the project work lasts. Quality circles focus on improving the effectiveness of production systems. Team building uses actual problems or simulations of problems to improve the decision making ability of work groups.

Section C: Answers to Essay Questions

1. In order to survive, organizations have to adapt and change. These changes may be good or bad but the way they are introduced is crucial, especially for the profitability of the company and the morale of the workforce.

   Organizational change may occur in response to either external or internal stimuli or both. To meet the challenge of externally induced change, organizations may follow several courses of action. First, they may change their goals and strategies. This may take the form of offering a new product or service or targeting new markets. Second, they may introduce new technology, perhaps involving the company in a downsizing exercise and therefore in detailed discussions with staff over redundancies or re-allocation of tasks. Finally, a decision may be made to redesign the organization transforming it from a functional to a product-design structure, for example. This change strategy may also involve decentralising into smaller operating units.

   When the stimulus for change is triggered by internal forces such as low productivity, high absenteeism, high labour turnover and increased grievance and discipline problems, organizations use other remedial devices. These may include redesigning jobs to include more variety, autonomy, feedback, significance and social interaction. The organization may alter its recruitment policies to bring new blood into the company or embark on a retraining programme to change the skill mix and the behaviour of its current workforce. Finally, the organization may refocus its appraisal and reward systems so as to encourage new behaviour patterns among its employees.

   Companies which can change their cultures quickly enough to meet new business requirements are likely to survive and prosper. However, there are three conditions which must be fulfilled in order for a successful corporate transition to be implemented. First, employees must be dissatisfied with the status quo. Second, the organization must have a vision for the future which will guide the redesign process and give the workforce a sense of purpose and direction. Third, the process of change has to be well managed in order to exploit the potential of the other two conditions.

   Successful planned change has several characteristics. For example, it is focused on a whole organizational unit. The "knock on" effect of changes to a sub-unit can be counter-productive if other parts of the unit are affected in ways which were not foreseen. It is also based on behavioural science knowledge. Change managers have to be aware of how the content, pace and extent of changes will affect and be affected by the behaviour of employees. Finally, the change requires its primary goal to be the improvement of organizational effectiveness.

   Levin has suggested that the planned change process should follow a sequence of organizational events. These events involve three stages which he has named, unfreezing, changing and refreezing. Unfreezing occurs when people in the organization realise that the current systems are failing to achieve strategic goals. In many cases it is the Chief Executive Officer of the company who decides the time is right for a transformation to be introduced. This is a top down approach and the focus then is to put procedures in place to involve the workforce in this process. However, sometimes the push for change comes from employees further down the chain of command and may have been uncovered during a regular employee attitude survey. Once unfreezing has occurred, action plans can be developed to move the organization and its workforce towards a new model. Refreezing occurs when the new model organization is fully functional and it is at this point that the company needs to review the whole process.

2. Participation is the active involvement of employees in making decisions about issues affecting them on the job. There are three major dimensions to this participation. One of these is connected with the psychological aspects of being involved. Encouraging employees to be mentally active in the decision-making process gives them the opportunity to think more creatively and to feel the sense of satisfaction that comes from contributing in a purposeful way to the challenges of the job. Their higher-order needs are being satisfied and they are unlikely to indulge in avoidance behaviour such as "looking busy". The purposeful element in participation is in itself a motivating device and is a second dimension of participation. It can encourage employees to make personal contributions to their organization. When the organization's social system meets the employee's belonging needs and the technical work system presents him or her with challenging and meaningful work, the conditions are right for creating the motivation to contribute. However, participation is a two-way process. Employees must want to participate and managers must be willing to share some of their decision-making powers. If participation is forced on the workforce by an over-zealous management, it will not achieve employee commitment and acceptance of organizational goals. The third dimension has to do with the acceptance of authority. When employees experience the greater control which accompanies participation they become more willing to accept delegated authority. Employees may then become more proprietorial over their jobs, deciding how and when particular tasks may be done and work teams may begin to develop.

   Managers who wish to use a participative style of decision-making more effectively must do so on an incremental basis, and the culture and climate must be right for this change. Managers cannot expect to move to autonomous work groups in one step, nor can participation be installed under emergency or crisis conditions. There must also be a strong belief that the benefits outweigh the costs, although attempting to cost changes in employee work behaviour is a difficult and lengthy procedure, if it can be done at all. The culture of the organization must underline the concept that employees are at the centre of organizational values values and that the company will benefit from developing the self-management skills of the workforce. Mission statements and published human resource management policies can reinforce in a public way the organizations commitment to its labour force.

   Employees, for their part, must view participation as central to their work and not as an intrusion. However, they must be given the training to tackle any problems which they are required to solve, and managers must be aware of the negative effect on morale and motivation of expecting employees to participate in solving problems which are over their heads. This issue may often be tackled by making information more user-friendly, for example, by using less technical jargon.

Finally it is important that neither managers nor employees feel that participation is a threatening step. It is inevitable that various interest groups, for example trade unions, may view the practice of participative management with some fear of its consequences; but once an employer has embarked on participation there is unlikely to be an opportunity to return to the status quo, and managers have to put into place procedures for anticipating and dealing with any problems arising from this conflict of interest.

3. Performance appraisal is the process which generates valid information about employee work-effectiveness for the purpose of making informed human resource decisions.

Few managers would question the organization's need to assess the performance behaviour of its employees. However, the process must produce results which are both fair and accurate. Errors can enter the process and it is important that these are recognized at an early stage so that steps can be taken to rectify these.

Errors, such as personal bias which may influence an appraiser's rating and the halo effect which can result in an employee being rated the same on all performance dimensions because of a general impression, may be rectified by training managers in the proper techniques of appraisal. Recency errors may be checked by more frequent recording of critical incident information relating to staff performance. Errors, such as strictness and leniency on the part of the appraiser or similarity errors where the appraiser has a performance quality in himself or herself which he or she looks for in the appraisee, may be corrected by awareness training. Central tendency errors occur when average ratings are assigned to all employees with little variations between them, and forcing the ratings to match other criteria occurs when sub-ratings are adjusted to justify an overall rating which has already been decided. These errors require constant monitoring of the appraiser's rating performance to ensure their early detection.

All of these errors are variations of the problems associated with validity in that they relate to how effective the components of the system are at measuring what they are supposed to measure. The errors also concern reliability in that they refer to the consistency and stability of the appraisal measures.

No appraisal system can eliminate all the threats to validity and reliability. However, the most prominent features of any performance appraisal system are the types of data-gathering instruments used, and it is here that we may find ways of at least enhancing the appraisal process.

First, there are absolute standards, where each employee is judged against a fixed and inflexible set of performance criteria. The absolute-standards system often results in leniency errors because appraisers prefer to give positive rather than negative feedback. A second type of data-gathering instrument is the graphic rating scale which lists performance criteria considered meaningful to both appraiser and appraisee. Use of this system highlights the differences in performance as between appraisees and encourages the appraiser to spread the ratings out along the scale. Since degrees of performance are possible for each dimension a great deal of information is generated which may be used by the appraiser during performance counselling sessions. Behaviourally anchored rating scales are a third form of data-gathering. This provides concrete examples of behaviour for different levels of performance. The participative procedure required to identify the items which describe effective and ineffective job behaviour helps to improve employee's understanding of what is required to achieve better performance on the job.

BARS emphasises how the work is performed versus the traits of those doing the work. This behavioural emphasis reduces the chances for extraneous employee-traits or peripheral job requirements to find their way into the employee's evaluation. BARS apply to a specific set of tasks. This may increase validity for the tasks in question, but it may require that multiple BARS be developed for other job groupings in the organization.

Reliability is a function of the number of dimensions in a performance appraisal system and the standardization of the administrative procedures. Reliability can be enhanced by using multiple raters to judge the performance of appraisees.

Performance appraisal aims to provide a mechanism for the assessment of performance so that appropriate rewards may be given and career paths identified. It is therefore important that any errors in the appraisal system should be identified and corrected.

PRACTICE FINAL EXAMINATION 2

Essay Questions

1. ***Compare and contrast* five *different methods of staff selection, particularly in terms of their utility. How can an organization determine which are the appropriate selection methods to use?*** **(60 marks)**

   Answers could include the use of biodata; references; interviews; simulations; personality tests; aptitude tests; assessment centres; peer evaluation; graphology; self-assessment. The utility of each of these devices is measured in terms of its validity, fairness, cost, and applicability. For instance, references have little validity, but are inexpensive and cover many types of job; interviews can produce moderate validity but can be unfair, and can be used by the applicant to gain information about the organization and job.

   The appropriate application of each method would be determined after a full job analysis, and the development of a personnel specification and of relevant criteria. The psychometric properties of the various methods would be considered before making a final choice. The accuracy of the selection tools would be examined retrospectively, and changes made to the procedures as necessary.

2. ***Management by objectives (MBO) is a practical application of the reasoning behind the notion of goal-setting theory. What are the assumptions upon which the MBO cycle rests? How can management ensure that their MBO system remains viable and meaningful to employees?*** **(60 marks)**

   Answers should include the following assumptions: employees perform better when they know what is expected of them; most employees prefer self-determination at work; employees can be motivated by timely feedback about their work methods and the results they achieve; employees prefer rewards commensurate with their performance.

   To ensure that the MBO system maintains its quality, there should be management commitment; the system should relate to routine managerial activities and responsibilities; it must emphasise organizational and personal development goals; there must be a commitment to training; MBO systems must be customized to suit different departmental needs; setting too many goals should be avoided; the system should provide cost benefits; discussion and evaluation should have equal value; the MBO system should be flexible.

3. ***"Conflict is a form of interaction between individuals or groups in situations that occur when one or both sides perceive that the other has thwarted or is about to thwart an important concern" (Vecchio,* Organizational Behaviour*). Compare the contemporary and the traditional views conflict and its place in the organization. What do you consider to be the sources of conflict within an organization?***

(60 marks)

Answers should discuss the traditional view, that conflict is harmful and unnecessary, and the contemporary view, that conflict is a natural and desirable state.

The sources of conflict can arise from poor communication factors; structural factors such as the organizational size, lack of staff heterogeneity, overmuch employee participation, line and staff distinctions, reward systems, resource interdependence, and the distribution of power, and from personal behaviour factors.

PRACTICE FINAL EXAMINATION 3

Essay Questions

1. ***Define the term "performance appraisal". Examine why organizations need to assess the performance of their employees and identify how the appraisal process affects the individual employee at work.***

Answer should include the following:

Performance appraisal is the process of generating valid information about the effectiveness of employees in their work for the purpose of making informed human resource management decisions. Organizations need to assess employee performance because:

- employees need to behave in a desired manner on the job and so require to have a clear understanding of what this involves
- employees' work needs to be evaluated for its contribution to organizational goals
- employees require to have feedback from the organization for motivational purposes
- managerial decisions about pay increases, promotions and training needs require accurate information about personal performance.

From the individual employee's viewpoint performance appraisal leads to:

- increased satisfaction with job, pay, supervision and promotion opportunities
- greater organizational commitment because the individual employee knows that the company is interested in, and wishes to treat him or her, fairly
- fulfilment of needs such as security and self-esteem
- increased self-awareness and willingness to accept responsibility which is important in times of growing empowerment of all employees.

2. ***What do we mean by "organizational culture"? Consider the factors which contribute to the development of a company's organizational culture and identify the liabilities associated with a strong organizational culture.***

Answer should include the following:

Organizational culture is a difficult term to define but in the formal sense organizational culture is about the shared beliefs and values which produce norms for employee behaviour. Two major factors contribute to the organization's culture. These are the role of the CEO or founder, and the management of the organization's socialization process.

The CEO's role is reflected in the way he or she has stamped his/her values on the company. Good examples of this are IBM, Ford and Apple Computers. Socialization is the process of passing on to successive generations of employees the culture of the organization. Companies which are efficient at achieving their goals/culture fit recognize that they have to be diligent in the management of their recruitment and selection, work design and employee development opportunities. Organizations with strong cultures operate a careful socialization process so that employees can understand the company culture. This socialization process includes such activities as:

- previews for jobs for job applicants
- debasement and indoctrination practices to develop humility
- employees learning to master the core areas of the business by being required to work for short periods of time at all levels of the business
- rewarding merit with pay increases and promotion
- using company officials as role models for the culture of the company
- encouraging folklore about the organization and its founder to use as a reinforcer of the company's culture
- identifying and nurturing young employees whose approach to the job fits with the company culture.

The liabilities associated with a strong culture are:

- the mission, goals and strategy of an organization may change faster than the culture so that there is a mismatch causing organizational and human resource problems
- there may be a clash between cultures when two firms merge
- succession planning has been ignored so that the first generation of management, often the founders, have not prepared for the orderly transfer of power to the next generation.

3. ***Describe the basic stages in the change process as identified by Kurt Lewin. Review the courses of action organizations might follow to meet the challenge of environmental change and examine how a company might evaluate the effects of its change programme.***

Answers should include the following:
Kurt Lewin identified three stages:

The **unfreezing stage** when employees recognize that the current culture and processes are outdated and undertake a "constructive destruction" of the organization.

The **changing stage** when an action plan is implemented to introduce a modified form of the old culture and encourage new work behaviour.

The **refreezing stage** when new behaviour, work designs, organizational structures and processes are adopted.

Companies have to change in response to changes in both the external and the internal environments. In response to external stimuli companies may:

- change their goals and strategies by introducing new products and services
- introduce new technology especially information technology
- modify their structure by changing from a functional to a product or territorial design and replacing centralized decision making with decentralized decision making.

In response to internal stimuli companies may:

- modify job design
- recruit new employees to bring new ideas into the organization
- use training and development programmes to build new behaviour patterns and skills into the current workforce
- change the performance appraisal and reward systems to encourage new behaviour among the current workforce.

Outcomes. This evaluation may be done by:

- assessing the reaction of employees in relation to their satisfaction with the changes, improvements in job involvement and company loyalty and the usefulness of their participation in the change programme
- assessing the amount of employee learning by identifying what new knowledge if any has been learned and how widespread this is
- assessing changes in employee behaviour and whether this is recognized by managers
- assessing organizational outcomes by investigating if there is any improvement in productivity, absenteeism, labour turnover and grievance rates.

Quantitative Methods

PRACTICE FINAL EXAMINATION 1 – WITH MCQs

Time allowed: 3 hours

Section A: Multiple choice.
Answer all 25 questions. Each correct answer receives 2 marks.
An incorrect answer or unanswered question receives 0 marks.
Total marks for Section A = 50 = 33% of total for paper.

Section B: Case studies.
Answer all 4 questions. Each question will be marked out of 25.
Marks for individual parts of a question are shown in the question.
Total marks for Section B = 100 = 67% of total for paper.

Section A

Multiple choice.

1. A toy manufacturer is putting together a financial plan for his business, but to do so he needs to estimate the Christmas demand for his newly developed children's board game. He knows demand will vary according to the price charged, but he does not want to set the price until nearer the Christmas season. However, he does have information on the two similar products he marketed last year. One was priced at £5 and sold 6 (thousands); the other was priced at £11 and sold 3 (thousands). Over this range he thinks the relationship between price and demand is linear. What is the straight line equation linking price and demand?

   (a) Demand = 3.5 + 0.5 × Price
   (b) Demand = 6 – 2 × Price
   (c) Demand = 8.5 – 0.5 × Price
   (d) Demand = 3.5 – 0.5 × Price

2. A furniture manufacturer is a supplier for a large retail chain. Amongst her products are a round coffee table and a square coffee table both of which can be made on either of two machines. Knowledge of the production times per table and the time per week each machine is available result in the following two equations showing possible production mixes for each machine.

   Machine A: 2R + 3S = 27
   Machine B: 5R + 4S = 50
   where R = number of round tables made per week
   S = number of square tables made per week

The solution to these simultaneous equations is the numbers of each product that must be made if all available machine time is used up. Which of the following production mixes is the solution to the equations?

(a) R = 5, S = 6
(b) R = 3, S = 7
(c) R = 10, S = 0
(d) R = 6, S = 5

3. Which of the following is correct? When analysing any management data the pattern should be found before considering exceptions because:

(a) exceptions can only be defined in the context of a pattern
(b) in management only the pattern needs to be considered
(c) finding the pattern may involve statistical analysis
(d) patterns are easier to find than exceptions

Questions 4 and 5 are based on the following data which refer to the number of customer complaints about the quality of service on one of an airline's routes in each of ten weeks:

11 20 12 11 16 13 15 21 18 13

4. Which of the following is correct? The range is:

(a) 6
(b) 10
(c) 11
(d) 21

5. Which of the following is correct? The Mean Absolute Deviation is:

(a) 0
(b) 3
(c) 3.3
(d) 15

6. Which of the following is correct? When randomness is incorporated into a sampling method:

(a) the sample will be representative.
(b) the sample will be as accurate as possible.
(c) the accuracy of the sample can be calculated.
(d) the cost of sampling is reduced.

7. An integrated factory production line fills, labels and seals 1-litre bottles of mineral water. Production is monitored to check how much liquid the bottles actually contain and that legal requirements on minimum contents are being met. A distribution is formed by taking a random sample of 1 000 bottles and measuring the amount of liquid each holds. The measurements are grouped in intervals of 1 millilitre and a histogram formed. To calculate how much of the production falls within different volume ranges, it is necessary to know what type the resulting distribution is. Which of the following is correct? The distribution is:

(a) normal
(b) binomial
(c) Poisson
(d) observed

8. In practice the binomial distribution is usually approximated by the normal if the rule of thumb, $np > 5$, holds. Which of the following is correct? The reason for following the procedure is that:

(a) it is easier to calculate probabilities.
(b) suitable binomial tables are not available.
(c) basic theory shows that the distribution is in reality normal.
(d) the Central Limit Theorem applies.

9. A medical consultant sees 100 patients per month in his office. In an attempt to optimize his appointments system he decides to analyse the time he spends with each patient. What type of standard distribution should he expect for the average time he spends with each patient over the course of a month?

(a) Normal
(b) *t*
(c) Binomial
(d) Poisson

Questions 10 to 12 refer to the following circumstances.

A supermarket is checking for the presence of bacterial infection in pre-cooked TV meals. To do this a sample of 16 is selected at random and given a laboratory test which gives each meal a score between 0 (completely free of infection) and 100 (highly infected). Tests on the sample of sixteen result in an average score of 10. It is known from investigations of other products that the infection score is likely to be normally distributed with a standard deviation of 2.

10. What is the point estimate of the population mean (the average score for all dinners)?

(a) 2
(b) 0.5
(c) 8 to 12
(d) 10

11. What are the 95% confidence limits for the population mean?

(a) 6 to 14
(b) 8 to 12
(c) 9 to 11
(d) 9.5 to 10.5

12. Which one of the following concepts did you have to use in answering question 11?

(a) Central Limit Theorem
(b) Variance Sum Theorem

(c) Sampling Distribution of the Mean
(d) Analysis of Variance

13. A consultant has made a presentation concerning the likely impact of a new quality control system on rejection rates. The production director asks why a significance level of 5% has been used. Which of the following is valid? It is:

(a) the definition of significance
(b) convention
(c) the boundary between an acceptable risk and an unacceptable risk
(d) part of normal distribution theory

14. A restaurant chain asks its customers to rate the service on a scale from 0 to 10 before they leave the restaurant. It is a corporate objective that an overall average of 8 should be achieved. To check how a particular restaurant compares with the corporate average, a random sample of the ratings of 36 customers is selected. The sample has a mean of 6.8 and standard deviation 3. A two-tailed significance test is conducted with the hypothesis that the overall mean rating is 8. Which of the following is correct?

(a) The test is inconclusive at 5% level
(b) The test suggests the hypothesis should be accepted at 5% level
(c) The test suggests the hypothesis should be rejected at 5% level
(d) The test suggests the hypothesis should be rejected at 1% level

15. A chi-squared test is used in testing customer attitudes to different brands of toothpaste. The value of chi-squared measured in the test is 23. What is the critical value in the upper 10% tail of a chi-squared distribution with 18 degrees of freedom with which to compare the observed value?

(a) 16.085
(b) 24.769
(c) 25.989
(d) 28.869

16. Which of the following is correct? Analysis of variance is a technique which:

(a) compares the variances of two samples
(b) compares the variances of several samples
(c) tests the hypothesis that there is no difference between the means of several samples
(d) calculates the combined variance of several samples

17. I. Correlation measures the strength of the linear relationship between two variables.
II. If high values of one variable are associated with low values of a second and vice versa, then the two variables are negatively correlated.
III. Regression measures whether changes in one variable cause changes in another.

Which of the following is correct?

(a) I only
(b) I and II only

(c) II and III only
(d) I, II, and III

Questions 18–20 refer to the following computer output from a regression analysis relating a company's annual revenue to three independent variables. The results are to be used to predict future revenue as part of the corporate plans.

Variable	*Coefficient*	*Standard Error*
Gross Domestic Product	6.4	0.8
Previous year's profit	0.6	0.1
Marketing expenditure	15.6	12.0
Constant	8.4	1.2

R-Bar-Squared = 0.94
Residual standard error = 1.2

18. Which of the following is correct? The value of R-bar-squared means that:
    (a) predictions of future annual revenue will be 94 per cent accurate
    (b) residual standard error should be reduced by 94 per cent to allow for degrees of freedom
    (c) the regression explains 94 per cent of the variation in the past record of revenue
    (d) 94 per cent of the residuals are within 2 residual standard errors of the regression line

19. Which of the following is correct? The *t* values for the three variables are respectively:
    (a) 8.0, 6.0, 1.3
    (b) 0.8, 0.1, 12.0
    (c) 6.4, 0.6, 15.6
    (d) 5.4, 0.5, 13.0

20. Which of the following is correct? Statistically, the variable "marketing expenditure" should be eliminated from the regression equation because:
    (a) it has the highest standard error
    (b) it has the lowest *t* value
    (c) its standard error is less than 2
    (d) its *t* value is less than 2

21. A company is trying to forecast its next two years revenue for a new venture in the Far East. Because of the lack of suitable data, it has been decided to use the Delphi technique. Six executives have been selected to take part. Which of the following is correct? The executives should:
    (a) all be at the same level of seniority
    (b) not talk to one another about their forecasts
    (c) adjust their forecast towards the mean at each iteration
    (d) continue making forecasts until a consensus is reached

Questions 22–23 refer to the following circumstances.

A mail order company has just installed a new computerized inventory control system. The stock levels for the first seven weeks under the new system were:

Week	1	2	3	4	5	6	7
Stock (£million)	13	15	14	10	8	11	12

22. For budgeting purposes a three-point moving average forecast for period 8 is calculated. Which of the following is correct? The forecast is:

    (a) 9.7
    (b) 10.3
    (c) 10.7
    (d) 12

23. In carrying out sensitivity analysis, an exponential smoothing ($\alpha = 0.2$) forecast for period 8 is prepared. Which of the following is correct? The forecast is:

    (a) 10.3
    (b) 11.7
    (c) 12
    (d) 12.7

24. Which technique should a confectionery company use to forecast quarterly ice-cream sales for the year ahead based on a ten-year data record?

    (a) Delphi
    (b) exponential smoothing
    (c) Holt's method
    (d) Holt-Winters method

25. A manufacturer of white goods has used two forecasting methods, 3-point moving averages and exponential smoothing, to make short-term forecasts of the weekly stock levels. The company now wants to choose the more accurate of the two and use it alone to forecast. To do this two measures of accuracy, the MAD (mean absolute deviation) and MSE (mean square error), have been calculated for each method over the last ten weeks. What conclusion should be drawn if moving averages has the lower MSE while exponential smoothing has the lower MAD?

    (a) Moving averages is superior
    (b) Exponential smoothing is superior
    (c) A calculating error must have been made because such a situation could never arise
    (d) Exponential smoothing is better on average but probably has more large individual errors

Section B: Case Studies

Answer all 4 questions.
Each question will be marked out of 25.

Marks for individual parts of a question are shown in the question.
Total marks for Section B = 100 = 67% of total for paper.

1. Are publishers suffering from under-exposure?

The UK publisher of a book on employment opportunities for business graduates measured the exposure the book was receiving as part of an investigation into marketing effectiveness. A survey of bookshops was carried out to determine, on average, how many copies of the book are displayed on shelves. To do this the publisher selected at random a sample of ten universities or colleges from all universities and colleges offering business degrees. Every bookshop near one of the selected campuses (within a two mile radius of the campus centre) was visited and the number of books on display counted.

(a) Which sampling method has been used? (5 marks)
(b) Why is this method preferable to simple random sampling? (10 marks)
(c) How might the sample be biased? (5 marks)
(d) How might the sampling method be improved? (5 marks)

2. **Can the envelope production problem be licked?**

Since introducing a new line in scented envelopes, production schedules have been continually changed because of substantial variations in demand from quarter to quarter. The production scheduling department is trying to improve the situation by adopting a scientific approach to forecasting demand. They have applied the decomposition method to quarterly data covering 1984–89. The separation of the elements of this time series revealed the following:

(i) The trend was: demand = 2 600 + 40t.
where t = 1, 2, 3, etc., and t = 1 represents Ql, 1984.
(ii) There was no cycle.
(iii) The seasonal factors (actual/moving average) were:

	Q1	Q2	Q3	Q4
1984	—	—	76	100
1985	113	109	73	104
1986	109	111	76	106
1987	110	110	72	104
1988	114	107	77	102
1989	114	108	76	108

Now, in the first quarter of 1990 the production scheduling department needs a forecast for the third quarter of 1990.

(a) What should the forecast be? (15 marks)
(b) Should the schedule be delayed until the results for the current quarter are available, i.e. is the actual demand for the first quarter likely to affect the forecast? (5 marks)
(c) If the method proves unsatisfactory in practice, what other forecasting methods would be used? (5 marks)

3. **Is advertising a driving force?**

Seven hundred motorists, chosen at random, took part in a market research survey to find out about consumers' attitudes to brands of petrol. The ultimate objective was to determine the impact of advertising campaigns. The motorists were presented with a list of petrol brands:

BP
Esso
Fina
Jet
National
Shell

They were also presented with a list of attributes:

Good mileage
Long engine life
For with-it people
Value for money
Large company

The motorists were then asked to tick the petrol brands to which they thought the attributes applied. A motorist was free to tick all or none of the brands for each attribute. The table below contains the results, showing the percentage of the sample which ticked each brand for each attribute.

			Brand			
Attitude	*BP*	*Esso*	*Fina*	*Jet*	*National*	*Shell*
Good mileage	37.1	61.5	7.6	11.9	22.6	85.3
Long engine life	12.2	19.2	3.8	5.0	8.5	19.0
For with-it people	6.9	10.0	1.2	3.1	12.4	10.9
Value for money	24.0	37.8	5.1	39.7	15.3	40.3
Large company	30.4	67.9	5.4	2.3	4.8	59.8

(a) Analyse this table. What is the main pattern in it? (10 marks)
(b) What are the exceptions? (5 marks)
(c) Can you explain the exceptions? (5 marks)
(d) What further information would be useful to understand the table better? (5 marks)

NB To analyse the table you will find it useful to re-present it first by rounding, re-ordering, etc.

4. **Can the government fuel the green debate?**

A national government analyst is investigating the fuel consumption of a popular make of car when it runs on a new "environment friendly" unleaded petrol. The preliminary data shown below were collected from twelve trips of similar length and in the same car. The evidence collected from each trip was the fuel consumption in miles per gallon, the average speed in miles per hour, the average altitude, in hundreds of metres and the total weight of passengers and luggage in the car in hundreds of kilos.

Trip	*Miles/ Gallon mpg*	*Average Speed mph*	*Altitude '00 m*	*Passenger Weight '00 k*
1	33	50	0	2
2	36	40	1	3
3	31	45	3	2
4	24	55	4	4
5	34	35	1	3
6	27	45	5	4
7	20	55	3	5
8	35	35	0	2
9	32	40	1	3
10	27	50	2	3
11	23	55	4	4
12	28	45	2	2

In an attempt to measure the effect on fuel consumption of speed, altitude and load, multiple regression analysis was used, relating fuel consumption to speed, altitude and load. The results were:

Variable	Coefficient	Std error
mph	–0.4	0.12
altitude	–0.8	0.58
weight	–1.5	0.92
constant	53.9	

R-bar-squared 0.82

Standard error of residuals 2.2

(a) What is the regression equation linking fuel consumption to the other variables? What consumption would you predict for a trip at an average speed of 45 mph, at an altitude of 200 metres and with total passenger weight 300 kilos? (5 marks)
(b) Calculate the values of the residuals. Is there a pattern in the residuals? (5 marks)
(c) Should any of the variables be excluded from the regression equation? (5 marks)
(d) Approximately, what is the accuracy of the prediction made in part (a)? What is the difference between the standard error of residuals and SE (Predicted) as a measure of forecasting accuracy? (5 marks)
(e) How could the analysis be improved? (5 marks)

Section A: Answers

1. (c) Demand = 8.5 – 0.5 × Price

The question is equivalent to finding the straight line linking the points (5,6) and (11,3), i.e. finding m and c in the equation

Demand = c + m × Price

The slope of the line is $\frac{3-6}{11-5} = -0.5 = m$

The intercept is then given by

Demand = c – 0.5 × Price

Putting demand = 6 and price = 5, c = 8.5

2. (d) R = 6, S = 5

Machine A: 2R + 3S = 27
Machine B: 5R + 4S = 50

Eliminate R from the equations by multiplying that for A by 5 and then subtracting 2 times that for B.

Machine A: 10R + 15S = 135
Machine B: 10R + 8S = 100

7S = 35
S = 5

Substituting in the original equation for A gives,

2R+ 15 = 27
2R = 12
R = 6

3. (a) exceptions can only be defined in the context of a pattern

(b), (c) and (d) may be true statements in some situations but (a) is always true.

4. (b) the range is 10

Range = highest value – lowest value
= 21 – 11 = 10

5. (b) the mean absolute deviation is 3

	11	20	12	11	16	13	15	21	18	13	mean = 15
Deviations from	–4	5	–3	–4	1	–2	0	6	3	–2	
Absolute deviations	4	5	3	4	1	2	0	6	3	2	mean = 3

6. (c) the accuracy of the sample can be calculated.

(c) is correct because randomness means that statistical theory can be used to measure accuracy through measures such as the standard deviation. (a) is not correct because, while randomness helps to make a sample representative, it does not guarantee it. (b) is not correct since, for example, methods such as stratified sampling increase accuracy by restricting randomness. As in opinion polls randomness by itself may increase sampling costs, so (d) is not correct.

7. (d) observed
The distribution is observed because the histogram is formed directly by measuring volumes rather than indirectly by making assumptions about the process which produces the data.

8. (a) Calculations are easier.
The approximation is simply so that calculating is faster. None of (b), (c) or (d) is correct.

9. (a) Normal
If the appointments are set at 30-minute intervals, the norm is that each appointment will take 30 minutes. However, there will be variations around this from patient to patient for many reasons, such as the nature of the problem, whether the patient is well known to the consultant, outside interruptions, etc. This is exactly the type of situation to which the normal distribution applies.

10. (d) 10
The point estimate of a population mean is the mean of the sample.

11. (c) 9 to 11
The population standard deviation is 2.
The standard deviation of the mean score of samples of 16
$= 2/\sqrt{16} = 0.5$
The 95 per cent confidence limits are therefore
$= 10 +/- 2 \times 0.5$
$= 9$ to 11

12. (c) Sampling Distribution of the Mean.
The concept of the sampling distribution of the mean is used in calculating the standard deviation of the mean score of samples of 16. The Variance Sum Theorem and Analysis of Variance have no direct relevance to the calculations. The calculations do depend on the sampling distribution of the mean being normally distributed but this follows from the fact that the underlying population is normal and the Central Limit Theorem need not be called on.

13. (b) it is convention
The decision-maker decides the significance level but 5 per cent is the usual level. Significance levels do define significance and they are the boundary between acceptable and unacceptable risks but they do not have to be 5 per cent. That is why (a) and (c) are not valid. Significance tests can be based on the normal distribution but they do not have to be, so (d) is not valid.

14. (c) Reject hypothesis at 5 per cent level
The sampling distribution of the mean has a mean of 8 (hypothesis) a standard deviation of 0.5 ($3/\sqrt{36}$) and is normally distributed (Central Limit Theorem). For a two-tailed test at the 5 per cent level the critical values are $8 +/- 2 \times 0.5 = 7$ and 9. The sample result was 6.8 therefore the hypothesis is rejected.

For a test at the 1 per cent level the critical values are $8 +/- 3 \times 0.5 = 6.5$ and 9.5. Therefore the hypothesis is accepted at the 1 per cent level.

15. (c) 25.989
The value is found directly from the chi-squared table.

16. (c) tests the hypothesis that there is no difference between the means of several samples
Analysis of variance works by measuring the ratios between variances but is a significance test on sample means.

17. (b) I and II are correct
I describes what correlation does; II describes negative correlation. III is untrue since correlation measures association and not necessarily causation.

18. (c) The regression explains 94 per cent of the variation in the past record of revenue.
R-bar-squared is the ratio between explained and total variance with allowance for degrees of freedom, therefore (c) is correct.

19. (a) 8.0, 6.0, 1.3
The t values are the ratios between coefficients and standard errors.

20. (d) Its t value is less than 2.
The decision to reject a variable from a regression equation is based, statistically, on a significance test which uses t values. The critical value, for t, at the 5 per cent level, is approximately 2. Therefore a variable with a t value less than 2 should, statistically, be omitted.

21. (b) not talk to one another about their forecasts
The Delphi process requires that the participators communicate only through the chairman to avoid factors such as rank and personality playing a part. Therefore (b) is correct. (a) is incorrect because one of the purposes of Delphi is that people at different levels of seniority can take part. Participators are under no requirement to adjust their predictions at each iteration in any direction or to adjust them at all so (c) is incorrect. This being the case, a consensus may not be reached therefore (d) is incorrect.

22. (b) 10.3

Week	1	2	3	4	5	6	7	8
Stock	13	15	14	10	8	11	12	
M Average	–	14	13	10.7	9.7	10.3		
Forecast				14	13	10.7	9.7	10.3

23. (b) 11.7
$\alpha = 0.2$

Week	1	2	3	4	5	6	7	8
Stock	13	15	14	10	8	11	12	
ES	13	13.4	13.5	12.8	11.9	11.7	11.7	
Forecast	–	13.0	13.4	13.5	12.8	11.8	11.7	11.7

24. (d) Holt-Winters method
Because ice-cream sales are to be forecast, a technique that can handle seasonality is needed. This suggests (d) rather than (b) or (c). A quantitative rather than qualitative technique is suggested by the lengthy data record, ruling out (a).

25. (d) Exponential smoothing is better on average but has some large individual errors
The MAD calculates the average of the absolute values of the forecasting errors, i.e. the average error size. Therefore exponential smoothing, having the lower MAD, is better on average. The MSE calculates the average of the squared forecasting errors. Squaring the errors has the effect of giving a heavy weighting to any large errors. Consequently if exponential smoothing has a higher MSE but a lower MAD, it is likely to have at least one more really large error.

Section B: Answers

1. Are publishers suffering from under-exposure?

(a) Two stage cluster sampling. It is two stage sampling because there are two levels in the sampling: universities/colleges and bookshops. It is cluster sampling because at the second stage all bookshops near the universities/colleges are included in the sample. **(5 marks)**

(b) It will be:

(i) *cheaper.* Only a limited number of locations need be visited since the sample is restricted to ten universities/colleges. Simple random sampling could mean visiting just one bookshop at many more locations.

(ii) *easier.* A list of universities/colleges from which to select is more likely to be available than a list of bookshops near campuses.

(iii) *more accurate*. The area near a university or college is likely to contain all types of bookshop (in terms of size, ownership, site, proximity to students, etc.). This diversity will be reflected in the sample whereas it might not have been with simple random sampling. **(10 marks)**

(c) Potential sources of bias are that:

(i) not all bookshops used by students will be less than two miles from a campus and they will be excluded.

(ii) the books will be of interest to groups other than students: graduates, potential employers, etc. The bookshops used by these groups will mainly be excluded from consideration.

(iii) two miles is an arbitrary radius. Large universities will be more spread out and specialist student bookshops could be at greater distances from the centre of a campus. **(5 marks)**

(d) Possible improvements.

(i) There are known differences among universities which might affect the number of copies on display and which are ignored. Stratified sampling would make the sample more accurate by recognising the differences between undergraduate and graduate schools, large and small schools.

(ii) More of the potential market would be included by having other strata, for example city centre bookshops.

(iii) Instead of a two mile radius, the "catchment areas" of the universities should be defined. **(5 marks)**

2. Can the envelope production problem be licked?

(a) First calculate the average of each quarter's seasonal factors to see if their level needs to be adjusted. Quarterly seasonal averages:

	Q1	Q2	Q3	Q4
1984	—	—	76	100
1985	113	109	73	104
1986	109	111	76	106
1987	110	110	72	104
1988	114	107	77	102
1989	114	108	76	108
Average	112	109	75	104

The average of these averages is exactly 100, so no adjustment is necessary.

Classical decomposition splits a time series into three elements:

Stage 1. Trend. For Q3, 1990, $t = 27$, and the trend factor is $2\,600 + 40 \times 27 = 3\,680$
Stage 2. Cycle. No cycle is found.
Stage 3. Seasonality. For the third quarter the seasonal factor is 75.
The forecast for Q3, 1990 is $3\,680 \times 0.75 = 2\,760$

(15 marks)

(b) Data from the first quarter of 1990 will affect the forecasts very little. First, the trend will be adjusted but since the record covers 24 quarters the effect will not be great. Second, the seasonal element will be unchanged since first quarter data cannot affect the third quarter seasonal factor. **(5 marks)**

(c) Other possible forecasting methods:
The series is a seasonal one therefore a method to handle seasonality is needed. Holt-Winters is a suitable time series method. If the main factors affecting demand can be found (perhaps a variable measuring economic activity, one measuring marketing expenditure, etc.) and measured, regression analysis can be used.

(5 marks)

3. Is advertising a driving force?

(a) The procedure is to follow the five stages for the non-technical analysis of data.
Stage 1. Eliminate irrelevant data: in this case there are no superfluous data.
Stage 2. Consider the seven guidelines for communicating data and represent the table.
Three changes can be made. They are to:
(i) round the percentages to eliminate the decimal points.

(ii) put rows and columns in size order. This can be done by calculating row and column averages and using these figures as the basis for ordering.
(iii) interchange rows and columns.

The table below is the product of these changes:

Brand	*Attitude* Good Mileage	Large Company	Value Money	Engine Life	With -it	*Average*
Shell	85	60	40	9	11	43
Esso	61	68	38	19	10	39
BP	37	30	24	12	7	22
National	23	5	15	8	12	13
Jet	12	2	40	5	3	12
Fina	8	5	5	4	1	5
Average	38	28	27	11	7	

Stage 3. Describe the overall pattern. The companies have approximately the same ranking whatever the attribute: Shell scores highly for all attributes, Fina lowly. **(10 marks)**

(b) *Stage 4.* Investigate the exceptions to the pattern. There are three main exceptions. They are that:
(i) Esso scores more highly than expected for "large company".
(ii) Jet scores more highly than expected for "value for money".
(iii) National scores more highly than expected for "with-it people". **(5 marks)**

(c) All exceptions can be explained in terms of the brands' advertising styles. Esso is known as a large company internationally, Jet as a retailer of cheaply acquired petrol and National has advertised to younger age groups. The conclusion is that the pattern is a good fit. **(5 marks)**

(d) *Stage 5.* Finally, additional information should be introduced. Is the response to the questions proportional to market share or to the size of the company? Does the pattern hold for other samples in other regions and at different times? It may even hold for other products besides petrol.

The information can be used to monitor the effectiveness of advertising campaigns. The impact of advertising does not depend upon the level of response but on the extent to which the response changes from the norm. **(5 marks)**

4. Can the government fuel the green debate?

(a) The regression equation is:

$$\text{mpg} = 53.9 - 0.4 \times \text{speed} - 0.8 \times \text{altitude} - 1.5 \times \text{weight}$$

When speed = 45, altitude = 200 and weight = 300,

$$\begin{aligned}\text{mpg} &= 53.9 - 0.4 \times 45 - 0.8 \times 2 - 1.5 \times 3 \\ &= 29.8\end{aligned}$$

(5 marks)

(b)

Trip	Residual
1	2.1 = 33 – (53.9 – 0.4 × 50 – 0.8 × 0 – 1.5 × 2)
2	3.4 = 36 – (53.9 – 0.4 × 40 – 0.8 × 1 – 1.5 × 3)
3	0.5 = 31 – (53.9 – 0.4 × 45 – 0.8 × 3 – 1.5 × 2)
4	1.3 = 24 – (53.9 – 0.4 × 55 – 0.8 × 4 – 1.5 × 4)
5	–0.6 = 34 – (53.9 – 0.4 × 35 – 0.8 × 1 – 1.5 × 3)
6	1.1 = 27 – (53.9 – 0.4 × 45 – 0.8 × 5 – 1.5 × 4)
7	–2.0 = 20 – (53.9 – 0.4 × 55 – 0.8 × 3 – 1.5 × 5)
8	–1.9 = 35 – (53.9 – 0.4 × 35 – 0.8 × 0 – 1.5 × 2)
9	–0.6 = 32 – (53.9 – 0.4 × 40 – 0.8 × 1 – 1.5 × 3)
10	–0.8 = 27 – (53.9 – 0.4 × 50 – 0.8 × 2 – 1.5 × 3)
11	0.3 = 23 – (53.9 – 0.4 × 55 – 0.8 × 4 – 1.5 × 4)
12	–3.3 = 28 – (53.9 – 0.4 × 45 – 0.8 × 2 – 1.5 × 2)

There is a pattern in the residuals in that the negative residuals are in the latter trips. However this is not linked to particular values of the independent variables. If the trips are numbered in time order, i.e. trip 1 was the first and so on, then the pattern could mean that fuel consumption worsened as the car became older.
(5 marks)

(c) To see if variables should be excluded, the *t* values have to be calculated:

Variable	Coefficient	Std error	*t* value
mph	–0.4	0.12	–3.3
altitude	–0.8	0.58	–1.3
weight	–1.5	0.92	–1.6

Speed has a *t* value that is less than –2 and is rightfully included. There is a doubt about altitude and weight since their *t* values are closer to zero. However, other evidence (on the working of internal combustion engines) suggests that they should be retained. **(5 marks)**

(d) Approximately, the accuracy of the forecast (95 per cent confidence limits) in part (a) is given by 2 × residual standard error,
i.e. + / –4.4
The standard error of residuals reflects error arising from the residuals only. SE (Predicted) reflects error from the estimate of the regression line as well as the residuals. **(5 marks)**

(e) Improvements to the regression would be to:
(i) include more data: 12 observations are too few when there are 3 independent variables.
(ii) ensure that the style of driving (or the driver) does not change from trip to trip.
(iii) ensure the terrain is approximately the same for each trip, i.e. the same mixture of urban and rural.
(iv) include a variable for wet or dry conditions. **(5 marks)**

PRACTICE FINAL EXAMINATION 2 – WITHOUT MCQs

Case Studies

Case Study 1

You have recently been appointed as a consultant in the cruising department of a large travel firm. Some market research has been carried out to determine the current price structures of Caribbean cruises offered by different shipping companies. The table below shows the information that has been collected by the market research agency.

Average cost per day for a Caribbean Cruise

Cruise Liner	*£*	*Cruise Liner*	*£*
Amerikanis (Chandris)	140	**Radisson Diamond** (Radisson)	315
Britanis (Chandris)	115	**Regal Princes** (Princess)	150
Caribe (Commodore)	110	**Regent Sea** (Regency)	170
Celebration (Carnival)	130	**Regent Star** (Regency)	170
Club Med I (Club Med)	185	**Regent Sun** (Princess)	180
Crown Dynasty (Crown)	125	**Renaissance Ships** (Renaissance)	340
Crown Jewel (Crown)	125	**Sagafjord** (Cunard)	185
Crown Monarch (Crown)	125	**Sea Goddess I** (Cunard)	510
Crown Princess (Princess)	150	**SeaBreeze** (Dolphin)	125
Cunard Countess (Cunard)	160	**Seaward** (Norwegian Cruise)	130
Dreamward (Nor' Cruise)	150	**Sky Princess** (Princess)	130
Ecstasy (Carnival)	130	**Song of Flower** (Seven Seas)	295
Encharted Seas (Commodore)	140	**Sovereign of the Seas** (R Carib')	150
Festivale (Carnival)	125	**Star Clipper** (Star Clipper)	170
Holiday (Carnival)	130	**Star Flyer** (Star Clipper)	195
Horizon (Celebrity)	205	**Star Princess** (Princess)	175
Majesty of the Seas (R Carib')	150	**Starward** (Nor' Cruise)	155
Meridian (Celebrity)	170	**Statendam** (H America)	185
Monarch of the Seas (R Carib')	185	**Sunward** (Nor' Cruise)	140
Nantucket Clipper (Clipper)	220	**Tropicale** (Carnivale)	125
Nieuw Amsterdam (H America)	155	**Vistafjord** (Cunard)	185
Noordam (H America)	150	**Westerdam** (H America)	155
Nordic Prince (R Carib')	140	**Wind Star** (Wind Ships)	272
Norway (Norwegian Cruise)	150	**Windward** (Nor' Cruise)	175
OceanBreeze (Dolphin)	140	**Yorktown Clipper** (Clipper)	230
Q Elizabeth 2 (Cunard)	175	**Zenith** (Celebrity)	175

The name of the company operating the cruise is shown in brackets.

Write a report to the manager of the department, summarising the main features of the price information for Caribbean cruises shown above.

You should include any necessary tables or graphs in your report, and should also comment on the limitations of your analysis and indicate any additional information you would require. **(50 marks)**

The answer should include summary statistics for the data given.

Number	52	
Mean	£174.4	
Standard Deviation	67.84	
Maximum	£510	(Sea Goddess I)
Minimum	£110	(Caribe)
Range	£400	
Semi-interquartile range	£25	
Median	£155	
Mode	£150	
Frequency Distribution	(see below)	

Graphs should include a histogram or a bar chart.

Data can also be summarized for each of the companies, e.g. Cunard, Crown, etc., to examine the price range covered by the companies. See table overleaf.

The report should question the cruise liners selected for the survey – what method of selection was used, were they all included? The basis for calculation of "average cost per day" should be examined, e.g. type of cabin, length of cruise, travel cost included, where did cruise start? Season and area of cruise may also be important determinants of price. Accuracy of the original data should be questioned, e.g. Nor' Cruise and Norwegian Cruise, Carnival and Carnivale.

Frequency Distribution

Grouped		*Ungrouped*			
Range	*Total*	*Value (x)*	*Frequency (f)*		
100–119	2	110	1		
120–139	11	115	1		
140–159	15	125	6		
160–179	9	130	5		
180–199	7	140	5		
200–219	1	150	7		
220–239	2	155	3		
240–259	–	160	1		
260–279	1	170	4		
280–299	1	175	4		
300–319	1	180	1		
340–359	1	185	5		
500–520	1	195	1		
	52	205	1		
		220	1		
		230	1	$\Sigma fx = 9\,067$	
		272	1		
		295	1	$\bar{x} = 174.4$	
		315	1		
		340	1	Upper Quartile	185
		510	1	Lower Quartile	135
			52	Difference	50

Ship	*Company*	*Cost*
Festivale	Carnival	125
Celebration	Carnival	130
Ecstasy	Carnival	130
Holiday	Carnival	130
Tropicale	Carnivale	125
Meridian	Celebrity	170
Zenith	Celebrity	175
Horizon	Celebrity	205
Britanis	Chandris	115
Amerikanis	Chandris	140
Nantucket Clipper	Clipper	220
Yorktown Clipper	Clipper	230
Club Med I	Club Med	185
Caribe	Commodore	110
Encharted Seas	Commodore	140
Crown Dynasty	Crown	125
Crown Jewel	Crown	125
Crown Monarch	Crown	125
Cunard Countess	Cunard	160
Q Elizabeth 2	Cunard	175
Sagafiord	Cunard	185
Vistafiord	Cunard	185
Sea Goddess 1	Cunard	510
SeaBreeze	Dolphin	125
Ocean Breeze	Dolphin	140
Noordam	H America	150
Nieuw Amsterdam	H America	155
Westerdam	H America	155
Statendam	H America	185
Seaward	Nor Cruise	130
Sunward	Nor Cruise	140
Dreamward	Nor Cruise	150
Norway	Nor Cruise	150
Starward	Nor Cruise	155
Windward	Nor Cruise	175
Sky Princess	Princess	130
Crown Princess	Princess	150
Regal Princes	Princess	150
Star Princess	Princess	175
Regent Sun	Princess	180
Nordic Prince	R Carib	140
Majesty	R Carib	150
Sovereign of the Seas	R Carib	150
Monarch of the Seas	R Carib	185
Radisson Diamond	Radisson	315
Regent Sea	Regency	170
Regent Star	Regency	170
Renaissance Ships	Renaissance	340
Song of Flower	Seven Seas	295
Star Clipper	Star Clipper	170
Star Flyer	Star Clipper	195
Wind Star	Wind Ships	272
Yorktown Clipper	Clipper	230
Zenith	Celebrity	175
	Tot	9067
	Mean	174.3654
	Var	4601.727
	Std	67.83603

Company Summary

	Lowest	*Highest*	*Average*
Carnival	125	130	128
Celebrity	170	205	183.33
Chandris	115	140	127.5
Clipper	220	230	225
Club Med	185		185
Comodore	110	140	125
Crown	125	125	125
Cunard	160	510	243
Dolphin	125	140	132.5
H America	150	185	161.2
Nor Cruise	130	175	150
Princess	130	180	157
R Carrib	140	185	156.25
Regency	170	170	170
Renaissance	340		340
Seven Seas	295		295
Star Clipper	170	195	182.5
Wind Ships	272		272
Radisson	315		315

Case Study 2

In a transportation system, managers wish to determine the relationship between travel time (TIME), the number of miles tavelled (MILES) and the number of deliveries made (DELIV). An additional variable (TYPE) indicating the type of vehicle, which is coded 0 if the vehicle is a pick-up and 1 if it is a van, has also been included in the analysis. The statisticians have used a multiple regression package for the analysis and this has produced the following output:

Variable	*Coefficient*	*Standard Error*	*t-ratio*
CONSTANT	0.534	1.22	0.438
MILES	0.04521	0.016000	2.826
DELIV	0.7123	0.2635	2.703
TYPE	0.8000	0.5392	1.484

R-bar-squared = 78.5%

Analysis of Variance

Source of Variation	*Degrees of Freedom*	*Sums of Squares*	*Mean Square*	*F-ratio*
Regression	3	20.5821	6.8607	12.0462
Error	6	3.4172	0.5692	
Total	9	23.9993	2.6666	

1. ***What is the estimated regression equation for the travel time?*** **(3 marks)**

   Regression equation

   TIME = 0.534 + (0.04521 × MILES) + (0.7123 × DELIV) + (0.8000 × TIME)

2. ***Test the significance of the regression coefficients and explain what this indicates.*** **(6 marks)**

   Testing the regression coefficients

   Null hypothesis: Coefficient = 0

   Alternative hypothesis: Coefficient ≠ 0

   Degrees of freedom = 6 (i.e. 9–3)

   Use *t*-statistics from tables Critical *t* at 5% = 2.447

MILES	$t = 2.826$	Significantly different at 5% level of significance
DELIV	$t = 2.703$	Significantly different at 5% level of significance
TYPE	$t = 1.484$	No significant difference

   This indicates that the variables MILES and DELIV have coefficients which are significantly different from 0, and both variables should be retained in the regression equation.

The variable TYPE has a coefficient which is not significantly different from 0. The regression should be run again omitting the variable TYPE. This will affect the values of the constant and the other variables, so the test of significance should be repeated.

3. ***What time would you predict for***

   (a) A van making 2 deliveries travelling 75 miles?
   (b) A pick-up making 3 deliveries travelling 50 miles? **(4 marks)**

Using the model given in the question:

(a) TYPE = 1
DELIV = 2
MILES = 75

TIME = 0.534 + (0.04521 × 75) + (0.7123 × 2) + (0.8000 × 1)

= 0.534 + 3.391 + 1.425 + 0.8

= 6.15 hours

(b) TYPE = 0
DELIV = 3
MILES = 50

TIME = 0.534 + (0.04521 × 50) + (0.7123 × 3) + (0.8000 × 0)

= 0.534 + 2.261 + 2.137 + 0

= 4.93 hours

4. ***What are the underlying assumptions of this regression model?*** **(4 marks)**

The errors are normally distributed and random.
The mean of the error terms is zero.
The error terms have a constant variance.

5. ***Write a short report on the results of the regression analysis. Include a critical assessment of the model used, together with recommendations or improvement.*** **(8 marks)**
(Total of 25 marks)

The model provides a reasonable fit to the data (R-bar-squared 78.5%) but could be improved. The fit can be examined using the F-ratio. The alternative hypothesis is that the model explains a significant proportion of the variation in the variable TIME.

F calculated = 12.0462
F critical = 4.76 at 5% from tables with (3.6) degrees of freedom
F critical = 9.78 at 1% from tables

Accept the alternative hypothesis; the model explains a significant proportion of the variation in the variable TIME at the 1% level of significance.

The model should be re-run omitting the variable TYPE as explained in Part 2 and its fit examined. The significance of the coefficients should be tested. A scatter diagram should be produced, and examination of the residuals and for collinearity should be made. More data should be collected. The model is only valid for data within the range sampled.

Case Study 3

The travel agent has recorded the number of bookings made for cruises in the last few months. He wants to use this information to produce a forecast of cruise bookings for the next month.

Year	*Month*	*Number of Bookings*
1992	January	3 250
	February	3 125
	March	2 350
	April	2 425
	May	2 275
	June	2 150
	July	2 375
	August	2 450
	September	2 825
	October	3 050
	November	3 500
	December	3 350
1993	January	3 325
	February	3 250

1. ***Make a forecast using a three-point moving average.*** **(6 marks)**

		Number	*3 Year Total*	*3 Point Moving Average*	*Forecast*	*Error*
1992	January	3 250				
	February	3 125	8 725	2 908.33		
	March	2 350	7 900	2 633.33		
	April	2 425	7 050	2 350.00	2 908	–483
	May	2 275	6 850	2 283.33	2 633	–358
	June	2 150	6 800	2 266.67	2 350	–200
	July	2 375	6 975	2 325.00	2 283	92
	August	2 450	7 650	2 550.00	2 267	183
	September	2 825	8 325	2 775.00	2 325	500
	October	3 050	9 375	3 125.00	2 550	500
	November	3 500	9 900	3 300.00	2 775	725
	December	3 350	10 175	3 391.67	3 125	225
1993	January	3 325	9 925	3 308.33	3 300	25
	February	3 250			3 392	–142

2. ***Make a forecast using exponential smoothing with α = 0.2. What does this value of α indicate?*** **(7 marks)**

		Number	*Smoothed* α = 0.2		*Forecast*	*Error*
1992	January	3250	3250			
	February	3125	3225	(2600 + 625)	3 250	–125
	March	2350	3050	(2580 + 470)	3 225	–875
	April	2425	2925	(2440 + 485)	3 050	–625
	May	2275	2795	(2340 + 455)	2 925	–650
	June	2150	2666	(2236 + 430)	2 795	–645
	July	2375	2607.8	(2132.8 + 475)	2 666	–291
	August	2450	2576.24	(2086.24 + 490)	2 608	–158
	September	2825	2625.99	(2060.99 + 565)	2 576	249
	October	3050	2710.79	(2100.79+ 610)	2 626	424
	November	3500	2868.63	(2168.63 + 700)	2 711	789
	December	3350	2964.90	(2294.90 + 670)	2 869	481
1993	January	3325	3036.92	(2371.92 + 665)	2 965	360
	February	3250	3079.54	(2429.54 + 650)	3 037	213

The value α = 0.2 shows that less reliance is placed on the most recent data than on the previous value in the series.

3. ***Compare the accuracy of the two methods using the Mean Squared Error.*** **(4 marks)**

Mean Squared Error

Calculated over period April 1992 to February 1993.

Moving Averages

$$\text{MSE} = \frac{\text{Sum of Squares Errors}}{\text{No. of months in the comparison}}$$

$$= \frac{(-483)^2 + (-358)^2 + \ldots\ldots + (-142)^2}{11}$$

$$= \frac{1\,540\,445}{11}$$

$$= \underline{\underline{140\,040}}$$

Exponential Smoothing

$$\text{MSE} = \frac{(-125)^2 + (-875)^2 + \ldots\ldots + (213)^2}{13}$$

$$= \frac{3\,390\,673}{13}$$

$$= \underline{\underline{260\,821}}$$

4. ***Which method is preferable and why?*** **(3 marks)**

Exponential smoothing has the higher MSE (influenced by the value of α used) and therefore Moving Average should be preferred.

5. ***What is the forecast for March 1993?*** **(1 mark)**

Forecast for March 1993 is 3 308, rounded to 3 300.

6. ***What reservations are there about this forecast?*** **(4 marks)**
(Total of 25 marks)

The reservations about the forecast are:

(i) No account has been taken of seasonal effects. The series is too short to identify these, although there appears to be a marked variation between the months.

(ii) A better forecast could have been obtained perhaps by using a different value of α in the exponential smoothing.

(iii) Other patterns may emerge for particular types of cruise, e.g. by location, duration, special offers, etc. These factors should be examined.

PRACTICE FINAL EXAMINATION 3 – WITHOUT MCQs

Case Studies

Case Study 1

At a crop research institute, four different varieties of wheat are grown so that the yields can be investigated. As it is thought that the location in the field (such as amount of sunshine, wind etc.) may also have an effect on yield, the field is divided into 4 equal strips. Yield figures are shown in the table below:

Yield
Wheat Strain

Location	*A*	*B*	*C*	*D*
1	11	15	11	11
2	15	17	14	14
3	15	18	14	13
4	13	16	15	12

1. ***Produce a two-way analysis of variance table for the above data.*** **(11 marks)**

2. ***Is there a significant difference in the average yield for the different varieties of wheat?*** **(4 marks)**

3. ***Is there a significant difference in the average yield produced by the different locations in the field?*** **(4 marks)**

4. ***Write a report on your findings. What qualifications would you wish to make to your conclusions?*** **(6 marks)**
(Total of 25 marks)

Solution

1. *Yield*
Wheat Strain

Location	*A*	*B*	*C*	*D*	*Total*	*Average*
1	11	15	11	11	48	12
2	15	17	14	14	60	15
3	15	18	14	13	60	15
4	13	16	15	12	56	14
Total	54	66	54	50	224	
Average	13.5	16.5	13.5	12.5		14

Total Sum of Squares (TSS) = $\Sigma (x_{ij} - \bar{\bar{x}})^2$

TSS = $(11 - 14)^2 + (15 - 14)^2 + (11 - 14)^2 + \ldots\ldots + (12 - 14)^2$

TSS = 9 + 1 + 9 + 9 + 1 + 9 + 0 + 0 + 1 + 16 + 0 + 1 + 1 + 4 + 1 + 4

TSS = 66

Sum of Squares between Treatments (SST) = No. of blocks $\times \sum_j (x_j - \bar{\bar{x}})$

$= 4 \times \{(13.5 - 14)^2 + (16.5 - 14)^2 + (13.5 - 14)^2 + (12.5 - 14)^2\}$

$= 4 \times \{0.25 + 6.25 + 0.25 + 2.25\}$

$= 4 \times 9$

SST = 36

Sum of squares between Blocks (SSB) = No. of treatments $\times \sum_i (\bar{x}_i - \bar{\bar{x}})^2$

$= 4 \times \{(12 - 14)^2 + (15 - 14)^2 + (15 - 14)^2 + (14 - 14)^2\}$

$= 4 \times \{4 + 1 + 1 + 0\}$

$= 4 \times 6$

SSB = 24

Analysis of Variance Table

Source of Variation	*Degrees of Freedom*	*Sum of Squares*	*Mean Square*	*F-ratio*
Treatments	3	36	12.00	17.91
Blocks	3	24	8.00	11.94
Error	9	6	0.67	
Total	**15**	**66**		

2. Testing differences in average yield for different varieties.

   Use F-ratio for treatments = 17.91 with (3,9) d.f.

   From tables at 5% level of significance F = 3.86.

   From tables at 1% level of significance F = 6.99.

   There is a significant difference in average yields for different varieties at the 1% level of significance.

3. Testing differences in average yield for different locations.

   Use F-ratio for blocks = 11.94 with (3,9) d.f.

   From tables at 5% level of significance F = 3.86.

   From tables at 1% level of significance F = 6.99.

   There is a significant difference in average yields for different locations.

4. The yields produced by four different varieties of wheat have been analysed. Observation of the data indicates that the yield from Variety B was higher than that from the other three varieties A, C and D. This difference was observed in each of the four locations used. Statistical analysis of the data using ANOVA indicates that the average yields for the four varieties were significantly different at the 1% level of significance.

   When the effect of location is examined, locations 2, 3 and 4 appear to produce slightly higher average yields than location 1. Location 1 produces the lowest yields for each of the varieties. Analysis using ANOVA shows that differences in average yield are statistically significant at the 1% level of significance.

Case Study 2

A local newspaper has a weekly section which advertises property for sale. Editorial comment is also included in this section. For their first issue in June the editors wish to comment on changes in property prices since the beginning of the year. It has been suggested that a property index should be calculated.

Properties sold in this area fall into three main categories: detached houses, other houses and flats. The table below shows the data for the first three months of the year (prices are given in £'000s and refer to the average price).

Month	*Detached Houses*		*Other Houses*		*Flats*	
	Price	*Quantity*	*Price*	*Quantity*	*Price*	*Quantity*
Jan	82	30	61.8	100	45.1	232
Feb	95	40	62.1	124	47.5	376
March	87	32	62.9	152	50.3	512

1. ***Write a short report on the trends observed in the above table.*** **(5 marks)**

2. ***Calculate three different types of aggregate price index for February using January as the base month.*** **(12 marks)**

3. ***Recommend the most suitable type of index for use in the property index, giving your reasons.*** **(2 marks)**

4. ***If the newspaper decided to make such an index a permanent feature, outline briefly the other factors that would need to be taken into account.*** **(6 marks)**

(Total of 25 marks)

Solution

1. The main types of property sold are considered in three groups, i.e., detached houses, other houses and flats.

   In the detached house sector there was in increase in sales in February, but sales in March returned to just above the January level. The average price rose to £95 000 in February but March sales showed in average of £87 000. Demand for this type of property can be quite variable as can the offer of properties for sale. There may also be considerable variation in the prices achieved for this group.

   For the "other houses" sector the quantity sold showed a steady increase from 100 in January to 124 and 152 in February and March respectively. Similarly the average price achieved showed an increase over the same period.

   In the "flats" sector there was a marked increase in the number of properties sold: 232 in January compared with 512 in March. Similarly the average price showed an increase from £45 100 in January to £50 300 in March. These data may reflect the preference of both buyers and sellers to move in the spring.

2. Possibilities are:

   Aggregate price index =

$$\frac{95 + 62.1 + 47.5}{82 + 61.8 + 45.1} \times 100 = \frac{204.6}{188.9} \times 100 = 108.3$$

   Equal weighting to different types of property, but change in price of flats will have less effect than same % change in detached houses.

   Laspeyes Price Index

$$= \frac{(95 \times 30)}{(82 \times 30)} + \frac{(62.1 \times 100)}{(61.8 \times 100)} + \frac{(47.5 \times 232)}{(45.1 \times 232)} \times 100$$

$$= \frac{2850 + 6210 + 11020}{2460 + 6180 + 10463.2} \times 100$$

$$= \frac{20080}{19103.2} \times 100$$

$$\underline{\underline{105.1}}$$

   Weighting relates to proportions occurring in the base year, but these may change.

Paasche Price Index

$$= \frac{(95 \times 40)}{(82 \times 40)} + \frac{(62.1 \times 124)}{(61.8 \times 124)} + \frac{(47.5 \times 376)}{(45.1 \times 376)} \times 100$$

$$= \frac{3\,800 + 7\,700 + 17\,860}{3\,280 + 7\,663.2 + 16\,957.6} \times 100$$

$$= \frac{29\,360.4}{27\,900.8} \times 100$$

$$= \underline{\underline{105.2}}$$

Weighting relates to proportions occurring in the current year. Total quantities required for the current year, often not known until well past the end of the year.

3. A fixed weight index might be the most appropriate using the stable weightings for the different sections. This may also be easier for ordinary house purchasers to understand and interpret.

4 – Choice of base year or month
- Categories to be included
- Weights
- Availability, timeliness and accuracy of data
- Uses to be made
- Changes in property market, effect of recession, mortgage rates, tax implications. etc.

Case Study 3

1. ***Describe briefly the characteristics of the normal distribution.*** **(5 marks)**

2. ***Outline the importance of the normal distribution in statistical inference.*** **(4 marks)**

3. ***In a factory producing soft drinks, there is a canning process to fill the cans. The content of the cans is normally distributed with mean 442.5 ml and standard deviation of 1.2 ml. The cans are all marked as containing 440 ml.***

   (a) ***What percentage of the cans contain more than 444 ml?*** **(5 marks)**

   (b) ***If the firm is found to have sold a can containing less than the stated content, the firm can be prosecuted. In a production run of 8 000 cans, how many cans would contain less than the stated content?*** **(6 marks)**

   (c) ***Between what limits does 92% of the production fall?*** **(5 marks)**

(Total of 25 marks)

Solution

1. **Characteristics of Normal Distribution**

   Continuous distribution, symmetrical, bell-shaped unimodal.

   Area under the curve represents a probability of 1.

68% of readings lie within ± 1 standard deviation of mean
95% of readings lie within ± 2 standard deviations of mean
99.7% of readings lie within ± 3 standard deviations of mean

Theoretical distribution can be calculated and tabulated.

2. **Importance of normal distribution in statistical inference**

If a series of samples are taken from a population then the distribution of their sample means follows a normal distribution. This relationship does not depend on the distributions of the population, providing that each of the samples is based on a sample size of 30 or more. The properties of the normal distribution can be used in the estimation of population parameters from the sample.

3. μ = 442.5 ml
σ = 1.2 ml

(a) **More than 444 mls**

$X = 444$

$$Z = \frac{X - \mu}{\sigma} = \frac{444 - 442.5}{1.2} = \frac{1.5}{1.2} = 1.25$$

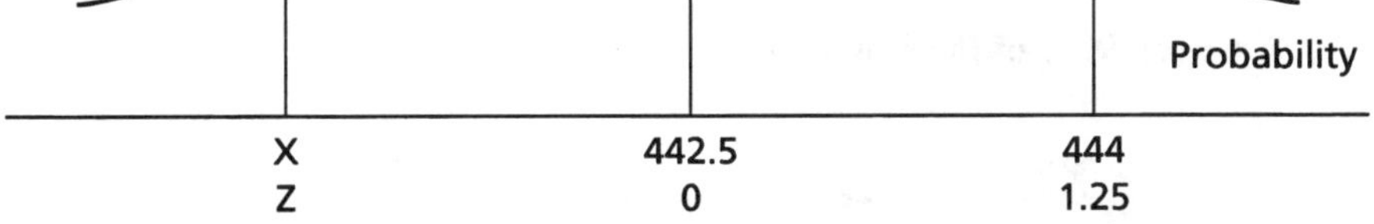

Prob [$Z > 1.25$] = 0.5 – 0.3944
= 0.1056

Prob [Can > 444 mls] = 0.1056

Percentage of cans containing more than 444 mls = 10.56%

(b) **Less than 440 mls**

$X = 440$

$$Z = \frac{X - \mu}{\sigma} = \frac{440 - 442.5}{1.2} = \frac{-2.5}{1.2} = 2.08$$

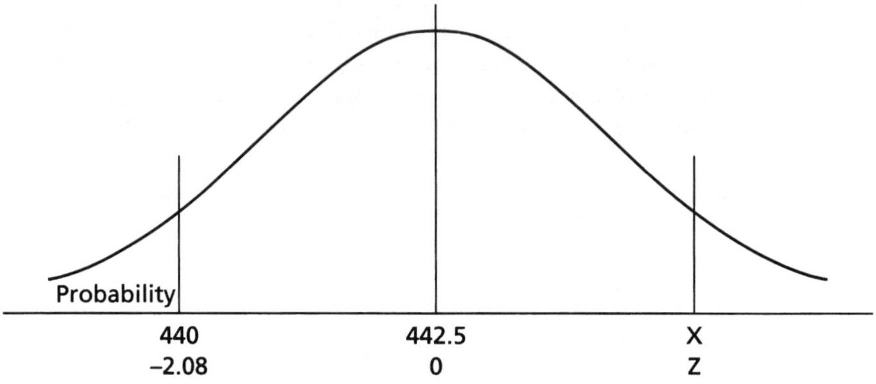

Prob [Z < –2.08] = 0.5 – 0.4812
= 0.0188

Prob [Can < 440 mls] = 0.0188

Percentage of cans containing less than 440 mls = 1.88%

Number of cans containing less than 400 mls = 0.0188 × 8 000
= 150.4

(c) **92% of the Production**

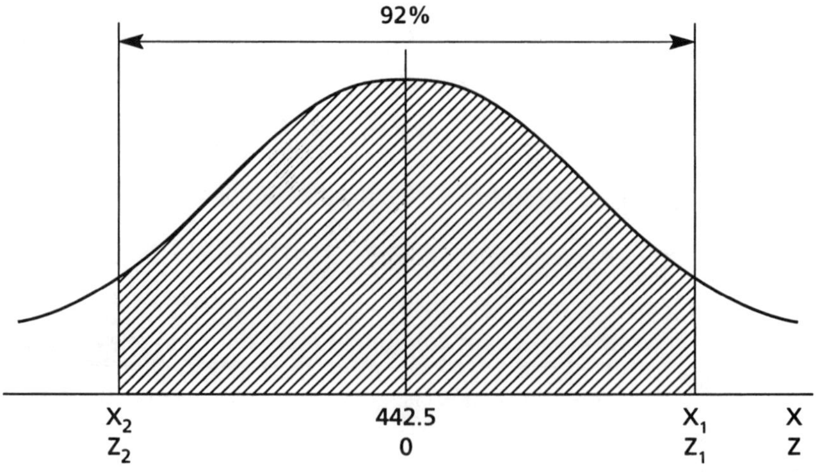

We need to find X_1 and X_2

Prob $[0 < Z < Z_1] = 0.46$

From tables $Z_1 = 1.75$

Since $Z_1 = \frac{X_1 - 442.5}{1.2}$ using $Z = \frac{X - \mu}{\sigma}$

$$\begin{aligned} \text{Then} \quad X_1 &= 1.2Z_1 + 442.5 \\ &= (1.2 \times 1.75) + 442.5 \\ &= 2.1 + 442.5 = 444.6 \end{aligned}$$

By symmetry $X_2 = -2.1 + 442.5 = 440.4$

92% of the cans produced contain between 440.4 and 444.6 mls.

Case Study 4

A brewery produces several different kinds of beer, together with its latest product, a low-alcohol beer. It supplies the retail market which includes ships, supermarkets and off-licences with its products. For this market the beer is usually sold in bottles or cans; these may be sold individually, or as multi-packs (4 or 6 cans), or in crates. The brewery also supplies the licensed trade such as hotels, restaurants, clubs, bars and pubs. In this sector, the beer may be supplied in cans, bottles, crates or casks.

The brewery needs to plan its future production, and requires forecasts of its sales in the different markets. The firm also needs to forecast sales for its various products and for the different types of packaging and distribution.

Describe how a suitable forecasting system could be developed for the brewery.

(Total of 25 marks)

Solution

Answers can be based on the forecasting guidelines given in the main text. The answer should, however, relate throughout to the brewery and its likely needs.

1. **Use of forecasting Model**

   Production includes:
   - raw materials
   - bottling/canning
   - storage

   Sales Force
   Promotion and Marketing
   Distribution

   Consider accuracy and details required

   Time period required

2. **Users of Forecast**

   Management
   Production
   Marketing
   Distribution

3. **Factors influencing the Forecast**

   (a) Internal
   Current production and demand
   Pricing
   Advertising/Promotion
   Brand image

   (b) External
   Taxation policy
   Disposable income
   Employment/unemployment
   Competitors
   Health image
   Drink/driving campaigns
   Seasonal factors
   Retail and licensed outlets

4. **Data Available**

   Some data available but not complete.

5. **Decide on the Technique**

   Possibly causal model with seasonal elements.

6. **Test Accurancy of Model**

   Use model to produce forecast and compare with actual demand.

7. **Incorporate Judgement**

   Use knowledge of market, competitors, taxation changes, etc., and incorporate in forecasts

8. **Implement**

   Gain agreement on implementation of forecasting system.

9. **Monitor**

   Monitor accurancy of forecast.
   Examine any deviations and investigate reasons for the deviations.

Strategic Planning

PRACTICE FINAL EXAMINATION 1

All 3 Sections should be attempted; the Sections carry equal marks. The pass mark is 50%.

Section 1

The accounts and product information in Exhibit 1 refer to a hypothetical company, Stratco Plc.

> THE FINANCIAL TIMES
> COMPETING IN A RECESSION
>
> The opinion of most forecasters is that the recession is now starting to bite and companies in the electrical and related sectors can expect their markets to be hit for the next 2 years. However, this does not mean that there are no opportunities for companies who are willing to look to longer-term prospects both in terms of productivity and product diversification. The changing nature of communications has led to market openings for a variety of new products; companies with resources and expertise in place will be ready to step into profitable markets when the business cycle begins its inevitable improvement. Experts vary on their opinion of when this may be, the most optimistic being 18 months and the most pessimistic being 3 years.

> MEMO
>
> FROM Marketing Director
> TO Board of Directors
>
> There has been a substantial increase in the number of small companies entering our market area where we are producing Links and Cutters. This has posed problems with some of our customers because these new entrants are able to offer products more closely tailored to their requirements. While the impact on the market shares of our existing products is likely to be marginal, it looks like we are going to face increasing difficulties in establishing market shares with new products from now on, and perhaps we should be reviewing the development potential of the Grinder.

On the basis of the limited information on Stratco plc in Exhibit 1, and the information above, assess the strategic prospects for the company by carrying out the following tasks.

1. Set up a profile of the company and its environment on which you would base recommendations for a strategic thrust. Pay particular attention to the incorporation of risk.
2. Suggest additional information which you would find useful. How might this information be obtained?

3. Assess your recommendations from the shareholder viewpoint.
4. The current operating surplus could have been increased from $1 409 000 to $2 454 000 by cutting research expenditure, development expenditure and company marketing by 50 per cent. What effect is this likely to have on company value in the short and long term?

Exhibit 1

Stratco plc

	Operating Account at end year: Production Cost, and Revenue ($000)		
		SALES REVENUE	8 954
COST OF GOODS SOLD	5 055		
		GROSS PROFIT	3 899
	Operating Account at end year: Overheads and Operating Surplus ($000)		
Factory Rents	300		
Owned Factory Overheads	100		
Research Expenditure	700		
Development Engineering	590		
Company Marketing	800		
TOTAL OVERHEAD	2 490		
		OPERATING SURPLUS	1 409
	Cash Flow Account at End Year ($000)		
	OUTLAY		INCOME
Material Purchase Costs	1 650		
		Interest on Assets	42
Wage Costs	2 592		
Assembly Line Costs	1 120		
Product Marketing	1 000		
Total Overheads	2 490	Sales Revenue	8 954
TOTAL OUTLAY	8 852	TOTAL INCOME	8 996
		NET CASH FLOW	144
	Balance Sheet at End Year ($000)		
FIXED ASSETS			
Factory	2 000		
TOTAL FIXED ASSETS		2 000	
CURRENT ASSETS			
Raw Materials	1 000		
Finished Goods	3 624		
Cash	3 500		
TOTAL CURRENT ASSETS		8 124	
TOTAL ASSETS			10 124
OWNERS' EQUITY		10 124	
DEBT			
Loan	0		
TOTAL DEBT		0	
TOTAL LIABILITIES			10 124

Company Value at End Year ($000)			
CASH	3 500	TOTAL DEBT	0
NET LIQUID ASSETS	3 500		
Operating Surplus Value*	9 545		
COMPANY VALUE	13 045		
POTENTIAL PRODUCT VALUES			
Production Models**	42 200		
Development Models**	7 300		

* Based on the market's view of the prospects of future earnings, derived from the company's Operating Surplus track record
** Based on the market's interpretation of the information in the product reports

Report on Products for year

Status: Production Models	Link	Cutter		Link	Cutter
Remaining Life (years)	9	5			
Composition of Demand			Composition of Supply		
Total Market	21 400	53 000			
Potential Market Share (%)	12.7	8.4			
Orders	2 715	4 437	Output	3 095	6 457
			Previous Inventory	1 643	1 453
Warranty Demand	79	115			
TOTAL DEMAND	2 794	4 552	TOTAL SUPPLY	4 738	7 910
Resource Productivity			Distribution of Supply		
Output/Line	515	645	Warranty Replacements	79	115
Output/Worker	10	18	Sales to Backlog	0	0
Output/Unit Material	0.97	1.96	Sales to Orders	2 715	4 437
Working Time (%)	100	101	Actual Market Share (%)	12.7	8.4
Labour Attrition Rate (%)	2.16	3.10	Excess Supply (Inventory)	1 944	3 359
Price ($/unit)	1 778	930			
Competing Price ($/unit)	1 778	1 000			
Account at end year					
Wage Cost ($000)	1 200	1 392			
Assembly Line Cost ($000)	420	700			
Cost of Material Used ($000)	829	857			
Product Marketing	300	700			
TOTAL COST ($000)	2 749	3 649	SALES REVENUE ($000)	4 827	4 127
Unit Cost ($1unit)	888	565	GROSS PROFIT ($000)	2 345	1 555
Cost of Goods Sold ($000)	2 482	2 572			
Labour Experience*					
1 quarters	10	20			
2 quarters		150			
3 quarters	290	65			
4 quarters		133			

*Number of quarters employees have worked on this product.

Report on Grinder for Year 5			
Status: Buying in Technology			
Remaining Life (years)	10		
Estimated Market Peak	50 000	Current Market Size	35 238
Competing Price ($/unit)	921	Forecast Warranty Returns (%)	3
Production Cost ($/unit)	712		
Forecast Market Share (%)	9.3	Remaining Development (years)	1
Development Expenditure			
Spending this Year ($000)	590		
Total to Date ($000)	1 180		

Section 2: The British Satellite Broadcasting Disaster

Background

The British television system comprises four terrestrial stations: two are run on the basis of an annual licence fee (which everyone who owns a TV set must pay); these are the British Broadcasting Corporation channels 1 and 2, and the commercial stations ITV and Channel 4. The first satellite TV licence was awarded to British Satellite Broadcasting (BSB) in December 1986; BSB had a number of apparent advantages. First, it was first in this new field serving the British market; its only rival Sky did not announce its satellite service until the middle of 1988. Second, BSB had the backing of some of Britain's richest media companies; on the other hand, Sky was owned and run by Rupert Murdoch, the proprietor of News Corporation, which at the time was labouring under the burden of an $8 billion debt. Third, BSB had what it considered to be a superior technology in D-MAC, which was supposed to provide clearer pictures and better sound than the PAL system used by Sky.

But by November 1990, after only three months of BSB transmissions, it had become clear that both satellite stations could not survive. Sky was making losses of about $8 million per week, while BSB was making losses of about $16 million per week. BSB was virtually taken over by Sky, which assumed complete management control of the combined company BSkyB. What went wrong with a company which was apparently in a situation with all the preconditions for success?

Getting to the Market too Slow

Despite BSB's 18-month lead in terms of licensing, Sky went on the air 15 months ahead of BSB. This was important because the two systems were incompatible, and the first to install a satellite dish and receiver was likely to keep the customer; it cost about $450 dollars to install or change a system. By the time BSB started broadcasting in April 1990 Sky had installed 750,000 dishes.

Defining the Product

The reason BSB was so late in actually starting broadcasting was that the superior technology could not be put into practice, and it was estimated that this delayed the BSB launch by eight months. Furthermore, BSB overrated the selling power of the D-MAC system, whose superior performance was only apparent on the newest TV sets and recorders. Viewers who had not committed themselves to Sky were therefore waiting for a product with a characteristic which they could not assess; once word started to get around that the difference between the two systems was minimal the advantage of D-MAC was lost.

Getting the Market Wrong

The market for Sky TV was largely the Cl-C2 socio-economic classes, which is not the higher spending middle and upper classes which appeal to advertisers. BSB could have aimed at the market niche which Sky had not exploited with "quality" programming, but it chose to fight Sky in the Cl-C2 market where Sky was already well ahead.

While, of course, it is impossible to know what lay in the minds of BSB executives, it seemed that they considered their competitor to be Sky, whereas in fact they also had to compete with the range of quality and popular programmes available free on the four terrestrial stations. Their problem was not just to attract a potential satellite customer from Sky, but to attract a satellite customer in the first place. Since Sky had already decided on the market and the level of programming, BSB was now competing for part of the market which had already been generated by Sky rather than adding to the total market by virtue of its unique characteristics.

Getting the Costs Wrong

On the cost side, BSB had various disadvantages. First, the D-MAC technology was more costly than PAL, which was already in existence and proven. Second, BSB bought and launched its own two Marco Polo satellites, while Sky rented time on the Astra satellite which was already in orbit. Third, BSB housed itself in lavish studios and offices in expensive central London; Sky was located in less ostentatious facilities in the cheaper suburbs. Fourth, it was well known that BSB had used relatively high salaries to attract executives from the terrestrial stations; Sky had not. Fifth, BSB was determined to outbid Sky for American films, and sent prices to unheard of levels. One explanation for the runaway costs at BSB was that it was a consortium, whose owners could not collectively act to control expenditure in the way in which Rupert Murdoch could.

1 Could BSB have been competitive if a different strategy had been adopted? Set out an argument which, on balance, suggests either YES or NO.
2 If YES

    Suggest reasons why the company followed the course which it did.

   If NO

    Suggest reasons why the enterprise was pursued to the disastrous extent which it reached.

Section 3

Imagine you have been hired to introduce strategic planning into a medium-sized company. The difficulty is that only the CEO believes that on balance there will be a payoff. The directors for Finance, Marketing and Production are sceptical because of the constantly changing environment within which the company operates. Set out the arguments you would use to justify your case for strategic planning, and do not ignore the potential drawbacks of the approach which are likely to be in the minds of your opponents.

Section 1: Suggested approach

1 Identify Strategic Thrust

The question requires you to **systemize** a quantity of diverse information in order to assess the current situation of the company and arrive at a reasoned conclusion on the strategic direction which it should follow. The Strategy Report in Appendix 1 provides a framework within which the problem can be tackled. Analytical tools such as supply and demand analysis, product portfolio analysis, financial appraisal and ratio analysis can be used to generate results to incorporate into an Environmental Threat and Opportunity Profile (ETOP) and a Strategic Advantage Profile (SAP); the profiles are then used in the identification of Strengths, Weaknesses, Opportunities and Threats (SWOT). It has been stressed in the Modules that there is no unique correct answer to strategy problems because of their wide ranging nature and the possibility of unknowable events occurring in the future; however, the following shows how factors can be fitted into a conceptual framework.

ETOP

Environmental factors relating to the economy as a whole and the market in which the company is operating can be gleaned from the newspaper article and observations in the company memo.

Threats

The recession is expected to last for up to 3 years; the newspaper refers to the "inevitable" improvement in conditions when the business cycle starts its upward trend. However, no one can predict the duration of the business cycle with any degree of accuracy. In the absence of any change in strategy by the company, the continuing recession will lead to

- reduced total market, depending on **income elasticity** for the products sold
- relatively low gross profit because of reduced sales and depressed prices
- potential action by competitors to attempt to protect existing sales; these actions might threaten the company's market share.

There appears to have been a reduction in **entry barriers**, resulting in increased competition from small companies. These increased competitive pressures could result in reduced profits.

The company is therefore faced with threats on two fronts: those due to the recession and those due to changed market conditions.

Opportunities

One view is that the upturn will eventually lead to an increase in market size. But to take full advantage of this it is necessary to get the timing right: this could be the right time to start building up market share in anticipation of the increased total market. On the other hand, because of the increased **differentiation** of products and **segmentation** of the market no company can afford to wait passively for better economic conditions to produce higher profitability. Specific action will have to be undertaken to exploit the changing characteristics of the market.

Ranking of threats and opportunities
The relative importance of the factors is open to interpretation. For example, in the **short run** the most important threat appears to be the recession and its potential impact on cash flows; in the **long run** the threat is in the form of a change in competitive circumstances. The most important opportunity seems to be in positioning the company to take advantage of the eventual end to the recession.

SAP
It is necessary to carry out a variety of analyses to determine where the internal strengths and weaknesses lie. An overall view of profitability can be obtained by analysing gross profit, operating surplus and cash flows. **Ratio analysis** can reveal the efficiency with which resources are being deployed. Measures include return on assets, overheads as a percentage of total cost and inventories as a percentage of total output. For example, operating surplus as a percentage of total assets suggests a **return on investment** of 14 per cent; it is a matter for debate whether this is an adequate return given the operating characteristics of the company.

Comparisons between products can reveal differences in the returns on the resources allocated to products. The Link is currently generating a gross profit of $839 (i.e. $2.345 million divided by 2 794) per unit sold, while the Cutter is generating $342 (i.e. $1.555 million divided by 4 437). Explanations for this difference can be found in costs and market position. On the cost side, the experience cohort suggests that the labour force has some way to go before the full benefit of the **learning curve** is achieved. On the market side the Cutter has a smaller market share in a bigger market, and is currently priced below the competing level. If the unit cost of the Cutter were 5 per cent lower, and the price set to the competing level then the difference between unit cost and price would be increased by about $100; at the current level of sales this would have added about $0.44 million to gross profit. This would have increased the gross profit per unit sold to about $450.

You can attempt to position the two products in the **BCG portfolio matrix**; for example, the Link has a higher market share, is on the market at the competing price, has a lower expenditure on product marketing and has a much higher gross profit than the Cutter. This suggests that the Link has characteristics of a Cash Cow, and that the Cutter may be a Star or Question Mark. The conclusions you reach on the position of the products have implications for the interpretation of the accounting cash flows and the future allocation of resources to the two products. For example, gross profit as a percentage of sales revenue is 49 per cent for the Link and 38 per cent for the Cutter. This accounting ratio might be taken to suggest that more resources should be devoted to the Link and fewer to the Cutter; however, the marketing department could argue that the difference between the two is a result of their position in the product life cycle and in the BCG portfolio matrix.

The product under development – the Grinder – can be analysed using **break-even, pay back** and **return on investment**. The projected difference between unit cost and competing price is currently $209; total development expenditure is likely to be about $2 million by launch date, and this suggests break-even sales in the region of 10 000 units. The forecast market share and market peak suggest maximum sales of about 4 500 per year; the break-even point is therefore well within the potential level of sales. However, the pay-back period is likely to be at least two years, given that the market is still growing and is currently at about 35 000 compared to the peak of 50 000, and a lot of things can happen during that time.

The return on investment for the Grinder can be approximated too by comparing the initial investment and the projected net cash flows. For example, selling 4 500 per year with a net contribution of $200 per unit would yield a cash flow of about $0.9 million per year; this results in over 40 per cent return on investment on the development costs of about $2 million.

The prospects for the Grinder can be assessed by using **scenarios** as a basis for investigating the **sensitivity** of cash flows to changes in assumptions; the information in the newspaper report and the internal memo can be used to derive a scenario. For example, the projected unit cost for the Grinder is currently $712, and the competing price is $921, while the Marketing Director's memo suggested that there are likely to be changes in competitive conditions. If the unit cost turned out to be 10 per cent higher and the competing price 10 per cent lower after launch, then the unit cost and competing price would be about $783 and $828 respectively, resulting in a net contribution of $45 per unit. This would reduce cash flows to less than a quarter of the estimate above, with severe effects on break-even, pay back and rate of return. The Marketing Director also stated that market share will be harder to win in the future; each 1 per cent loss of market share would cost about $0.1 million in annual gross profit. The combination of higher cost, lower price and lower market share could be fatal for the Grinder.

Advantages

- The company has built up expertise in existing product markets, and has already climbed well up the experience curve for the Link.
- The gross profit figure suggests that the company is effective at making money in existing markets.
- Currently there is no debt and the company is cash rich.
- The potential product values suggest that the company has a sound basis for long-term survival.

Weaknesses

- The high gross profit is not translated into a high operating surplus because of the level of overheads.
- Resource management could be improved; the Cutter could have higher labour productivity, and inventories of the Cutter increased by over 100 per cent.
- The Grinder does not seem to be well positioned for stiff competition.

Ranking of advantages and weaknesses

Again it is necessary to exercise judgement to assess the relative importance of different factors. For example, it appears that the company has been good at selling products and establishing market shares, but poor at resource management and cost control.

SWOT

The objective is to find a match between the market potential and the strengths of the company, as well as identifying where the company is likely to be under threat.

Strengths
- Existing products and expertise
- Unused cash
- Potential cash flow

Weaknesses
- Cost control
- Potential competitive position of Grinder

Opportunities
- Deploy cash: boost existing market shares
  spend more on Grinder
- Use spare capacity when Grinder launched and sell Cutter from inventory.

Threats
- Increased competition in declining total market

Strategic Options

In order to reduce the possibilities to a set of potentially viable and feasible options, it is useful to think of these initially in terms of **generic** possibilities. The following are examples of how the options might be presented.

Stability: carry on and hope that upturn will compensate for increased competition.

- Risk: market share may decline further.
- Contingency: be ready to protect market share by price reductions and/or increased marketing effort.

Retrench: abandon the Grinder, increase cash as a buffer, reduce overheads such as research, and devote some more resources to the Cutter and Link; reduce capacity.

- Risk: Competitive advantage will pass to other companies who may eventually compete us out of the market. Lower research expenditure may lead to a lack of prototypes in the long run.
- Contingency: be ready to use cash aggressively in the light of competitive reaction.

Expand: position company for expected upturn; meet competition head on and use cash to consolidate position.

- Risk: the company may run out of cash before returns accrue.
- Contingency: ensure that sources of credit are available.

General risk considerations
- Length of recession unknown
- Emerging competitive pressures may be stronger than predicted
- Getting the timing right is crucial

Choice

It is necessary to come down in favour of one of the options. In arriving at a choice give some indication of the trade-offs you are willing to make in terms of threats, opportunities and risks.

2 Additional information

By this stage you have identified potential opportunities and threats, and additional information on these would enable a more informed choice of strategy.

The likely timing of the changes in economic activity are clearly important, and additional insights can be obtained from published forecasts, stockbrokers, consultants. A constant watch needs to be kept on the unemployment rate, the inflation rate, changes in consumer expenditure and the general state of the world economy.

Additional market research into product life cycles would help in refining the composition of the product portfolio. For example, it looks like the Cutter will require a higher market share in order to generate a competitive advantage which will enable higher profits to be made; if the market has reached maturity it will be difficult to achieve this.

The new entrants are segmenting the market, therefore more market research on the characteristics of these segments would be valuable.

It is not clear whether the Grinder is viable, given the likelihood of increased competition, and a rigorous financial appraisal is required, together with additional research into its market potential.

3 Shareholders

The impact on shareholders depends on the market view of the risks and the potential returns. Put yourself into the position of a shareholder and consider whether the strategy you have proposed would cause you to sell your shares. Currently, the market value of the company is greater than the total asset value suggested in the balance sheet. However, the values of the development products come to a total of $49 500 000 which is far in excess of the current company value. This suggests that the company value could be increased by splitting it up into the SBUs represented by the individual products, although this may not be possible in practice. The gross profit is, in fact, nearly three times the operating surplus, on which the company value is largely based. If the overheads were reduced and the gross profit increased as a result of the proposed strategy, operating surplus could well be doubled; this alone would have the effect of increasing company value by about $10 million.

Another way of looking at this is that a strategy based on stability would leave the share value largely unchanged in the short run, but with little chance of long-term growth; a strategy based on retrenchment could increase share value in the short run, with less certain long-term prospects; a strategy based on expansion might reduce value in the short run, depending on the view the market takes of risk.

4 Reduce overheads

The point here is to distinguish between short- and long-run effects. In the short run operating surplus would be increased, as would the Operating Surplus Value; however, the market may take a dim view of the long-term consequences. The Grinder would go out as a marginal product in a competitive market, market shares would fall, and fewer prototypes would be generated in the long run.

Section 2: Suggested approach

Could BSB have been competitive?

The events leading up to November 1990 suggest that both companies had made a major strategic blunder, because the market which they targeted was not large enough to support two major satellite stations. It looks unlikely that controlling costs on its own would have been sufficient to generate success for BSB, because even the much leaner Sky was losing heavily by the time of the takeover. However, it is possible that BSB might have been successful if it had controlled its costs **and** developed a different segment of the market; for example, BSB had not exploited the A and B socio-economic groups.

The BSB experience can be expressed in terms of the **process model**. The **strategists** were apparently not a cohesive group because of the consortium structure, and a clear set of **objectives** in terms of intended market, type of programming and so on does not seem to have been spelt out. The company was weak on **analysis and diagnosis**, and did not appear to understand the **competitive environment** well. The **choice** of strategy seemed to have been dictated by Sky. Finally, in the **implementation** stage BSB was very poor. **Resource allocation** was poor: resources were unnecessarily costly, and there was no control mechanism.

BSB can be positioned in the **perceived price differentiation matrix**. Once perceived differentiation disappeared BSB dropped into the failure likely part of the matrix. In terms of the **familiarity matrix** BSB was moving into new familiar markets with new unfamiliar technology. Competition between the two companies led to a **zero sum game**, where one could benefit only at the expense of the other; the problem for BSB was that Sky already held a strong position by the time BSB started playing. The claimed superiority of the BSB product can be analysed in terms of the **dimensions of quality**.

If YES

If the conclusion is reached that a viable success strategy existed, then it is interesting to ascertain why BSB did not recognize it. This is probably to do with managerial perceptions, and the conviction that the BSB product had the quality to overcome Sky competition. The lack of an analysis of the company's own strengths and weaknesses (SWOT) compared to Sky probably led to managers being unaware of how precarious their position really was.

Because of the resource allocation BSB was unable to exploit potentially profitable avenues, such as product **differentiation** and **market segmentation**.

If NO

Once the course of action had been decided on then no individual seemed to be able to stop it. There seems to have been a lack of **feedback** from the control and monitoring stage which would have led to a re-evaluation of the strategy choice.

It is possible that the BSB management was not **risk averse**, and was willing to push ahead despite the lack of any immediate indications of success.

Section 3: Suggested approach

There are various ways of tackling the essay, and high marks would be awarded for a discussion which covered the following points.

The central issue is that Strategic Planning has been promoted by the general manager (CEO) but opposed by the specialists, each of whom is likely to be concerned with protecting his own interests (the principal/agent problem). There are many arguments which can be advanced both for and against strategic planning systems. The question is concerned with the potential benefits and costs to:

Individual specialists

Benefits:

- Opportunity to contribute within a recognized structure
- More information on other areas in the company
- Constraints on resources made explicit
- Opportunity to contribute to objective setting

Costs:

- Potential loss of control
- More accountability

The company

There is, of course, no empirical evidence from real life studies that planning itself will increase profitability. However, an explicit recognition of objectives, the allocation of resources consistent with these, and the development of control and feedback systems may increase the probability of success. The attempt to identify performance gaps, pursue a general strategic thrust and consider contingencies can help provide the company as a whole with a sense of common purpose.

PRACTICE FINAL EXAMINATION 2

Case Studies

Case Study 1

ACME PLC
SHAREHOLDERS' REPORT

The new Board of management has succeeded in dramatically turning the company round since being appointed just over two years ago: the company is now making an operating surplus of $2.5 million compared with a loss of $1.3 million. We have completed a $16 million plant upgrading programme, and have instilled new life into a product which was falling behind the times and being seen as increasingly unreliable.

FINANCIAL TIMES
ECONOMIC SURVEY

The past two years have seen a significant increase in GNP. But there are now signs of "overheating" in the economy: the inflation rate has soared, and the interest rate has increased from 9% to 12%; the demand for luxury goods has risen dramatically, with some sectors showing growth of 20% over the period; because of short term supply bottlenecks this has been accompanied by price increases of up to 25%. There are signs that the government is becoming concerned about the state of the economy, and a package of deflationary measures is expected in the near future.

The accounts and product reports in the Appendix on pp.4/179–4/180 show the situation **before** and **after** the new management Board took over

1. ***Analyse the before and after situation to determine how the company's profitability has improved. To what extent has the "turn round" been due to the new management Board? Do you have any reservations about this "turn round"?***

   A set of ratios, such as return on investment, gearing, etc. will show the extent to which company performance has changed between the two periods. The accounting conventions adopted could have an impact on the appearance of the company.

   The improvement in operating surplus has been due to changes in both revenues and costs. Part of the "turn round" was due to the Board, i.e. internal factors, and part to changing market conditions, i.e. external factors.

   On the revenue side, the increase in marketing, setting the price below the competing level, and the expenditure on product development have led to an increase in market share. To assess the impact of the new Board's policies it is necessary to estimate what would have happened in the absence of their actions. Both the market and the market price have increased by about 20%, therefore if nothing had been done then revenues would have increased by 1.2*1.2=1.44, i.e. by about 40%. The remaining increase of 60% can be attributed to the Board.

   There are a number of difficulties in attributing cause and effect, i.e. in attempting to determine what worked and what did not. For example, the price elasticity of demand versus the impact of advertising and product improvement is unknown; there may be a significant "kink" in the company's demand curve. However, there seems little doubt that the effect of the Board's actions has been significant.

   On the cost side a more efficient resource management approach has eradicated undertime working, reduced warranty returns, reduced inventory, and fostered productivity gains, with a reduction of about 10% in unit cost. The net result was that while sales revenue increased by about 80%, COGS increased by less than 50%. However, a 10% reduction in unit cost might be regarded as modest given the investment undertaken, and the company presumably has further cost reduction potential. A major contribution to the increase in operating surplus has been the control of overheads despite the increase in output: the increase in development expenditure has been compensated by the reduction in hiring and firing costs.

The increase in development expenditure can be viewed as evidence of the longer term view of the Board: investing in the future.

The management has succeeded in strengthening the competitive position with a higher market share and a lower unit cost. However, there are a number of reservations about the "turn round". The cash flow position is still negative; this is due to continued inventory accumulation, heavy debt charges and material purchases in excess of usage. Furthermore, part of the improvement was due to favourable general market and economic factors, which the *Financial Times* suggests might not continue. The company is highly geared now that the investments have been undertaken; the debt interest payments and the repayment of the loans will comprise a burden for some time. The company is vulnerable to a deterioration in market conditions. For example, sensitivity analysis can reveal the likely impact of a downturn in demand to previous levels.

2. ***Assess the company's prospects for the next two or three years.***

This **must** be tackled using a profile approach which makes it possible to systemize the various factors. A SWOT framework will identify several potential threats, together with a number of weaknesses in the **after** situation. Scenario and sensitivity analysis can be used to discuss likely outcomes.

Case Study 2

Lufthansa has a rough landing

The well known German airline fell on hard times after a period of expansion in the 1980s, and the following table shows how profits declined from DM260 million in 1989 to a loss of DM301 million by 1991.

	1987	*1988*	*1989*	*1990*	*1991*
Turnover (DMm)	10961	11845	13055	14447	16101
Pre-tax profit (DMm)	207	241	260	142	–301
Employees	47150	49056	51942	57567	61791
Seat kilometres offered (m)	57000	61700	65000	75500	81700
Seat kilometres sold (m)	40000	42500	44900	50600	52300
Seat load factor (%)	70	69	69	67	64
Number of aircraft	151	155	197	220	275

Source: *Financial Times* 1/9/92

Capital spending in the three years up to 1991 was DM8 billion. In 1992 Lufthansa intended to take 26 aircraft out of service, and was looking for a partner to help develop the US market.

The total market for air travel during the period was as follows:

	1987	1988	1989	1990	1991
Passenger kilometres flown (billions)	1 600	1 700	1 800	1 900	1 800
% change from previous year	10	7	4	6	–4

Lufthansa was not alone in making losses in 1991. Four major airlines made bigger losses, the largest loss for the year being 30% higher than Lufthansa's. The world's scheduled airlines in total made a loss of 0.5% on revenues in 1991, compared with a loss of 0.8% on revenues in 1990).

Lufthansa was the 10th largest airline in the world by 1991 in terms of the number of passenger kilometres travelled (excluding Aeroflot). However, it is small (40%) in comparison with the large US carriers American and United.

Rank	*Airline*	*Million Km*
1	American	132 500
2	United	132 400
3	Delta	108 400
4	Northwest	86 800
5	Continental	66 700
6	British Airways	65 900
7	USAir	54 900
8	Japan Air Lines	54 700
9	Air France	53 400
10	Lufthansa	52 300

Source: *Airline Business* magazine

Analyse the Lufthansa strategy, assess why it is making losses, and suggest what it might do in the future.

Strategy

From 1989 Lufthansa embarked on an **expansionary** strategy, and in 1992 it was in the process of **retrenchment**. The expansion in its capacity between 1987 and 1991 was very substantial: 30% increase in employees, 80% increase in aircraft, and 43% increase in seat kilometres offered. Unfortunately the expansion on the supply side was not matched by increase in the volume of sales, which went up by 30%. This meant that each employee was still selling the same number of seat miles, while the aircraft were running at 36% empty, compared with 30% empty in 1987.

The attempt to increase market share was successful:

	1987	1988	1989	1990	1991
Market share (%)	2.5	2.5	2.5	2.7	2.9

Compared to the rest of the industry, Lufthansa's losses were not all that bad.

The Lufthansa situation could be characterized as a Dog or Question Mark.

Reason for losses
Lufthansa expanded at precisely the time when the market entered a recession. This could have been due to poor prediction, the construction lag for airplanes and a lack of an effective control system.

Lufthansa was very susceptible to a marginal increase in its costs in relation to its revenues. **Ratio analysis** shows this very clearly: from 1987 to 1989 profits were about 2% of turnover, and this dropped to 1% in 1990; in 1991 the loss was about 2% of turnover.

The **market structure** suggests that competition is fierce. Even the largest carriers have no more than 7% market share and Lufthansa has about 3% market share.

Lufthansa has been looking for a partner, possibly to achieve economies of scale and/or horizontal integration. Could be evidence of a prospector approach.

Future prospects
A SWOT framework can be used to systemize Lufthansa's prospects. There are various strategic possibilities, such as to aim at cost leadership or differentiation. But there is limited scope for action. The product is largely **homogeneous**, therefore **differentiation** is difficult. The market is **mature**, therefore it is difficult to increase market share because of the strength of the larger companies. It may be possible to **segment** the market and target specific **niche** sectors. But since the market is declining, it is to be expected that the **competitive reaction** will be fierce. The industry is dominated by a relatively small number of large companies, therefore it is to some extent **oligopolistic**, and as a result the demand curve is likely to be kinked, making price competition even more problematical. Trying to increase market share is a **zero sum game**, because of the static market size. Since Lufthansa is only 40% of the size of the largest company, it cannot easily pursue a low cost strategy because it does not have the advantage of **economies of scale**. Furthermore, since **marginal costs** of passengers are very low, price competition at the margin is going to be difficult. In order to achieve a **competitive advantage**, it needs to reduce its capacity and hence its costs in line with its projected sales, which will get its capacity up to the level it was at and will once again ensure that profits are made. It should use the marginal cost and revenue approach when assessing which routes to cut, and get rid of the planes with the highest operating costs.

Case Study 3

What is the role of formal investment appraisal techniques in arriving at a strategic thrust? What are the limitations in relying only on these techniques?

Formal investment appraisal is typically used to allocate resources within the company; it is the basis for making selections among competing alternatives. Strategic decisions about the company's future can be assessed within the net present value framework, given that the overall objective of the company is to maximize shareholder value.

The contribution of formal investment appraisal techniques include:

- They make explicit the assumptions which are made in arriving at the evaluation of alternatives.
- They force managers to be explicit about factors such as risk premiums, time horizons, revenues, costs, cash flows, market share.

- They make it possible to compare completely different options.
- They enable choices to be made among competing projects within a strategy.
- The appraisal framework can be used as the basis of scenario evaluations which can show the sensitivity of different strategies to changes in key variables.

But it is inadvisable to rely on formal techniques alone in arriving at a strategic thrust. Reasons include:

- The raw data may be suspect because it is necessary to use information about the past, which may be suspect if it is based on accounting conventions.
- Formal appraisal techniques can evaluate what might happen, but they cannot take into account the unknowable; the assumptions about the future may be wrong.
- Different projects may have completely different implications for personnel management through their impact on job satisfaction and incentives.
- While risk can be incorporated in the formal analysis, managers vary in their risk aversion and the desire to maintain contingency.
- Although it is important to quantify the options confronting the company as far as possible, decisions are often based on qualitative rather than quantitative factors.

The overall limitation of formal techniques is that they can give the impression that strategy is a mechanical process which can be solved.

Appendix 1

Acme Plc
Operating Account at end year: Production cost, and revenue
($000)

	Before	After		Before	After
			SALES REVENUE	11 700	19 600
COST OF GOODS SOLD	11 278	15 297			
			GROSS PROFIT	422	4 303

Operating Account at end year: Overheads and Operating Surplus
($000)

	Before	After		Before	After
Factory Overheads	500	500			
Hiring and Redundancy cost	750	250			
Development Expenditure	500	1 000			
TOTAL OVERHEAD	1 750	1 750			
			OPERATING SURPLUS	–1 328	2 553

Cash Flow for year
($000)

	Before	After		Before	After
OUTLAY			INCOME		
Material Purchase	7 500	9 000			
Loan Interest	220	1 290	Interest on Assets	450	120
Wage Cost	4 200	4 640			
Line Cost	1 500	1 620			
Product Marketing	500	1 500			
Total Overhead	1 750	1 750	Sales Revenue	11 700	19 600
Total Outlay	15 670	19 800	Total Income	11 250	19 720
			Net Cash Flow	–3 520	–80

Balance Sheet at end year
($000)

	Before	After
FIXED ASSETS		
Factory	4 000	4 000
Plant	8 000	16 000
TOTAL FIXED ASSETS	12 000	20 000
CURRENT ASSETS		
Raw Materials	4 000	4 000
Finished Goods	3 677	1 050
Cash	5 000	1 000
TOTAL CURRENT ASSETS	12 677	6 050
TOTAL ASSETS	24 677	26 050
OWNERS EQUITY	22 677	17 050
DEBT		
Short Term Loan	2 000	1 000
Long Term Loan		8 000
TOTAL DEBT	2 000	9 000
TOTAL LIABILITIES	24 677	26 050

Report on Product for year

	Before	After
Composition of Demand		
Market share (%)	3.0	4.0
Orders	9 000	14 000
Warranty demand	540	280
TOTAL DEMAND	9 540	14 280
Working time (%)	88	109
Labour attrition rate (%)	8	3
Price ($/unit)	1 300	1 400
Competing price ($/unit)	1 300	1 500
Account at end year		
Wage cost ($000)	4 200	4 640
Assembly Line Cost ($000)	1 500	1 620
Cost of Material Used ($000)	6 390	8 051
Product Marketing ($000)	500	1 500
TOTAL COST ($000)	12 590	15 811
Unit Cost ($/unit)	1 182	1 071
Cost of Goods Sold ($000)	11 278	15 297

	Before	After
Composition of Supply		
Output	10 650	14 760
Inventory	2000	500
TOTAL SUPPLY	12 650	15 260
Distribution of Supply		
Warranty Replacements	540	280
Sales to orders	9 000	14 000
End Year Inventory	3 110	980
SALES REVENUE ($000)	11 700	19 600
GROSS PROFIT ($000)	422	4303

PRACTICE FINAL EXAMINATION 3

Case Studies

Case Study 1

THE FINANCIAL TIMES
INFLATION RETURNS

The past two years have seen the fastest growth in the economy in 20 years, with real GNP increasing by over 4% each year. But there are signs that this is causing extreme inflationary pressures, the unemployment rate has dropped to its lowest level for 12 years, and wage claims are up to 12%.

MEMO ACME Plc
FROM Managing Director
TO All Board Members

The accounting department has expressed severe misgivings about the performance of the Liqueur and the Blend. The marketing department suggests that we need to look at the performance of our products against the background of a growing economy. It seems to me that the Malt commands a strong competitive position reflected in its high profitability. We have spent a lot trying to generate market share for the Liqueur, but despite the fact that sales have risen by 20% in the past two years market share has stayed very low. The Blend has been around for a long time, but the market is likely to decline as tastes change in favour of the Malt and the Liqueur.

Information on the accounts and products for Acme Plc is contained in Appendix 1.

1. ***Compare the views of a marketing specialist and an accountant on the three products.*** **($5\frac{1}{3}$ marks)**

   The accountant is concerned with efficiency of resource allocation and would look at the ratios: price to unit cost, profit to production cost, profit per unit sold, sales per employee, inventories, etc.; the analysis would be based on historical data and trends. The marketer is concerned with the development of products with a competitive advantage and would look at product position and prospects for the future. The marketer would look at product life cycles, and attempt to place the three products in the BCG matrix, and could conclude that the Malt is a cash cow, the Blend is a dog, and the Liqueur is a question mark, i.e. it has a small market share in a fast growing market. The accountant and the marketer would have similar views about the Malt and the Blend, but would differ on the Liqueur. Of course, not everyone would agree that accountants are so narrow minded.

   Accounting conventions can be misleading: e.g. the hiring costs may be due to attrition on Liqueur, and hence should be allocated to that product. The COGS approach can conceal poor performance in terms of current resource allocation.

2. ***How would you reallocate company resources to increase profits in the short and the long term, bearing in mind the newspaper report and the memo?*** **(14 marks)**

There is a great deal of scope for answering this question. The macroeconomic situation is ominous: the high growth in sales for the Liqueur has probably been partly due to a high GNP elasticity, and it is likely that the government will take action to deflate the economy as a result of worsening inflation. Tight labour markets have two implications. First, it may be difficult to avoid overtime working in the future because labour will be scarce; second, an increase in labour cost of 12% could have serious implications for profitability.

When reallocating resources the general principle is to evaluate the impact of changes on marginal cost and marginal revenue.

In the short run there are various overhead costs which could be reduced. For example, Hiring and Redundancy cost is likely to be a one off and material purchases are far higher than material consumption. The price of the Liqueur could be increased to the competing level (depending on price elasticity), and marketing expenditure on the Blend could be reduced to at least the same level as for the Malt ("harvest" the Blend for the remainder of its life cycle). Resources currently allocated to the Liqueur could be reduced to get rid of the inventory – bearing in mind the likely prospects for GNP growth; in the extreme, the Liqueur could be abandoned.

In the long run the objective is to utilise resources more efficiently and transform the Liqueur into a cash cow. At the same time, there is a need to ensure that more products are developed for the future portfolio, and at the moment nothing is being spent on R&D. The problem is that these long term objectives are not necessarily consistent with short term profit maximisation.

Sensitivity analysis can be carried out to indicate the rough impact of measures such as increasing the price of the Liqueur, reducing marketing expenditure, introducing, JIT and so on.

3. ***Imagine that the company decides to issue 1 million shares. What information would you use in deciding how much to pay for a share? Approximately how much would you be willing to pay?*** **(14 marks)**
(Total of 33⅓ marks)

The share price is determined by the expectation of future cash flows, and is found by discounting expected cash flows using the cost of capital. Each share would generate $1.4 in operating surplus at the moment. Assuming the cost of capital is 10% this would give a share price of $14 approximately. However, the expected future cash flows depend on the company's prospects, the market will make use of all information available such as ratios, the company's track record, gearing, cash flow, which will provide an indication of likely future profits and the degree of risk associated with the company. The candidate has already made some suggestions for improving profitability, and the sensitivity analysis will suggest a maximum price which he would be willing, to pay given this "insider" view of the company.

Case Study 2

The TV Guide Price War
The events in 1991 show how competitive pressures come into play when a legal monopoly is terminated. Until the end of February 1991 in the UK television pro-

gramme listings were published weekly by two magazines: *TV Times* (which published **only** commercial channel listings) and *Radio Times* (which published **only** British Broadcasting Corporation channels, which are funded by an annual licence fee); beside providing listings, these magazines contain the type of article found in all popular magazines: articles about stars, personalities, programmes and films, letters to the editor, horoscopes and so on. When the monopoly was terminated *TV Times* was selling about 3.2 million copies per week, and *Radio Times* sold about 2.4 million copies per week. *Radio Times* was priced at 50p, which it did not change for the rest of 1991; *TV Times* was also priced at 50p. When the monopoly was removed both *TV Times* and *Radio Times* started to publish both commercial and BBC channel listings.

The history of sales in the early stages of competition is set out in Table 1, and illustrated in Figure 1.

Table 1 Sales of TV Guides (millions)

	TV Times	*Radio Times*	*TV Plus*	*What's on TV*	*TV Quick*	*Total*
February	3.10	2.35	0.50			5.95
March	2.20	2.10	0.40	0.70		5.40
April	1.60	1.70		0.70	2.00	6.00
May	1.65	1.70		0.75	2.70	6.80
June	1.70	1.70		0.90	1.30	5.60

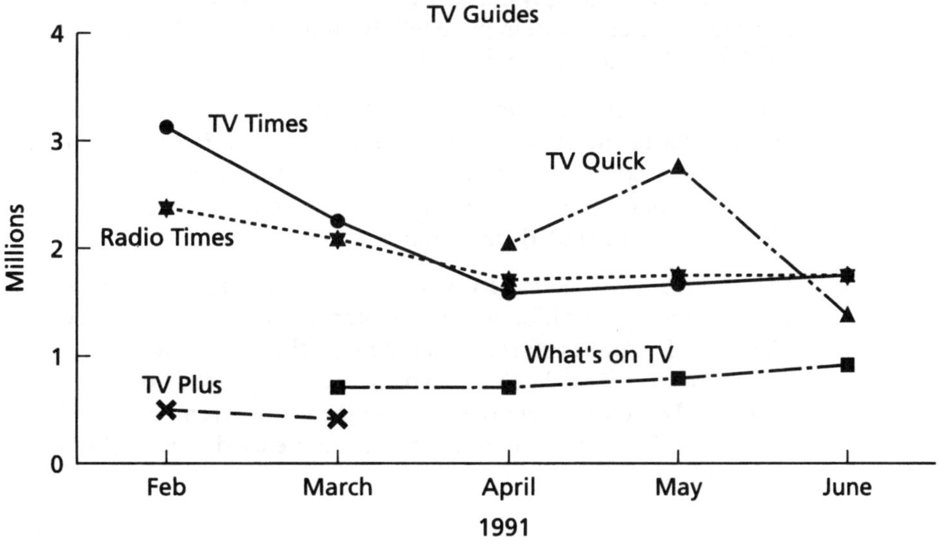

Figure 1
Source: *Sunday Times* 16 June 1991

The first entrant to the market was *TV Plus*, priced at 50p, which took less than 0.5 million sales and lasted one month before going into liquidation.

The second entrant was *What's on TV*, which went on sale at 25p. Soon afterward the price was increased to 35p, then reduced to 10p. It then put the price back up to 35p. Sales of *What's on TV* started at 0.7 million in March and rose marginally for the next four months.

By the end of April the sales of both *TV Times* and *Radio Times* had fallen to about 1.6 million, despite the fact that *TV Times* had reduced its price from 50p to 25p for two short periods in March and April. This was partly due to the fact that the next entrant appeared on the scene with a bang in April: *TV Quick*. It was estimated that *TV Quick* spent about £20 million in initial advertising; during April it was the biggest individual spender on TV advertising in the UK, and it came on to the market priced at 10p for 10 weeks. It started with sales of 2 million, and quickly increased to 2.7 million, taking market leadership away from *TV Times* and *Radio Times*. *TV Quick* then quadrupled its price to 40p, and sales immediately fell by half to 1 .3 million.

Assess the strategic moves by the new entrants, and the effectiveness of the response by *Radio Times* and *TV Times.*

(Total of 33⅓ marks)

The Market Environment

This is an example of monopoly being replaced by competition among the few, or oligopoly. Some candidates argued that the homogeneous product, coupled with the ease of entry and knowledgeable consumers actually approximate to a perfect market. In this case firms could expect to make the opportunity cost of capital, and all monopoly profits would disappear. Other candidates represented the "big picture" in terms of supply and demand: the supply curve for TV guides moved out to the right, and since demand is inelastic the equilibrium price fell. By June the price had fallen from an average of 50p to about 44p (the average of the four prices).

The more or less fixed market size (subject to short run fluctuations) means that in strategic terms the oligopoly was a zero sum game. Gains in market share could only be made at the expense of competitors, and of course consumers must be given some reason to switch from one TV guide to another. Thus individual producers were likely to be faced with a "kinked" demand curve.

Despite the fact that the TV guides are homogeneous in terms of their main content, there is scope for differentiation in terms of the articles accompanying the listings. Then the TV guides start to encroach on the general magazine market; in fact, at the height of the *TV Quick* advertising campaign the total market size appeared to increase. There was therefore some scope for differentiation and market segmentation; the perceived price and quality matrix can be used to identify the prospects for each of the competitors.

The problems confronting new entrants were formidable. The two existing competitors, *TV Times* and *Radio Times*, had large market shares and hence had the potential benefits of economies of scale and experience effects, together with a degree of consumer loyalty. Some candidates pointed out that advertising revenues were not included in the data, and if these were significant they could help account for the behaviour of competitors.

TV Plus

TV Plus appeared to have no particular strategy; it entered as undifferentiated in terms of quality or price and could not generate sufficient sales to generate profits; it is likely that it incurred much higher costs than *TV Times* and *Radio Times*, and had little financial backing.

What's on TV

What's on TV could be classified as a prospector, and adopted a low cost strategy. It was differentiated on price alone, and apparently tried to test the market by varying price significantly. The outcome suggests that demand was inelastic in the range 10p to 35p.

TV Quick

TV Quick attempted to enter the market as a highly differentiated low cost producer. The objective was to grab market share and then increase the price and hope for a low elasticity of demand. Some candidates felt that the act of quadrupling the price was catastrophic, since demand fell by about half. However, demand was inelastic, and the fact that half as many were sold at four times the price meant that total revenue increased. Compare the revenue generated by the two prices: at 10p the revenue on 2.7 million copies was £0.27 million per week, while at 40p the revenue on 1.3 million copies was £0.52 million per week. Clearly the higher price is preferable, and the losses made up to that point can be regarded as the cost of establishing a 20% market share. This suggests a total revenue of about £26 million per year, which puts the initial £20 million advertising budget in perspective. For example, if *TV Quick* made 20% gross profit on sales revenue, this would generate about £5 million profit per year, giving a pay back period on the initial advertising outlay of about 4 years. This makes no allowance for the losses incurred in the period when price was set at 10p, and any advertising revenue should be included in the final evaluation.

TV Times* and *Radio Times

There are many ways of classifying their response. One argument is that they had no strategy because they were used to a monopoly and were paralysed by a bureaucratic management; this would be particularly true of the *Radio Times*, with its long term association with a government owned service. If they had had any foresight, they would have attempted to erect barriers to entry at an early stage. However, because of their monopoly position they might not in fact have been low cost producers, and may have had to take action to become more efficient after the advent of competition.

Another view is that *Radio Times* adopted a Defender stance in the sense that it did not indulge in the price war because of the zero sum nature of the contest, and decided that a market share loss was the lesser of two evils; on the other hand, *TV Times* was a Reactor, and entered the price war before realising what the Radio Times had seen from the beginning. *TV Times'* foray into the price war possibly cost it a great deal in foregone revenue without achieving a significant impact on market share.

Case Study 3

What differences in the approach to strategy are there likely to be in small compared to large diversified companies? Frame your answer in terms of a strategy process model.

(Total of $33\frac{1}{3}$ marks)

A strategy process model is intended to clarify the elements of strategy making, and usually takes the form of objective setting, analysis and diagnosis. strategy choice, implementation and control, evaluation and feedback.

There is plenty of scope for discussion on where differences are likely to arise in the two types of organizations. The quality of the argument rather than being "right" or "wrong" is the important feature of the answer. Some candidates argued that all companies, whatever their size or composition, ought to do much the same under each of the elements, and that differences were really a matter of degree, or that the elements were more apparent in a large company because procedures are more formalized.

Objective setting
There is centralized control in the small company, and with the limited product range there is likely to be a more definable set of objectives. The large company devolves a great deal of strategy making to the SBUs. There is a difference between corporate and SBU policy which does not exist in the small company, and the means/ends distinction is particularly important. It is necessary to disaggregate objectives and make them meaningful and achievable to those who implement them.

Analysis and diagnosis
The large company is likely to have more specialists and a lot more information available than small companies. Analyses by functional experts may be conflicting and the CEO must integrate them. Some candidates argued that large companies are more likely to be affected by general economic factors, changes in competition, etc.

Strategy choice
Techniques such as SWOT ought to be employed by both; some candidates argued that the options are not so clear cut for the large company, since it has to make decisions for a number of products in a number of markets. There may be conflicts of interest among the SBUs.

Implementation and control
The large company has less direct control over its resources, and it may be difficult to relate resource use and deployment back to the original strategy choice. This makes it necessary to utilise sophisticated monitoring systems, financial controls, internal pricing and so on. The principal agent problem is particularly apparent in the large company, starting with the separation of ownership and control and pervading all levels of the organization. It can be argued that there is more flexibility in small companies because there are fewer formal controls, a smaller hierarchy and less bureaucracy.

Feedback
Because of the size, complexity, hierarchy and bureaucracy of a large company communication is a particular problem. Unless there is a formalized structure for communication it may not occur.

Appendix 1

Acme Plc
Operating Account at end year: Production cost, and revenue
($000)

		SALES REVENUE	10 119
COST OF GOODS SOLD	6 825		
		GROSS PROFIT	3 294

Operating Account at end year: Overheads and Operating Surplus
($000)

Factory Rents	200		
Owned Factory Overheads	100		
Hiring and Redundancy cost	750		
Company Marketing	800		
TOTAL OVERHEAD	1 850		
		OPERATING SURPLUS	1 444

Cash Flow for year
($000)

OUTLAY		INCOME	
Material Purchase	3 000		
Loan Interest	750	Interest on Assets	100
Wage Cost	2 820		
Line Cost	1 470		
Product Marketing	1 400		
Total Overhead	1 850	Sales Revenue	10 119
Total Outlay	11 290	Total Income	10 219
		Net Cash Flow	–1 071

Balance Sheet at end year
($000)

FIXED ASSETS			
Factory	4 000		
TOTAL FIXED ASSETS		4 000	
CURRENT ASSETS			
Raw Materials	4 000		
Finished Goods	2 964		
Cash	1 000		
TOTAL CURRENT ASSETS		7 964	
TOTAL ASSETS			11 964
OWNERS EQUITY		6 964	
DEBT			
Loan	5 000		
TOTAL DEBT		5 000	
TOTAL LIABILITIES			11 964

Report on Products for year

	Malt	Liqueur	Blend
Composition of Demand			
Orders	7560	2550	1500
Warranty demand	151	128	30
TOTAL DEMAND	7711	2678	1530
Working time (%)	100	117	100
Labour attrition rate (%)	2	6	2
Price ($/unit)	900	800	850
Competing price ($/unit)	900	1000	850
Account at end year			
Wage cost ($000)	1540	720	560
Line Cost ($000)	770	420	280
Materials Used ($000)	976	825	250
Product Marketing	200	800	400
TOTAL COST ($000)	3486	2765	1490
Unit Cost ($/unit)	446	838	745
Cost of Goods Sold	3442	2243	1140

	Malt	Liqueur	Blend
Composition of Supply			
Output	7810	3300	2000
Inventory	500	2000	200
TOTAL SUPPLY	8310	5300	2200
Distribution of Supply			
Warranty Replacements	151	128	30
Sales to orders	7560	2550	1500
Actual market share (%)	28.0	5.0	5.0
Excess supply (Inventory)	599	2623	670
SALES REVENUE ($000)	6804	2040	1275
GROSS PROFIT ($000)	3362	–203	135

The elective courses

Decision-making Techniques

PRACTICE FINAL EXAMINATION 1 – WITH MCQs

The examination is in 2 sections:

(a) **Section A: Multiple Choice Questions.** 25 questions each worth 2 points. Total points available in Section A: 25 × 2 = 50.

(b) **Section B: Case Questions.** 4 questions each worth 25 points. Points for individual parts of a question are shown in the question. Total points available in Section B: 4 × 25 = 100

Total points available for examination = 150
Pass mark: 50% of 150 = 75

Section A: Multiple Choice Questions

Do all 25 questions.

Each correct answer receives 2 marks.
An incorrect answer or unanswered question receives 0 marks.
Total marks for Section A = 50 = 33% of total for paper.

Questions 1 to 5 refer to an armaments manufacturer who is deciding whether to embark on a major project, the development of a new main battle tank.

If the tank is to be sold successfully worldwide, new weaponry must be developed which can pierce a new type of armour with which opposing tanks will soon be equipped. The R&D Group has estimated that there is a 60% chance that this breakthrough can be made. If so, the overall payoff of the project is a profit with a present value of £100 million. A second possibility is that the new weaponry might be only partially effective. In this case limited sales would be made and the profit of the project would be reduced to £10 million. The probability of this outcome is 20%. A third possibility is that no effective weaponry is developed and then the project would make a loss of £30 million. The decision tree representing the decision to go ahead or not is given in Figure 1.

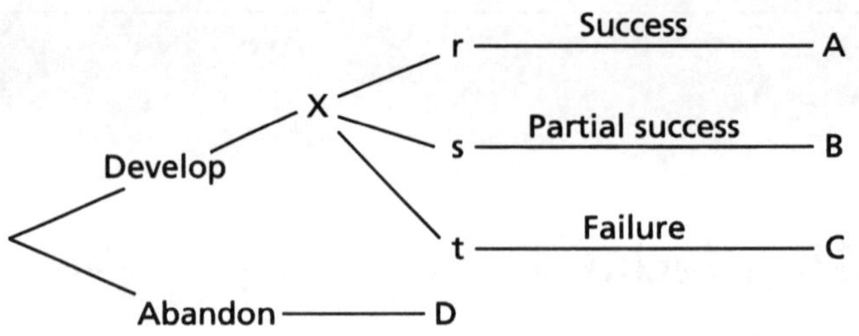

Figure 1

1. What are the payoffs at the ends of each branch of the tree, the points A, B, C and D, assuming all costs incurred up to the present time are ignored as sunk costs?

   A 0, –30, 10, 100
   B 100, 10, –30, 0
   C 100, 10, 0, 0
   D 100, 10, 30, 0

2. What are the probabilities on the branches marked r, s and t?

   A 0.2, 0.2, 0.6
   B 0, 0.2, 0.6
   C 0.6, 0.2, 0
   D 0.6, 0.2, 0.2

3. What is the expected monetary value at the chance event node X?

   A 0
   B 34
   C 56
   D 60

4. What decision should be taken and what is its expected monetary value?

   A Abandon, 0
   B Develop, 10
   C Develop, 56
   D Develop, 60

5. What is the expected value of perfect information?

   A 4
   B 6
   C 62
   D 100

Questions 6 and 7 refer to the estimated profit of a major oil company.

The company is to announce its profit for the last financial year in two weeks' time. An analyst has solicited opinions about what the profit is likely to be and uses the information to construct a cumulative "greater than or equal to" probability distribution:

Probability (%)	100	80	60	40	20	0
Profit (£billion)	12	20	26	30	36	52

For example, it is thought that there is an 80% chance that the profit will be £20 billion or greater.

6. The distribution breaks the total profit range into five equi-probable ranges relating to 0–20%, 20–40%, etc. What is the bracket median of the last of these ranges for 80–100%?

   A 12
   B 16
   C 20
   D 44

7. What is the expected value of the profit?

   A 28
   B 28.8
   C 29.3
   D 32

Questions 8 to 10 are based on the following information, relating to a craft consortium and one of its products, wooden dolls.

The consortium manufactures two types of wooden doll, male and female. Production of the dolls requires three operations: assembling, finishing and dressing. A limited amount of time is available on the machines that carry out these tasks in any one-week planning period. There are maximum and minimum sales requirements for each type of doll for the week. A recent recruit to the consortium is an MBA graduate who has moved on from his career in financial services. He thinks doll production for the week can be planned using linear programming. In questions 8–10 which of the following is correct?

8. The decision variables should be:

   A The total number of dolls to be produced (i.e. 1 variable).
   B The numbers of each type of doll to be produced (i.e. 2 variables).
   C The amount of time taken up by each production operation (i.e. 3 variables).
   D The amount of time taken up by each production operation on each type of doll (i.e. 6 variables).

9. The objective function should be to:

   A Maximize revenue.
   B Maximize contribution (price minus variable costs).
   C Minimize costs.
   D Minimize time spent on production operations.

10. The number of constraints should be:

A 3
B 7
C 9
D 12

11. In considering a linear programming problem, which of the following is correct?

A If the objective function is in £s then the constraints must be in £s.
B Each constraint must be of one of two types, $\leqslant$ or $\geqslant$.
C For a $\leqslant$ constraint having a right-hand side in hours, the expression on the left of the $\leqslant$ must be in hours.
D Decision variables must have the same unit of measurement as the objective function.

12. In the following formulation, which constraint is redundant?

$$\begin{aligned} \text{Max.} \quad & 7x + 9y \\ \text{Subject to} \quad & x + 3y \leqslant 12 \\ & 2x + y \leqslant 18 \\ & x \leqslant 15 \\ & x, y \geqslant 0 \end{aligned}$$

A $x + 3y \leqslant 12$
B $2x + y \leqslant 18$
C $x \leqslant 15$
D $x \geqslant 0$

13. The following statements refer to the dual values of a linear programming problem.

I Each constraint has a dual value associated with it.
II The dual value of a resource is equal to the price paid for it.
III If the solution to an LP problem does not require all of a resource to be used up, the dual value of the resource will be zero.

Which of the following is correct?

A I only
B I and III only
C II and III only
D I, II and III

14. A linear programme which maximizes profit is used to help plan the facilities at a fast-food restaurant. The output from the computer package includes the line below which refers to the constraint for a barbecue grill on which 100 hours per week are available:

Constraint	*Slack*	*Dual*	*RHS range*
Grill	0	5	50 to 180

If an additional grill were purchased, making 100 more hours available, what would be the additional profit?

A 0
B 400
C 500
D 900

15. Consider the following statements:

I Simulation generally needs a smaller amount of data than optimization techniques.
II Simulation can be applied to a wider range of situations than optimization techniques.
III Simulation selects the best possible decision.

Which of the following is correct?

A I only
B II only
C I and II
D II and III

Questions 16 to 18 refer to an airport authority which is assessing new manning levels for check-in desks.

A Monte Carlo simulation is being carried out based on the arrival pattern of passengers. The random numbers between 00 and 99 have been allocated to the distribution below, which is the number of passengers arriving per minute during the afternoon period.

No. of arrivals/minute	*Probability*
8	0.02
9	0.03
10	0.05
11	0.10
12	0.15
13	0.20
14	0.25
15	0.15
16	0.05
Total	1.00

16. Which random numbers relate to 12 arrivals?

A 10–19
B 20–34
C 21–35
D 35–54

17. What is the arrival rate associated with the random number 80?

A 14
B 14.5
C 15
D 80

18. For each possible staffing arrangement, the Monte Carlo simulation is run many times and the average queue length, waiting time, etc., calculated. These averages, along with other information such as costs, are used to choose the preferred staffing level.

    What is the reason for running the simulation many times?

    A It checks that there are no mistakes in the calculations.
    B The central limit theorem has to be applied.
    C Any distortion caused by a particular random number stream not being representative will be averaged out.
    D Inaccuracies in any assumptions made will be removed.

19. The following statements refer to activities in a network diagram:

    I An activity is represented as a line connecting two nodes.
    II Two activities can have the same starting node and the same finishing node.
    III An activity can have more than one immediate predecessor.

    Which of the following is correct?

    A I only
    B III only
    C I and II only
    D I and III only

20. Dummy activities are used in a network to represent:

    I Optional activities.
    II Activities taking a very short time to complete.
    III Delays in the project.

    Which of the following is correct?

    A I only
    B II only
    C II only
    D Not I, II or III

Questions 21 to 23 refer to the application of critical path methods to the complex build sequence of a microprocessor.

The duration of the activity of securing chip LS43 has been estimated as:

Optimistic 2 minutes
Most likely 4 minutes
Pessimistic 12 minutes

21. In analysing the network, what number of days should be used as the single estimate of the activity's duration, i.e. what is its expected duration?

    A 4 minutes
    B 5 minutes
    C 6 minutes
    D 12 minutes

22. What is the variance of the activity?

A 1.67
B 2.77
C 4
D 34

23. When the variances of the activities are used to calculate confidence limits for the project, the following assumptions are being made:

I The activity durations conform to a beta distribution.
II The critical path remains unchanged.
III The central limit theorem applies.

Which of the following is correct?

A II only
B I and II only
C II and III only
D I, II and III

24. There has been a trend for computing power to be distributed throughout an organization rather than being centrally located because:

I It is necessary if large-scale computer systems are to be developed.
II Central computer departments are not always able to respond quickly to local needs.

Which of the following is correct?

A I only
B II only
C I and II
D Neither I nor II

25. Which of the following is correct?

The major management application of microcomputers is:

A Databases
B Spreadsheets
C Statistical methods
D Word processing

Section B: Case Studies

Do all 4 questions.

Each question will be marked out of 25.
Marks for individual parts of a question are shown in the question.
Total marks for Section B = 100 = 67% of total for paper.

1. How to stop the bad vibes

Modern electronic musical instruments use computer technology. Technomusic Ltd manufacture the basic microelectronic components and sell them on to a number of customers who use them in a wide range of instruments, including keyboards and percussion kits.

A particular component, the R210 circuit, which is used in electronic vibraphones and similar instruments, is currently causing some difficulties. Under the present manufacturing process 25% of the units produced turn out to be defective when assembled in the instruments. The problem is that the defect affects the quality of the sound produced and this is not known until the instrument is finished.

The contribution of this component has been calculated at £40 but, according to the contract with the customer, Technomusic must refund £60 for each component found to be defective because the customer has to remove the component and replace it with a substitute.

One of Technomusic's engineers has recently developed a simple test to evaluate this component before shipping. For each component the test registers "positive", "negative" or, occasionally, "inconclusive". While the test is not totally accurate in that it sometimes gives the wrong result, it is consistent for each component, i.e. repeated testing always gives the same result for any one component.

To check the testing device it was tried out on a number of components which were known to be either satisfactory or defective. The results were:

Instrument	*State of component*	
reading	*Satisfactory*	*Defective*
Positive	80%	5%
Inconclusive	10%	20%
Negative	10%	75%

For example, of the components known to be satisfactory, 80% gave the test result "positive" 10% "inconclusive" and 10% "negative". The test cost £2 per component.

Technomusic could rework any components thought to be defective at a cost of £30 per component (regardless of whether it was defective or not). This would guarantee that a component was satisfactory and so it could be sold at normal price.

(a) What is the expected monetary value per component of continuing with the current practice and not using the test? (5 marks)

(b) For any given component what are the probabilities that the test will give a reading of "positive" "inconclusive", or "negative"? (10 marks)

(c) Should Technomusic use the test and, if so, how should they use it? (10 marks)

2. Can the berth rate be increased?

A port has two berths, where ships of various sizes arrive for unloading and loading. The amount of cargo to be unloaded and loaded depends upon the size of the ship. The maximum number of gangs needed for unloading and loading also depends upon the size of the ship. The rate of unloading and loading depends on the number of gangs used. The total number of gangs available each day varies and is allocated to the ships by given allocation rules. Only one shift is worked by the gangs per day. Ships vacate berths immediately after loading.

A simulation is to be carried out to investigate the amount of congestion and to find ways of allocating manpower to reduce ships' waiting time at least cost. Assume that the number of days to load or unload a ship takes integer values only. Information on the mean number of ships queuing for berths, the average queuing time and the amount of idle time for berths is required.

(a) Draw a flowchart showing the main stages in a simulation of port operations. (20 marks)

(b) State any assumptions made. (5 marks)

3. Can a garden equipment company unearth greater profits?

Leisure Products produce garden equipment. The main products of their garden furniture division are a lawn chair, a bench and a garden table. Currently the contribution received from the manufacture and sale of one unit of each is £30 for a chair, £30 for a bench and £50 for a table.

There are two stages in production: tube bending and welding. The table below gives the total capacity for each stage and also the times (in hours) required by each item for each stage:

	Capacity			
	Chair	*Bench*	*Table*	*Time (hours)*
Tube bending	1.2	1.7	1.2	1 000
Welding	0.8	0	2.3	1 200

The company is confident that it can sell any number of all three products. However, for the coming season, production is limited by a shortage of the main raw material, tubing, because of a long strike. Currently, 2 000 lb of tubing are available, the requirements being 2 lb per chair, 3 lb per bench and 4.5 lb per garden table.

In an attempt to decide the best production mix, the production manager has produced the following linear programming formulation:

Let x_1, x_2 and x_3 be the numbers of chairs, benches and tables produced.

To maximize contribution $3x_1 + 3x_2 + 5x_3$

Subject to constraints
1: $1.2x_1 + 1.7x_2 + 1.2x_3 \leqslant 1\,000$ bending
2: $0.8x_1 + 2.3x_3 \leqslant 1\,200$ welding
3: $2.0x_1 + 3.0x_2 + 4.5x_3 \leqslant 2\,000$ supply

The computer output for the solution of this LP is:

Objective function: 27666.7

Decision variables:	1 Chair	700.000
	3 Table	133.333
Slack in constraints:	2 Welding	333.333

Shadow price for constraints:

1	Bending	11.667
3	Supply	8.000

Reduced costs for decision variables:

2	Bench	–13.8333

All items not listed above have zero value.

Ranges on coefficients in objective function:

Variable	*Lower bound*	*Current value*	*Upper bound*
1. Chair	22.2	30.0	50.0
2. Bench	Unbound	30.0	43.8
3. Table	30.0	50.0	67.5

Ranges on constraint limits:

Variable	*Lower bound*	*Current value*	*Upper bound*
1. Bending	533.33	1 000.00	1 200.00
2. Welding	866.67	1 200.00	Unbounded
3. Supply	1 667.67	2 000.00	2 556.67

(a) What is the best production mix and what contribution will it bring? (5 marks)

(b) Leisure Products has been offered an additional supply of tubing at £6 a pound over and above the normal price. Should they buy it? If so, by how much would the contribution increase if 500 pounds were bought? (5 marks)

(c) The marketing manager suggests that at least 100 benches should be made to balance the production line. How would this affect contribution? (5 marks)

(d) Leisure Products can sell some of its capacity in tube bending at a fee of £15 per hour. How would contribution be affected if it sold 200 hours at this price? (5 marks)

(e) Because of a promotional campaign, contribution on chairs will drop to £25. What will be the optimal production mix and what contribution will result? (5 marks)

4. How to make a carphone go faster

Speed in getting a new product to the market-place is of critical importance to high technology companies. Southern Communications has been very successful in developing, manufacturing and marketing a range of telecommunications products but suffered a recent failure when a competitor was faster in making a new carphone available to consumers. SC decided to look at the process of bringing new products to market and have decided to monitor all such initiatives by means of critical path planning methods.

The process of bringing a new product to market involves the following activities:

(i) The first two activities can be carried out simultaneously:

(A) R&D product design
(B) Carry out market research

(ii) Once the R&D is complete, two activities can take place:

(C) Build prototypes
(D) Plan marketing material

(iii) When the prototype is available, two further activities can be started:

(E) Large-scale production planning
(F) Rigorous testing

(iv) After the production methods have been finalized and market research is complete, the pricing can be decided and likely production levels decided (activity G).

(v) The availability of marketing material and prices means that a full marketing plan can be prepared (activity H). This activity also depends upon the completion of product tests.

(vi) When the marketing plan is available and production levels decided, full production can commence (activity I).

The product can be made available to the market once inventory has reached a certain proportion of the expected first year sales.

The durations of the activities have been estimated by assessing an optimistic, most likely and pessimistic time for each. These estimates are shown in the table below:

		Duration (weeks)		
	Activity	*Opt*	*ML*	*Pes*
A	R&D	15	20	25
B	Market research	5	15	25
C	Prototype	2	3	4
D	Marketing material	1	4	7
E	Production planning	1	2	9
F	Testing	1	6	17
G	Pricing	1	2	3
H	Market plan	1	2	9
I	Full production	4	5	12

ML = Most likely
Pes = Pessimistic
Opt = Optimistic

(a) Draw a critical path network for the project. (5 marks)

(b) Make a schedule of the earliest and latest start and finish times for the activities, including their floats. (15 marks)

(c) What are the variances for the individual activities and for the whole project? What are the 95% confidence limits for its completion time? (5 marks)

Section A: Solutions

1. **B is correct: A = 100, B = 10, C = –30, D = 0**
   A represents a fully successful project (£100 million profit), **B** a partial success (£10 million), **C** a failure (a loss of 30 million). **D** is zero because this is the payoff for not attempting the project, ignoring sunk costs.

2. **D is correct: 0.6, 0.2, 0.2**
   The probability that effective weaponry will be developed is given as 60%, hence r = 0.6. Likewise the probability of a partially effective solution is given as 20% therefore s = 0.2. The only other possibility is that the project fails and so the remaining probability t, must be 0.2 (= 1.0 – 0.6 – 0.2).

3. **C is correct: EMV = 56 million**

   $$\begin{aligned}\text{EMV at chance node X} &= (100 \times 0.6) + (10 \times 0.2) - (30 \times 0.2)\\ &= 60 + 2 - 6\\ &= 56 \text{ million}\end{aligned}$$

4. **C is correct: develop, 56 million**
   The decision node at the first point of the tree presents the choice between "develop" with an EMV of 56 and "abandon" with an EMV of 0.

5. **B is correct: EVPI = 6 million**
   Perfect information would say whether the outcome was effective weaponry, partially effective weaponry or failure.

Information	*Action*	*Payoff*	*Probability*
Effective	Develop	100	0.6
Partial	Develop	10	0.2
Failure	Abandon	0	0.2

Expected value of project with perfect information

$$\begin{aligned}&= (100 \times 0.6)+(10 \times 0.2)+(0 \times 0.2)\\ &= 60 + 2 + 0\\ &= 62 \text{ million}\end{aligned}$$

To find the expected value of perfect information, the expected value of the project without perfect information must be subtracted from this amount, i.e.

$$\text{EVPI} = 62 - 56 = 6 \text{ million}$$

6. **B is correct.**
   The range of profits relating to 80–100% is 12 to 20. The bracket median is the midpoint of the range, 16.

7. **B is correct.**
   The expected profit is found by multiplying the bracket medians by the probability associated with them. Since each equi-probable range covers 20% this probability is 0.2.

Expected profit $= (16 \times 0.2) + (23 \times 0.2) + (28 \times 0.2) + (33 \times 0.2) + (44 \times 0.2)$
$= 3.2 + 4.6 + 5.6 + 6.6 + 8.8$
$= 28.8$ million

8. **B is correct.**
The decision variables are the numbers of each type of doll to produce. Answer **A** is not possible since it does not allow a distinction to be drawn between the different costs, prices and production times of the two types of doll. Answers **C** and **D** would make it difficult to devise algebraic expressions for the objective function and the constraints.

9. **B is correct.**
The objective function would be to maximize contribution. **A** is incorrect because it ignores costs. The maximum revenue does not usually equate to the maximum profit. **C** is incorrect because it would lead to a solution for which only the minimum sales requirements were produced, ignoring the fact that higher production levels will be more profitable. **D** is incorrect because minimizing time on the machines is unlikely to lead to greater financial returns. In any case we have no information that any machine time saved can be used for anything else.

10. **B is correct.**
The constraints are:

	Contraints
Times available for each operation	3
Minimum sales requirements for each type of doll:	2
Maximum sales requirements for each type of doll:	2
Total	7

Note that non-negativity constraints are not required since they are covered by the minimum sales requirements.

11. **C is correct.**
The left-hand side of a constraint expresses the amount of a resource used up (in terms of the decision variables), whilst the right-hand side is the total amount of that resource available. Therefore both sides must be in the same units.

A is false. An objective function can be to maximize profit (in £s) whilst constraints could be the availability of time (hours), the level of demand (in whatever the unit of production is) and many other things. **B** is false. A constraint could be an equality. **D** is false. For example, a decision variable could be in tonnes of production, with an objective of maximizing profit in £s.

12. **C is correct.**
$x + 3y \leqslant 12$ means that x must be less than 12 ($x \leqslant 12$ when $y = 0$);
$2x + y \leqslant 18$ means that x must be less than 9 ($x \leqslant 9$ when $y = 0$).
Consequently $x \leqslant 15$ is a weaker constraint than the other two and is redundant.

13. **B is correct.**
There is a dual value for each constraint so I is true. A dual value measures what an extra unit of a resource is worth in the context of the decision problem. Therefore it

is only by chance that it would be equal to the price paid for it and II is wrong. If some of a resource is not used up its dual value must be zero and so III is correct.

14. **B is correct.**
The LP output shows that all 100 hours are used up (slack is 0) and that an additional hour will add 5 to the objective function which is profit. However, the RHS range shows that the dual value applies up to a total of 180 hours, i.e. an extra 80 hours. Only 80 of the 100 hours made available by the new machine would be used and the extra profit would be 400 (5 × 80).

15. **B is correct.**
Optimization techniques can only be applied to a limited set of problems with particular characteristics whereas simulation is a less structured method. I is wrong since the amount of data depends upon the situation rather than the technique. III is untrue: optimization techniques select the best decision.

16. **B is correct.**
The numbers should be allocated as follows:

Demand	*Probability*	*Numbers*
8	0.02	00–01
9	0.03	02–04
10	0.05	05–09
11	0.10	10–19
12	0.15	20–34
13	0.20	35–54
14	0.25	55–79
15	0.15	80–94
16	0.05	95–99

17. **C is correct.**
The random number 80 is in the range 80–94 which refers to a demand of 15.

18. **C is correct.**
Since the numbers are chosen at random they could, by chance, present an arrival pattern not representative of what happens in practice. Several simulation runs using different random number streams help to average out any resulting bias.

19. **D is correct.**
I is correct since it describes how activities are depicted on a network. However, they are not allowed to have exactly the same starting and finishing nodes, therefore II is incorrect. III is correct since an activity may have several immediate predecessors.

20. **D is correct.**
There are two situations in which dummy activities are used and neither is described by I, II or III. First, they enable two activities having exactly the same starting and finishing nodes to be represented separately. Second, they are devices which are sometimes needed so that the logical sequence between activities can be represented in network form.

21. **B is correct.**
The average or expected duration is calculated as:

$$\begin{aligned}\text{Expected} &= (\text{Optimistic} + 4 \times \text{Most likely} + \text{Pessimistic})/6\\ &= (2 + 4 \times 4 + 12)/6\\ &= 5 \text{ minutes}\end{aligned}$$

22. **B is correct.**

$$\text{Variance} = \left(\frac{\text{Pessimistic} - \text{Optimistic}}{6}\right)^2$$

$$= \left(\frac{12 - 2}{6}\right)^2$$

$$= 2.77$$

23. **D is correct.**
All three assumptions have to be made in calculating confidence limits. The calculation of the variances are based on the beta distribution. The confidence limits can only be calculated if the critical path has not changed and if the central limit theorem is applied so that the overall time for the project is normally distributed.

24. **B is correct.**
Large computer systems have always been and in general continue to be developed by central computer departments with access to the whole organization. Therefore I is not correct. Concentration on large-systems and a consequent inability to provide speedy solutions to smaller, local needs has been one of the factors in the trend to greater decentralization of computers. Therefore 11 is correct.

25. **B is correct.**
The biggest selling software packages are word processors. However, this is usually but not always a clerical application. The software that managers use most is spreadsheets.

Section B: Solutions

1. How to stop bad vibes

(a) Without the test, Technomusic have two options:

(i) Ship all components without reworking:

$$\begin{aligned}\text{EMV} &= \underset{\text{(satisfactory)}}{0.75 \times 40} + \underset{\text{(defective)}}{0.25 \times (40 - 60)}\\ &= £25\end{aligned}$$

(ii) Rework all components before shipping:

$$\begin{aligned}\text{EMV} &= \text{Contribution for all components}\\ &= 40 - 30\\ &= £10\end{aligned}$$

(5 marks)

(b) If the test is used, Bayes' theorem is the means of calculating the probabilities of the different test results. The resulting Venn diagram is given in Figure 2.

Prob("positive") = 0.60 + 0.0125 = 61.25%
Prob("inconclusive") = 0.075 + 0.05 = 12.5%
Prob("negative") = 0.075 + 0.1875 = 26.25%

(10 marks)

(c) The Venn diagram in Figure 2 also gives some other probabilities:

Prob(satis | positive) = 0.60/0.6125 = 0.98
Prob(defective | positive) = 0.0125/0.6125 = 0.02
Prob(satis | inconclusive) = 0.075/0.125 = 0.6
Prob(defective | inconclusive) = 0.05/0.125 = 0.4
Prob(satis | negative) = 0.075/0.2625 = 0.29
Prob(defective | negative) = 0.1875/0.2625 = 0.71

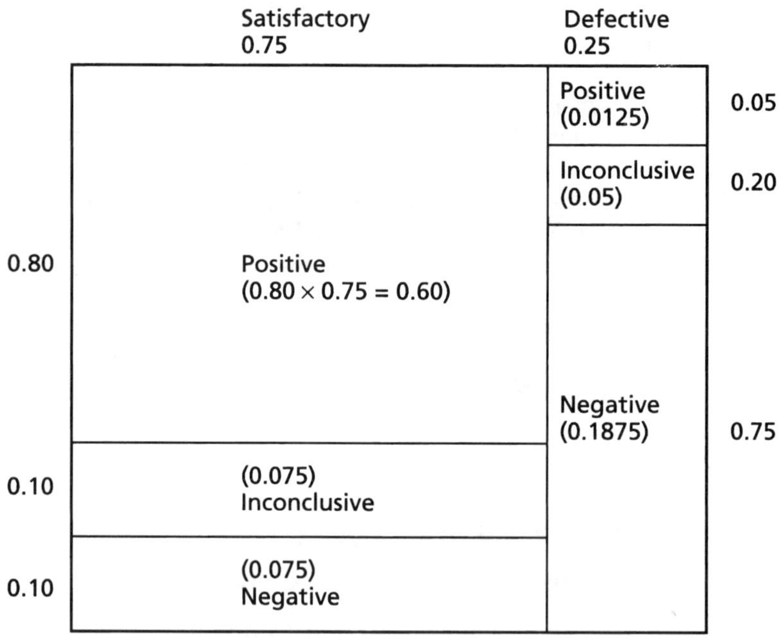

Figure 2

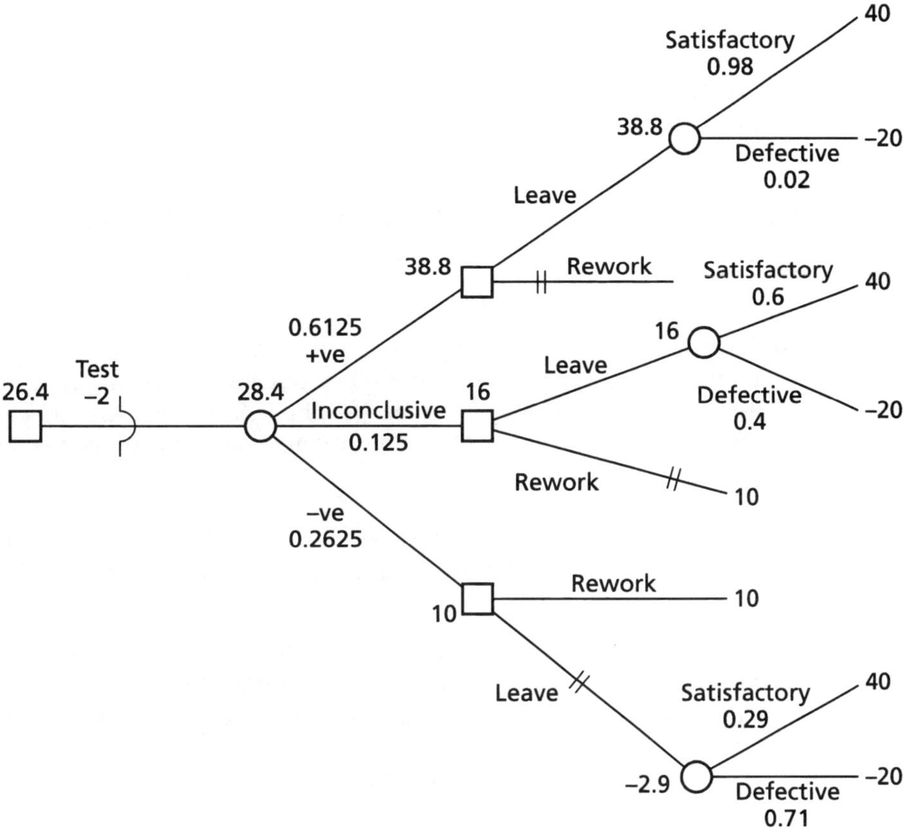

Figure 3

These can be used in the decision tree for the situation in which the test is used in Figure 3.

The EMV of using the test is £26.4. This is better (slightly) than the EMV when the test is not used, £25, therefore Technomusic should use the test.

If for any component the test is "positive" or "inconclusive", the component should be shipped. If the test is "negative" the component should be reworked. **(10 marks)**

2. Can the berth rate be increased?

(a) Figure 4 is a flowchart of a simulation of dock operations. It is important that the essentials of the physical operations (docking, allocating a gang, loading, etc.) and the recording of information for the simulation (waiting time, queue length, etc.) are included. However, not every flowchart need be exactly like Figure 4.
(10 marks for port operations, 10 marks for simulation activities)

(b) Assumptions:

(i) Once started a gang will complete work on a ship.
(ii) There are seven working days a week.
(iii) All days are the same working length.
(iv) There is no seasonal variation in port operations. **(5 marks)**

3. Can the garden equipment manufacturer unearth greater profits?

(a) The optimal production mix is 700 chairs, 133 tables and no benches. This will give a contribution of £27 667. **(5 marks)**

(b) The shadow price for tubing is £8, compared with the purchase price of additional tubing of £6. Therefore some should be bought. The constraint ranges show that an additional 556.7 pounds can be bought before the dual value changes. Leisure Products should buy all 500 pounds offered and the extra contribution will be:

$500 \times (8 - 6) = £1\,000$ **(5 marks)**

(c) The optimal mix suggests that no benches should be made but the marketing manager is insisting upon at least 100. The reduced cost for benches is £13.83, consequently making 100 will reduce the contribution by £1383. **(5 marks)**

(d) The shadow price for tube bending is £11.67 per hour. Since this resource can be sold for £15 per hour, Leisure Products can sell it profitably. The constraint ranges table shows that the available time can be reduced from the present 1 000 hours to 533 hours without affecting the dual values. Therefore Leisure Products can sell 200 hours and increase contribution by:

$200 \times (15 - 11.67) = £667$ **(5 marks)**

(e) Coefficient ranges show that the contribution on chairs can be reduced to £22.2 before the optimal production mix will change. If the contribution is reduced to £25 the optimal production mix will not change but the overall contribution will decrease by:

$700 \times (30 - 25) = £3\,500$ **(5 marks)**

4. How to make a carphone go faster?

The stages in a network analysis are:

1. **List** all activities in the project.
2. **Identify** the predecessors of each activity.
3. **Draw** the network diagram.
4. **Estimate** activity durations as average times or, if uncertainty is to be dealt with explicitly, as optimistic/most likely/pessimistic times.
5. **Produce an activity schedule** by making a forward then a backward pass through the network.
6. **Determine the critical path** by calculating activity floats.
7. **Measure uncertainty** by calculating activity variances, the variance of the whole project and finally confidence limits for the duration of the project.
8. **Draw cost–time curves** for each activity.
9. **Crash the network** and construct a cost–time graph for the project.

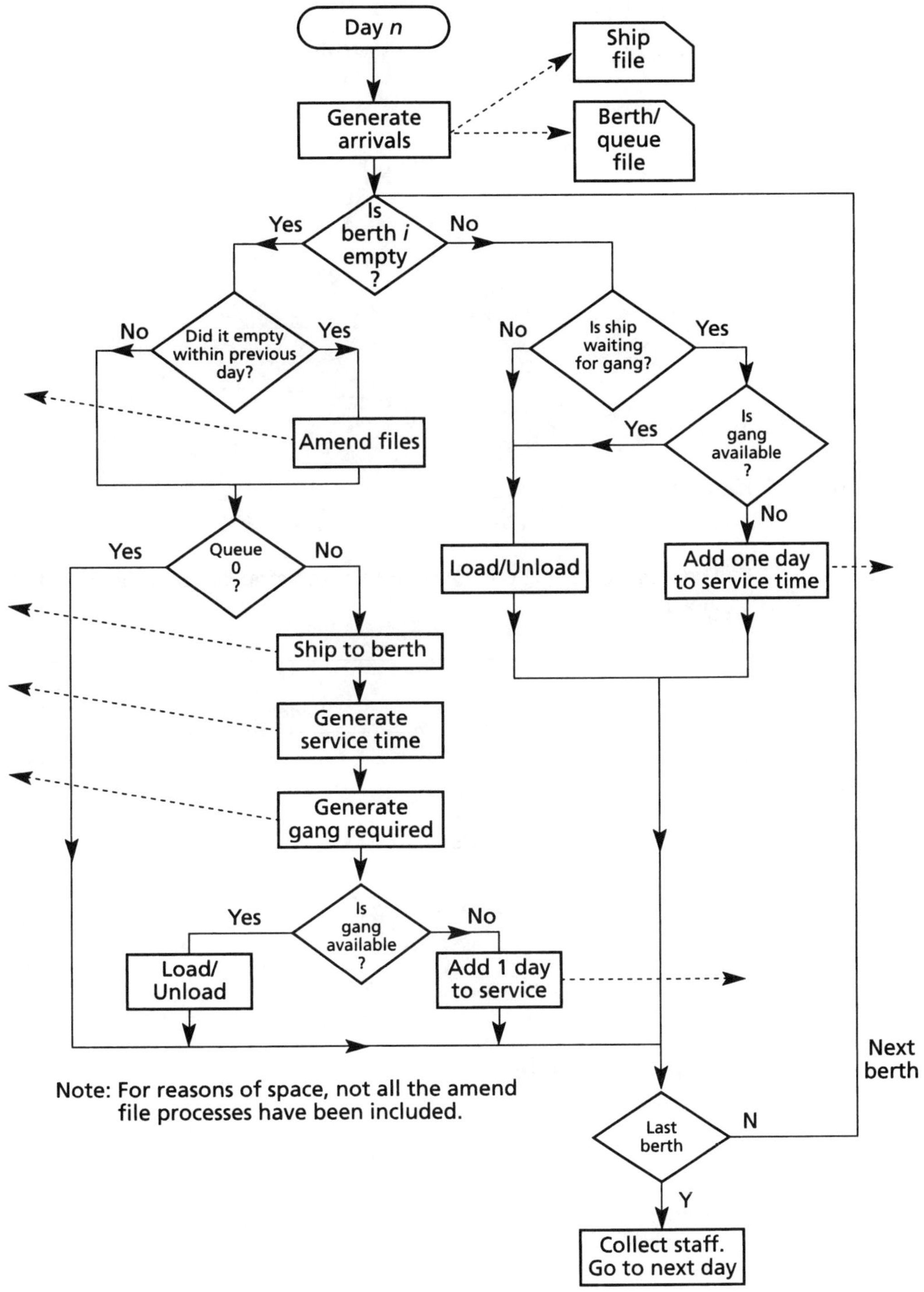
Day n
Ship file
Generate arrivals
Berth/ queue file
Is berth i empty ?
Yes
No
Did it empty within previous day?
No
Yes
Amend files
Is ship waiting for gang?
No
Yes
Is gang available ?
Yes
No
Queue 0 ?
Yes
No
Load/Unload
Add one day to service time
Ship to berth
Generate service time
Generate gang required
Is gang available ?
Yes
No
Load/ Unload
Add 1 day to service
Next berth
Note: For reasons of space, not all the amend file processes have been included.
Last berth
N
Y
Collect staff. Go to next day

Figure 4

Steps 8 and 9 are not relevant to this case since crashing the network is not required. Following steps 1–7:

1. A list of the activities is already available.

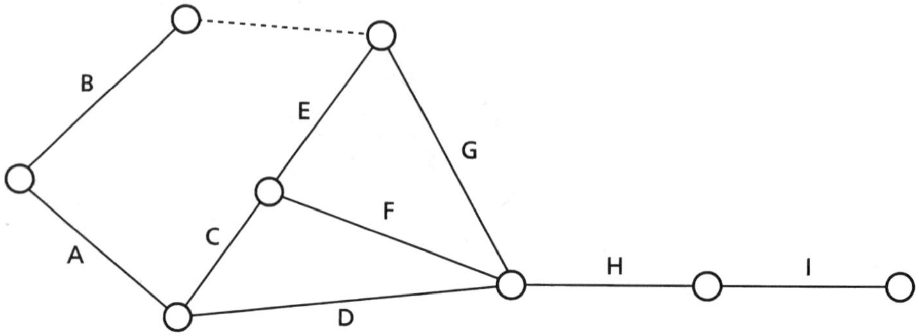

Figure 5

2. The immediate predecessors can be taken straight from the case description and are shown below:

	Activity	Predecessors	Duration (weeks) Opt	ML	Pes
A	R&D	–	15	20	25
B	Market research	–	5	15	25
C	Prototype	A	2	3	4
D	Marketing material	A	1	4	7
E	Production plan	C	1	2	9
F	Testing	C	1	6	17
G	Pricing	B, E	1	2	3
H	Market plan	D, F, G	1	2	9
I	Full production	G, H	4	5	12

Opt = Optimistic
ML = Most Likely
Pes = Pessimistic

3. The network diagram is shown in Figure 5. **(5 marks)**

4. Estimates of the durations of the activities are given in the case but an expected duration has to be calculated from the optimistic, most likely and pessimistic estimates. This is shown below:

	Activity	Predecessors	Opt	Duration (weeks) ML	Pes	Expected
A	R&D	–	15	20	25	20
B	Market research	–	5	15	25	15
C	Prototype	A	2	3	4	3
D	Marketing material	A	1	4	7	4
E	Production plan	C	1	2	9	3
F	Testing	C	1	6	17	7
G	Pricing	B, E	1	2	3	2
H	Market plan	D, F, G	1	2	9	3
I	Full production	G, H	4	5	12	6

5. A forward followed by a backward pass through the network gives the results shown in Figure 6.

   The results can be used to produce the activity schedule shown below, giving the earliest and latest starts and finishes of each activity.

	Activity	ES	Earliest/latest LS	Start/finish EF	LF	Float
A	R&D	0	0	20	20	0
B	Market research	0	13	15	28	13
C	Prototype	20	20	23	23	0
D	Marketing material	20	26	24	30	6
E	Production plan	23	25	26	28	2
F	Testing	23	23	30	30	0
G	Pricing	26	28	28	30	2
H	Market plan	30	30	33	33	0
I	Full production	33	33	39	39	0

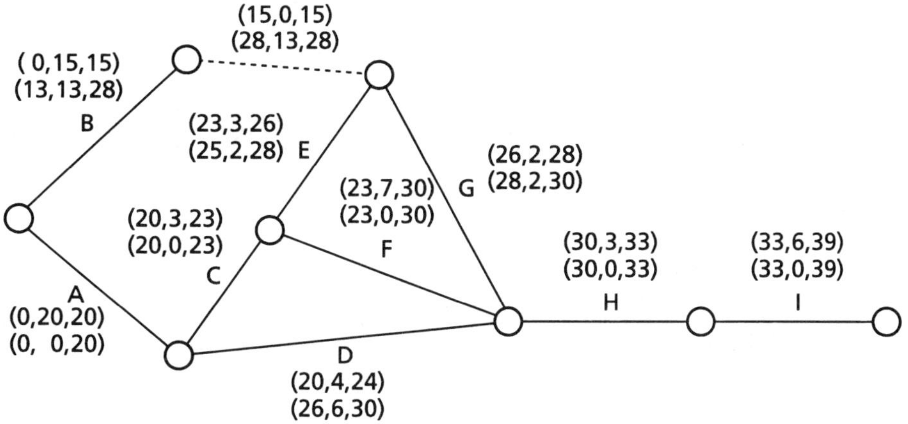

Figure 6

6. The float for each activity (Earliest start – Latest start) is shown above. The critical path is those activities with zero float and is therefore:

A–C–F–H–I **(15 marks)**

7. The variance of each activity is calculated from the formula:

$$\text{Variance} = \left(\frac{\text{Pessimistic} - \text{Optimistic}}{6}\right)^2$$

The results are shown below:

	Activity	*Opt*	*Duration (weeks)* *ML*	*Pes*	*Expected*	*Variance*
A	R&D	15	20	25	20	2.8
B	Market research	5	15	25	15	11.1
C	Prototype	2	3	4	3	0.1
D	Marketing material	1	4	7	4	1.0
E	Production plan	1	2	9	3	1.8
F	Testing	1	6	17	7	7.1
G	Pricing	1	2	3	2	0.1
H	Market plan	1	2	9	3	1.8
I	Full production	4	5	12	6	1.8

The variance of the whole project is calculated as the sum of the variances of the activities on the critical path:

$$\begin{aligned}\text{Variance of project} &= 2.8 + 0.1 + 7.1 + 1.8 + 1.8 \\ &= 13.6\end{aligned}$$

Therefore, the standard deviation is $\sqrt{13.6} = 3.7$.

The 95% confidence limits for the duration of the project are the expected completion time plus or minus two standard deviations:

$= 39 \pm 2 \times 3.7$
$= 31.6$ to 46.4 days **(5 marks)**

PRACTICE FINAL EXAMINATION 2 – WITHOUT MCQs

Case Studies

Case Study 1

A theatre director has identified the activities which need to be completed before his play can be staged at the Edinburgh Festival. The table below indicates the activities, their dependencies, normal durations and costs, together with the crash durations and costs.

Activity	*Dependency*	*Normal Duration (Weeks)*	*Normal Cost (£)*	*Crash Duration (weeks)*	*Cost(£)at Crash Duration*
A	–	6	18 000	4	24 000
B	–	5	20 000	3	32 000
C	–	4	16 000	3	20 000
D	B, C	7	28 000	6	33 000
E	C	7	21 000	5	27 000
F	A	6	35 000	5	38 500
G	F	3	18 000	2	22 500
H	D, E	6	15 000	5	19 000

1. ***Draw the network.*** **(6 marks)**

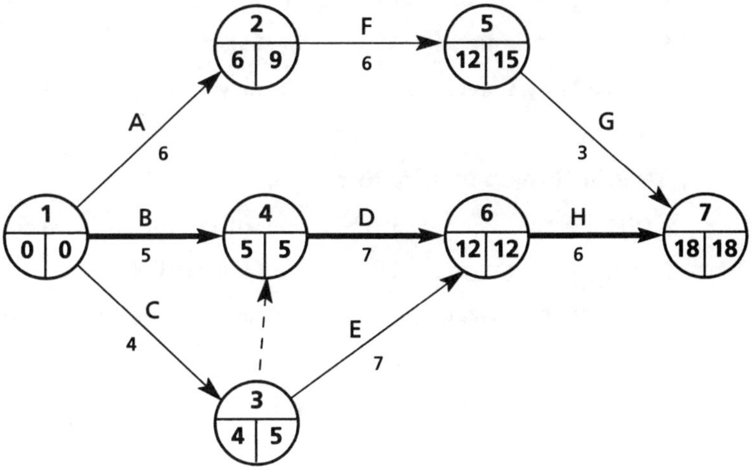

2. ***Find the critical path.*** **(5 marks)**

Activity	*Total Float*	*Earliest Start Time*	*Latest Finish Time*	*Weeks Saved*	*Extra Cost(£)*	*Extra Cost per Week Saved (£)*
A	2	0	9	2	6 000	3 000
B	0	0	5	2	12 000	6 000
C	1	0	5	1	4 000	4 000
D	0	5	12	1	5 000	5 000
E	1	4	12	2	6 000	3 000
F	2	6	15	1	3 500	3 500
G	2	12	18	1	4 500	4 500
H	0	12	18	1	4 000	4 000

Critical Path: B–D–H (i.e those activities where total float = 0)

3. ***Calculate the minimum project duration.*** **(1 mark)**

Minimum Project Time: **18 weeks**

4. ***Find the cost of reducing the overall project duration by***

(a) one week
(b) a second week
(c) a third week
(d) a fourth week
(e) a total of four weeks

Show your working. **(13 marks)**
(Total of 25 marks)

Calculate the Extra Cost per week saved as in the table above.

Reducing Project by 1 Week

Critical path: B-D-H

Cheapest option: H Cost: £4 000

Reduce H by 1 week new duration 5 (crashed)

Cost: *£4 000*

Reducing Project by 1 Further Week

Critical path: B-D-H with duration 17 weeks

Cheapest option: D Cost: £5 000

Reduce D by 1 week new duration 6 (crashed)

Cost: *£5 000*

Reducing Project by 1 Further Week

Critical path: B-D-H with duration 16 weeks
C-E-H

Cheapest options: B Cost: £6 000
and E Cost: £3 000

Reduce both B and E by 1 week

Cost: *£9 000*

Reducing Project by 1 Further Week

Critical path: B-D-H 15 weeks
C-E-H
A-F-G

Cheapest options: B Cost: £6 000
E Cost: £3 000
A Cost: £3 000

Reduce each of B, E and **A** by 1 week

Cost: *£12 000*

Total Cost of Reducing Project by 4 Weeks

	£
1st week	4 000
2nd week	5 000
3rd week	9 000
4th week	12 000
	30 000

Case Study 2

A bicycle manufacturer has three factories in the UK which produce bicycles, at Axbridge, Birmingham and Cambridge. The bicycles are then collected and stored at four warehouses which are near to the major retail outlets, i.e. at London, Manchester, Newcastle and Oxford.

The factory production is normally 300, 450 and 400 bicycles per month at Axbridge, Birmingham and Cambridge respectively. The warehouse demands are for 500, 250, 150 and 250 bicycles per month at London, Manchester, Newcastle and Oxford respectively.

The costs associated with transporting one bicycle from the factory to the warehouse are shown in the table below.

Cost (£) Per Unit Transported

	To Warehouse			
From Factory	*London*	*Manchester*	*Newcastle*	*Oxford*
Axbridge	5	7	9	6
Birmingham	5	4	6	6
Cambridge	4	6	8	5

The logistics manager has to decide the cheapest way of transporting the requisite number of bicycles from the factories to the warehouses.

Explain how this decision can be made by the use of linear programming, giving examples.
(25 marks)

(This is similar to the example on pages 85–8 of the main text.)

Decision Variables

Number of bicycles/month along each route.

12 routes (3 factories × 4 warehouses).

x_{AL}, x_{AM}, x_{AN}, x_{AO} are the numbers taken from factory A to warehouses L, M, N and O.

x_{BL}, x_{BM}, x_{BN}, x_{BO} from factory B and x_{CL}, x_{CM}, x_{CN}, x_{CO} from factory C.

Objective Function

Minimise $5x_{AL} + 7x_{AM} + 9x_{AN} + 6x_{AO}$

$+ 5x_{BL} + 4x_{BM} + 6x_{BN} + 6x_{BO}$

$+ 4x_{CL} + 6x_{CM} + 8x_{CN} + Sx_{CO}$

Subject to the following constraints:

Constraints

Factory Production	$x_{AL} + x_{AM} + x_{AN} + x_{AO}$	$\leq$	300	(Factory A)
	$x_{BL} + x_{BM} + x_{BN} + x_{BO}$	$\leq$	450	(Factory B)
	$x_{CL} + x_{CM} + x_{CN} + x_{CO}$	$\leq$	400	(Factory C)
Warehouse Demand	$x_{AL} + x_{BL} + x_{CL}$	$\leq$	500	(Warehouse L)
	$x_{AM} + x_{BM} + x_{CM}$	$\leq$	250	(Warehouse M)
	$x_{AN} + x_{BN} + x_{CN}$	$\leq$	150	(Warehouse N)
	$x_{AO} + x_{BO} + x_{CO}$	$\leq$	250	(Warehouse O)

Non-negative $x_{AL}, x_{AM}, \ldots\ldots, x_{CO} \geq 0$

Solution

Use linear programming to find optimal solution. Note that all the coefficients are 1 or 0 in the constraints and the "transportation method algorithm" could be used to simplify the calculations. These calculations would normally be performed using a computer program.

Case Study 3

A manufacturer of tennis rackets is evaluating whether to launch a new model.

Your firm of consultants has been asked to provide advice on the decision-making process, and on the assessment of the likely demand for the new model during its first year of production.

Write a report detailing the stages of discussion, and the information that would be required for this process. **(25 marks)**

(This is similar to the example given on pages 36–41 of the main text.)

The required stages are:

(i) Set the context for the discussion.

(ii) Review previous experience and knowledge.

(iii) Estimate median.

(iv) Estimate 25% + 75% fractiles.

(v) Check for consistency.

(vi) Estimate other fractiles.

(vii) Check for consistency.

(viii) Draw demand distribution.

(ix) Obtain bracket medians and use these in decision tree.

The report should detail the above stages. It should highlight the information on likely demand which can be obtained from the manager using the concept of equally likely parts. It should be based on the manager's previous experience and knowledge of market conditions, budget constraints, etc. Terminology should be restricted to terms that the manager is happy with, e.g. probably avoiding terms like median, fractile, etc.

Information should also be obtained on factors likely to affect demand, e.g. nature of market, competitors, market saturation, customers' profiles, etc.

Case Study 4

A small craft workshop produces hand-made patchwork cushions in two designs, the Arran and the Bute. The Arran cushion costs £30 to produce and sells for £45, while the Bute cushion costs £24 to produce and sells for £36. The workshop aims to maximise its profit.

Cutting out and making the patches for one cushion takes a total of 50 minutes for the Arran design and 25 minutes for the Bute design. Sewing the patches together takes 40 minutes for the Arran design and 80 minutes for the Bute design. Stuffing the cushion and sewing it up takes 30 minutes for each design.

Different skills are required for these tasks and workers are only available on a part-time basis. During a normal week only 1 000 minutes are available for cutting the patches, 1 600 minutes for sewing the patches together, and 900 minutes for the final stuffing and finishing process.

1. ***Construct the linear programming model for the weekly production of these cushions.*** **(5 marks)**

Let A be the number of Arran cushions produced per week.

Let B be the number of Bute cushions produced per week.

Objective function

Maximise 15A + 12B

Subject to Constraints

50A + 25B	≤	1 000	Cutting
40A + 80B	≤	1 600	Sewing
30A + 30B	≤	900	Finishing
A	≥	0	
B	≥	0	

2. ***Draw the graph showing the feasible region and the contribution line.*** **(5 marks)**

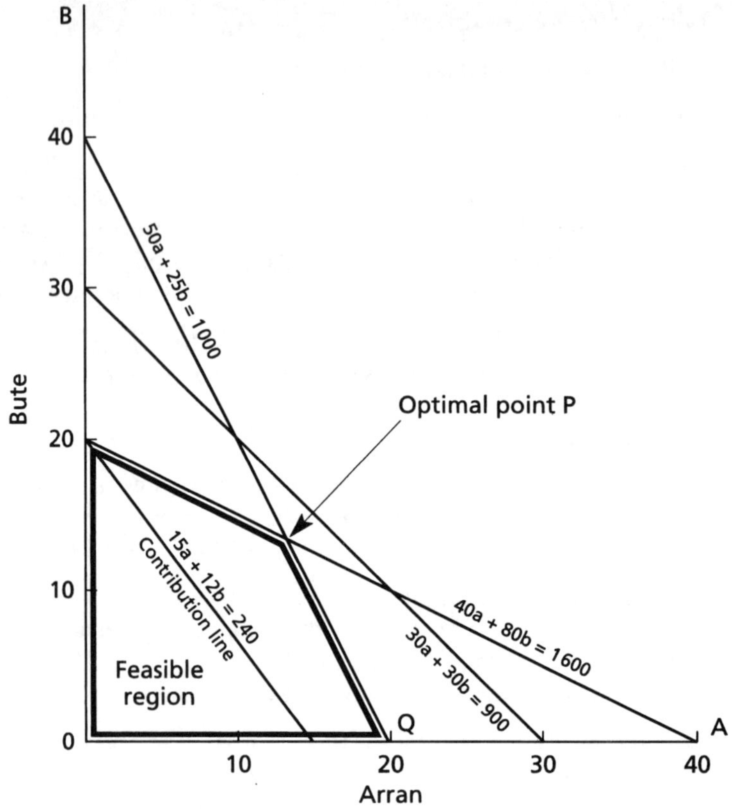

3. ***Find the optimum number that should be produced for each cushion.*** **(4 marks)**

40A	+	80B	=	1 600	Sewing	.... (1)
50A	+	25B	=	1 000	Cutting	.... (2)

(1) × 5	200A	+	400B	=	8 000	.... (3)
(2) × 4	200A	=	100B	=	4 000	.... (4)
(3) – (4)			300B	=	4 000	
			B	=	13.33	

In *(1)*

40A + (80 × 13.33) = 1 600

40A = 1 600 – 1066.4

$$A = \frac{533.6}{40} = 13.34$$

The firm should produce 13.34 Arran cushions and 13.33 Bute cushions.

4. ***Calculate the profit that this would produce.*** **(1 mark)**

Profit this would produce

= (15 × 13.34) + (12 × 13.33)

= 200.10 + 159.96

= £360.06

5. ***Find the increase in the selling price of an Arran cushion that is required to change the optimal mix.*** **(5 marks)**

(Total of 25 marks)

Let c_{ai} be the new contribution from an Arran cushion.

$$\text{Slope of objective function} = \frac{c_{ai}}{12}$$

If contribution of A increases then the slope of objective function increases until it is parallel to the line PQ, i.e. the line 50A + 25B = 1 000.

So Slope of Objective Function = Slope of PQ

$$\frac{c_{ai}}{12} = \frac{50}{25}$$

$$c_{ai} = 24$$

New contribution of A is £24.

This is an increase of £9 from the previous contribution of £15.

Hence, contribution of A must increase by > £9 to change the optimal mix.

PRACTICE FINAL EXAMINATION 3 – WITHOUT MCQs

Case Studies

Case Study 1

A baker makes speciality loaves for an outlet, each loaf costs 80p to make and retails at £1.50. The probabilities of a daily demand at this outlet for 6, 7, 8, 9 or 10 loaves are estimated to be 0.15, 0.22, 0.26, 0.24 and 0.13 respectively. Any loaves remaining at the end of the day's business cannot be sold.

1. ***Draw the decision tree and calculate the Expected Monetary Values.*** **(15 marks)**

Profit Obtained (£)

	Demand				
Number Made	*6*	*7*	*8*	*9*	*10*
6	4.20	4.20	4.20	4.20	4.20
7	3.40	4.90	4.90	4.90	4.90
8	2.60	4.10	5.60	5.60	5.60
9	1.80	3.30	4.80	6.30	6.30
10	1.00	2.50	4.00	5.50	7.00

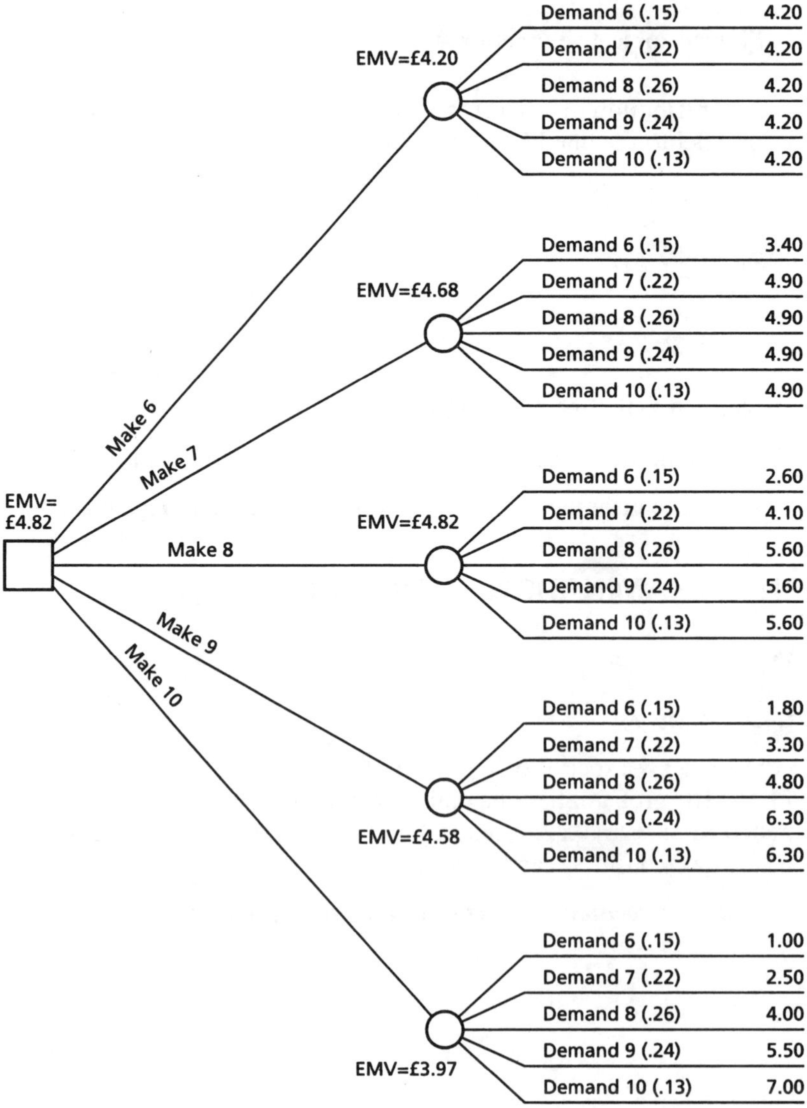

2. ***What number of loaves should the baker produce for this outlet? Show your reasoning.*** **(2 marks)**

   The baker should make 8 loaves for this outlet since this produces the highest Expected Monetary Value (EMV) of £4.82.

3. ***Construct the risk profile for the optimal path.*** **(3 marks)**

   The risk profile for the optimal path is:

Outcome	*Payoff*	*Probability*
Demand 6	£2.60	0.15
Demand 7	£4.10	0.22
Demand 8	£5.60	0.26
Demand 9	£5.60	0.24
Demand 10	£5.60	0.13

4. ***Write a short report explaining your findings to the baker.*** **(5 marks)**
   (Total of 25 marks)

Dear Sir

I have examined the profit you would expect if you were to make between six and ten speciality loaves daily for this outlet. Based on the information that vou have given me on the likely demand for these loaves at this outlet, I recommend that you should make eight loaves daily. This would result in a likely profit of £4.82 per day in the long run.

You may, however, not wish to disappoint other customers with a probable adverse effect on future trade. If you were to bake nine loaves daily the average profit is likely to be £4.58 but you may gain more satisfied regular customers. An alternative approach would be to bake only six loaves. This would generate a likely return of £4.20 and there would be no waste.

If you require any further information please do not hesitate to contact me.

Yours faithfully

Case Study 2

A firm has analysed the steps needed in the implementation of a new data-base system. The activities, their dependencies and the durations in days are summarised in the table below.

Activity	*Dependency*	*Duration (days)*
A		5
B		4
C		3
D	B	7
E	A and B	10
F	B and C	8
G	B and C	9
H	F	6
I	E and D	2
J	G	4

1. ***Draw the network.*** **(8 marks)**

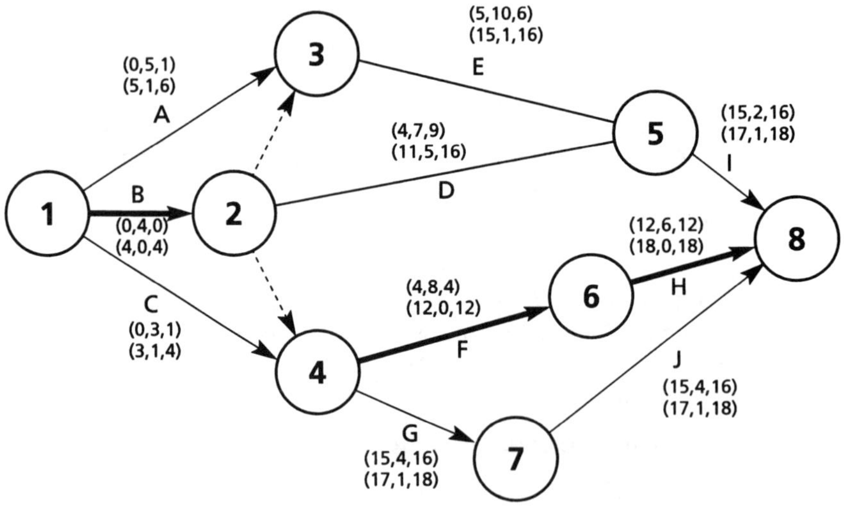

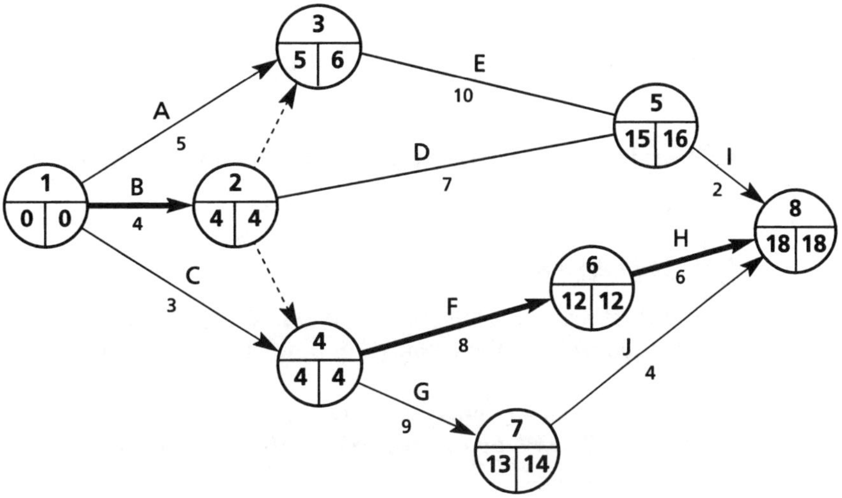

2. ***Construct a table showing for each activity the earliest and latest start and finish times, together with the floats.*** **(8 marks)**

Activity	*Earliest Start*	*Lastest Start*	*Earliest Finish*	*Latest Finish*	*Float*
A	0	1	5	6	1
B	0	0	4	4	0
C	0	1	3	4	1
D	4	9	11	16	5
E	5	6	15	16	1
F	4	4	12	12	0
G	4	5	13	14	1
H	12	12	18	18	0
I	15	16	17	18	1
J	13	14	17	18	1

Earliest Finish = Earliest Start + Duration

Latest Start = Latest Finish – Duration

Float = Latest Start – Earliest Start
= Latest Finish – Earliest Finish

3. ***Find the critical path and explain what this indicates.*** **(2 marks)**

Critical Path B-F-H

If these activities are delayed or their starts are delayed, then the completion of the whole project will be delayed.

4. ***What is the minimum duration for completion of this project?*** **(2 marks)**

Minimum duration of project = 18 days.

5. ***Explain the meaning of "float".*** **(2 marks)**

The float measures how much the start of the activity can be delayed or its duration extended without the completion time of the project being affected.

6. ***The project manager has discovered that he can reduce the time required for each of activities B and F by one day. What effect does this have on the network, and what are the implications?*** **(3 marks)**

(Total of 25 marks)

If Activity B reduced by one day, duration of B = 3 days.

If Activity F reduced by one day, duration of F = 7 days.

The network should be re-drawn and the start and finish times and floats should be recalculated. This will alter the critical path through the network.

Reduced durations for B and F

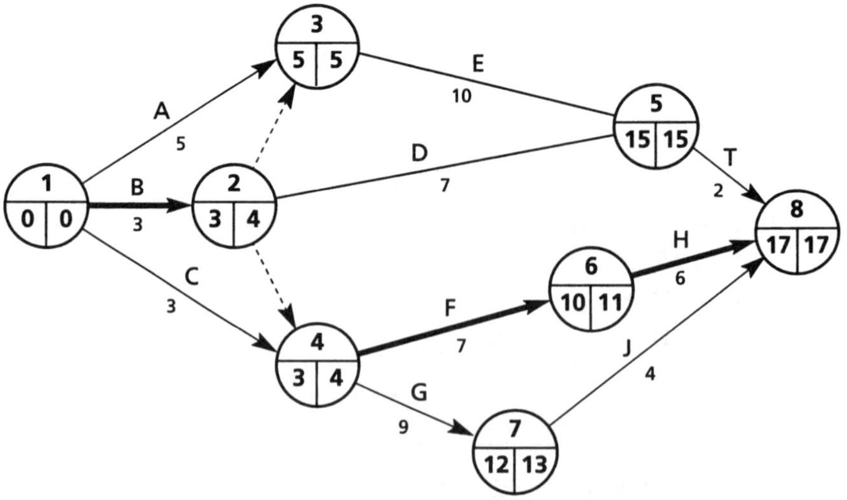

The critical activities will be A, E and I. The new duration is 17 days.

A delay in any activities on the critical path can affect the final completion date of the project.

Case Study 4

A garden centre produces many different types of plant. In this week in March, the manageress intends to pot-up the conifers and the rhododendrums. However, she is restricted by the amount of labour available, a maximum of two workers each working a 35 hour week, and by the amount of potting compost that has been delivered, i.e. 1 000 kilos. To pot-up a rhododendrum plant requires 3 kilos of compost and takes 20 minutes. A conifer requires 5 kilos of compost and takes 15 minutes to pot-up. The manageress has only 200 rhododendrum plants and 150 conifer plants that are ready to be potted-up.

The cost of producing plants ready for sale is £1.80 for a conifer and £2.60 for a rhododendrum. The plants retail for £3.60 and £4.60 respectively.

The manageress needs to decide how many of each type of plant she should pot-up in order to maximise her profit

1. ***Construct the linear programming model.*** **(6 marks)**

	Number	*Cost*	*Retail Price*	*Contribution*	*Maximum*
Rhododendrum	R	£2.60	£4.60	£2.00	200
Conifer	C	£1.80	£3.60	£1.80	150

Objective function Maximise $2.0R + 1.8C$

Subject to constraints

$3R + 5C \leq 1\,000$	*Compost (kilos)*
$20R + 15C \leq 4\,200$	*Labour (mins)*
$R \leq 200$	*Rhododendrums*
$C \leq 150$	*Conifer*
$R \geq 0$	
$C \geq 0$	

2. ***Show this graphically.*** **(5 marks)**

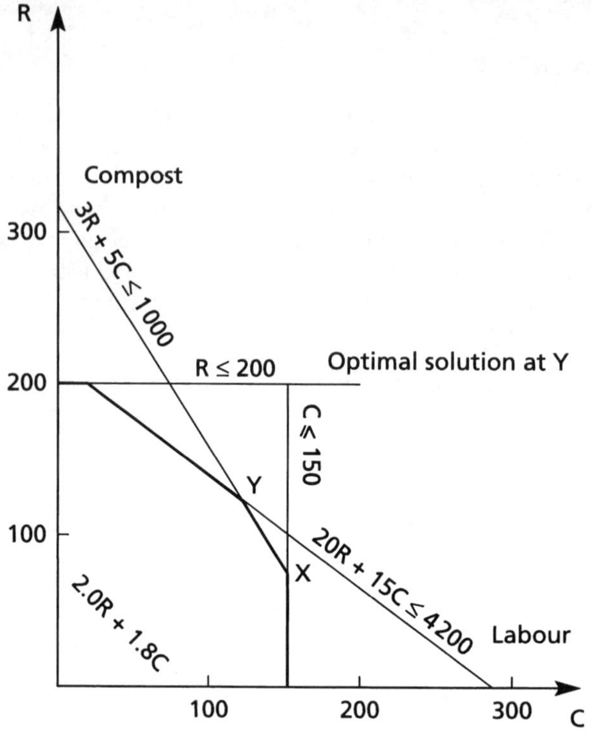

3. ***Find the optimal mix and calculate the profit that this would produce.*** **(8 marks)**

Optimal solution occurs at intersection of constraints

	3R	+	5C	=	1 000	..........❶
	20R	+	15C	=	4 2000	..........❷
❶ × 3						
	9R	+	15C	=	3 000	..........❸
❷ – ❸						
			11R	=	1 200	
			R	=	109.09	

In ❶

(3 × 109.09)	+	5C	=	1 000
		5C	=	1 000 – 327.27
		5C	=	672.73
		C	=	134.55

The optimal mix is 109.09 rhododendrum plants and 134.55 conifers.

This would produce a profit of

$$\begin{array}{rcr} 109.09 \times £2.00 & = & 218.18 \\ + \; 134.55 \times £1.80 & = & + \; \underline{242.19} \\ & & \underline{\underline{£460.37}} \end{array}$$

4. ***By how much could the sales price of the conifers be increased without affecting the optimal mix?*** **(6 marks)**
(Total of 25 marks)

$$\text{Slope of objective function} = \frac{\text{Contribution of Conifer}}{\text{Contribution of Rhododendrum}}$$

Let new contribution of a conifer be C_c

$$\text{Then slope of objective function} = \frac{C_c}{2.0}$$

If sale price of a conifer increases, contribution increases and slope of objective function increases.

When slope of objective function = slope of line the optimal solution will be on the line.

The contribution from the optimal mix will be constant on the line, but the optimal mix will vary.

When slope of objective function = slope of line

$$\frac{C_c}{2.0} = \frac{5}{3}$$

$$C_c = \frac{10}{3} = 3.33$$

Therefore, if the contribution of a conifer is £3.33 or more the optimal mix will change.

Hence, if the sales price of a conifer is £5.13 or more the optimal mix will change.

Note that if the sales price of a conifer is > £5.13 the optimal solution will be at point X where only 150 conifers will be produced together with some rhododendrums.

The sales price of a conifer can be increased by up to £1.53 without affecting the optimal mix.

Case Study 4

A university wants to introduce the use of information technology into its administrative functions. This would enable information on accounts, students and staff, etc., to be input and accessed by the central administrative department, staff in departmental offices and also by academic staff.

In the past, departments have pursued their own strategies on hardware and software purchases. This has resulted in a great variety of different computers (e.g. PC-compatibles, Apple Macintoshes and Sun workstations). Similarly numerous different software packages are used in the university, and staff with the same kind of software are often using different versions. The range of staff expertise ranges from expert to zero. Some departments do not use computers at all.

1. ***Outline the factors that should be taken into account when introducing the new policy.*** **(10 marks)**

Factors to be taken into account:

Different backgrounds of users – computer expertise
– hardware
– software
– communications, e.g. networks

Different levels of interest
Likely usage
Interest in project
Involvement of management, departmental and university
Cost/benefit analysis
Training
Data input and conversion
Changeover period and method
Access and security
Back-up facilities
Interfaces with other systems
Compatibility with corporate strategy

2. ***Describe the strategy required for successful implementation of the new information technology system in the university.*** **(15 marks)**
(Total of 25 marks)

Strategy

High level management support
Involvement of users from beginning
Realistic evaluation of options, cost and timing
Standards for software, hardware, networks, etc.
Bulk purchases
Training
User support and motivation
Keep users informed and consulted
Monitoring of new system
Security and control of system, e.g. access
Future expansion
Evaluation
Effective changeover policy and conversion of existing data
User "champions"
Strong project management and leadership
Ensure confidence in new system by careful testing prior to changeover

Government, Industry and Privatization

PRACTICE FINAL EXAMINATION 1

Answer all five questions. Time allowed: Three hours

1. (a) Explain and illustrate the difference between a positive and normative approach to the study of government measures designed to influence the behaviour of industrial companies. **(10 marks)**

   (b) What connection, if any, can be established between the growth in government spending and the following variables:

   (i) Population growth.
   (ii) Growth in GDP per head.
   (iii) The proportion of government employees in total employment? **(10 marks)**

2. (a) Define and illustrate the meaning of any **two** of the following terms:

   (i) Natural monopoly.
   (ii) Contestable markets.
   (iii) "RPI–X".
   (iv) A Demsetz auction. **(10 marks – 5 marks for each component)**

   (b) A firm is considering two mutually exclusive investment projects. The following comparative information is available:

Project I	
Capital cost (incurred immediately)	£5 million
Operating costs per year	
Employment:	100
Average wage:	£25 000 per year
Maintenance and raw materials	£1.5 million per year
Capacity output per year	1 million units
Price of output per unit (in the absence of regulation):	£5 per unit
Project II	
Capital cost (incurred immediately)	£9.33 million
Operating costs per year	
Employment:	50
Average wage:	£25 000 per year
Maintenance and raw materials	£2.35 million per year
Capacity output per year	1 million units
Price of output per unit (in the absence of regulation):	£5 per unit

   In answering the following question assume (for ease of computation)

   (i) A 50 week year.
   (ii) An indefinitely long life for each project (assume that the capital does not depreciate or that the yearly expenditure on maintenance is sufficient to maintain its value constant).

(iii) That revenues and operating costs relating to each year occur on the last day of that year.
(iv) A discount rate used by the firm for investment appraisal of 10 per cent.

The firm is assumed to undertake the project with the higher net present value.

Description of Regulatory System
The firm is restricted to a rate of return on capital invested not exceeding 15 per cent. A higher rate of return will result in regulatory intervention and a reduction in the price of the output until the 15 per cent limit is satisfied. Assume that the regulators are not concerned about possible shortages or queues which may develop at controlled prices.

Question
Using the above information, examine the effect of rate of return regulation on the firm's investment decision. Is the result consistent with the existence of an Averch–Johnson effect? **(10 marks)**

3. (a) Explain what is meant by the "asymmetric information problem" and show how it arises in the case of any **two** of the following:

(i) Government purchasing contracts.
(ii) Selective government subsidies to industry.
(iii) Government bureaucracy.
(iv) Control of environmental damage.

(10 marks – 5 marks for each component)

(b) How close is the parallel between monopolistic and bureaucratic behaviour? Use a diagram in answering this question. **(10 marks)**

4. (a) Distinguish a public enterprise as an economic entity from

(i) A "bureau".
(ii) A private enterprise. **(5 marks)**

(b) Analyse the problems that arise in attempts to compare the productivity of public and private enterprises. **(5 marks)**

(c) Use principal–agent analysis to illustrate the difficulties encountered by government in seeking to impose "rules" on the operations of public enterprises. **(10 marks)**

5. (a) Using examples, distinguish between

(i) Privatization.
(ii) Deregulation.
(iii) Liberalization. **(5 marks)**

(b) Define and illustrate the difference between

(i) Technical efficiency.
(ii) Productive efficiency.
(iii) Economic efficiency. **(5 marks)**

(c) A certain good can be produced using three possible processes. Each process involves a different capital to labour ratio. Below are recorded the number of units of capital and labour required to produce a single unit of output for each of the three processes.

	Capital	*Labour*
Process A	4	1
Process B	2	2
Process C	1	4

The wage rate is £10 and the rental rate on capital (i.e. the price to hire a unit of capital per time period) is also £10.

Company I uses process C. Its labour costs are £600 per unit time and its capital costs are £150 over the same time period. It produces 10 units of output. Company II uses process B. Its labour costs are £200 and its capital costs are £200. Output is also 10 units.

(i) Compare Companies I and II with respect to both technical and productive efficiency.

Suppose that some policy change results in a new, more competitive, environment. The price of labour falls to £5. Company I continues to use process C and produces 10 units of output. Labour costs are £300 and capital costs £150.

(ii) Does the fall in measured costs of production represent an improvement in either technical or productive efficiency? Explain your answer.

(10 marks)

Answers to Practice Final Exam

1(a) Positive and Normative

It is a matter of fact that governments attempt to influence the actions of industrial companies with a range of objectives in mind. Some illustrations make this clear. Governments frequently express concern about the rate of growth of the economy and seek to influence the rate of growth of industrial output by measures designed to raise the level of industrial investment and to improve the efficiency of factor inputs, for example by supporting technical education and research and development expenditure. They respond to political pressures from different regions by measures designed to iron out differences in economic growth between them, for example by allocation of government purchases. The present-day concentration of interest on the "diseconomies" created by environmental pollution has produced a response by government in the form of anti-pollution regulation and the use of fiscal measures.

A positive approach to the study of government industrial policy seeks to identify the policy objectives of government which are actually operative and to use economic analysis to examine whether or not the measures adopted achieve the stated objectives. No judgement is passed on the objectives themselves. A normative approach evaluates the objectives themselves. A set of policies are classified as "good, or "bad", according to whether or not they conform to a particular "norm". Thus economists frequently argue that satisfying consumer wants is the main function of the economy and that industrial policy measures ought to conform to and therefore are to be judged by that aim. However, while disagreements over the effects of a government measure can be resolved by appeal to facts and logic, in principle at least, whether the measure is "good" or "bad" is a matter of personal opinion. The fact that there may be a consensus view amongst economists identifying some policies as "good" does not mean that "good" policies can be derived from economic expertise.

In practice, it has to be accepted that a separation between normative and positive approaches to industrial policy may be difficult. It is often not possible to prove beyond question that a particular policy measure will achieve its objective; in which case analysts may be biased, consciously or unconsciously, in favour of the evidence which supports their normative position. Again, one's normative position might be influenced by positive analysis. A strongly-held view that a high rate of economic growth is desirable, might be modified if it were shown that it entailed the use of industrial policy measures which made the distribution of income more unequal.

1(b) Determinants of Government Expenditure Growth

In answering this question, it is assumed that all the variables can be identified and clearly defined. The dependent variable, **government spending**, could be defined in a number of ways. Here it is taken to refer to expenditure on goods and services and transfers and refers to all layers of government: public enterprises are excluded. This definition influences the choice of the independent variable. For example, the proportion of government employees in total employment, which is taken to include employees in all layers of government, but excludes those employed in public enterprises. The remaining independent variables may be assumed to be capable of clear definition.

A further preliminary point is to establish the relevant time period, for the influence of the independent variables may be different in the long and in the short run. It is assumed in this answer that the time period is determined by the availability of reliable statistical data which suggests concentrating on the last thirty years.

(i) The common-sense view would be that the growth in population would increase the demand for government services: more children means more schools, larger working population means more transport facilities and social benefits, more retired people means more pensions. This view neglects the possibility that there could be a "scale effect" – the extra output of government services need not require a proportional increase in inputs. It would also have to be modified in the light of the speed of population growth. For example, slow-growing populations are associated with an ageing of the population. The connection between (p) and (G) then becomes more complicated. The growth in the demand for educational resources could fall, whereas the growth in the demand for pensions and social services for the aged would rise.

(ii) Historically, the income elasticity of demand for government spending with respect to GDP is positive, though this is not to say that government spending has risen purely in response to the rise in average incomes. Nevertheless, it would be reasonable to expect that a rise in living standards would be associated with a rise in standards of provision of government services including increases in the real income of transfer receivers.

(iii) A growing proportion of working population employed by government might have two positive effects on government spending. The first is that government employees presumably have a vested interest in government spending and their growth in numbers relative to the size of working population makes them a growing proportion of the electorate. The second is that they are under less pressure to be "cost conscious" if they are producing services which are not priced. Empirical evidence is sparse.

2(a) Natural Monopoly

An industry is said to be a natural monopoly if a single producer can supply the entire market at lower total cost than any conceivable combination of two or more producers whose aggregate output sums to the same quantity as the single supplier. An industry for which this condition holds is said to have a cost structure which is "sub-additive". More formally this can be expressed as follows:

$$C(Q) < C(qi) + C(qj) + \ldots + C(qk),$$

for all qi, qj, qk, such that $Q = qi + qj + \ldots + qk$, where C(qi) represents the total cost of producing output qi, etc. The most obvious situation in which this condition will be satisfied is when average costs of production decline continuously because of economies of scale. However, such continuously declining average costs are not necessary for a natural monopoly to exist even though in the single product case they are sufficient.

Natural monopoly is most often associated with public utilities such as gas, electricity and water, or with the area of public transport such as the railways. In these industries large fixed costs are incurred in laying down networks of pipes, cables, wires, or permanent ways. Costs are therefore expected to decline over fairly large ranges of output.

2(a) (ii) Contestable Markets

A market is perfectly contestable if it is impossible for incumbent firms to leave a profit opportunity without a new entrant taking advantage of it. Contestability represents a situation of "ultra-free" entry into, and exit from, an industry. Any attempt by a monopolist to make high profits will be instantly thwarted in a perfectly contestable market by an entrant supplying the whole or part of the market at a lower price. The incumbent simply loses customers who transfer to the new supplier.

The condition of costless exit from an industry implies that there can be no sunk costs incurred upon entry. All costs can be recovered. Physical capital can be costlessly transferred to some other use, or sold on the market for its original value less any economic depreciation. In these conditions an entrant always faces the same cost calculations as an incumbent, even if the length of time the entrant plans to serve the market is extremely short. The industry is vulnerable to "hit and run" entry.

Entry will not occur, even in the conditions described above, if a potential entrant expects the incumbent to respond instantly by adjusting his price to match that of the new entrant. For a market to be perfectly contestable therefore, it is necessary that there exists some positive time-lag in the response of the incumbent, during which the new entrant can reap the benefits of entry into the market.

Although the conditions for perfect contestability will not in practice be satisfied in any industry, the force of potential competition in disciplining incumbent firms will often be important. Conditions in the civil air transport industry have been considered to be contestable by some analysts.

2(a) (iii) RPI – X

RPI – X refers to a regime of price regulation devised for natural monopoly industries. Under this system, the price of the product cannot rise by more than the rate of increase of the retail price index (RPI) minus some factor "X" to take account of expected productivity improvements in the regulated industry. Clearly "X" is subject to negotiation, and will change from time to time. If adverse changes (such as the rise in price of some important input) are possible, they may be taken into account by adjusting the formula to RPI + Y – X, where Y is the rate of increase in the price of the important input.

This regime of regulation was first introduced in the UK in the case of British Telecom, and in the form of RPI + Y – X in the case of British Gas. The advantage over regimes of regulation based on profits, rates of return or costs, is that the firm has an incentive to pursue productivity improvements knowing that these will not be followed immediately by more stringent price regulation. However, in practice, the factor X must be reassessed at intervals, so that in the long term a high rate of productivity improvement might be likely to result in a higher value of "X" and hence a more stringent regime.

2(a) (iv) The Demsetz Auction

The Demsetz or Chadwick auction is a method of introducing competition into areas of natural monopoly by using competition **for** the market to make up for the absence of competition **in** the market. Potential suppliers of a good or service would bid for the franchise. They would do so **not** by offering a lump sum or a royalty to the government in return for the right to act as a natural monopoly supplier, but would instead bid by quoting **prices** at which they were prepared to supply the market. Other things equal, the supplier quoting the lowest price would be offered the franchise. In principle, competing bidders would drive the price down to a competitive level and no monopoly profit would be made by the eventual producer.

Theoretically attractive, the Demsetz auction faces considerable problems of implementation including defining product quality in the franchise contract, coping with failure to comply with the contract conditions, setting a suitable length of contract, valuing capital at contract termination, and adjusting to changes in conditions over time. Nevertheless the mechanism is being used in the area of some local authority services, and in varying degrees of purity in television broadcasting and cable television.

2(b) First calculate the net present value (NPV) of the two projects in the absence of regulation

Project I

Labour costs per year	£m
(employment × average wage)	2.5
Maintenance and raw materials costs per year	1.5
Hence: operating costs per year (C1)	4.0
Revenue from sales per year (R1)	5.0
Capital investment (Kl) (incurred immediately)	5.0

Thus (over an infinite time horizon)

NPV(1)= –Kl +(R1 – C1)/0.1 = 5, where the rate of discount is 0.1.

Project II

Labour costs per year	£m
(employment × average wage)	1.25
Maintenance and raw materials costs per year	2.35
Hence: operating costs per year (C2)	3.60
Revenue from sales per year (R2)	5.00
Capital investment (K2) (incurred immediately)	9.33

Thus (over an infinite time horizon)
NPV(2) = –K2 + (R2 – C2)/0.1 = 4.67, where the rate of discount is again 0.1.

Clearly, in the absence of regulation, project I is preferred to project II. NPV(1) – NPV(2) = £0.33m.

Now consider the impact of regulation:

Project I
In the case of project I, the observed rate of return on invested capital will be (Rl – C1)/K1 = 0.2. This 20 per cent return exceeds the permitted maximum, and the regulators will reduce the price of output to £4.75 per unit in order to restrict the company to a 15 per cent return on capital invested. R1 will thereby be reduced to £4.75m and the NPV of the project in the presence of regulation NPV' (1) will be £2.5m, i.e.

NPV' (1) = – 5 + (4.75 – 4.00)/0.1 = 2.5

Project II
In the case of Project II, the observed rate of return is 15 per cent even without the interference of regulators. The excess of revenue over operating costs in each period is £1.4m and this is precisely 15 per cent of the £9.33m invested. Thus the regulated price of the output would remain unchanged at £5. It follows that the NPV of the project to the firm is unchanged by regulation. NPV'(2) is £4.67m.

Conclusion
The regulatory system will indeed affect the investment decision of the firm. The firm will prefer Project II under regulation but Project I when not constrained by the regulators. This result is consistent with the Averch–Johnson effect. Project II involves a greater investment of capital, greater maintenance expenditures, but less reliance on labour compared with Project I. Both projects result in the same output, but their cost structures differ. The more capital intensive cost structure is preferred under rate of return regulation.

3(a) Asymmetric Information

In examining economic relations between government and a firm, it has become common practice to regard the government as the "principal" which enters into an agreement with the firm, as its "agent", to carry out some agreed courses of action. In principle, a contract can be drawn up between the principal and agent, but, in practice, it may not be possible for the government to detect if the contract is reasonably specified or, is being adhered to once specified, if the agent's activities are not perfectly observable. This is called the "asymmetric information problem", for the problem is how far a firm is tempted to obtain more generous terms in the contract than would be possible if its activities could be closely monitored, and how far the government, as principal, will wish to invest resources in improving information in order to enforce the contract more completely.

The problem of asymmetric information can be exemplified in a number of different situations, (two) of which are now considered.

(i) Government purchasing contracts
The existence of the problem depends on the market environment. If the government is a monopolist faced with competing suppliers of a clearly specified product, competition between firms will ensure that they will have an incentive to reveal information about their activities in order to obtain the contract. Where the government is faced with only one seller, the government cannot compare the offers made by one seller against another and has to rely on the sole seller for information on its costs which will form the basis of the sales contract. The government purchaser may be faced with inflated cost estimates and checking these requires the use of resources which have alternative uses, e.g. post-costing of contracts and delay in final payments to the seller until final cost estimates are agreed.

(ii) Selective government subsidies to industry
Such subsidies are usually given to alter the value of some "target" variable of interest to the government such as an increase in a firm's investment, output or employment. The precise link between the amount of subsidy in the movement of the target variable(s) in the desired direction depend on information supplied by the firm. For example, the firm's incentive to increase output will depend on whether its profits will increase, but profit estimates will be a function of the information supplied to the government about the change in costs incurred in increasing its output to the desired level. The firm is in a position to exercise strategic behaviour not only because it is the sole source of information about costs but also because the firm itself may not have a precise idea of the costs that it will incur.

(iii) Government bureaucracy
A government "bureau" may be regarded as a "firm" supplying services to the government in power though it does not price its output. A government allocating a budget for a particular service may be assumed to wish for "value for money", in the sense of obtaining the maximum output from a given budget. This would entail minimizing the cost per unit of output. However, the sole source of information on the nature of output and the "production function" is the bureau and, as bureaux are prevented from making profits, the incentives to minimize costs per unit of output are weak. The principal is again faced with the problem of whether or not to invest resources in checking on the information on cost per unit of output provided by the agent.

(iv) Control of environmental damage
Regulation of environmental damage caused by pollution, for example, can take several forms, but the asymmetric information problem is clearly demonstrated in the case where government agencies rely on enforcement of regulations. Successful regulation depends on the ability to calculate the damage from a particular pollutant which entails estimating both the physical effects and their translation into "welfare loss". The physical effects of the pollution of any one plant may be uncertain and can depend on climate and posi-

tion and the existence of other pollutants. The costs of corrective measures undertaken by firms may be uncertain. Experts may not be able to agree amongst themselves on the measurement of both effects. Firms will have both the incentive and the opportunity to bargain with government regulators about the enforcement of anti-pollution measures and can rely on the asymmetric information problem to raise the costs to the regulators of obtaining agreement about the anti-pollution measures, the costs of which have to be incurred by the firms themselves.

3(b) Monopolistic and Bureaucratic Behaviour

The standard analysis of the economics of monopolistic behaviour and that of bureaucratic behaviour draws a contrast between the motivation of the monopolist and bureaucrat respectively. The former maximizes profits but the latter is precluded by the contract of service from appropriating any surplus over and above the cost of producing any given level of output. Accordingly, the motivation of the latter is usually taken to be that of maximizing the size of the budget of the bureau. These motivation assumptions are rather extreme, but serve as a first approximation in exploring the behaviouristic parallel.

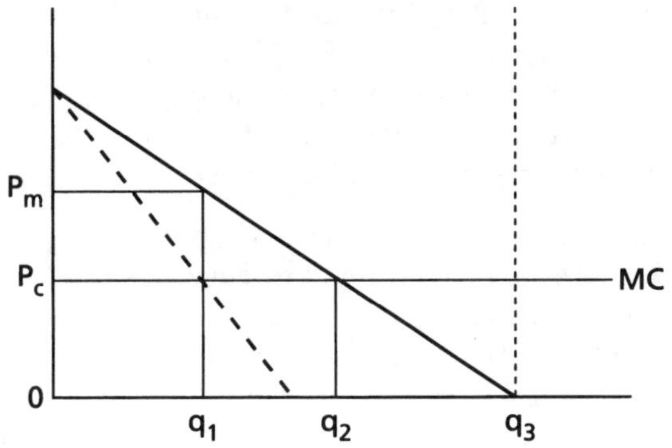

Figure 1

The diagram shows that both monopolistic and bureaucratic behaviour lead to a deviation from the "social optimum", which is taken to be the equation of marginal cost with the "price" or "marginal evaluation" (P_c with output q_2). However, using this criterion, the monopolist "under-produces" by equating marginal cost with marginal revenue (with output $q_1 < q_2$) whereas the bureaucrat "over-produces" (with output q_b where $q_2 < q_b \leq q_3$). The limitation facing the latter is the point (q_3) where the marginal evaluation of his output is zero. The bureaucrat exploits the existence of asymmetric information (see answer 3(a)) in order to obtain the maximum size of grant which is compatible with the credibility of the estimates submitted to those providing him with finance.

The contrast between monopolistic and bureaucratic behaviour in this analysis rests heavily on the behaviouristic assumptions. These are often questioned. The theory of the firm employed above does not distinguish ownership from control and therefore does not distinguish between shareholders' and managers' objectives. Managers exploiting monopoly power may seek to appropriate any gains by increasing their own emoluments, subject to the constraint of paying dividends which satisfy shareholders. Bureaucrats may eschew the prestige and power, and possibly promotion, associated with maximizing their output and use their control over information to enable them to inflate costs which makes their jobs more comfortable. In the technical jargon, managers and monopolies and bureaucrats may share the characteristic of being "X" or technically inefficient, as well as promoting an allocation of resources out of keeping with the objective of maximizing consumer surplus.

In the long run even the simple presumption that monopolists' and bureaucrats' actions are out of line with consumers' wishes may offer an incentive to governments to devise methods for controlling their actions. How effective these are likely to be in modifying the behaviour of both parties is a complex matter beyond the scope of this analysis.

4(a) (i) The Public Enterprise and the Bureau

A "pure" public enterprise may be defined as an enterprise which produces some marketed output using assets that are vested in the state, or an agency of the state. The assets of a pure public enterprise are therefore collectively held, and there are no privately exchangeable rights to the profits deriving from the enterprise's activities. A bureau uses assets which are similarly vested in the state, but it does not market its output. The revenue of the bureau is received out of taxation and depends on the decisions of government ministers responsible to Parliament.

In practice, the distinction between a bureau and a public enterprise can become blurred. This is because the proportion of revenue generated from sales of the output of an enterprise will not necessarily be either zero or 100 per cent. A public enterprise which receives a significant flow of subsidy from the government for specific activities, or to cover general losses, becomes more bureau like. Conversely, a bureau which begins to market specialized services becomes more like a public enterprise. The sale of weather forecasting services by the meteorological office, for example, could be seen as a transformation from a bureau type of economic entity to a public enterprise type of economic entity.

4(a) (ii) The Public Enterprise and the Private Enterprise

The main characteristic which defines a "private" enterprise is the existence of exchangeable claims to the profits of the enterprise which may be held by private individuals. This definition implies that co-operatives and non-profit firms would not be classed as private enterprises. For example, a workers' co-operative might give its members rights to a share in the profits. These rights would not normally be exchangeable, however, and therefore a co-operative would not be considered a private enterprise. Similarly, a non-profit or charitable enterprise would not be considered part of the private enterprise sector, under the definition given above, because there are no exchangeable residual claims.

Once again, the distinction between public and private enterprise is not always perfectly clear cut. The state may hold a proportion of the shares of a public company thereby creating a "mixed enterprise". At what precise point a private enterprise is transformed into a public enterprise by the state's acquisition of shares cannot be determined with perfect objectivity.

4(b) Comparing Productivity of Public and Private Enterprises

Productivity comparisons aim to show whether property rights matter. Is it the case that the absence of exchangeable property rights in a public enterprise depresses incentives and results in a lower level of productivity compared with a private enterprise? The main problems which arise in attempting to answer this question are as follows:

(i) Somehow it is necessary to try to isolate the influence of differing property rights from all the other factors which may affect the performance of an enterprise. Thus it is necessary, in principle, to compare enterprises of the same size, in the same industry, using the same technology, facing the same degree of competition in the product market, in an attempt to see whether **other things equal** a different property rights structure results in a different level of performance. This is done on the, probably false, premise that factors such as size, technology and competition, are themselves not affected by the property rights structures characteristic of the enterprises which make up the industry. The study by Davies (1971) of two Australian airlines, and the study by Caves and Christensen (1980) of two Canadian railroads, are examples of attempts to compare public and private enterprise in situations which are as closely comparable as possible.

(ii) The second problem is that productivity comparisons require agreed measures of inputs and outputs. The output measurement problem can be particularly acute if the very purpose of public ownership is to change the quality or type of output from what it might otherwise have been under private enterprise. Further, it is always open to an enterprise to claim that unfavourable productivity measures simply reflect some underestimated or unmeasured component of their output. A private enterprise running a reliable luxury coach service may seem to have a lower productivity than a public enterprise running an unreliable and extremely basic one if the output is measured simply in terms of passenger miles travelled. Conversely a private supplier who pollutes the environment may appear more productive than a public supplier who invests in cleaner technology if the "output" is not properly identified.

4(c) The Control of Public Enterprise

Principal–agent analysis can be applied to any situation in which one party (the agent) agrees to act on behalf of another party (the principal). If the interests of the agent and the principal diverge, and if the principal is unable at low cost to determine what effort the agent is supplying, the problem of devising a suitable incentive scheme arises. In the context of the public enterprise, managers of the enterprise can be viewed as agents, and the responsible minister in the government can be regarded as the principal.

An agreement between principal and agent will specify a fee schedule such that the reward to the agent will vary with the final "outcome" achieved. The more the agent's reward depends upon the final outcome, the greater is the incentive to the agent to exert effort on the principal's behalf. In the case of public enterprises the problem is in defining a simple "outcome" measure. In public companies, managers can be paid profit bonuses, given stock-options, and other benefits linked to profitability. Managers may also fear take-over by other more profitable firms, and they face the possibility of bankruptcy if profits fall too far. These incentive devices depend upon a simple measure of "success" – the profits of the enterprise – and the existence of tradeable claims to the profits.

In the case of a public enterprise the specification of the desired outcome is more difficult. In cases where the enterprise has monopoly power, the maximization of profit is not likely to be acceptable to voters as a suitable objective. Linking managerial rewards to the achievement of gains in "economic efficiency" might be attractive to voters and politicians in principle, but measures of such gains are extremely difficult to devise. The absence of a clear summary measure of "success" led in the 1967 White Paper *Nationalised Industries* to the imposition of "rules" on the operation of public enterprises. These rules included the marginal cost pricing rule, and an investment rule based upon the calculation of the net present value of a project at a given "social" rate of discount. These rules could be defended as a means to achieving economic efficiency. However, there existed no way of knowing, given high monitoring and information costs, whether or not the management of an enterprise was complying with these rules. There was no clear incentive for managers to do so, and as it was possible to reconcile virtually any results with some plausible interpretation of the rules, they became discredited as a means of public enterprise control.

More recently the pricing and investment rules have been replaced by financial and productivity targets. These are observable and measurable but may direct managerial effort in ways which do not always correspond to the principal's interests. For example, financial targets can be achieved by exploiting monopoly power, and productivity targets can be achieved by ignoring dimensions of output which are not specified by the target.

5(a) (i) Privatization

The privatization of assets occurs when collective property rights held by the state are replaced by exchangeable private rights. Examples include the flotation of British Telecom and British Gas.

5(a) (ii) Deregulation

Deregulation occurs when the direct intervention in economic decisions by government or its agents using non-fiscal instruments is reduced. The removal of control on the wellhead price of natural gas in the US is an example of deregulation.

5(a) (iii) Liberalization

Liberalization occurs when competitive forces are permitted to operate where they have hitherto been inhibited. Usually this will involve reducing restrictions on the ability of competitors to enter an industry, trade, or profession. The competitive determination of brokerage fees and the abolition of the minimum brokerage commission in the UK in 1986 is an example of liberalization.

Liberalization may often accompany deregulation (for example the abolition of restrictions on entry into long-distance coach services), but some measures of liberalization may require regulatory enforcement (for example facilitating entry into gas or electricity supply by using the network as a "common carrier"). Similarly, privatization may increase (as in gas and water) or decrease (as in British Steel) the importance of regulation.

5(b) (i) Technical Efficiency

An enterprise is technically efficient if it is producing the maximum physical output possible with the available resources. It is a concept which requires knowledge of purely technological possibilities.

5(b) (ii) Productive Efficiency

An enterprise is productively efficient if it is producing a given output at the lowest possible total cost given the prevailing prices of inputs. Technical efficiency is a necessary but not a sufficient condition for productive efficiency.

5(b) (iii) Economic Efficiency

Economic efficiency requires that the price of the product in the market reflects its social cost of production at the margin. Social costs include all the costs incurred in the production process, including those experienced by "outsiders" through pollution or other "spillover effects".

Productive efficiency is a necessary but not a sufficient condition for economic efficiency. A monopolist, for example, may be productively efficient, but the price and output level chosen by the monopolist is unlikely to be economically efficient.

5(c) (i)

Company I uses 60 units of labour and 15 units of capital to produce 10 units of output. Using process C it should be possible when technically efficient to produce 10 units of output with 40 units of labour and 10 units of capital. The company is therefore not technically efficient. Total costs of £750 exceed the technically efficient level of £500.

Company II uses 20 units of labour and 20 units of capital to produce 10 units of output. This is the minimum input level required to produce 10 units of output using process B. The company is therefore technically efficient.

Total costs in Company II are £400. This is £100 less than could be achieved using process C, even if process C were operated in a technically efficient way. Thus, of the £350 cost advantage achieved by Company II over Company I, it is possible to attribute £250 to greater technical efficiency, and £100 to greater productive efficiency.

5(c) (ii)

With labour costs of £300 and capital costs of £150 Company I is still using 60 units of labour and 15 units of capital to produce 10 units of output. It is therefore as technically inefficient as ever, despite a drop in measured costs of production from £750 to £450. The £300 difference represents a redistribution of income away from labour rather than a gain in efficiency.

The new lower price of labour may, however, lead us to reassess our conclusion that Company II was initially more productively efficient than Company I. At the new factor prices, process B has no advantage over process C with respect to productive efficiency. If the new prices are assumed to represent the true costs incurred by owners of factor inputs, it is possible to argue that the lower costs initially associated with process B were illusory, and that no real efficiency gains accrued to the use of process B over process C.

PRACTICE FINAL EXAMINATION 2

Questions

Question 1

(a) ***Explain what is meant by a "normative" approach to the study of industrial policy.*** **(5 marks)**

A normative approach to industrial policy offers a prescription to government about the content of that policy. For example, it might be laid down that the government ought to ensure a "sound" manufacturing base. It is to be contrasted with a positive approach to industrial policy which analyses what the effects of that policy are likely to be, e.g. whether particular policy measures will achieve the aim of ensuring a "sound" manufacturing base.

(b) ***Which of the following statements is normative?*** **(5 marks)**

P = positive
N = normative

(i) ***A tax on the value of output raises the price of a commodity and lowers the amount supplied.***

clearly P

(ii) ***There is a general consensus amongst economists that governments ought to control monopoly.***

P

(A tricky one. The statement does not say that government ought to control monopoly, but makes the positive statement, which could be verified, that economists support such a policy.)

(iii) ***Environmental quality is best achieved by regulating industrial pollution.***

clearly P

(iv) ***The aim of industrial policy should be to improve economic growth.***

clearly N

(v) ***If one laid all the economists in the world end-to-end, they would not come to a conclusion.***

clearly P

(c) ***Outline briefly the characteristics of the growth of government expenditure in post-1960 industrial economies and consider how far this growth can be explained by demand factors.*** **(10 marks)**

Interest presumably attached to the growth of government expenditure in relation to the growth of the economy for absolute figures will give no idea of the resources absorbed by government and of the relative importance of government transfers as a source of personal income. It is also important to distinguish between government expenditure on goods and services and government expenditure on transfers.

There are four characteristics of the growth of government expenditure between, say, 1960 and 1990:

(i) On average, government expenditure on goods and services as a proportion of GDP has increased by a modest amount.

(ii) When transfers are included the rise in G/GDP is more rapid.

(iii) The dispersion of G/GDP between countries appears to have diminished through time, if we exclude Japan.

(iv) The indications are that G/GDP may have stabilized.

Demand factors appear to be the motive force for expansion of government expenditure. As the economy grows, a complementary demand is set up for services which have normally been undertaken in the first instance by government, such as transport and communication services, energy, waste disposal and education and training. The growth in transfers could be explained as the "cost" of rapid economic growth, notably the incidence of unemployment, and this growth would be promoted by the growth in the enfranchisement of those in lower income groups. If "demand" is a necessary condition, it is not a sufficient one. The fact that governments have a monopoly of government business suggests that supply factors play a part in the expansion process. Furthermore, it is claimed that government services are not subject to the same productivity gains that accompany economic growth, because of the importance of personal services in the public sector.

(Total of 20 marks)

Question 2

(a) ***Explain what is meant by the "efficiency losses" of monopoly and outline the difficulties encountered in removing these losses by price regulation.*** **(10 marks)**

The candidate is expected to reproduce Figure 3.1 from page 32 of the main text (shown below).

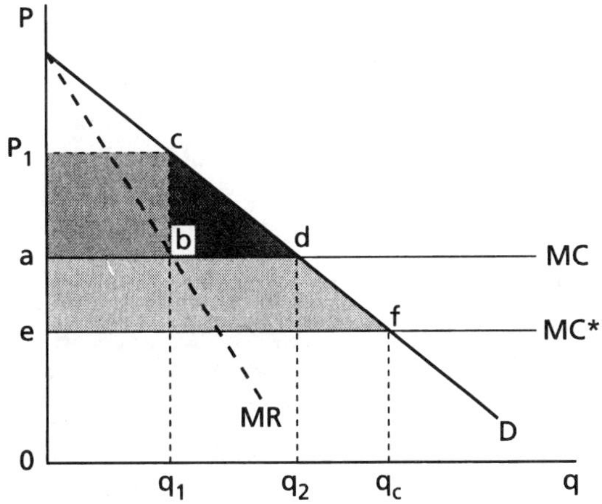

Referring to the diagram, for a given demand schedule a profit maximizing monopolist producing at constant costs will equate Marginal Revenue with Marginal Cost such that output would be less and price higher than in the case where pure competition prevails $q_l < q_2 : OP_l > 0a$. The efficiency losses are represented by the shaded area bcd, i.e. the extra benefits denied consumers from the absence of competition.

The implication of the above analysis is that price regulation will induce a monopolist to produce at higher output and at a lower price. Two major problems arise in any attempt to implement such a policy. The first is that the source of information on the monopolist's cost curve is the monopolist, offering an incentive to distort projections of future costs. The second is the potential variation in the quality of output which could allow skimping on quality as a method for reducing the burden of regulation. Accordingly the price administration may have to incur extra costs of negotiating and policing cost estimates and quality specifications.

(b) **Define and illustrate the meaning of any TWO of the following:** **(10 marks)**

(i) ***A Demsetz auction***

One way of approaching the natural monopoly problem is to institute competitive bids for the monopoly rights, with the object of "bidding away" monopoly profits so that they approach competitive levels. The Demsetz approach is to make bidders tender prices at which they would be willing to supply the market, in expectation that price would be bid down to average cost while leaving the winner enough incentive to supply the product. While this system avoids the necessity for prior knowledge of cost conditions, it does not avoid the problem of defining quality. In addition, it does not circumvent the problems of defining the duration of the contract and of reaching agreement on the treatment of the valuation of assets which are specific to the franchised activity.

(ii) ***The polluter pays principle***

The reduction of pollution is an industrial policy objective which is internationally accepted and a variety of measures may be used ranging from subsidies to pollution reduction schemes and taxes on polluters' products to the banning of the use of pollutants. PPP requires that prices should reflect all costs of production including environmental, and therefore pollution, costs. The common example of a measure which invokes this principle is a tax on products which embody the use of pollutants. Clearly the effectiveness of this measure will depend on the technical link between the output and the amount of pollution. This is not always easy to find. In the UK, petrol containing lead is taxed at a higher rate than unleaded petrol. However, there are many important examples, such as electricity, where the input of pollutant would not be affected by charging a higher price for the final product.

(iii) ***External costs of production***

The production of many goods and services may frequently result in costs which are not reflected in the producers' cost curves of which pollution (see (ii) above) is an obvious example. Producers in a given industry may impose costs on one another as in the "over-fishing" case where unrestricted communal use of an unpriced resource, i.e. the stock of fish, may raise costs as fishing stocks diminish.

(Illustration of the external costs problem by correct explanation of Figure 4.1, page 57 of the main text, would ensure high marks.)

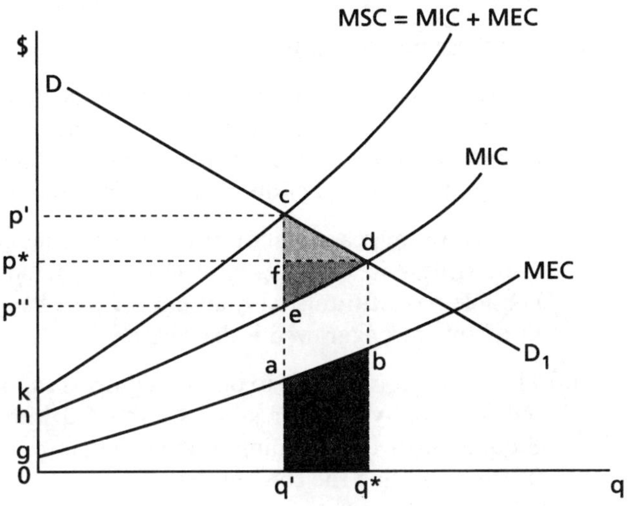

(iv) ***"RP1–X"***

"RPI–X" is shorthand for a price regime used to control the activities of natural monopolies. The rise in the product price is restricted to the rate of increase in the retail price index (RPI) minus some factor "X" which takes account of any expected productivity gains in the regulated industry. This appears to be a more effective alternative than attempting to specify "satisfactory" rates of return or the use of marginal cost pricing which are beset by the principal–agent problem, and has the advantage of offering an incentive to pursue productivity gains, once the regime is fixed. In practice, the formula has to be subject to fairly frequent review to take account of unanticipated influences on price and productivity, and therefore to negotiation between the regulator and the regulated monopoly.

(Total of 20 marks)

Question 3

(a) **Critically consider the case for limited entry by bidding firms in tendering for government contracts. (10 marks)**

Given the aim of minimizing the cost of contracted work, economic analysis would suggest that competitive tendering would achieve that aim. It is claimed that while selective tendering may be contrary to the aim, limitation on the number of those able to tender would better fulfil it than open competition for the following reasons:

(i) The transaction costs would be reduced if details of contract, examination of tenders and informing bidders of the result were restricted to a limited number of bidders.

(ii) Search costs are high if the financial circumstances of a large number of firms have to be investigated, especially if new firms of unknown competence make bids. Therefore, confining investigation to firms of known reliability seems sensible.

(iii) Tendering costs may be high for individual firms so that the longer the tender list the higher the total costs incurred in "abortive tendering" by unsuccessful firms. With only a few firms, fewer resources will be wasted in preparing tenders and false expectations of success are minimized.

Each of these points can be questioned:

(i) Transaction costs are bound to rise with the number of bids but the marginal cost seems likely to fall. The specification of the contract is a fixed cost and does not increase with the number of firms. Any extra costs incurred could be outweighed by the extra benefits of obtaining full information about potential bidders.

(ii) Concentrating search on firms of known reliability must introduce an element of arbitrariness in deciding who shall be included or not included in the bid. Possible new entrants with an incentive to be price and quality conscious may justifiably feel aggrieved if they are denied the chance to bid.

(iii) There is no compulsion to bid so that firms can make their own judgement about the probability of their success, provided purchasing agents follow the rules. Bidding involves a learning process so that even unsuccessful bidders may benefit from entering the competition.

(b) ***Explain what is meant by the "principal–agent problem" and illustrate your answer with reference to government subsidies to private industry.*** **(10 marks)**

The "principal-agent" problem arises from the difficulties encountered when the government (the principal) seeks to induce a firm or industry (the "agent") to carry out its policies, given the instruments at its disposal. The practical importance of this problem may be judged by outlining the conditions necessary for the principal to be able to achieve its policy aims. First the agent's activities must be perfectly observable so that any departure from a contract between the parties can easily be detected. Second, the production costs and the demand conditions facing the regulated firm can be determined in advance with reasonable certainty.

Government subsidies to private industry are normally designed to induce firms to produce additional output and employment, and the government has an interest in minimizing the amount of subsidy necessary to achieve the desired objectives. The calculation of the amount of subsidy runs into the "principal–agent" problem, as illustrated by the direct, narrow-based output subsidy case. The appropriate policy would appear to be to offer a marginal output subsidy sufficient to induce the producer to increase output by the desired amount. The government, as principal, can only obtain the necessary information on which to base the subsidy from the company itself so that the fortunes of the company are a function of the information which it supplies to government. In the light of the uncertainties attached to calculating future costs and prices, the company has a strong incentive to behave strategically by overstating the amount of subsidy that it considers is necessary to induce it to fulfil the government's objectives. In short, a bargaining situation can develop in which the government has to trade-off minimization of the amount of subsidy against the costs of obtaining and assessing the additional information that it seeks from the firm if it rejects the latter's estimates. **(Total of 20 marks)**

Question 4

(a) ***Analyse the similarities and differences between the position of a private monopoly supplier and that of a government bureau supplying a non-marketed product.***

(10 marks)

A monopolist may be defined as the sole seller of a product, and a government bureau may be in a similar position as the sole provider of a service. The parallel may be explored by the use of the familiar diagram (see Figure 7.1, page 101 of the main text). This shows that the loss of consumer surplus as a result of the monopolization of the sale of a given product will be equal to cbd, with output lower and price higher than in the competitive case. Is there a parallel here in the case of the bureau's supply of a service?

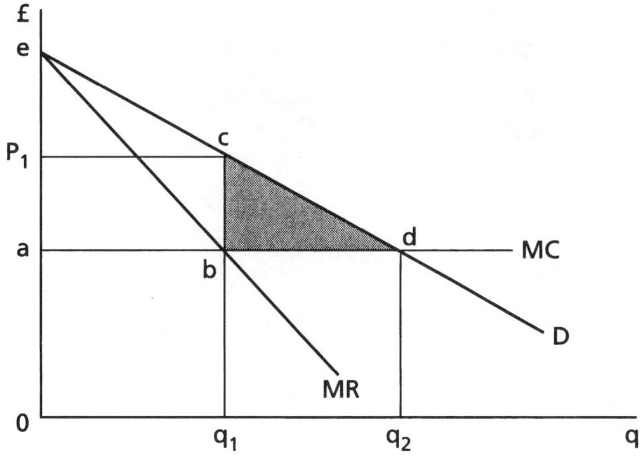

First, there are certainly cases where the government is the sole supplier of a service, and the extent of monopoly power will also depend on the actual or potential availability of alternatives. Thus a potential "rival" to the police service in reducing crime could be social work departments. At the same time, defining and measuring the output of a service which is not marketed presents a substantial difference with the private monopoly case.

Second, the reactions of a monopolist, e.g. to a fall in his costs, would depend on the shape and location of the demand curve. There are two differences in the case of a bureau: it is faced with only one "buyer" (a bi-lateral monopoly situation) and output is not priced. This is not to say that the "buyer", the sponsoring department or agency, has no method of evaluation of the service – presumably it would prefer a higher output to a lower one, for a given budget allocation to the bureau.

Third, bureau managers cannot appropriate net profits over and above the cost of producing any given level of output. This is a crucial difference with the private monopoly case. The bureau manager has to maximise utility, often translated into a desire to maximize the size of his budget.

(b) ***Explain the "marginal cost pricing rule" as applied to public enterprises and examine the difficulties in applying it.*** **(10 marks)**

The marginal cost pricing rule states that, given that the price of a good or service can be taken to be a measure of marginal social benefit, the most efficient system of pricing is to set its price equal to the marginal social costs of production. Attempts to apply this rule to public enterprises have run into a number of problems:

(i) Where there are considerable variations in demand by season or time of day, and the product could not be stored, e.g. electricity, the rule would require the institution of a complicated pricing structure in order to take account of the greater social costs imposed by "peak load" consumption.

(ii) "Social costs and benefits" are notoriously difficult to calculate and inevitably lead to interference in pricing decisions by governments.

(iii) Where economies of scale are significant, as in the case of natural monopolies, the rule results in the making of losses.

(Here extra marks would be gained by demonstrating this result by reproduction and explanation of Figure 8.1, page 119 of the main text.)

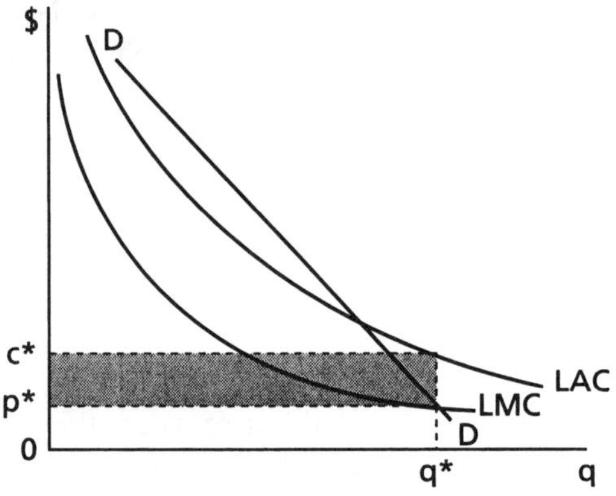

One solution to this problem is a "two-part tariff" in which the consumer pays a lump-sum independent of the quantity purchased and in addition a price per unit equal to marginal cost which would enable the enterprise to break even. This may not always be easy to implement and any attempt to avoid efficiency losses by lump-sum payment may be resisted by governments sensitive to its distributional effects.

(iv) As an answer to Question 3b would indicate, policing the "rule" can run into the "principal–agent" problem if the public enterprise is a monopoly and the sole source of information on its costs.

OR

(b) ***Examine the criteria used to assess economic performance and consider how far they can be translated into controls over public enterprises.*** **(10 marks)**

Two criteria are usually advanced to assess economic performance:

(i) productive efficiency entailing that a public enterprise has to produce any given output at minimum cost at prevailing factor prices; and

(ii) allocative efficiency which, while assuming productive efficiency can be achieved, also requires that prices to consumers maximize net social benefits.

As public enterprises are frequently monopolies in which managers are restricted in fixing their own remuneration there are no built-in incentives to meet these criteria.

The government can devise rules for managers to follow such as marginal cost pricing, subject to the constraint that costs must be minimized. However, such rules assume that the activities of the enterprise are perfectly observable.

This is not likely to be the case when the public enterprise is the sole source of information on costs and alternative sources of information which would offer a check on costs are unobtainable.

It is for this reason that governments have tried to restore incentives by indirect and crude means that "work" rather than to use "rules" which are conceptually correct but unenforcable. These have included attempts to improve productive efficiency by allowing private firms to compete with public enterprises, and the use of financial criteria such as a required rate of return on investment and the Littlechild "RPI–X" formula designed to protect consumers from monopolistic exploitation and to give incentives for enterprises to look for cost-reducing improvements.

(Total of 20 marks)

Question 5

(a) ***You are asked by the Government Department concerned with law and order to write a memorandum in reply to a Government Minister's question: "Why should we not privatize our prisons?"***

Ministers being busy people, your reply must be no more than 500 words. **(10 marks)**

(Note: The candidate clearly could not be expected to have a detailed knowledge of prison services and is being tested on the general ability to apply analytical techniques explained in Government, Industry and Privatization. It must be emphasised that the answer below is only one example of how the question might be tackled.)

To Minister "X"

The Minister presumably accepts that law and order is the essential "public good" provided by his government. Protection of private property and person can be carried out by private enterprise but would be denied to those who could not afford protection. It could also lead to breakdown of law and order itself, as Mafia situations demonstrate. The Minister presumably has in mind that the supply of law and order does not necessarily entail that imprisonment of offenders need require that prisons be run by government itself. He no doubt knows of cases in other countries where privatization of some parts of the prison service has occurred.

It will be agreed that your Government has an interest in seeing that prisons are efficiently run. The Department lays down performance indicators for the service which are designed as a check on costs of manpower, materials and capital investment. It is well known that we encounter what we have described to you as "principal/agent problems" in agreeing budgets and in monitoring results. In principle, therefore an "internal market" might be constructed by which the prison service or parts of it, could be open to competitive bids both from outside security agencies and the existing nationalized service.

In my view it is doubtful if this restricted form of privatization could be made to work, and for the following reasons:

(i) If a private agency offered to supply the services on a lower budget, we would still have to monitor quality of service closely.

(ii) Lower budget costs might be offset by an increase in costs of regulation, particularly if privatization entailed use of the services of a number of suppliers.

(iii) As there is at present no "private competition" in prison services, private operators would have to buy or lease existing government properties and employ existing government staff. This would cause considerable short-term disruption as terms of sale and employment are negotiated.

(iv) Prison service work is highly specialised and staff exchange specificity of occupation for long-term contracts. Private firms could find it difficult to provide staff training and long-term contracts without government subsidy.

The conclusion is that privatization of the whole service would be incompatible with the government's own objectives.

OR

(a) ***What safeguards are necessary in order to ensure that a privatized public monopoly is prevented from exploiting its monopoly power?*** **(10 marks)**

It is assumed that the object of privatization is to benefit the final consumer of the monopoly's product so that the basic concern of government is to produce conditions where either the monopoly can be made subject to competition or that it operates as if competitive conditions were in operation.

The first method must be to remove barriers to competition with the privatized public monopoly. The success of this method clearly depends on the availability of new entrants. Provided that the public monopoly is not a natural monopoly, de-regulation may achieve the desired object. Where national suppliers of the product are not strong enough to compete, barriers against foreign importation may serve as an alternative. Lastly, in the course of privatization of the industry, the government may introduce structural changes to separate out the stages of production. Thus distribution of electricity may be separated from production, and the distributors allowed to buy electricity from alternative sources or generate their own.

The second method is more appropriate in the case where it is likely that the industry will remain a natural monopoly or where the competitive challenge will take time to develop. The nationalized industry is permitted to operate more or less like a private corporation with private shareholders responsible for the election of a board of directors. The government may regulate its activities through such devices as

"RPI–X", as a way of ensuring that consumers are not faced with monopoly pricing. The monopoly's pricing practices may also be subject to scrutiny by government agencies with the duty of preventing restrictive practices. A more extreme measure, which raises the question of how "privatization" is to be defined, is for the government to retain a "golden share" in the corporation which gives it control over the appointment of Directors. This may be used only as a temporary, precautionary measure until alternative regulatory arrangements are able to operate satisfactorily.

(b) ***Two firms have these common characteristics:***

(i) ***they produce the same amount of output per period;***
(ii) ***their wage rate and rental rate of capital (i.e. the price of hire of a unit of capital per time period) are the same.***

They differ in one important respect:

Firm 1 needs 1 unit of capital and 4 units of labour to produce a unit of output.

Firm 2 needs 2 units of capital and 2 units of labour to produce a unit of output.

You are asked to:

(i) ***define technical and productivity efficiency; and***
(ii) ***compare Firm 1 and Firm 2 with respect to both technical and productive efficiency.***

(10 marks)

(i) Technical efficiency is achieved when an enterprise produces the maximum physical output with available resources, given the technological possibilities.

Productive efficiency is achieved when an enterprise produces a given output at the lowest possible total cost, given the prevailing prices of factor inputs.

(ii) It is not possible to compare technical efficiency given that capital and labour are complementary inputs. This would only be possible if one firm used more of one or both inputs to produce the same output as the other.

(iii) We can rank the firms according to productive efficiency for particular values of the wage rate and price of capital. For example:

x = wage rate = 1
y = rental value of capital = 3

Then for

Firm 1: total cost = $4 \times 1 + 1 \times 3 = 7$
Firm 2: total cost = $2 \times 1 + 2 \times 3 = 8$

Firm 1 is productively more efficient.

However, as capital and labour are employed in fixed proportions, this is not a general solution. We could equally well produce examples with the opposite result.

Any result will depend on the ***relative*** prices of capital and labour.

(Extra marks are given for devising a simple formula to prove this using the fixed factor inputs in the question:

if $(2x + 2y) = (x + 4y)$

then $\frac{x}{y} = \frac{2}{1}$

In the example given, only if the wage rate is twice the rental rate will the productive efficiency be the same in both cases.) **(Total of 20 marks)**

PRACTICE FINAL EXAMINATION 3

Questions

Question 1

(a) ***Explain what is meant by a "positive" approach to the study of government policies towards industry.*** **(5 marks)**

A positive approach to the study of industrial policy seeks to identify the policy objectives of government which are actually in operation and to employ economic analysis to examine whether or not the measures adopted promote the stated objectives. Therefore, no judgement is passed on the objectives themselves. In contrast a normative approach evaluates the objectives and decides whether which objectives are, in some sense, preferable to others, according to whether they conform to some particular "norm".

(b) ***Identify which of the following statements is "positive":***

(i) ***A government subsidy to an industrial firm normally results in an increase in output and reduction in price.***

Positive – the objectives are given.

(ii) ***The aim of industrial policy should be to foster competition between firms.***

Not positive – a judgement is made in favour of competition policy.

(iii) ***Many economists believe that it is their task to distinguish "good" from "bad" industrial policies.***

Positive – what economists believe is a question of fact.

(iv) ***The interest of consumers should be paramount in the design of economic policies.***

Not positive – see (ii) above.

(v) ***There are several difficulties encountered in designing pricing rules for public corporations.***

Positive – the statement is based on analysis of pricing rules but does not judge the rules themselves. **(5 marks)**

(c) ***"Improving productivity in the government sector is more difficult than in the private sector and therefore government expenditure tends to grow more quickly than Gross Domestic Product."***

Appraise this statement.

It has been claimed that technical factors limit the growth of productivity in the public sector relative to that of the private sector. This is alleged to be the result of the importance of personal services which place limitations on the substitution of machines for people. Therefore, if there is an increasing demand for public services in line with GDP, expenditure on government services will have to increase at a faster rate than GDP, unless, as seems unreasonable to suppose, public servants accept wage rates less than those in comparable occupations in the private sector.

There are a number of reasons why this proposition cannot be accepted uncritically.

(i) A major element in the growth of government expenditure in Western countries has been transfer expenditure, which is not part of government-produced services.

(ii) There appear to be areas of government where at least some new technology could be introduced, notably given the wide use of office equipment and communications.

(iii) An alternative explanation for the relative growth in government expenditure on goods and services could be the greater opportunities for resistance to technical change in government departments which are monopoly suppliers and do not price their services.

The last two objections could be tested empirically – in principle. One obvious problem in devising tests is the difficulty of defining government output and therefore the relation between inputs of labour and machinery and the services provided.

(10 marks)
(Total of 20 marks)

Question 2

(a) ***Define and illustrate the meaning of ANY TWO of the following terms:***

(i) ***Natural Monopoly***
(ii) ***Contestable Markets***
(iii) ***A Pigouvian Tax***
(iv) ***Efficiency Losses***

(i) It is usual to think that natural monopoly exists where it would be "wasteful" to employ more than one producer. Examples include the public utilities such as gas, water, and electricity distribution. In each of these cases large fixed costs must be incurred in establishing networks of pipes, cables, or permanent ways, and average costs to customers are expected to decline over a very large range. Duplication of these facilities by competing firms is unlikely to happen in the cases just cited, but if such an event did occur, the cost of the services would be greater than technically necessary.

A more precise definition of natural monopoly is provided by the concept of sub-additivity. If the costs incurred by a single producer at a given output are lower than the sum of the costs of a set of competing producers whose combined output is the same as that of the single producer, the industry's cost structure is said to be sub-additive. An industry can be a natural monopoly even if economies of scale have been exhausted and average costs are rising. In the figure below (Figure 3.2 from the main text), for example, average costs are lowest at output levels q'. If more than q' is demanded (say q*) it would not follow that another firm would enter and produce the additional output.

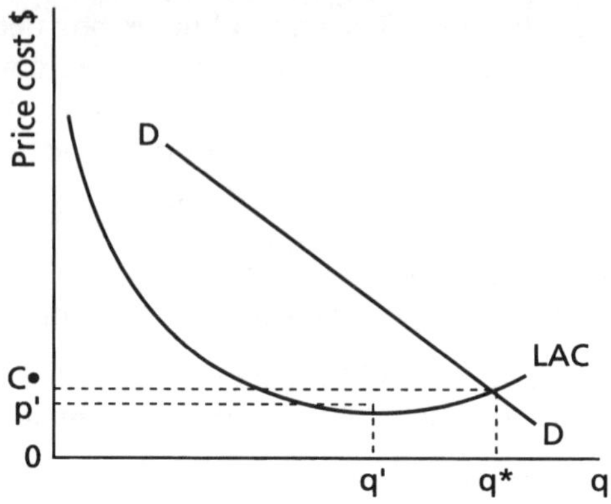

(ii) If economies of scale enable a single firm to dominate a particular market, the question arises as to whether such a firm is immune from competition. The problem for a potential entrant lies in the costs incurred in investing in overhead capital. Contestable markets are ones where such costs can be retrieved by those leaving the business and used for some other purpose and where the incumbent firms would only be able to lower prices with a time lag long enough to allow new entrants to set up in business. Civil aviation is often given as an example. A particular route may be monopolised by a single carrier able to operate at lower costs than any other airline. However, a new entrant may be able to capture part of the market given that the capital, aircraft, are not specific to any particular route and could, if necessary, be switched to another route if the challenge were to fail.

(iii) Pollution may be controlled by regulation, by subsidies for its reduction and by taxing pollution emissions. The last-named method was first explored by A. C. Pigou, hence the name of the tax. In the normal presentation of the effect of the tax it is assumed that the pollution and output rise and fall together in the same proportion and are technically inseparable. Using Figure 4.1 (see page 57 of the main text) the marginal cost curve of the industry is raised from MIC to MSC, the effect being to reduce output and to raise price. Pollutees certainly benefit (see area abg" q') and government revenue increases enabling government expenditure to increase or other taxes to be reduced. It is to be noted, however, that consumers will pay a higher price for the product and firms will receive a lower (after tax) price for their output.

(iv) Efficiency losses are associated with monopolistic behaviour. In Figure 3.1 from the main text shown below, a profit maximising monopolist with constant costs produces output q_1 and sells at a price P_1. The shaded area bcd is an approximate representation of the efficiency losses associated with monopoly. In addition to restricting output and charging higher prices, the absence of competing firms may enable monopolists to operate "wastefully". If this is true, costs of production will be higher for a monopolist than for a competitive firm.

Consumers lose out but managers and workers in the monopoly will benefit. Suppose, for example, that a competitive industry were able to produce at constant cost MC* in the figure below, then assuming that the lower cost level does not simply reflect lower prices of inputs, there are extra efficiency gains associated with competition of the area adfe accruing to consumers.

(10 marks)

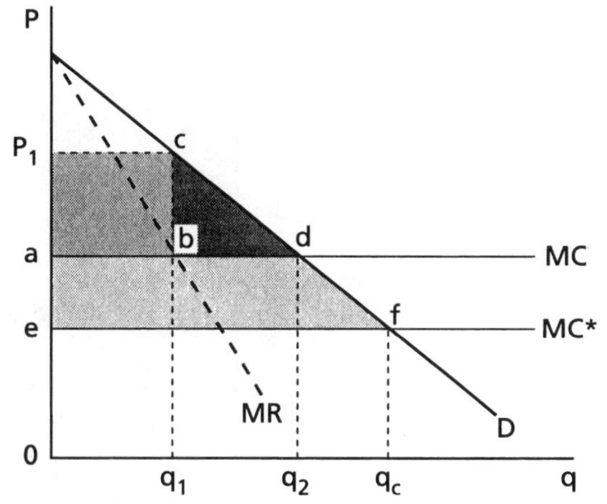

(b) ***"The general problem with regulatory systems attempting to control the rate of return is that perverse incentives are created and a complex bargaining situation develops."***

Discuss and illustrate this statement with particular reference to regulation of the rate of return on capital.

Consider a monopoly which is permitted to earn more than a given rate of return on capital. This situation is illustrated in Figure 3.3 from the main text, shown below. The upper part of the diagram shows the monopolist minimising costs for a given level of output by using the combination of labour and capital at θ. Suppose that the monopolist's profit at this point is π_m and that the output level is the one the monopolist would choose if there were no regulatory constraint. Clearly the production of q_m using any alternative factor combinations would involve higher costs and lower profits. If the firm operated at point *e* on the isoquant, for example, costs would be higher as shown by the isocost line *cd*. The lower quadrant of the diagram plots the profit of the firm for the given output level q_m but using different inputs of capital and labour. As K increases above or falls below K_m, profits decline.

The regulatory constraint is represented by the straight line through the origin labelled π_r. Because the rate of return on capital is controlled, the total profit the monopolist is permitted to keep will be directly related to the amount of capital employed. The best the firm can now do is to operate at the point where the constraint intersects with the profit curve (point *f*). Regulation would in these circumstances influence production methods rather than monopoly profits.

As this analysis shows, there is an incentive for a firm regulated in this way to "waste" capital. However, this would be true if regulators were fully informed of the firms' activities, but this need not be the actual situation. Firms will have an incentive to mislead regulators about their capital stock and may conceal information about the productivity of capital employed. Regulators will therefore be faced with monitoring costs in trying to expose the firm's strategy and, if this information is costly to acquire, they may prefer to accept the firm's version to being involved in continuous bargaining and in the intervention of "third parties" such as politicians with an interest in the industry.

(10 marks)
(Total of 20 marks)

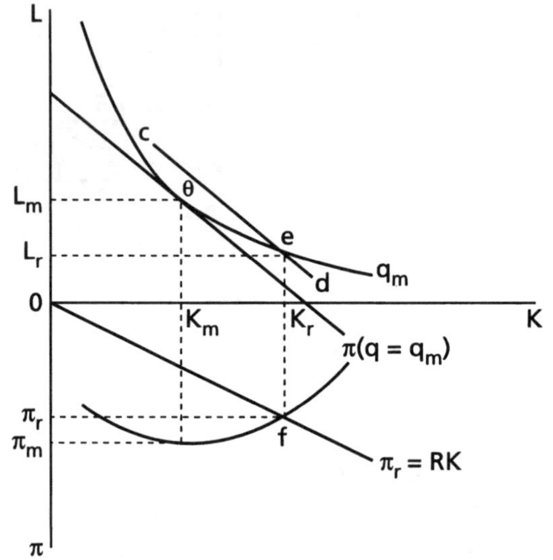

Question 3

(a) ***Identify and illustrate the problems facing a government purchasing authority trying to minimize costs when it decides to make a contract with a single firm.***

In making a contract with one firm only, the market position is one of bi-lateral monopoly. Different problems arise depending on the type of contract proposed.

With a fixed price contract agreement has to be arrived at on the number of units of output required, their quality, the delivery dates and the profit margin, the latter is usually based on the rate of return on capital employed or on some percentage of outlays. However, with the spur of competition absent, the inducement of firms to provide full and reliable information is missing, as the government has no alternative source of information or would incur considerable costs in obtaining it. If the government makes an error in the estimated costs, e.g. because of the lack of incentive or opportunity to institute careful cost checks, firms may be cost efficient for thereby they make large profits. However, if the government institutes some form of profit constraint in the form of a maximum rate of return, firms are likely to waste capital in the attempt to maximise profits [see answer to 2(b)].

With a cost-plus contract, commonly used in defence contracting, the government may agree a target cost per unit of output and a profit rate based on these costs. This kind of contract or a variant of it may by the only feasible way to induce firms to accept contracts when there is considerable uncertainty about cost estimates. The target cost can be used as a benchmark such that if actual costs exceed the target, only an agreed percentage of the excess is paid by government, whereas if costs are below target then the government "taxes" the excess profit. However, the same monitoring difficulties arise as in the case of fixed price contracts so that the government cannot be certain that it obtains output at the minimum consistent with profits which will just induce the firm to undertake the contract. Accordingly, in monitoring such contracts other aspects of them become important. These include penalties for late delivery and sharing of property rights such as patents on development work in the contract. Sharing of property rights which could be used to award contracts to other suppliers beyond development states may act as a useful "threat" to induce co-operation from the incumbent firm. **(10 marks)**

(b) ***Outline and illustrate the policy problems arising from the use of direct subsidies to an individual form designed to increase its output and employment.***

Subsidies to industry can take several different forms, but the main policy problems can be illustrated by considering the case where a single firm and sole producer of a particular product is offered a direct subsidy per unit of output. The policy interest may be in increasing employment in a particular area or occupation and encouragement to import substitution.

The case may be illustrated diagrammatically (see Figure 6.1 in the main text). This depicts a firm competing in an international market in which it has no control over price (Pw = B). To increase market share, the government could provide a subsidy per unit of output which would lower the MC curve and induce the firm to increase output and employment. In principle this requires the offer of a subsidy only on the extra (marginal) output desired, but this may not be a practical possibility.

The subsiding authority would run into several difficulties in matching its policy aims with the subsidy methods, of which the principal ones are:

(i) the asymmetric information problem as presented by the fact that information on costs depends on the firm's co-operation. The subsidising authority has to trade off minimisation of the amount of subsidy required against the cost of obtaining accurate information and agreeing on the information basis of the subsidy contract. Part of the subsidy per unit may be "wasted" because of the opportunity for the firm to inflate cost estimates.

(ii) The subsidy measure assumes that overseas firms in its international market will be passive adjusters to its effects. Such firms may be able to persuade their own governments to offer them subsidies in order to restore their competitive position. This is likely to nullify the effects of the original subsidy measure.

(10 marks)
(Total of 20 marks)

Question 4

(a) ***Explain what is meant by the "principal–agent problem" and illustrate your answer EITHER with reference to enforcement of environmental standards OR with reference to monitoring the activities of a government bureau applying a non-marketed product.***

The "principal–agent" problem arises from the difficulties encountered when the government (the principal) seeks to induce a firm or industry (the "agent") to carry out its policies, given the instruments at its disposal. The practical importance of this problem may be judged by outlining the conditions necessary for the principal to be able to achieve its policy aims. First the agent's activities must be perfectly observable so that any departure from a contract between the parties can easily be detected. Second, the production costs and the demand conditions facing the regulated firm can be determined in advance with reasonable certainty.

Enforcement of Environmental Standards

The enforcement of environmental standards represents a fairly extreme case. First of all, even if the government had full information on the nature and volume of emissions of pollutant, it may be technically difficult to measure the environmental damage caused, and the cost of controlling emissions. This violates both the conditions necessary to solve the principal–agent problem for there will inevitably be arguments between regulator and regulated about such technical matters. Second, if polluting firms are to be controlled by taxing emissions or by regulating them, technical uncertainties and costs of compliance with regulations will offer an incentive to bargain over and even to evade taxation and regulation so that monitoring costs of government may be high in relation to the desired effect.

Governments may be unwilling to incur sufficient costs in order to enforce strict compliance with legislation and prosecution of offenders will be used only as a last resort.

The Government Bureau Case

A government department may be depicted as the sole supplier of a non-marketed product to the government in power, indicating a situation akin to bilateral monopoly. However, a major difference is that the bureau chief cannot appropriate net profits over and above the costs of providing the agreed amount of the service supplied. A common assumption is that a bureau chief derives extra utility over and above that indicated by his/her salary from maximising the bureau's budget.

The result of these assumptions can be shown in the figure below taken from Figure 7.2 of the main text.

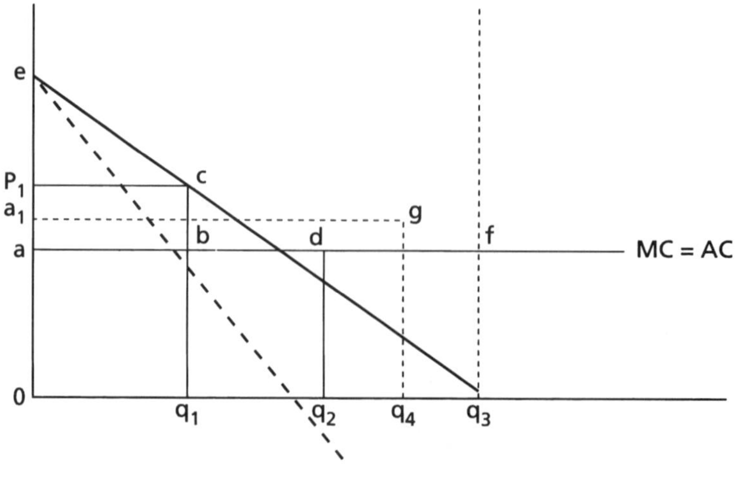

The bureau chief will negotiate the maximum grant for the output provided compatible with estimates of cost given as Oeq_3. Assuming asymmetric information and therefore high monitoring costs the bureau chief will be able to decide both the amount of output and the cost of it, within the budget constraint, which is compatible with his desire to maximise utility. He/she will maximise output if he/she is interested in prestige and power, or inflate costs and produce a lower output if interested in a "quiet life". The result will be allocative and/or technical inefficiency. **(10 marks)**

(b) ***Consider how far financial targets can be used to affect the economic performance of public enterprises.***

The question requires a definition of "economic performance". Economists usually identify three criteria of performance: technical efficiency; productive efficiency and allocative efficiency. Technical efficiency requires producing the greatest output from a given input; productive efficiency achieving a given output at lowest cost: allocative efficiency ensuring that prices to consumers reflect the social costs of production.

Various financial targets may be used alone or in conjunction with each other. A public enterprise may be required simply to "break-even", but usually this entails taking account of the cost of capital by supplementing this measure by some required rate of return (RRR). It may well be asked why public authorities do not simply instruct public enterprises to equate prices with marginal costs and to produce at lowest cost where the measures of economic performance are strictly interpreted. The difficulty is that of identifying costs and therefore of being able thereby to determine "lowest cost". A financial target does not identify the measures of performance but its rationale must therefore be that it offers an inducement to the enterprise to operate efficiently.

The claimed advantages of financial targets are:

(i) clarity in targeting;

(ii) improvement of management morale by both the clarity of the objective and removing the psychological disadvantages of managing loss-making concerns; and

(iii) clear, if crude, accounting information made available to indicate that costs of production are in line with consumer benefits.

The main problem with financial targets is that, by themselves, they do not prevent exploitation of a monopoly situation. Where monopoly obtains, then a public enterprise can still set prices which are allocatively inefficient and may be tempted to "pad out" costs. Additionally, determination of financial targets is likely to involve bargaining between government and public enterprises in which strategic behaviour is evident.

Accordingly, financial targets are usually supplemented by other targets such as efficiency targets which embody target unit costs. **(10 marks)**

(Total of 20 marks)

Question 5

(a) ***Distinguish between***

(i) ***Privatization***

Privatisation occurs when collective property rights held by the state are replaced by exchangeable property rights. This is commonly done by sale of rights by government to private citizens but the terms of sale may be conditioned by political objectives.

(ii) ***Deregulation***

Deregulation occurs when there is a reduction in the use of non-fiscal instruments used to control the economic activities of private enterprises as, for example, in the abolition of price controls.

(iii) ***Liberalization***

Liberalisation occurs when controls which restrict competition are removed, usually taking the form of removing barriers to entry into a trade or profession.

(5 marks)

(b) ***What are the two main characteristics of public goods?***

The two characteristics are:

(i) non-rivalness – consumption of the good by one person does not preclude consumption by another;

(ii) non-excludability – the service cannot be denied to those not prepared to pay or it would be difficult to deny it to them.

Give an example of

(i) ***a government service with both characteristics;***

defence/law and order/fire prevention.

(ii) ***a government service with one characteristic;***

national parks/motorways.

(iii) ***a government service with neither characteristic.***

free elementary education/waste collection/public housing.

It is worth noting that the fact of "publicness" cannot offer a sufficient explanation for the amount and composition of goods and services provided by government.

(5 marks)

(c) ***A local government service is provided "in house". There are two inputs – labour and capital. Employment is 200 and the wage per unit of employment is 200 per time period. The cost of capital (interest plus depreciation) over the same time period is 2 000.***

Now suppose that the service is contracted out. It is observed that employment falls to 120, the wage per unit of employment remains unchanged but capital costs per time period rise to 8 000. (The rise in capital cost is the result of extra investment in capital equipment, the interest rate remaining unchanged). Output is unchanged.

(i) ***Has productive efficiency increased and is it possible to tell if technical efficiency has improved?***

(ii) ***Suppose that the results of contracting out were different. Employment falls to 120, capital costs rise as before to 8 000, but the wage per unit of employment falls to 150. Output is unchanged.***

In this case, has productive efficiency increased?

Stage 1. "In-House" costs are labour costs of 200 × 200 = 40 000 + capital costs of 2 000, making a total of 42 000.

Stage 2. Contracted out costs are labour costs of 120 × 200 = 24 000 + capital costs of 8 000, totalling 32 000.

Stage 3. Definitions:
Productive efficiency = given output at lowest cost.
Technical efficiency = maximum output per given input.

Stage 4. First question.
Yes. Contracting out produces given output at 10 000 cost units less. (42 000–32 000).
Yes. Contracting out inputs per unit of output are lower in contracted out case.

Stage 5. In alternative contracting-out case, labour costs incurred are 120 × 150 = 18 000 which, together with capital costs of 8 000 = 26 000.

Stage 6. Contracting out produces given output 14 000 cost units less (42 000–26 000).

It will be noted that technical efficiency is unchanged or physical inputs of labour and capital are the same in "in-house" and "contracting-out" cases. **(10 marks)**

(Total of 20 marks)

International Trade and Finance

PRACTICE FINAL EXAMINATION 1

The examination is in 3 sections:

Section A Multiple Choice Questions	30 questions each worth 2 marks
Section B Case Study	1 question worth 40 marks
Section C Essay Question	1 question worth 40 marks
Total marks available for examination	= 140
Pass mark: 50% of 140	= 70

Section A: Multiple Choice Questions

Do all 30 questions. Each correct answer receives 2 marks.
An incorrect answer or unanswered question receives 0 marks.

1. If two countries' opportunity costs of production differ, then:

   I one country will have a comparative advantage in both products
   II one country will have an absolute advantage in both products
   III each country will have a comparative advantage in one of the products.

   Which of the following is correct?

   A I only
   B II only
   C I and II only
   D III only

Questions 2 and 3 relate to the following information:

Output	*Wheat*		*Wine*
Country:			
Home	500	or	2 500
Foreign	100	or	1 000

2. At which set of relative prices would the home country enjoy all the gains from trade?

   A 1 unit of wheat exchanges for 8 units of wine
   B 1 unit of wheat exchanges for 5 units of wine
   C 1 unit of wheat exchanges for 6 units of wine
   D 1 unit of wheat exchanges for 10 units of wine

3. Which change in production would result from mutually beneficial trade between the two countries?

   A Wine production would increase in the foreign country
   B Wheat production would increase in the foreign country

C Wine production would decrease in the foreign country
D Wheat production would decrease in the home country

4. According to the factor price equalization theorem, if country X is labour-abundant which of the following will happen if trade opens with country Y?

A Wages and the return to capital should rise in country X
B Wages should rise and the return to capital should fall in country Y
C Wages should fall and the return to capital should rise in country Y
D Wages should fall and the return to capital should rise in country X

5. Leontief reconciled his results by arguing that:

I foreign capital was more efficient than US capital
II US labour was more efficient than foreign labour
III US wages were higher than foreign wages

Which of the following is correct?

A I only
B II only
C I and II only
D I, II and III

6. The simultaneous export and import of automobiles by the United Kingdom is an example of which of the following?

A Increasing returns to scale
B Imperfect competition
C Intra-industry trade
D Interindustry trade

7. The imitation gap arises because:

I some countries do not have access to advanced technology
II it takes time to reallocate resources in response to new technology
III it takes time to put new technology into effective operation

Which of the following is correct?

A I only
B II only
C III only
D II and III only

8. A prohibitive tariff is one which:

I consumers cannot afford to pay
III maximizes government tariff revenue
III results in zero imports of the protected products

Which of the following is correct?

A I only
B II only
C III only
D I and III only

Questions 9 to 11 are based on the following diagram.

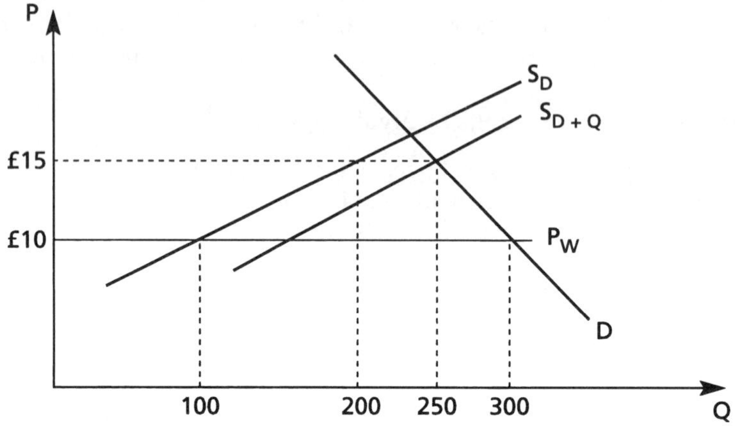

S_D = Domestic supply
S_{D+Q} = Domestic supply and quota
P_W = World price

9. The quota restricts trade by the same amount as:

A a tariff of £10
B a tariff of £5
C a tariff of £15
D there is insufficient information to determine the equivalent tariff

10. If the government were to auction quota licences it would receive revenue of:

A £1 000
B £500
C £250
D £1 250

11. The quota in the diagram reduces imports by:

A 100 units
B 150 units
C 200 units
D 50 units

12. New protectionism describes a situation of:

I increased use of tariff barriers
II increased use of quotas
III increased use of voluntary restraints

Which of the following is correct?

A I only
B I and II only
C III only
D I, II and III

13. Under a voluntary export restraint agreement, the gap between the domestic price and the export price is captured by which of the following?

A Consumers in the importing country
B The organization with the right to import
C The government of the importing country
D Foreign exporters

14. Under the GATT, the most favoured nation clause means that:

I one country may give favourable treatment to another
II a country which unilaterally reduces tariffs has special status in the GATT secretariat
III a tariff concession given to another country must be given to all member countries

Which of the following is correct?

A I only
B II only
C I and II only
D III only

15. Which of the following constitutes an improvement in the terms of trade?

A A reduction in tariff barriers
B A balance of trade surplus
C A rise in export prices relative to import prices
D An increase in the value of the currency

16. Economic integration which gives rise to trade diversion means that:

I domestic production is substituted for imports
II there is an improvement in the balance of trade
III there is an increase in consumer surplus

Which of the following is correct?

A I only
B I and II only
C I and III only
D I, II and III

17. Which of the following is correct?

Current options sold on the Philadelphia Exchange:

A contain a commitment to the owner and are standardized
B are tailored to the requirements of the owner
C contain a right but not a commitment to the owner
D can only be exercised at the date of maturity

18. The spread which is quoted for a foreign exchange transaction reflects:

I the profit earned by the foreign exchange dealer
II the degree of competition in the foreign exchange market
III the degree of market instability

Which of the following is correct?

A I only
B I and II only
C III only
D II and III only

19. Which of the following is correct?

Profitable locational arbitrage is possible if:

A one bank's ask price for a currency is greater than another bank's bid price for the currency
B one bank's bid price for a currency is less than another bank's bid price for the currency
C one bank's bid price for a currency is greater than another bank's ask price for the currency
D one bank's ask price for a currency is less than another bank's ask price for the currency

20. Which of the following is correct?

If a Japanese firm is due to receive 1 million dollars in 90 days' time and wishes to avoid exchange rate risk it could:

A take a 90-day forward contract to buy 1 million yen
B sell 1 million dollars 90 days from now at the spot rate
C take a 90-day forward contract to sell 1 million dollars
D purchase 1 million yen 90 days from now at the spot rate

21. A Eurobank is one which:

 I is located in a European financial centre
 II is governed by European Community regulations
 III accepts deposits in the currency of the country in which it is located

 Which of the following is correct?

 A I only
 B I and II only
 C III only
 D Not I, not II, not III

22. Which of the following is correct?

 If the forward rate of exchange of sterling against the dollar is lower than the spot rate and the expected future spot rate was lower than the spot rate and higher than the forward rate, a speculator would:

 A sell sterling now and take a forward contract to buy sterling
 B sell sterling now and take a forward contract to sell sterling
 C buy sterling now and take a forward contract to buy sterling
 D buy sterling now and take a forward contract to sell sterling

23. The supply schedule of US dollars will shift to the left if:

 I there is an increase in US exports
 II there is a decrease in US imports
 III the US restricts capital outflows

 Which of the following is correct?

 A I only
 B I and II only
 C III only
 D II and III only

24. Which of the following is correct?

 The monetary theory of the exchange rate suggests that:

 A if domestic money supply decreases then the exchange rate for domestic currency will depreciate
 B the exchange rate adjusts to the demand for exports and imports
 C if the demand for domestic currency decreases then the exchange rate for domestic currency will depreciate
 D if the demand for foreign money decreases then the exchange rate for domestic currency will appreciate

25. Which of the following is known as absolute purchasing power parity?

 A The percentage change in the exchange rate is equal to the percentage change in relative prices

B The percentage change in money supply in one country is equal to the percentage change in money supply in the other
C The exchange rate is the ratio of domestic and foreign price indexes
D The level of expenditure in one country is equal to the level of expenditure in the other

26. Under a pegged exchange rate system which of the following options is available to a government when the exchange rate is at the floor?

A Buy foreign currency
B Reduce taxation
C Raise domestic interest rates
D Increase government expenditure

27. Under a system of floating exchange rates, the exchange rate will depreciate if:

I there is a downward adjustment in expectations of inflation
II there is a reduction in domestic rates of interest
III there is an upward adjustment in expectations of foreign inflation

Which of the following is correct?

A I only
B II only
C I and II only
D I, II and III

28. In the European Monetary System:

I each country's currency is given a weight in the ECU currency basket
II each country's currency has an agreed value against the ECU
III the Deutschmark acts as the reserve currency in the system

Which of the following is correct?

A I only
B I and II only
C III only
D I, II and III

29. International borrowing can lead to an increase in actual output if:

I the money is used to finance consumption
II the money is used to finance a balance of payments deficit
III the money is used to finance government expenditure

Which of the following is correct?

A I only
B II only
C I and II only
D I and III only

30. Which of the following features characterized the Bretton Woods system?

    A The International Monetary Fund acted as the world's banker
    B Free movement of international capital
    C Exchange rates reflected market forces
    D Exchange rates were agreed between governments and the International Monetary Fund

Section B: Case Study

The newly elected government of a large industrial economy won over public opinion on the basis that it would implement policies to address the domestic economic problems of high unemployment and falling output. Supporters of the new government argue that a crucial element in the economic strategy to create jobs and raise domestic output must be policies aimed at increasing exports and lowering imports, although there is no suggestion that formal import controls in the form of tariffs or quotas should be used. Instead, government policy should target specific subsidies at a few key productive sectors in the economy – those where the opportunity for export growth is greatest and which contribute most to economic growth. Advocates of this approach reject the claim that they are latter-day mercantilists. Instead they point to similar practices being carried out by governments elsewhere in the world to justify their demands for this type of policy. You have been asked to advise the new government of the likely consequences from adopting this activist trade policy stance. What issues would you highlight in your report?

Section C: Essay Question

Why do many firms spend large amounts of money purchasing foreign exchange rate forecasts or devote considerable resources to the preparation of 'in-house' forecasts? Assess the use of forecasts as against the forward rate of exchange.

Section A: Answers to Multiple Choice Questions

1. The opportunity cost of producing one good is the quantity of another good which must be sacrificed. If one country has to sacrifice less of product X to get an extra unit of product Y, then it has a comparative advantage in Y. If this is so then the converse is true and the second country must have a comparative advantage in X. One country could have an absolute advantage in both products – we do not have that information – but as long as opportunity costs differ, the second country must have a comparative advantage in one of the products.

   Correct response is D

2. In the absence of trade, if the home country sacrifices one unit of wheat, it can get five units of wine while the foreign country can get ten bottles of wine by giving up one unit of wheat. If trade were to take place on the basis of one unit of wheat exchanging for ten units of wine, then the home country would specialize in wheat production, receiving ten units of wine for every unit of wheat traded. The foreign country neither

gains nor loses since the terms on which trade takes place are the same as its pre-trade domestic terms. The home country enjoys all of the gains.

Correct response is D

3. With the opening up of trade, countries gain through specializing in the production of the product in which they have a comparative advantage. As the answer to question 2 indicates the home country has a comparative advantage in the production of wheat and the foreign country has a comparative advantage in the production of wine. Mutually beneficial trade would result in an increase in wine production in the foreign country.

   Correct response is A

4. If country X is labour-abundant then the price of labour relative to capital is cheap and the price of capital relative to labour is dear. If trade leads to the equalization of prices of factors of production, then wages in country Y will fall and come into line with country X and the return to capital in country Y will rise for the same reason.

   Correct response is C

5. When Leontief carried out his study of the composition of US trade it was generally accepted that the US was a capital-abundant country. This was thought to be particularly true given his data were for 1947 and the US economy had not experienced the wartime damage of the European and Japanese economies. The Heckscher-Ohlin theory would predict that US exports would be capital-intensive and US imports would be labour-intensive. Leontief's empirical study suggested completely the reverse. In seeking to explain this apparent paradox Leontief argued that US labour was much more efficient than foreign labour and if the US labour supply was adjusted to take account of this productivity differential then the US was in practice a labour-abundant country.

   Correct response is B

6. Early theories of international trade, e.g. Ricardian Comparative advantage and Heckscher–Ohlin, suggested that countries would specialize in particular products. The pattern of trade would be characterized by inter-industry trade. One country would specialize in, and export, automobiles while another would specialize in, and export electronic goods. The pattern of international trade as it has changed over time shows that trade in manufactured goods increasingly involves a country both exporting and importing the same (though normally differentiated) products. The UK exports Rolls-Royces and imports BMWs. It is an example of intra-industry trade.

   Correct response is C

7. We may consider innovation in terms of a new product or a new production process which makes the production of an existing product more efficient. In the first case the innovator has, for a period of time, a competitive advantage. Competitors will seek to eliminate these advantages. Technology is internationally mobile, but it does take time to react to the new situation and reallocate resources accordingly. Effective operation of new technology also involves a learning process.

   Correct response is D

8. As tariffs increase it will be true that some consumers will be forced out of the market. This cannot be true for all consumers or else there would be no domestic industry producing the protected product. A prohibitive tariff is one which makes it no longer profitable for a foreign producer to sell in the domestic market, and demand would be fully met by domestic suppliers. There would be zero imports of the protected product and consequently zero government tariff revenue.

   Correct response is C

9. The world price is £10. A tariff of £5 raises the price to £15, at which price demand is 250 units, of which 200 comes from domestic suppliers. A tariff of £5 results in imports of 50 units which equals the quota.

   Correct response is B

10. Prior to the introduction of a quota the product would sell at a price of £10. The successful bidder in an auction has the right to import 50 units which he can sell at a price of £15. In a perfect auction he would be prepared to bid up to, but not beyond £250 the £5 price increase on the 50 units.

    Correct response is C

11. Before the imposition of the quota, the product sells at the world price of £10, at which price the demand is 300 units of which domestic producers supply 100 units and 200 are imported. The quota reduces imports by 150 units.

    Correct response is B

12. Tariff barriers and quotas are traditional forms of protecting domestic markets. New protectionism should not be confused with increased protectionism. New protectionism refers to new approaches to protecting domestic markets. These include market entry barriers, administrative practices, technical requirements and the use of fiscal instruments. Voluntary restraints (normally the result of duress) represent market entry barriers.

    Correct response is C

13. A voluntary export restraint by foreign producers results in fewer imports of the relevant product into the domestic economy and therefore reduces supply and leads to higher prices in the domestic economy. The export price of the foreign producer is unchanged though he now finds he gets a higher price for his product. For the exporter there is an increase in producer surplus. He is now receiving a higher price than the price at which he would have been willing to supply the product.

    Correct response is D

14. The most favoured nation clause is the principal way in which the GATT aims to remove discriminatory trade practices. In essence it says that any reduction in tariffs granted to one or more countries must be granted to all member countries – essentially there should not be 'favoured' nations.

    Correct response is D

15. The terms of trade reflect the relative price at which products are traded. They show the number of units of imports which can be purchased by one unit of exports, or conversely the number of units of exports which you need to sell to buy one unit of imports. A rise in the relative price of your exports means that each export can buy more imports than was previously the case, and the terms of trade have improved. You should not confuse this with the balance of trade which could, at the same time, deteriorate if export demand were price-elastic, resulting in a fall in export receipts.

    Correct response is C

16. Trade diversion occurs when demand is switched from a low cost to a higher cost supplier. Prior to integration a member country may have imported a product from a relatively low-cost producer anywhere in the world. With integration and the imposition of a common external tariff that lower-cost supplier may no longer be competitive inside the integrated union and the demand switches to higher-cost union producers. Domestic production (and domestic shall be thought of as anywhere in the union) is substituted for imports. Consumer surplus will be reduced while we do not have enough information to know what will happen to the balance of trade.

    Correct response is A

17. American currency options sold on the Philadelphia Exchange are for standardized amounts of money (yen etc.) and can be exercised at any time in the life of the contract. The owner of a put option has the right, but is not committed, to sell the currency and conversely to buy the currency with a call option.

    Correct response is C

18. The spread is the difference between the price at which a bank or foreign exchange dealer is prepared to buy a currency and the price at which it is prepared to sell. Buying at a lower price than selling does of course generate profit, but it is not the sole determinant of profit since we need to know about the volume of transactions, the dealer's operating costs and so on. If the dealer had a monopoly position, he would be able to exploit profit by widening the spread; the spread, in part, reflects the degree of competition. If the market is unstable, then there is an increased chance that the dealer will get the price wrong and face losses. Thus having bought the currency at a particular price he may find that he cannot resell it at a higher price. The spread will widen in periods of market instability, essentially as dealers seek to insure their interests.

    Correct response is D

19. Profitable, locational arbitrage occurs when there is a differential between the price at which you can buy something and the price at which you can sell it. When banks are asked for a quotation on the price of foreign currency they will quote the price at which they will buy the currency and the price at which they will sell it. If one bank is prepared to sell a currency at a lower price than another bank is prepared to buy it, then provided the difference is greater than any transaction costs, profit can be earned by exploiting the differential.

    Correct response is C

20. Taking a forward contract to buy 1 million yen presupposes that the forward rate is on a one-to-one basis between the dollar and the yen, and we do not have this information. Waiting 90 days to transact at the future spot rate means that the firm is willing to accept exchange rate risk. Only by taking a forward contract to sell their future receivables of 1 million dollars does the firm know with certainty the yen value of its export receipts.

    Correct response is C

21. The term Eurobank was coined to describe banking practices which have emerged over the last forty years. The term is a reflection of the fact that these practices first appeared in Europe in London and Paris. Today similar banking practices are carried on around the world. Eurobanking is still dominated by the European financial centres, but has nothing to do with anything European. Eurobank activity involves accepting deposits and making loans in currencies other than the currency of the country in which the bank is located – originally US dollars deposited and loaned in London and Paris. Thus an overseas branch of a foreign bank which accepts deposits and makes loans in local currency is engaged in conventional domestic banking activity, not Eurobanking activity.

    Correct response is D

22. Speculation may be carried out in terms of both spot and forward transactions. In this instance a speculator may profit by selling sterling now (provided he possesses sterling) and buying it back at the lower expected future spot price. Equally he may profit by taking out a forward contract to buy sterling and selling it at the higher expected future spot price.

    Correct response is A

23. The supply schedule of US dollars is based upon the actions of economic agents supplying dollars in exchange for foreign currency. A decrease in US imports means less foreign currency is required to pay for them, hence fewer US dollars are supplied A restriction on capital outflow also reduces the demand for foreign currency to invest overseas with a consequent reduction in the supply of US dollars on the market.

    Correct response is D

24. The monetary theory of the exchange rate emphasises the demands and supplies of different monies as the key to the determination of the exchange rate. Other things being equal, increases in supply will reduce price, and vice-versa. Equally, increases in demand will lead to an increase in the price, and vice-versa. If the demand for foreign money decreases then, other things equal, the price of foreign money will fall. Domestic currency has increased in value; the exchange rate for domestic currency has appreciated.

    Correct response is D

25. Purchasing power reflects what we can buy with a given sum of money. Absolute purchasing power parity is a concept which says that if a particular basket of goods costs 10 US dollars in America, and the same basket of goods costs 5 Australian dol-

lars in Australia then the exchange rate would be A$1 = US$2. The exchange rate is the ratio of domestic and foreign price indexes.

Correct response is C

26. If we consider the options, two of them (reducing taxation and increasing government expenditure) are likely to be expansionary in terms of the domestic economy. Such expansion typically sucks in more imports which results in an increase in the supply of the currency, putting further downward pressure on prices. Buying foreign currency will push up the price of foreign currency, i.e. lowering the price of domestic currency. By raising domestic interest rates a government can hope to attract a capital inflow, boosting demand for the currency and pushing up the price.

Correct response is C

27. If there is a downward adjustment in expectations of inflation then domestic prices are thought to rise less than was previously the case. In adjusting their expectations transactors now have a more optimistic view of the future course of events, and in acting upon their revised expectations the exchange rate will appreciate. Equally if there is an upward adjustment in expectations of foreign inflation then foreign prices are expected to rise more rapidly and the exchange rate for the domestic currency will appreciate. A reduction in domestic rates of interest reduces the return on domestic currency denominated assets relative to foreign currency denominated assets. The associated capital outflow will lead to depreciation of the exchange rate.

Correct response is B

28. The European Currency Unit is at the centre of the European Monetary System. It is the accounting unit of the European Community, the reserve base of the European Monetary System and the numeraire of the Exchange Rate Mechanism. Its valuation is based on a basket of currencies in which each member country's currency is weighted on the basis of its relative economic importance. In the Exchange Rate Mechanism each participating currency has an agreed control rate against the ECU, from which are derived bilateral exchange rates. While it is true that the Deutschmark has traditionally been the strongest currency, it has no official function and is treated the same way as any other currency.

Correct response is D

29. If international borrowing is used to finance any expenditure in the domestic economy, then provided the additional expenditure does not have a 100 per cent import content there will be an increase in actual output. This should not be confused with an increase in potential output, which is the result of an increase in the quantity or quality of factors of production. If the borrowed money is simply used to pay for an existing balance of payments deficit, then there is no net impact on the domestic economy.

Correct response is D

30. The Bretton Woods system was one in which exchange rates were pegged at an agreed par value around which there was a permitted band of variation. Exchange

rate fluctuations within this band were a reflection of market forces, but whenever the floor or ceiling of the band was reached, then governments had to intervene to offset market forces. During the Bretton Woods period controls on international capital movements were commonplace. While the IMF could provide assistance to countries with balance of payments difficulties, it was not the world's banker, and was never a lender of last resort.

Correct response is D

Section B: Solution to Case Study

The question of what constitutes a policy of protection in today's world is a difficult one, and this ambiguity in definition has provided an opening for supporters of protectionism to advance their cause. In the orthodox approach to international trade, protectionism was clearly defined as the imposition of formal barriers to free trade. These usually took the form of tariffs and quotas on imports, and economists from David Ricardo onwards agreed that trade barriers of this type undermined global economic efficiency and reduced consumer welfare. This was due to the fact that such trade controls distorted the global pattern of production, denying consumers access to the lowest cost source of supply and engineering a distortion in the allocation of resources as countries were producing certain goods which could be more efficiently produced elsewhere. The law of comparative advantage dictated that, as all countries had a comparative advantage in the production of some goods, only universal free trade would maximize global welfare.

However, in recent times the matter of the costs and benefits to protection have become less straightforward. There are a number of reasons for this, and each in its own way has raised the demands for governments to intervene and influence, through policy, the international flow of goods and – increasingly – traded services.

The first reason is quite simply that during episodes of recession the clamour for protection against imports and measures to increase exports intensify. This is always the case and, to the extent that the present agitation can be traced to the current state of the economic cycle, we can expect it to be short-lived. Once economic recovery is under way, output and employment will rise and the public will be less concerned with trade policy. Moreover, to the extent that any action we should take in the area of trade policy will upset our trading partners, this could delay economic recovery as the international economic co-operation required to induce economic recovery would be undermined. After all, the demand for our exports crucially depends on the economic health of our trading partners. Perhaps the best approach would be to discuss common measures to accelerate the economic upturn.

The second cause of the revival of protectionism is altogether more problematic as it relates to the public's perception that our trading partners have in place a range of economic policies that undermine free or fair trade and which bestow upon them an unfair advantage in global markets to the detriment of our firms. This suspicion is given credibility by the apparent inability of the General Agreement on Tariffs and Trade (GATT) to take effective action against those countries which are found to be contravening both the letter and the spirit of international trade agreements. And if the GATT cannot stop abuses that are occurring, how can it hope to prevent new abuses arising? There is much truth in this claim. There is considerable evidence that a range of protectionist policies are in place in many countries. These policies are difficult to detect, involving as they do subtle means of impeding imports and encouraging exports. These non-tariff barriers to trade include technical barriers, preferential public procurement policies, administrative barriers to imports, and providing subsidies to production and investment in export industries. Experience has shown that even when governments can prove the existence of such unfair trade practices they can do little to stop them through the usual channels of international commercial diplomacy. Consequently, this supports the protectionist claims at home that the only response is to introduce similar policies here – that is, to retaliate. The third problem is that some economists claim that active trade policies can actually improve domestic economic welfare. As you will recall the common argument is that protectionist policies affect everyone as those countries affected by your policy will retaliate in kind. So, whilst a country may reduce the flow of imports, it can expect exports to fall as retaliation occurs. However, a new school of thought says that if policy targets specific industries, then domestic welfare might rise. There will be no retaliation. The reasoning is as follows. In many new, high technology markets there are cumulative advantages to be derived from early entry, what economists call 'first-mover' gains – e.g. familiarity with the technology and marketing, and the acquisition of reputation ahead of competitors. Moreover, these markets are global. Consequently, if a government in one country intervenes to assist domestic producers to be the first entrants to that market, we can expect these producers to take a large share of the global market. In turn, this increases that country's share of world value-added in production. If the gains from early entry are cumulative, the initial subsidy can be repaid at some future date. The upshot is that economic welfare in the home country has risen and nobody is worse off. There is no incentive for other countries to retaliate as you have not forced any of their existing firms out of business. It appears to be the perfect case for trade policy – in fact the logic of the argument is very powerful.

None the less, trade policy carries with it distinct risks. Introducing policy as a response to practices elsewhere is a weak case, especially if we are to avoid becoming embroiled in a full-blown trade war. Even where it can be demonstrated that unfair trading practices are being undertaken by trading competitors would it not be preferable to rely on the existing mechanisms for resolving trade disputes? Indeed, perhaps the most effective retaliation would be to propose that these rules be strengthened by giving formal powers to police world trade to the GATT. The risks of non-co-operation with economic partners are extremely high.

The case for subsidies to assist early entry to world markets as yet underdeveloped is superficially attractive, although again we should be cautious. It is not clear that government is capable of identifying the appropriate industries to target with such support. It is worth recalling that countries such as the UK and France have, in the past, attempted to 'pick winners' with no real success. In short, domestic subsidies follow domestic subsidies into a potentially bottomless pit. At the same time a powerful pressure group is created on the basis of national prestige which is well placed to demand further support. And if we rely on industry itself bringing forward eligible proposals then we run the risk of being 'captured' by those we are seeking to support. Further, subsidies can and do attract in applicants who otherwise would not be involved. If we agree to support a novel technology or project, we cannot be sure that companies coming forward for assistance are ever likely to be able to produce results. In this event the subsidy simply is a burden on public expenditure. Finally, nothing in this argument guarantees that we will not become involved in an out-and-out 'subsidy war' with other countries. If there are gains associated with 'first movers', why should other countries not move first? In that event world welfare will deteriorate as an excess of global resources will be allocated to the same area. The market, if left to itself, would not produce this situation.

In conclusion, while there are superficial reasons for introducing a more active trade policy, there are inherent dangers that this policy will become, and will be perceived as, little more that protectionism. This would be to the long-term detriment of our economy.

Section C: Suggested Answer to Essay Question

Your answer should follow a cohesive logical structure. You should start by explaining the possible impact of exchange rate changes on the domestic currency value of a firm's future payments and receipts. Such exchange rate changes can affect the profitability of any international transactions and the present value of a firm's future cash flows. Your answer should therefore include a consideration of types of exchange rate exposure and the associated risk. You should draw a distinction between the degree of exposure and the degree of risk, since they are not one and the same thing. A firm may have a large proportion of future payments denominated in a foreign currency and hence has a high level of exposure. If, however, the relevant foreign currency is closely tied to the domestic currency, then the degree of risk is small. The converse is also true. Having established the scenario faced by firms, you should emphasize the possible problems they face by referring to the considerable instability of exchange rates in recent years.

The second part of the essay requires that you show an understanding of the determination of the forward rate of exchange, and the extent to which it may be a good predictor of future spot rates of exchange. You should then explain the different approaches to forecasting and demonstrate an understanding of what constitutes a good forecast – it is not necessarily the most accurate. You should conclude by indicating the relative merits of different approaches.

PRACTICE FINAL EXAMINATION 2

Case Study

As a rising star in the financial management staff of a Japanese multinational company you are on your first "solo" mission to Spain. You have been asked first, to carry out an in-depth assessment of current operating performance of the Spanish subsidiary and, second, to evaluate the prospects for additional investment in Spain. Having taken a three day break in Paris en route to Spain you arrive at your Barcelona hotel to find a fax from Tokyo headquarters. It reports that the Japanese press carries reports that the latest statistics on Spanish trade performance and inflation are such that the Spanish government may have to seek a realignment of the peseta within the European Exchange Rate Mechanism.

You are asked to report urgently on three issues.

1. ***An assessment of the likelihood of a realignment.***

2. ***An assessment of the likely impact on costs, prices and sales of the Spanish subsidiary should a realignment take place.***

3. ***An assessment of the prospects for Spanish monetary policy should a realignment take place.***
(40 marks)

You should note that you are not told whether the latest economic indicators suggest a strong trade performance and low inflation or vice-versa. Accordingly, you may consider an upward realignment (revaluation) or a downward realignment (devaluation). You do not need to deal with both scenarios. Arguments put forward for one case are, to all intents, simply reversed for the other case. Take the case of a possible downward realignment.

1. **Likelihood of a Realignment**

   The likelihood of a realignment will depend upon both economic and political factors. Among those you might identify are:

   (a) How severe, and perhaps more important, how persistent is the deteriorating Spanish economic performance?

   (b) How willing is the Spanish government to target domestic economic policy to the exchange rate? In particular, will it be prepared to accept high rates of interest to attract a capital inflow or deter a capital outflow, given the likely adverse effects on domestic output and employment levels.

   (c) To what extent can (will) the Spanish government directly intervene in the market as a purchaser of its own currency to keep the price up? This will depend on the level of Spanish foreign exchange reserves and the willingness of the government to draw credit through the VSTF.

   (d) How likely is it that other member countries will be prepared to intervene to support the peseta?

   (e) How likely is it that changing economic performance and/or policies in other member countries will operate in a way which benefits the peseta?

2. **Costs, Prices and Sales**

   (a) **Costs**
   This is perhaps the most complex of the issues. The devaluation will raise the peseta price of imported inputs, so the impact will depend upon the extent to which the subsidiary relies on imported inputs. It may not be quite so simple however; the imported inputs could be intra-company, i.e. from other subsidiaries around the world. The MNC may decide not to alter the predevaluation set of transfer prices for imported inputs. To what extent will Spanish suppliers face increased costs and to what extent will they seek to pass them on in higher prices which the subsidiary would have to pay? Finally there are labour costs. If the devaluation leads to increased inflation – dependent in part on the import content of total domestic expenditure – some labour may seek compensating wage increases. Whether they are unsuccessful, partially successful or fully successful will each have implications for your costs. It is, as suggested, a complex issue.

(b) **Prices**
The devaluation, in itself, does not alter the peseta price of the output of the Spanish subsidiary. This will only happen if any increased costs resulting from the devaluation ((a) above) are passed on through higher prices. The extent to which this may happen will reflect the significance of any such cost increases and any decisions made about profit margins. The devaluation will change (increase) the peseta price of the products of any foreign producers on the Spanish domestic market and decrease the foreign currency price of the output of the Spanish subsidiary in foreign markets.

(c) **Sales**
Clearly what happens to sales depends on the issues discussed above. The subsidiary may look to increase sales in the Spanish market at the expense of foreign producers, though not of any Spanish based competitors who face the same issues in (a) and (b) above. They may also look to increase sales in foreign markets. The outcome will depend upon the cost and price issues discussed, price elasticities of demand and whether foreign competitors will change pricing/profit-margin policies to negate any competitive advantage which the Spanish subsidiary might gain.

3. **Monetary Policy**

There are three possibilities:

(a) No change.

(b) If the devaluation is expected to make inflation even worse, then monetary policy may have to be tightened.

(c) If inflation is not perceived as a problem then the devaluation allows the opportunity to relax monetary policy (lower interest rates) in an attempt to boost Spanish economic activity and reduce unemployment.

Essay Question

What motivates international economic integration? **(40 marks)**

It is true there may be political motives for integration but we are concerned with the economic factors. The principal motivating factor is the desire to exploit more fully the gains from trade. Possible gains from trade were first identified by Ricardo. You do not have to deal with trade theories (Heckscher–Ohlin, product life cycle, etc.). They are attempts to explain why trade takes place and to explain the pattern of trade. Here you are concerned only with any gains which might be derived. In a world economy characterised by barriers to trade it was increasingly seen that benefits might be realised by forming regional trading blocs in which barriers between member countries would be dismantled. Benefits would accrue provided trade creation outweighed trade diversion. These are so-called static effects of integration. Empirical evidence suggests that there will be net benefits but the size of the effects is relatively small. The significant gains are seen to come from the so-called dynamic effects of integration. These include fuller exploitation of economies of scale in the larger market; increased competitiveness; opportunity for greater R&D activity; and so on. The outcome should be an increase in consumer surplus and increased economic growth, hence such arrangements are seen as welfare enhancing. You should also distinguish between positive and negative integration.

Your answer should also identify and distinguish between the different levels of integration which may exist, i.e. free trade area, customs union, common market, economic and monetary union.

PRACTICE FINAL EXAMINATION 3

Case Study

Some years ago a group of neighbouring countries, which are your major trading partners, formed a customs union which evolved into a common market. After fierce debate, and a referendum, your country decided not to join the union. There were political reasons – a strongly held view about independence and sovereignty – but also economic reasons. Your country was a major oil producer, and oil prices were high. As a result, the balance of payments was healthy, the currency was strong – making imports relatively cheap – and government oil tax policies ensured substantial government revenue which financed a high level of social expenditure.

It is true that the countries which formed the union were highly successful, with sustained growth rates at a historic high. Until two years ago this did not seem to matter, as your economy was also extremely successful. Since then the mood has changed. First, oil prices have slumped, the external balance has moved into deficit and the high level of social expenditure is leading to an increasing budget deficit. Second, there is growing awareness that oil reserves are being rapidly depleted. Third, there is a growing concern over the erosion of the domestic industrial base as a result of the relatively cheap imports during the period when the currency was strong.

As a result of these developments there is now an increasingly vocal lobby in favour of reversing the earlier decision and seeking membership of the union

As economic consultant to one of the major domestic engineering companies still in business you are asked to prepare a report for the board of directors setting out the arguments for and against a move towards membership, as the board wishes to decide whether or not to join – and help finance – the lobby.

Your report should deal with the costs and benefits at a microeconomic level – you are, after all, employed by a company – and also at a macroeconomic level since, for example, any implications for changes in government economic policies will have an impact on your company.

Your report should start with an outline of the features of a common market. Not all of the directors will necessarily understand! You don't need to go into a lot of detail about different levels of integration, the basics will suffice. There are three important elements. First, the absence of barriers to trade between member countries Second, the existence of a common external tariff against non-member countries. Third, free movement of labour and capital across member countries.

At a microeconomic level you should deal first with the static effects associated with integration. Your company will have access to a larger tariff-free market. Against this, the company may face increased competition in the domestic market. You can't judge the extent of this factor since you don't have information about any present tariff imposed upon member countries' products but you should certainly point out the possibility. Equally your company may or may not face increased costs associated with trade diversion. Thus your company may currently import some inputs to the production process – raw materials, semi-manufactures, etc. – from low cost non-member countries The imposition of a common external tariff may make these sources of supply uncompetitive and you have to purchase from higher cost member countries.

Perhaps more important than the static effects are the dynamic effects, and your report should emphasise this. In particular you should deal with the economies of scale argument and the competitive pressures for increased efficiency

At a macroeconomic level you should show an awareness that membership will result in increased interdependence of the economy with other member countries and this will constrain the degree of independence in national economic policy making. This is particularly true in respect of monetary – interest rate – policy given the free movement of capital. Whether you view this as a beneficial outcome depends of course on whether you consider your country's monetary policy to be more, or less, "responsible" than that pursued by other member countries.

Essay Question

In what ways are firms exposed to exchange rate risk?

Analyse the different ways in which they may deal with such risk.

Exchange rate risk in the situation that the economic "well being" of a company may be reduced by an adverse movement of the exchange rate. Since there is a time lag between ordering and payment the profitability of trade deals currently in the pipeline can be adversely affected. The domestic currency value of export earnings may be lower than anticipated, but more commonly the domestic currency costs of imports may be higher than anticipated. (Most exports are invoiced in domestic currency.)

Your essay should explain the three ways in which firms can be exposed to exchange rate risk. These are transaction exposure, economic exposure and translation exposure. The first relates to the profitability of trade deals as indicated above. The second makes clear that even firms who do not engage in international trade are nevertheless exposed to exchange rate risk. If the domestic currency appreciates, then foreign goods become more competitive and the firm may lose part of its share of the domestic market. You should make clear that what is at stake in these two instances is the present value of future cash flows.

Translation exposure occurs in the case of multi-national companies when the foreign currency activities of subsidiaries are converted to the national currency of the parent company. The impact is on the balance sheet of the MNC and can affect the valuation of stockholders' equity.

While you should show an awareness of the different ways in which firms may deal with risk, you would not be expected to deal with all of them in detail. An acceptable answer would involve an explanation of, say, two possibilities, e.g. forward contracts and options with only a passing reference to the existence of futures, swaps, invoicing techniques, etc., or an explanation of any other combination.

Negotiation

PRACTICE FINAL EXAMINATION 1

Part 1: Case Study

Read the following case study and answer the questions that follow in the form of short essays. Each answer in the Case Study is worth up to 8 marks. Total possible marks for the Case Study = 40.

"Unauthorized Variations"

Holt Plc, an offshore contractor specializing in weather-proofing of production platforms in the North Sea, won a contract to clean and repaint one of Conto Oil's six production platforms against some stiff price competition. Conto Oil specified that time was of the essence and that in no circumstances was the weather-proofing to interfere with production, or production-related maintenance work, and that the job had to be completed in 35 days.

Holt's bid was £1 250 000 and included all labour and material costs but excluded transport to and from the rig and offshore board and accommodation of the crews. The work, however, was not completed on time – it took 47 days – though it passed Conto's quality inspections and did not disturb production.

Holt submitted its invoice for the contract as follows:

Original bid as agreed	£1 250 000
Variations and delays	£123 000
Additional materials	£15 000
	£1 388 000

Conto returned this, unpaid, with a letter stating its refusal to pay for extras that were not authorized by the Purchasing Controller, and requested that they be re-invoiced for the original bid price.

Holt's Managing Director felt unable to accept Conto's response and decided to call in a consultant to prepare a reply and a negotiating case. He briefed the consultant with the following information.

The delays on the Conto platform were occasioned entirely by Conto and not by any slackness on Holt's part. For example, the platform's flaring boom had to be shut down for several days, while Conto's safety and maintenance people surveyed its structure and undertook some repairs. This prevented Holt from following its prepared work-pattern and caused some considerable rescheduling to occupy its crews in other work elsewhere on the platform. In addition, another contractor caused a major spillage of solvents on the production deck of the platform, affecting two lower decks that had been cleaned and primed by Holt, necessitating rework and replacement of stored materials that were contaminated both in the original spillage and the preventative hosing down of the entire area by Conto's Safety Teams, plus those materials that were required to redo the partially completed work.

Other minor delays were caused by production and production-related maintenance work by other contractors, though these are normal in this industry and an allowance is usually made in the agreed timetable for completing the contract. However, in this case all delays had knock-on effects. Most of the variations in the work schedules were agreed verbally on the spot between Holt's and Conto's production staff. Sometimes this entailed agreeing to interrupt a particular task, which meant dismantling and setting up the painters' rigging elsewhere on the platform. The working culture on an oil platform is one of 'get the job done and argue later', and while Conto had established variation procedures, pressure is always on a contractor to get on with the work and sort out paperwork at the end of a job. Conto's production people certainly did not adhere strictly to procedures and with shift changes – and sometimes entire personnel changes as men went ashore on leave – variation procedures sometimes were let slip. Rearranging Holt's crews, including rescheduling onshore and offshore leave and personnel movements, to make up for lost time involved Holt in additional direct expense in personnel costs (including overtime and additional people on extra shifts), and in indirect expense in, mainly, managerial overheads to supervise on-site and ashore the rescheduling and the work rate of the offshore extra shifts.

Holt's internal breakdown on the additional costs were:

Extra materials	£15 000
Additional crew costs due to delays	£119 500
Premium for managerial time due to rescheduling	£13 500
	£138 000

Holt was not willing to compromise too far on the invoice, in view of the high proportion of actual costs to Holt involved in completing the contract.

Assume that you have been engaged by Holt's as a consultant and they have presented you with this problem as your first assignment. Using the above information, answer the questions that follow with short essay-type answers.

1.1 What is the first task you would want to undertake before making any recommendations on possible courses of action?

1.2 What would you estimate the interests of Holt Plc to be in this case?

1.3 What issues can you identify in this case from Holt's point of view?

1.4 What would you perceive Conto Oil's interests to be from what you know of the problem?

1.5 What does Holt need to know from the debate phase before it can make a proposal for solving the problem?

Part 2: Essay Questions

Write essay answers to the following questions.

Each essay answer is worth up to 20 marks.

Total marks for Part 2 = 60.

2.1 What alternative methods could a manager use when a decision has to be made?
2.2 Why is a Red negotiating style so common?
2.3 What are the common and dissimilar characteristics of a proposal and a bargain?

Model Answers to the Case Study

1.1 *What is the first task you would want to undertake before making any recommendations on possible courses of action?*

	Marks
Emotional approach to conflicting beliefs leads to strife	2
Data is more persuasive than unsubstantiated opinions	2
Data must be collected and analysed	2
Evidence that supports credibility of data useful	2
	8

This type of dispute is often charged with the potential of emotional conflict. Conto Oil appears to believe that Holt is trying to extract additional income at its expense; Holt believes that it is entitled to the additional charges and that Conto Oil is trying to evade its responsibilities. If these beliefs persist there is not likely to be a basis for a negotiated solution and it might come down to either brute strength and ignorance or to litigation.

Holt needs to know the exact details of the events that caused it to suffer the extra expenditures outlined in its invoice. It is not sufficient for Holt to attack Conto Oil on a broad front with charges of delays and incidental anecdotes of what happened on some occasions with Conto's production people. Holt needs data on each and every delay and the details of the cost consequences, and the more specific the data the better. If this data has been logged by Holt's on-site management it can build its case and substantiate the bulk of its claim for variation payments; if it cannot do this, or if the data is patchy, it may have to accept a less favourable compromise. In the absence of data we are down to opinion and impression, neither of which is as convincing in a negotiation as data.

A detailed examination of the documentation, including the work schedules, all the associated paperwork (instructions to staff, reassignment memos, booked and cancelled trips, overtime requests, payslips and so on), stores requisitions, project diaries and such like should be undertaken by those personnel likely to be involved in the negotiations. Some preliminary analysis is also useful, including the drafting of line or bar charts and diagrams representing the raw data. Wherever possible, the names of Conto Oil staff who authorized individual variations should be collected, and, of course, any Conto Oil official paperwork must be brought into the picture. In addition, examples of Conto Oil breaching their own variation procedures (especially involving senior Conto Oil personnel) could be useful in presenting Holt's case.

In summary, Holt requires data as this case is likely to turn on the credibility of Holt's claims for variation payments.

1.2 *What would you estimate the interests of Holt Plc to be in this case?*

	Marks
Define interest as a motivator	2
Identify interests as:	
– economic survival	1
– good relations with customers	1
– customization of work opportunities in North Sea	1
– proper authorization of variations to avoid disputes	1
– protection of commercial reputation	1
– timely resolution of dispute	1
	8

Holt has more than one interest in this case. An interest is a motivator that leads the negotiator to prefer one solution over another. For instance, Holt wishes to survive economically as a going concern engaged in profitable business. To this end, Holt requires it to be paid for work it has undertaken, which payment must include compensation for its direct and indirect costs plus some contribution to its annual profit. It also has an interest in maintaining good relations with its customers, and Conto Oil in particular. A failure to resolve this dispute amicably could lead to its exclusion from future work with Conto on its other five North Sea rigs.

The dispute itself has shown that Holt has an interest in ensuring that all variations in work, however occasioned, must be properly authorized and documented, for while it might achieve something satisfactorily in this dispute without formal authority for variations, it could also do so at some expense to its reputation (word soon gets round about these things), or to its relationship with Conto. This interest in proper procedures is joined to its broader interest in protecting its commercial reputation. Any notion that Holt is 'padding its accounts' for undeserved gain could damage it severely in a highly competitive market. How it might meet this interest is open to discussion but it might be possible to negotiate some agreed and workable procedure for the future that could benefit both Conto and Holt.

Holt presumably has an interest in resolving the invoice at the earliest moment. It is fair to assume that Holt has already paid out the personnel element of its costs, which stand at £119 500 or 87 per cent of the invoice, and the material costs at £15 000, or 11 per cent of the invoice. This combined proportion of 88 per cent of the invoice represents Holt's direct costs of working for Conto Oil and currently are a drain on its cash flow. A timely settlement would ease that burden and is plainly in the interests of Holt.

1.3 *What issues and positions can you identify in this case from Holt's point of view?*

	Marks
Define issues as agenda of negotiation	1
Define position as quantitative measure of issue	1
Issues include:	
– future contracts	1
– authorization of variations	1
– payment of invoice	1

Positions include:	
– exact terms of future contracts	1
– detailed procedures for authorizing variations	1
– how much of invoice is to be paid	1
	8

Issues are the agenda of decisions that address the negotiator's interests. To survive economically, the issue of the payment of the invoice has to be settled. How much of the invoice is paid is a position. Presumably, Holt would enter with a position that demands payment in full; its exit point would be determined by circumstances, including how it prioritized the issues to serve its perception of its interests.

Future relationships with Conto Oil in particular, and other major oil companies in general, might create an issue out of future contracts and the terms under which they are accepted. The individual terms constitute an agenda of issues and we would expect that terms relating to authorization of variations would feature in the negotiations. Clearly, whatever the procedures for authorizing variations the current work practices on the platform do not conform to them. This could be, as Holt would argue, because Conto production staff evade procedures that jeopardize production, or as Conto would claim because Holt personnel evade the procedures to pad their invoices. A practical and fully applied procedure for authorizing variations is required that meets both production requirements and protects the contractor from undertaking work for which it is not compensated. The negotiation might centre on this issue, or it could break down in a welter of emotional accusations of cheating, with Holt in a pompous defence of its integrity and Conto hiding behind bureaucratic rules.

Another issue would be the integrity of the data that support Holt's claims and Conto's challenges of them. Conto need to be convinced of Holt's integrity and this requires detailed information of each and every expense; Holt require assurance that in disclosing the data it can convince Conto to make payment. This creates a problem for Conto because in accepting the principle of paying for unauthorized variations it both signals to higher management a failing of its platform managers to operate established procedures and sets precedents for other contractors that Conto is a "soft touch" for variation payments. This issue could be the most significant to come out of the negotiation. Naturally, Conto and its contractors might adopt different positions on the details, with the contractor anxious not to get entangled in too tight a system that builds in avoidable delays while a variation is cleared by Conto management with the contract clock still running towards the scheduled but now impossible completion date. Similarly, Conto must prefer to eliminate uncontrolled variation claims from contractors to avoid spurious claims but would not want to so restrict decision-making by local management that it made the platforms inefficient.

The positions that Holt would take would depend entirely on how it prioritized the issues. A position is subordinate to a negotiator's interests for there is no point taking a firm position on an issue that jeopardized an interest. For example, to demand full payment, irrespective of what the data reveal, might ensure payment but could cause the contractor to be eliminated from future bids. Likewise, to refuse payment of genuine variation claims under the guise of a failure to conform strictly to procedure might cause contractors to refuse any variation even when it was manifestly in Conto's interest to agree to it or to insist on full procedures being carried out even when by doing so Conto's production interests were jeopardized. Managerial time spent in 'cat and mouse' games is always wasted.

1.4 *What would you perceive Conto Oil's interests to be from what you know of the problem?*

Conto's interests include	*Marks*
– establishing current integrity of variation procedures	2
– financial consequences of current and future procedures	2
– professional competence of Conto's purchasing managers	2
– continuous and safe production	2
	8

Conto has an interest in establishing just how leaky is its current variation procedure as applied by local platform managers (though whether its negotiators spot this is another matter) and this should lead it to welcome the side-effect of the Holt negotiation in that it provides a detailed case history of the failure of its procedures in a specific instance. If Conto see benefit in pursuing the truth and can refrain from only wanting to punish a contractor for technical breaches of procedures it could find itself with the basis of a workable and leak-proof authorization procedure for variations.

There are financial interests of Conto to be considered. Contract procedures require careful budgeting of maintenance work, which is one of the reasons for the use of a tendering system. Having accepted Holt's bid against stiff competition, Conto's contract managers would not want to see a rise in the cost of the work in case this reflected on their purchasing abilities. The managers would feel threatened if they allowed contractors to up their prices against their bids. Indeed, many companies judge the performance of their purchasing managers entirely on their ability to secure lower prices than those budgeted. Containing costs is an important element of a manager's job and the Holt invoice would fall foul of that interest. Suppose, for instance, that the Holt cost overrun coincided with a promotion contest in purchasing? Would not this introduce a new, though personal, interest into the negotiations?

Financial interests are constrained, however, by other interests, such as those of continuous and safe production, which must take precedence over the containment of a contractor's costs for a £1 250 000 job. Failing to secure the safe operation of the flaring boom, for example, could cost many times the £138 000 involved in the Holt cost overrun. This precludes the platform management from adhering to impractical procedures or permitting contractors to insist on the strict terms of their work schedules.

The negotiated settlement would have to take account of these sometimes conflicting interests.

1.5 *What does Holt need to know from the debate phase before it can make a proposal for solving the problem?*

Holt needs to know:	*Marks*
– the basis for Conto rejecting the invoice to identify Conto's interests	1
– is rejection merely bureaucratic legalism?	1
– what does Conto want and why?	1
– do they accept the principle, if not the current invoice amount, that variations should be paid for?	1
– is it a question of substantiating the claim or a fact of outright rejection irrespective of the claim's merits	1
– is it possible to agree that variations should be paid for if they are genuine?	1
– can Conto's concerns about escalating costs be met by agreeing a workable variation procedure for the future?	1
– if Conto recognizes that its current procedures were defective, can this be used to justify payment for Holt's current invoice?	1
	8

Holt needs to know a lot more about the basis of Conto's rejection of the invoice. Is Conto hiding behind a bureaucratic procedure for authorizing variations and taking a purely legalistic stance, or is it rejecting the invoice until it has been convinced by data that the variations, though not strictly authorized, were in fact occasioned by the production requirements of its platform management? In short, Holt negotiators would want to know what interests were motivating Conto's contract staff.

The answers would emerge from questioning Conto's negotiators and listening to their statements and their reactions to Holt's statements and documentation. There would be absolutely no point in formulating a proposal to reduce the invoice before discovering what Conto wanted. Their interests might preclude them wanting to have the invoice reduced if this would expose the local management to criticism from head office that they are not managing their affairs effectively. What they might want instead is assurance (and detailed evidence) that Holt's charges were soundly based. To jump the gun could be disastrous for Holt and its future relationships with Conto.

Holt's negotiators would want to use the debate phase to secure agreement with Conto that genuine variations in contracted work are legitimate claims for payment. The question comes down to whether a formally authorized variation is the sole criterion for payment independent of whether the actual variation was genuine or not. If the Conto principle was that it cannot allow unauthorized variations to be paid because this would expose it to abuse by contractors, Holt could shift the focus to whether the current procedures for authorizing variations met Conto's production needs and gave contractors an incentive to co-operate with the platform management. It could be that the details of the case would help to convince Conto that its procedures required amendment to secure both these objectives. From here Holt could make proposals on the authorization procedures, and on the basis that Conto recognized that changes were necessary, Holt could justly claim payments for work done which was not authorized under what is agreed to have been an inadequate procedure.

Model Answers to the Essay Questions

2.1 *What alternative methods does a manager have when a decision has to be made?*

	Marks
Recognition of range of decisive options	1
No method superior to another – each depends on circumstances	1
For explanation of the following:	
– Persuasion	2
– Coercion	2
– Give in	2
– 'No'	2
– Postpone	2
– Chance	2
– Arbitration	2
– Problem-solving	2
– Negotiation	2
	20

The manager has several options, each of which involves a different method of making the decision. He selects the method appropriate to the circumstances, sometimes unconsciously and by experience and sometimes after consideration of the people involved in the decision, the people affected by it, the urgency of the decision, and the relative costs and benefits of different methods in respect of the outcome.

No particular method is superior to any other; each method is appropriate to different circumstances and to different considerations of these circumstances. Given that different managers might consider different aspects of the circumstances to be important to their interests, it is likely that more than one method may be attempted, either sequentially by a manager or simultaneously by different managers. In the absence of a source of overall authority, the decision-making process could shift between different methods during the course of a meeting and managers wishing to influence the outcome should consider this possibility when making any remarks.

Managers could try persuasion to reach a decision that they favour. This has the advantage that it only costs an articulation of either good sense or sympathy. If the person is persuadable by virtue of a willingness to decide on the basis of reason or emotion, the use of persuasion is a sound technique. Most of the techniques of selling are based on persuasion. Sellers highlight the benefits of using their product, rather than its particular features, because most people are prone to respond to a benefit rather than the technicalities of how the benefit is brought about (unless they are themselves technical experts and they are interested in the features). When managers use persuasion they try to marshall all the good reasons why a decision should be made this or that way; sometimes they overdo the list of good reasons and include less convincing reasons which are weaker and vulnerable to contradiction by other managers who have alternative ideas about the right decision. Managers who have an interest in the outcome are not easily persuaded if the proposed decision affects their interests in what they perceive to be a negative way. Hence, persuasion can lead to a deadlock, and with it, frustration, and because persuasion is based on politeness, rather than fear, the tone of the meeting can change for the worse and managers can slip into threats. Persuasion then is a fragile form of decision-making: when it works it can be good for all concerned; when it does not work it can be destructive.

Coercion is the opposite method to persuasion. Managers who use coercion are generally taking advantage of some overwhelming power they feel they have in the situation that will force the other decision-makers to concede or give in. Coercion can be as simple as a reminder of the consequences of not taking a line of action ('we will miss this one great opportunity') and as risky as a direct and specific threat of the consequences of not agreeing to the decision ('if you do not support me on this issue, you can forget about your career prospects here').

Coercion differs from instruction in that the instructed are not directly threatened with awful consequences of disobedience and they carry out their instructions because that is what they are paid for or have agreed to do. Both the victims of coercion and the instructed give in (say 'yes') but they do so for different reasons: the victims do so because the consequences of saying 'no' are unbearable; the instructed do so because it is their role to accept instructions.

Giving in is a form of decision-making. When we buy goods at their marked prices – set by somebody else – we give in. When we obey the law – perhaps made by people who were long dead before we were born – we give in. We do so because the cost and consequences of saying 'no' by trying to get something off the price, or ignoring the courts, are disproportionate to the benefits we might obtain. To say 'no' might mean doing without the goods that are on sale at a set price or doing without our liberty for transgressing the law. There is an implicit coercion in set prices (and laws) that leads managers to give in.

Where managers are unconvinced of the appropriate decision and when they have time to consider their options, they can decide to postpone their decision. This could permit a more searching examination of the options, in which various factions or proponents of conflicting decisions can marshall evidence, support, or coercion to get their way later, or the time taken to reconsider might permit tempers and passions to cool. Events sometimes move decisions on. A hotly contested managerial dispute over whether to take over a company could wither as an issue if the market turns downwards suddenly and managerial attention is switched to survival.

Where managers are evenly divided between two equivalent options, or there is not all that much at stake, it is possible for the decision to be made by some form of chance mechanism – toss of a coin for example. In more sophisticated versions of chance, managers could develop probability measures to estimate which decision to take dependent upon a comparison of the probability of a particular outcome and its value against the probability of another outcome and its value.

Faced with a definite conflict of choice, in which management is divided on which course to take, the issue would be referred to some form of arbitration. Commercial disputes are often settled by arbitration, providing the parties can agree on an arbitrator and undertake to accept the decision. Industrial relations also use arbitration, though it is open to abuse when one side deliberately fails to agree to a final offer and wants it sent to arbitration to get a 'split the difference' outcome. The system of 'pendulum' arbitration overcomes this abuse; here the arbitrator cannot compromise between the rival claims but most choose one or the other only (or in a modification of this system when dealing with numerous issues, the arbitrator can choose either side's final offer on each issue, thus avoiding an all-or-nothing outcome).

Problem-solving is applicable when the parties to the decision have a high degree of personal and corporate trust between them and they also agree that they all share the problem. In the absence of either of these conditions, the managers would be unable to take advantage of problem-solving techniques. These techniques include an openness to consider, and propose, as many options as possible that are not rejected, no matter who is adversely affected by them, but are considered as suitable for discussion on their merits. It is implicit in problem solving that if somebody in the management team is adversely affected by a proposed outcome to a common problem then that person's problem is shared by the whole group and worked through to an agreed solution.

Negotiation is appropriate where the conditions for it exist. These include the requirement that the decision must be agreed by the parties to the decision. Each side's negotiators have a veto on the proposed outcome. Agreement cannot be imposed. If the negotiators step out of the process to carry out threats, they are attempting to resort to coercion as an alternative to deciding the issue by negotiation or as a means of forcing some movement in the negotiators' most recent positions. Negotiation itself cannot involve coercion because in negotiation the decision is one that the parties volunteer to accept (they can say 'no', and take the consequences – though the experience of the consequences might amend their resolve to continue with a 'no').

Negotiation is distinguished from the alternative methods of decision making by its basis in trade or exchange. Managers exchange things, tangible or intangible, for their common consent to the final outcome. Negotiation is above all a trading exercise. Without something to trade, a manager would be unable to negotiate an outcome acceptable to both, or all, parties. The manager would have to resort to some other method – perhaps persuasion – to achieve his goals.

2.2 *Why is a Red style so common in negotiation?*

	Marks
Identifies two styles: Red and Blue	1
Defines Red style	1
Defines Blue style	1
Describes extent of both styles	1
Describes implication of Prisoner's Dilemma game	4
Explains why people act in Red style to protect themselves or to cheat	4
Explains Negotiation Dilemma in terms of dependence on other negotiators' actions	4
Shows how negotiation deals with Red styles by measured risk taking on Blue style	4
	20

There are two main styles of negotiation, Red and Blue. These can be thought of as the opposite ends of a continuum of styles running from extreme Red – the bombastic, aggressive approach to negotiation – through to its opposite, extreme Blue – the submissive, cringing approach. In between the extremes, there are various shades of Red and Blue, with a Purple hue where the two colours overlap in the middle. Colours are used to designate different approaches in order to avoid any moral overtones implied by words like competitive or collaborative: Red is a sign of danger, indicating a competitive approach; Blue, a more peaceful, cooler style, indicating a co-operative approach.

While for some people their negotiating style reflects their perceptions of business or their personalities, for most people their approach is mainly determined by the situation they find themselves in and by how they perceive themselves vulnerable to potential actions by the other negotiator.

The Red stylist perceives business as a highly competitive contest between himself and everybody else – the prizes go to the toughest not the meekest and from this perception he views every negotiation, or indeed, every decision, as one in which he must push for the largest slice of whatever is going, and be seen to get the largest slice too. This is summed up in the statement that 'more means less': more for me means less for you. He does not seek to share, he seeks to win, and if this is at the expense of the other negotiator, that is just too bad (losers deserve to lose).

The Blue stylist, in contrast, is uncomfortable with the losses that arise from conflict and seeks to avoid clashes of interest disrupting the possibilities of both sides gaining from co-operation. In its extreme form the Blue stylist (like his extreme Red counterpart, though for different reasons) can be hopelessly inadequate as a negotiator because he will give in rather than fight for his own interests and would rather have peace on somebody else's terms than be too confrontational (his Red counterpart would rather fight than compromise).

The moderate Blue stylist sees the virtues and the benefits of collaboration rather than competition with the people with whom he does business (he is no less competitive than the Red stylist with his rivals in business, but unlike the Red stylist he does not see himself in competition with his suppliers or his customers). His approach can be summed up as 'more means more': more for me means more for you. Instead of fighting over a single pie, 'let us see if we can create several pies and share them equitably according to our interests'.

Setting aside the minority of Red or Blue stylists who act because of their personalities, we must explain why people are often driven by the situation to behave in a Red manner, even though they might be clear on the benefits of co-operation and would prefer to be Blue.

Prisoner's Dilemma games have demonstrated that people can adopt a Red rather than a Blue style because their perceptions of the situation force them to act Red, irrespective of their general awareness of the benefits of co-operation. Faced with a choice of co-operation or defection, in circumstances where a player is at risk of a defection by the other player, the rational choice is to defect to protect oneself.

People perceive the game as a competitive contest. There is a risk of 'losing' and a hope (temptation?) of 'winning'. The co-operative choice of both sharing the available gains is seldom attractive enough, because it requires that the players have a basis for mutual trust (which Prisoner's Dilemma games either eliminate by prescribing non-communication between the players or do not make explicit as a goal for them in the briefing). The result for most plays of these games is for one, or both, to defect (play or behave in a Red style), which reinforces the doubts of all the players about the efficacy of trustworthiness (playing or behaving in a Blue style) in such situations.

The games highlight the negotiator's dilemma: 'I do not behave in a Red style because I want to, but because I must.' But by behaving in a Red style for whatever reason, be it motivated by fear of vulnerability to Red play by the other negotiator, or by an attempt to win at the other negotiator's expense, this reinforces the perception of vulnerability felt by the other negotiator, who cannot easily distinguish between the other player's motivations, and, naturally, he comes to the worst conclusion: you set out to cheat me!

It is the vulnerability of the negotiator that promotes Red style behaviour. This behaviour does not necessarily have to be of the Red bombastic and aggressive type. Red styles encompass all kinds of behaviours well short of such extreme examples of the style. Any signs of unwillingness to trust the other negotiator can have elements of the Red style, either explicitly or implicitly, in them. For example, the negotiator must assume that other negotiators have Entry positions that are different from their Exit positions; in short, that they have padded their demands or shaved their offers. The degree to which the negotiator believes the respective Entry positions are unrepresentative of the other negotiator's Exit positions will influence the tone by which he or she reacts to hearing them. If they believe that they are totally unrepresentative, it is likely that they will use abrasive language in challenging them, which encompasses Red style manners and provokes Red style responses.

Moreover, the negotiator who has presented what is in fact an Entry position close to his Exit position and who receives a Red response has no way of knowing whether the apparently Red response is caused by the other negotiator's genuine belief that there is more padding or shaving than there is, or whether such behaviour is part of his normal (Red) tactics with everybody. Is this a mistaken perception or a tactical ploy? To avoid the dilemma of not knowing what the other negotiator is up to, the negotiator can open with a padded or shaved Entry position and see what sort of reaction he gets. If it is Red he has negotiating room; if it is Blue he has lost nothing (perhaps he has made a Red gain as well). Thus negotiators tend to open Red because they expect the other negotiator to do so too, or they expect them to react in a Red way to any Entry position – so they get their retaliation in first. However, by opening in such a way, the negotiator risks that his padded or shaved Entry position, because it is unrealistic, will drive a Blue style negotiator into a Red reaction.

The Prisoner's Dilemma games are one-off, all or nothing, outcomes. Negotiation seldom requires such a sudden-death decision. Nevertheless, negotiators face the dilemma of trust because they do not have a reliable mechanism for knowing exactly what the other negotiator is up to ('is he exploiting me?' – a Blue concern – or 'is he exploitable by me?' – a Red motivation). The situation leads commonly to some degree of Red style behaviour, and this can escalate into a vicious circle of destructive argument, leading to deadlock, or to a distributive bargaining contest over the division of a single pie, leading to a less than open stance by both negotiators, which reduces the possibilities from a more open Blue style and a mutually beneficial trade-off between different shares of different pies.

2.3 *Which are the common and which the distinguishing characteristics of proposals and bargains?*

	Marks
Defines proposal as a tentative suggestion	2
Can only negotiate proposals	2
Shows difference between a signal and a proposal	2
Identifies two components of proposal as condition and offer	2
Shows condition as non-specific or specific and offer as always non-specific in a proposal	2
Identifies assertive format of proposal as If – Then	2
Defines bargain as a solution	2
Identifies components of bargain as a condition and offer	2
Shows difference between proposal and bargain as specific condition and specific offer	2
	20

A **proposal** is any form of tentative statement that makes a suggestion about how to proceed during the negotiation, or which indicates what might be a solution to an issue under discussion. The key adjective is **tentative**. Proposals are not explicit solutions and cannot sensibly be treated as such. They crop up all the time, from the proposal on the order of an agenda – 'lets deal with the accident rate first and then with warehouse thefts' – to an outline of a solution –- 'if you pay for safety training we could **consider** accepting random inspections at the warehouse gates.'

Debates, and their components, cannot be negotiated. We can only negotiate proposals, which are remedies or solutions to whatever we are debating. It is not possible to offer an explicit solution to a problem and to expect it to be accepted without debate or amendment in those circumstances where a negotiation is the appropriate method of reaching a decision (i.e the parties to the debate require each other's consent if a solution – an agreement – is to be implemented). If one party's solution must be implemented then it is not a negotiation. Therefore, negotiators explore possible solutions – naturally proposing their own preferred solutions when it is appropriate to do so – and also they explore the possibility of a solution that is different from the ones first proposed by the other negotiator, and they consider, and reconsider, how to amend their own preferred solution to make it more acceptable to the other party.

Proposals are tentative because it is never clear what is actually acceptable to the other negotiator, if only because each negotiator attempts to present his or her own solution as the basis for agreement. Starting off with two solutions to the same problem – one from each negotiator – they move towards finding out if there is a common solution.

A **signal** is the most tentative of indicators that a solution is possible which is different from whatever has been suggested or indicated to that point (including the case where what has been indicated is a total opposition to any solution). Signals are the antechamber of the proposal phase of the negotiation. If responded to positively they can lead to a tentative proposal; if rejected, they usually lead back to the debate phase.

Proposals consist of two parts: the **condition** and the **offer** (note that offers without conditions are not proposals, they are give-aways). In the proposal phase, the condition can either be specific or non-specific but the offer is always non-specific. For example a proposal could take either of these forms:

> 'If you were to show some flexibility on weekend coverage, then we could consider some improvement on shift premiums.'

or

> 'If you accept our contingency profit scheme, then we could consider reducing the qualifying payback period of the loan.'

In the first example, the condition is non-specific ('show some flexibility') and so is the offer ('we could consider'); in the second example, the condition is specific ('accept our contingency profit scheme') but the offer is non-specific ('we could consider'). Note, however, that both are linked in the assertive format of 'If you – then I' which places the condition first and follows with the offer.

The proposal can be presented in as tentative a form as is suitable for the occasion. A negotiator could use words such as 'Supposing that . . .'; 'Just for arguments sake . . .'; and 'What if . . .?' Clearly the more tentative the proposal the more exploratory is the need of the moment, particularly if the negotiator is trying to move the focus of discussion from a difficult and tense mood towards a more flexible stance by both sides.

As the negotiation moves from debate towards solutions, as each negotiator acquires a clearer understanding of the other's interests and flexibilities on issues and positions, the proposal phase is likely to see a firming up in the conditions attached to each proposal, though there should be an element of non-specificity remaining in the offer. By presenting alternative or complementary proposals, or blends of the two, the negotiators are repackaging their solutions to take account of each other's interests and inhibitions.

At some point, one of the negotiators, or both together, will recognize the outlines of a solution that should be acceptable to each side, at least in general terms if not yet in detail. The proposal phase slides into the bargaining phase and the format of the proposal changes.

A **bargain** keeps to the assertive format of 'If you – then I' (or its equivalent words) but shifts from being non-specific to specific. For example, a bargain would take the form of:

> 'If you pay our legal costs, then we will accept your price of £3.5 million.'

The specific condition, 'pay our legal costs', is the price of the specific offer, 'accept your price'. Bargains are always specific in both the condition and the offer. They are final, in the sense that if the other negotiator says 'yes', then there is an agreement; if he says 'no' they go back to debate, perhaps to be followed by an amended bargain. A bargain, if accepted, closes the negotiation. The parties need only to write up the deal and to arrange its implementation.

In the case of a proposal, a negotiator who accepts the proposal and says 'yes' has some work left to do, because while the condition might be specific or unspecific, the offer is not yet and the least that requires to be done is for the negotiator to establish what is meant by the unspecific offer. For example, a negotiator would want to know what is meant by 'show some flexibility' (an unspecific condition) and what is meant by 'some improvement' (an unspecific offer) in the following proposal:

> 'If you were to show some flexibility on weekend coverage, then we could consider some improvement on shift premiums.'

He or she would want to know what is meant by 'consider reducing' (an unspecific offer) in the following proposal:

> 'If you accept our contingency profit scheme, then we could consider reducing the qualifying payback period of the loan.'

Saying 'no' to a proposal leads both back to debate, as does saying 'yes' (asking questions to what is meant by a condition or an offer returns the negotiation to the debate phase).

In the bargain phase, the terms of the bargain are specific. Saying 'no' must return the negotiators to the debate phase, making a statement about why the bargain is unacceptable returns them to the debate phase, while proposing an alternative bargain keeps them in or returns them to the Bargain phase. Saying 'yes' closes the negotiation, at least on that issue.

A proposal is a tentative solution which requires more work; a bargain is a specific solution which can decide the outcome. They both, however, must be presented assertively (If –Then).

PRACTICE FINAL EXAMINATION 2

Case Study

Twelve months ago, a bank negotiated with a mail order firm an arrangement that provided free banking services in exchange for the client firm maintaining a credit balance in its account of a minimum of \$400 000. Due to a change in local management, the firm's account was not monitored as closely as it should have been and the new manager has noted that in the past quarter the account has not been maintained at \$400 000 but has fluctuated below that and is currently as low as \$100 000. At the same time activity in the account has increased from an average of 6 000 cheques per week passing through the account (average amount per cheque is \$80) to 9 000 a week.

Using the client firm's credit balances earns income to the bank, which usually more than pays for the firm's use of the bank's facilities. On the original arrangement the bank made a small profit. With the drop in credit balances (presumably to finance expansion in the client firm's business), the income earned by the bank has fallen below the cost to the bank of the facilities it provides to the client firm. For the last quarter, the bank estimates it is losing \$12 000 on this account, i.e. it is costing it \$12 000 more than it can earn from using the \$100 000 credit balance in financial markets.

The bank manager has several options available, not all of them compatible, and he must decide quickly what he is to propose as he has a meeting with the client in two hours to renegotiate the agreement. Among these options he could:

(a) Abandon the free banking approach (linked to the maintenance of a fixed amount in the client firm's account) and pay interest on the firm's credit balance at the usual rates and charge the firm for actual use of banking services; consisting of at least $12 000 per quarter plus an amount up to a profit of $6000 a quarter, i.e. up to $18 000 a quarter.

(b) Maintain the free banking approach with some form of financial charge on the client firm to reflect the size of the actual credit balances it maintains, if they fall below an agreed minimum, and charge for its use of banking facilities if they rise above the current levels of 9 000 a week.

The manager also faces the issues of the bank's own failure to monitor the original agreement and what to charge the firm for the bank's losses in the most recent quarter.

1. ***Define the bank's interests in this case.*** **(8 marks)**

An interest is a motive in wanting a specific outcome in a negotiation. An interest is why the negotiator wishes to achieve certain wants by negotiation. The wants are expressed by the issues and positions adopted by the negotiator.

The main interest of the bank in this case is to maintain a profitable income from the account. The bank was making money on the account before the client defaulted on the agreed arrangements (which the bank failed to monitor).

A second interest of the bank is to maintain its professional credibility. The bank had an agreement with the client and will have to change it from a position of relative weakness. The bank has an interest in maintaining good customer relations. By negotiating a just settlement with this account, the bank stands to enjoy a profitable relationship with this customer in future. A poorly handled negotiation could cost the bank this account.

The bank's interests are, therefore, to:

(a) make a profit from conducting business with its client;
(b) introduce a workable monitoring system to avoid potentially damaging disputes with clients;
(c) conduct its affairs with professional integrity;
(d) assist clients to become profitable and to maintain sound financial arrangements.

2. ***How would you prioritise the negotiable issues from the client firm's point of view?*** **(8 marks)**

Negotiable issues make up the agenda of the negotiation. They are the main points of the negotiation that both parties must jointly decide upon. The NEGOTEK® Preparation Planner is a useful tool when prioritising issues. The planner breaks the issues down into HIGH, MEDIUM and LOW. A HIGH priority is an issue that must be achieved or almost certainly you will decline to reach an agreement. A MEDIUM priority is important, but not so important that you would walk away from an agreement. A LOW priority is important in that it may have some value in a trade with the other party but you would be unlikely to fail to agree if you could not achieve it. It is important not to rank something as of HIGH priority if it is not crucial enough to you to be a 'deal breaker'.

(NB: The method of prioritising that is demonstrated in the answer is more important than the specific contents. Views will vary and differing contents are acceptable. What follows is one version. Students must demonstrate understanding of the method.)

The priorities from the client's point of view include:

HIGH

- Cost of servicing for amounts over an agreed minimum
- Avoiding compensating the Bank's losses in the previous quarter

MEDIUM

- Size of credit balance to be maintained
- Level of service
- Number of cheques per week before higher charges are triggered

LOW

- Interest earned on credit balances

Cost of services is categorised as of HIGH priority because the client firm's main interest is low cost banking. If the bank charges too much for the level of services provided, then the client might move to another bank if it has lower costs.

The bank's losses on a previous quarter is a high priority because the company does not feel it should pay for a bank monitoring error. They agree they should have known they were slipping on the agreed £400 000. However, the bank should have monitored the situation better; it is more a matter of principle than money (or a plausible excuse to avoid extra costs).

The medium rankings are related to the level of service the bank is providing. It is important to the client, but not as important as the cost of these services. The reason for this is there are many banks that can supply the same level of service and by switching banks the service to customers would not be altered in such a way as to prove detrimental to the client.

3. ***Which of the two options might be more acceptable to the client firm?*** **(8 marks)**

Because the high priority is to keep the cost of bank service at a minimum, the agreed option that will achieve this is Option 2. The client and the bank need to agree on the minimum balance and the number of cheques written without triggering higher charges. If the client agrees on a minimum level of balance, it is because they believe they can maintain that level. If they agree to a number of cheques it is because they believe they can achieve that level. If they maintain these levels then they will have their free banking (the foregone interest on their credit balances contributing to the bank's costs of servicing their account). The first option would charge them a minimum of \$12 000 per quarter and could go as high as \$18 000. For this reason alone, number 2 is attractive. The client should try to negotiate some flexibility into the contract. If the client were to grow substantially, then they might be in danger of higher bank fees or of having to maintain higher credit balances. This flexibility would allow them to alter the agreement so they are not tied in.

(NB: A discussion putting a contrary view in favour of Option 1 is acceptable providing it is argued credibly by relating the answer to the client's interests.)

4. ***How would you prioritise the negotiable issues from the bank's point of view?*** **(8 marks)**

(NB: If the description of the prioritising of the negotiable issues is outlined in Question 2 it need not be repeated here.)

The prioritised negotiable issues from the bank's point of view would be as follows:

HIGH

- Minimum credit balance

MEDIUM

- Interest paid on credit balances
- Level of services provided
- Cost of services for amounts over agreed minimum number of cheques

LOW

- Number of cheques per week
- Bank's loss in previous quarter

The minimum credit balance is ranked of HIGH priority. It is the balance that determines how much money the bank can make on the financial markets, which is one of the bank's main interests in the case. This income nets against the cost of providing the client with banking services. If too low (as is now the case) the bank loses from servicing this account.

The bank's loss in the previous quarter is of LOW priority. Although it would be nice to recover this money, it is not of high priority. Because one of the bank's interests is to maintain customer relations and credibility, an attempt to force recovery of these losses might provoke the client to walk away to another bank for similar services which would not, of course, make an issue about recovering this bank's losses.

5. ***Select one of the options available to the bank and produce Entry and Exit proposals to meet bank profit objectives.*** **(8 marks)**
(Total of 40 marks)

Entry Proposals are opening offers, while Exit Proposals are the position at which the bank would prefer to withdraw from the negotiation (as things currently stand).

For an agreement to be made, it is important for the Exit points of both parties to overlap, or at least meet. This is the negotiators' settlement range and it produces the negotiators' surplus. It is this surplus that the bank and the client in effect will distribute between themselves. In negotiations one does not know where the other's exit point is.

Staying with the second option, the bank's entry and exit proposals could be as follows:

	Issue	*Entry*	*Exit*
1	Minimum balance	400 000	100 000
2	Banks loss on previous quarter	12 000	0
3	Interest paid on credit balances to client	2%	what could be earned
4	Level of service provided	minimal	high standard
5	Cost of services	5p per cheque	15p per cheque
6	Number of cheques per week	9 000	12 000

(NB: A similar statement covering Option 1 is acceptable – the main point is the demonstration of what Entry and Exit points are plus a credible example from the case.)

Essay Questions

1. ***How should negotiators prepare for a negotiation?*** **(20 marks)**

Preparation is absolutely essential if we are to gain an optimal outcome.

Preparation ensures that:

- Wasted time and effort are minimised.
- We approach negotiation with confidence through our command of the detail. This has a psychological effect on the other party.
- We put forward credible arguments because we have based them on well-researched data.
- We have prepared for most things that the other negotiator may raise (though always expect surprises).
- We have an idea on the likely issues and positions to be raised by the other party, their interests, and their entry positions.

When preparing, follow these steps:

Step 1
Collect and analyse data relevant to our case. Data may be qualitative or quantitative, and should be objective and factual.

In this situation, an element of trust may be built as the other negotiator sees us as reliable and honest.

Step 2
We must establish what our interests are, and focus on them during negotiation. By doing this we will ensure that we make positive steps towards our interests and that we are not distracted by peripheral arguments.

Step 3
We must identify the issues, and our desired positions on these issues, to meet our objectives/interests.

The acid test of an issue is how important it is to the other party (to allow linkage of tradables).

Step 4
Prioritise the tradables (issues and position).

In negotiation, movement is essential. In single issue negotiation it is often difficult to obtain movement if we focus exclusively on one issue/position.

However, with multi-issue negotiations we are able to obtain movement by linking tradables and switching between different issues and positions.

The NEGOTEK® Preparation Planner, although devised for complex negotiations, can also be used in more simple circumstances.

Issues are identified and prioritised as HIGH, MEDIUM and LOW.

We must determine our entry/exit points and assess likely prioritised issues for the other party, as well as their anticipated entry points (the other party's exit points are unlikely to be known).

Party 1 *ISSUES*	Party 1 *ENTRY*	Party 1 *EXIT*	Party 2 *ENTRY*	Party 2 *ISSUES*
HIGH				HIGH
X	1 per week	2 per week	2 per week	A
Y	6 per week	8 per week	7 per week	B
Z	5 per week	10 per week	8 per week	X
MEDIUM				MEDIUM
A	11 per week	15 per week	12 per week	Y
LOW				LOW
B	10 per week	19 per week	16 per week	Z

Step 5
In Step 5 we briefly demonstrate the NEGOTEK® Preparation Planner.

Step 6
Anticipate as much as we can about the other party:

- their interests;
- likely issues which they will raise;
- likely positions on issues (entry points);
- the character of the negotiator (red or blue stylist);
- past negotiation experiences with this negotiator;
- reputation.

Although step six is very much based on estimation, we seek to have some idea of the other negotiator's strategy – we can amend once more information is available.

2. ***What are the main features of the Karass tactical ploy approach?*** **(20 marks)**

Dr Chester Karass advocated tactical or, more correctly, manipulative negotiation. He published a book in which over 200 tactics for differing situations were detailed.

The tactical ploy approach suggests that there is always a winner and a loser – it is very much a Red Style approach (competitive "more for me means less for you" type approach). This style lends itself to short-term, quick win, situations and is not ideal to form long-term relationships and trust.

However, it is important that we are aware of these tactics as a ploy identified is a ploy disarmed.

Many negotiators are attracted to this tactical approach because they feel it gives them an immediate practical, 'streetwise' knowledge.

Some of Karass's more common ploys are:

BOGEY

Where we persuade the seller that we love his product but do not have the budget to buy.

Karass argues that "how can someone be angry with you when you love his product?"

The seller may open up to us on his pricing structure providing valuable information.

The bogey can be combated/tested by:

1. Offering a cheaper version of the product.
2. Offering to examine the buyer's budget.
3. Asking to speak with the person who controls the budget.

NIBBLE

Where we do not go for the whole deal, but a smaller part of it.

Again, a destructive ploy as it involves sending overnumbered orders, providing inferior products, delaying orders, delaying bill payments, etc. This is a controversial ploy which raises ethical issues.

KRUNCH

Where we ask the question: "Is that the best you can do?"

Karass argues that there is always some padding in prices. The danger is that sellers will always pad their prices in anticipation of a Krunch ploy.

Tactical ploys rely on bluffs, counter-bluffs, deceit and coercion. To this end they are not really suitable for progressing negotiations so that both parties maximise their benefits.

A knowledge of tactical ploys is not sufficient without knowing more about the 'game of negotiating' as a whole – just like knowing the various clubs and what they are used for in golf does not make a successful golfer.

3. ***What are the significant differences between a proposal and a bargain?*** **(20 marks)**
(Total of 60 marks)

Although bargaining follows on from proposals, it is essential to note that **A PROPOSAL IS NOT A BARGAIN.**

A proposal is a tentative suggestion which highlights a possible way forward in a negotiation.

A bargain is a possible conclusion to the negotiation.

Both proposals and bargains are structured in the following manner:

CONDITION + OFFER
(IF .... THEN ....)

However, the fundamental differences are as follows:

	CONDITION	OFFER
PROPOSAL	Non-specific or specific	Always non specific
BARGAIN	Always specific	Always specific

Some examples can be detailed to illustrate the above.

(a) If you raise volumes, then we will look at your commission again.

NON-SPECIFIC CONDITION + NON-SPECIFIC OFFER = PROPOSAL

(b) If you raise volumes to 5%, then we will look at a commission again.

SPECIFIC CONDITION + NON-SPECIFIC OFFER = PROPOSAL

(c) If you raise volumes to 5%, then we will raise your commission to 10%.

SPECIFIC CONDITION + SPECIFIC OFFER = BARGAIN

Proposals are tentative suggestions. By their nature they are non-committal in the offer.

Bargains are specific proposals, and we must therefore be specific with our wording because they commit us to a specific solution which, if accepted by the other negotiator, close the negotiation with an agreement.

To be effective, both proposals and bargains should be phrased in the format of *CONDITION + OFFER.*

Early in a negotiation, the negotiators make frequent tentative proposals. As the negotiation progresses these become firmer and firmer, until the negotiation slides into the bargaining phase where offers become much more specific.

Proposals are likely to invite further questions and debate whereas bargains tend to focus on conclusion (proposals invite 'open' answers, whereas bargains invite 'closed' answers).

PRACTICE FINAL EXAMINATION 3

Case Studies

Question 1

Read the following Case Study and answer the questions below.

Michel Satran is an electronic engineer who has developed from his own resources a completely new processor for mini-computers. From a technical point of view the processor is a long way ahead of anything in production and, also, anything in progress by the major players in this market, who are sticking with refining existing technology. What Satran does not have is capital to turn his prototype into a mass product for the market.

Satran has been turned down by the usual sources of banking funds (they are very risk-averse having made major losses during the recession and through defaulting Third World debtors). He is now engaged in negotiations with Rich Investment Bank (Jersey) Ltd. who see the potential for the new processor as balancing the undoubted risks, and who are willing to advance the necessary finding (US$ 15 million) if they can secure their investment. They have suggested that they hold a majority share of the equity of Satran's company. They have asserted that they are only interested in making a profit from their involvement and have no long term plans to maintain their holding.

Satran plans to exploit his invention, possibly by licensing it to one or two of the major producers of computers with, perhaps, some in-house production in France and joint ventures with Far East manufacturers. Satran is considering the proposal to give to Rich Investment Bank a majority of his company's equity, because he is desperate to gain access to funding. He is convinced that once the new processor is adopted as standard it will produce millions of dollars profit for all concerned.

M Satran has asked you, as a consultant negotiator, to assist in the negotiations to find a way to secure the funding and protect his and Rich Investment Bank's legitimate interests. He is also interested in any general advice you can give in forthcoming negotiations.

1. ***Where is Satran vulnerable in the proposal from Rich Investment Bank (Jersey) Ltd?*** **(8 marks)**

Satran is in the weaker negotiating position because his options are few. He has a potential winner but has no capital to develop and produce it; the Bank has capital and numerous options to place its funds. Therefore the Bank proposes to secure its investment by majority ownership of Satran's company. True, it claims only to have limited objectives, largely confined to making a profit, and not to maintaining their holdings.

Satran is vulnerable because without control of his company he cannot enforce a limited duration for the Bank's involvement. The Bank could change its mind and stay in control, thus taking the larger share of future profits. They could interfere in the marketing and future development of Satran's product, such as turning to profit churning through licensing – with the attendant risks of technological leakages to rivals – or they could enforce a decision to sell Satran's technology and patents to a major player for short-term cash, cutting out any longer term intentions that Satran might have about staying in the business.

The Bank could tire of the technology and sell out to a third party without considering Satran's interests, which party could fall out with Satran and marginalise his involvement.

In summary Satran needs to maintain control of his company or have in place a mechanism for ensuring that he can take control back from the Bank should circumstances arise to make this advisable.

2. ***What are Satran's longer term interests?*** **(8 marks)**

Interests are the reasons why a negotiator wants something. They are the motivators, the concerns or the benefits and drawbacks that arise from agreeing to certain positions on the negotiable issues.

Satran's longer term interests are to ensure his ownership of future income streams arising from the commercial exploitation of his invention, to protect his patents and rights in the product so that he can continue to develop them commercially, and to protect his reputation as the person who changed the technology of a key industry.

Whatever he agrees to now will affect the future. A careless agreement could jeopardise his longer term interests. Hence he should identify them in order to take account of them in the negotiations.

The computer industry, however, is open to rapid technological change and his short-term interest is to get an early agreement to establish his product before somebody else discovers and exploits the same technology. He needs control of his company – or some mechanism for establishing it – to ensure his future interests but short-term pressures could force him to compromise in the area and thus deny him his longer-term interests.

3. ***What proposal could you suggest to reconcile Satran's and Rich Investment Bank (Jersey) Ltd's interests?*** **(8 marks)**

Satran needs to test the Bank's intentions and his proposal should accomplish this objective. He could set out a formula that takes his and the Bank's interests into account. How they react to it would test their intentions.

Satran's proposal could include the following elements:

(a) A division of the equity starting with a majority (ratio to be decided) held by the Bank and gradually shifting (time table to be decided) to a majority owned by Satran as the Bank's initial investment is reduced from Satran's share of the profit stream from sales, royalties, and general income from the exploitation of the product.

(b) Commitment that initial profits would be used to earn-out the Bank's shares with an option for Satran at any time during the agreement to buy-out the Bank for a sum, such as some multiple of the profits.

(c) All development, production, licensing and joint venture decisions to be taken by Satran.

(d) Satran to have first option to buy the Bank's equity, at the lesser of the price established by some multiple of the profits or the price offered by the third party, should the Bank want to sell to a third party.

4. ***What are the basic elements of an agreement that he should consider when deciding whether to license his product?*** **(8 marks)**

Licensing is an alternative to establishing one's own manufacturing operations in the other territory or to exporting to that territory. The relative costs of each method of commercially exploiting his product needs to be considered. Exporting directly or through agents is the simplest consideration; setting up wholly owned manufacturing is more risky. Licensing a local manufacturer is also risky if Satran loses control but less costly to Satran if it works. If the balance favours licensing, Satran should consider some of the following:

(a) Protection of his intellectual property rights, including local patents, in the product and future derivatives.
(b) Protection of his technology.
(c) Strictly and exactly what he is licensing to avoid doubts about future developments.
(d) The division between himself and the licensee of the net revenue from sales in the defined territory.
(e) What share of the costs are the responsibility of each party.
(f) How much of the development costs Satran can recover from the licensee.
(g) The conditions under which the licence can be terminated.
(h) Should exports to third countries by the licensee be permitted and if so under what conditions?

5. ***What kind of BATNA could Satran develop to strengthen him in his negotiations?***

(8 marks)
(Total of 40 marks)

BATNA means the Best Alternative to a Negotiated Agreement and was introduced as such by Fisher & Ury in *Getting to YES*. Economists call it the opportunity cost. Briefly, it defines the negotiator's alternative option to agreeing to the present terms for agreement offered by the other party. BATNAs provide data on the 'walk-away' or 'take-it' positions open to the negotiator. They strengthen the negotiator to the extent that the BATNA is credible to the other party; they underscore the weakness if there is no BATNA at least as good as the current deal on offer.

Satran is relatively weak in negotiations with the Bank. Time spent considering – or developing – an alternative to accepting these terms could strengthen his negotiating position. For instance, if he can establish a better offer from a major player to buy up his invention he might be able to improve the Bank's offer into his favour because the Bank would not want to be cut out from the profits from his invention. However, if the best alternative offer is worse than that offered by the Bank he will have to seriously consider accepting the Bank's offer, albeit after he makes a considerable effort to improve its terms.

In negotiating with potential licensees Satran can improve his position by developing a strong BATNA, such as better terms from rivals to the licensee, or fully costing the alternative of local manufacturing.

Possibilities for Satran's BATNA include: offers from other Jersey type banks; funding from public bodies (the European Union's various R&D schemes, for example); possible joint ventures with major players or manufacturers; and selling out to somebody else.

Question 2

1. ***How does the negotiator's surplus assist in understanding the dynamics of a negotiation?* (20 marks)**

Negotiation implies movement because unless the negotiators move from their opening or entry positions, they cannot reach agreement (unless their entry points coincide!). The gap between the negotiators' entry points is the negotiation range.

That they are prepared to move does not mean they are prepared to move indefinitely. The implication is that they are prepared to move up to a point. Further movement beyond this point – their exit point – is precluded in the existing circumstances.

The negotiators' exit points determine whether a negotiated outcome is likely. The exit points may not meet, in which case there is a gap. The most the buyer will pay is less than the least the seller will accept. In this case, unless one or both move their exit points an agreement will not occur.

For agreement, the exit points must at least meet. The least the seller is willing to accept must equal the most the buyer is willing to pay. Most cases where agreement is possible involve the exit points of each negotiator overlapping – the seller is willing to accept a lower price than the most the buyer is willing to pay.

Negotiators do not normally know the exit points of each other. They know their own, of course, but can only guess at the other's exit point. Much of negotiation consists of each negotiator trying to convince the other that they have reached their exit point, though this is seldom true.

The overlap in exit points constitutes the negotiators' surplus. Consider a situation where the seller opens at 5 000 and the buyer at 3 000. The negotiating range consists of 5 000–3 000 which equals 2 000.

Suppose the least the seller would accept (s) is 3 800 and the most the buyer would pay (b) is 4 300, then the negotiator's surplus is 4 300–3 800 which equals 500. Whatever price they agree upon between 3 800 and 4 300, for necessarily the price must be bounded by that range unless somebody moves their exit price, the agreed price will divide the 500 surplus into two parts, i.e. effectively dividing 500 between them.

For example, suppose they agree on a price of 3 900. This is 100 more than the least (3 800) the seller was prepared to accept and 400 less than the buyer was prepared to pay (4 300). The buyer's surplus is 400 and the seller's surplus is 100. Similarly, for any other price between 4 300 and 3 800 (inclusive).

It is possible that the negotiation will result in the buyer being forced to go to his or her exit price of 4 300. In this case the buyer receives zero surplus and the seller captures all 500 of it. Negotiation is about dividing the available surplus, usually under conditions in which neither knows if a surplus is available. Exit points are not disclosed though each gives the impression that their exit is wherever they are at a particular moment.

For an agreement price (p^*) to exist, it is necessary for $s = b$ or $s < b$. When $s > b$, p^* is not possible. Yet negotiations open with the condition that $s > b$. The dynamics of negotiation consist of exploring whether there is a surplus by transforming incompatible prices in the range where $s > b$ into price p^* in the range $s = b$ or $s < b$.

In general, single issue negotiations make the process of finding p* relatively difficult. By increasing the number of tradables in a negotiation, finding p* for each issue is assisted by the negotiators trading between each issue to find an overall p* which consists of larger surpluses on some issues and smaller or zero surpluses on issues such that there is a win–win solution.

2. ***Why does the principle of assertive conditionality enable a negotiator to deal with any of the four Red or Blue negotiating styles?*** **(20 marks)**

Assertive proposal language centres on conditionality, or the IF–THEN format: 'If you do . . . x . . . for me, then I will consider doing . . . Y . . . for you.' While loose proposal language is better than making no proposals at all, assertive proposal language is better all round. Unassertive language can give the wrong signal to the other negotiator, namely that you are not sure of your case, that you are not fully committed to your ordered solutions and that, perhaps, you will retreat if pushed or resisted. What you invite is usually provoked.

Weak unassertive language uses words such as 'like', 'wish', and 'hope'. It often gets the conditionality principle round the wrong way. For example, instead of making a proposal statement (IF you . . . then I . . .) it asks a proposal question: IF I . . . will You? Asking permissions invites a refusal or a conditional acceptance which squeezes out another concession ('Only if you' . . .).

Weak language convinces few negotiators of your seriousness. In negotiations with an aggressive red style negotiator, it can be positively fatal. The red stylist seeks to exploit the weaker negotiator. Weak language gives the image of overall weakness, which encourages anybody with a proclivity for red behaviour to be more red than usual.

The two extremes of style are Red ('more for me means less for you') and Blue ('more for me means more for you'). Between the extremes there is a continuum running through moderate red and moderate blue. Effective negotiators are able to work in the moderate range of red and blue behaviour, sometimes referred to as the purple style. This means they can be assertive but short of aggressive, and accommodating but short of submissive. The use of assertive conditionality ('IF–THEN') is appropriate in dealing with either extreme of red and blue and the moderate ranges between them. The recommended strategy for dealing with red players uses tit-for-tat, which is a purple strategy because the blue player responds with a red play if the red player plays red and with a blue play if and when the red player switches to blue.

The bombastic, aggressive red stylist – usually wanting something for nothing – is unable to intimidate the assertive blue stylist who insists on the principle: 'give me some of what I want and I will give you some of what you want'. The aggressive red cannot get anything from the assertive blue in the same way that he/she gets something for nothing from the submissive blue. The more subtle red stylist – charming, devious, manipulative – also wants something for nothing but he/she cannot ruffle the insistence on assertive conditionality. As the conditionality principle is the basis of all assertive blue proposals, the subtle red stylist is stuck with either revealing their red nature or in accepting that the decision is going to be made only by trading ('IF–THEN').

A normally extreme blue stylist – the submissive, the cringing and the weak – expects little from the negotiation and is usually not disappointed. But assertive blue stylists do not behave differently with submissive types – to do so could be to exploit them in the way a red stylist attempts. By consistently applying the conditionality principle of 'IF–THEN' the submissive is treated no differently. For once they are treated as partners and they are offered something back for what they give in exchange. By showing the submissive how to trade conditionally they also learn how to stand up to the red stylists who normally dominate them.

This leaves the assertive blue negotiator up against another assertive blue negotiator. As both are using the same conditionality principle (IF–THEN) they experience no problems of understanding what each is about. Both expect to get something back for what they give and both formulate their tentative proposals in the same way. Negotiations can proceed to a conclusion without either of them being exploited (though the terms they settle upon can vary).

3. ***How would you apply the main features of the negotiator's preparation planner to a hypothetical negotiation case?*** **(20 marks)**
(Total of 60 marks)

Their preparation planner requires an input of relevant data, collected and analysed by the negotiator. It requires that the negotiator assesses the interests of both parties and identifies the negotiable tradables applicable to the case. On the basis of this work, the preparation planner can be completed, saving the time and energy usually wasted in unstructured preparation.

A hypothetical example can be used to illustrate the process. (NB: Any reasonable example would be suitable here.) Consider the case of the owner of a football club which is in debt to the bank but, excluding the cost of its debts, makes an operating profit. The owner of 75 per cent of the shares wants to sell, and a buyer is willing to buy, if they can agree terms. Suppose you are the buyer.

The buyer's major problem is that with the club in debt to the tune of £3 million and a need to service the debt (£300 000 a year approximately), money paid to buy the shares reduces his ability to cover the debt, because the payment to the majority shareholder takes money out of the club. Hence, he has to find a way of paying for the shares a price acceptable to the owner but structured in such a way as to minimise an immediate cash outflow. The present owner is eager to sell (but not at any price) because the bank is pressing for a reduction in the overdraft debt and he needs the money for other ventures.

The negotiable tradables include the price to be paid for the shares, when and how that money is paid, the question of current owner's personal guarantees to the bank for the debt, and how the new owners will reduce the bank's overdraft.

Prioritising the tradables, you might decide that the price per share, while important, is less important than when payment is made. Thus, when payment is made is of High priority (a walk-away decision), while price per share is of Medium priority (it might be a walk-away position). Keeping the current owner's guarantees in place is more important (medium) than reducing the overdraft (low – unlikely to be a walk-away decision) because the former allows latitude on the latter.

Setting out the negotiable tradables in a planner format produces:

Tradables	*Priority*	*Entry*	*Exit*
Payment timing	H	All of it spread over 10 years	Some now, rest over 7 years
Price per share	M	£1.20	£1.90
Owner's guarantees	M	Maintained for 10 years	Maintained for 3 years
Reducing the overdraft	L	Delayed 3 years	Delayed 12 months

Entry and Exit terms must be set for each tradable. Negotiators decide on their entry points by a judgement as to what is credible to the other negotiator in the circumstances. The entry point must be defensible when challenged. Their exit point is determined on the basis that anything beyond it is unacceptable and could cause a walk away decision depending on the importance of the tradable.

The negotiator aims to spread payments over ten years but recognises that he will probably have to split the payments between so much now and the balance spread over a number of years; how big a split and how long the spread are both negotiable. A 50% split is possible, which, if agreeable would raise the importance of settling the price per share, though it is likely that the negotiator would have to iterate between these two tradables to achieve the acceptable combination. In effect the total price paid for the owner's shares, say £2 million, would produce an immediate income for him of, say, £1 million now and the balance over 8 years of £125 000 per year.

There is also the possibility that you would recognise that what you need is control (51 per cent) and not total ownership, which would reduce the demand for cash now to £500 000, perhaps even paid up on a split basis, assuming the owner could be persuaded to accept such a deal (which depends on how badly he needed cash). If an option to buy the rest of his shares, or some proportion of them, was also agreed, the new owners could meet their main targets and have cash available (£500 000) to lower the overdraft from the bank. By reducing debt charges they increase the likelihood that the operating profit can become a trading profit.

The need on the part of the new owners for the current owner to keep in place his personal guarantees to the bank, at least for some time ahead, puts him in a strong position for which he can trade on other issues. However, his desire – perhaps of high priority – to be relieved of these guarantees to the bank puts the new owners in a stronger position to achieve movement on the price and the payment terms.

Using the preparation planner to set out the negotiation issues in this way assists in the planning of the negotiation and highlights in a structured way how the negotiator might proceed to achieve his or her objectives.

Strategic Information Systems

PRACTICE FINAL EXAMINATION 1 – WITH MCQs

The examination is in 2 sections:
Section A: Multiple Choice Questions. 25 questions each worth 2 marks.
Section B: Case Study. 2 questions each worth 50 marks.
Total marks available for examination = 150
Pass mark: 50% of 150 = 75

Section A: Multiple Choice

Do all 25 questions. Each correct answer receives 2 marks.
An incorrect answer or unanswered question receives 0 marks.
Total marks for Section A = 50 = 33% of total for paper.

1. True or False? The role of IT has changed because of the combined effects of competitive pull and technological push.

2. In which cell on the Strategic Grid would you locate an international management consultancy?

   A Strategic
   B Turnaround
   C Factory
   D Support

3. Which type of information system is described by this statement: The system takes selected information from the financial systems of the organization's subsidiaries and is used by the group chairman to control the finances of the whole group.

   A MIS
   B DSS
   C EIS
   D MSS
   E SIS

4. True or False? The basic functions of IT are conversion, processing, printing and storage.

5. You want to check upon your rivals' financial performances over the last ten years. You go to a business library to carry out a computer search. A personal computer system allows you to search through all annual accounts published in the last ten years. On what medium is the data most likely to be held?

   A Floppy disc
   B Cassette tape
   C CD-ROM

6. A car manufacturer wishes to streamline the exchange of documents between itself and its main suppliers and implements an EDI network. An appraisal report lists the business benefits including:

   I improved accuracy of invoices.
   II improved product design.
   III improved information on deliveries.
   IV reduced stock levels.

   Which of these benefits normally result directly from EDI?

   A I only
   B I and II only
   C I, III and IV only
   D All of I–IV

Questions 7–9 refer to the following situation.

A computer company has produced a small personal computer with appropriate software which is used in the home for a range of services: making travel arrangements, home banking, ordering groceries, etc. When it is plugged into the telephone socket, the user can look through the menu at the services on offer and can choose what he or she wants to do, for example, transfer funds from one account to another. The computer company has signed up the travel agents, banks, retailers, etc., to participate in the system and charges them a fee every time their services are used.

7. To which "Era" of IT application does the system belong?

   A Era 1
   B Era 2
   C Era 3

8. Which cell of the Index matrix best describes the benefits the system is likely to bring to the computer vendor?

   A Process automation
   B Functional enhancement
   C Role expansion
   D Functional re-definition
   E Product innovation

9. Which of the Five Levels of transformation best describes the level at which the computer vendor is operating in respect of this system?

   A Level 1
   B Level 2
   C Level 3
   D Level 4
   E Level 5

10. True or False? An electronics manufacturer has devised software which enables it to design its products to be more sophisticated and more customized. This is an example of "Product Innovation" in the Index matrix.

Questions 11 and 12 refer to the following situation.

A chain of medium-price restaurants has developed a new strategy, an important part of which is to reduce costs by streamlining the ordering of raw materials. Goals relating to this are established, and the chain changes its organizational structure in order to implement the strategy. When this has been done, the IT manager is asked to report on how IT could help achieve the strategic goals.

11. What parts of the overall strategy appear to be in alignment?

 A the business domain
 B the IT domain
 C the external aspects of strategy
 D the internal aspects of strategy

12. What parts of the overall strategy are not likely to be in alignment?

 A the business domain
 B the IT domain
 C the external aspects of strategy
 D the internal aspects of strategy

13. Which of the following evaluation techniques seems most appropriate for a project to computerize a warehouse in order to reduce staff costs?

 A Boundary values
 B Information economics
 C MOMC
 D Return on investment
 E Return on management

14. A retailer of do-it-yourself products uses IT to a very limited extent, but knows it must invest in IS projects because that is what the rest of the industry is doing successfully. However, it finds it difficult to measure the benefits. Which of the following techniques would help it to decide on general expenditure levels?

 A Boundary values
 B Information economics
 C MOMC
 D Return on investment
 E Return on management

15. True or False? The main reason that there does not appear to be a single technique that can handle the evaluation of all IS projects is that the circumstances in which IT investments are made are so different.

Questions 16 to 19 refer to the following situation.

An organization providing health care is an extensive user of IT but its IT projects have all been at Level 1 (localized exploitation). Its latest project is to computerize the information links between the consultants (the experts in the different fields of medicine) and the pathology laboratories (where blood tests are carried out). The system will reproduce the present manual reports in an electronic form. A main justification for the system is that it will speed up the treatment of patients.

16. The feasibility stage of the project is when:

    A a rough estimate of how the system would work and its costs are made.
    B the software is written.
    C the hardware is chosen.
    D the IT department tries out the software for the first time.

17. True or False? The system is low technology relative.

18. Into which cell of the Implementation Risk matrix would you put the system?

    A high tech/low structure
    B high tech/high structure
    C low tech/low structure
    D low tech/high structure

19. What type of project manager is most appropriate?

    A senior health care manager
    B medical consultant
    C inexperienced project manager
    D a project manager with technical expertise

Questions 20–24 refer to the following situation.

The UK division of a worldwide pharmaceutical organization develops, produces and markets products ranging from prescribed drugs, through listed branded products to off-the-shelf items. Manufacturing, management, marketing and registration/licensing take place in different locations in England. Group Head Office, in the USA, exercises tight control over UK activities and dictates IT policy, setting computing standards and recommending the brands of equipment and software that can be bought.

One of the major tasks of the Medical Department is creating the documentation for registering and licensing new drug products. A variety of reports are consolidated, bringing together text, tables, graphics, etc. from the different parts of the company, into one document. This final report, which can run to thousands of pages, is sent to relevant government department in London for approval. The drug cannot be sold until this department has registered and licensed it. This process is lengthy and can take years to be completed.

The existing system was rudimentary involving stand-alone word processors and manual preparation of diagrams. Medical Department staff (qualified medical doctors) wrote reports in longhand and gave them to secretaries working on the word processors. The idea to change came from the UK President who was looking for means to implement the corporate strategy of getting new products to market faster. He wanted a publishing system which could integrate the whole document production process, and include facilities to produce sophisticated tables, charts, graphics, etc. The UK President saw such a system in operation and personally supervised the MIS and Medical Departments as they carried out a joint cost benefit study.

The resulting Justification Report took nine months to complete and included experiments to find how much manpower and paper would be saved. This lengthy procedure did result in the request being approved, with little opposition, and the system was installed. Within six months the planned manpower savings had been achieved. Also, 90% of the medical staff were happily keying in their reports themselves. However, neither the president nor the MIS Department were aware of this when, three years later, the computer vendor carried out an audit of the system.

Answer the following questions 20–24 from the evidence available.

20. How would you describe the link between strategy and IT?

    A there is a link
    B there is no link
    C can't tell

21. How would you rate top management support?

    A good
    B poor
    C mixed
    D can't tell

22. How would you rate the evaluation of IT investments?

    A good
    B poor
    C mixed
    D can't tell

23. How would you rate the way the transition to the new system was handled?

    A good
    B poor
    C mixed
    D can't tell

24. How would you rate the way this IT investment was monitored?

    A good
    B poor
    C mixed
    D can't tell

25. True or False? The emerging view of IT is not as a cost but as an investment.

Section B: Case Study

Answer both questions. Each question will be marked out of 50.
Marks for individual parts of a question are shown in the question.
Total marks for Section B = 100 = 67% of total for paper.

AB is a firm of Chartered Accountants whose main business is carrying out financial audits. However, management consultancy has recently been added, and this is expanding rapidly. There are offices in several locations, including London and Birmingham, but the head office is in Leeds.

AB used to have a central computer department, but because of its growing computer consultancy work, it has become a subsidiary. This group imposes policies relating to the choice of equipment and of software, but it is still possible to make a case for bending the rules. Overall the policy is to standardize on personal computers. There is no long-term plan covering the development of IT usage within the company.

The Administrative Manager wanted a new system to produce the 3 500 annual accounts (75% of the workload of her department), reports relating to consultancy (currently 20% of the workload but increasing) and other documents such as marketing material where high quality output was required. The existing system was a series of stand-alone word processors which had been very successful, but were limited in the range of functions they could tackle. They produced text only and accounts/tables had to be input as if text.

The general process for producing a set of accounts is:

1a. (If the company is a new client.) On receiving a request from an accountant, produce a skeleton set of accounts and forward to the accountant. Dummy accounts are available and they form the template for the skeleton. If the company is very small it may be simpler for the accountant to produce the skeleton in longhand.
1b. (If the company is an existing client.) Retrieve the skeleton from the archives, print and forward to the accountant.
2. The accountant fills in the figures in longhand and returns to the Administrative Manager's department for printing.
3. Four months after the accounts are issued the skeleton is updated ready for the next financial year and archived.

Stage 3 involves some tricky procedures for manipulating accounting documents and any new system would have to be able to handle these efficiently. It would also have to handle other tables and graphics and integrate them with text.

The IT committee (several partners plus IT experts from the computer group) agreed with the Administrative Manager that a new system was needed. However, they also wished to support the computer group policy of standardizing on pc systems for all functions throughout the firm. Accordingly the committee recommended that the Administrative Manager's department be upgraded to a pc system, allowing two years for the change to be made.

The Administrative Manager thought a pc system would be inadequate for the task, since the software available was not particularly suitable for producing accounts, nor for improving presentational quality. She wanted some form of specialized Desk Top Publishing system using sophisticated workstations.

The IT committee continued to press for pc standardization, and also that the Leeds headquarters should take the lead. The Administrative Manager continued to press the view that a pc system was not right for her department, and that the inadequacy of a pc system would result in an explosion in staff numbers.

Eventually a subcommittee was set up to look into the issue. It took the views of a range of people and looked at alternative systems. A Desk Top Publishing system was brought in on trial on the grounds that its manufacturer was that of the existing successful system. This DTP system seemed to dominate others in terms of its ability to produce a table of information and of its user friendliness.

The Administrative Manager then produced a Review Document stating the reasons for acquiring the system. The subcommittee, especially the Director of Finance and the Director of Personnel, became the sponsor of the DTP system, and recommended it to the senior committee of partners. The senior committee approved the DTP system.

Several months later the system was installed and comprised a network of workstations, fileservers and high quality printers. It was used for tables (in accounts and also in reports which may run to over 100 pages and usually have many tables), graphics, maps and logos. Similar systems were eventually installed at other locations with the capability of communicating with AB's offices across the country.

The system also produced semi-glossy booklets, usually financial help for clients. An example is the immediate post-National Budget Day document which is jointly produced by Leeds and London. This has to be finished in time to be on clients' desks at 9 a.m. the next morning. All chartered accounting firms aim to be first on the grounds that a client will only read the first to arrive. The text was input on workstations in London, the artwork and appendices in Leeds. There was continual swopping of files between Leeds and London until the complete document was ready. It could then be transmitted to a variety of locations for printing.

There had long been a problem in that staff in London were more expensive than those elsewhere in the country, particularly Leeds. In addition, staff turnover was much higher in London. The success of the Budget Day operations gave birth to a new method of operating which solved these problems. The basic idea was that work originating in one place no longer had to be completed in that place. In other words, the IT infrastructure made it possible to have documentation carried out where it could be done most cheaply and where there was spare capacity. Information generated as a by-product by the system allowed the organization to know where spare capacity existed. For example, the preparation of a report for consultants working in London could be done by clerical staff in Leeds, at much lower cost. The net result was that staff in London decreased, staff in cheaper locations increased.

(a) (i) Use the Strategic Grid to assess the importance of IT to organization AB.

(ii) Use the Index matrix to categorize the business benefits of the system.

(iii) Use the Five Levels of Transformation graph to pinpoint the transformation level organization AB has reached.

Each part of question (a) carries an equal mark.

(b) Carry out an audit of AB's development of the system described in the case. Assume the objective of the audit is to take stock of the current situation as preparation for constructing an IT strategy. Assume also that the collection of evidence has been carried out, resulting in the information presented in the case. The case does not have sufficient information for a thorough investigation to be undertaken so confine your attention to the pro formas in Figures 1–6. For each topic assess AB's performance as:

Good – where there is evidence of good performance
Poor – where there is evidence of poor performance
Mixed – where the evidence is mixed
Not Applicable – where there is no evidence at all

Auditing IT developments

Strategy

ISSUE	COMMENT
• Top management support	
• Opportunity identification	
• Corporate/IT strategy	
• Strategic alignment	
• IT in the organization	

Figure 1

Auditing IT developments

Planning

ISSUE	COMMENT
• Decision-making	
• Business risks	
• Change management	
• Change manager	

Figure 2

Auditing IT developments

Project management

ISSUE	COMMENT
• Implementation policy	
• On time	
• Within budget	
• Resource balance	
• Who involved	

Figure 3

Auditing IT developments

User involvement

ISSUE	COMMENT
• Liaison	
• Users/project	
• Users/implementation	
• Users/influence	
• Attitudes	

Figure 4

Auditing IT developments

Operations

ISSUE	COMMENT
• Information	
• Users/access	
• Ease of use	
• Hardware	
• Software	

Figure 5

Auditing IT developments

Monitoring

ISSUE	COMMENT
• Ex post evaluation	
• Benefits harvest	
• Use of info	
• Achieved *vs.* expected	
• Problems	
• Potential	

Figure 6

For each topic add a comment indicating the evidence on which you have based your assessment. Since the information available in the case is limited, and since there are often no right or wrong answers, the comments you make will be critical in determining the mark.

Section A: Solutions

1. **True.**
   Both events have influenced the changing role of IT.

2. **D is correct.**
   An international management consultancy will use IT to support its activities but it is unlikely to be dependent upon it hour by hour. Nor is IT one of the 3 or 4 things it must get right if it is to be successful in the future.

3. **C is correct.**
   An EIS is a system holding top level information for use by senior management.

4. **False.**
   The basic functions of IT are conversion, storage, processing and communication.

5. **C is correct.**
   Ten years of all published annual accounts is a lot of data. Of the above storage media, only CD-ROM is likely to have the necessary capacity, and to offer a suitable speed of access.

6. **C is correct.**
   I, III and IV are typical EDI benefits. Improved design of supplies (II) is not a benefit stemming directly from EDI.

7. **C is correct.**
   Essentially the system changes the way people do their banking, shopping, etc., and so is a transformation which belongs to Era 3.

8. **E is correct.**
   The system is a new product for the computer company since it is charging the retailers for participating in the scheme. From the point of view of banks and retailers or the individual home users the system might belong elsewhere, because it brings these groups different types of benefits.

9. **E is correct.**
   The system transforms the business scope of the computer company and gives it a new product. The company is therefore operating at the level of "business scope re-design".

10. **False.**
    This is an example of using IT to improve existing products not to create entirely new ones. It could better be described as "functional re-definition" where the function is that of design.

11. **A is correct.**
Changing the organizational structure is seen as a necessary part of achieving strategic goals. In this regard, therefore, the corporate strategy and the organizational structure, which constitute the business domain, are in alignment.

12. **C is correct.**
The IT manager is only brought into the process after issues to do with the corporate strategy and the organization have been settled. The IT strategy is, therefore, not likely to be in alignment with the business strategy, i.e. the external aspects of strategy are not in alignment.

13. **D is correct.**
Return on Investment is the usual method for evaluating a straightforward project with efficiency benefits. The other techniques listed are generally more appropriate for less well-defined projects.

14. **A is correct.**
The organization has no specific project in mind and so ratios which compare overall expenditure levels with that of its competitors would be a useful guide.

15. **True.**
The main reason it has proved hard to find a single all-purpose evaluation technique is that the whole context in which IT investments are made can differ so widely.

16. **A is correct.**
The feasibility stage is the first step in determining how and whether the project will work. **B** is the programming stage; **C** is the specification stage; **D** is the testing stage.

17. **False.**
The organization is a sophisticated IT user, but has not operated at Level 2 (integration). The consultant/pathology system is likely to involve communication technology with which the organization is not yet familiar, and it may present technical challenges.

18. **B is correct.**
The relative technology of the system is high. The output of the system is an electronic version of the present manual reports and is therefore highly structured.

19. **D is correct.**
The project is in the medium risk category and, because of the high relative technology, requires a project manager with technical expertise. Senior managers and health care consultants will have to have some involvement with the system, but using them as project managers would not be a good use of scarce resources.

20. **A is correct.**
There is a link: the president sought to introduce the new system in response to his strategic objective of getting new products to market sooner.

21. **A is correct.**
The system was the president's idea and he personally supervised the first stages of its introduction.

22. **A is correct.**
The justification report appears to have been thorough and was compiled by users and MIS department jointly.

23. **A is correct.**
Within six months of its first being implemented the system seems to have been working well – to the extent that the professional medical staff were keying in reports themselves.

24. **B is correct.**
Until the computer vendors carried one out, no audit was undertaken. This is reinforced by the fact that both the president and MIS department did not know the extent to which professional medical staff were using the system.

25. **True.**
The emerging view of IT is as a business investment, to promote business benefits such as increased revenue and market share, as well as increased efficiency.

Section B: Solutions

(a) (i) *Use the Strategic Grid to assess the importance of IT to organization AB.*

IT plays a big part in Organization AB's current activities. However, if IT systems failed to operate, fatal damage would not result. AB would be able to continue its work with manual operations for weeks or months, albeit at greater expense and with considerable difficulties. The dependence axis should be assessed as "low".

In the future IT will continue to be important to AB, but it is not likely that IT will be one of the three or four things that AB **must** get right if it is to prosper. The impact axis should be assessed as "low".

The net effect is that AB is in the "Support" cell, as shown in Figure 7.

DEPENDENCE	Low **Impact**	High **Impact**
High	Factory	Strategic
Low	Support **Organization AB**	Turnaround

Figure 7 Strategic grid

(ii) *Use the Index matrix to categorize the business benefits of the system.*

Era I. *Process Automation.* (Function/efficiency cell.) There are benefits here. The greater sophistication of the system should enable tables and diagrams to be produced with fewer clerical staff.

Functional Enhancement. (Function/effectiveness cell.) There are benefits here. The greater sophistication of the system should enable better documents to be produced.

Era II. *Task Mechanization.* (Individual/efficiency cell.)
Work Improvement. (Individual/effectiveness cell.)

The same efficiency/effectiveness benefits at the functional level also apply at the individual level.

Era III. *Role Expansion.* (Individual/transformation cell.) The Administrative Manager's role has expanded, as she now has the vital role of allocating work to offices across the whole country.

Functional Re-definition. (Function/transformation cell.) The system also belongs to this cell, since the process of producing documentation has been transformed.

Boundary Extension. (Organization/efficiency cell.) There is no boundary extension.

Service Enhancement. (Organization/effectiveness cell.) There is a small benefit here, assuming that customers regard the improvement in the presentation quality of their accounts and reports as improved service.

Product Innovation. (Organization/transformation cell.) There is no product innovation.

(iii) *Use the Five levels of Transformation graph to pinpoint the transformation level organisation AB has reached.*

Basically, the system is at Level 1 – a localized exploitation of the document producing system, aiming at improved efficiency and effectiveness. However, the later development of using the system to move work from one part of the country, according to the availability of resources, involves a re-design of a management process. It is therefore at Level 3.

(b) *Carry out an audit of AB's development of the system described in the case. Assume the objective of the audit is to take stock of the current situation as preparation for constructing an IT strategy. Assume also that the collection of evidence has been carried out, resulting in the information presented in the case. The case does not have sufficient information for a thorough investigation to be undertaken so confine your attention to the pro formas in Figures 1–6. For each topic assess AB's performance as:*

Good *– where there is evidence of good performance.*
Poor *– where there is evidence of poor performance.*
Mixed *– where the evidence is mixed.*
Not Applicable *– where there is no evidence at all.*

For each topic add a comment indicating the evidence on which you have based your assessment. Since the information available in the case is limited, and since there are often no right or wrong answers, the comments you make will be critical in determining the mark.

Figures 8–13 show how AB's performance might be assessed.

Auditing IT developments

Strategy

ISSUE		COMMENT
• Top management support	*MIXED*	*Good at the end but the Administrative Manager had to fight.*
• Opportunity identification	*GOOD*	*The opportunity to use the system for resource allocation was grasped.*
• Corporate/IT strategy	*GOOD*	*Although we know little about the strategies, both were dealt with at top level.*
• Strategic alignment	*POOR*	*The IT strategy seems technology-based, bearing little relationship to the business.*
• IT in the organization	*MIXED*	*IT seems to be well regarded and is a separate business but as such may be isolated.*

Figure 8

Auditing IT developments

Planning

ISSUE		COMMENT
• Decision making	*GOOD*	*A small organization with the flexibility to treat each situation on its merits.*
• Business risks	*NOT APPLICABLE*	
• Change management	*MIXED*	*See below*
• Change manager	*GOOD*	*The change process seems to have been successful, but mainly through the accident of the Administrative Manager being closely involved.*

Figure 9

Auditing IT developments

Project management

ISSUE	COMMENT	
• Implementation policy	*GOOD*	*The system was up and running in a short time.*
• On time	*NOT APPLICABLE*	
• Within budget	*NOT APPLICABLE*	
• Resource balance	*NOT APPLICABLE*	
• Who involved	*GOOD*	*Senior management, IT and users all seem to have been involved in the project.*

Figure 10

Auditing IT developments

User involvement

ISSUE	COMMENT	
• Liasion		
• Users/project	*GOOD*	*"Good" but only because of the principal user, the Administrative Manager who was the "champion" of the project.*
• Users/implementation		
• Users/influence		
• Attitudes	*GOOD*	*Because of the involvement of the Administrative Manager users "owned" the system.*

Figure 11

Auditing IT developments

Operations

ISSUE		COMMENT
• Information		
• Users/access		
• Ease of use	GOOD	*There is little information in the case but as far as we know everything worked well. The capability to use the system for resource allocation suggests that the operationable aspects of the system were good.*
• Hardware		
• Software		

Figure 12

Auditing IT developments

Monitoring

ISSUE		COMMENT
• Ex post evaluation		NOT APPLICABLE
• Benefits harvest		
• Use of info	GOOD	*Resource allocation based, in part, on information from the system.*
• Achieved *vs.* expected		NOT APPLICABLE
• Problems		
• Potential	GOOD	*The opportunity for resource allocation was seized.*

Figure 13

PRACTICE FINAL EXAMINATION 2

Case Study

H, an engineering company in the defence industry, produces weapons systems, usually computerised, for a wide range of military equipment. Extensive technical documentation of a highly complex nature is published to support the products. In addition, a substantial amount of documentation and presentational material is involved in bidding for new contracts and reporting on progress on existing contracts. The existing system relied on word-processing for text and the drawing-board and cut-and-paste for the charts, diagrams and graphics.

There is a two stage standard procedure for justifying new systems. First budget provision must be made. Then the proposal document is considered by the Computer Steering Group on which senior management is represented. The document must deal with two major issues: engineering and costs. A project should either contribute to engineering objectives, obtaining and completing projects; or to reducing overheads. Benefits and costs must be quantified where possible.

There was general dissatisfaction with the existing system. It was felt to be slow, inefficient, inflexible and providing poor quality output. In addition, the increasing complexity of documentation was making it difficult to control costs and quality. It was decided to introduce a new computer system which was already in use elsewhere in the company. The system would integrate different parts of the documentation process.

The following benefits were planned for the new system:

- allow technical publishing to keep up with increasing complexity;
- document production time to be reduced to a third of previous levels, saving the time of clerical staff and engineers;
- engineers to have continuous control over documentation, and link it to design and production work.

In addition, other benefits, not planned for, were achieved:

- improved quality;
- improved quality of viewfoils.

However, the most remarkable benefit was the impact of the system on how the engineers worked – this exceeded all expectations. They used the new system to control the flow of work and manage projects themselves, giving leadership to the rest of the company. Previously they had done their work reactively, waiting for someone else to shout when deadlines were in danger of being missed.

(1a) ***Describe the Index Matrix of IT benefits, explaining what the axes represent and giving examples for each cell.*** **(20 marks)**

ERA I

Process Automation	(Function/efficiency cell) Payroll.
Functional Enhancement	(Function/effectiveness cell). Sales/ordering, to give availability, delivery information.

ERA II

Task Mechanization	(Individual/efficiency cell). Word-processing.
Work Improvement	(Individual/effectiveness cell). DTP.

ERA III

Role Expansion	(Individual/transformation cell). Office manager's role expanded to include work flow control.
Functional Re-definition	(Function/transformation cell). Sales function expands as integrated system allows it to monitor progress of an order through manufacturing, distribution, finance, etc.
Boundary Extension	(Organization/efficiency cell). Benetton.
Service Enhancement	(Organization/effectiveness cell). Insurance brokers have information on all policies/insurers.
Product Innovation	(Organization/transformation cell). American Airlines.

(1b) ***To which "Era" of IT application does organization H's system belong and which cell of the matrix best describes the benefits the system is likely to bring? Give reasons.*** **(20 marks)**

The case states that the major impact is on the way the engineers work so "Role Expansion" is probably the best answer. "Work Improvement" is an alternative. However, the system also provides efficiency and effectiveness benefits for the documentation process so "Functional Enhancement" is another alternative.

(1c) ***What might be the limitations in using the matrix in practice?*** **(10 marks)**

Limitations: Systems may cover several cells; cells do not give an exhaustive range of benefits; a system might cover most or even all cells at any one time; organisations are likely to move about the matrix quickly as time passes.

(2a) ***Describe the "Five Levels" Transformation Graph, explaining what each level means and giving examples for each cell.*** **(20 marks)**

Describe levels giving examples such as:

(i) Payroll
(ii) Sales/stock/finance link
(iii) Health Service/M & S merchandiser
(iv) Auto manufacturer-supplier links, publishing
(v) AA.

(2b) ***Which of the Five Levels of Transformation best describes organisation H's situation, particularly with regard to the system described? Give reasons.*** **(20 marks)**

Level 2. The system integrates several functions. There is no transformation of processes, networks or business scope so an answer of Levels 3–5 would be wrong. The only transformation is at an individual level.

(2c) ***For what purposes might organisations use the matrix?*** **(10 marks)**

Uses. Understanding roles of existing systems and their potential for transformation, generating ideas, creating awareness.

PRACTICE FINAL EXAMINATION 3

Case Study

A division of a large engineering company G produces computerised industrial controls. A typical example would be a system for running an automated manufacturing plant. Sales are made throughout the world including recent major deals in Russia and Central Europe.

The technical documentation associated with the controls is extensive and increasingly complex. In addition, a substantial amount of documentation has to support the process of bidding for new contracts and the associated presentations. The existing system for producing all this documentation relied on stand-alone word-processing for text and cut-and-paste for the charts, diagrams and graphics.

The management of the product documentation section and that of the central Business Systems Group were aware that the latest publishing technology could make document publishing much more efficient. In addition, imminent legal changes meant that documentation had to accompany products rather than follow them. The documentation process was, therefore, going to be critical in meeting delivery dates.

There was no standard procedure for justifying new IT investment within the company although a rigorous proposal document had to be prepared. This was essentially economic, dealing with cost and manpower reductions and other efficiency benefits. The exhaustive quantification was based on a four-year write-off period. The proposal had to be approved by the Business Systems Group, the Site Director and the Group General Manager.

The proposal envisaged the following benefits:

- faster production to meet product delivery dates;
- manpower cost reduction/avoidance by reducing clerical staff by almost half;
- reduction in outside printing costs of £57 000 by bringing all printing in-house;
- improving control of projects by bringing printing in-house;
- storage cost reductions by printing on demand instead of to store;
- income increase by doubling price of manuals because of their better presentational quality.

In addition, the following unplanned benefits were achieved:

- The system was a significant factor in gaining a large Russian contract because of the speed with which the proposal documentation was prepared.
- Cost reductions were achieved even though the throughput was almost doubled.
- The system acted as a catalyst to a re-organisation of the management structure.

The general user reaction has been favourable and the system has had a real business impact "The Russian contract would probably not have been achieved without it."

(1a) ***Describe McFarlen's Strategic Grid, explaining what the axes represent and giving examples for each cell.*** **(20 marks)**

Describe the grid. Give examples such as:

Factory:	credit card company
Support:	management consultancy
Turnaround:	oil company, retail marketing
Strategic:	airline

(1b) ***Where is organization G on the Strategic Grid? Give reasons for your decision.*** **(20 marks)**

Support. Organisation G does not appear to be heavily reliant on IT at the present time and IT is not one of the 3 or 4 things it must get right to survive and prosper in the future.

(1c) ***What are the limitations of the Grid in assessing the importance of IT to an organization?*** **(10 marks)**

Imprecise allocation to cells; the Grid can only be used as a guideline or for increasing IT awareness; different parts of an organization may be in different cells; rapid changes over time are hard to represent.

(2a) ***Describe the Index Matrix of IT benefits, explaining what the axes represent and giving examples for each cell.*** **(20 marks)**

Describe the matrix. Give examples such as:

ERA I

Process Automation	(Function/efficiency cell). Payroll.
Functional Enhancement	(Function/effectiveness cell). Sales/ordering, to give availability, delivery information.

ERA II

Task Mechanization	(Individual/efficiency cell). Word-processing.
Work Improvement	(Individual/effectiveness cell). DTP.

ERA III

Role Expansion	(Individual/transformation cell). Office manager's role expanded to include work flow control.
Functional Re-definition	(Function/transformation cell). Sales function expands as integrated system allows it to monitor progress of an order through manufacturing, distribution, finance, etc.
Boundary Extension	(Organization/efficiency cell). Benetton.
Service Enhancement	(Organization/effectiveness cell). Insurance brokers have information on all policies/insurers.
Product Innovation	(Organization/transformation cell). American Airlines.

(2b) ***To which "Era" of IT application does organization G's system belong and which cell of the matrix best describes the benefits the system is likely to bring? Give reasons.***
(20 marks)

The system does produce different types of benefit but they seem to be centred on "Process Automation", "Functional Enhancement" is the best alternative.

(2c) ***For what purposes might organizations use the matrix?*** **(10 marks)**

Understanding business purposes of systems checking no potential benefits are missed, creating awareness of what systems can do, preparation for investment appraisal.
(Total of 100 marks)

Strategies for Change

There is no choice in the selection of questions to be answered. Each examination is in two sections: multiple choice questions and essay questions.

Multiple Choice Questions

20 questions each worth 1 point for a correct answer.		
Total points available in Section A	20 × 1 =	20

Essay Questions

4 questions each worth a maximum of 20 points.		
Total points available in section B	4 × 20 =	80
Total points available for each examination		100

PRACTICE FINAL EXAMINATION 1 WITH MCS

Section A: Multiple Choice Questions

Each question is worth one point.

1 Human resource management is concerned with creating an environment which enables companies to:

A Obtain, motivate and retain the people they need.
B Reduce operational costs by reducing staff levels.
C Develop a culture which emphasizes customer satisfaction.
D Ensure the minimum of quality control problems.

2 Which of the following information is *not* usually produced by an environmental audit?

A Local unemployment levels.
B Changes in social norms and values.
C Availability of part-time workers.
D Current salary levels.

3 The Hay Scheme is one of the most widely used traditional job evaluation schemes. It relies on three factors, namely:

A Know-how, problem solving, and accountability.
B Accountability, job analysis, and qualifications.
C Management position, accountability, and budget responsibility.
D Difficulty of job, skills needed, salary level.

4 Empirical evidence suggests which of the following about profit-related pay?

A It cushions employees against recession.
B It makes employees more aware of business.
C It changes the motivation levels of employees.
D Companies using it appear to perform better, though it is uncertain why.

5 The homeostatic view of stress:

A Emphasizes the importance of the sources of stress, which may be internal or external to the individual.
B Concentrates on the sexual orientation of the individual.
C Encompasses the sources of stress, the resources available to the individual, the ways in which the individual appraises the demand–resource gap and the coping methods used.
D Is concerned with the problem of the man–machine interface.

6 Those things in the environment which might result in the triggering of stress are defined as:

A Strains.
B Stressors.
C Pressures.
D Hormonal reactions.

7 The emphasis in Employee Assistance Programmes has been:

A To provide employees with financial support.
B To assist employees with alcohol problems.
C To provide employees with blood pressure control and smoking reduction programmes.
D To offer employees lifestyle workshops on diet, hobbies, etc.

8 Which of the following is *not* a feature of a bureaucratic organization?

A Vertical communication.
B Heavy reliance on instructions and decisions issued from managers to subordinates.
C Network structure of control.
D Precise definition of rights and duties throughout the organization.

9 An organization which tends to be free from favouritism and bias may be characterized as:

A A bureaucracy.
B An organic organization.
C A matrix organization.
D A post-bureaucratic organization.

10 The "temporary organization" of Warren Bennis was a creation with the twin themes of:

A Technology and adhocracy.
B Environment and matrix organizations.
C "Organization man" and technology.
D Technology and environment.

11 Which of the following is *not* an aspect of technology in Schon's terms?

A Products.
B Physical equipment.
C Techniques.
D Finance.

12 Subcontracting a function to another organization rather than developing it in-house is an example of:

A Virtual solution.
B Divisibility.
C Implementation complexity.
D Non-technical solutions to business problems.

13 The search process for new technologies depends upon:

A The amount of finance available.
B The quality of advertising of the product under consideration.
C Whether an "off-the-shelf" or an R&D solution is preferred.
D The awareness of top management of new technologies.

14 In most developing countries the government:

A Pursues protectionist industrial and economic policies.
B Encourages free trade.
C Tends to be decentralized.
D Plays little part in the management of the economy.

15 In comparing the commitment of British and Indian managers, it is found that:

A Indian managers are less committed than their employees.
B British managers are less committed than their employees.
C British and Indian managers both have greater commitment than their employees.
D There are no differences between the commitment of managers and employees in either country.

16 The typical Japanese company has:

A Workers represented by a number of unions.
B A single union representing all workers.
C A policy of no union recognition.
D Craft-based union recognition.

17 Which of the following is *not* a fundamental quality characteristic?

A Holistic nature.
B Focus on prevention.
C Just-in-time.
D Customer focus.

18 In Crosby's view "there is no such thing as a quality problem", since the prime cause of quality problems is:

A Management.
B Employees.
C Performance standards.
D Measurement.

19 The particular norms or beliefs that are supposed to govern conduct in a social group or society are known as:

A Morals.
B Normative ethics.
C Philosophy.
D Applied ethics.

20 Game theory can be applied to business ethics to show that:

A Human nature does not have a universal component.
B Rules are unable to determine action.
C Co-operation can lead to greater gains for everyone.
D Ethical codes are unlikely to improve moral conduct.

Section B: Essay Questions

Each question is worth 20 points.

1 How does the strategic model of human resource management view the role and potential contribution of the employee, and what are the principles which develop from this approach?

2 Describe 5 methods of stress management which might be used by an individual employee, and the aspects of stress which they have been shown to affect.

3 Describe how changes in the age distribution of workers, the increasing number of women employees, and the growth in "professional" workers, are affecting contemporary bureaucracies.

4 Explain what is meant by "technology" and why organizations need new technology. Give an example of new technology and its use for competitive advantage, and outline the dangers associated when considering the use of new technology.

Section A: Answers to Multiple Choice Questions

1 D	8 C	15 C
2 D	9 A	16 B
3 A	10 D	17 C
4 D	11 D	18 A
5 C	12 A	19 A
6 B	13 C	20 C
7 B	14 A	

Section B: Answers to Essay Questions

Question 1

The strategic model of human resource management considers that employees should should be invited to share in the strategic perspective of the organization and to become active in its development. Human resource management focuses on company policies involving all levels of the workforce, in determining and working towards the achievement of the organization's strategic goals. Formerly this was the domain of senior management only. This approach to human resource management emphasizes the development of five main principles:

1 *Integration* Integrating human resource policies on selection, pay, training and employee relations, with marketing, production and finance policies. In addition, harmonizing the pay and conditions of all sections of the workforce. This involves a shift at the operational level in responsibility for "people" issues from human resource managers to line managers.

2 *Commitment* This implies the use of company policies and procedures to bind employees to the organization so that they use their skills and effort for the achievement of organizational goals and at the same time satisfy their own individual aspirations.

3 *Flexibility* It is necessary to develop the organization's capacity to adapt to changing business environments and to be receptive to new and innovative ideas.

4 *Involvement* With the strategic model of human resource management it is necessary to replace collective procedures in favour of direct individual relationships, to include consultation with and the participation of all the workforce in strategic issues.

5 *Empowerment* More power should be devolved to individual workers in areas such as how they carry out their duties and in questions of appraisal and performance-related pay.

Question 2

Five methods which might be used by an employee to help deal with stress-related illness are relaxation training, biofeedback, the application of cognitive techniques, exercise, and time management skills:

1 *Relaxation training* This covers such techniques as breathing exercises, muscle relaxation, meditation, autogenic training (which is a combination of muscle relaxation and meditation), and mental relaxation strategies. Relaxation training has been found

to reduce the individual's levels of anxiety and alcohol intake, and also to reduce the levels of the perceived symptoms of stress.

2 *Biofeedback* Through biofeedback, certain bodily functions can be brought under voluntary control, and these include brain waves, heart rate, muscle tension, stomach acidity and blood pressure. Biofeedback is reported as reducing anxiety, controlling both tension and migraine headaches, reducing stress-related hypertension, and modifying Type A behaviour.

3 *The application of cognitive techniques* These are used to enable the individual to re-appraise or restructure situations so that they are no longer considered to be stressful. This is done by removing cognitive distortions, such as overgeneralizing, magnifying and personalizing negative events, and by introducing assertiveness training. The aim is to give individuals more control over their reactions to stressors. Cognitive techniques have been successful in reducing at least one aspect of Type A behaviour, and in reducing blood pressure.

4 *Exercise* Moderate exercise of as little as 5 to 30 minutes' duration has been found to produce significant tranquillizing effects, and routine vigorous exercise can reduce the intensity and duration of anxiety.

5 *Time management skills* Poor use of time management has been shown to be a source of many work-related negative health outcomes. Time management skills should encompass both work and extra-employment activities. For instance, employees can be shown how to identify the key areas in their life, develop priorities and recognize and deal with those events which continually "rob" them of their valuable and limited time.

Question 3

1 In Western Europe, the "baby boom" of the immediate post-war years is in decline, with the consequence that the balance of older people in the working population is on the increase. The consequences of this are that organizations may be forced to consider the needs of older citizens in ways which have not been immediately obvious in the past; for instance, in the provision of geriatric medicine. More and more specialists in geriatric medicine are being appointed With shrinkage in the number of people in the workforce under 25 years old we are also beginning to witness the growth in attractiveness of older people as employees. Some supermarkets in the United States and Britain, for example, are now boasting that they are employing only people over 50 as they are considered to be more thoughtful and reliable than their youthful counterparts.

2 More and more women are returning to work after having a family. Equal opportunities legislation in Britain, Europe and the United States now makes it illegal to discriminate against individuals on the grounds of race, religion or gender in hiring and employment terms. Such legislation will undoubtedly lead to the employment of more women and so-called minority groups in contemporary organizations. Some commentators claim that the bureaucratic organizations of industrial society stress masculine values, such as superior/subordinate relationships, that they are relatively uncaring and punitive; and that they are overly committed to success. Organic organizations on the other hand can stress "feminine" values such as greater care of and compassion for staff, and a much greater stress on co-operation rather than competition in the work environment. The general rise in the number of female workers in the labour force (a

trend in "developed" countries) is matched by a change in the nature of job categories. There has also been a general decline in the number of blue collar jobs (the traditional bastion of male employment) in favour of the growth of "white collar" work.

3 There has been a growth of "professional" groups of workers. These are often self-employed, have high educational qualifications and similarly linked status. They are members of groups which are typically self-regulating to a high degree in that they set their own entry standards and attempt to ensure their groups' quality assurance and the maintenance of standards. They may be employed in large bureaucratic organizations but they provide a parallel organization-within-an organization which is only loosely controlled by the career bureaucrats without their specialist knowledge. Hospital doctors are an example. They owe allegiance to their professional "calling" and are subject to general management rules but they can still retain considerable autonomy in their work environment.

Question 4

One definition of technology is: "any tool or technique, any product or process, any physical equipment or method of doing or making, by which human capability is extended". "Technology" is usually seen as having two components: first, a hardware component, that is, the tool embodying the technology as a physical or material object; and second, a software aspect, consisting of the information base for the tool. For example, the hardware aspect of the fax machine is the piece of plastic and metal and its connections. The software aspect of the fax machine is the internal programming which makes it work, and the manual or other information or training which instructs the user. It is only when the user is able to use the tool effectively that the technology has been integrated effectively into the organization. Without appropriate knowledge and skill the hardware alone cannot extend the organization's capability, and its potential cannot be exploited. This is why the information in the manual must be transferred to the mind of the user as part of the process of acquiring a technological capability.

Organizations need new technology because they operate in a highly competitive environment which obliges them continually to seek ways of offering either greater satisfaction to their customers or clients or the same satisfaction more cheaply. These objectives can be achieved in a number of ways. A company can make its products or services more attractive to customers by reducing their charges or improving their speed of service. Internal reorganization to improve efficiency may be able to meet some of the need. However, technological solutions can sometimes offer much greater gains. For instance, the fax (facsimile) machine has provided a very convenient solution to the problem of providing speedy written communication to clients and/or suppliers. A note can be sent around the world as quickly as a telephone message. It is immediately turned into hard copy, including signatures. If the recipient lives at the other side of the world, twelve hours time difference away, it is even more useful than the telephone since he or she is not likely to be at work at the same time as the sender and there may be no one answering the phone and accepting messages at that time. The fax machine offers a speedy and reasonably reliable way of sending a message.

Because of success stories such as the fax, organizations are aware that new technology may offer them opportunities to gain competitive advantage. This awareness carries its own danger. It often leads to the unconsidered assumption that acquiring new technology always solves problems and saves money. This assumption is not justified by the experiences of many organizations. Recent studies of many industries and technologies show very high failure rates with a wide range of causes, including inappropriateness of the technology, lack of necessary skills, etc. Technological solutions to problems are not necessarily cheap or quick. Nor is it easy for an organization to understand the difficulties it may be creating for itself when it makes a commitment to a particular technical solution. Until it has become skilled in using a new technology, the organization has to make decisions about the unknown, a risky process at any time. In order to minimize the risks, it is important to adopt a systematic approach towards making decisions about technology. Technology should not be acquired for its own sake, or just because competitors have done so.

PRACTICE FINAL EXAMINATION 2 – WITH MCQs

Section A: Multiple Choice Questions

Each question is worth one point.

1 The most effective level at which pay bargaining should take place is:

A Industry-wide.
B Enterprise level.
C Plant level.
D Dependent upon the particular environment.

2 Job evaluation refers to:

A The ways in which the relative worth or value of different jobs is established.
B The procedure used to determine promotion within an organization.
C The technique used to assist in the selection of staff for vacant posts.
D The practice used during the pay bargaining process.

3 Performance-related pay has become popular in recent years because:

A It allows organizations a means of keeping pay rates at a low, and thus competitive level.
B It fits with the development of a results-oriented culture.
C Performance criteria cannot be derived from business objectives.
D It enables employers to dispense with unnecessary and unco-operative employees.

4 One estimate (from the US National Institute for Occupational Safety and Health) suggests that the number of industrial accidents related to stress is:

A 30% to 50%.
B 40% to 60%.
C 60% to 80%.
D 80% to 90%.

5 Job burnout is associated with:

A Shop-floor workers doing boring, repetitive jobs.
B Professionals who deal with other people.
C Employees who have to endure job overload.
D Cultural and ethnic attitudes to stress.

6 Type A coronary-prone behaviour is found to be higher:

A Among poorly educated employees at low levels within an organization.
B In the unemployed.
C Amongst those of higher socio-economic status.
D In those employees over the age of approximately 40 years.

7 Bureaucracies:

A Are always a poor way of organization design.
B Flourish in a static environment, with clear-cut goals and clear tasks.
C Are unsuitable for the demands of mass assembly production.
D Are suitable for organizations which exist within a rapidly changing environment.

8 The matrix organizational form:

A Encourages participation and teamworking.
B Results in the reduction of ambiguity in reporting lines.
C Is very suitable for the accomplishment of numerous small-scale tasks.
D Fails to make better use of the contributions of specialist staff than do bureaucratic organizations.

9 One response by the private sector to the pressures of a changing and more competitive marketplace is to implement:

A Administrative perestroika.
B Telematics.
C Discontinuous paradigms.
D Corporate re-engineering.

10 The first step towards a satisfactory technological solution of a business problem is:

A To determine how much the organization can afford to invest in the technology.
B To define the organization's needs clearly.
C To decide whether an "in-house" or "off-the-shelf" solution is preferred.
D To recognize the organization-wide effects of the technology.

11 Subcontracting the acquisition of a required functional capability is known as:

A Implementative complexity.
B A non-technical solution.
C Benchmarking.
D The virtual solution.

12 The appropriate sequence for technology acquisition is:

A Identify need, plan, implement, audit and modify.
B Plan, identify need, implement, modify and audit.
C Identify need, plan, implement and audit.
D Identify need, plan, audit, implement and modify.

13 In countries such as the People's Republic of China, trade unions:

A Are rubberstamping puppets of the regime.
B Are either non-existent or are repressed.
C Are encouraged and flourish.
D Are highly political and tend to engage in class struggles.

14 Which of the following is *not* a feature of human resource management in India?

A Labour-intensive technologies are encouraged.
B Managers can sack those manual workers who do not carry out their tasks properly.
C There are minimum wage regulations.
D Quotas are set by which organizations must recruit workers from among the lower castes.

15 Statistical quality control:

A Was introduced to the Japanese by W. H. Deming.
B Was introduced to the Japanese by General MacArthur.
C Was well known to the Japanese before the Second World War.
D Was introduced to the Japanese by J. M. Duran.

16 Philip Crosby's approach to quality is based on four quality absolutes. Which of the following is *not* one of Crosby's quality absolutes?

A System.
B Performance standard.
C Inspection.
D Measurement.

17 The Japanese quality expert Kaoru Ishikawa suggests that in order to determine what variations require control, organizations should use:

A Shewhart's control charts and graphs.
B Histograms.
C Check sheets.
D Pareto charts.

18 Which of the following is *not* advocated by Deming as a means of increasing employee participation in decision making?

A Emphasize mass inspection.
B Concentrate on long-term deployment of resources.
C Replace numerical quotas with statistical methods.
D End the practice of awarding business solely on the basis of price.

19 Ethical egoism is the view that:

A Different situations may require different acts.
B Actions can be right in themselves regardless of the consequences.
C A certain act must be performed regardless of circumstances or consequences.
D Whether an action is right or morally wrong depends upon how good or bad the results of the action are for oneself.

20 Which of the following is *not* one of the core virtues identified by Bernard Williams in his advocacy of virtue theory?

A Courage.
B Utilitarianism.
C Temperance.
D Wisdom.

Section B: Essay Questions

Each question is worth 20 points.

1 Describe and comment on the changing role of the line manager in relation to human resource management and the human resource specialist.

2 Among the cultural values and attitudes which are relevant in organizations are employee attitudes towards power and authority and their tolerance for ambiguity and uncertainty, and individualism/collectivism. Discuss these factors, and how they vary between national cultures.

3 Three of the fundamental quality characteristics are need for commitment, culture change, and customer focus. Discuss these characteristics in terms of managing quality.

4 Should ethical behaviour apply to business? Can a corporation be held to be ethically responsible? How can the use of ethical theories help in an analysis of business practices?

Section A: Answers to Multiple Questions

1 D	8 A	15 C
2 A	9 D	16 C
3 B	10 B	17 A
4 C	11 D	18 A
5 B	12 A	19 D
6 C	13 A	20 B
7 B	14 B	

Section B: Answers to Essay Questions

Question 1

It may be said that all line managers are their own human resource managers. Line managers are able to observe, in a direct way, the performance of their staff. Persistent lateness or absenteeism, low morale, lack of training and poor work performance may all be observed at first hand by the line manager. Moreover, new models of motivation, for example, as expounded by Alderfer, emphasize the importance of individuals and their needs. This means that managers have to focus on individual workers, recognizing the differences between them. It is the line managers who are in a position to observe these distinctions and who therefore have responsibility at the operational level for the management of people.

New techniques in people management have also affected the role of the line manager. For example, performance appraisal, which many line managers have formerly treated with mistrust, has developed into the wider concept of performance management. Since this has now become a central activity associated with learning at the workplace, it will require the skill of the line manager to direct and influence the performance of individuals at work so that they can contribute effectively to organizational goals. Coaching and counselling are best done by line managers trained in the techniques, who have an intimate knowledge of individual workers acquired from daily contact with them.

Line managers have also a part to play in the development and management of reward systems. Many of the more traditional compensation schemes are mechanistic and inappropriate for the following reasons. They become obsolete as working conditions change. They take control away from the line managers and they lack flexibility. They reflect a mechanistic image of the organization where employees are treated similarly if not identically in terms of pay. The more modern systems, such as performance-related pay, require detailed knowledge of the unique contribution of each worker to organizational goals. The line manager is able to collect this information because he or she is in a position to observe the work performance of individual workers at first hand.

These changes may affect the relationship between the line manager and the human resource specialist in that many of the human resource activities will be transferred from the human resource manager to the line manager. The extent to which this may happen is likely to be influenced by the nature and characteristics of the particular industry or organization. Top management has the responsibility for determining the underlying philosophy of the organization and this philosophy is embodied in the statement of core values. These statements require to be followed up by clear terms of reference for the human resource manager. Within this framework the human resource function may operate at a number of different levels. At the operational level the human resource specialist may act in an administrative capacity to the line manager, and this requires good teamwork and co-operation between them. If the human resource function is to be effective, it has to be a shared responsibility between line management and the human resource department. This will require companies to adopt a new training strategy in relation to line managers emphasizing the importance of their role and rewarding them for their human relations skills and competencies. It may also require a refocusing of the role of human resource specialists as their traditional territory changes.

Question 2

Attitude towards power and authority is defined by the amount of power that each of the two sides in an organization – management and employee – has and exercises over the other.

In a culture where people respect their seniors and are even afraid of people in positions of power, it is less likely that as employees they challenge their superiors. Decisions tend to be taken by a few senior managers and carried out by subordinates. Iran is an example of this type of culture. In cultures where people are brought up to share power with others, organizations may be more decentralized, managers may delegate their authority lower down the hierarchy, and there will be more consultation and communication among employees. The United States and United Kingdom belong to a large extent to this cultural category.

Tolerance for ambiguity and uncertainty as a cultural trait is especially relevant to risk taking and decision making in an organization. Social institutions such as family, religion and education can encourage or discourage risk taking and accepting responsibility for one's own action. The ability or inability to cope with uncertainty can thus be learned at an early age in any cultural group. This trait can then be manifested in their behaviour in work organizations. Employees who have less tolerance for uncertainty, and are unwilling to face ambiguity and risk, are more likely to avoid making decisions on their own and without direction from above, and prefer procedures and regulations, which involve sharing responsibilities with others. The Japanese practice of collective decision making, *ringi*, may be due to the Japanese people's high uncertainty avoidance. It has been argued that the rise of Nazism in Germany earlier this century was because of the German people's relatively low degree of tolerance for ambiguity.

Individualism/collectivism is another aspect of national culture which has been demonstrated to have a significant implication for management–employee relationships. Individualism can be defined as self-interest or as selfishness, and collectivism can be defined as self-sacrifice. An individualistic culture is generally characterized by a high value placed on one's independence, autonomy and privacy, with a belief in one's own worth and confidence in one's own ideas and opinion. In a collectivist culture the group to which one belongs, such as family, community, or even work organization, takes priority over one's individuality. Britain and many Western European cultures are considered individualistic cultures, and India and Japan as collectivist. In individualistic cultures the relationships between employees and work organizations are on the whole less emotional and may well be hostile. Industrial relations in Britain are characterized by mutual hostility and distrust. In Japan, industrial relations are characterized by apparent harmony and co-operation.

Question 3

Need for commitment

Commitment in total quality terms means that the organization must win the battle for the hearts and minds of the workforce. The way this change process is introduced will have a decisive impact on the outcome. In one example, that of Hewlett-Packard, all staff came to believe that they could contribute to the betterment of the quality of their products. Commitment by management to its people and product is considered essential. For instance, an MD might attend and participate in all the training sessions held to introduce total quality to the entire workforce. Commitment demands a basic change in attitude at all levels and across all functions in the organization. It is a key element in enabling pride in the job to be generated, and it is the nature of that commitment and the way in which it is transmitted throughout the organization which are critically important. The impact on the nature of the organization's culture is profound.

Culture change

Culture change is also associated with commitment. The nature of the linking is critical but the impact of a beneficial change in organizational culture can be dramatic. There is a substantial body of evidence in Europe and in the US supporting the view that four out of five of total quality initiatives will fail because management believe a simple quality system is sufficient to stimulate change. Overemphasis on systems at the expense of establishing the appropriate culture will fail to secure the full benefits from a quality initiative. Organizations that become good examples of "total quality" do so because they have realized the importance of creating a culture favouring the development of quality improvement initiatives. Among the appropriate aspects of organizational culture relevant to quality management, and which managers should attempt to introduce to the organization, are a belief in the importance of enjoying one's work, a belief in being the best, a belief that people should be innovators and take risks without feeling that they will be punished if they fail, a belief in the importance of attending to details, a belief in the importance of people as individuals, a belief in superior quality and service, a belief in the importance of informality to improve the flow of communication, a belief in the importance of economic growth and profits, a belief in the importance of "hands on" management, and a belief in the importance of a recognized organizational philosophy developed and supported by those at the top.

Customer focus

The idea of customer focus or service is reinforced by a study which reported that most large companies in the area studied had introduced total quality management without surveying their customers' reactions. Consequently, much total quality management was not sufficiently concerned with what customers want, which is the very opposite of what the quality process is supposed to be about. Total quality management should start with the external customer. Only when that is the case does total quality management provide real total customer satisfaction. Quality means meeting customer requirements exactly. However, many organizations begin the improvement process with problem solving rather than with focusing on the customer. To achieve customer orientation it is necessary to ask questions such as "Who are our customers?", "What do they do with our outputs?", "What are our customers" precise requirements?", "Do our products and/or services match their needs?", "How far have we gone in acting as an informed supplier?" To answer these questions, companies should commission a customer satisfaction study.

Question 4

Business ethics is the study of the conduct of people in business. This raises the question of whether this behaviour should be judged by the same standards of ethical behaviour normally applied to the rest of life. Some commentators claim that personal ethics are unrelated to business ethics. But ethical conduct should be consistent in all contexts and there is no fundamental difference between personal and business ethics. Ethical problems are part of business life, but today they are more complex, as business has expanded and become global. The Bhopal disaster, the *Exxon Valdez* oil spill, the BCCI banking fraud, the Ivan Boesky scandal, the Guinness affair, are all concerned with business ethics and the morals of businessmen. Ethical issues are also part of everyday business life and ordinary transactions could not be performed if certain moral norms did not prevail. For example, the making of contracts, while legally enforceable, depends for its efficacy upon the ethical behaviour of truth telling, keeping promises and acting in good faith. It is impossible to think of an employment contract purely as a legal contract, for it would be meaningless and quite useless as a contract unless it is built upon the moral and social norms which both parties leave unacknowledged in the contract.

Can a corporation be held to be ethically responsible? Some commentators argue that only people are ethically responsible and that a corporation is not a person and so is not a responsible moral agent. Others argue that corporations are organizations that are recognized under the law as legal persons and so can be treated as moral agents for the purposes of making them accountable for the deeds and misdeeds committed in their name. The question of whether there is a corporate social responsibility is also the subject of debate. One view holds that the separation of ownership from control in the corporation is an undeniable fact and that the accountability of the modern firm is increasingly tenuous in terms of shareholders and nation-states, but the corporation is a structure of enormous power in society and so should recognize its responsibilities to its various stakeholders which are dependent upon and subject to the actions of the corporation. Therefore, to maintain a social mandate, the managers of the corporation need to be mindful of these responsibilities and act accordingly.

Any business issue that relates to human values is of interest to business ethics. Its scope of concern can be divided up into four levels of analysis:

1 the ethics of the social system;

2 the ethics of the business organization;

3 the ethical issues which arise in the course of business activity; and

4 the personal values that people have in business life.

The analysis of such issues requires the use of ethical theories to investigate in a systematic way specific business practices. The language, concepts and arguments of those facing ethical dilemmas can be examined and the moral choices identified. Not all moral dilemmas are resolvable, nor can ethical analysis provide solutions about what to do. But they can make clear what we are doing when we act, what the contending viewpoints are, and how they are being justified.